Webmaster's Guide
to
Internet Server
Connectivity

Leon Salvail with Steven K. Besler and Sacha Mallais

New Riders Publishing, Indianapolis, IN

Webmaster's Guide to Internet Server Connectivity

By Steven K. Besler, Sacha Michel Mallais, and Leon Salvail
Published by:
New Riders Publishing
201 West 103rd Street
Indianapolis, IN 46290 USA

Printed in the United States of America 1 2 3 4 5 6 7 8 9 0

Library of Congress Cataloging-in-Publication Data

```
Salvail, Leon, 1971-
Webmaster's Guide to Internet Server Connectivity/ Leon
Salvail
p.      cm.
Includes index
ISBN 1-56205-574-7
1. Internet (Computer network)
2. HTML (Document markup language)
I. Title
TK5105.875.I57S355      1996
004.6'7—dc20               96-13066
                           CIP
```

Warning and Disclaimer

Publisher	Don Fowley
Publishing Manager	Jim LeValley
Marketing Manager	Mary Foote
Managing Editor	Carla Hall

Product Development Specialist
Julie Fairweather

Acquisitions Editor
Ian Sheeler

Development Editor
Suzanne Snyder

Project Editor
Christopher Cleveland

Copy Editors
Susan Christophersen,
Lillian Duggan,
Sarah Kearns, Cliff Shubs

Technical Editor
Rick Fairweather

Associate Marketing Manager
Tamara Apple

Acquisitions Coordinator
Tracy Turgeson

Publisher's Assistant
Karen Opal

Cover Designer
Karen Ruggles

Cover Production
Aren Howell

Book Designer
Anne Jones

Production Manager
Kelly Dobbs

Production Team Supervisor
Laurie Casey

Graphic Image Specialists
Steven Adams, Dan Harris,
Clint Lahnen, Laura Robbins

Production Analysts
Bobbi Satterfield
Jason Hand

Production Team
Heather Butler, Kim Cofer,
Aleata Howard,
Krena Lanham, Joe Millay,
Beth Rago, Erich Richter,
Christine Tyner,
Megan Wade, Christy Wagner

Indexer
Christopher Cleveland

About the Authors

Steven K. Besler lives in Vancouver, British Columbia, where he is a working partner in Global Village Consulting, which he co-founded in January of 1995. When he finds the time he enjoys surfing, traveling, and photography.

Mr. Besler received his education from the University of British Columbia Department of Computer Science, where he specialized in distributed systems and computer language theory. Prior to working for Global Village Consulting, he developed distributed software systems for academia, government, and the telecommunications industry.

Sacha Michel Mallais has been working on, playing on, loving, and hating computers for fifteen years. His latest endeavor is Global Village Consulting, a computer consulting firm based in Vancouver, British Columbia. Sacha no longer has any time for any of his other pursuits (which include skiing, swimming, and photography).

Sacha received his education from the University of British Columbia Department of Computer Science, where he studied database design and implementation.

Leon Salvail is a graduate of the University of British Columbia in Political Science, where he specialized in local government and aboriginal affairs. Leon has been involved with computers and communications for the past fifteen years. Leon is currently a working partner in Global Village Consulting, a computer consulting firm based in Vancouver, British Columbia. Global Village specializes in providing custom computer solutions for clients, ranging from online database search engines to CD-ROM development.

Leon brings with him to Global Village three years of information systems experience working for the Union of BC Municipalities, where he helped to develop an Internet pilot project for local governments. At Global Village Consulting, Leon works to manage projects from the transition period to implementation, and his attention to good customer relations ensures that all projects will be completed to the clients' satisfaction. Working with the GVC technical staff, Leon is able to provide complete solutions for networking problems, including the assessment and management of computer networks.

E-mail: gvc@cafe.net

Trademark Acknowledgments

All terms mentioned in this book that are known to be trademarks or service marks have been appropriately capitalized. New Riders Publishing cannot attest to the accuracy of this information. Use of a term in this book should not be regarded as affecting the validity of any trademark or service mark.

Dedication

To all of the wonderful people and their sites that are available on the Internet.

Acknowledgments

When I first started this book, I was not really certain what to expect. In the end, the experience was both more and less than what I had dreamed. On the positive side, I was able to learn a considerable amount while writing this guide. Obviously some sections were easier than others, and I hope that I have not made any (horrendous) errors. On the negative side, the project took much more time and effort than expected, and as a result, I must first acknowledge all of the help that my two partners,

Steven Besler and Sacha Mallais, provided. Not only did they contribute to the actual writing of this book, but they also provided invaluable technical assistance. At the same time, Sacha worked diligently to maintain our company's direction while I was distracted elsewhere—Thanks Sach!

To the NRP staff, thank you for all the time, effort, and support that you provided. You took a chance on a small, little-known company to write this book, and I hope that the faith you have shown in us will be rewarded. A special thanks goes out to Jim for his "author" review of some of the chapters. To Chris and Suzanne, thank you for helping me through this process and kicking my butt when needed! To all of the other NRP staff involved, thanks a bunch! I look forward to working with you all on another project.

Finally, I would like to acknowledge all the assistance that the members of the Internet community provided. While not all of you are aware of your impact, I appreciate all of the useful suggestions and information provided. A special thanks must go out to Paul Celestin, who generously allowed us to use his ISP listings for our appendix.

Without this kind help, the appendix would not have been nearly as comprehensive nor as easy to compile.

One last note. Thank yous go out to all my family and friends (you know who you are) that have given me moral and physical support over the years. Without your special care and attention for me, I would not be the person I am today, and would not have had the confidence and skills necessary to write this book.

Contents at a Glance

Introduction

Table of Contents

INTRODUCTION

INTRODUCTION INTRODUCTION INTRODUCTION INTRODUCTION INTRODUCTION INTRODUCTION INTRODUCTION

As communications expert Marshall McLuhan said,

"The new electronic interdependence recreates the world in the image of the global village."

The Internet and information distributed on the World Wide Web (WWW) has brought this theory closer to reality. As the second millennium moves toward completion, the need for connectivity—and, thus, the need for this book—becomes more apparent.

What is This Book About?

Simply speaking, this book is about connecting to the Internet. It is not, however, about the process of setting up the software on a single user's computer for dial-up Internet access, nor does it provide advice or specific instructions on installing or configuring the software on a WWW server. Instead, this book deals with the myriad issues surrounding the decision to gain connectivity for a WWW site, and addresses how organizations and individuals should select their connectivity solutions.

Given the desirability of having a WWW site available 24 hours a day (a good idea since the "World" in WWW means that people from around the world and across time zones may access your site), this book looks at the methods that provide global 24 hour connectivity. By providing discussions about the technology, costs, benefits, and limitations of each connection option, this book provides the details you will require in order to choose the connectivity method that best suits your needs.

Who Should Be Interested in This Book?

Often the decision of what resources to consult for a specific problem can in itself be an issue. In the case of this book, we would like to simplify the issue by providing some direction to your information search (just think of us as the book equivalent to a WWW search engine). In our opinion, this book should be of interest to five types of individuals:

- The manager or CEO, who makes the final decision about Internet connectivity for his or her company

- The Information Systems manager who makes and implements connectivity decisions

- The WWW professional looking to solve his or her own connectivity options

- The Internet consultant

- Anyone with a serious interest in Internet connectivity

The Corporate Decision Makers

The first group that should find this book of interest includes the corporate managers and CEOs of companies that are considering setting up a WWW site. Although CEOs are unlikely to be among company personnel responsible for directly implementing the chosen connectivity option, the decision to connect will probably be theirs. This book provides a wealth of background information on connectivity so that the CEO can make this decision with confidence. Even though some sections of this book are somewhat technical, the overall result is a book that is easy to read and useful for a variety of users.

The Connectivity Implementors

The second group that this book should interest are the Information Systems experts and professionals charged with choosing and implementing Internet connectivity for the purpose of establishing a WWW site. For these individuals, the technical information and checklists included in this book provide a measured assessment of the various connectivity options. The result for you, if you consider yourself part of this group, is that you will be able to make a more informed and appropriate decision for your company's connectivity.

The WWW Site Creators

The third group of individuals targeted in this book includes the actual creators of Web sites. The WWW professional, or Webmaster, often has the task of providing WWW connectivity for a number of clients. This may include setting up a site to house a client's WWW infomation. This book provides the information necessary for you—the Webmaster—to determine the best solution for your problem: rented space, a server in a server park, or a dedicated connection. As well, this book will help you answer questions about the amount of bandwidth required for a WWW site.

The Facilitating Consultant

The fourth group of individuals that will find this book useful consists of Internet consultants (like the authors of this book). As you well know, if you are a consultant, the Internet explosion via the WWW has created a large demand for connectivity solutions. Although it is sometimes difficult to keep up-to-date with the technological changes related to Internet connectivity, this book attempts to provide a snapshot of current options and an overview of developing. If the term "Internet consultant" applies to you, the book should provide a useful reference for your work.

The Interested Observer

Even if you are not directly connected (pun intended) to the Internet and WWW issues, you may find this book interesting. We have attempted to provide some useful insights into the world of communications and computers. By reading this book, you will have a greater understanding of how a communications connection works, including the phone on your desk, or the server you have connected to via your Web browser. Moreover, because the WWW may eventually be considered one of the creations that defines this present Information Era, understanding how to connect is a noble pursuit.

Why is This Book Important?

The *Webmaster's Guide to Internet Server Connectivity* is an important tool for learning and action. A thorough read of the book will give you an in-depth understanding of the issues surrounding connectivity decisions. At the same time, the book has been organized in a way that enables you to come to a quick decision on connectivity and implement your decision.

The decision-making process for connectivity is an area that publishers of Internet-related books have long ignored, although information about configuring software and programming WWW sites has been discussed in a number of excellent books. This book addresses that deficiency.

A Note from the Author

This book assumes that you have identified a need for a WWW site, and as a result, you require some level of connectivity. What is not addressed in this book are the "ifs and whens" of connectivity. Should you connect to the Internet or create a WWW site? When is a good time for a company to start a WWW site? What types of businesses are better suited for Internet connectivity (or WWW exposure)? If you have questions such as these that still need to be addressed, we suggest that you read New Riders Publishing's Internet Commerce, available at your local bookstore.

Conventions Used in This Book

> ❈ *Italic* is used to indicate new words or phrases that are followed by a definition.

> ❈ A regular bullet ❈ precedes any text lists that are non-specific.

> ❈ A checklist bullet precedes a user checklist item summarizing a point in the chapter.

Also used in this book are icons that illustrate notes, tips, warnings, and notes from the author. The author made an effort to set these aside for your added information.

Note

A note includes extra information that you will find useful. It complements the discussion rather than being part of it.

Tip

A tip provides quick instructions for getting the most from your Internet server connectivity.

Warning

A warning cautions you to be aware of certain situations that can occur when making your connectivity decisions.

A Note from the Author

A note from the author shares the author's insight and personal experiences with regard to establishing Internet server connectivity.

With these special fonts, bullets, and icons in mind, you will be able to read through this book with more subjective and evaluative information that will aid you in making your connectivity decisions.

New Riders Publishing

The staff of New Riders Publishing is committed to bringing you the very best in computer reference material. Each New Riders book is the result of months of work by authors and staff who research and refine the information contained within its covers.

As part of this commitment to you, the NRP reader, New Riders invites your input. Please let us know if you enjoy this book, if you have trouble with the information and examples presented, or if you have a suggestion for the next edition.

Please note: New Riders staff cannot serve as a technical resource for the *Webmaster's Guide to Internet Server Connectivity* or for questions about software- or hardware-related problems. Please contact your service provider or onsite technical advisor for support.

If you have a question or comment about any New Riders book, there are several ways to contact New Riders Publishing. We will respond to as many readers as we can. Your name, address, or phone number will never become part of a mailing list or be used for any purpose other than to help us continue to bring you the best books possible. You can write us at the following address:

New Riders Publishing
Attn: Publisher
201 W. 103rd Street
Indianapolis, IN 46290

If you prefer, you can fax New Riders Publishing at (317) 581-4670.

You can also send electronic mail to New Riders at the following Internet address:

```
jfairweather@newriders.mcp.com
```

NRP is an imprint of Macmillan Computer Publishing. To obtain a catalog or information, or to purchase any Macmillan Computer Publishing book, call (800) 428-5331.

Thank you for selecting *Webmaster's Guide to Internet Server Connectivity*!

Bandwidth and Internet Connectivity

Connectivity can have many different meanings. Connectivity can be as simple as two people joining together to develop and share ideas. When discussing connectivity and computers, the general definition in the past has been the development of links between processing power and users. The connections have changed to accommodate improved connection methods, and changed work methods and environments. Connectivity is no longer contained at the LAN level, but has grown to include WAN connectivity for a large number of users through the Internet. This book examines the impulse behind connectivity to the Internet with the specific purpose of determining and obtaining the proper level of connectivity for World Wide Web (WWW) information provision.

This chapter contains a basic discussion of the potential reasons for connecting to the Internet. Obviously, not everyone needs an Internet connection. This book is for companies who have identified a specific need that the Internet can help them address: information distribution. With the advent of the WWW, and the resulting explosion of commercial Internet activity, an increasing need exists for companies to promote themselves and provide information to the growing consumer base on the Internet. In general, the information is being provided through WWW sites, either private or commercial. This chapter examines the factors that determine Internet connectivity needs and the providers of Internet connectivity, and briefly touches on the future trends in connectivity.

A Note from the Author

I know this might seem like blasphemy in a computer book, but here is my opinion:

Although the Internet can be a useful tool, and information and entertainment source, it is not required for everyone.

As a consultant, I see businesses that want to "get connected" to the Internet without any particular reason. Although the Internet can serve to increase the communicative capabilities of a company, this connectivity has a cost, both in financial and human resource terms. I feel that the days of connectivity for all enterprises will come, but that time is a few years away yet. Staying on the cutting edge can be beneficial and give a company a leg up on their competition, but the "bleeding edge" can be costly.

The World Wide Web, or the "New" Internet

When the Internet was first envisioned, the creators were concerned about the security and reliability of communications (see Chapter 3, "The Historical and Technical Background of the Internet," for a brief history of the Internet). Soon after the first set of connections was established, users quickly discovered that the Internet could easily be used to exchange information and collaborate on projects. Even so, Internet usage grew slowly, being mainly contained in larger organizations and universities. The major change came with the development of the *World Wide Web* (WWW) project by CERN, a Switzerland-based organization for physicists, in 1990 (official launch date).

Working from the idea of hypertext as developed by Ted Nelson of Stanford Research Institute (SRI) in the 1960s, the CERN group developed an implementation of a markup language named *HyperText Markup Language* (HTML). The concept behind this language was to provide a mechanism for organizing data and information for collaboration between physicists. Because this collaboration occurred on a global basis, the CERN Institute developed a language that could be used over the Internet, and at the same time made the specification public. Between 1990 and 1992, the WWW grew slowly, with servers and text-based browsers being developed (and made available for free—the first of which were developed by CERN itself).

The change in the Web's growth came with the development of a graphical WWW browser (a client program that enables the user to view HTML in a standard manner). In 1992, Marc Andreessen was working on an information collaboration project for the National Center for Supercomputing Applications (NCSA). Aware of the project developed by CERN, he worked to develop a Web browser that used the same specification, but incorporated the use of a graphical interface for use with Graphical User Interface (GUI) systems. This first graphical browser included the capability to view text and graphics, as well as to launch other programs for the utilization of sound and high-resolution graphics ("helper applications," as they have become known).

With the advent of the first graphical browser, the WWW blossomed. The capability to publish information worldwide with very little cost caught the attention of users and businesses. The potential for graphics, sound, and video methods of portraying information created an explosion of users and providers. At the same time, Web browsers have continued to develop and progress, including more and more features (currently, the most popular browser is Netscape by Netscape, Inc.). Today, some of the most exciting developments for the WWW include Virtual Reality Markup Language (VRML), Java (a scripting/programming tool that allows applications to be embedded in HTML code), and narrow-casting audio and video.

Tip

Narrow-casting audio and/or video in the context of the Internet is the use of specialized software to provide real time audio and video services via the WWW. Since this software only sends the information to those who request it, this is often referred to as narrow-casting. The name stems from the contrasts between this distribution method and that of broadcasting, which sends all information to all users at all times (like cable TV).

The development of graphical and specialized uses for the WWW not only has provided for the rapid growth of the Internet, but also has created the need for greater connectivity. Because of the possible applications of the WWW, the need for bandwidth and Internet connectivity is based on the following three major factors:

- The information you provide

- The reason to provide the information

- To whom you provide the information

Information: The Determining Factor

The type of information you provide for your clients is one third of the equation that determines whether or not, and to what degree, you need to be connected to the Internet. If you are providing basic textual information applicable to only a small set of users, then your needs will be modest. Large quantities of useful high-bandwidth information increase your needs greatly, by increasing the traffic to your site, in terms of the number of clients and volume of information that your site serves. The first task of any potential WWW site manager is to determine what type of information to provide, how often to update the information, and to what level to maintain historical data.

Types of Data Provided

Early in the planning process, a prospective WWW site manager must determine what type of information his or her site will carry. In general terms, this information can be broken down into three main categories:

* Text

* Graphics

* Time-based multimedia (sound and video)

Each category is discussed in the following sections to create a more detailed picture of the bandwidth implications of these data types.

Text

Text is the simplest of all the information contained on the WWW and is the base for the entire Web. No matter how fancy and interactive the WWW becomes, the basic means of distributing information is text. As browsers and the HTML standard are modified to include more formatting functionality, the use of text will become even more popular. In no other form can vast volumes of information be contained and distributed with such a small bandwidth requirement.

A well-designed page of text in HTML format might consist of as much as 3 to 4 KB of data, for example. This book could be contained in a set of HTML documents (with hyperlink references throughout the document) consisting of 400 (pages) × 4 KB = 1,600 KB (or 1.6 MB). A video file 30 seconds long compressed using a lossy compression (a high efficiency method of compression that discards data not required for optimal human viewing via monitors) method also might take 1.6 MB of space.

In this example, the 400 pages of text would provide a much greater level of information, but unfortunately, given the human desire for color, sound, and motion, the Web site probably would not be well utilized. Although content is important in a WWW site, the truth is that presentation and usability are just as important. One of the best methods of increasing the usability of information is to incorporate graphics into your Web pages.

Graphics

Graphics in WWW pages can increase the visibility of a site and enable you to create better designed pages (currently HTML provides very limited formatting capabilities, although this is changing with the revisions to the standard). Simple headers can give a consistent look to your pages, and with the addition of CGI-scripting, images can become maps to other HTML documents.

Although the added functionality of the images can increase interest in your page, the cost of these images is the additional bandwidth they require to be transmitted. A simple logo banner across the top of a page can greatly increase the size and consequently the bandwidth cost of a page. Take an image 4.5" by 1" in diameter. This image before compression contains $4.5 \times 1 \times 72 \times 72$ bytes of information, or approximately 28KB. Even after compression using GIF format (one of the formats generally used for images not requiring picture-like colors), this image could still be as large as 20 KB. As a result, for every image this size used in a Web page, the bandwidth requirements could increase by a factor of five to seven. Consequently, a text-based WWW site that required a 28.8 connection may require an ISDN connection if graphics are used instead of text.

Putting all WWW information into graphical format is not cost effective. This book digitized into graphics takes up as much as 75 MB of space on a server (7" by 6" $\times$ 72 bits per inch $\times$ 72 bits per inch $\times$ 400 pages). As a result, a WWW site manager has to decide how much information to store as graphics and how much to maintain as text. As well as static text and graphics, the site manager can use a third type of information: time- or motion-based information.

Time-Based Multimedia

No matter where you turn today, you hear talk about *multimedia*. Generally this term refers to the integration of sound and video with the everyday text and graphics of our published world. Due to the digital nature of WWW information distribution, these types of information can be incorporated into the WWW. In fact, the incorporation of this information happens today.

Unfortunately for a Web site manager, the use of these formats of information can be very bandwidth-intensive. A 30-second video clip compressed with an advanced compression routine, such as the AVI format (a common

Windows-based video compression format), can take as much as 3 MB of space and bandwidth. Video broadcasts via the Internet are based on compression routines that are lossy (data is actually lost in the process) and work on the basis that the human brain is able to provide the missing steps in the pattern. Even so, video conferencing via the Internet is limited to 10 frames per second on ISDN-level bandwidth.

Like the information that you provide on your WWW site, the time between updates also plays a role in determining your connectivity needs.

Time between Updates and Historical Data Caches

A second major factor in determining your bandwidth requirements is the degree that your site provides updated information, and the amount of *data caching* (maintenance of historical data over a period of time) that you provide. Because the WWW, and most browsers, provide information caching, information that has not changed is not reloaded across the Internet. The limitations of caching, the degree that you change your site, and the level of historical data that you store have heavy impacts on the bandwidth requirements of your site.

Changing Information

Although information on the WWW is easy to manipulate and update, changing information is one of the main sources of bandwidth usage. Changing information increases your site's bandwidth in two ways. First, the information that changes is reloaded by browsers, and individual WWW users on a regular basis so that users are able to maintain data integrity (i.e., their data continues to match the data supplied by your site).

Although a number of organizations are providing data caching for entire organizations through proxy servers (the CERN server in proxy mode supports this function), this data caching does not reduce demand on a server that has changing information (proxy servers are discussed in more detail in Chapter 3). Every time the site is queried, even through a proxy, the information about that site is verified to not have been altered. If the site has been changed, or the server is unable to verify, the information is reloaded.

A Note from the Author

An example of this condition is a database structure Global Village Consulting has implemented. Providing online stock information through a WWW site, our company linked a database to a set of C programs that interfaced with a set of WWW pages. Because these databases are updated on a daily basis and each information search is different, the information is not cached by browsers or servers, thus increasing the bandwidth draw because of this application.

Maintaining Historical Data

Not only does updating information add to your bandwidth by increasing the traffic to your site, but so does the maintenance of historical data. You have to decide whether to maintain old data after new data is added to the site. The maintenance of stored historical data dramatically increases the amount of bandwidth used by each new client for your site because instead of accessing only new information, any added client may download both the new and old information.

You can find an example of this situation at any number of Webzine sites. A *Webzine site* is any site that provides an online magazine functionality. Although any such site wants to provide some past issues online rather than only introduce new issues, each old issue adds potential bandwidth requirements for new clients. When logging onto a site that includes 12 back issues of an online magazine, you have the opportunity to download all 12 issues. If the number of issues stored continues indefinitely, the bandwidth requirements would also increase. (The increase in bandwidth assumes that the data being maintained retains its value as time elapses and is still requested by clients.)

A Note from the Author

As I have mentioned before, Global Village Consulting has had some experience with continually updated data. The stock database scenario provides an example of not only increasing usage through changing data, but also the demand increase due to historical data.

The stock database archives the data from each day so that clients can analyze the data over time. Not only does this increase the bandwidth requirements, but as a result of the historical requirements, the database requires a more robust server. Due to the increasing hardware requirements (especially memory), the historical data is limited to six months worth. To see this site in action, visit **http://www.visions.com/stocks**.

Why You Provide the Information on Your Site

The second of the three determining factors for providing information via the WWW, and for the way your activities impact your connectivity requirements, is the *why* of your information equation. Generally, WWW information is provided for one of three reasons:

- As information about your enterprise for future benefit (such as advertising information for a company, or a demo of your current software)

- As information of a direct benefit to the client (generally provided as a commercial service or to reduce costs)

- As a general public service

Company Information

By far the most prolific use of the WWW by enterprises is the publishing of company advertising in an electronic format. This information can be presented in a number of possible methods, but generally reflects current printed literature with a few of the benefits of hypertext incorporated. As a result, the number of people who visit the site is limited to at least vaguely interested clients; therefore, the number of clients and the direct cost of bandwidth is low. Although employing this style of advertising helps keep costs down, it also limits the benefit of the site. After all, no one can force clients to visit the site, a fundamental difference from television and the Internet. As a result, many sites combine this functionality with the second reason for service provision: information that provides direct benefit to the clients.

Direct Benefit Information

The following are the two basic types of information that provide a direct benefit to the client:

- Cost-elimination services

- Commercial services

In both cases, the goal is to provide information that the client needs in some way. This information has the purpose of generating more traffic to the site or generating revenue to offset site costs.

The first situation—eliminating costs while providing information the client needs—is a common aspect of computer-oriented sites. Most major software companies have WWW sites that are used to distribute bug fixes and demos, and provide additional documentation for their software products. Not only are these sites of great use to clients, the services also decrease distribution and production costs.

The second method of direct benefit services is to provide a service for which great demand exists, but to charge a fee for the service. In general, the site must provide a service that is of great value to users and is easy to access. In other words, the service's collection methods must be based on a simple method, either credit card (securely transferred) or a prepayment registration. An example of this type of WWW site is the Canadian Open Bidding Service (OBS). The OBS provides bidding information to companies about possible contracts with the federal government. Access to the service is controlled via passwords, and the fees are fairly steep considering the cost of transferring files electronically. Even so, the service is well used because of the high potential gain for the clients.

Public Service

Unlike the OBS, there are a number of sites that exist simply as a public service and charge no fee. These include a number of information sites by private individuals and vary in size from a simple page to a complete index of the WWW. Key examples are the WWW search engines (as an example, check out New Riders' WWW Yellow Pages at **http://www.mcp.com/newriders/wwwyp**). Generally, these search engines are free to users and to the companies and organizations listed within. The sites operate on the principle that the publicity the search engine draws provides the traffic needed to sell advertising banners on search results pages. Companies pay fees to advertise their site or product to the millions of searching clients.

Targeting Your Clients?

The third of the three factors that determine your connectivity needs is the "who" of your clients. Depending on the type of information you provide, your clientele can change, and different clientele will use your site in different ways. In general, your site will attract one of two types of clients: the professional looking for specific information, and the surfer just checking out the site.

The Professional

When referring to the concept of the professional WWW client, I am not talking about a business professional necessarily, nor any class of people in general, but only about the way in which these clients use the Internet. The professionals know what they are doing, and generally come to your site for a reason: You have the information they want. As a result, the professional tends to jump right to the area of information required and download only what is needed. The result of professional users for a well-designed site is the elimination of redundant downloading of information, consequently reducing bandwidth usage. Typically, sites that provide information that has a specific purpose, such as software bug fixes, attract this type of client.

The Surfer

Unlike the professional, the surfer has no true purpose in his or her Web activity other than the exploration of the WWW. As a result, the surfer is attracted to sites that are cross-linked in many places, provide an interesting variety of information, or keep up with the latest new WWW fad (or a few old standbys such as image archives). In general, surfers use a haphazard approach to site access, which generally results in a deeper and more random penetration of your site. The surfer might download that 3 MB video clip of your cat just because the clip is there.

Providers of Connectivity

After considering the type of, reasons for, and clients of your information to determine whether you have a connection need, and your bandwidth requirements, a WWW site manager must next examine the options for Internet connectivity. This section discusses general service providers and the benefits each type of provider brings to the business.

In general, the Internet services you require as a WWW information provider are split into two types: bandwidth usage over the Internet in general, and local loop service to the bandwidth provider.

Internet Service Providers (ISPs)

Although the Internet is a collection of interconnected networks that no single company owns, the main backbones of bandwidth are owned by a number of larger providers. These providers in turn sell access to their backbones to smaller providers, who in turn resell the bandwidth again. The whole food chain of bandwidth is based on the principle that not all users use all their bandwidth at once. The policy of oversubscribing bandwidth is similar to an airline overbooking flights. As a result, a number of minor lags can develop in networks, although because communications are so slow at the local link level (limited to modem speed), clients are not truly affected.

Internet access providers are divided into the following two main types:

　❀　Dedicated Internet access providers

　❀　Commercial network services that provide a platform for access to the Internet

The difference between the two is that dedicated Internet providers provide your site with a direct link to the Internet, whereas commercial network services provide a home for your home page, site, or server.

Note

Although commercial networks such as America Online, CompuServe, and others provide an alternative for client access to the Internet, they do not provide the access required for WWW site development. Therefore, "commercial providers" in this chapter refers to the Internet Service Providers that provide commercial services such as home page/site hosting along with design, markup, and promotional services.

Dedicated Internet Service Providers

Internet Service Providers (ISPs) that provide dedicated Internet access come in many different sizes and types. The types of access are discussed in more detail in Chapters 4 through 10. The key to choosing a provider is to identify the types of service providers that can accommodate dedicated connections, and some issues that influence the quality of the service provided. ISPs can be divided into the following two main designations:

⊛ Local providers

⊛ Regional or national providers

Local Providers

Local providers provide access to a variety of clients in a relatively local area. In general, local providers gain network access from larger regional or national providers. Because local ISPs resell bandwidth acquired from national providers, their price-to-bandwidth ratio is likely to be higher that that of the national providers. In theory, the use of a local provider should always be rejected. In practice, however, local service providers can fulfill the valuable role of providing technical expertise in your WWW site. Depending on the ISP you choose, the service might include the provision of routers, installation, and other technical services. These services might cost you more than just purchasing bandwidth, but if your organization does not have the technical expertise required to set up the site, then the cost may be worthwhile. Again, the extra level of bureaucracy of a local provider is costly, but the smaller size and personal attention can be beneficial.

A Note from the Author

In our first year of having a WWW site, Global Village Consulting used a small local provider (at a slightly higher rate than the rates offered by larger providers). At this point we had chosen to locate our site on rented server space, but the principle of choosing a smaller provider remains the same. Although bandwidth issues occasionally were a problem (due to a high level of overbooking), the provider was very flexible in handling our account. The service provider allowed us access to CGI-bin directories, to install software on the server, and helped with some of the technical aspects of our site. As a result, our company learned a number of useful lessons, including how servers and custom software can interact. We recently moved our site to our own server in a server park, and we hope that the knowledge we learned serves us well in the future. For more information on server parks, refer to Chapter 2.

Regional or National Providers

With the recent increase in Internet popularity due in large part to the WWW, the market for bandwidth has become more competitive as larger companies acquire or create regional or national service providers. The market for national service provision currently is dominated by the backbone companies and other large corporations. In the case of the backbone companies, or infrastructure maintainers (Sprint, MCI, ANS, and so on) access is provided through commercial companies that have spun off the parent (Sprintlink and so on).

Although these national infrastructure providers also sell bandwidth, the account size required is very large. Because few companies need full T1 or T3 access, there is little demand for these providers. Also, smaller accounts have less influence with larger national providers because they contribute little to the profit of the larger companies (any single account is unimportant to the larger provider because it manages so many). As a result, even though using a large national provider eliminates the extra layer of bureaucracy and (possibly) cost of a local provider, you can lose some of the personal touch and fringe benefits available from a smaller ISP.

Commercial Providers

Commercial providers are companies that provide commercial services for WWW sites in addition to providing the simple pipe to the site. Instead of only selling bandwidth to a client, the provider provides one of two types of services:

✺ Housing services

✺ Parking services

Housing Services

Generally speaking, the provision of housing services is better suited for a smaller WWW site of an enterprise that does not require strong control over their site. The service can be as simple as a place to have a home page (technically can be a small site of a couple of pages), or as complex as a full-blown site including scripts and online databases. The key to a good housing service consists of the following:

✺ Site Access

✺ Technical Support

Because your site is part of the active WWW server run by the service provider, your site access is limited to what the provider allows. Generally, scripts have to be approved by the systems administrator prior to installation, and changes to HTML also might have to be performed by the service provider's HTML staff.

Tip

Because the rules for access can vary, shop around to find the provider that best suits your needs. A service provider should be willing to allow you unlimited shell access to your files (in a private directory). Do not accept a limited number of changes to your files per period, because you could end up paying hidden markup charges. Try to find a provider that allows you to choose your own HTML authors, or even perform the markup yourself.

The provider should be willing to set up a virtual CGI-bin directory for your organization. The presence of this directory simplifies the task of adding and removing scripts for your site. If the service provider is unwilling to provide CGI-bin access, then it should institute a standard method of script checking that enables you to know exactly when your script is installed. The existence of such a procedure ensures that both groups know their obligations, and enables you to better schedule necessary changes to your site.

Even though having access to your site enables you to perform your own maintenance and upgrades, the service provider also should be able to provide you with technical services. If a provider is unable to supply CGI-bin, markup, and backup services then reconsider your choice. Most of these services are required by the provider to maintain its site, and although fees for such services can be expected, failure to provide the services should concern most managers. Lack of technical support may indicate a lack of trained personnel and, therefore, available backup resources in the event of a network crisis.

Parking Services

Parking services simply refers to allowing the placement of your server (generally one host) on the local area network (LAN) of the ISP. After it is configured properly, the host will be accessible from throughout the Internet. The LAN connection should be high speed (at least Ethernet speeds), and your server configuration and uses should be determined by you. The three main issues with a server park are:

❀ Access to the physical server

❀ Dial-up or dedicated access to the server for maintenance

❀ Bandwidth charges

Any server park agreement should contain some provision for site access to your server. In general, access during normal business hours should be free and unrestricted. The caveat is that limiting access to simply the maintenance of the server is understandable—organizations should not expect an office with their server park. During off hours and weekends, emergency access should be available. Such access undoubtedly is limited in scope and a number of providers charge a time-based fee. Use the privilege sparingly, or your welcome will be worn out.

Although physical access sometimes is necessary, you can perform most work on a server remotely using a telnet or rlogin service (see Chapter 3 for more information about rlogin security). To accomplish this, a server park must provide you with one of the two following access methods:

⚛ Dial-up

⚛ Dedicated modem link

The charge for a dial-up link should be included in your server park fees because it limits the amount of physical tinkering you have to do on the server. Dedicated link fees should be limited to the telephone company line and the bandwidth you use over the link. The company already charges you for bandwidth used by your server (see below and Chapter 12, "Server Park: Cost Effective High Bandwidth Access?"), therefore the dedicated connection bandwidth can be routed through your server for the cost of the local loop.

The bandwidth your server uses depends on the type of site you have; however, you should at least be provided with a flat amount of bandwidth per month, with clearly defined prices for extra bandwidth. The fees charged should be no higher than those fees charged for WWW housing services. Also ask to see the rates charged by your ISP's bandwidth provider. If the profit margin on the fees you pay is too high (more than 50 percent), either switch providers or renegotiate the deal. Service providers that are unwilling to provide these figures should be avoided. If the provider has flat fees for bandwidth, ask how the current fees were determined. If the provider refuses or the calculations are not convincing, move. The provider is the single most important link for your site, and if trust cannot be established, then the relationship will fail.

Telephone Companies and the Local Loop

After you arrange for service provision in terms of bandwidth access, you must still look to your local telephone company for the local loop between you and your ISP. Whereas the telcos also can provide bandwidth, your ISP cannot provide you with the local loop (unless you happen to have an office next door). The type of loop you require depends on the type and size of service you are using. The main types are local lines, ISDN lines, and dedicated switched services.

Local Lines

At a bare minimum, your local telephone company provides any telephone lines you need for your service. The lines can be for simple dial-up access to a server in a server park, or for a dedicated SLIP or PPP connection. In either case, the service is limited to 28.8 Kbps because of modem technology. Due to the slow speed of such modem connections, the usefulness for basic line services is minimal.

Warning

Consider the possibility that your telephone company does not allow dedicated use of regular telephone services. As a result, the company could dump your line periodically. For a management circuit between your office and a server park, this would not cause a big problem; but if your line is your WWW site's only connection to the Internet, any interruption is devastating. To avoid situations like this, refer to some of the strategies mentioned in Chapter 4, "SLIP and PPP."

ISDN Services

Integrated Services Digital Network, or ISDN, provides a more robust method of closing the local loop between you and your service provider. As Chapter 6, "Integrated Services Digital Network (ISDN) Connection" discusses, the ISDN service generally consists of two 64 Kbps data channels and one 16 Kbps control channel. As a result, ISDN can provide you with a larger local loop pipe down which to send your data. Again, be careful about the "camping" policies of the telephone company (camping is the telephone company term for using a line as a dedicated circuit when it is not licensed for such use).

Switched Services

Although ISDN provides an alternative method for providing the local loop, the tried and tested method is to lease a switched circuit from the local telephone company. The simple explanation is that the telephone company provides the requisite number of switched pairs of copper wire to equal your bandwidth needs (each pair can carry 64 Kbps fully duplexed). Because these circuits are dedicated to your organization, the telephone company expects (and allows) full utilization. The drawback to switched circuits is that their installation and monthly charges can be expensive.

Future Internet Connectivity Options

Current methods of obtaining bandwidth and local loops depend on the telephone companies and ISPs (ultimately the network or national backbone companies), however a couple of trends look promising for future provision. One is a general technological infrastructure upgrading occurring through the introduction of optical cabling at the local loop level. As well, the introduction of Internet services by satellite and cable companies could lead to savings on Internet access.

Optical Cabling

As long as the communications infrastructure of an area is based on older copper lines, the costs of Internet access include a fairly large local loop charge. As more telephone companies and cable companies (see the next section, "Satellite Internet Access") begin installing optical cabling into developments, the cost for high bandwidth access will fall. The falling costs will result from an infrastructure capable of carrying the higher bandwidth without an increase in the number of lines required.

Whereas copper lines can carry 64 Kbps per pair using existing technology (see Chapter 8, "Frame Relay," for an example of a technology to extend this figure), optical cables can carry an unknown quantity. According to Nicholas Negroponte in *Being Digital*, we literally do not know how many bits per second we can send down a fiber. Recent research results indicate that we are close to being able to deliver 1,000 billion bits per second. This means that a fiber the size of a human hair can deliver every issue of the *Wall Street Journal* in less than one second—roughly two thousand times faster than the theoretical maximum of twisted pair (Nicholas Negroponte, *Being Digital,* Alfred A. Knopf, New York, 1995, p. 23).

Also, optical cabling has recently become cheaper to install and maintain than traditional copper wires. As a result, the telephone and cable companies are moving to replace aging infrastructure with optical cabling. As the infrastructure is upgraded, so will be the ability to transmit data from a local loop to an ISP. If anything, bandwidth costs will fall rather than climb. The question is when—the near complete replacement of the infrastructure could take as long as 20 years.

Satellite Internet Access

Satellite technology is just beginning to move into Internet provision, however most consumers are familiar with the concept of satellite TV. In fact, the smaller mini-satellite disks for satellite TV are basically the same ones used for satellite Internet. As Chapter 10, "Cable and Satellite: User Connectivity?" details, the satellite Internet has some major problems as a connectivity solution for WWW sites, but the service might be useful in certain circumstances.

Cable Modem Internet Access

Cable modem connections are covered in greater detail in Chapter 10. They deserve a brief mention here as a technology that has great potential for future expansion. Other than the telephone companies, the cable modem companies and broadcasters have one of the few infrastructures capable of providing high levels of throughput for data transmissions. The current infrastructure can carry approximately 500 Kbps fully duplexed.

The problem with cable access lies with the switching technology currently in place. As a result of the historical uses of switches in broadcasting, the switches in place are one way, making the upstream bandwidth much smaller than the downstream bandwidth. The cable companies aim to upgrade the switching infrastructure, and in the near future, the changes might result in a viable option for Internet local loop and bandwidth services.

Summary

Now that you have some idea of the bandwidth requirements of your WWW site, and the various bandwidth factors influencing your bandwidth choices, you are in a better position to assess your WWW needs. After deciding that some level of connectivity is required, the next issue is how to obtain this connectivity. The next chapter discusses this by presenting three types of connectivity: rented space, leased connections, and server parks.

Checklist

The following are concerns that should be addressed at the conclusion of the chapter.

- ☑ Need for WWW site?

- ☑ Reasons:

  promotion

  information distribution for cost savings

  public service

- ☑ Internal Network needs access to Internet?

- ☑ What type of data will you need on WWW site?

  text

  graphics

  time-based multimedia

- ☑ How often will the information change (times per year)?

- ☑ Will your site maintain historical data?

  how many revisions kept

- ☑ What type of clients do you expect?

  professional

  "surfers"

Initial Discussions: Renting versus Leasing, or Cohabit?

Given the discussion in Chapter 1 regarding the whys, hows, and whos of connectivity, this chapter further develops a framework for evaluating the various connectivity options. Naturally, you must examine a number of criteria to determine the most effective connection method for your WWW site. The decision of whether your site should be connected through rented space, leased bandwidth, or a parked server is determined by your requirements, the costs involved in each method, and the potential limitations of each connectivity option.

After reading this chapter, you should be able to determine the general level of connectivity your site requires (rent, lease, or co-habit). Future chapters examine these options in technical detail to provide you with the technical background to select your Internet Service Provider (ISP), hardware, and personnel.

Renting WWW Server Space

Renting space on an existing WWW server is in many ways the technically simplest of the connectivity options. You do not have to worry about hardware setup or maintenance, and your level of expertise can be limited to HTML and Internet navigation. Even so, renting server space is not necessarily the best solution for all sites. To illustrate this fact, this section examines the following issues:

❀ The requirements for renting WWW space

❀ The costs involved with renting

❀ The potential difficulties of renting server space

Determining Requirements

In general, the process of determining your WWW site requirements depends on the preferred type of connection method. If you are considering renting space on a WWW server, for instance, you have to be concerned about the amount of storage space that will be available to you (after all, you cannot just add a drive). As well, all connection methods depend on the amount of bandwidth you need: not the amount of bandwidth you will necessarily use, but the minimum bandwidth that your provider should have available to ensure a sufficiently fast download time. (See this chapter's later section on leased bandwidth for formulas to determine bandwidth usage.) Finally, you must decide what level of connectivity your office requires, and if connectivity is necessary at all.

Space Needed

The issue of WWW server storage space requirements is determined by the amount of information that will be stored on the server at any one time. This amount is not just that of your initial site, but should include some room for enhancements and growth. Because disk storage is relatively inexpensive for your service provider, the amount of space you require should not heavily affect your costs.

Use the following formula to determine the appropriate additional disk storage needed for your site, to minimize costs while providing you with some degree of flexibility:

$i + k + (i+k)g - b$ = total space required

where

i = initial site size in MBs

k = known enhancements to site in MBs

g = growth factor

b = basic WWW space

In this equation, the formula adds all the known factors (site size, enhancements to site, and basic space available for the WWW account) and then adds in a site growth factor. The ratio of growth you expect over the next contract period depends on the type of site you have developed. If your site will maintain continual historical data for the entire year, your site will grow rapidly. If the site is a simple company profile page, then growth may be limited to 10 to 20 percent.

A Note from the Author

An example of a site that Global Village Consulting developed as rented space is our original company site. Because we had clients who purchased space from us along with their WWW markup, we had a significant initial space requirement. We realized that the site would grow because of our largest client's growth (doubling in the first year) and because of our company's increased clientele. As a result, we chose a growth factor of 200 percent. This figure allowed our largest client to double (which took up approximately 75 percent of the initial site), provided room for our development site (where we test our technological advancements), and allowed us to sign on future clients without re-negotiating our rental agreement.

Bandwidth Needed

Not only must you consider the amount of WWW space you need, but you must also decide what level of connectivity (bandwidth) your provider must have available to provide your clients with reasonable download speeds. The two main issues in determining the required bandwidth are

❋ The amount of overbooking in which the provider has engaged

❋ The average size of the data your site is providing

Bandwidth Overbooking

Most ISPs provide bandwidth at a price equal to the cost recovery, and oversubscribe the amount of bandwidth available in order to make a profit. The subscriber might have enough bandwidth to support 40 dialup lines at 28.8Kbps. Normally, you would expect that the provider would have more bandwidth to cover the access requests from the rest of the world for the information on your WWW site. This is not necessarily the case.

The provider acts on the assumption that the 40 dialup lines will not necessarily be fully utilized at any one moment in time. This could mean

❋ Not all are in use

❋ Not all are requesting data from outside the local network

❋ Not all are actively receiving the requested information at an instant in time

The ability to hedge their bandwidth bets enables providers to resell bandwidth and still make a profit.

Given that all providers oversubscribe their bandwidth, you should still ask for an explanation of the amount of bandwidth used and the sources of use. Compare the use information to the amount of bandwidth the provider leases. Comparison should be made at specific high watermark periods during the day (business hours and late evening). If the amount of use is near or at the maximum throughput available through the leased bandwidth, then you should demand an explanation of how the provider plans to accommodate your extra traffic. The closer to the maximum throughput a provider is, the greater the possibility that a client will experience a delay.

Figure 2.1

A look at the bandwidth chain.

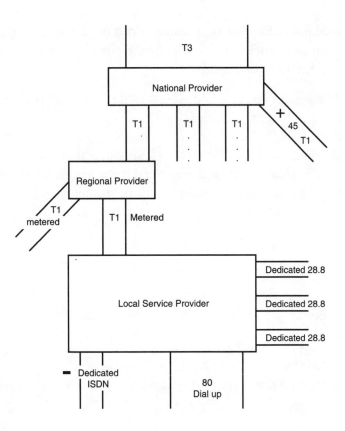

Average Data Size

Although the availability of bandwidth is important, the actual impact of low bandwidth on your clients' performance depends on the size of data you are providing. If the average size of data provided by your WWW site is small (for example, your site is a collection of small documents hyperlinked together), then the impact of lower bandwidth availability lessens. On the other hand, if your data consists of large pieces of data that are self-contained (cannot be used until the entire download is completed), then the lower bandwidth has a greater impact on the performance your clients experience.

Imagine a site that is an Internet version of this book. The site can be implemented in at least two methods. In the first method, the book is broken down into individual documents that correspond to the pages of a book. The text is marked up in HTML, the pages are loaded one by one, and at the bottom of each page a forward/back icon is added to enable reading of sequential pages. In the page method of this book, the download time the client has to wait is limited to a few seconds per page.

The second example is designed to limit the online time required to read the book. The entire book is designed as a *Portable Document Format* (PDF) document. To read any part of the book, the client has to download the entire file (likely a few MBs of data). If the connectivity of your site is oversubscribed, the client can experience considerably noticeable delays. Although the cumulative delay in the first example may be greater than in the second example, the client would not notice the longer delay because of its periodic nature.

Tip

The example of the online version of this book illustrates the potential benefit of good design for WWW sites. To take the example a step further, the publisher would likely insulate the book site further from delays by designing the book as slightly larger chapter files. Most WWW browsers display the loaded text as it occurs. The client could then start reading the first part of a chapter while the rest of the chapter loads. As a result, the overall number of server accesses, and delays, is minimized.

Office Connectivity Needed

Even though your site resides on the service provider's server, you still may need connectivity to your office. To make any changes to your WWW site, for example, you need a direct line to the site. If you rely on the link for internal office Internet access, then you may consider obtaining greater connectivity than that provided by a dialup line (see this chapter's later section on leased bandwidth for formulas to determine bandwidth usage needs). Eventually, as your site grows, you may decide that time and costs justify moving to a different level of connectivity.

Determining Costs

Generally speaking, renting space on a WWW server can be cost-effective. Unfortunately, the range of prices is astounding. Although any number of geographical differences exist, the following section outlines some common charges for renting WWW space. Some providers only charge a flat rate instead of charging by service requirements. Although this flat rate may be beneficial for budgeting for your WWW site, you might pay higher charges for services that are unnecessary for your site. Specifically, site costs are based on the following items:

- Setup fees

- Monthly storage

- Bandwidth use charges

- Service "extras"

- Local loop charges

Charges for Setup

In most cases, charges for WWW site setup should not be tolerated. The notable exceptions to this rule are charges for setting up a virtual domain (such as www.your_org.com) and any programming and markup. The fee for domain registration with InterNIC ($100 U.S. for a two-year registration) and setup for the virtual domain should be no more than a few hundred dollars. As for programming and markup services, the rates vary between $15 per hour to $150 per hour. In general, a set of high-quality services are available in the $60 to $80 per-hour range.

In any case, programming and HTML services should be optional for your site setup. You should be permitted to choose your own personnel or perform the task yourself. Any programs and scripts have to be checked by the systems administrator, but other than this restriction, the provider should be reasonable.

Monthly Fees for Space

In general, charges for storage space are included in the flat fees of most WWW space rentals. Only after the size you are consuming progresses to a critical mass do most providers consider selling you additional space. With that said, the option of purchasing bulk storage is generally cheaper than paying for storage rental on a per page basis. As a basic metric, some providers are willing to provide bulk space for as low as $75 for 100 MB up to $100 for 5 MB. The difference in cost is generally due to the inclusion or exclusion of bandwidth charges, and the extras provided by the service provider.

Paying for Bandwidth Usage

Bandwidth used by smaller rental sites is generally included in a flat fee. For larger sites whose throughput is much higher, service providers charge a basic fee that includes only small throughput, and charge rates based on the throughput costs they pay. Some ISPs provide bandwidth only up to a certain level (for example, the first 100 MB of throughput is included), and then charge fees for each additional MB of throughput.

A number of providers have a wide variety of bandwidth charges; in general, the rate varies between $2 and $25 per 100 MB. The method service providers employ to determine these figures is somewhat magical; a simple division of T1 charges by throughput available over a one-month period reveals a much lower rate:

1.5 MB/sec × 60 sec × 60 min × 24 hrs × 30 days ~ 3,800 GB

3,800 GB per month / $3,000 per month ~ $1 per GB

This rate does not include the cost of technical support for the connection and hardware acquisition; however, the current rate of $2 to $25 seems higher than necessary. The discrepancy may be attributed to cross-subsidization for dialup accounts (which rarely have bandwidth charges) and added levels of bureaucracy for smaller local providers. The general level for throughput averages between $50 and $100 per GB. Charges that are more expensive should be questioned.

A Note from the Author

I have personally experienced the variance of bandwidth charges. In our area, prices generally fall within the range mentioned in this section, but one provider quoted considerably higher rates. The higher rate would have increased our throughput charges $120 per month. As a result of our knowledge of the local market, Global Village Consulting was able to negotiate a lower rate with this particular provider, one more consistent with general market trends.

Occasionally, providers themselves do not know what the going rate is, and therefore do not offer proper prices. Shop around and request detailed quotations from a number of providers before choosing one. As the following section, "The Extras" details, price is not always the final determining factor for choosing a service provider, but it definitely plays an important role.

The Extras

One area that may distinguish one provider as being better than another is the quality of service in areas other than bandwidth. The benefits of each "extra" depend on your technical knowledge, though some basic extras always are necessary. The "basics" should include the following items:

- ❁ Shell access

- ❁ An online editor (for small updates)

- ❁ Access to a CGI-bin directory (either direct or indirect)

For services that provide a "complete" package, including updates (not a recommended course unless you truly do not work with UNIX), your account should include a minimum number of scripts and HTML updates each month (suggest at least one, preferably bankable) and a defined cost for additional services.

Tip

Another common extra that service providers include in quotations for WWW site rentals is the placement of your site in a virtual mall. The selling point of virtual malls is that they have a large presence on the Internet in general, and by being a part of the mall, your site receives more exposure and traffic. Asking questions about the number of search engines with which the mall is registered, the monthly traffic, and other promotional activities taken by the mall will give you a better idea of whether the charges are warranted. If you find the charges unwarranted, the provider should be willing to unbundle the service. If not, you should be willing to walk away.

Remember that each extra is likely to involve a hidden charge. Such hidden charges might not be high, but you should compare similar accounts when price shopping. Ask each provider for a quote on a specified set of services. Also, clearly state that you will not take into consideration additional services not requested when choosing a supplier. After all, if you have not identified a service as useful to your site, why should you pay for that service? Requests for Proposals also should include an estimate of the amount of space and bandwidth you need, and should request the various charges for additional space/bandwidth.

Local Loop Charges

As with any type of Internet connection, renting server space may require you to pay local loop charges. In general, the charges should be as simple as the account charge you pay the provider and the telephone access charge you pay your local telephone company. You probably do not need a dedicated connection; a standard telephone line/modem combination should be sufficient.

Tip

Any site that needs a continuous connection for a majority of the day should consider a dedicated line or server park instead of renting space.

Limitations of Renting WWW Space

Renting WWW space can offer some cost advantages. Several major drawbacks of renting WWW space must be addressed. The three main difficulties of renting a WWW site stem from the following items:

❋ The security concerns of the ISPs

❋ The charging policies of ISPs

❋ The remoteness of the site

Security and Control of Site Changes

Because your site runs under the HTTPd of the service provider's Internet server(s), any scripts your site calls are implemented by the provider's WWW server, and any security holes in your work become security holes in the provider's security plan. As a result, most providers are reluctant to offer free and open access to CGI-bin directories or to allow the installation of software for your site. This reluctance is understandable, but flexible providers are willing to work with your staff to solve the problems. Generally, the provider needs to view the source code of programs and scripts, and may require non-root executables. Service providers likely have automatic kill functions that react when a program executes improperly due to bad programming or malicious misuse.

Tip

Remember that all the hurdles you are required to cross to enhance your site exist for your protection as well. A badly designed program with memory leaks can bring even the most powerful server to its knees. (Ah, the joy of swapping!) If a provider is not concerned about your scripts/ programs, then you should be. With no restraint on your actions, what restraint limits other clients' actions?

Budgeting Predictability

A major concern on the business end of a WWW site is the cost. With the pricing mechanisms currently in place, the price of budget stability is high. Site managers can either accept the unknowns of bandwidth payments, or agree to a flat fee that may provide more throughput than needed. Companies requiring that site costs are below a firm ceiling price can benefit from the flat fee approach. Take care to ensure that the flat fee for bandwidth does not include services your site does not use. For sites willing to accept some budget risks, generally prepurchasing larger bandwidth blocks can be cost-effective, as can spreading the average bandwidth over longer periods.

Lack of Internal Benefits

The final limitation of renting WWW space that this section addresses is the lack of spin-off benefits for internal operations. Generally, the link to the WWW site is a simple dialup SLIP or PPP link that does not enable your office to easily set up internal LAN access to e-mail, WWW, and other Internet services. These services are difficult, if not impossible, to set up without further costs. Access accounts generally provide only one e-mail account, with additional accounts available only for a fee. Network routing and multiplexing SLIP or PPP access over a dynamic link are even more difficult technical challenges with respect to both setup and use. Finally, providers do not usually allow more than one concurrent login through dialup ports on one account, because multiple logins limit the availability of ports for other paying customers.

Leasing Bandwidth

Renting WWW space on a provider's server is the best course of action for certain sites and situations; however, the benefits in accessibility and cost can make a dedicated access link more attractive. While there are many different methods through which dedicated access can be achieved, some basic issues determine the level (if any) and means of connection. (The various connectivity technologies are discussed in detail in Chapters 4 through 10.) Again, the issues are determined by your site requirements in terms of the following items:

- ❀ Bandwidth use

- ❀ Multihoming/redundancy

- ❀ Costs of service

- ❀ Potential limitations of the connectivity methods

Determining Requirements

One of the most difficult issues in determining your WWW site requirements is the question of a dedicated link versus renting space serviced by a dedicated link (such as space rental and server parks). As a general rule, the choice to provide a dedicated link for your WWW site depends more on your need for internal access and control than your need for bandwidth. After you establish the necessity of a dedicated connection, the questions of bandwidth requirements, upgrading, and redundancy all become issues.

To Dedicate or To Not Dedicate

Given the possibility of using a server park or rented space to provide the world access to your WWW site, the issue of a dedicated connection generally is resolved by issues other than bandwidth. Commercial providers of space and server parks can usually meet or beat any cost-per-bandwidth-unit metric that a dedicated connection provider can. The reasons to acquire a dedicated link then can be resolved into two:

- ❀ Spin-off benefits

- ❀ Control issues

Spin-Off Benefits

One of the most persuasive reasons to move to a dedicated connection for a WWW site are the benefits that such a connection can provide for an internal network. Advantages such as universal LAN access to Internet services and personalized e-mail access are key to most decisions to acquire a dedicated line.

The capability to exchange files and information seamlessly with other branches and organizations provides the impulse for many other companies. Whatever WAN communications your company requires, the implementation of such services at a LAN-wide level are easier with a dedicated link.

Given the small nature of many WWW sites, the capability to use the link for cost recovery (e-mail versus fax is one great method; file transfer versus disk couriers another) makes the WWW site affordable. Even so, the issue of setting up a dedicated link is a fairly major one, because the link is technically challenging and could prove to be a security risk.

The way cost recovery through a dedicated link works can be illustrated by the hypothetical scenario of a small computer consulting firm with a small WWW site. Because the computer consulting company needs to communicate with a number of clients worldwide, the staff (six) all need access to Internet e-mail. As well, the development staff (four) regularly needs access to Internet-based discussions and developer tool sites (WWW and FTP). Normally, the access required for each staff member is $210 per month. The cost for renting space for the company's WWW site (mainly a company promotional site) equals $120 per month. The company also has to provide a network modem, which is costly, or lines for each staff member. Because at any one time at least two staff members need access, the company has to provide at least two dial-out ports (two telco lines at $60 each). The total for the rented space scenario is $450 per month.

Now consider the following alternative. The computer consulting company brings in an ISDN connection and dedicated Internet access of 128Kbps. The local loop costs $120 per month, and the bandwidth costs are $400 per month. The total cost is $520 per month, slightly higher than the previous scenario. Although complete cost recovery is not achieved, the benefits of internal access do provide a significant degree of recovery. Further recovery may be achieved through access control, by which the dedicated link is more cost-effective than the rental scenario.

The preceding example does not take into consideration the extra management time required for servers or the security risks of a dedicated link, the scenario illustrates the process of determining whether a dedicated link is a cost-effective solution due to spin-off benefits.

Control Issues of a Dedicated Link

The spin-off benefits of a dedicated link can provide cost recovery for some WWW sites. The increased access (or ease of access) to the WWW server the dedicated link provides also can justify the increased costs. An examination of the access process (using the example from the previous section) illustrates the benefit of the dedicated connection.

At first glance, the dedicated scenario appears weaker than dialup accounts with rented WWW space. You must, however, consider the hidden costs of rented space, such as access to your WWW site. Access is difficult and time-consuming over a 28.8Kbps dialup link. The dedicated connection provides quick, hassle-free access via the local network. Second, programmers occasionally need to access the Internet simultaneously. In the rental solution, access is impossible or slow (if line sharing is available). With the dedicated solution, the entire office can access the Internet at the same time with little delay.

Formulas for Bandwidth Use

After deciding to acquire a dedicated connection, the next task is to determine how much bandwidth is sufficient. This problem is complex, but the following formula provides a general idea of the amount of bandwidth used in any one time period:

$$wo + wi + eo + ei + is + ms - ch = tb$$

where

wo = WWW output (information sent to external requests)

wi = WWW input (information retrieved for internal requests)

eo = e-mail out

ei = e-mail in

is = Internet services (news, telnet, ftp, audio and video, and so on)

ms = management services (DNS, routing information, and so on) *ch* = caching (via WWW browsers or servers, or a local news server)

tb = total bandwidth

The bandwidth usage for the small computer consulting firm example is as follows:

6 staff @ 20 e-mail in per day = 120 e-mail messages

6 staff @ 10 e-mail out per day = 60 e-mail messages

4 development staff with WWW access = 6 MB access per day

2 support staff with WWW access = 2 MB access per day

Complete Usenet feed = 60 MB

Telnet sessions to clients = 500 KB per day

FTP of files to/from clients = 1.5 MB per day

FTP files for demos/bug fixes = 4 MB per day

Management services = 20 bytes/datagram $\times$ ~370,000 datagrams

Accesses to WWW site per day = 75

Total size of WWW site = 3.2 MB

Average Amount of WWW site viewed = 40%

Caching = little other than Usenet news feeds—each person works in a separate development area

Therefore, the total bandwidth used in one day is:

wo = 75 $\times$ 3.2 MB $\times$ .4 = 96 MB

wi = 6 MB + 2 MB = 8 MB

eo = 60 $\times$ 8 KB ~ .5 MB

ei = 120 $\times$ 8 KB ~ 1 MB

$is = 60 + .5 + 1.5 + 4 = 66$ MB

$ms = 20 * {\sim}370{,}000 \sim 7$ MB

$ch = $ NA

$tb = 178.5$ MB

Bandwidth via a 28.8 connection per day is, therefore:

28,800 bps×60s/min×60min/hr.×24hrs. = 2,488,320,000 bits

2,488,320,000/8 bits/B×1,024 B/KB*1,024 KB/MB ~ 296 MB per day

At first glance, a 28.8 dedicated connection seems sufficient for the consulting firm. Unfortunately, the actual usable bandwidth for staff activities is much lower:

296 MB × (7.5/24) = 92.5 MB per work day

The lower amount of bandwidth is due to the limited number of work hours per day. All activity based on human access in the office and the local area generally takes place in a 7.5-hour period. As a result, the total bandwidth used during each business day is better estimated as follows:

$wo = 75 \times 3.2$ MB $\times .4 \times .7 \sim 67$ MB

$wi = 6$ MB $+ 2$ MB $= 8$ MB

$eo = 60 \times 8$ KB $\sim .5$ MB

$ei = 120 \times 8$ KB ~ 1 MB

$is = .5 + 1.5 + 4 = 6$ MB

$ms = 20 \times {\sim}160{,}000 \sim 3$ MB

$ch = $ NA

$tb = 85.5$ MB

In the revised usage table, the amount of WWW output is reduced by 30 percent to account for after-hours accesses, and the Internet services value is reduced by the entire Usenet feed. Because the feed can take place at one time during off-peak hours, the amount need not be included in the daytime bandwidth usage. Consequently, the management services overhead is reduced due to the lower number of datagrams required to handle the information.

In this example, the total utilization is 85.5 MB/92.5 MB or ~92 percent. This level of utilization probably is sustainable, although staff and clients will likely experience slow-downs during peak periods of the day (8:00 to 9:30 a.m. and 1:00 to 2:30 p.m.). The actual degree of lag depends on the work habits of both your staff and clients.

When Should You Go to a Higher Bandwidth Level?

When to upgrade to a higher bandwidth level is a question that is very difficult to answer. You cannot rely on any solid percentage usage rules, but a few factors will influence your decision:

- Resources available for the link

- Dependency of your staff on connectivity

- Role your WWW site plays in company revenue generation

- Patience of your WWW clients

Obviously most of these factors depend on a subjective evaluation on your part. One fact to remember is that the amount of lag time does not linearly increase as you approach 100-percent utilization. Because the probability of a scheduling conflict increases as you approach maximum utilization, performance drops drastically over the last portion of utilization. Exactly where the drop occurs depends on your usage patterns.

If your staff relies on connectivity to perform valuable work for your organization, remember that wasted staff time is wasted money. A faster link may enable you to save money through greater staff productivity. If the site is a public service (free of charge), most WWW clients are patient with small lags. If the site is commercial and the main source of revenue, lags of any kind are unacceptable.

Finally, the amount of resources available may determine the amount of bandwidth. If you can afford only a 28.8Kbps connection, then 28.8Kbps will have to do. If the site needs more bandwidth, find a way to scale down the site, increase available funds, or perhaps reexamine the rental versus leased bandwidth debate.

Multihoming and Redundancy

One final issue that the leased-line solution brings forward is bandwidth redundancy and multihoming. In simple terms, *multihoming* is the provision of multiple network connections for one site. The theory is if one access point goes down, the other link(s) will provide the necessary connectivity while the down link is repaired. The main questions with this approach are whether redundancy works, and to what level your bandwidth should be mirrored.

Does Redundancy Work?

Theoretically, multihoming and demultiplexing IP datagrams over two separate network connections is supported by the specification. Nonetheless, two main problems can arise in practice

- ⚛ Implementations fail to support features

- ⚛ Redundant connections fail redundancy tests further up the bandwidth chain

Failure to support the multiplexing feature is mainly theoretical because of the general desirability of such features in routers. As a result, as long as a router has more than one network interface (other than the local connector), the router generally supports demultiplexing of some sort.

To illustrate the second potential problem whereby redundant connections fail redundancy tests, consider the following example: A WWW site acquires connectivity from two ISPs (A and B). The links are equal in size to avoid the difficulties that result from relying on any one link. Unfortunately, a problem occurs because both local ISPs obtain their bandwidth from regional provider Y. As a result, your site is vulnerable to a complete outage of connectivity if the external connection(s) of the regional provider fail (see fig. 2.2).

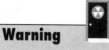

Warning

Remember, your connectivity is only as good as the weakest link in the bandwidth food chain!

Figure 2.2

Redundancy flaws in network connectivity.

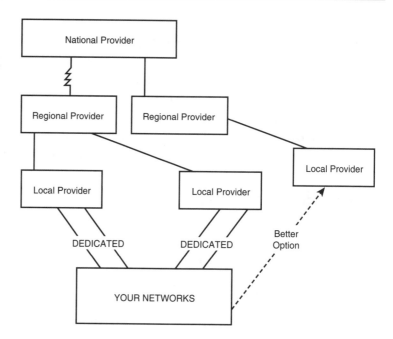

How Much Is Sufficient Redundancy?

If your connection consists of only one 28.8Kbps line, redundancy will cost you at least twice as much as a standard link. Because any of your links could theoretically fail, any redundant links should be the same size to avoid reliance on any one link. The amount of redundancy that is sufficient depends on the critical nature of your work. If a complete loss of connectivity would cost you a million dollars a day, then obviously the issue is moot: redundancy should be as high as physically possible (the limit being the number of independent providers in your area). For most sites, a brief loss of connectivity is not critical. In this case, the redundant connectivity can be more limited. Because usage is funneled over the remaining redundant links in the event of a failure, the greater the number of links, the less degradation of service results from the failure of any one link.

Consider the following connectivity example for a multihomed connection equivalent to a T1 (1.5 Mbps). The site's router is connected to 12 ISDN basic channels (128Kbps per channel) to two different service providers (that have 12 different regional providers). The internal network is connected to the router by a 10Mbps Ethernet connection. The router takes information from the internal network and multiplexes the data onto the Ethernet connection. The router demultiplexes the same information from the Ethernet port and allocates the datagrams equally to the 12 network ISDN connections. The IP datagrams may take different routes, but they all reach the correct destination(s). Should one ISDN connection fail (or become overloaded from outside data flowing in), the router reallocates the datagrams to the other 11 connections.

This type of solution does have a price. Regarding this connectivity example, not only is it unlikely that 12 completely independent ISPs exist in one area, but the total cost for 12 ISDN access channels is likely to be greater than the cost of one T1 digital trunk connection.

Costs for Leasing Bandwidth

Of all the costs of your WWW site, the cost of a dedicated connection is the major factor in determining the appropriate level of connectivity. Four main factors determine the overall cost of the dedicated connection

- ❀ Local loop charges
- ❀ Bandwidth charges
- ❀ Hardware costs
- ❀ Technical support costs

Local Loop Connection

Local loop connectivity is the connection between your site and the local ISP point of presence. The method of connectivity depends on the level required. For low levels of connectivity via modems, the local loop can be as simple as a local telephone line (usually requiring a data-quality line or a business line due to the high level of use that such a line must provide). For higher levels of connectivity, the local loop requires a digital connection of some sort. This connection can be either an ISDN line(s) or a leased digital circuit(s) (each circuit provides 56Kbps of bandwidth). In some cases, the cost of the connection is included in your ISP's bandwidth charges; otherwise, you are required to arrange service with your local telephone company.

Bandwidth Charges from ISP

Along with the charges for the local loop connection between you and the ISP, you are responsible for paying for the bandwidth designated for your connection. The bandwidth charges from your ISP are the costs to transmit your information across the major trunks. Actually, the cost is for the possibility of transmitting data across those trunks, because even the larger bandwidth reservations can include some oversubscription. Although prices can vary considerably depending on the amount of bandwidth allocated, in general they range from $300 for a 28.8 dedicated connection to $3,600 for a T1 connection (1.544 MB).

Hardware Purchases or Rentals?

Along with the monthly charges for local loop and bandwidth, users also must either buy the required hardware or lease or rent from the telephone company or service provider. For organizations that are technically proficient, the purchase route can provide cost benefits. On the other hand, most rentals and leases include some level of maintenance and support. Technical expertise is still needed to manage the connection, but at least hardware failures and problems of rented or leased hardware can be resolved by the provider.

Technical Support

Aside from hardware and access, the other main cost of a dedicated connection is the requirement for a systems administrator and possibly a network administrator. The skills needed include UNIX systems administration and a strong background in TCP/IP networking. At the same time, the personnel should have an understanding of the networking infrastructure used to obtain your connection. If the connection is via a leased T1 with a DSU/CSU, then your technical staff should be able to perform troubleshooting on the equipment. In the event that the equipment is provided by the ISP, then a service contract could eliminate the need for hardware-specific skills, although a general knowledge of the technology always is useful.

Potential Limitations

For any connectivity solution, a number of potential limitations might make a dedicated connection less beneficial in your particular situation. Issues you should carefully examine before deciding to pursue a dedicated connection include:

- Bandwidth utilization

- Technical requirements

- Limited bandwidth scenarios

- A decrease in security

As a result of these four factors, the dedicated connection may become either too expensive, difficult, slow, or insecure.

Full Bandwidth Payment for Off Periods

One of the first severe limitations of having a dedicated Internet connection is that the connection is dedicated to your use. As a result, the bandwidth in general cannot be oversubscribed to as great a level as with dialup consumers (after all, you are paying for X Kbps of throughput). You pay the majority of the connection's bandwidth costs even when you are not using any of the through-put.

Consider the computer consulting company used in the previous example. As a result of the usage patterns of their WWW site and internal staff, the company almost fully utilizes the bandwidth 7.5 hours per day, five days a week. On the other hand, for 16.5 hours a day, for five days plus weekends, the bandwidth is greatly underutilized. The underutilized bandwidth is paid for even when not used. If the company's needs exceed a 28.8 connection for office hours because of WWW access, then they would need even greater bandwidth but would incur even greater losses during off hours.

In a situation in which bandwidth usage takes place mainly during the day for certain services, with a better spread of bandwidth requirements for other services, then a two-fold approach might be a better course. If the computer consulting company were to move its WWW site to a server park (see the following section on server parks) with a 28.8 link to support the internal office, for example, its bandwidth needs might be met for less cost.

Technical Requirements

As the section on dedicated lines costs indicates, the technical requirements to manage a dedicated connection can be staggering. Even with the relatively simple solution of a 28.8Kbps link maintained by a hardware router, running the WWW server generally requires at least an understanding of UNIX systems administration (or some other stable operating environment such as Windows NT). Not only is the cost of external support costly, but the potential for service delays might not be acceptable to your site. As for an in-house administrator, the costs can only be justified if your company has a need outside of Internet connectivity, or is very big.

Note

Although numerous WWW servers and other services for non-UNIX-based operating systems exist, UNIX is the standard and base for most Internet servers. The reason for UNIX's high level of market penetration is two-fold. First, the Internet networking protocol TCP/IP also is the networking protocol of UNIX, meaning that all flavors of UNIX include with the operating system most, if not all, Internet services. The second reason for the dominance of UNIX is that most other operating systems do not provide the strong degree of memory protection and security provided under UNIX. Windows (3.x and 95) is neither stable nor secure enough to be trusted as an Internet server. The same is true for the Macintosh operating system.

As these other operating systems are upgraded and improved, the dominance of UNIX might fade, but for now UNIX remains the backbone of the Internet. (Even now a few brave souls are using both Windows 95 and Macintosh for Internet servers, but for mission-critical servers, I would not recommend taking the risk.)

Lower-Level Insufficient Bandwidth

Because your dedicated connection likely is the smallest connection available to meet your needs (due to costs), you are more likely to acquire only a fairly small connection. As a result, the amount of access the rest of the Internet has to your site will be limited. Your need for bandwidth might indicate that you can support a dedicated connection; however, other methods of connectivity might provide better Internet access to your site while meeting your internal needs.

A Note from the Author

Our computer consulting company could rent space on a commercial server that has T1 access to the Internet. At the same time, the company could obtain a dedicated 28.8 connection for internal access. As WWW site bandwidth usage increases, the office need not jump to 56Kbps access, because the WWW site has T1 access for Internet purposes. Instead of increasing costs and wasting greater evening bandwidth, the company is able to maintain stable costs and response times.

Security

If your site is connected via a dedicated connection, security becomes an important issue. (The issue of WWW server security is addressed in Chapter 3 in greater detail.) Under the space rental solution, most security issues are the responsibility of the provider. You need only maintain password security, and the internal network remains secure regardless. When you add a dedicated connection, the internal network's security becomes an issue. Now, no matter what precautions you take, the risk of a hacker breaking into your system is greater (except, of course, if your WWW server is completely isolated from the internal network, in which case you forfeit the benefit of internal WWW connectivity). In certain cases, the risks of access or the costs of preventing security breaches may be too high to justify a dedicated connection.

Parking a Server

As mentioned a couple of times prior to this section, space rental and dedicated connections are not the only options for connectivity. A third option is a server park. The concept behind a server park is that the tenants of the park pool their resources to gain the benefits of higher bandwidth (through cheaper bulk rates) and greater technology (uninterruptible power supplies, backups, and physical security are a few common examples). When evaluating the options of a server park for your server, determine your requirements for space, control, and physical access. With respect to costs, pay close attention to monthly fees, bandwidth charges, local connection charges, and physical access charges. Finally, consider the potential limitations of a server park, including controlling costs, physical access, and internal Internet access requirements.

Determining Requirements

Like any connectivity method, the server park option is beneficial only if you have certain requirements. If your site is only one small part of an entire internal network need for Internet access, a server park is not likely to provide an adequate level of connectivity because it provides Internet access to only one server rather than an entire network. If your site's needs greatly outweigh internal needs (if any exist), there is a question of whether a server park provides the best option. Examine the following issues prior to choosing the server park option:

※ Whether space on a commercial server will suffice for your needs

※ The level of control over scripting and programs you require

※ To what level you need to support a local access link

The Space versus Server Debate

Essentially, the deciding factor between participating in a server park and renting WWW space from a commercial server is the degree of complexity of your site. For any site, no matter how large or how popular, space rental can be as beneficial as space sharing, if not more so, depending on the level of control and complexity your provider allows. Practically speaking, the more complex the site, the less likely your provider is willing to offer server park service. Even in the event that the provider is willing, the costs may be prohibitive. Because server parks and rented space generally should be charged a similar bandwidth charge, the benefits of a server park only become apparent with respect to control and local access issues.

Control over Your WWW Scripting and Programs

The more the HTML specification evolves and supports additional functionality, including additional scripting and programming interfaces, the more robust WWW sites will become. Already, sites include complex databases and scripts for search functionality and greater information management. All of this functionality causes an increased need for access to CGI-bin directories, and increases the number of auxiliary programs you might want installed on a server. If your site includes (or you plan to include) a number of technological advancements, a server park may provide you with the necessary level of control.

Take, for example, the imaginary computer consulting firm. Suppose the company decides to run a search engine as a public service for its customers (access controlled by passwords) that searches identified software sites for the latest upgrades. Because of the popularity of this service, the company decides the increased bandwidth requirements require the presence of a T1 connection to the Internet. Because the company's internal needs do not justify the cost of a dedicated T1, the company considers the options of rented space, and a server in a server park.

With the rented space option, the company quickly discovers that the service providers in its area are cautious about allowing processes for rental customers to run on their servers. Because the search engine requires a significant amount of memory and processing to function, the providers intend to charge the company a price premium. As well, any modifications of the programs, as well as the initial installation, have to be performed by a programmer that works for the provider. The install bill alone could be as high as $1,500.

With the server park option, the company finds that the service provider is willing to provide the option for approximately the same rate as rented space would require. Because the company does not have to deal with the costs of installation and maintenance, the option has significant benefits. As well, the company can add future developments and increase the size of its site at no extra cost and without first clearing the procedures with the provider. As a result, the computer consulting company is better off with the server park solution.

A Note from the Author

Although the example of the server park decision on the basis of control issues might seem contrived, I assure you that a similar situation can, and in fact did, occur.

Our company originally rented space for our WWW site from a local provider. Because the site was a testing ground for some of our Internet-based technology, we required a fairly high level of access from the provider. At first, while our activities were confined simply to the use of scripts and HTML, the provider checked the scripts and then installed them for us. Unfortunately, as our technology progressed, we were confronted by the reality that the service provider was no longer willing to have our site located on its server at the current rate. The provider's change in attitude was due mainly to the amount of resources our technology testing required. As a result, the provider canceled access to certain tools and generally degraded the amount of control we had over our site.

In response to our situation, and to an increase in the need for internal office access to the Internet, our company examined the possibilities of a server park. Because the computer would be fully controlled by our partners, the issue of installing programs and testing technology was eliminated. As well, the cost of our dialup access and WWW space rental had increased to a level whereby the server park was only slightly more expensive. Due to the potential for a local dedicated link to our server at a low cost, we chose the server park option (see the following section "Local Access Requirements").

Local Access Requirements

Not every company requires access to the Internet for its internal network; however, a great many develop these needs as their WWW sites develop. Because a site needs to be maintained either in rented space or on a server in a server park, the need for access increases as your site grows. Although dialup access can provide access to sites, the dialup connection has a certain amount of time overhead for employees, and use is generally limited to one user at a time. A dedicated 28.8 connection generally costs $300 per month, but with the server park solution, another option is available.

Because your server is being charged for bandwidth used, most providers that offer a server park also allow you to connect a modem to your server to provide a link from the server to your office. The cost of the link is a telephone line at the provider's site; therefore, this type of dedicated link is an inexpensive method of gaining full internal access to the Internet. At the same time, your WWW site gains the benefit of T1 Internet access, and you do not have to pay for wasted bandwidth during off hours.

Costs

The costs associated with a server park solution are dependent on the variety of services that come bundled with your server park. The services could include server maintenance, UPS services, backups, or advertising. Whatever is included, the basic formula for costs is the aggregate of the monthly fees, bandwidth charges, local loop charges, and emergency access charges.

Monthly Parking Fees

Monthly server park fees vary according to the quality of connection and the amount of service provided along with the connection. In general, the bandwidth available to the server park should be a T1 connection at the minimum. Accepting anything less results in higher bandwidth charges. As well, the monthly fee should include a reasonable amount of bandwidth free of charges. Not only does the monthly bandwidth provide you a degree of security in cost control, but the bandwidth allocation helps your ISP manage the total amount of bandwidth required by its network.

As for services, at the very minimum, the provider should offer the support needed to attach your server to its LAN via its internal network (Ethernet or the equivalent). As well, you should be allowed access to your server, free of charge, during regular office hours. Other services you might want are switching of backup tapes and attachment to the local power supply (UPS). Charges for the monthly fee depend on configuration, but generally should be equal to or only slightly more than a 28.8 dedicated connection from the provider.

A Note from the Author

When looking for a local provider for our server park, we found a number of possibilities that varied greatly in price. All ISPs provided a minimum T1 bandwidth via Ethernet connection, and allowed access during office hours. The provider we chose also provided after-hours emergency access.

In our case, the bandwidth supplied for the monthly rental fee was the equivalent of the bandwidth we would use with a 28.8Kbps connection, and the final cost was only slightly higher than a dedicated connection of 28.8Kbps. On the plus side, we could access our site at a much higher speed, and our internal office had the same level of connectivity (actually, the response for the office was better because the WWW traffic was traveling over the same 28.8Kbps connection).

Bandwidth Fees

Due to the variable nature of WWW access to your site, bandwidth charges can become a serious financial burden. As a result, any server park arrangement should include the installation of a bandwidth tracking program on your server. Also, the provider should provide you with the necessary training to obtain a current month's total of bandwidth used. You also might ask that the provider notify you when you expend your monthly bandwidth allotment.

One of the key benefits (or at least key future benefit) of a server park is its capability to provide a relatively inexpensive low-speed dedicated link to your office. As a result, the monthly bandwidth included with the server park should include an amount equal to that used by a 28.8Kbps connection during working hours (approximately 1 GB). If you require less bandwidth, then you should reconsider your server park option completely. If your site and office uses so little bandwidth, perhaps you should rent space instead with a local dialup connection.

Local Loop Charges

As stated previously, most server park solutions require some level of local loop access for management purposes. Although you can gain the access through a standard dialup account, using your server to provide a dialup port is a more cost-effective method. At most, the cost of this solution is the price of a local line at the provider's site. As well, with some technical effort or hardware, the link can be made dedicated for no additional cost. In fact, many versions of UNIX support multiplexing over multiple serial connections (SLIP or PPP). Your internal office can have a virtual 56Kbps connection for the price of four telephone lines (two at each end).

Emergency Access Charges

Some service providers might hesitate to give you keys to their site; however, you should insist on some method of guaranteed access in the event of an emergency. If emergency access is included in the base price, so much the better. A fee for service is more common. In most cases, this fee covers the staff member who supervises your access to the site. As a result, common fees range from $100 to $300 per access.

Potential Problems

Although the server park option has many strengths, it also has several limitations you should consider before making a decision. First and foremost are the possible impacts of high bandwidth uses on your budget equation. Second, consider the limitation of physical accessibility to your server. Finally, you must consider which type of Internet access your office requires.

The Bandwidth Cost Equation

A dedicated link of a fixed size has a limited amount of bandwidth available at any one time, and it also has a limited total bandwidth available in one month. The price of the link reflects both conditions, as well as the standard average utilization of dedicated links of a particular size. As a result, your ISP generally provides the dedicated connection at a fixed price per month, and your costs are stable.

In a server park, the bandwidth available to you over time is usually more than your site needs and more than any dedicated link you purchase would provide. The main purpose of the server park solution is, after all, to enable your site to be accessed at a faster rate to avoid delaying your clients. The speed increase is accomplished, but the performance gain comes at a potential budgetary risk. Because the bandwidth available to clients is virtually unlimited (in the scope of your site's needs), the site can end up costing huge sums in bandwidth charges.

Imagine a site that was 50 MB of data, for example, contained in 10 files (sample video files). Each download results in slightly more than 5 MB of bandwidth use billed against your site. If limited to a 28.8Kbps connection, each download would take 25 minutes, assuming only one is accessed at a time. Two would double the time. In a server park solution, the bandwidth speed limitation occurs at the client's site. If the example site becomes popular under the 28.8Kbps connection, the costs do not rise, only the delays. With a server park solution, the costs would soar. At $50 per GB, for example, the 10 files would have to be downloaded only 20 times each to result in an additional $50 in cost.

A very popular site could accumulate hundreds if not thousands of extra charges as a result of bandwidth usage. To avoid this problem, you can provide a hard limit of bandwidth usage to the service provider. After you exceed the limit, the site becomes unavailable for a period of time. Although this solution limits the cost potential, it is only makeshift.

Accessibility

One key issue with regard to a server park is the level of accessibility. Your provider is not likely to allow you to move your office into the site (at least not without a larger fee for space!), though it should be willing at least to allow you occasional access as needed during office hours. If the server goes down during off hours, the emergency access clauses should cover you. Even so, accessibility to your server might be inconvenient. If your provider is located a large distance from you, the time required to drive to and from the server becomes a cost associated with the solution. As well, travel time can be a factor in the length of service interruption. Therefore, try to find a provider located relatively close to your main office, and consider possible troubleshooting options by the provider.

Local Internet Access Requirements

Possibly the greatest limitation of a server park is in providing high levels of connectivity for your internal network. Because the bandwidth charges of a server park likely have a premium associated with them, high levels of use result in a larger overall cost than using a large dedicated connection. In cases in which the needs of an office are in the order of a partial T1 or T1 of bandwidth during the day (for e-mail, file transfer, and internal WWW access), having a WWW site attached to the connection would not likely change the overall bandwidth requirement.

Therefore, the use of a server park would result in bandwidth charges greater than those of the appropriate dedicated connection. Also, the connection provided with a server park might provide only a small amount of bandwidth at any one time. Even though this amount is greater in the aggregate than the required amount, the download time could be greater than that of a dedicated connection large enough to support both internal and WWW access.

Which One Is Right for You?

Which connection methodology is best for your WWW site depends in large on the services and issues that are important to you. In every case, examine the following factors to determine their importance to your organization:

- Internal connectivity needed

- WWW bandwidth needed

- Type of information provided

- Tolerance for delays or failures

- Technical expertise available

- Complexity of the WWW site

- Availability of connectivity options

- Costs of connectivity options

- Security issues
- Site size

If in examining these factors you find that you require a high level of connectivity, the site is large, the technical expertise is low, the complexity is high, and your internal network needs little connectivity, then the server park option is likely the best solution.

If your organization has no need for internal connectivity, a major concern about internal security, few technical resources, and a simple site, then the rented WWW space option provides the most complete and cost-effective method.

Finally, if your site and office require high levels of bandwidth, the site is complex and requires close control and physical access, and the technical expertise to manage a dedicated connection exists in-house, then a high-bandwidth dedicated connection is the appropriate solution.

Checklist

The following are concerns that should be addressed at the conclusion of the chapter.

- ☑ Office connectivity needed?

  Space for Site Needed: i+k+(i+k)g-b=total, where:

  > *i* = initial site size in MBs
  >
  > *k* = known enhancements to site in MBs
  >
  > *g* = growth factor
  >
  > *b* = basic WWW space

  Average Size of Data: Number of items in site? Total size of site? Average size of items (size divided by number of items)?

- ☑ Do you need physical access to site server?

☑ Are you needing a large number of scripts and custom applications?

☑ Site changes often?

☑ Bandwidth needed for site/office: wo+wi+eo+ei+is+ms-ch=tb, where:

> wo = WWW output (information sent to external requests)
>
> wi = WWW input (information retrieved for internal requests)
>
> eo = e-mail out
>
> ei = e-mail in
>
> is = Internet services (news, telnet, ftp, audio and video, and so on)
>
> ms = management services (DNS, routing information, and so on)
>
> ch = caching (via WWW browsers or servers, or a local news server)
>
> tb = total bandwidth

☑ Tolerance for delays or failures?

☑ Technical expertise available?

☑ Availability of connectivity options?

WWW space?

Server Park?

Dedicated Lines (speeds)?

☑ Costs of connectivity options

Monthly

Bandwidth (based on estimate)

Local Loop Costs

☑ LAN security an issue?

The Historical and Technical Background of the Internet

Now that you have a general idea about the types of connectivity available, and the problems and costs associated with each one, the discussion turns to the technical underpinnings of the Internet. By providing you with an understanding of the historical and theoretical basis of the Internet, this chapter enables you to evaluate the technical connectivity options covered in later chapters with a clearer picture of how your choices affect the addressing, routing, naming, and security of your network.

ARPAnet and the History of the Internet

With the number of articles and books currently available about the Internet, the recollection of how the Internet came to be has become rather confused and muddled. As a manager in charge of the information systems of a large corporation or a small home-based business, you might wonder why a guide to Internet connectivity has a section on the Internet's history. The answer is simply that the historical development of the Internet has affected the protocols and conventions that govern the Internet today. Understanding the Internet's history will not provide a miraculous insight into if, when, and how to connect, but it will make the technical discussions to come much more relevant.

The Early Days before TCP/IP

As with any large evolving project, the Internet has been claimed by a number of creators. In some ways, all the competing tales are valid—after all, the Internet is, simply put, a network of networks. As the networks that make up the Internet were invented, so was the Internet. Even with the fluid, international, and independent nature of the development of the Internet, at the very least the roots of its technological base can be traced back to a project by the U.S. Department of Defense Advanced Research Projects Agency (DARPA) in 1969. The tale is one of classic Cold War paranoia. In an era of global mistrust, the U.S. Department of Defense desired a method of communications that could withstand the elimination of a portion of the network. The often referred to scenario is that the network had to be able to deal with a partial destruction due to a nuclear attack.

A Note from the Author

As a young entrepreneur in 1996, I find the paranoia that led to the development of Internet technology to be amazing. Needless to say, today we have very little worry about a nuclear war disrupting our communications networks. In fact, I wonder if the original system designers really felt that the network would ever be tested by nuclear attack. A much more plausible reason for the Net's origin is the designers' desire to build a technically superior network. Yet, the idea that the networking method should be able to handle partial collapse is valid. I can easily imagine a number of natural and manmade disasters (such as an errant road construction crew digging up the wrong cables) that could damage a section of the network. Naturally a networking architecture/protocol that can handle these types of disruptions better serves our business needs.

As a result of the Department of Defense's requirements, ARPA (along with a number of universities, professors, and students) created a network with four nodes—University of California Los Angeles (UCLA), Stanford Research Institute (SRI), University of California Santa Barbara (UCSB), and the University of Utah in Salt Lake City. The resulting network—dubbed *ARPAnet*—is often perceived as the fledgling Internet. A better description, however, is to call ARPAnet one of the ancestors of the Internet. After all, the packet-switching protocol first used on the ARPAnet was the *Network Control Protocol* (NCP, which later resulted in the x.25 standard) rather than the now familiar TCP/IP protocol suite.

Eventually, the military recognized the need for a protocol that did not rely on virtual circuits, as is the case with NCP. Because these circuits can fail, the military reactivated ARPA's routing and networking project. (The reactivation possibly was due to a real failure of the packet-based NCP communications network to reach the USS *Pueblo* when the ship was threatened by an impending North Korean attack.) In networking terms, the Department of Defense had the following requirements:

- ❀ **Independence from host computer hardware and software.** The protocol standard must be implemented on any number of computer platforms and within any number of computer operating systems.

- ❀ **Independence from network (or subnetwork) hardware.** The protocol must be usable over virtually any kind of physical network media (Ethernet, telephones, satellites, and so on).

- ❀ **Capability to route data between networks.** The protocol must be able to recognize and deliver a data packet to a number of networks or subnetworks.

- ❀ **Tolerance of routing errors in networks or subnetworks.** The protocol must be able to dynamically recognize that a particular route does not work and adjust to find an alternative route.

⊛ **Failure recovery.** The protocol must be able to recognize a data failure (either data corruption or loss) and provide a mechanism that recovers from the failure in a timely and efficient, yet robust, manner.

⊛ **Capability to add new subnetworks.** The protocol must be able to handle the addition of new subnetworks without the disruption of services.

The Addition of TCP/IP and the Growth of the Internet

The need for a protocol that could guarantee reliable delivery for packet-based routing brought the Department of Defense back to the ARPA networking project, and brought two computer scientists/electrical engineers into the forefront of the development of a new protocol. Vinton Cerf and Robert Kahn (along with a number of other researchers at Stanford, BBN, and University College of London) released the first version of what was then the Transmission Control Protocol (TCP). The first version of this protocol did not separate the guarantee of delivery with the routing functionality. Only after experiments with packet voice was it noticed that the TCP protocol needed to have TCP separated from IP (Internet Protocol). This development allowed for the creation of the User Datagram Protocol (UDP), which allows packet transmission with less concern for reliability.

After the TCP/IP protocol suite was developed, the officials at ARPAnet decided to make the switch from NCP to TCP/IP. All of ARPAnet was completely converted in 1982.

During the ARPAnet conversion to the TCP/IP protocol suite, a number of other networks were being developed by other organizations, mainly universities. The first major breakthrough, and really the first internetworking project, was the development of the *Computer Science Research Network* (CSnet). Again Vinton Cerf entered the picture and suggested that the two networks be linked through a gateway and the TCP/IP protocols. This linkage is truly the birth of the Internet: a collection of networks linked together by a common protocol suite—TCP/IP. By 1982, researchers on the two networks could exchange mail.

After these two networks were linked, a number of other independent networks developed (including FidoNet and Bitnet). Near the end of the 1980s, with fears of technological obsolescence, the U.S. government stepped in and created the National Science Foundation Network (NSFnet). Although the main purpose of this network was to allow researchers access to a number of supercomputers spread across the United States, researchers quickly began using the network's high-speed cross-country connections for communications. By the beginning of the 1990s the original networks that made up the early Internet (ARPAnet and CSnet) were both retired from service, supplanted by NSFnet (and its regional portions).

In the last five years, the Internet underwent another tremendous revolution. This revolution resulted in the creation and addition of numerous commercial networks (CompuServe, Prodigy, and America Online to name a few). In fact, these networks so completely took hold that on April 30, 1995, the NSFnet was retired. In the place of NSFnet now exists a linked set of commercial networks that include MCInet, Sprintlink, and ANSnet (the networks connect a variety of other networks through their infrastructure links). Added to this is a variety of private networks, satellite connections, UUCP links, and basic mail exchanges (either FidoNet bulletin board systems or private LANs).

TCP/IP: How Does It Work?

A discussion of how the TCP/IP protocols work to connect the networks that comprise the Internet is in order. This section details how the two protocols—TCP and IP—ensure that information sent from your network to a remote network is reliably transmitted.

The OSI Model

The TCP and IP protocols use the standard Open Systems Interconnection (OSI) model shown in figure 3.1.

Figure 3.1
The OSI model.

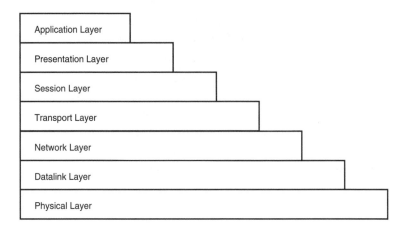

The OSI Layers
Table A.1

Layer	Function
Physical	Handles the transmission of (unstructured) bits across the physical medium; dealing with the issues of the mechanical, electrical, and functional characteristics.
Data Link	Provides data synchronization, error control, and flow control, including sending blocks of data (frames) for reliable transport.
Network	Allows independence from the lower two layers so that the communications do not depend on similarities of data transmission and switching. Ensures/Monitors proper setup, maintenance, and termination of connections.
Transport	Provides a method of transportation transparent to applications, between the two endpoints created by the network level. Also provides error correction and flow control.
Session	Controls the communication between applications.
Presentation	Enables applications to seamlessly handle differences in data syntax.

Layer	Function
Application	Allows users access to the OSI model and to distributed information services.

The next section relates the OSI model to the TCP/IP protocol suite. The entire internetworking process fits within the OSI model. The TCP/IP protocols comprise only two levels of the model, with connectivity methods accounting for two other levels.

Transmission Control Protocol (TCP)

The TCP portion of the TCP/IP protocol suite corresponds with the transport layer of the OSI model. As a result, the TCP protocol is responsible for handling and managing the stream of data from applications. TCP must break the data stream into manageable chunks of data (called *datagrams*), reorder the datagrams, reassemble them at the other end, and resend lost or damaged datagrams.

Creating Datagrams

The first task of the TCP layer is to break the datastream into datagrams of the appropriate size. When transferring data between two networks, the TCP layers must determine what datagram size both networks can handle. The lowest common denominator is the determining factor.

Note

A datagram might have to pass through any number of networks before reaching its destination. Again the lowest common denominator determines datagram size. The 576-octet datagram is the minimum that every implementation is required to support. Portions of the Internet require datagrams of no more than 1000 octets (8 bits), whereas Ethernet can handle 1500-octet datagrams. An obvious problem can occur when the two ends of a connection both support 1500-octet datagrams, but a hop between them supports only 1000-octet datagrams. To respond to this problem, IP can fragment a datagram that is too large to travel over a particular section of the route. Because larger datagrams are more efficient when transferring large files, you want to use the largest possible size. Nevertheless, a number of TCP/IP implementations settle for 576-octet datagrams when any section of the route is in doubt.

The TCP Header

After TCP establishes an acceptable datagram size and breaks up the data into datagrams, the protocol puts a header in front of each datagram (see fig. 3.2). The TCP header contains at least 20 octets of data, including source and destination port numbers, sequence number, acknowledgment number, window, checksum, and urgent pointer. This data manages the reordering, reassembling, and resending of datagrams, and is described in the following sections.

Figure 3.2

The TCP header.

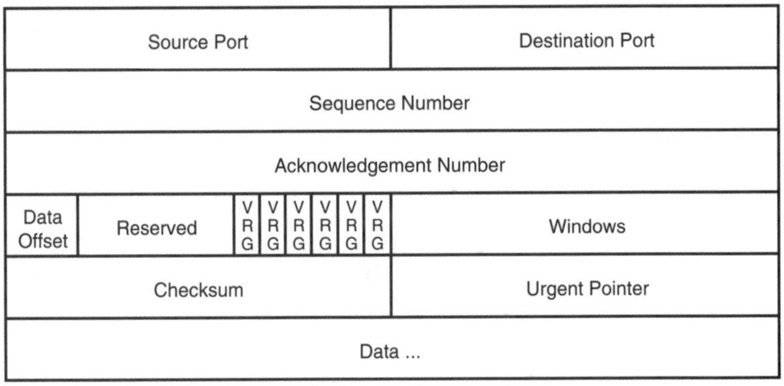

TCP Source and Destination Port

When the TCP protocol establishes a connection, each side has to know to what port the datastream should be directed. The sending host assigns the source port number, and the receiving host designates the destination port. A port number enables each host to manage a number of connections without confusing the datagrams. If the source port for an ftp transfer is set to 1000, for example, and another to 1001, by sending any replies regarding the first ftp transfer to port 1000, the recipient can inform the sending host correctly on the status of reception.

Sequence Number

The *sequence number* enables TCP to recognize the correct order in which to reassemble the datagrams after they reach their destination. Because the communication route to a particular site might be different for individual datagrams, it is possible for the datagrams to arrive out of sequence. The sequence number enables the receiving TCP to recognize the proper order, as well as whether any datagrams were lost in transport. TCP assigns sequence numbers to the datagrams according to the number of octets sent. If the TCP protocol uses a 1000-octet datagram, for example, the first might be numbered 0, and the second 1000 (indicating up to what octet should be received prior to the current datagram).

Acknowledgment Number

The *acknowledgment number* enables the receiving TCP protocol to acknowledge the receipt of datagrams. The value in the field indicates the number of octets successfully received. In the case of our 1000-octet transfer, for example, the receiving TCP would send a datagram with the value 2000 in the acknowledgment number field to indicate that up to the 2000th octet has been successfully received (the second datagram).

If a sending host does not receive an acknowledgment of a specific datagram within a set period of time, the host automatically resends that datagram. The automatic resending is based on the principle of a data life cycle (see the section "Internet Protocol (IP)" for more details), which assumes that after a set period of time, a packet likely will not reach its destination.

Window

The *window* field in the TCP header controls the flow of data over the connection. The number in this field represents the amount of data in octets that the host is able to process. As more data is received, the number decreases, and as more data is processed, the number increases. If the number in this field reaches zero in an acknowledgment datagram, the sending host stops sending data until it receives another acknowledgment datagram indicating that the receiving host can process more data. The window field therefore enables communication between hosts with dissimilar power. The window value prevents a fast computer from overwhelming a slower computer.

Checksum

The *checksum* field in the TCP header enables the TCP protocol to ensure data integrity for each datagram. Simply put, the checksum is computed by adding all the octets in a datagram. The resulting sum is put in the checksum field of the datagram's header. At the receiving host, TCP recalculates the octets received and compares its result to the value in the checksum field. If the values do not match, the receiving TCP rejects the datagram and requests the sending TCP to resend that specific datagram (the request can be implied through failure to acknowledge receipt of a specific sequence number). If the value matches, the receiving TCP accepts the datagram and sends an acknowledgment datagram.

Urgent Pointer

The *urgent pointer* is a mechanism that enables the two TCP protocols to process events asynchronously. A value in this field tells TCP to process a specific datastream before processing others. As a result, a control character in the datastream that interrupts the datastream can be identified by the urgent pointer. As a result, the receiving TCP can stop its output more quickly than if the octets were processed in sequence.

Note

TCP/IP is the most commonly used protocol of the Internet transportation and network layers. The TCP portion of the model can be substituted for another datagram method called the *User Datagram Protocol* (UDP). UDP is a much simpler transportation protocol that simply attaches to a header a source and destination port number, length information, and a checksum. Missing are the sequencing, flow control, and acknowledgment data available in the TCP header. As a result, UDP normally is used only to send data that does not require guaranteed reliability. Usually, if a piece of data can fit completely into one datagram (such as a Domain Name Request), the lower overhead UDP is used.

UDP was developed because certain applications are more dependent on receiving data on an ongoing basis rather than in a specific order or with a high degree of integrity. The need for this type of transportation layer was first realized in the mid 1970s by Danny Cohen, who was working with packetized voice over networks. Cohen argued that the delay due to resending datagrams because of suspect reliability had greater consequences than losing or destroying them. The data included in one datagram, for example, does not necessarily alter the final sound in such a way that the human ear can hear. Unlike a computer, the human brain can interpolate missing or damaged data.

Internet Protocol (IP)

The preceding sections covered all the data that directly control the functionality of TCP, although the TCP header usually contains other data also. After the data is broken into datagrams, the header handles sequencing, flow control, and error correction required of the transportation level of the OSI model. The transportation layer, however, only manages data sent over an established connection. Establishing, maintaining, and closing connections is the responsibility of the network layer of the OSI model, called the *Internet Protocol* (IP) in the TCP/IP suite. IP must ensure that datagrams (passed to IP by TCP) are correctly routed to their destination.

Getting the Address

The network layer of the OSI model establishes the correct route from origin to destination, but to accomplish this feat, IP must receive three pieces of information from the transportation layer: the source IP address, the destination IP address, and the type of service. The *source IP address* is the IP address that corresponds with the medium used to deliver the datagram. This information is important because hosts have multiple IP addresses, one for each interface, such as Ethernet, serial line, and so on. The *destination IP address* comes from TCP, which either received it from the application layer or resolved it through Domain Name Services (DNS). Finally, IP needs to know how to send the datagram: over the coaxial, the serial line, or satellite; and how fast to send it.

The IP Header

After IP receives the required information, it places a header in front of each datagram. The IP header contains at least 20 octets of data, including type of service, checksum, time to live, fragmentation information, protocol, source IP, and destination IP. The header contains the data to manage the routing of datagrams from source to destination and is placed like a larger envelope around the already present TCP header (see fig. 3.3).

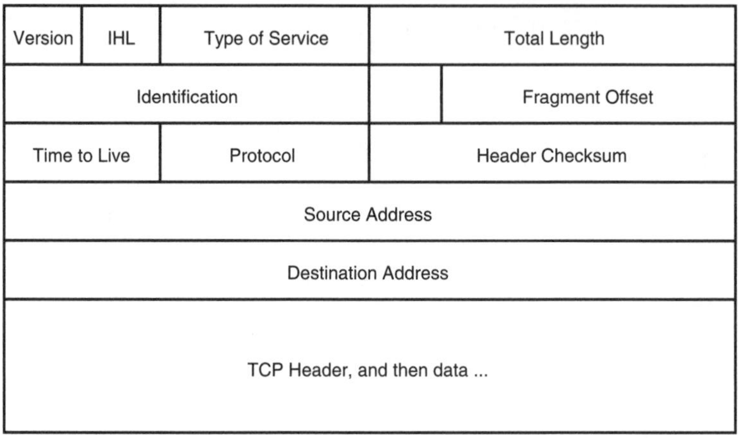

Figure 3.3
The IP header.

Version	IHL	Type of Service		Total Length	
Identification				Fragment Offset	
Time to Live		Protocol		Header Checksum	
Source Address					
Destination Address					
TCP Header, and then data ...					

Type of Service

The 8-bit type of service information field in the IP header shows how to deliver a specific datagram. The information includes what medium and speed to use. This type of service information helps to establish the datagram's preliminary route in terms of medium.

Checksum

Like the TCP header, the IP header contains a checksum that enables the destination IP to verify that the IP header has not been damaged. A damaged header could contain an incorrect destination/source IP address.

> **Note**
>
> The IP checksum is simply a sum of the 20 or more octets in the IP header, rather than the entire checksum of the TCP layer and the actual data. To maintain the separation between routing and integrity protocols, the IP checksum only deals with routing verification.

Time to Live

The *time to live* value ensures that datagrams are not stuck in routing loops due to poor network design. The number in the time to live field decreases every time a datagram passes through a system. When the time to live value reaches zero, the datagram is discarded.

Fragmentation Information

The fragmentation offset and flags provide the information needed by IP to fragment and reassemble datagrams in the event that a section of its route cannot handle the datagram size established by TCP. As mentioned in the section "Transmission Control Protocol (TCP)," some networks (such as ARPAnet, which is limited to 1000-octet datagrams) cannot handle the 1500-octet standard supported by Ethernet. As a result, if two Ethernet-based hosts are communicating via the Internet, the intervening sections of the route might not be able to accept the 1500-octet datagrams. IP uses flags and fragmentation offset fields to fragment datagrams into an acceptable size and reassemble them at the destination.

Protocol

The IP header contains information about to which protocol the datagram should be passed at the destination. Internet communications (other than protocol level requests) generally use the TCP protocol, although this field could indicate UDP or another protocol able to use IP as a networking layer.

Source IP Address

As mentioned previously, the source IP address is simply the address assigned to the source interface. Common interfaces include Ethernet, serial (for a SLIP, PPP, or null modem connection), satellite, or local loopback. Each of these interfaces must have a unique IP address (see the section "IP Addressing and Routing" later in this chapter for more information). The DNS system helps to resolve domain names with the IP addresses associated with the domain name.

Note

Although IP addresses indicate a specific interface on a specific host (when taken as a full 32-bit number), not every data link layer understands IP addressing. Commonly, the IP address is simply a logical address that must be resolved into a physical-hardware-dependent address. Ethernet uses the Address Resolution Protocol (ARP) to discover the unique Ethernet address (the 64-bit address unique to any Ethernet card) for that interface. The datagram is then passed to the data link layer for transportation across the physical Ethernet before being handed back to the IP network layer.

The OSI model provides independent layers to deal with address resolution. Each layer works independently of the others and passes the datagram to the next layer after it completes its task.

Destination IP Address

Unlike the source IP address, the IP layer cannot take the destination IP address from the host computer. Instead it relies on the transportation layer (TCP) for this information. The TCP protocol in turn relies on the application layer, which supplies either the actual IP address (rare) or the domain name (common). In the event that the application layer passes on a domain, the TCP protocol uses the DNS system to resolve the address into its 32-bit version (123.23.12.12, for example).

While the IP header can (and usually does) contain other data, the previous sections dealt with all of the data that directly controls the functionality of IP. While the basic functionality of the IP layer can be seen by examining the use of the header information, the issues of addressing and routing are of such importance to Internet networking that these issues are dealt with in greater depth in the following section.

IP Addressing

This section covers the theory behind the current IPv4 addressing method, some problems that have developed as a result, current temporary solutions, the proposed long-term solution—IPv6, and how to obtain an address.

Because of the connection between the IP address and routing, this section also discusses the theories used in IP routing and their implications. Finally, this section looks at some potential problems with IP routing methods and discusses real network issues that pressure the basis for Internet routing.

The Class-Based Theory

The current IP addressing system was designed around the assumption of a variety of network sizes. The designers of the addressing systems expected the addressing needs of each network to vary. They anticipated a few very large networks (millions of hosts), a moderate number of medium-sized networks (thousands of hosts), and millions of smaller networks (maximum of 254 hosts). The designers designated the large address blocks Class A networks, the medium blocks Class B networks, and the small address blocks Class C networks.

Note

Binary numbering systems are based on a base-2 numbering system rather than the standard base-10 system we use in everyday mathematics. To read binary numbers, you must first establish the grouping methodology. IP addresses, for example, are grouped into four octets (groups of eight bits). In this case you can read an octet in a manner similar to how you read an eight-digit number in base 10:

11111111base 2, or binary number

33333333base 10, or decimal number

The far right column contains the base to the power of zero. As a result, the base-10 number is 10 to the 0 power, which equals 1. The same is true for base-2, where 2 to the 0 also is 1. The second column is the base to the power of 1; therefore in base-10 this is the 10s column, whereas in base two it is the 2s column. Similarly, the third column is the base to the second power, giving 100s or 4s for base-10 and base-2, respectively.

You can write the binary number in decimal form by adding all the bits based on their power:

1×1

1×2

1×4

1×8

1×16

1×32

1×64

1×128

255

Using this system, a network address of 255.255.255.0 also can be represented as four octets:

11111111 11111111 11111111 00000000

Obviously, humans find it easier to understand the decimal version of this number, so as a result, the IP addressing system is constructed to allow both methods (since computers think in binary, this number system makes sense for computers).

Class A Addresses

Class A addresses are the large address blocks designated by either a binary 32-bit address that starts with 0:

0YYYYYYY XXXXXXXX XXXXXXXX XXXXXXXX

or a decimal address containing a number from 0 to 127 in the first octet:

Y.X.X.X

The first bit indicates the address class, the next 7 bits (Y from above) indicate the network, and the final 24 bits identify the host. From this configuration, millions of hosts are available to each Class A address (16,777,214 possible combinations exist because hosts 255.255.255 and 0.0.0 are reserved), but only 128 possible (2E7) networks. To further reduce this number, the 0.X.X.X, 10.X.X.X (Private Network Addresses), and 127.X.X.X addresses are reserved. As a result of the limited quantity of addresses, Class A addresses are no longer available.

Note

Most literature states that IP addresses identify a host. Strictly speaking, this designation is not entirely correct. The IP address actually identifies an interface of the host. The interface can be the Ethernet port, a serial line, or any other communications connection. Routers are devices that have multiple interfaces and the capability to transfer datagrams between them. A router with an ISDN modem and an Ethernet interface, for example, has two IP addresses. One identifies the ISDN interface, and the other identifies the Ethernet interface. Generally the ISDN IP address is part of a service provider's network address block, whereas the Ethernet is a separate address block (see the section "Subnetting" later in this chapter).

Class B Addresses

Class B addresses are the address blocks for medium-sized networks designated either by a binary 32-bit address that starts with 10:

10YYYYYY YYYYYYY XXXXXXXX XXXXXXXX

or a decimal address containing digits from 128.1 to 191.254 in the first two octets:

Y.Y.X.X

The first 2 bits indicate the address class, the next 14 bits (Y from above) indicate the network, and the final 16 bits identify the host. From this configuration, 65,534 hosts are available to each Class B address, and thousands of possible networks. To further reduce this number, the 128.0.X.X, 172.16.0.0 to 172.31.255.255 (Private Network Addresses), and 191.255.X.X addresses are reserved. Due to the flexibility of the Class B addresses for subnetting, larger organizations have shown a preference for Class B addresses, and as a result, addresses in this class no longer are available.

Class C Addresses

Class C addresses are the address blocks for the smallest networks designated either by a binary 32-bit address that starts with 110:

110YYYYY YYYYYYY YYYYYYY XXXXXXXX

or by a decimal address containing digits from 192.0.1 to 223.255 to 254 in the first three octets:

Y.Y.Y.X

The first 3 bits indicate the address class, the next 21 bits (Y from above) indicate the network, and the final 8 bits identify the host. From this configuration, 254 hosts are available to each Class C address, and millions of possible networks. The 192.0.0.X, 192.168.0.0 to 192.168.255.255 (Private Network Addresses), and 223.255.255.0 addresses are reserved. Due to the large number of possible Class C addresses, they are the only addresses still assigned by InterNIC.

Address Space Running Out?

As the previous discussion indicates, the current addressing system is not unlimited in the number of networks and hosts it can accommodate. In fact, the class-based system severely limits the number of available addresses. As a result, the increase in popularity of the Internet has placed the current addressing system under pressure.

While current addresses are running out, the Internet Engineering Task Force (IETF) is currently using *Private Address Blocks* and *Classless Inter Domain Routing* (CIDR) to alleviate the problem in the interim. In the long run, the IETF is looking for a solution that increases the number of available addresses without increasing the load on routers (through the increase of routing table size), and that will be implemented in router hardware rather than at the host level.

Currently, the IETF is considering the IP-NG or IPv6 model to solve addressing and routing problems.

Note

The class system was in part designed to limit the size needed for routing tables. Their size is limited by associating whole networks with one routing table entry. A Class A network, for example, can be subnetted through the use of subnet masks to create virtual networks within the organization. To the rest of the world, the address and all subnets are simply entries in a routing table. Any packets for the network, say 12.X.X.X, are routed to the specific router for that network, such as Network 12. From there, the internal router directs the datagram to the appropriate network and host.

Private Address Blocks

As mentioned in the discussion of Class A, B, and C addresses, a set number of these addresses is set aside for the use of enterprises that require IP addresses but that are not part of the Internet. According to Request for Comment (RFC) 1597, the definition of networks and hosts that can use the private address blocks is as follows:

* Hosts that do not require access to hosts in other enterprises or the Internet at large

* Hosts that need access to a limited set of outside services (for example, e-mail, FTP, netnews, and remote login) that can be handled by application layer gateways

If the hosts and networks of an organization fit within these categories, then the network administrator is asked by the Internet Assigned Numbers Authority to address hosts and networks using addresses from the following blocks:

* 10.0.0.0 to 10.255.255.255

* 172.16.0.0 to 172.31.255.255

* 192.168.0.0 to 192.168.255.255

The private address solution enables enterprises to use TCP/IP networking with internally unambiguous, but externally ambiguous, addresses. Any enterprise can use these address blocks without coordinating with any Internet authority.

Hosts acting in a firewall capacity through the use of application layer security are still required to use completely unambiguous IP addresses. Still, the use of private IP addresses reduces the demand for addresses, because portions of the networks of many enterprises never directly (via network layer connections) access the public Internet.

Of possible concern for IS managers is the need to renumber hosts should a host's or network's access requirements change. Although renumbering can be troublesome, the current use of Classless Inter Domain Routing (CIDR) makes renumbering more common (see the following section, "Classless Inter Domain Routing"), and InterNIC's more stringent address allocation rules necessitate this solution. As a result, tools continue to be developed to facilitate the task (see RFC 1541, "Dynamic Host Reconfiguration Protocol").

Classless Inter Domain Routing

As mentioned earlier, the main concern with using a classless method of IP addressing is that the resulting increase in routing tables would overrun the capability of routers to store the routing information. To deal with this routing problem and to free up addresses for use, the IETF has developed and implemented an interim solution called *Classless Inter Domain Routing*, or CIDR.

CIDR is based on the principle that Internet routing must be made hierarchical to constrain the growth of the information that must be contained within routing tables. CIDR works on the basis of routing aggregation at the subnet, subscriber, and provider level. A router with one large enterprise does not need to keep routing tables for each host on each subnet, but simply the routing information for each subnet. Likewise, the provider to that enterprise does not keep detailed information about each subnet, but simply adds an entry in the router for the subscriber. At a provider level, the providers do not add entries for each other's subscribers, but simply provide entries for each service provider.

The need for hierarchical routing aggregation raises the question of the usability of the CIDR system with pre-CIDR address allocation policies. In organizations that have already been allocated IP addresses, only small possibilities exist that address aggregation can occur. Addresses within a certain block managed by service providers can be used for aggregated routing tables, but addresses outside these blocks do not easily lend themselves to this approach.

RFCs 1518 and 1519 recommend that the CIDR system be used to allocate addresses, and that providers and clients work together to establish hierarchical routing. As a result, address "lending" from service providers has become common. *Address lending* is a system by which service providers assign addresses to their customers for the duration of the time service is provided. The lending of addresses takes place on all levels of service provision. A national provider such as Sprintlink, "lends" a set of IP addresses from its address block to an Internet Service Provider (ISP) that obtains leased service from Sprintlink (T1 service, for example). The ISP then subnets that set of addresses to its dedicated customers (such as an enterprise with a dedicated ISDN connection). If either the ISP or the enterprise changes service providers, then it has to renumber its hosts with newly lent IP addresses. (If the ISP changes providers, the enterprise also has to renumber, thus making careful selection of an ISP important.)

For enterprises that require or already use IP addresses allocated under a non-hierarchical routing methodology, certain difficulties exist in acquiring routing support. Service providers might refuse to provide or change for the provision of routing services for "owned" IP addresses. As a result, an enterprise that relies on privately acquired IP addresses finds it difficult or expensive to maintain full routing connectivity to the Internet at large. Larger enterprises that acquire service through a national-level provider and who provide hierarchical routing information within their own Intranet are an exception.

Given the potential problems associated with the acquisition of IP addresses from InterNIC (or the Canadian IP registry office), enterprises benefit by using both interim solutions recommended by the IETF working groups. Use private addressing within an enterprise wherever possible (the private addressing method is particularly well suited to enterprises that require application-level firewalls; (see the section "Firewalls" later in this chapter) and fulfill addressing needs for fully public hosts through your service provider. Although the IPv6 model provides increased address space, IPv6 currently is designed around the hierarchical routing principle, so that any networks designed under the current CIDR model will be applicable under the new regime.

IPv6 or IP-NG

The IP version 6 Addressing Architecture is intended to replace the current version—IPv4. The IPv6 model is based on a 128-bit address system that uses CIDR style hierarchical routing. Recipients can read the address as different addresses depending on their intelligence. Simple hosts see the address as a contiguous 128-bit address:

```
| 128 bits |


| node address |
```

A more sophisticated router sees the same address as follows:

```
| x bits            | 128-x bits |


| subnet prefix     | interface ID |
```

The preceding router knows to which subnet the address was going and can perform simple routing between the subnets.

A slightly higher-level router can read the following address designations:

```
| x bits            | 80-x bits    | 48 bits |


| subscriber prefix | subnet ID    | interface ID |
```

This address format probably is common because the 48-bit interface ID corresponds to the IEEE-802 MAC address (associated with the specific Ethernet interface). The subscriber interface refers to the subscriber, and the subnet ID to a particular subnet of that subscriber.

Finally, provider-based unicast addresses (similar to CIDR addressing and routing under IPv4) appear as follows:

```
|3   |z bits      |y bits      |x bits       |125-z-y-x bits    |


|010 |registry ID  |provider ID |subscriber ID |intra-subscriber |
```

Provider-based addresses implement routing solutions that take advantage of the hierarchical model established under CIDR. A number of IP registries (designated by the registry ID) are established, for example, who in turn assign addresses from within their blocks to service providers in their areas. These providers (designated by the provider ID) then assign portions of their IP blocks to individual subscribers. All these addresses are then assigned on the "lending" principle, so that the routing table can be simplified to a regional or at least a provider level.

If host (address 1) of subscriber 1 of provider 1 of the A region, for example, sends a datagram to host 1 of subscriber 1 of provider 1 of the B region, the only difference between their addresses is the registry ID. Routers in the A region ignore all other information and simply route the datagram to region B. After the datagram arrives at region B, the routers route the datagram to provider 1, whose routers route the datagram to subscriber 1. At this point, the subscriber's router sends the datagram onto the appropriate subnet router (if one exists), and the datagram then is forwarded to the specific interface of the host.

Under this addressing system, each router needs to know only the next level up and down from its level. Regional routers, for example, need to know only the providers of their region and the routing addresses for the other regions. The providers need to know only their regional router and the subscriber-level routers. The subscriber routers need only know their provider's router and the subnet routers on their network. Subnet routers in turn need to know only their subscriber router and the host of their subnet.

The IPv6 specification proposal also incorporates anycast addressing. With anycast addressing, multiple routers are assigned the same address, which enables redundancy in routing. Which of the multiple routers receives the datagrams is determined by the level of network traffic on any one route.

Implications of the IPv6 for Connectivity

Due to the compatibility of the proposed IPv6 with the CIDR format of IPv4, the conversion to the new addressing system will be relatively painless. When you set up your network with Internet connectivity, remember to follow proper IPv4 procedures, such as private addresses and the CIDR addressing method. Although enterprises might be required to change addresses when changing ISPs, the capability of IPv6 to encapsulate IPv4 addresses limits most renumbering of routers and tables. In combination with CIDR procedures, the enterprise-level changes should be limited to small router adjustments for gateway addresses.

Obtaining an Address

As discussed in the preceding section, how you obtain addresses greatly affects your networking and routing. You can obtain addresses using two methods: by a "loan" from an ISP, or from your national coordinator (either InterNIC in the United States or the Canadian IP registry office in Canada).

Obtaining Addresses from an Internet Service Provider

Generally the preferred method for obtaining addresses for your Internet host(s) is through your ISP. The type of addressing that the ISP provides you with depends on both your addressing needs and your level of connectivity.

When you begin to plan your Internet connectivity, keep in mind the issues of security and future scaling. If you intend to implement a firewall system that relies on application-level proxies, then the recommended course of action is to use the private addressing scheme to address the majority of your network. You can obtain an IP address for the firewall host through your ISP. This address can be one of a few available through a small subnet, which is optimal because it offers you future scalability to add further Internet servers, or through a single IP host address. Remember, if you plan to eventually change to a packet filtering method of security, you will have to renumber your hosts.

The determining factor of the addressing that an ISP is willing to allocate to your enterprise is the level of connectivity you require. ISPs are generally required to utilize the IP addresses assigned to them in the most productive manner. Therefore, they must ensure a certain level of usage for all of their addresses. As a result, ISPs carry only a small percentage of IP addresses that are surplus to their current needs. The smaller the service provider, then the smaller number of available addresses. As a result, if you have the need for more than a couple of addresses, you must seek a larger regional or even national provider.

Providers generally only dynamically allocate addresses to dial-up nondedicated customers. For smaller dedicated customers, they might allocate only a small number of IP addresses (a dedicated 28.8 link cannot reasonably accommodate a large number of hosts). After you obtain either a dedicated 56 KB or 128 KB ISDN line, your provider can offer a reasonable number of IP addresses (generally, one Ethernet can support a mid-sized enterprise of 60 to 100 computers by one 56- to 128-KB link; see Chapter 2, "Initial Discussions: Renting versus Leasing, or Cohabit" for more information). If the ISP is reluctant to supply the appropriate number of IP addresses, consider other service providers, including national providers, or apply to InterNIC or the Canadian Registry for allocated addresses.

Applying to the National Coordinator for Addresses

Generally speaking, the national coordinating bodies have become more strict in allocating IP addresses over the past few years. As address depletion and routing issues grow, the rules governing allocation will become even more stringent. In general, an enterprise is required to be very large, to be multihomed (see Chapter 2), or to have no intention of connecting to the Internet.

Because addresses assigned by regional allocating agencies are not automatically contained within routing tables, these addresses are the least likely to be routable across the Internet. Although an organization can contract with an ISP for upstream routing services, no guarantee exists that other ISPs carry multiple entries in their routing tables. Therefore your addresses might be dropped from certain tables, possibly causing a loss of connection to certain portions of the Internet.

A Note from the Author

I cannot stress enough the benefits of working together with the Internet community to maintain address and routing viability. If you fail to follow these simple procedures, your network connectivity will suffer. Generally, ISPs are not only better connected to major routing ports, but they also have the technical expertise needed to ensure that the routing needed for your network (as their customer) is properly distributed. In fact, the blocks of addresses assigned to ISPs in general already are associated with the ISPs' routing systems. As a result, most routers already recognize IP addresses as belonging to a particular provider, and the only addition needed is that of your domain to the DNS system (a much quicker process than ensuring routing information distribution).

If your organization determines that the need for unique, "owned" IP addresses outweighs the difficulties these regionally allocated addresses present, then apply to your regional body for allocation. In the United States, you apply to InterNIC, and in Canada to the Canadian IP Registry.

Internet Routing

The majority of Internet routing is performed by the IP protocol. The fact that the IP layer of the TCP/IP stack provides routing makes the issue of IP addressing even more important. In fact, with the sudden influx of activity on the Internet since the commercialization of the World Wide Web (WWW), extreme pressure has developed around the number and routing of these addresses.

The Theories

In general, the routing method used by the Internet depends on the part of the network over which your datagram is traveling at any particular time. The method options include the complete routing table method, the hierarchical core model, and the coequal routing domain system.

Complete Routing Table Method

When the Internet was simply a small collection of hosts and networks, each machine kept a routing table listing all the possible routes to each host. Needless to say, this routing method is not able to scale to any extent. In fact, the complete routing table method generally is used only for small internal network routing; the size of the routing table would be extreme if this method were implemented Internetwide.

When you send data from your local computer to a coworker's computer across the hall, the datagram is sent by the routing table method. Because these hosts reside on the same network, it is pointless for them to use router time and resources. Your computer looks up the information in a local routing table to discover the coworker's computer on the same network. The datagram is then broadcast over the Ethernet and accepted by your coworker's host.

A Note from the Author

A *router* is a computer (or "black box" machine) dedicated to routing datagrams to specific destinations. Originally this task was handled by the gateway hosts of networks (and still is in smaller enterprises), but as routing became more difficult and intensive, the task was handed over to routers.

The Hierarchical Core Model

The complete routing table method was replaced by the *hierarchical core model*, which allows a greater degree of scaling. In the core model, the core network of the Internet (originally ARPAnet and then NSFnet) maintains routers that collect information about all the networks of the Internet. This information is shared among core gateways through the Gateway to Gateway Protocol (GGP). Attached to the core Internet is a collection of independent networks called *autonomous systems.* These systems each maintain their own routing information and pass the network information (called *reachability information*) through their systems. The autonomous systems use the Exterior Gateway Protocol (EGP) to pass reachability information to the core gateways (see fig. 3.4).

Figure 3.4

The core gateway model.

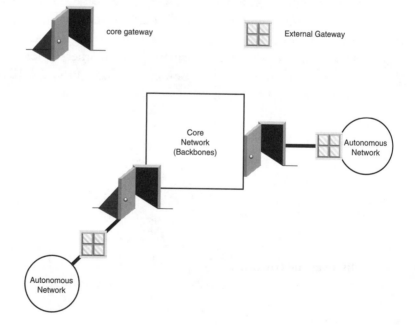

core gateway

External Gateway

Core Network (Backbones)

Autonomous Network

Autonomous Network

If a host on virtual.net (an autonomous system connected to the Internet through the reality.net core gateway) sends a datagram to nonsense.net (an autonomous system connected to the core Internet through paradox.net), using the hierarchical core model, the host system routes the datagram to an external gateway (default gateway), which then passes the datagram to the reality.net core gateway. Reality.net then analyzes the complete routing tables and determines the best route to virtual.net. Because in this model the only external gateway to virtual.net is the core gateway reality.net, paradox.net then routes the datagram to reality.net, which in turn passes the datagram to the external gateway for reality.net.

The main problem with the core routing model is that it requires the core gateways to contain and process routing information for the entire Internet. As well, each routing request external to a particular autonomous system must be handled by a core gateway. As a result, this system does not react well to increases in Internet size, and core gateways are susceptible to failure (which could isolate an autonomous system under this routing model).

The Coequal Routing Domain System

In response to the limitations of the hierarchical core model a new routing system is being utilized: the *coequal routing domain system*. In this new method of routing, autonomous systems collect into regions or domains of equal networks. Within these networks, the systems determine together the best routes. As well, these domains exchange information with other regions that overlap. The regions either use EGP or Border Gateway Protocol (BGP) to exchange information (see fig. 3.5).

Figure 3.5

Coequal routing domains.

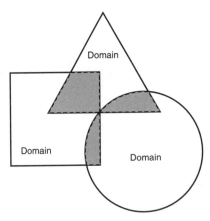

Imagine a series of three overlapping domains of autonomous networks. Each network in the region works to provide routing information about that region, and border networks exchange this information with neighboring regions. If a datagram is sent from region A to a host in region B, the routing tables of any of the border networks can be used to determine the best route to region B (depending on traffic or other performance factors). After the datagram is passed to any number of the border gateways of region B, the datagram routes to the network gateway and on to the host.

Does the Theory Match Practice?

No matter which routing method is used, the IP protocol's main function is to react to damage to a portion of the network. If you recall the Department of Defense's nuclear attack scenario, you remember the capability of IP to route around the damaged portions. The question is whether this theoretical capability of the protocol is translated into a practical reality.

Dynamic Routing and Redundancy: Myth and Reality

As mentioned previously, IP is designed to choose the best route to a particular host. Unfortunately, the way this is accomplished is dependent on the particular implementation of the protocol. In many cases, due to the difficulty of maintaining up-to-date routing tables, some smaller gateways are equipped with only a single routing path from their internal networks to the rest of the Internet. If this route becomes damaged, datagrams on this network become trapped and excluded from the outside world.

One method of avoiding this problem is to establish connectivity through a provider that has multi-homed access to the Internet at large. Unfortunately, depending on where you are located, this can be costly or impossible. Further, even if a provider has multi-homed access, the end result might not be any different. If a provider has two T1 connections, one to regional provider A and one to regional provider B, and both regional providers acquire their access from national provider X, should the link between national provider X and the region of A and B become damaged, then the service provider is unable to route any traffic to the rest of the Internet.

Look for a provider whose system is multi-homed with two distinct service providers and that maintains a routing method that identifies the two routes and uses both regularly (thus maintaining more up-to-date routing information through Internet Control Message Protocol (ICMP) datagrams).

An IS manager can do little to limit disruptions. Although the service providers at the top of the scale generally are well staffed and maintain their connectivity with few or no interruptions, as you travel further down the bandwidth chain the issue of redundancy arises. The fact that only a limited number of providers exist and rely on an even more limited number of national and international links means that disruptions are a constant threat. The network topography makes these problems an issue.

Domain Name Servers

The 32-bit addressing system is difficult for specific hosts to remember. The affinity of humans for textual names resulted in a process of mapping addresses to more memorable names. Address mapping originally assigned names based on the syntax *user@host*; however, eventually a more complex system called the *Domain Name Server* (DNS) was established. Thirty-two bit addresses rarely are seen because of this system. This section explains DNS and the process of registering a name.

Historical Naming Methods

To help people remember addresses, a system of naming hosts was established. Originally when the Internet was the ARPAnet project, hosts were named by system administrators without any coordinated plan. The names were mapped to IP addresses through a simple system of a *hosts.text* file on one machine. As the Internet grew, this file-based system quickly became too large for one file on one machine to handle. As well, because any system on any network could choose any name, the possibility of name conflict existed, which could invalidate the whole system.

The Domain Name Server (DNS)

The system for naming hosts was changed from the *hosts.text* format to a distributed database of hierarchical domain names called *Domain Name Server* (DNS). A hierarchical naming convention was established based on the premise that as long as names were unique within each level of the hierarchy, no name conflict would occur. The distributed database enables a distributed client-server approach to share the name-resolution load across servers.

The DNS Hierarchy

The DNS naming convention is based on a hierarchical tree structure. At the top of the tree is the root domain. Below the root domain are seven top-level domains:

edu	Educational institutions such as Michigan Institute of Technology (mit.edu)
com	Commercial organizations such as Macmillan Computer Publishing (mcp.com)
gov	Government institutions such as the National Science Foundation (nsf.gov)
mil	Military organizations such as the U.S. Navy (navy.mil)
net	Networking organizations such as Sprintlink (sprint.net) and MCInet (mci.net)
org	Noncommercial organizations such as the Electronic Freedom Foundation (eff.org)
int	International organizations such as the United Nations (un.int)

As well as these top-level domains, which are specific to the United States, geographically based top-level domains also exist that are based on international two-letter country codes, such as ca (Canada), nz (New Zealand), and us (United States). Countries usually have a subdomain hierarchy below the geographical top-level domains based on the organizational model of the seven U.S. top-level domains.

In Canada and the U.S., the subdomains are slightly different. Below the top-level ca or us domain are subdomains based on provincial or state designations. The subdomain in Canada for Ontario is on.ca, and for British Columbia bc.ca. This domain structure also can be extended to the city level—vancouver.bc.ca—similar to the postal addressing system.

Figure 3.6

DNS Hierarchy.

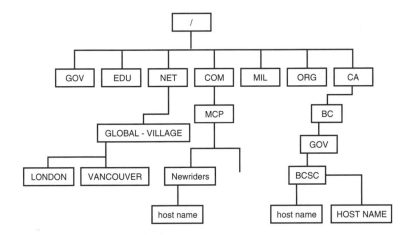

Figure 3.6 illustrates the hierarchical nature of the DNS naming system. The figure shows several top-level domains, one of which, the com domain, branches off to the Macmillan Computer Publishing domain (mcp.com). The mcp domain branches to the New Riders Publishing subdomain (newriders.mcp.com). The domain newriders.mcp.com establishes the name of a particular network of computers (or networks). This name can be further qualified by adding the host name bob to the domain name. In DNS language, a domain name that has been resolved to the host level (bob.newriders.mcp.com) is a *fully qualified domain name* (FQDN).

The hierarchical nature of the DNS naming system suggests that DNS provides routing information, however it does not. The system of names simply provides a convenient label for IP addresses (which do provide routing information). At any one level, the domain names can refer to machines around the world (com), one corporation (mcp.com), or one subsidiary (newriders.mcp.com). Although a logical connection exists between the machines in all these domains, a physical connection is not necessary for routing information. In contrast, single networks of IP addresses must be physically connected (through a cable-based or wireless connection).

The DNS Distributed Database

The *name server* is the process that manages the information within a zone. A *zone* is a body of information within a domain over which authority has not been delegated. When a name server completes information about a zone, the server then has *authority* for that zone. Whereas a domain contains all the information within that domain (for example, the mcp.com domain contains all the data about all the nodes within mcp.com, such as newriders and so on), a name server contains information about a zone. The name server at Macmillan Computer Publishing can either contain all the information about the entire domain in its DNS server, or the DNS server can delegate authority over the newriders.mcp.com subdomain to a separate DNS server at New Riders Publishing.

When a DNS process is set up, the server contains a list of information about the authoritative zone and a list of name servers to consult in the event the domain queried was not contained in the DNS files. Queries are handled through a *name resolver* that contains information on where to look for addresses not contained locally.

The following is an /etc/resolve.conf file:

```
; Default domain:
domain global-village.net
; Name servers:
ASTERIX.HELIX.NET    205.233.118.2
WHISTLER.SFU.CA      142.58.103.1
```

This resolve.conf file provides our system information about the way to perform name resolution for our server. The first piece of information, *default domain,* provides information to append to a non-fully qualified domain name (a host name only, for example).

The second entry is the list of domain name servers to consult to resolve the name. The first DNS is the local provider's name server. Because we do not run a DNS server on our World Wide Web machine's network, name queries are sent first to helix.net, and should that name server fail to respond, to sfu.ca (Simon Fraser University, in Burnaby, British Columbia). The redundancy of the name servers can be increased by adding a third server to the list.

If a resolver request is sent to the asterix.helix.net name server, the server looks in its helix.net.hosts file to see if it can provide an authoritative response to the query. If helix.net.hosts contains an address for the requested name, then the name server resolves the name in the IP address and sends that address to the name resolver process on our WWW machine. If the name server cannot resolve the address, it makes a request to a higher-level name server, the root name server.

Note

The seven root name servers of the Internet (as of 1992, as contained in Albitz & Liu, O'Reilly & Associates, Inc.) contain information about authoritative name servers for all the top-level domains and authoritative information about the top-level United States domains.

The root name server either authoritatively resolves the domain request, or provides the domain name server address of the authoritative name server for that top-level domain. The originally queried name server then requests information from the second name server, which either resolves the address or provides the address of an authoritative name server for the subdomain. The process of delegation continues until the domain is resolved and the address is passed back to the original name server (asterix.helix.net) and then to the resolver on our server. The resolver then passes the address back to the process that requested the name resolution.

Registering a Domain Name

Domain names for distribution are limited to at least the first subdomain (such as global-village.net), and in some areas to the sub-subdomain (such as organization.bc.ca). How you register a domain name depends on the country in which you live. In the United States you must register with InterNIC; in Canada the registration is handled by caNET.

The easiest method of registering for a domain name is through your service provider. A service provider can easily identify all the relevant technical information, and likely is one of the two required domain name servers for your domain.

Registering a Domain: The Official Process

To register your name yourself, start by checking the availability of your preferred domain by running the whois process from a UNIX system attached to the Internet. Most systems point to the InterNIC name server and return results regarding the requested name. If no entry is available on InterNIC for any of the seven root-level domains (gov, edu, mil, int, org, net, com), then the domain is available.

At this point you gain access to the InterNIC WWW site and use its online registration form:

```
http://rs.internic.net/reg/reg-forms.html
```

This form collects the necessary information and e-mails it to you for verification. You then return the form to InterNIC at HOSTMASTER@internic.net, otherwise your registration is not processed. As mentioned in the InterNIC home page, the domain name servers listed on your application must contain the authoritative information about your domain or your application will not be accepted.

The registration process for a ca domain is slightly different, and can be found at **http://www.canet.ca**.

Registering a Domain: Finding Domain Name Servers

In most cases, your service provider acts as your primary domain name server. As well, your provider might give you the address and name of an established secondary name server for your use. If not, you must arrange for another organization to act as your secondary domain name server. A good source of servers are the universities in your area. In most cases, university DNS systems act as secondary servers without charge. Another possibility is to use a second service provider, although service providers might charge a fee.

Internet Security, Firewalls, and Encryption

As with any type of security, be it personal or domestic, the likelihood of an Internet security breach depends on one's degree of preparedness and use of the proper prevention tools.

Internet Security

Often the debate surrounding Internet security focuses on protecting data through the use of complex and technical computer software. Although these tools can be useful (see the "Firewalls" section later in this chapter), you can obtain a great deal of security simply by preparing your system and users. If a network is not portrayed as a weak yet valuable commodity, "hackers" will not waste their time trying to break in.

The Risks to Your Network

You network is at risk if a hacker perceives a benefit from breaking into it. If your server is simply a stand-alone server with no client or corporate public information and no access to another network or system, then the motivation to hack the system does not exist. In this case, either vendetta or pure chance is your enemy. After all, your house can be robbed by mistake or by a former employee. To avoid attack by a former employee, thoroughly clean house after an employee leaves.

If the Internet provides access for your staff, as well as providing information for the world, security is even more important. Over the past eight years, as the popularity of the Internet rose, so did the number of security incidents. Although paranoia about hackers is not necessary, risks are real. You can manage the risks with a serious approach to network security and by formulating an Internet Security Plan.

The Internet Security Policy

The idea of maintaining a security plan for your network comes from the IETF Site Security Handbook Working Group that is developing a site security manual to help system administrators plan security on their networks. The guide is currently in draft form and can be found at:

```
gopher://ds.Internic.net/00/rfc/rfc1244.txt
```

In short, the document discusses the need to make authoritative decisions about security issues: services offered versus security provided, ease of use versus security, and cost of security versus risk of loss. In the case of Internet security, all three tradeoffs and your decisions regarding them affect your choices among the different firewall security methods.

Note

Security can be gained via a number of means. First, you can simply remove risky service. If ftp is vulnerable to security breaches, then as a systems manager, you can decide not to offer ftp service. Obviously standard services such as e-mail, the World Wide Web, and ftp are your reason for connecting to the Internet. You can gain security by making them more difficult to use (for internal network clients), or by limiting Internet access to your network to non-critical and less valuable information. In most cases, you use the triad of options.

After you identify your network security goals, establish the methodology to implement the plan. Then consult with stakeholders to formulate a network security policy and make sure the policy is effectively distributed to system users. The policy should identify specific security processes and tools for ensuring the policy's effective implementation. When tools for maintenance of a specific policy do not exist (for example, a policy that employees not use WWW services to connect to non-business-related sites), sanctions should be clearly identified.

Firewalls

The most common security approach is to implement a firewall between you and the Internet. In traditional terms, a *firewall* is a barrier erected to prevent the spread of a fire. In the case of computers, connectivity, and security, a firewall prevents the spread of a security breach. More specifically, a firewall is a host, or a system of hosts and routers, that limits or at least hinders access to the core of your network. See the following figure for a visual representation.

As shown in figure 3.7, a firewall provides a common front against Internet hackers. With a firewall, the security features of a network can be concentrated on the one machine that the Internet can access. While in theory this strong defense provides a deterrent, more than one type of firewall exists. This section examines three of the more common configurations: the bastion host and proxy servers, packet filtering, and password/encryption methods.

Figure 3.7
Firewall placement.

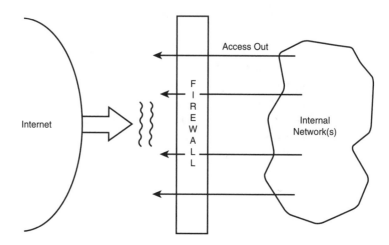

A Note from the Author

Some debate exists over the "hard shell/soft core" model of Internet security. In general, the idea that the enterprise is secure behind a firewall leads to severe security risks within the inner network. When employees fail to practice "safe" computing, they can provide the hole in a firewall a hacker seeks. When a hacker breaks into a network in this manner, they have a virtual carte blanche in the internal network.

Many security officials therefore recommend a security policy that is comprehensive and pervasive through your network (an "extra-hard-on-hard" model). The firewall's role in this model is to monitor and provide information about attempted and successful breaches in security, like an early warning system.

Bastion Host and Proxy Servers

Probably the most common firewall configuration for smaller networks is the *Bastion Host* configuration (also called *a dual-homed gateway*). The primary goal of the bastion host configuration is to provide one access point to the Internet and to limit direct IP access between the Internet and the inner network.

The term *bastion host* refers to the security function of this particular host, which is like that of the defensive positions (bastions) on medieval castles. A bastion host has a minimum of two network interfaces. One interface contains an IP address on an Internet-accessible network, either one of your ISP's subnets, or a subnet of your own address block. The second interface is addressed as part of the internal IP network (or subnet). See the following figure on bastion host topology.

Figure 3.8

Bastion host topology.

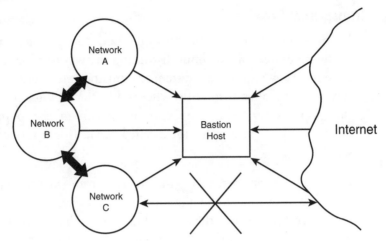

The main purpose of the bastion host is to prevent IP packets from moving between the Internet and the inner network. In the simplest setup, the bastion blocks traffic of IP datagrams in both directions. If the Internet connection allows your network access to the Internet, then a completely blocking host will prevent the access you need. To overcome this problem, you can use the bastion host to run proxies for the inner network. The two configurations of proxies are traditional and transparent.

Traditional Proxies

The original method to provide the inner network access to the Internet (and in certain cases to enable hosts on the inner network to provide services to the Internet) is by *traditional proxy.* In a traditional proxy system, inner network users are required to first access the bastion host, and then access the external host. To telnet to an external host, a user must telnet to the bastion host, and then telnet to the external host. Similarly, WWW services must be delivered through a simple text-based Web browser on the bastion host.

A Note from the Author

Although it is possible to use an X Windows-based system to run a graphical browser on the bastion host, from all the literature available on this topic, I understand that this can be a severe security risk. As a result, I do not recommend using X Windows as a solution to inner-network access, especially given the more reliable proxying systems available for WWW services.

Transparent Proxies

In contrast to the traditional proxy method, *transparent proxies* provide services to the inner network without disrupting the way services are provided. Such a system usually requires the system administrator to modify the clients for proxy service, install already modified clients (like the SOCKS package), or use clients that support proxying. The current version of the popular Web browser Netscape provides support for proxied service for ftp, gopher, http, and wais servers.

In the transparent proxy system, the user from the internal network runs the modified software or a client that points to a proxy. The proxy server handles the request and passes it to the external network. The external network thinks it is communicating with the bastion host, whereas the user sees the connection as direct to the external host.

Packet-Filtering Firewalls

Packet-filtering topology uses a router to control the flow of information to and from the internal network. Normally, the router enables datagrams that originate from within the internal network to pass freely to the Internet. The router examines the SYN and ACK bits of the TCP header to determine if the packet is internally originated. At the start of connection, both are set, and if the source address is internal, the datagrams are allowed to pass.

Figure 3.9
Packet filter placement.

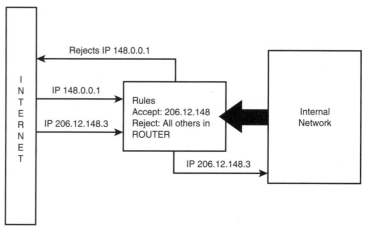

As figure 3.9 shows, the packet-filtering firewall usually relies on a bastion host as well as on the router. The router can be configured to allow only connections from certain external hosts or ports from internal networks. As well, all these requests are passed not to the internal hosts, but to a bastion host that provides these services (http, ftp, and so on). This configuration can include measures as sophisticated as only allowing DNS connections from the two DNS servers (based on IP addresses) responsible for maintaining name resolution for the external network.

Passwords and Encryption Methods

Passwords and keys ensure a great level of security on any network, including the Internet. A password (either a reusable or one-time password) helps to verify that a request to a server comes from an authorized source. Passwords and keys are not useful for all applications (such as a public Web site), but they increase internal security and that of commercial online services.

Passwords

By now, most people are familiar with password-protecting a document or an account on a host. Most people do not realize that using reusable passwords is inherently risky (in comparison to using once passwords with an encryption key) because these passwords are maintained for a set period of time during which they are vulnerable to a systematic attack. Because most systems only recognize the first eight characters of a password, and because most passwords are not very secure, 20 to 25 percent of all passwords can be broken with readily available software (such as the CRACK program).

To ensure the greatest level of security for passwords, IS managers should enforce the following rules for password creation and use:

- Do not use a password that is related to your username (in reverse, doubled, or any other form).

- Do not use personal information such as birthday, phone number, social security number, driver's license number, SIN, and so on.

❀ Do not use your name or that of a friend, relative, or pet—first, last, cat's, wife's, and so on.

❀ Do not use words in the dictionary.

❀ Do not use a series of the same character, such as 11111111 or eeeeeeee.

❀ Do not write down your passwords.

❀ Use different passwords for different accounts.

❀ Use a password of six or more characters. Remember that most systems only use the first eight characters, and that these characters must not be easy to break.

❀ Use mixed cases in your passwords—AeAddId, for example.

❀ Use non-alphabetic characters, such as SatI%twO.

Encryption Methods

As mentioned earlier in this chapter, encryption is not a security solution for services available to the public. Even so, as an extra level of protection for the internal network, encryption can provide a hard inner network beneath the hard shell of a firewall. Encryption schemes generally rely on one of two methods: *secret key* or *public key*. Unfortunately, each method has its problems. As a result, the encryption of files can provide greater security, not perfect security.

Secret Key Encryption

Secret key encryption relies on the generation of a secret key used by both the sender and receiver. The secret key method requires that the receiver be informed of or sent the key by mail, courier, or phone. As a result, if anyone intercepts the key, they can decode any messages sent using that key. Key transmission and storage is the main hazard of secret key encryption.

Public Key Encryption

In public key encryption, both sides generate two keys: public and private. The public key is published (or sent to the recipient), whereas the private key remains contained on each system. The users can send information back and forth, encrypted with the recipient's public key. The resulting encrypted message can only be decrypted with the private key exclusive to the recipient.

The main difficulties with public key encryption are its lack of speed (100 to 10,000 times slower than secret key), no registry of public keys exists for widespread use, and the storage of keys is dependent on computer security. A registry is necessary because of the threat of impersonation and distribution of public keys. Little can be done, however, to solve the storage problem.

Public key encryption addresses only transmission problems while sacrificing speed. Therefore, it typically is used to transmit keys for private key encryption, removing the transmission risk without the loss of speed.

Checklist

The following are concerns that should be addressed at the conclusion of the chapter.

☑ Technical resources available for setup of option?

☑ IP addressing in place (if needed)?

☑ Domain name registered (if needed)?

United States Domains: InterNIC

Canadian Domain Hierarchy (.ca): caNET

☑ Routing in place (if needed)?

☑ DNS? Local versus Provider supplied

☑ Security policy in place?

☑ Firewall in place?

Proxies?

IP Filtering?

Encryption?

☑ Password training for users?

☑ Internal passwords have been tested?

$\mathscr{S}$ LIP and PPP

This chapter discusses the use of Serial Line Internet Protocol (SLIP) and Point-to-Point Protocol (PPP) as methods of connecting to the Internet. Background information on both protocols will be discussed with a further examination of the merits and availability of each. The chapter continues by discussing the cost and hardware requirements of using SLIP and PPP. Finally, it describes the setup requirements for your connectivity solution.

Background Information on SLIP and PPP

Understanding SLIP and PPP will help you make an informed decision on their use in your connectivity solution. To aid in your understanding, the following sections present some general information on SLIP and PPP as they apply to setting up a continuous dedicated connection over normal analog telephone lines. In this context, SLIP and PPP fit in the layer between the TCP/IP protocol suite and the serial connections established between computers and modems or dedicated devices such as routers.

The History of SLIP

In the late 1970s, geographically separate TCP/IP networks were generally connected using special dedicated digital links and leased lines. A need arose to use a cheaper and more widely available transport mechanism—serial lines connected via modems through the public telephone network. SLIP originated from an early 1980s implementation of 3COM UNET TCP/IP. It was conceived as a very simple solution to the problem of sending IP over serial lines (such as telephone lines or hard-wired RS232 connections). Even its name (Serial Line IP) parallels this simplicity. It is important to note that there is no "standard" SLIP specification today. Luckily for users, most, if not all, SLIP implementations manage to work together anyway.

Technically speaking, SLIP is a packet-framing protocol. Details on packet framing will be discussed in the next section. The important thing to note here is that SLIP does not provide addressing, packet type identification, error detection, or error correction. Originally, it did not even provide compression, although this has been added recently in CSLIP (*Compressed* SLIP). It was SLIP's simplicity that probably led to the ease of its implementation and its subsequent proliferation.

The widespread use of SLIP is usually attributed to Rick Adams' implementation of it around 1984. His software was implemented for both 4.2 Berkeley UNIX and Sun Microsystems workstations and released to the world. At the time, both Berkeley UNIX and Sun's workstations enjoyed widespread use in the Internet community, and Adams' software quickly caught on because it was an easy, reliable way to connect hosts and routers via serial lines using TCP/IP—the cornerstone of the Internet.

Inside SLIP

How SLIP works is remarkably simple. SLIP implementation conceptually does the following two things (see fig. 4.1):

- ⚛ Continuously takes in a stream of bytes from a serial line and transforms it into a stream of IP datagrams (A in fig. 4.1).

- ⚛ Continuously takes in a stream of IP datagrams and transforms it into a stream of bytes, which it sends across a serial line (B in fig. 4.1).

Figure 4.1

SLIP's simple processes.

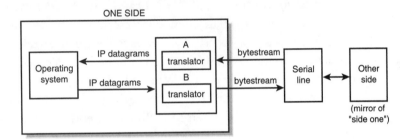

These processes indicate why SLIP is known as a *packet-framing* protocol. An implementation of such a protocol takes data packets from one networking source and formats them for another, and vice versa.

Now that you know what a SLIP implementation does conceptually, it is time to explain the details of how SLIP operates. Serial lines send and receive data one piece at a time; that is, they send and receive data in a "serial" fashion. The pieces of data transported are of a specific size and in a specific order. At the lowest layer, they are only one bit in size, and so can have a value of either one or zero.

By the time these pieces of data have reached a SLIP implementation, they have been grouped into bytes, also known as *characters*. SLIP defines two special characters, "END" (which signifies the end of a frame) and "ESC" (which signifies escape). These are defined so that everyone uses the same values to mean the same thing. The END character corresponds to the (decimal) number 192 and the ESC character corresponds to the (decimal) number 219. These values were probably chosen because they are easy to remember when written as octal numbers: 300 and 333.

A Note from the Author

Don't worry if these numbers don't look particularly memorable to you—this probably just means that you're not a protocol implementer, systems programmer, or another form of digital numerologist!

When sending a frame, a SLIP implementation starts sending an IP datagram and normally just sends the characters unmodified down the serial line. The exception is when SLIP encounters an END or ESC character in the datagram. In order to not confuse the SLIP END and ESC, SLIP uses the following process to "escape" or encapsulate these characters: When SLIP encounters an END character, it sends a special two-character sequence (referred to as a *framing character*) in its place—ESC followed by octal 334 (decimal 220), which happens to be the value of END plus 1. When SLIP encounters an ESC character, SLIP sends another two-character sequence instead—ESC followed by octal 335 (decimal 221). Finally, when SLIP finds the end of the datagram, it sends the END character, marking the end of the SLIP frame.

On the receiving side of the serial line, the corresponding SLIP layer knows about all this numeric trickery. The SLIP implementation on the receiving side reverses the process by replacing the two-byte sequences with the original characters. If SLIP receives an END character from the serial line, SLIP knows it is finished with this frame and can start with the next one. Hence, the part of SLIP receiving the serial line transmission reconstructs the same data packets that the other end was sending.

There is one more special number used by SLIP. In theory, SLIP could send frames of any length using the method described previously. In reality, computer programmers (and hardware designers) tend to store groups of data in fixed-size chunks, called *buffers*. The "classic" implementation of SLIP (the Berkeley UNIX SLIP drivers) limits the size of a packet to 1,006 characters (not including the framing characters). In accordance with this limitation, other disciplined programmers have maintained compatibility by designing their SLIP implementations to accept 1,006-byte frames and by not sending frames exceeding this size.

SLIP is an ad hoc protocol that solves the problem of sending IP over serial lines, but that is all it does. In addition to not being a standard, SLIP also did not originally even have a formal specification other than source code. SLIP is now documented in Internet RFC 1055, "A Nonstandard for Transmission of IP Datagrams Over Serial Lines: SLIP." That said, it may still fulfill your needs.

The History of PPP

By the late 1980s, members of the Internet community began to realize that the Internet was experiencing explosive growth, and that serial connections to the Internet were becoming more and more important because it was impractical for some people to use other means of connection. These Internet users also knew that existing point-to-point protocols (such as SLIP) were not official Internet standards and did not fulfill their needs well enough to become Internet standards.

The Network Working Group of the Internet Engineering Task Force (IETF) shouldered the task of first defining the requirements for an appropriate standard, and then creating the standard. The group succeeded in producing the requirements in the form of a Request For Comment (RFC) document in June of 1989. Its present form (at the time this book was written) is known as Internet RFC 1547. The standard itself was produced later, and its present form is RFC 1661. The PPP standard was designed to be extensible and companion documents exist to describe these extensions, which are also standards (RFCs 1220, 1332, 1333, 1334, 1337, 1338, and 1376).

Note

All documents are available on the Internet from: **ftp://ds.internic.net/ rfc/rfcXXXX**, where XXXX is the RFC number.

Inside PPP

The Internet Standard Point-to-Point Protocol (PPP) is considerably more sophisticated than its predecessor, SLIP. It was designed to fulfill a different set of requirements, many of which SLIP did not. The full set of requirements includes the following:

❀ Simplicity

❀ Transparency

❀ Bandwidth efficiency

❀ Protocol processing efficiency

❀ Protocol multiplexing

❀ Multiple physical and data link layer protocols

❀ Standardized maximum packet length

❀ Support for switched and non-switched media

❀ Symmetry

❀ Connection liveness

❀ Loopback detection

❀ Misconfiguration detection

❀ Network layer address negotiation

❀ Extensibility

❀ Option negotiation

That is a lot of requirements to meet! Luckily, the complexity of using or configuring PPP is not proportional to the feature set in the preceding list. The following paragraphs explain what these requirements mean, and how they are fulfilled. In some cases, multiple requirements are fulfilled by a single feature. In these cases, the feature will be explained in some depth later in this section.

❀ **Simplicity** has two main benefits. First, it stops PPP from needlessly implementing functionality that is already in higher-level protocols such as TCP. Thus, no error correction, sequencing, or flow control are necessary parts of the PPP protocol. Additional features needed to boost performance are optional. Second, simplicity decreases the likelihood of programming errors by the implementers of a given PPP implementation. This has the pleasant side effect of increasing the likelihood of interoperability—a primary goal of standardization.

❈ **Transparency** means that the protocol must not place any data constraints during transmissions. This makes it unnecessary for the higher-
level protocols it carries to be modified in any way, or even be aware
that they are being transmitted over PPP. The PPP implementation
achieves transparency by treating the data it is sending as if it were
opaque (that is, PPP cannot or does not read the data). It does not need
to read data in most cases, and when it does, it puts the data back the
way it was before entering the PPP layer.

❈ **Bandwidth efficiency** means getting the most out of the bandwidth
available. The overhead for the PPP protocol may only consist of a few
percentage reductions in the raw link bandwidth. PPP implementations
achieve this by compensating for protocol overhead by using data
compression.

❈ **Protocol processing efficiency** means that PPP headers must be inherently easy for processing by typical computers. PPP achieves this by not
normally requiring complex field checking to be performed, and by
aligning the information along 32-bit boundaries. The reason that
alignment produces a speed-up—which is surprising because it often
causes the data to be larger—is that most modern processors store data
in 32-bit words. The hardware of a processor is optimized to work most
quickly on pieces of data the size of a word, or a multiple of the size of a
word.

Note

This is also related to why most operating systems in existence (for
example OS/2, VMS, Windows NT, BeOS, Plan 9, and various products
based on UNIX) often perform better on today's computers than do
software products such as Microsoft DOS, Microsoft Windows 3.x, and
Microsoft Windows 95. These software products are all still stuck in the
past by being either partially or completely based on 16-bit technology.

Meanwhile, companies that make higher-end computers (such as Sun
Microsystems and Digital Equipment Corporation) are already beginning to sell systems based on 64-bit technology, and are updating their
operating systems accordingly.

❀ **Protocol multiplexing** is the capability to support multiple higher-level protocols. Unlike SLIP, which can only support at best one protocol at a time or at worst just IP, PPP supports multiple protocols simultaneously. While the Internet community is mainly interested in IP, it is often necessary to support other protocols such as AppleTalk, DECnet, or IPX. This is because point-to-point links between gateways for geographically diverse Local Area Networks (LANs) should simultaneously support all protocols implemented on those LANs. PPP achieves this goal by transmitting and interpreting a large protocol type field (usually either 8, 12, or 16 bits in width), as well as sending the packets of a given protocol.

❀ **Multiple physical and data link layer protocols** enable PPP to operate over a wide variety of commonly used point-to-point link technologies, whether they are serial or parallel, synchronous or asynchronous, low-speed or high-speed, electrical or optical. PPP does this by not being tied to the specifics of any set of physical or data link protocols. The PPP standard even allows implementations over new link types as they become available.

❀ **Standardized maximum packet lengths** define a standardized default packet length for each type of point-to-point link. This defaults to 1,500 octets, which allows efficient transmission of common LAN-sized packets. This value is known as the *Maximum Receive Unit* or MRU. The MRU can also be negotiated by both ends of a PPP connection via the Link Control Protocol (discussed later in the chapter). The capability to use default MRUs ensures interoperability, while the capability to negotiate a better MRU on a given link improves efficiency.

❀ **Switched (dynamic) and non-switched (static) point-to-point links** are supported by PPP. An example of a non-switched link would be an RS232 serial cable connecting two host computers. An example of a switched link would be a modem connection between two computers via the telephone system. In the second example, the connection itself may traverse several telephone switches, but it doesn't matter to PPP, much like the connection method doesn't matter to a human speaking to another via the telephone.

※ **Symmetry** is embodied in the capability for a given PPP host to act as either a gateway to another host, as a host itself, or as a server or a client. The PPP protocol does this by not defining any preassigned static roles to a host running PPP. Any host that is capable of running PPP could act in either role, and this role could change dynamically as time goes on. PPP hosts can be connected to the Internet on a full-time basis, or transiently, whenever the operator requires it.

※ **Connection liveness** can be monitored on a PPP link by means of the Link Control Protocol. This enables either end of a PPP link to automatically determine when the link is working properly, and when it is essentially dead. At this point, corrective action can be taken, or a peer can simply give up, saving resources. It could even attempt to start a new connection with another available peer. As well, connection liveness features can be disabled in situations where they are deemed as "expensive," such as when a service provider charges for bandwidth utilization.

※ **Loopback detection** automatically senses if the underlying communication equipment (such as a modem) is in a self-testing mode. This allows routing to operate sanely in such a scenario by PPP telling the higher-level protocols (for example) that the local end of the connection is reachable, but the remote end is not. This behavior is implemented using the Link Control Protocol, which is discussed later.

※ **Misconfiguration detection** is the capability of PPP to quickly detect improper link configuration. A misconfigured link is declared to be down once it is detected. An example of misconfiguration is when a gateway has multiple point-to-point links and the cables get swapped due to operator error. PPP detects this through a simple verification of the peer's identity before marking an interface as operational.

※ **Network layer address negotiation** is the capability to dynamically determine one's own address, or the address of one's peer. This is done in PPP by using a Network Control Protocol (NCP) such as Internet Protocol Control Protocol (IPCP), which is extremely useful when a PPP host or terminal server is being used as a dial-up server. Multiple hosts can then connect to the server and be dynamically allocated one of a set of addresses. Users on the dial-up hosts can then access the full range of Internet services. Even e-mail can be accessed by connecting to a Post Office Protocol (POP) daemon located on the server, or anywhere else on the Internet.

❀ **Data compression negotiation** is the capability for peers to decide what sorts of compression algorithms (if any) they can use while communicating. Peers may even simultaneously use multiple, independent data compression schemes. PPP enables, but does not require, peers to use data compression, and it does not specify a fixed set of data compression schemes. The use of compression algorithms is negotiated using the Link Control Protocol.

❀ **The extensibility requirement** is very general, but is probably the single most important requirement. A protocol with the built-in capability to be extended should be flexible enough to adapt to the unknown conditions of tomorrow's Internet. PPP achieves extensibility by enabling groups of companion protocols, such as Network Control Protocols and Authentication Protocols, to exist. These companion protocols can develop separately from PPP, while enabling higher-level protocols to benefit from enhanced security or routing capabilities. The purpose of these protocol groups is discussed later in this section.

❀ **Option negotiation** is the capability for the peers on both ends of the link to automatically come to an agreement on the best parameters for the Data Link Layer. Options to be negotiated include: network layer addresses, data compression schemes, maximum packet length, and encryption schemes. PPP achieves this through the use of the Link Control Protocol, which satisfies both the requirement for option negotiation and the requirement for extensibility. The protocol itself is extensible and allows the use of other types of point-to-point links and encapsulation schemes.

The *Link Control Protocol* (LCP) is the portion of PPP that ensures that the protocol is sufficiently versatile to be portable to a diverse set of environments—LCP is possibly the main advantage of PPP over SLIP. LCP enables the peers on a given link to negotiate important parameters that will affect the link's viability and performance. Luckily, the process of negotiation occurs independently of the actions of a user or system administrator, greatly easing link maintenance in the ever-changing network environment. LCP provides a channel of communication between the peers so that they may transparently and automatically agree upon encapsulation format options, handle changing limits on sizes of packets, detect common network configuration errors, and terminate the PPP link cleanly. SLIP, on the other hand, has no capability analogous to PPP's Link Control Protocol. Any negotiation for SLIP is done manually by people, or even worse, by trial and error experiments by a single person.

The most important implication of LCP is that it enables a very simple PPP implementation to communicate with a more sophisticated peer. While sophisticated peers may be able to reap the benefits of various PPP options, and see a subsequent increase in performance, they are still fully compatible with simpler peers and can automatically communicate effectively (if not as efficiently) with a less capable peer. No conforming PPP implementation becomes a second-class network citizen. Higher-level protocols such as IP operate seamlessly, no matter what set of options the peers agree upon. PPP leaves configuration options that are specific to the network layer to network configuration protocols (NCPs).

Figure 4.2

PPP Protocols.

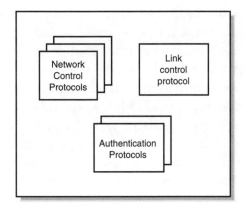

The set of options negotiated by peers using LCP include the following:

- ❀ MRU

- ❀ Authentication protocol

- ❀ Quality protocol

- ❀ Magic number

❄ Protocol field compression

❄ Address and control field compression

Option types are represented as one octet in an LCP packet, which corresponds to 256 options. One option (0) is reserved, and the rest are available for use. Existing option types are documented as part of the PPP standard in the Internet Standard document known as "STD 2." For example, STD 2 states that the MRU option type is represented by the number 1. There are fewer than 255 option types defined at this point, which leaves some room open for future option types. The Maximum Receive Unit (MRU) has been explained. The other options are explained in the following:

❄ **The authentication protocol** enables the PPP implementation to choose a way of verifying the identity of the peer on the other side of the link. When the peers agree on an authentication protocol to use, authentication is attempted. If authentication fails, the link is terminated. Two examples of authentication protocols are the Password Authentication Protocol and the Challenge Handshake Authentication Protocol. In cases where the peers agree that authentication is not necessary, no authentication need take place at this level. This is common when authentication has occurred previous to when the PPP implementation takes control. One very common example of authentication occurring independently of PPP is when authentication is handled by an underlying operating system, such as UNIX. PPP is initiated either interactively by a human user, or by a simple program (often known as a *script*) only after that user has supplied a valid name and password to the system. This is so common that it appears to be the rule, rather than the exception. Use of this "manual" authentication may fade in the future because it requires considerably more user intervention (at least to set up) than using a real authentication protocol.

❄ **The quality protocol** is another option negotiated by peers via the Link Control Protocol. Link quality protocols monitor when, and how often, the link is dropping data. Link quality monitoring is disabled by default.

❄ **The magic number configuration option** enables PPP implementations to automatically detect loopback conditions. By default, a magic number of zero is used to indicate that the implementation does not want to negotiate a magic number. A *loopback condition* occurs when both sides of the link are actually the same—that is, the peer is talking to itself. It is important for PPP to be able to recognize this condition, because loopback is often used as a self-testing mechanism by underlying hardware, such as modems. The magic number scheme works by one side sending a random number to its peer. The other peer looks at the number, and if the number matches its own magic number, the peer requests a new magic number from the first peer. This happens several times. It is very unlikely for this process to not succeed eventually in the case where the two peers are different. In the loopback case, it is very likely that identical magic number pairs will be generated again and again. After identical numbers appear several times, the PPP implementation concludes that the link is indeed in the loopbacked state and it can take corrective action, such as notifying the human operator.

❈ **Protocol field compression** enables peers on a PPP connection to send one octet, rather than two octet protocol fields in each and every frame they send. This increases the efficiency of PPP links, which often operate on relatively low-speed network media. LCP packets themselves are never sent with protocol field compression to guarantee recognition of link control packets by peers that do not implement protocol field compression.

❈ **Address and control field compression** is another form of compression negotiated by the peers via LCP. If the peers are both capable, they agree to allow the compression of data link layer address and control fields. This is a very successful form of compression because these fields usually have constant values for point-to-point links.

Another important family of protocols used by PPP are called *Network Control Protocols* (NCPs). In general, such protocols exist for every type of network layer that can be transported via PPP. Before a network layer link can be established, the peers negotiate parameters to be used in one or more network layer protocols using the appropriate NCPs.

An important example of an NCP is the *PPP Internet Protocol Control Protocol* (IPCP). Through IPCP, peers can negotiate compression formats to be used within the IP layer. Peers can also use IPCP to discover their peer's IP address, and they can even ask that the peer give them an address. This is a very important capability of PPP, especially for the transient connections typical of an Internet service provider's dial-up server. In this environment, users who do not have dedicated connections to the Internet can dial into a server and be dynamically allocated an address, at which point they become connected to the Internet. When they disconnect, the address can be reused by someone else. The consequence of this is that they may get a different address each time, but their PPP software is automatically able to handle this situation. IPCP frees humans from having to write complicated scripts to discover their address from their PPP server.

The preceding paragraphs reveal a great deal of information about PPP, a complex and extensible protocol. A great deal of thought and planning went into its definition and its various implementations. Luckily, you don't have to remember all of this information. Configuring and using PPP is generally simple because a great deal of the process has been implemented for you.

Deciding When to Use SLIP or PPP

At some point, you must decide whether a SLIP- or PPP-based solution is the right way to solve your Internet connectivity problem. First of all, you must know when such a solution is appropriate. Second, you must know the implications of using SLIP or PPP for such a solution. Finally, you may want to know some alternatives to using either a SLIP- or PPP-based solution.

Typical Uses for SLIP and PPP

SLIP and PPP's main benefit is that they provide interactive access to Internet services, such as the World Wide Web, gopher, electronic mail, and file transfer. They are often considered as offering the lowest common denominator for connecting to the Internet. They provide a way for users to access the Internet through temporary connections established by dialing into a service provider. When you set up a site on the Web today, the vast majority of those accessing it will probably be using either SLIP or PPP. The other side of the coin is that these technologies can also enable companies, organizations, and individuals to be self-contained providers of interactive Internet services. In addition, SLIP and

PPP can be used to connect geographically diverse local area networks in a transparent way.

Benefits of SLIP

SLIP is capable of delivering all the benefits of being connected to the Internet —accessing and providing Internet services such as file transfer, gopher, electronic mail, and the World Wide Web. Due to the simplicity of its design, SLIP is available for most computer platforms in active use today. SLIP connections are usually offered by dial-in and dedicated line providers before they offer PPP.

Problems with SLIP

The design of SLIP is so simple that it moves some of the complexity into the user or system administrator's lap. SLIP implementations often require more complex dial-up scripts and provide a lower level of robustness. When problems occur—and they will—it is often difficult to diagnose the problem because SLIP itself does not address issues such as monitoring the quality of a connection, checking authentication, or providing a built-in way of dynamically discovering your address.

Benefits of PPP

PPP was defined with SLIP's deficiencies in mind. Many describe PPP simply as "a better SLIP." While this is certainly true, it is a gross oversimplification. The main benefits of PPP are in areas that are not even addressed by SLIP, such as quality monitoring, authentication, and dynamic address negotiation. These technical benefits translate into time savings in setup, performance tuning, and troubleshooting. It is interesting to note that despite the benefits derived from PPP, the speed of PPP has not been sacrificed—PPP operates as fast as SLIP (approximately 2.1 to 3.3 Kbps over a 28.8Kbps modem connection).

Problems with PPP

The most significant problem associated with PPP (and SLIP as well) implemented on 28.8Kbps connections is that it is not fast enough. This problem is not really a result of PPP, but of the underlying connection technology generally used: normal analog phone lines. The telephone network was optimized for the transmission of human voices, not data.

Another problem is that PPP is still not a turn-key solution in most cases. Because most providers do not use PPP-based authentication protocols, someone still must write the scripts that are capable of sending a user's name and password before establishing the connection.

Recommendations

On a technical level, PPP is superior to SLIP. This should not be surprising, considering that PPP was defined later than SLIP, and that those who were defining it had the opportunity to learn from SLIP's design oversights. The bottom line is that if you have the choice between PPP and SLIP, choose PPP. In choosing PPP, it is possible that you will gain nothing, but it is extremely likely that it will save you a great deal of headaches and effort.

Alternatives to SLIP and PPP

It is possible that you do not require the full set of capabilities that SLIP and PPP offer. Pricing of available services can also be prohibitive if you are located in a sufficiently remote or undeveloped area. In this case, however, you still may have some alternative technologies at your disposal.

One example alternative would be to connect to Internet electronic mail via a store-and-forward system such as *Unix to Unix CoPy* (UUCP). You could then set up a piece of computer software known as a mail-bot (short for "mail robot") to serve documents to Internet users. At intervals of your choosing, your mail-bot-equipped computer could retrieve e-mail requests and respond to them. When you eventually move to a direct connection to the Internet, your mail-bot could continue to serve its purpose. This would enable you to serve information to users worldwide who only have e-mail access to the Internet. Although the Internet is growing at a remarkable rate, there are still a significant number of users, especially in remote or less-developed areas, who only have e-mail access to the Internet.

Availability and Usability

Now that you know some background information on SLIP and PPP, it is important to bring up issues that will affect your choice more directly— availability and usability. Availability refers to the chances of there being SLIP or PPP service in your area. Usability refers to the ease of use inherent in SLIP and PPP implementations.

Current Availability

Presently, both SLIP and PPP connections to the Internet are available on a widespread basis. In large urban centers, you likely have a choice between several competing service providers. Even beyond these urban centers, service providers exist anywhere the market is large enough to support them. If you are lucky enough to live in one of these areas, SLIP and PPP connections to the Internet are only a local telephone call away.

Future Availability

As time goes on, SLIP and PPP connections will probably become increasingly available in cities with small populations. In large urban areas, the amount of access available will increase, but extrapolating from current business trends, the number of service providers will likely decrease as large companies buy up smaller ones. In the future, wherever there is a demand for SLIP and PPP connections, there will be a supply.

Demand will show a sharp decrease when affordable, higher-bandwidth connection options become available. In the very near future, conventional telephone line-based PPP and SLIP connections will simply not be fast enough for even the smallest Internet content providers to justify the associated costs. Content providers will not be willing to invest in a technology that is considered to be on the verge of becoming obsolete.

Bandwidth Issues

A typical SLIP or PPP connection enables data to pass through it at a rate of 28.8 Kbps. This relatively low data rate has important ramifications if you plan to use such a connection to put your Web server on the Internet.

The problem is simple. If multiple users access your Web site at exactly the same time, and they are all connected to the Internet at 28.8 Kbps, they will experience a delay—the Web site can *only* fulfill their requests by sending data to them at a maximum combined rate of 28.8 Kbps. If this delay is large enough to make the users feel annoyed or inconvenienced, then your Web server is failing to satisfy its audience.

There are two further points to take into account when discussing this scenario:

1. Users tend to access a Web page, and then spend some time reading or viewing its contents.

2. The distribution of accesses to a Web server over time is probably not uniform.

The first point works in the Webmaster's favor. While one user is viewing a Web page, the server is completely free to satisfy the requests of another user's Web browser. The second point works against the Webmaster's cause because it is likely that at certain times of the day (even when users exist in multiple time zones), many users will be accessing your site, while at other times very few will be.

It is hard, if not impossible, to predict what the access rates of your Web site will be. What is certain is that as interest in your site increases, it is likely that the bandwidth of your PPP or SLIP connection will become saturated.

For Web sites that have a potentially small or infrequent viewership, a SLIP or PPP connection can be quite adequate. In many cases, however, low-speed connections such as SLIP or PPP are used as a stepping stone—they are better than nothing while a higher-speed solution is being sought.

In many areas, especially large urban centers, a SLIP or PPP connection simply is not cost effective. Using another type of connection, you may be able to receive twice the bandwidth (or more) for less than twice the cost, for example. You could then recoup your costs by renting out Web space on your server to others, or even by reselling one or more dedicated or dial-up lines.

Reliability Issues

Another potential drawback of using a PPP or SLIP telephone line-based solution lies in the area of reliability. Reliability problems tend to crop up at two points in the life of a connection:

⌘ When the connection is established

⌘ During the connection

A SLIP or PPP connection is established by first creating a telephone connection to the remote site. At this point, many things can go wrong: the phone line may give no dial tone, a busy signal, or a fast busy that indicates an error on the phone network. In the first two cases, an intermittent problem may have occurred in the telephone network. This is quite unlikely, but can happen at peak periods of telephone usage. In all the preceding cases, the only recourse is to try to dial again.

The telephone network itself can become congested because it is only possible for a limited number of telephone lines (as low as ten percent in some areas) to be used at any one time. This is important to realize when you consider a PPP or SLIP connection that is always connected. You should ask your telephone company about their policy on data lines. Attempting to circumvent this policy to save a few dollars in the short term is probably a poor idea. It is advisable to establish a good working relationship with your telephone company in order to maximize your chances of receiving good service from them.

The software that you use should be able to detect the various failures that can occur when establishing a telephone connection. By using these capabilities, you can generally solve the problem by having your system retry until it succeeds in establishing a telephone connection.

During the connection, other problems may arise that cause the line to become disconnected. Again, at this point, your software should be set up to automatically reconnect. In this case, if the problem persists, the root of the problem may be that the quality of the telephone connections you are establishing is very poor. To a human, this level of quality would appear as static on the line. To the modem, router, or PPP/SLIP software, this static would either seem like random garbage data, or just the loss of the real data. The best course of action in this case is to speak with your telephone company. They can either fix the problem, or perhaps set you up with service of a higher quality.

Spending the time to set up your software to detect failures and act appropriately will save you a great deal of trouble in the future. This is usually accomplished through writing small programs (called *scripts*). It is important to realize that the input to your scripts will vary depending on the state of your telephone connection, the state of the modem, what speed is achieved by the connection, and other factors. It is advisable to design your scripts to be flexible enough to handle this varying input.

Appropriate Uses of SLIP and PPP Connections

It was mentioned previously that in many cases, a SLIP or PPP connection may not be fast enough to support a popular Web site. This does not mean that this connection type is useless to you. For instance, a very useful and common scenario is the idea of a server park.

A Note from the Author

Global Village Consulting's external Web server, **www.global-village.net**, is currently being moved to a server park, where it will also serve as a gateway to our head office's network and to customer networks. We fully endorse a server park-oriented solution!

The server park is a service that you can purchase from your Internet Service Provider. It enables you to "park" your server hardware at their site. Typically, you could then connect your hardware to your provider's Ethernet network. The provider's network is probably connected to the Internet at a minimum of T1 speeds. If you choose the server park option, discussed in greater detail in Chapter 12—congratulations, you have just increased the bandwidth between your Web server and the user by one or more orders of magnitude, at a considerably less bandwidth to cost ratio. They may even be able to offer you backups or other administration services.

Once your server is in a server park, SLIP or PPP connections are then an excellent way to connect your server to other sites.

Tip

At this point, you can proceed from being an Internet content provider to an Internet service provider. You can sell dedicated lines to other organizations or even sell dial-up lines to individuals. The funds gained from this reselling could then help pay your server park fees.

SLIP or PPP connections could be used to connect one or more of your organization's local offices to the Internet. Remote offices that are also connected to the Internet could even be set up in such a way that you could provide file sharing or other services by "tunneling" through the Internet. Tunneling creates a point-to-point link that uses the Internet as the transport layer. Protocols such as AppleTalk or IPX can travel through this tunnel as if the link was a normal LAN connection.

After you have your Web server in a server park, it can fulfill a variety of useful purposes in addition to serving Web pages, as follows:

⚛ Serves as your office's gateway to other offices and to the Internet itself.

⚛ Acts as a firewall between the Internet and your organization's internal networks.

⚛ Serves as a USENET news server, a Domain Name Server, or a POP (Post Office Protocol) server.

⚛ Acts as a caching Web proxy server, saving you bandwidth charges.

When more affordable and higher-bandwidth connectivity options become available, you can proceed to replace your PPP or SLIP links at a comfortable pace. When an increase in bandwidth occurs, the architecture of your network can remain the same, but you can enjoy the benefits that increased bandwidth brings!

Hardware Requirements

In addition to your host computers and SLIP or PPP software, you will need to purchase the equipment that transports the serial link over the telephone system. Essentially, this is performed by modems, or by dedicated devices that have both routing and modem functions, called "routers."

Modems versus Routers

When planning your PPP or SLIP connection to the Internet, there are two hardware solutions to choose from—modem-based or router-based. Note that there is no requirement that you use the same solution on both ends of the connection. Each has its own benefits, as discussed next.

Modem Benefits

Modems must be used in conjunction with a computer in order to connect your LAN to the Internet. The modem is used to establish the physical layer of the connection, while the computer runs the PPP or SLIP software. The computer also routes packets between hosts on the LAN and hosts on the Internet. If you only have one computer, then it will act as its own gateway. While it may seem cumbersome that you must use a computer along with your modem, the following benefits are present:

1. You will probably be able to use a computer that you already own.

2. Even if you have to buy a computer to be your gateway, you will be able to use it to do other things as well—its gateway operations should not take up much of its computing power.

3. Using a modem with an existing computer as your gateway is much cheaper than buying a router.

Router Benefits

Routers are dedicated devices that connect to your LAN as a complete turn-key solution. Routers are generally more expensive than transforming an existing computer into a gateway via a modem and SLIP or PPP software. If you have to buy an extra computer or extra software to make the computer and modem act as a gateway, however, it may be cheaper to purchase a router (which range from $400 to $1,500). Routers are also much easier to set up and maintain, and you will probably receive better support from your vendor than if you connect via a modem. Using a computer, some software, and a modem, moreover, has many more possible points of failure than does a router. Even if it costs you more up front to purchase a router, you may save money in the long run, because you probably will have to tinker with it less.

Selecting a Modem

Taking care to select a high-quality modem will save you a great deal of hassle in the long run. Low-quality modems are not necessarily slower—they are just less reliable due to software and hardware bugs. They also are often difficult or impossible to upgrade. Don't assume that well-known modem manufacturers necessarily have the highest quality of modems; the opposite is often the case.

Avoiding Known Problems

To find a high-quality modem, read multiple reviews of modems written by independent third parties. You can find such reviews in the trade press, on the Web, or in USENET (**comp.dcom.modems**, for example). Keep in mind that reviews are often aimed at the consumer market, rather than at using the modem for a dedicated connection. In addition, it is important to find out if a given modem works with the software, operating system, and hardware you intend to use.

Some large, well-known modem manufacturers sell modems at a cost that is quite low, compared to their lesser-known competitors. People buy these modems due to name recognition, and the fact that "everybody else" seems to be buying them.

A Note from the Author

This consumer "herd mentality" is also present in the personal computer software industry. Consumers base their purchasing decisions too heavily on a lower price and name recognition rather than on the technical merits of the product. The result is that a software giant will get their product to market early, sell it at a lower price, and worry about quality later. At this point, these larger companies have captured significant market share.

Consumers later are surprised to discover that their modem is unstable, and that the manufacturer is offering a "free upgrade" to the modem's firmware, which fixes the problem(s). Essentially, the customer is paying money to test a product for the company. Eventually, the product becomes stable after several "upgrades." You probably want to avoid such a situation—your time is better spent getting real work done for yourself or your company.

Information about upgrades and bug fixes is generally available from the modem manufacturer's telephone support line, BBS, or Web site.

Compatibility with Service Provider

To ensure that you get a reliable, high-quality connection to your service provider, you must ensure that you are communicating in a compatible manner. You must make sure that your modem and PPP/SLIP software are configured properly with respect to the other end of the link. It is often the case that if you use the same kind of modem on both sides of the link, you receive a more reliable and perhaps faster connection. This may be because the modem manufacturer tests the modems it makes primarily using its own brand of modems. Using proprietary features of the modems may also enable you to achieve a connection at a higher data rate, such as 34 Kbps rather than 28.8 Kbps.

Don't Overpurchase

Today's modems come with a wide range of features, from fax capabilities to being able to store the phone numbers of incoming calls, to dial back capability. Given that you are using your modem for a dedicated connection, many of these features are of very limited use to you. One feature that can prove invaluable, however, is the capability to perform upgrades to the modem's software. This enables you to fix bugs in the modem's software quickly, and possibly even for free. The bottom line is just common sense: never pay extra for features that you don't need, if you have the choice.

Selecting a Router

If you can justify the cost of a router, it is probably worth it. Routers also come with a varying number of features. In contrast to modem features, chances are very good that some of the router's features will be extremely valuable to you. Even if you don't use them initially, they are available for future use. Some useful router features, such as those presented in the following list, are discussed in this section:

- Dial on demand
- Dynamic redial
- Administration tools
- Expandability

Dial on Demand

Dial on demand is the capability of the router to establish a telephone connection only when necessary. This is only useful when both ends of the link have this capability. When a packet arrives at the router on one end of the link and the telephone connection is down, the router will bring up the link. The link will then stay up until some set of criteria is met, such as some period of inactivity, and then the link will be brought back down. This can be useful in scenarios where telephone connection time is at a premium, because it is a long distance call, or if your telephone company is charging you less with the understanding that the line will not be used 24 hours a day.

Dynamic Redial

Dynamic redial is the capability of the router to sense that the telephone connection has been broken, and to automatically attempt to reestablish the connection. This could be useful if you occasionally or frequently receive noisy telephone connections or have other problems, such as power outages. Dynamic redial has even been known to keep TCP/IP connections alive when the building hosting one end of the connection was struck by lightning.

Administration Tools

Routers are specialized systems. They serve one purpose, and do it well. Router administration tools should be simple to use, and generally are. You will probably only need to set up your router once, and then leave it to do its job on its own. Probably the only maintenance that you will need to do is when you need to reconfigure your network.

Expandability

Expandability is an extremely useful capability of a router. For instance, you may be able to use your SLIP/PPP router over normal telephone lines, and then upgrade to another datalink technology, such as ISDN or leased lines, when it becomes available or affordable. It is also a good idea to purchase a router that can have its software updated easily, just in case you need to receive updates from your vendor.

SLIP/PPP-Based Dedicated Internet Connection Costs

When making the decision on whether to use a SLIP- or PPP-based connection, it is important to consider all the costs. The following sections will examine the various products and services for which you will have to pay to make your connectivity solution complete.

Telephone Company Costs

Depending on the policy of your Internet service provider, you will have to pay for one or two telephone lines, one for each end of the connection. It is important to note that telephone companies charge for telephone lines based on their intended use. This is why business lines are more expensive than residential lines. Your telephone company may have a different rate for data lines. To avoid hassles, get the kind of phone line appropriate for use with a dedicated data connection. In addition to this monthly charge, you may also have to pay a one-time set-up charge, or installation fee.

Internet Service Provider Costs

Your service provider may also charge you both one-time setup fees and ongoing fees. The one-time setup charge may include services such as routing configuration at their site, domain name registration, domain name service, and so on. The ongoing fees may include administration costs when you need your provider to maintain these services.

The main ongoing cost will be for bandwidth. Your service provider will either charge you a flat rate or a rate based on your usage. In the case of a dedicated 28.8Kbps connection, it is likely that your provider will charge you a flat rate; even if you continuously transferred data over your connection, this would not impact the provider or other customers. In the server park scenario, you will most likely get some bandwidth for free, and then pay for any additional amount used at a fixed dollar rate. For example, you may be able to transfer 1 GB of data for free, with any additional data costing you $50 per GB.

Hardware Costs

Hardware costs include any hardware you will need to purchase. You will need a modem or a router at each end of the connection.

If you're lucky, the service provider will pay for the equipment needed for their end. If you aren't planning on using a router on your end, but need to connect your whole LAN to the Internet, you will also need a computer to act as a router. If you don't have a capable machine, you will need to purchase one. 28.8Kbps modems will typically cost between $150 and $300 dollars, while routers can cost between $400 and $1,500 dollars. A computer capable of acting as a gateway will range in cost from $700 to $1,200 (and up).

Software Costs

You may need to purchase additional software. PPP and SLIP software will sometimes, but not always, come free with the operating system you are using for your gateway. Excellent free software is also available for most platforms. Even if the operating system for your gateway supports TCP/IP, you may need to purchase a separate "server" version in order to perform routing functions. The required software is generally included free, or is available as a free add-on with UNIX-based operating systems.

Setup Requirements

There are several things you will have to do to get your SLIP or PPP solution up and running. These include the items in the following list:

- Acquiring telephone lines
- Configuring the link
- Picking a service provider
- Acquiring the expertise necessary to set up and maintain your solution

These items are discussed in detail in the next section.

Telephone Lines

First of all, you must make sure to order your telephone lines as soon as possible. Depending on the telephone company, it can take weeks to get the lines set up, especially if the company needs to perform actual line installation. The last thing you want is to have to wait for the telephone company when you are ready to go with the rest of your solution.

Configuring the Connection

Configuring the connection may take a considerable amount of tinkering. It is worth your time to set it up properly the first time, to lessen the problems you run into later. Your connection should be tested for stability before officially going online. Configuration of the connection hinges on using provided or constructed robust connection scripts, and testing your system as thoroughly as possible.

Using Provider Scripts

If you are lucky, your service provider will provide you with the scripts you need in order for your software to establish a proper connection. Because your provider has many customers all doing the same task, their staff can alleviate much pain and suffering by facilitating the distribution of knowledge of how to connect to its system. Unfortunately, not all service providers provide scripts, or the scripts provided won't work for you. If this is the case, you will have to write your own connection scripts.

Connection scripts are small "programs" that tell your computer how to initiate your connection. A script first sets up your modem by sending the proper initialization string. The script then sets up the telephone connection by dialing the telephone. The script then has to detect a login prompt (if using SLIP, or PPP without an authentication protocol) and send a user name and password. If the last step succeeds, the script must be able to set up routing (PPP does this for you), and set into motion the PPP or SLIP software.

Figure 4.3

Connection script functionality.

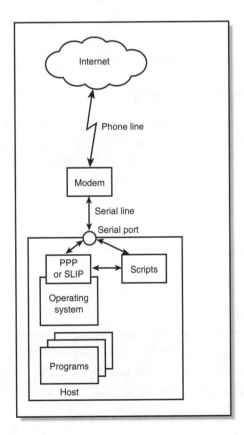

Creating Custom Scripts

Creating scripts is a little bit tricky and somewhat time-consuming. Scripting languages used for this generally have a construct that enables you to specify a set of expect-send pairs, which are executed in order. The trickiness comes in because the input you receive can differ somewhat each time you connect.

The best strategy for creating scripts is to perform the connection task manually (using a terminal emulator) several times. At this point, you know what input to your script to expect, and how the input can differ from time to time. It is a good idea to find out what modem initialization string to use by reading the documentation that came with your modem. Reading the documentation and examples provided with your SLIP or PPP software, and asking others who have set up connections before, can help you a great deal.

Your custom scripts should be set up in such a way to handle various failure points, such as telephone busy signals or excessive ringing. When such a failure occurs, your script should try to reestablish the connection. The script should be run when your computer starts up, so that after maintenance or other disruption, the connection will be established when you reboot your system.

Picking a Provider

You will probably have more than one Internet Service Provider to choose from. There is no precise recipe for choosing the perfect ISP. In general, you should see if it provides the services that meet your needs, and try to avoid a provider who oversells bandwidth. Choosing a provider carefully is especially important with a SLIP/PPP dedicated solution, because of the potential unreliability of the connectivity method. As a result, a provider's assistance will likely be more necessary for SLIP/PPP than for more turn-key solutions such as ISDN and T1 connections.

Required Services

Your service provider must be able to provide you not only with a connection, but also some level of initial and ongoing support. Don't base your choice only on low setup and bandwidth charges at the expense of acceptable support. A good ISP will also have good customer service. Both when you are first setting up your connection and later on, the service provider should be able to give you some help in diagnosing any problems that crop up. Most service providers will do this, although some also charge a great deal of money for support. Make sure that you at least get some degree of free support. The service provider must also set up routing to your network and propagate this routing information to the Internet at large.

Optional Services

You may also want some additional services from your service provider. Some examples include the following:

- ❀ Providing you with addresses

- ❀ Creating your Internet domain

- ❀ Maintaining Domain Name Service

- ❀ Granting you access to their USENET news server

- ❀ Renting "space" in their server park

- ❀ Administering and backing up your server (for server park solution)

You may receive some of these optional services for free, but you will probably be charged a hefty sum for anything that is labor-intensive, such as constantly having to update the name service entries, or restoring lost files from backups.

Bandwidth Overselling

Some service providers will sell more dedicated lines than are appropriate to the amount of bandwidth they have coming in. Stereotypically, this occurs in small companies that are attempting to cash in on the Internet hype that is so prevalent today. You should steer clear of providers that do this—check on a provider's reputation, or even ask the ISP directly if it oversells bandwidth. The result of having a bandwidth overselling service provider is low data throughput. Make sure that if you are paying for 28.8 Kbps of bandwidth, you are actually getting it.

Personnel Requirements

Your connectivity solution using SLIP or PPP will require not only software and hardware gadgets and an ISP, but also someone to configure and maintain your end of the connection. The personnel that implements your solution should have:

[1] the technical skill set necessary to implement your solution.

[2] the ability to maintain your solution on an ongoing basis.

Types of Skills and Optional Sources

In order to set up your connectivity solution, you will need people with the skills to do so. They should have a good understanding (gained through experience) of the configuration and troubleshooting of computer hardware and software. Familiarity with modems and networking is also desirable. There are three main sources for these personnel, as follows:

- ✺ In-house

- ✺ From your ISP

- ✺ From an independent consultant

In-house personnel may need to be trained or learn as they go. They may be a cost-effective choice simply because your organization retains their expertise. If you already have someone acting as your LAN administrator or computer-support person, he or she will probably be very capable of setting up your Internet connection.

Some ISPs offer their services in this area. They are often highly skilled, and will get the job done quickly and very well. Unfortunately, your ISP will probably charge you a high hourly rate for this service. If you need things done correctly the first time and very quickly, hiring experts could be worth the expense.

Another option to consider is to hire a computer consulting company, or an individual consultant. A consultant should be willing to sign a contract for a fixed cost, with some money paid out before the project is complete, and the balance paid when the project is complete. This can be quite beneficial for you, because you will know how much the project will cost up front, rather than paying an hourly rate and being surprised at how long it took.

Maintenance

You should ensure that you have the resources to maintain your Internet connectivity solution. One benefit of in-house workers setting up your solution is that they will be around later to maintain it. If you use a consultant, you should include maintenance as part of your setup contract. Otherwise, if you have problems later, he or she may be unwilling or unable to help you. You should also keep this in mind if your ISP set up your solution, or you may be charged hefty hourly rates for maintenance. Keep in mind as well that you may want to change service providers in the future, and your current ISP may not be thrilled about you paying them for the switch-over.

Summary

Now that you know what is involved in setting up a PPP- or SLIP-based solution, you can start working on planning and implementing it. Good luck! You may also have come to the conclusion that a SLIP or PPP connection-based solution is not for you because it is too expensive, too complex, or too slow. If this is the case, do not despair. The next chapter offers information on a faster technology—leased lines. In addition, Chapter 10 offers information on renting Web space on someone else's site. Chapter 11 offers information on server parks, which gives others access to your site at a very good speed to cost ratio.

Checklist

The following are concerns that should be addressed at the conclusion of the chapter.

☑ Dedicated 28.8 Kbps available?

☑ SLIP or PPP?

☑ Modem or Router?

Modem Selection: Reliable? ISP uses compatible modem? Modem does not have functions not needed?

Router Selection: Dial on demand supported? Redial functionality? Expandable to support higher speed connections? Administrative tools available?

☑ Telephone company costs:

☑ ISP costs:

☑ Hardare costs:

☑ Software costs:

☑ Provider configuration scripts available?

☑ Telephone policy on line usage:

☑ Solution in place for dropped lines?

☑ Requirements for ISP selection: Bandwidth available from ISP? Setup support free? Routing and propagation in place? Ongoing support offered?

☑ Options for ISP selection: Address provision? Domain name registration? Domain name service provided? USENET news server access? Upgrade options available?

CHAPTER CHAPTER CHAPTER CHAPTER CHAPTER CHAPTER CHAPTER CHAPTER CHAPTER

5

Stepping up to 56 Kbps:The "Old" Digital Connection

Although the basic connection of SLIP or PPP relies on the older technology inherent in the analog communication systems, a number of different connection methods exist that take advantage of the digital telecommunications infrastructure. Unlike the older analog service, digital telephone service allows much higher speeds of connection over the same twisted-pair wiring available in most locations today. This chapter examines the simplest form of digital connection: a 56Kbps dedicated or switched connection. After discussing what having a dedicated 56Kbps service entails, the chapter examines the availability and limitations of this connection method, and then moves on to discuss the equipment and cost requirements for such a connection. Finally, the chapter examines the issues specific to dedicated 56Kbps setup.

After reading this chapter, you should understand the basics behind digital telephone services at 56 Kbps. Not only does this chapter explain the theory of digital telephony, it also provides a basic understanding of the equipment controlling the use of digital telephone connections for Internet connectivity. Finally, this chapter helps you assess the service providers that offer 56Kbps service so that you can determine whether the service and providers will meet your WWW site needs.

Understanding 56Kbps Dedicated Service

The previous chapter examined the use of an analog connection to the Internet via modem and telephone line as one of the possible methods of Internet connectivity. Because of the limitations of analog communications, however, the maximum data transfer rate available via modem today is 28,800 bps (due to the limits of analog signals to deal with the "noise" of copper lines).

The speed limitation is viewed as one of the main drawbacks to analog communications, and is mainly a function of the rapid degradation of analog signals. A system of digital communication has developed over the past 40 years to overcome this limitation. This section details the history of digital telephony, focusing on the basic digital connection—the 56Kbps connection. After detailing the history, the section defines the various categories of 56Kbps connections, and reviews the technical background behind the digital communications.

History of Digital Telephony

Before discussing the basic technology behind the digital telephone system that includes 56Kbps lines, a bit of history of the system explains why digital phone systems developed. In order to understand their development, the basics of the older analog systems are covered in detail, followed by a discussion of the reasons behind the switch to digital telephone connections.

Analog Telephone Basics

Before examining the digital telephone system that provides the 56Kbps connectivity option, it is useful to examine the historical analog telephone system. The history of the analog system provides a basis for the reasoning and purpose of the digital system that provides for 56Kbps lines. Historical analog systems are comprised of two main divisions:

❈ Local loop

❈ Trunk lines

The Local Loop

The history of digital telephone systems actually has its roots in the earlier analog telephone system. Analog telephone systems work on the principle of frequencies transmitted over a single twisted pair of copper wires. The twisted-pair wiring connects your receiver to the central office of the telephone company, carrying voltage to your phone (approximately 48 volts of direct current). Because of the power transmitted by the copper wires, the telephone can continue to operate even in the event of a local power failure.

A Note from the Author

The term *twisted pair* refers to the fact that the pair of copper wires used to transmit the analog signal is twisted together. The twisting of the wires reduces the amount of line noise, enabling the signal to travel farther in the circuit without becoming degraded to the point of being unusable.

The explanation of the local loop connection between standard phones illustrates the main connection in local telephone calls within one exchange. One of the parties calls the number and the signal travels to the central office where switches determine if the called number is available. If the number is not available, a busy tone is received. Otherwise, a connection is made, and the phone at the receiving end rings. For this type of connection, the entire call takes place over local loop cabling.

Figure 5.1

A local call through a central office.

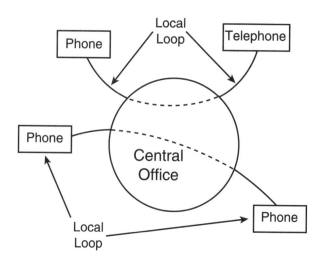

The main difficulty with local loop connections occurs when the telephone call is placed from a number in one exchange to another number in a different exchange. Because the multitude of possible connections between individuals involves considerable areas and distance, the telephone companies developed a process of connecting local exchanges with telephone lines that could carry more than one call over the twisted-pair cabling. Twisted-pair lines used in this way are refered to as *trunk lines*.

Trunk Lines

Because the distance required to connect exchanges is lengthy, the cost for connection is prohibitive. To better provide the trunk service without a large cost, the telephone companies used a technique called *frequency division multiplexing* (FDM) to combine 12 lines onto a single set of twisted-pair wires.

Frequency division multiplexing refers to a concept of utilizing the complete analog frequency available on a copper wire. Because telephone conversations require frequencies only between 300 Hz and 3,300 Hz (this range provides enough range for human vocal communication, such as a telephone call), the telephone company limits voice calls to this frequency. Frequency division multiplexing enables the telephone companies to stagger a number of individual voice communications over the entire spectrum of bandwidth available on the twisted pair (48,000 Hz are available on twisted-pair wiring).

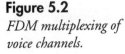

Figure 5.2

FDM multiplexing of voice channels.

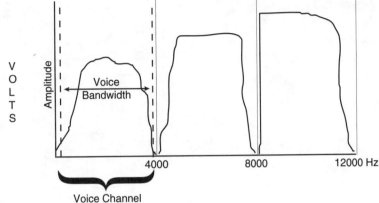

As figure 5.2 illustrates, the telephone companies modulate the individual telephone calls to higher frequencies. For example, one call is modulated from the 44,000 Hz to 48,000 Hz frequency band. The extra 1,000 Hz frequency (because only 3,000 Hz is required for the actual sound) is provided as a *guard band* between each frequency. A guard band is unused frequency around each signal that prevents the individual signals from overlapping and creating crosstalk on the line.

By using frequency division multiplexing, the telephone company is able to develop a set of carrier designations. The lowest level of analog trunk lines is the Channel Group, which provides for the multiplexing of 12 signals over one line. Larger trunks are used to provide for the transmission of even larger numbers of voice signals over long distances. Although the analog trunk system provided an increased capacity for telephone companies, analog systems degraded over distance, and the addition of repeaters could provide only limited corrective benefit, because noise was also amplified by the repeaters. As a result, the companies could multiplex only a finite number of telephone signals over analog trunks without adding more trunk lines. As telephone usage proliferated, the number of lines required became prohibitive. A new system was then adopted to allow even greater utilization of the existing infrastructure—digital telephone.

Figure 5.3

Frequency division multiplexor groups hierarchy.

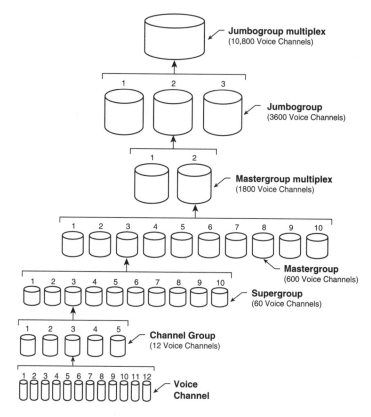

Making the Switch to Digital

Back in the 1960s, AT&T ran into the problem of having to support too much cable. Each new subscriber added another local loop to the system, which required additional trunk lines. As a solution, AT&T converted all its analog trunk lines to digital trunks. The conversion process, completed by the end of the 1960s, enabled AT&T to greatly increase the amount of voice channels that could be carried over any one trunk line. To better understand the reasons for the increase of carried voice channels that resulted from digital lines, the technical background behind digital telephony is examined.

The Technical Background of Digital Telephony

This section examines the basis of the digital telephone system to provide a more comprehensive overview of the benefits and limitations of a digital 56Kbps connection. After providing the theoretical basis, this section looks at where your 56Kbps connection fits into the picture, and how communications over a 56Kbps line work. Finally, this section takes a brief look at the issue of switched versus dedicated 56Kbps lines and the implications of each for WWW site managers.

The Theory of Digital Communications

Whereas analog communications use electrical frequency waves to represent the sounds of telephone conversations (hence the need for modems to convert the digital information of computers to the frequency or sounds that can be transmitted over analog lines), digital telephone systems convert sounds into a stream of information represented as bits (either zeros or ones). The process goes through a number of stages, starting with the analog-to-digital conversion, signal sampling, and two types of modulation. The result is a digital signal that creates the standard digital voice carrier.

Analog-to-Digital Conversion

The first process in digital telephone systems is the conversion of information from sound waves to digital sound. The conversion is accomplished through the use of a codec (coder/decoder). In terms of communications, the codec provides the opposite functionality of a modem. Modems take digital data and convert it into analog data, whereas codecs take the analog sounds and convert them into digital data.

Signal Sampling and Pulse Amplitude Modulation

The process of digital conversion is accomplished by the codec through sampling of the analog source. The number of times the codec must sample an analog source depends on the frequency of the original signal. Because telephone conversations are limited to 4,000 Hz per signal (including the guard band), the codec must sample the source 8,000 times per second.

The sample process represents the first step in converting the analog signal into a source that can be transmitted over digital telephone systems. Through the use of *pulse amplitude modulation*, the samples are converted into digital signals that have amplitudes corresponding with the original amplitudes of each analog sample. Because of the inclusion of amplitudes in the digital representation of the analog signal, the signal created by pulse amplitude modulation does not yet provide the necessary structure to be transmitted efficiently over the digital lines. At this point, the signal is still subject to many of the same problems as the original analog signal. To avoid these problems, the codec provides a second level of conversion—*pulse code modulation.*

Pulse Code Modulation

Pulse code modulation takes the pulse amplitude signal (which represents a variety of amplitude values) and converts the information into binary digital signals. The result is a signal that is not prone to the degradation analog signals encounter. The cost to transmit these signals and to regenerate the signal along the transmission lines is therefore less than when using analog communications.

Figure 5.4

Pulse amplitude and code modulation for analog signals.

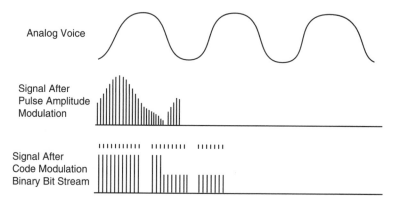

The conversion of pulse amplitude signals to pulse code signals is based on the principle of quantized levels. To regenerate an analog signal so that it can be understood at the receiving end, a minimum of 128 amplitude levels must be represented. Because 7 bits are needed to represent 128 discrete levels of amplitude, each sample of the analog source must be converted into 7 bits of information by the pulse code modulation. Because the samples are taken 8,000 times per second, the resulting bit rate of the channel is as follows:

8,000 samples per second $\times$ 7 bits per sample = 56,000 bps

The bit rate of a standard digital communication channel (for one voice communication) is actually higher, because the channel requires an extra 8,000 bps for system control. Although the 64Kbps channels provide the basis for each telephone call, the real benefit of digital telephony is not realized until the channels are combined into the digital trunks.

Digital Telephone Hierarchy

As previously mentioned, the main problem that AT&T faced in the 1960s was the large cost and wire requirements of the analog telephone trunk system. Because the trunks were created using frequency division multiplexing, the limit of the trunk lines was 12 channels per twisted pair. Increased capacity could be generated only through an increase in wires. The digital trunk system was created to increase the amount of channels that could be multiplexed over a single wire. The process of multiplexing digital trunks explains the final piece of technology behind digital telephone systems, giving you an understanding of why digital trunks can have variable capacities.

The How of Digital Trunks

Digital trunks are created through a process of multiplexing multiple digital signals into one wire. Unlike analog signals, which utilize frequency division multiplexing, digital systems utilize *time division multiplexing*. Under time division multiplexing, the multiple individual sources are each assigned a time slot within a frame of information. Frames consist of a number of slots equal to the number of sources being multiplexed (there is a limit to the amount of sources that can be successfully sampled). Each source provides 8 bits of information to the multiplexor each time it is sampled. Again, the sources are sampled at a rate of 8,000 times per second. The entire "train" of information is framed with 1 control bit at the front, and sent down the wires as a unit.

24 sources × 8 bits per source per sample × 8,000 samples per second + 1 bit = 1,537 Kbps

Note

The amount of sources that can be successfully sampled depends on the multiplexor used. For example, over twisted-pair copper wiring, T2 speeds can be sent.

The 1.544 Mbps resulting channel is the T1 digital carrier designation. The channel carries 24 individual voice communications including control information over a single line. Multiple T1 trunks are then multiplexed into T2, T3, and T4 channels (for a more in-depth discussion of the T1 and T3 carriers, see Chapter 7, "Entering the Global Arena: A T1/T3 Leased Line").

Variable Trunk Capacity on Single Lines

One of the main benefits of the digital telephone system is the capability of providing a greater utilization of the existing copper wires. For example, the standard trunk lines are now 24 signals instead of the 12 signals provided by the analog system. The technology behind the multiplexors also enables the telephone company to support a T2 (96 voice channels or 4 T1 channels) over the same copper wiring, consequently reducing the need for more wiring. The process is controlled by the number of sources that the multiplexor can sample over 1/8000th of a second.

Where Does 56 Kbps Enter the Picture?

Now that the basis for the digital telephone system has been established, the role of a 56Kbps connection needs to be examined. Because the digital telephone system was primarily designed to increase the capacity of the trunk lines, the standard local loops were not digitized (although these loops are now being digitized as a result of the ISDN developments; see Chapter 6, "Integrated Services Digital Network (ISDN) Connection," for an in-depth discussion of ISDN). Even so, telephone companies are willing to provide 56Kbps connections for organizations that desire more reliable and higher bit rate digital connections. Although the digital connection provides a number of benefits for trunk transmissions, communications also benefit, some of which are detailed in the next section.

A Note from the Author

As discussed in the previous sections, the basic digital carrier is actually 64 Kbps, but 8 Kbps is used for system control. The system control bandwidth is mainly a result of the lesser technology that was a product of the original digital networks. As telephone companies upgrade their facilities, the full 64Kbps bit rate will become available.

Communications and 56 Kbps: The Benefits of Digital Communications

As mentioned previously, digital communications have a number of advantages over the earlier analog communications. One of the most obvious benefits is the lack of signal degradation in digital communications. This feature is a result of the discrete nature of digital signals. Because only two values for a digital signal are possible (zero and one), the electrical noise on a transmission line must be very great to provide degradation enough to damage the signal (as long as the discrete values differ enough in amplitude). Digital signals are also easier and less expensive to restore and repeat through the use of a simple digital repeater that can remove all noise and replicate the signal.

What digital signals provide in terms of distance support and quality of communications results in the most important benefit to communications for a manager of a WWW site. In terms of connectivity issues, a digital connection provides a mechanism for much higher bandwidth over copper telephone wires than the modem connectivity provides. At the base level of a 56Kbps connection, the service provides for the two basic configurations (discussed in the following sections) that influence the pricing structure and usability of 56Kbps services.

Configurations of 56Kbps Connections

Telephone companies generally offer two categories of service for digital connections. The type of service depends on the usage patterns that are being supported; as a result, the costs and billing methods vary. At the 56Kbps level, the service can be either a switched connection or a dedicated connection.

Switched 56Kbps Connection

Switched 56Kbps connections are provided by the telephone company on an "as needed" basis. The telephone company creates a virtual circuit between your site and the requested site. As a result, the bandwidth becomes available only when requested, and you pay only for the amount of time online. This is beneficial for site connectivity dealing with intermittent bulk data transfers. Because WWW sites need to be connected to the Internet at all times, the use of a switched 56Kbps connection is not feasible. Instead, the connectivity of a dedicated 56Kbps connection should be considered.

Dedicated 56Kbps Connection

A dedicated 56Kbps connection is simply a digital connection that is dedicated to your communications from point x to point y. Because the connection is always open and available for you, the telephone company charges you for the full utilization of the circuit. As a result, a dedicated 56Kbps connection generally is more expensive than a regular telephone line. Also, the cost of the connection depends on the distance between the two points that need to be linked. Because connections that travel over a longer distance require that trunk space and possibly even intercontinental carrier space be reserved, the costs associated with the dedicated circuit can increase rapidly.

A Note from the Author

In general, the costs for any telephone connection increase as the distance between you and the destination increases. Although this may not make too much difference when the connection stays within the same city, large increases in costs can occur if your connection travels through other exchanges. To minimize your costs, you should attempt to decrease the amount of distance between you and your ISP. All other things being equal, the smaller the distance, the better (it does not hurt in terms of onsite support, either!).

Understanding Dedicated 56 Kbps Availability and Limitations

Now that the technological basis of 56Kbps digital connections has been detailed, this section looks at the current availability of dedicated 56Kbps services. Although 56Kbps connections are widely available, the age of the system calls into question the long-term viability of the service. The section concludes with a brief discussion of the bandwidth issues that govern WWW sites, and ways in which dedicated 56Kbps services match up with other connectivity options.

Current Availability

Given that the digital telephone system behind 56Kbps service was designed for use over the existing infrastructure of twisted-pair copper wiring, it is not surprising that the service is available from virtually all telephone companies in all areas. The exception to this availability is in certain rural areas. One other concern regarding the availability of 56Kbps service is the support for this service by ISPs. Generally, the 56Kbps connection is well supported, but in some areas, the distance of the connection can create price disincentives. Although the current availability of service is plentiful, some of the trends mentioned below are raising concerns about future availability.

Trends and Future Availability

The main concern with 56Kbps connections is the capability for thirty-plus-year-old technology to continue to evolve and adapt with time. The age of this technology has produced a number of concerns about how well 56Kbps service will continue to meet client needs in light of the new advances in internetworking and the new services demanded by Internet users (such as sound and video). Given the limitations of 56Kbps connections, two main factors should be considered in evaluating 56Kbps connections for your WWW site:

* The age of the technology

* The developments of other technologies

An Aging Service? Competition from New Technology

As mentioned previously, the technology behind 56Kbps lines is now more than 30 years old, and telephone companies have discovered that the needs of the consumers have continued to expand over time. As telephone companies continue to examine new ideas to replace current technology, the digital system is slowly being phased out and replaced by new advances in technology.

New techniques for utilizing the existing copper infrastructure such as ISDN (see Chapter 6) and ADSL (see Chapter 9, "Emerging Technologies: ADSL and B-ISDN/ATM") provide methods of utilization that lend themselves to be more cost-effective and simultaneously providing higher capacity levels to the telephone clients. Also, the telephone companies are experiencing new competition, both from cable companies and as a result of the breakup of the telephone industry into the regional Bells. As the competition increases, the companies turn to even more efficient communications media, such as optical cabling, to provide even greater capacities at lower costs.

The result is that traditional digital services may not provide a sufficient long-term path for newly connected companies. As technological advancements ments change the industry, support for the older technology, in terms of ISPs, continued hardware availability, and upgrade paths, could decrease. Before choosing traditional 56Kbps service for WWW site connectivity, site managers should seriously consider the long-term expectations of this site.

Bandwidth Issues

Along with the questions concerning long-term viability of service with the traditional 56Kbps dedicated service, questions exist regarding the bandwidth provided by such a connection. To detail the problems inherent with the relatively low level of bandwidth provided by a 56Kbps connection, this section discusses three main issues:

  ❀ Bandwidth requirements for a LAN-to-LAN connection

  ❀ Bandwidth requirements for WWW sites

  ❀ Cost of 56Kbps bandwidth versus other possible connection methods

Bandwidth Requirements for LAN Connections

To illustrate the nature of bandwidth usage, it is useful to examine the data flows between two LAN sites. For example, take two offices connected by a dedicated 56Kbps link—one office in Vancouver, and the other in New York (ignoring the Internet for the moment and instead concentrating on the more expensive long distance dedicated point-to-point connection). Because the majority of the work performed in most offices is of local concern only, most LANs today require the bandwidth available from a 10Mbit Ethernet connection.

A Note from the Author

Given the ever increasing reliance on computers and network-based applications, the bandwidth requirements of our local area networks has been continuously expanding. Originally, serial connections of 9,600 and even 2,400 bps was sufficient for local networks (a link to the mainframe or printer to transfer text). As our needs expanded and the volume of personal computers became even more prevalent, the connections increased to high-speed serial connection such as Apple's LocalTalk connections (256 Kbps). Finally, the connections in most offices have increased to the Ethernet level of bandwidth. This started with the relatively narrow 10Mbit Ethernet, and is now progressing to the higher-speed 100Mbit connections.

For a long time since the connection of the computers via local networks, the amount of data flowing offsite has been relatively small. The bandwidth gradient has been identified and accepted by many industry experts for a number of years, and as a result of the gradient, the overall bandwidth required for inter-LAN data flows has been limited to that available from the 56Kbps connections. The trend of the bandwidth gradient appears to be changing. Because more and more of our activities on computers have become cooperative and collaborative, the amount of data flow between LANs has increased dramatically. By looking at the new data flow, some predict that inter-LAN requirements will rise to fractional T1 (a portion of a T1 less than 1.544 Mbps in multiples of 64 Kbps) or T1 levels by the turn of the century (estimates of current requirements are between 96 Kbps and 128 Kbps). (Netwatcher (ISSN 0890-5800), April 1995, Volume 13.4.)

Note

Actually, the fact that bandwidth requirements are increasing for LAN-to-LAN connections should not be surprising to anyone who is currently working in the industry, or who even uses the Internet. Connectivity requirements are increasing rapidly. Groupware, video conferencing, or even real-time sound transmissions over the Internet greatly increase the amount of data flowing to and from the LAN.

Bandwidth Requirements of WWW Sites

Although the bandwidth flow generated for a LAN-to-LAN link is interesting, the hard fact of the matter is that most WWW managers will not have to deal with the issue of LAN communications links. The beauty of the WWW is that the requirements to set up a site are low enough that small organizations can set one up without the side connection requirements of LAN communications being needed for justification. Even so, the changes in our work habits that have altered LAN data flow have affected how the Internet is used. Take the WWW for example, the collaborative nature of the WWW is exactly the type of change in our working habits that results in the increase of LAN data flow. In fact, the entire principle behind the WWW is for collaborative information distribution. As a result, the total bandwidth required to support the WWW increases as the types of data change (for example video and audio instead of text).

In estimating the bandwidth requirements for a WWW site, serious attention must be paid to the future expandability of your site's connection. Because Internet technology is evolving quickly, the bandwidth requirements for such technology also is evolving quickly. Two years ago, real-time audio communications via the Internet was an interesting test. Now, that technology has been widely distributed over the Internet. The result is a much greater draw on the bandwidth of sites that deploy this technology.

One of the main limitations of WWW traffic (believe it or not, traffic could be much higher) is the small size of the local loop for most users. The local loop limitation is changing rapidly. Technological advances such as cable connections and satellite connections (see Chapter 10, "Cable and Satellite: User Connectivity?") are quickly increasing the amount of bandwidth available for the casual user. Simultaneously, the number of users accessing the Internet is growing at a tremendous rate (conservative estimates are that the number of users with full Internet access will go from 9 million in the U.S. to 15 million by the end of 1996). Combined, these trends make the bandwidth requirements of a WWW site even more important. To maintain the interest and traffic on your site, you will have to maintain a significant level of service. If the site is too slow, clients will not access the site and will find the information they need at another site (and trust me, there is *always* another site).

Price to Bandwidth versus Options

Although this section does not go into the details of pricing for 56Kbps connections (see later in this chapter), the key point here is the cost of 56Kbps dedicated connections versus the alternatives. On a price-to-bandwidth ratio, the cost for a dedicated connection decreases as you increase the size of the link purchased. This fact holds true regardless of whether you are discussing the cost of local loop connections or the cost of Internet connectivity. Because the 56Kbps connection is the lowest level of digital dedicated connection available, the price point is quite high. Also, the newer digital connection methods such as ISDN (see Chapter 6, "Integrated Services Digital Network (ISDN) Connection") provide bandwidth at an even more cost-effective level, even at the same size of pipe. As a result, the cost to upgrade from a 56Kbps connection is generally considerably less per increment of bandwidth.

Determining Hardware Requirements

Despite the limitations of the dedicated 56Kbps connectivity method, a large number of ISPs exist that provide this level of connectivity. Consequently, a considerable amount of equipment has been developed and perfected with cost-effective availability. As newer technologies emerge, the price of older technologies may increase (or availability may drop). Even so, until that time, the required equipment should be relatively inexpensive and easy to acquire. Before choosing 56 Kbps as a connectivity method, however, you should understand the hardware requirements and related issues. This section discusses the two main pieces of equipment required—CSU/DSUs and routers—and where they can be obtained.

What Are CSU/DSUs and Routers?

The primary equipment required to connect a network to the Internet via a dedicated 56Kbps digital connection is the Channel Service Unit/Data Service Unit (CSU/DSU) and a router. This section defines each piece of equipment and describes the tasks handled by each piece. This section should help you understand the importance of the equipment and determine whether to buy or rent your equipment from a provider.

CSU/DSU

The first piece of equipment, the CSU/DSU, provides the interface between the telephone company's network and yours. The features of the units partially depend on the required connection speed and the characteristics of your network. Although the CSU/DSU is generally considered one piece of equipment (often, it's actually a box that can perform either function), explaining their functions separately is useful.

Channel Service Unit

The *Channel Service Unit* (CSU) is a simple device that interfaces with the telephone company's network. Issues such as signal transmission quality, making sure that signals meet network specifications for bipolar signals, and network timing are not handled by a CSU. The CSU assumes that the client's network equipment is providing an appropriate signal to the CSU. In general, this type of interface connects directly to a network device that already provides this functionality. The simplicity of the CSU makes the basic CSU relatively inexpensive.

CSUs provide an interface to the client's network that depends on the required connection speed. In general, for speeds of 56 Kbps and higher, CSUs provide the ITU-T V.35 interface. The type of pin connector depends on the manufacturer of the CSU. An example of a network connected via a simple CSU is a computer containing a built-in digital interface (such as a digital signal processor, or DSP). Such computers generally can add an adapter that will provide them with an appropriate V.35 interface. Some routers also provide digital signal capabilities that make the CSU sufficient.

Data Service Unit

The *Data Service Unit* (DSU) is a much more complex piece of equipment that not only provides an interface for the telephone company's network, but also filters the digital signal, synchronizes the signal with the network clock, and provides network control codes (timing for signal control and how the information is coded). The DSU provides communication over a digital network that is transparent to the communicating computer. In this way, a DSU fulfills a function similar to the modem, although the modem is obviously an analog equivalent. In general, the DSU is more expensive than the simpler CSU.

Like the CSU, the performance of the interface provided by the DSU is dependent on the manufacturer and the speed of the connection. Again, the ITU-T V.35 interface is commonly used. When is the DSU used instead of the CSU? If the computer system or network device connecting to the digital network does not provide the necessary functionality for the signal regeneration and timing, then the DSU must be used. For instance, a number of routers do not provide the appropriate digital signals, consequently requiring you to use a DSU rather than a CSU.

Routers

In a nutshell, the router is a piece of equipment that reviews each IP datagram and decides if and where that datagram should be sent. Connecting your local network (or computer) to the CSU/DSU enables a router to make decisions about the sending options of each datagram it receives. As discussed in Chapter 3, "The Historical and Technical Background of the Internet," the routing information can be provided via a static table, or via a more dynamic routing protocol.

Because the router is simply examining the headers of individual datagrams and deciding whether to send the datagrams out to the Internet, the functionality of routers can be provided by a properly configured host (usually running UNIX). Although UNIX hosts can provide a significant amount of routing capabilities, the software-based routing of UNIX hosts is considerably slower than the hardware routing that is performed via stand-alone routers. Only slower-speed connections are effectively routed via the host method. For higher-speed connections, a hardware router is recommended.

In either case, the setup of a router can be somewhat complicated. In the case of a host router, the process requires considerable knowledge of TCP/IP networking and systems administration in order to configure the router with routing algorithms, gateways, and subnets. In the case of a hardware router, the process is somewhat simplified, although a good understanding of the TCP/IP mechanism is recommended.

Sources of Equipment

Given that a 56Kbps dedicated connection requires a CSU/DSU and an IP router for use with an Internet connection, one serious concern for any WWW site manager is where to get this equipment. In the case of the 56Kbps dedicated service, you can either rent or lease equipment from the telephone company and ISP, or you can buy the equipment yourself. Each method has its own benefits and drawbacks.

Telephone Company Equipment

The first source that you should examine for a CSU/DSU is the telephone company that is providing you with the dedicated circuit. By leasing the equipment from the local loop provider, you will gain the benefit of the telephone company's technical expertise. Moreover, the company likely will replace the equipment in the event of a malfunction, which will reduce the amount of time that your site is unavailable. Unfortunately, unless the local loop provider also has ISP services, you will have to look elsewhere to rent an IP router.

Telephone companies are also more likely to charge you a higher rate for the CSU/DSU unit than if you buy the unit outright. Although the support and guarantee that you gain through this arrangement may more than make up for the extra cost, you should be aware of the increased monthly cost of this solution.

ISP Equipment Packages

The second possible means of obtaining the necessary equipment for a dedicated 56Kbps connection is through your ISP. A number of Internet Service Providers offer complete packages of Internet service, dedicated circuits, and all hardware. Because the ISP will be responsible for the installation, maintenance, and management of all the hardware, the overall cost of this solution on a per month basis will be higher than if you use the ISP only for access purposes. The main factor in deciding whether to choose this solution should depend on the technical resources available in your own organization. If your staff understands all the equipment and the networking required, then a complete contract arrangement with the ISP will create unnecessary costs.

Purchase of Equipment

The final method used to obtain the necessary equipment is to purchase it outright, either from the telephone company (in the case of the CSU/DSU), or from the suppliers (for either routers or CSU/DSUs). Although purchasing reduces the overall costs of the connection over the long run, it has two main drawbacks:

❋ High up-front costs

❋ Lack of maintenance and support

High Up-Front Costs

The first drawback with the direct purchase of a CSU/DSU and a router is that you have to carry the costs of the equipment right away. Renting the equipment may cost more in the long run, but it provides you with the security of not being locked into the connection method or a particular brand of equipment should a better option exist in the near future. With a purchase, you commit to your connection choice with little chance of cost recovery should you want to change either connection methods or equipment type (because of a change of ISP or local loop provider).

Lack of Maintenance and Support

The second major drawback of purchasing 56Kbps equipment is the need for support and maintenance. Generally, leased equipment is maintained by the company that supplies it. If you purchase the equipment, you are responsible for its maintenance and repair. Moreover, you will likely have to install and support the equipment with your own personnel, which can be very difficult without good network administrators and technicians.

A Note from the Author

The decision to purchase and support network equipment in-house is a very difficult one, even for a computer consulting firm. For example, when our company was examining the options for our own WWW site, we considered some of the package services for the connection. Unfortunately, the services generally included hardware that was beyond our relatively simple needs. As a result, the services would have cost us considerably more than purchases and internal support. Because PVC has a number of good technical resources, we ended up managing the equipment ourselves. In this case, we used a host-based router for our office-to-server park connection.

Finally, the equipment upon which your WWW site depends will not have the luxury of replacement units in the event of a breakdown. In the case of leased equipment, the repairs are completed quickly or a replacement unit is provided while more time-consuming repairs are made. Although some warranties may also provide this type of service, most will not, which means that a malfunction with your networking hardware will keep your WWW site offline for the duration of the repairs, resulting in the potential loss of clients or business contacts.

Evaluating Costs

Now that the hardware requirements have been detailed, it is time to look at a key factor in evaluating any connectivity methods: the costs. In the case of 56Kbps connections, as with most connections, the costs are broken into four categories:

⚜ Local loop charges

⚜ Bandwidth charges

⚜ Setup charges

⚜ Hardware costs

Local Loop Charges

The first charges that you will incur are the local loop charges—the cost from the telephone company for providing the circuit from your site to the ISP site. Because your site requires continuous connection, the cost of the dedicated service for the local loop is a necessary expense. Even so, a brief discussion of both the switched and dedicated local loop costs are included for comparison.

Switched Service Costs

Switched 56Kbps service costs depend not on the location and distance between the two sites, but rather on the length connection time. This service allows the telephone company to support a number of customers with the same resources (because not all of the customers will require a link at any one time), so one would expect that the service would be cheaper than the dedicated service. This is not necessarily the case. Generally speaking, switched service costs a small monthly fee—about $0.06 per minute. The service allows a connection between your site and the dialed site, and the circuit is established only for the duration of the transfer.

So far, so good. The interesting part about the switched service is that the pricing structure assumes that a portion of the connections will be of a certain distance, requiring a certain amount of trunk lines and interexchange lines. As a result, the pricing for switched service is generally higher for communications over short distances than it is for the dedicated counterparts *at the same short distances* (assuming a reasonable usage). It is only when you start looking at longer distance dedicated connections, multiple connection points, or very small usage that the switched service becomes cost-effective.

Dedicated Line Costs

Dedicated 56Kbps service makes more sense as a WWW site connection method. Unlike switched service, the dedicated service charges are based on the distance between the two points of the connection, although the price varies according to where you are and what telephone company services your area. A good rule of thumb is that the price will be in the $60–$110 per month plus a $6–$10 per mile distance charge. These charges allow you to connect two sites, and only two sites, with a dedicated 56Kbps digital link. For example, you could have a server in a server park and a 56Kbps link to your office for maintenance of the WWW server and LAN access to the Internet. If your office is 12 miles away from the server park, then the total charge per month would be between $132 and $206 U.S. currency.

Bandwidth Charges

Over and above the charges by the local telephone company for local loop connections from your site and the ISP, you will also be charged fees by the ISP for Internet access. In the case of a dedicated digital 56Kbps connection, the charges from the ISP will consist of two parts:

✻ A port charge

✻ Network access fees

Port Costs

The first component of dedicated 56Kbps service is the ISP charge for the connection of your 56Kbps line to its router. Because this utilizes one of the ports available on ISP router, you will receive a monthly rental fee for the port. Even in the event that the port fee is not listed separately, the final price for the overall service will include some hardware fee.

In addition to the port charge for the router usage, the ISP may or may not charge for the CSU/DSU at its site. If the ISP supplies the CSU/DSU, then there will either be an explicit charge for the rental of this unit, or the cost will be rolled into the overall price. If you are required to provide the CSU/DSU on both ends of the link, then the ISP will not (or at least should not) include any hardware charge for this equipment. It is very important when comparing ISPs to ask for a detailed breakdown of all the charges you are paying, and to find out what you will be responsible for on your own. This will allow you to confidently assess the ISPs and compare their costs.

Tip

In a lot of cases, the port charges of the ISP can be the hidden cost that catches you unaware. Be very cautious with providers that offer rates that are substantially lower than their competition. Do not be afraid to ask the ISP how they are able to offer such a better rate. In some cases, the lower rate may be the result of a higher rate of bandwidth over subscription. In others, the lower rate may be due to a price that does not include any service or port charges. Unless a provider is offering a rate to encourage growth (which means that it may not last), or it buys its bandwidth at a larger bulk rate (that is, the ISP is bigger than its competition), then the prices should be close. Higher prices indicate likely profit taking, and lower prices indicate cut corners. Buyer beware!

Service Fees

The second component of dedicated 56Kbps ISP charges is the service fee charged by the ISP for Internet access. As with most connection methods, the fee can be based on one of two methods:

※ Flat rate

※ Metered bandwidth

In the case of flat-rate bandwidth, the ISP provides a simple monthly fee for the transmission of data to and from your port and the Internet at large. Because the amount of data transmitted to and from your connection is limited to a theoretical maximum of 56 Kbps, the ISP is able to provide a reasonable estimate of the amount of its bandwidth that your connection will utilize. The ISP will therefore charge you a fee equal to the bandwidth used plus a margin for profit. Current rates can vary greatly, depending on your geographic location (and the amount of high connectivity present), but should range between $300 and $450 per month.

Tip

If a flat rate is negotiated, you should ensure that you are getting a guaranteed data rate, and not a variable rate. A number of providers offer 56Kbps connections for which they only guarantee a rate of less than 56 Kbps but provide a theoretical maximum of 56 Kbps. If their other customers are not using the bandwidth, your connection will operate at 56 Kbps. As more customers utilize their connections, your effective bandwidth will drop (although never below the guaranteed rate).

In the case of metered bandwidth, the ISP will charge you a fee for each unit of bandwidth used (generally GB). Unfortunately, the fees charged for throughput (bandwidth used) vary greatly, depending on your ISP. On a per GB basis, the rates can range from $4 to $40. In general, you should expect a rate of approximately $10 to $20 per GB.

Setup Charges

The setup charges for a dedicated 56Kbps circuit can amount to a significant expense when first establishing a WWW site. This particular method of connectivity therefore should generally not be considered as a viable method for a short-term or pilot WWW site. The types of charges vary by area, but will fall into two main categories:

- ✿ Provider-based setup charges

- ✿ Hardware installation and setup charges

Provider-Based Setup Charges

Provider-based setup charges include both your local loop provider and your ISP. Both providers will charge a fee to set up your service. In the case of the local loop provider, the charges ($250 to thousands of dollars) can include a number of different services, ranging from installing lines into your premises to configuring provided local loop equipment.

In addition to incurring any local loop installation charges that may occur at their office, your ISP will also charge a fee for the installation and configuration of your connection. This can include the establishment of a domain name (because InterNIC charges $100 for the first two years of registration, the ISP will charge you at least this fee), routing setup, port configuration, and support for your site administrator. Because the total costs will depend on the types of services offered, you should pay very close attention to what your setup fees provide rather than the total setup fees. Try to have a plan that includes only the service you need, and excludes extras that are not cost-effective for you. For example, if your administrator is experienced at setting up the necessary hardware and software on your end, it does not make any sense for you to pay for setup charges for ISP technical support.

Installation and Configuration Charges

As with any Internet connectivity method, the type of solution you choose will determine the amount of installation and configuration that will be required. In the case of a dedicated 56Kbps connection, you will be required to set up your WWW site and routing from your host to the ISP's network. Also, domain name servers will need to be updated, and telephone interface hardware may need to be installed and configured. A router may need to be purchased and configured, or your host may need to be set up to act as your router.

In all of these instances, you may or may not receive assistance from either of your providers. Keep in mind that, although packages that include setup services will ease the startup of your WWW site, you will be paying for these services one way or another. If you have a number of onsite technical resources, you may be able to handle most technical issues, but personnel inexperienced with this type of connectivity will be faced with some new difficulties.

A Note from the Author

Even computer consulting companies will experience a number of different problems when setting up Internet connection solutions. For example, when our company first set up a dedicated link to the Internet, our technicians experienced a number of difficult problems, each requiring considerable time to resolve. In our case, taking the time to train our technicians was worthwhile, because the investment can be reapplied for future installation procedures. In the case of a single connection for an organization, trained external help may allow you a more cost-effective method of setting up the Internet connection. Moreover, the added training for your staff may allow you to realize savings in future maintenance of the connection.

Hardware Costs

One of the largest costs associated with the 56Kbps dedicated connection is that of hardware. Both the CSU/DSU and router required for 56Kbps connections can cost upwards of several thousand dollars, depending on the functionality of the equipment. A relatively simple set of equipment could cost as little as $1,000, whereas a router that is able to perform firewall security features (such as packet filtering) could cost as much as $10,000! As a result of the large capital costs associated with this solution (and most other dedicated solutions), the 56Kbps connectivity option does not lend itself readily to short-term or pilot WWW sites.

Tip

Some ISPs are willing to rent or lease hardware with your Internet connectivity package. If you require the bandwidth of a 56Kbps connection for a pilot site, and the provider does not require a long-term commitment, then this option may provide a method of utilizing a 56Kbps connection. Keep in mind that the setup charges for the connection will still have to be paid.

Understanding Setup Requirements

If you choose the dedicated 56Kbps connection as your method of Internet connectivity, you will have to address a number of setup requirements. First, you must order a local loop connection. Second, you need to assess ISPs before choosing one; and finally, you must ensure that sufficient technical expertise is available to set up and maintain the connection.

Subscription of the Local Loop

Local loop subscriptions will most likely start with a telephone call to your local telephone company. Given the infrastructure that this company has in place in your area, it will be able to offer you some rates and information about the services that it offers. Even so, you may want to investigate the larger exchange carriers (such as AT&T, MCI, and Sprint) because they also might offer services in your area. Regardless of who you decide to approach for your local loop connection, the following actions need to be carried out:

⊛ Measuring the local loop

⊛ Installing the line

Measuring the Local Loop Distance

Because the total cost of your 56Kbps connection will partially depend on the distance between the ISP site and your WWW site, the first setup requirement for the local loop provider is to measure the local loop. In addition, the provider will establish whether it can offer service to you between those two points. Although 56Kbps service is generally available everywhere, the company may not have the capacity available in a particular area. Because the hardware required for additional capacity can be expensive, the local loop provider will probably not be willing to increase capacity. At this point, it may be worth investigating other providers or connectivity methods.

If the local provider has the capacity to carry your connection, the loop length will be taken into consideration, and they will give you a price quote. The price will include the monthly cost of the connection and the charges required for installation. Make sure to confirm whether you or the local provider will be supplying the necessary CSU/DSU. After a price is confirmed, you will be able to place your order.

Installing the Line

After the 56Kbps dedicated circuit has been ordered, the next step in the setup process is the installation of the line at both sites. Depending on where the service is connecting, the installation may require the coordination of a number of telephone companies (for example, a connection between two cities). In most cases for Internet connectivity, only the chosen local provider will be involved. Again, depending on the companies available in your area, the installation can take as little as two or three days, or stretch into a couple of weeks. In either case, you will have to coordinate the installation of the circuit with the ISP that you have chosen.

Choosing an ISP

The process of selecting an ISP is covered in more depth in Appendix A, "Listing of ISPs," but this section briefly touches on some of the main issues that you should keep in mind when selecting an ISP for dedicated 56Kbps connections. The four main issues to carefully consider are as follows:

- Flexibility of services provided

- Bandwidth subscription of the ISP

- Technical knowledge of the ISP staff

- Upgrade paths available from the ISP

Reasonable Flexibility

One of the most important aspects of the relationship between you and your ISP is the degree of flexibility that your ISP provides. Does your ISP simply have one standard package for all customers, or is your account treated as a custom connectivity solution? The degree of ISP flexibility greatly impacts the quality of the service that you will receive. For example, if your ISP is willing to provide options of leasing or buying equipment, you will be able to make the best financial decisions for your company and alter those decisions over the course of time. In addition to the overall level of flexibility, in the area of pricing policy, the level of flexibility can have impact on the cost-effectiveness of the service. Your ISP should be willing to offer both metered and flat-rate dedicated 56Kbps accounts.

The main advantage of having the option of metered or flat-rate accounts lies in the ability to manage your connectivity growth and costs. For a smaller new site, a metered account can provide you with a cost-effective method of accessing mid-level bandwidth without paying for throughput not being used. As the level of usage increases (resulting in bandwidth charge increases), you can entertain the idea of switching over to the flat-rate plan. At a certain point, the flat-rate feature may become more cost-effective.

Tip

A number of service providers allow for the equivalent of a flat-rate yet metered account. This type of account allows you to have a metered account that charges you only for the bandwidth that you utilize. The benefit with this type of account is that the bandwidth charges only equal the same cost per GB as if you had ordered a flat-rate 56 Kbps.

Obviously, this connectivity option allows for the best of both worlds. The only problem can be in finding a provider that offers this type of billing option.

Bandwidth Subscription

The second major issue when selecting an ISP is the level of bandwidth subscription of the ISP. This criteria has two separate parts:

- The total amount of bandwidth leased by the provider

- The total amount of bandwidth leased from the provider

In the case of the provider's bandwidth, the reality of Internet access is that the larger the bandwidth leased by the provider, the more likely the provider is able to realize economies of scale.

On the other hand, you should at least get a good idea of the amount of bandwidth that the provider has leased out. Has the provider leased out more bandwidth than it has? To what level of oversubscription is its network? No matter what your provider says, you have a right to receive answers to these questions. An ISP that is not willing to answer questions about its connectivity should not be trusted to provide for your connectivity.

Technical Knowledge

Even if you have a number of technical resources available onsite to manage your side of the dedicated connection, the ISP's staff will have a major impact on your link's performance. You should question your ISP about the qualifications of its staff, and the number of staff members available. Also, ask the ISP what plans it has for network outages from its provider. Are there truly redundant links in place, or, at the very least, is there a reaction plan and is the staff trained to respond accordingly?

One possible method of assessing the technical capabilities of the technical staff of the ISP is to ask about using ISP staff on contract. If the ISP does not have staff to provide for contracting, this may indicate a shortage of personnel. On the other hand, an ISP that provides staff for contracting may do so at a risk to network efficiency. Either way, pay close attention to how the ISP answers any of your inquiries. Only with a relationship built on strong trust and ability can you rely on the connectivity provided.

Upgrade Paths

No matter what your bandwidth needs are today, or your expectations for tomorrow, the likely result of new technologies and uses for the Internet will result in an increase in your needs. Therefore, the options that your ISP provides for stepping up the bandwidth curve can be very important. For example, the ISP should offer one or two other options beyond the 56Kbps options selected. This could be fractional T1, T1, or ISDN service.

The importance of the upgrade path is a direct consequence of the difficulties presented in moving your connection from one provider to another. Any move will result in a somewhat time-consuming process involving changing routing tables and possibly IP addresses when switching ISPs. A poorly managed change could even result in a loss of service, either completely for a short period of time, or partially over a longer duration as routing information repropagates to the rest of the Internet.

Knowledge of Telephony and Networking

The final setup requirement that you should ensure before ordering a dedicated 56Kbps connection is having the appropriate technical personnel. In some cases, this could be the personnel from your service providers. In others, the technical expertise could already exist within your organization. Whatever the case, close attention should be paid to the issue of technical support for the connection. The ongoing costs of Internet connection support can be considerable, either in man hours or money.

Summary

The dedicated 56Kbps connections have long been the traditional medium level of connectivity for Internet connectivity. As a result, the technology is well established and supported. On the other hand, new applications and uses of the Internet (and computer communications in general) have resulted in an increasing need for higher bandwidth connectivity. This has consequently resulted in a push for a newer digital connection to replace the aging 56Kbps connection.

In the next chapter, the newest digital kid on the block is examined: ISDN. ISDN provides a modern connectivity option in the medium bandwidth range. In addition, the lowest level of ISDN connectivity is more than twice the bandwidth of the older 56Kbps connection. These features, combined with the expandability of ISDN to support even higher levels of bandwidth, have resulted in some people looking to ISDN to solve the pressures of bandwidth.

Checklist

The following are concerns that should be addressed at the conclusion of the chapter.

- ☑ 56Kbps service available?

- ☑ Newer options available that could be cheaper?

    ISDN

    ADSL

    Cable

- ☑ Frame Relay available for link?

- ☑ Router provision?

    ISP costs

    Leasing costs

    Purchase costs

- ☑ CSU/DSU provided by telephone company?

☑ Length of local loop:

☑ Local loop ordered?

☑ Cost of local loop:

☑ Port costs at ISP:

☑ Service fee for bandwidth:

☑ Setup costs for ISP/Telephone company:

☑ ISP requirements:

Flexibility?

Bandwidth available?

Technically proficient?

Upgrade path offered?

6

Integrated Services Digital Network (ISDN) Connection

Although the 56Kbps (kilobits per second) connection discussed in Chapter 5 is the traditional and widely available digital service, one of the newest members of the digital club is Integrated Services Digital Network (ISDN). ISDN is only recently becoming widely available in both the United States and Canada. Before choosing an ISDN connection for your Internet solution, a manager should examine a number of issues surrounding the technology. This chapter will detail these issues, which include an explanation of ISDN and a look at the ISDN availability, benefits and limitations, hardware requirements, costs, and setup requirements. After reading this chapter, you should be able to properly assess ISDN service in your area as an option for your connectivity.

Understanding ISDN: Digital to the Doorstep

As mentioned previously, ISDN stands for Integrated Services Digital Network. In general, ISDN is the provision of a completely digital connection from the local user right to the Central Office of the telephone company. Using the existing wiring (except in certain low grade areas), the service provides a basic channel of 64 Kbps from one end to the other through the upgrading of switches. Through the use of multiplexing, multiple devices are able to simultaneously use the same standard telephone service that is available in most homes. This section examines in detail the following topics:

❈ The history of ISDN

❈ The classifications of ISDN service

❈ The technical background of ISDN technology

The basics of this section will enable you to positively understand the use of ISDN as a connectivity option for Internet access.

The History of ISDN

ISDN has been available as an international standard since 1984. At that time, the UN organization CCITT (now known as the ITU-T, or *International Telecommunications Union—Telecommunications Standardization Sector,* a body whose primary objective is to standardize telecommunications at an international level) established guidelines for the implementation of ISDN. Unfortunately, for most of the time since 1984, most telephone companies in the United States and Canada have proclaimed their support for ISDN, but have not gone far in implementing the service. Originally, this problem of implementing ISDN was due to the conflicting implementations of ISDN switches by Northern Telecomm and AT&T. As a result of the conflicting implementations of switching methodology, the equipment for end users must be compatible with the switching equipment used.

In 1992, the impasse between technology for implementation and the provision of service was somewhat relieved. At a conference on telecommunications, telephone companies and equipment vendors demonstrated the use of ISDN across the continental United States to establish the interoperability of services and equipment. Simultaneously, telephone companies agreed upon a standard for the implementation of ISDN—NISDN-1. The national ISDN standard was created to address three main issues of standardization: equipment and services, procedures for operation, and communication among central offices. Unfortunately, some problems exist with the acceptance of the standard in western U.S. states.

Classifications of ISDN Service

The three classifications of ISDN service—Basic Rate Interface (BRI), Primary Rate Interface (PRI), and Broadband-ISDN (B-ISDN)—are based on both geographical area and the amount of bandwidth provided. The following section details the standards of classifications used by North America and Japan. Europe uses a different standard of classification. In the first two classifications (BRI and PRI), the basic technological principles behind the classification are similar. These principles are discussed presently. The third classification (B-ISDN) is a future implementation of ISDN that is not in widespread use at this time.

Basic Rate ISDN (BRI)

Basic Rate ISDN (BRI) is what is traditionally referred to when speaking of ISDN as a technology that will bring a digital connection to your doorstep. As a result, the BRI service will be the most common ISDN service implemented, although any area that can support BRI service may also support PRI service with proper switching.

As figure 6.1 illustrates, the BRI service is made up of two 64Kbps bearer channels (referred to as B channels) and one 16Kbps delta channel (referred to as the D channel). The bearer channels are used to carry either voice or data, whereas the Delta channel is used for signaling or coordination among the channels. In certain situations, the two bearer channels can be bonded together to provide a virtual 128Kbps channel for communication.

Figure 6.1

A Basic Rate ISDN interface.

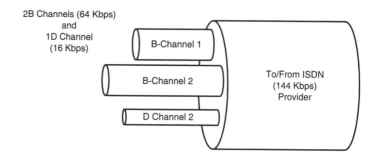

> **Note**
>
> BRI service is also often termed the 2B+D service, after the two bearer and one Delta channels.

The BRI interface is provided via the two twisted pairs of copper wires that are common in most areas. One set of two wires provides the incoming data and the other two wires provide the outgoing data transmission, providing for full duplex ISDN service. The capability of ISDN to provide a higher level of bandwidth than analog modems over the same copper infrastructure is a function of time division multiplexing. Due to the digital nature of communications, time division multiplexing allows for greater granularity because of the conditioning of signal that is possible on digital signals.

Although the BRI interface provides for up to 144 Kbps of bandwidth, the use of bonding, as mentioned earlier, can provide higher bandwidth when available from the telephone central office. One common connection is the 6B interface, or H0, which provides 384 Kbps of bandwidth. In each case of higher bandwidth, the central office allocates a greater level of bandwidth to the local loop to your residence. The transmission continues to take place over the same copper infrastructure in place today.

Primary Rate ISDN (PRI)

The Primary Rate ISDN (PRI) interface is similar to the BRI interface, except that the PRI interface provides 23 bearer channels and one Delta channel, all of which provide 64 Kbps of bandwidth (see fig. 6.2). All the channels can be bonded together to provide T1 bandwidths (see Chapter 7, "Entering the Global

Arena: A T1/T3 Leased Line"), with the D channel providing the signaling required to support the "services" of ISDN (such as caller ID, request services, report transmission status, and so on).

Figure 6.2

A Primary Rate ISDN interface.

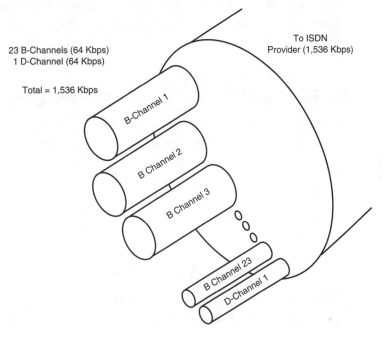

23 B-Channels (64 Kbps)
1 D-Channel (64 Kbps)

To ISDN
Provider (1,536 Kbps)

Total = 1,536 Kbps

B-Channel 1

B Channel 2

B Channel 3

B Channel 23

D-Channel 1

Because of the much higher bandwidth available to a PRI interface, the service is generally reserved for head offices or larger organizations. Although there are 23 B channels, the channels can be used separately or in combination, as required. For example, a Primary Rate interface can provide 12 channels for data transmission (for 756Kbps bandwidth), one fax line, two dial-up lines, and eight phone lines. As more bandwidth is required, the system can dynamically allocate lines to the data bandwidth. If a phone call is received (signal carried in by the D channel), the bandwidth would release a B channel, and the phone would ring.

Broadband ISDN (B-ISDN)

Broadband ISDN is a variation of the ISDN standards that relies on frequency multiplexing to provide higher than PRI interface bandwidth over a completely optical connection (end to end). Because of the higher rate of switching required for the high bandwidths envisioned under B-ISDN, the switching will be required to be handled by hardware, as opposed to software. As a result, the ATM standard is being touted as the primary technology for B-ISDN services. Because B-ISDN relies on a completely different technology than the BRI and PRI interfaces, the rest of the chapter refers to these traditional methods. B-ISDN is discussed in more depth in Chapter 9, "Emerging Technologies: ADSL & B-ISDN/ATM."

The Technical Background of ISDN Connections

Although the standard interfaces for ISDN (BRI and PRI) provide an indication of the types of bandwidth rates available under ISDN, a discussion of them does not explain how the services work or what is possible using ISDN. The following section discusses the technical underpinnings of ISDN wiring, and the technology behind time division multiplexing. The section also details some of the possible uses of ISDN service.

How Does ISDN Work? The Wiring

ISDN is provided according to the standards set out by ITU-T, and provides for the connection of both ISDN intelligent and standard interfaces.

As figure 6.3 illustrates, the ISDN service is connected to the customer's residence via a two-wire link from the local telephone company switch. The maximum length that the U loop can be is 18,000 feet. The U loop can be only two wires because of the loop nature of the bus. Data comes into the bus from a point on the bus, and travels in one direction. The U bus terminates at the customer's house at a device called the NT1 (Network Termination 1), which is the ISDN equivalent of a modem. (It's not truly a modem, however, because the NT1 provides CODEC (COding and DECoding), as opposed to modulation/demodulation.)

From the NT1 junction, a four-wire full duplex bus, referred to as the T bus, connects to a second device called NT2 (Network Termination 2). The second device can be a number of different devices, such as a Private Branch Exchange (PBX), a bridge/router, or a multiplexor (for multiple BRI interfaces). In general, for Internet access, the NT2 will be a digital router that provides the BRI interface on one side and the Ethernet or token ring interface for the network on the other.

Figure 6.3

The architecture of ITU-T ISDN.

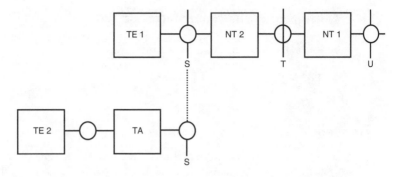

ITU-Ts ISDN Architecture

Another bus can come out of the NT2—the S bus, which is still a four-wire full duplex bus used to connect your ISDN stations to NT2. Stations can be of two basic types: ISDN-aware and the older, less-advanced variety. ISDN-aware stations are referred to as TE1 (Terminal Equipment 1) and can be connected directly to the S bus. TE2 (Terminal Equipment 2) stations are not ISDN-capable (including dumb terminals or telephones that cannot use the D channel for signaling) and must be connected to the S bus with a TA (Terminal Adapter).

The junction between TE2 and TA is the R junction. TAs can be stand-alone units or an interface card for a computer. In general, TAs are serial devices and are therefore limited to slower speeds (19.2 Kbps or slightly higher). TAs emulate asynchronous communication over the B channels and replace a modem in the communication scheme.

Communication via ISDN: Understanding Time Division Multiplexing

Although the physical infrastructure of ISDN is important to the implementation of ISDN for Internet connectivity, the true magic of ISDN lies in the use of time division multiplexing to provide greater bandwidth out of existing copper wiring. To better understand what an ISDN connection depends on, and what it provides to you as a connection method, this section examines the physics and theory behind the following ISDN issues:

- ❀ Frequencies and communications

- ❀ CODEC methods and sampling

- ❀ Time division multiplexing

Frequencies and Communications

Sound waves have long been the main method of telecommunication, and the principles of sound govern the ability of humans to hear the sounds emitted. Because human hearing is limited to frequencies between 20 Hz and 20 KHz, the phone systems need not be concerned with supporting anything less or more. In fact, telephone communications support a considerably smaller set of frequencies—between 300 Hz to 4,000 Hz. The reason that the phone can support such a smaller set of frequencies and still provide understandable sound to the listener is that the majority of human-created sound is within this range. So, most telephone systems support 4 KHz frequencies for analog communications.

Figure 6.4

The telephone frequency spectrum.

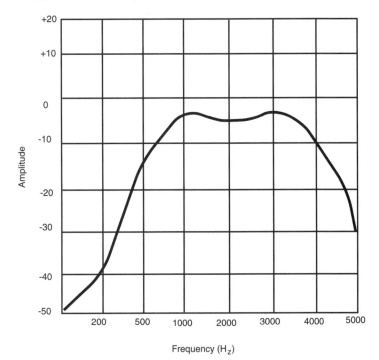

CODEC Methods and Sampling

What about digital communication? After all, we are discussing IS**Digital**N. The use of the telephone infrastructure for digital communications is based on the use of coder-decoders (CODEC) to convert analog signals to a digital signal and then back to an analog signal.

Note

The process of converting analog signals into ones and zeros of digital communication was first developed by Harry Nyquist in the 1920s. The process of providing information about the analog signal is referred to as *sampling*.

The CODEC measures the analog signal and encodes the measurement as a sample of 8 bits of information. To provide enough samples for the receiver to reconstruct the analog signal correctly, the CODEC must take samples at twice the level of the maximum frequency. Because telephone communications have been limited to 4,000 Hz, the CODEC for digital voice samples is 8,000 times per second. As a result, the bandwidth provided for and required for a digital voice communication is 8,000 times 8 bits, or 64,000 bps (bits per second).

Time Division Multiplexing

Now that you understand how digital communications are used to convert analog signals, the question of how ISDN provides 128 Kbps of bandwidth via a set of copper lines that supports only a maximum of 56 Kbps via analog communications can be addressed. Recalling the process of coding analog information (mentioned previously), you will remember that the coder samples the signal 8,000 times per second. This is the same principle used by time division multiplexing.

As shown in figure 6.5, the time division multiplexing relies on a multiplexing unit to sample X number of sources for 8 bits per source. The multiplexer then adds either a framing bit and the beginning or end of the frame. The total value of the frame depends on the number of sources, but for an example, in a T1 communication structure (see Chapter 7 for more details), 24 sources are sampled to give a frame size of 193 bits (8 × 24 plus 1). The multiplexer repeats the whole process 8,000 times (again, the frequency of the media makes this required) to gather a sufficient number of samples.

Figure 6.5

Time division multiplexing and the data frame.

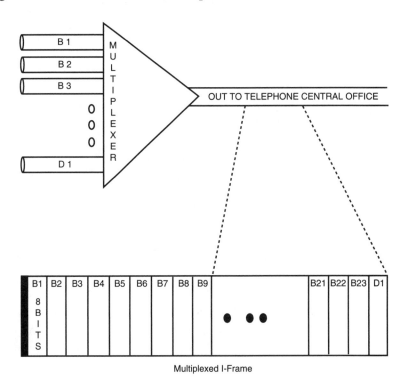

Multiplexed I-Frame

In the case of ISDN, the type of connection determines the number of sources that are included in each frame. With the Primary Rate Interface, the total number of sources equals 24, with each bearer channel supplying 8 bits, and the one D channel also providing 8 bits. The case of the Basic Rate Interface is slightly different, as the sources are sampled a disproportionate number of times. The first bearer channel is sampled for 8 bits, then one bit from the D channel, 8 bits from the second B channel, and finally one bit from the D channel. The complete frame is repeated the 8,000 times necessary. As a result, the BRI ISDN configuration can provide a total bandwidth of 144 Kbps (8,000 cycles × [8+1+8+1] = 144,000 bps).

Note

The total available bandwidth is dependent on the number of sources that are polled and the frequency of polling. Because the frequency is dependent on the media used for communications, the main way of increasing bandwidth under this scheme is to increase the number of sources polled for each frame. With the ISDN specification, the maximum defined number of samples (in North America) is the 24 channels of a Primary Rate Interface. As a result, only T1 speeds are available over the copper ISDN infrastructure.

Different media and source numbers have been defined for B-ISDN and, as a result, that standard allows for much greater bandwidth possibilities.

Because the multiplexer controls the number of sources sampled, and the demultiplexer does the reverse at the other end, the switch from a Basic Rate Interface to a Primary Rate Interface generally requires changing local and Central Office equipment (or, at least, the Central Office would be required to identify the change in sources in each frame).

What Can ISDN Do?

With all that bandwidth available from the ISDN configurations, what can you do with ISDN? The following list might give you some ideas:

Keep in mind that the ISDN B channels can be bonded together to provide a 128Kbps channel for communications. Even if the connection is not required simply for Internet communications, the router could be placed as a TE1, and TE2s could be added for use of the B channels for voice and fax communications (among other things).

Refer to figure 6.3. In that diagram, the S/T bus that holds TE1s and TE2s (via TAs) can accommodate up to eight devices. These devices can be any number of devices, including fax machines, digital telephones with call display, integrated voice and terminal, your electricity controls, or even your VCR. As a result, the ISDN D channel can be used for signaling for any or all of these services.

In fact, the D channel is the key to all the services available under the ISDN services. For example, the fact that you can use the 64Kbps B channels for bandwidth to a service provider, bonded as one virtual channel of 128 Kbps, does not preclude you from using the D channel to handle signaling for other ISDN services. If the ISDN service was attached to a telephone number as well as a connection to the Internet, for example, the D channel would be utilized to indicate the incoming call or fax. The ISDN service would free one B channel to handle the phone/fax and, when finished, would reallocate the B channel to again provide greater bandwidth.

A second example of the ISDN D channel used for signaling is in the case of electricity control of your office. Here, the D channel can be used to provide the signaling for the control of temperature and lights of your office. In this way, the D channel would enable you to lower the heat and turn off lights in the office from a remote location (or even have the electric company do it for you, saving you money on your electrical bill!).

Considering ISDN Availability and Liabilities

Now that the benefits and technical details behind ISDN have been discussed, the question of ISDN availability quickly becomes the issue. Considering that the technological knowledge and theories behind ISDN have been available for the last twenty years, it is surprising that the services are not already widespread in most homes. Nonetheless, ISDN is not available in all areas, with the main determining factor being the distance of your location from the Central Office (the local telephone switching center). This section discusses the issues of the current availability, and two opposing views of ISDN trends in availability. It also looks at the question of interoperability, the issue of bandwidth, and the long-term viability of ISDN service.

Current Scenarios: Are You in the Loop?

One of the most difficult issues surrounding the use of ISDN for Internet connectivity is the availability of service. Even given the twenty-year history of ISDN, the availability of service is dependent on the issue of local loop distance. Given that the local loop distance from the Central Office to your site must be less than 18,000 feet long (as mentioned earlier), the only limitation is the location of your site in relationship to the central office. Because the equipment necessary for the central office is very expensive, the lack of a close central office means that ISDN will not be available for your site.

A Note from the Author

Just because your office is located in a major city does not ensure that ISDN service will be available. For example, our company is located in Vancouver, BC, the third largest city in Canada, and an area of intense high-tech industrial development. As a result, ISDN is available in certain areas of the city, including the area where our office is located. Unfortunately, the distance between our office and the telephone company's central office is greater than 18,000 feet, and we are therefore unable to get ISDN service to our office.

Trends and Future Availability

Although in most urban centers ISDN services are available to at least some areas (generally 70 to 85 percent of the larger urban centers), the trends in bandwidth usage calls into question the usefulness of the ISDN service for World Wide Web services. Because ISDN can provide only 128 Kbps on the copper cables running into most sites, the question is raised of whether ISDN is a savior or just a step in the process. Whatever the case in urban centers, users must also be aware that most nonurban areas still do not have ISDN services, and may not anytime soon. Given the potential of ISDN that has been touted by many industry representatives, the question of the future of ISDN remains.

ISDN Provides Solutions

ISDN provides a larger utilization of the existing telecommunication infrastructure and provides a larger level of bandwidth availability to both users (basic interface) and service providers (primary interface). As a result, for many years, ISDN has been viewed as a long-term solution for telecommuting and even video conferencing. Without the need to spend incredible amounts of money on capital improvements, telephone companies are able to offer high bandwidth alternatives at prices equal to or better than traditional digital connections. As a result of these strengths, a case can be made for ISDN as the wave of today and the future. In fact, the recent level of popularity with both Internet clients and service providers appears to confirm this view. Unfortunately, this view has a few flaws, and as a result, ISDN has a number of critics for whom ISDN is simply an interim solution.

ISDN Wiring Overhead

ISDN as it is currently provided depends on the copper infrastructure (with a few modifications) already in place. Although this is a benefit in terms of the telephone companies providing service, it is also the main flaw of considering ISDN as a long-term solution. Because the use of copper wiring limits ISDN to 128 Kbps of bandwidth per set of four wires, the wiring overhead for ISDN is fairly large in order to provide larger bandwidth (such as T1). As a result, the critics of ISDN point to the very services that are touted as ISDN's strengths (video conferencing and telecommuting) as being its downfall. Although both of these activities are available to ISDN subscribers, the truth of the matter is that the level of bandwidth required for video conferencing and telecommuting, not to mention the bandwidth that is needed to provide most of the breaking WWW services (real-time audio and video), is much higher than 128 Kbps. As a result, most critics see ISDN as an intermediate step while optical cabling is extended to more areas (see Chapter 9 for Broadband ISDN and ATM).

Interoperability

Resolving the argument of ISDN as a bandwidth option will take time. Meanwhile, a more critical issue is the difficulty of maintaining a defined standard for equipment, switching, and transfers between central offices. Although an ISDN standard was established by the ITU-T (formally the CCITT), the individual switch companies have established switches that implement the standard in their own way. Each manufacturer's switch does not necessarily operate in the same manner; therefore, ISDN equipment (including NT1s) is not portable between switches. As a result, ISDN services have not been compatible across the country, limiting the growth of ISDN equipment and leading to higher prices for consumers.

The Solutions of Today

Given the problems that the switching companies have created through the variety of implementations, it is not surprising that the equipment manufacturers of ISDN equipment have been slow to develop products. After all, the equipment designed to work with one telephone company's implementation of ISDN may not work with another's. As a result of these complications, the spread of ISDN was very slow up until 1992.

National Agreement

As was mentioned in the section on the history of ISDN, in 1992, the telephone companies and equipment manufacturers got together to show customers that ISDN service was a viable option for communications across the United States. As a result of this meeting, the companies made a national agreement that established standards for the ISDN services, equipment, and switching standards. Although it has not been fully implemented due to difficulties with existing infrastructure, this agreement has created a high level of stability and computability within the ISDN providers. Consequently, ISDN service has become much better utilized, which in turn has resulted in lower prices and greater service provider options for Internet access.

X.25, PPP, and Frame Relay: Communication Standards

In speaking about Internet access and ISDN, the issue of communications over the ISDN link comes into play. In general, the use of TCP/IP over an ISDN link requires an encapsulation method—just link most other media types (for example, Ethernet requires Ethernet packets to be created while IP datagrams travel over the Ethernet). In the case of ISDN, three main encapsulation methods are favored, as follows:

- X.25

- Point-to-Point Protocol (PPP)

- Frame relay

X.25 is an older standard that requires a considerable amount of overhead for reliability. The overhead stems from the history of X.25 in that the methods of communication when the standard was developed were less reliable than current communication devices. Even so, the X.25 standard is support for data communication over ISDN links. In fact, the control information transmitted over the D channel is a variant of the X.25 protocol.

While X.25 has evolved historically, and is accepted by the ITU-T, both the Internet Working Group and the ITU-T recommend the use of the Point-to-Point Protocol (PPP) for IP encapsulation over an ISDN link. This standard that originally developed to replace SLIP for modem communications has evolved into the standard method implementing ISDN Internet connectivity.

The final method of accomplishing IP over an ISDN link is fairly recent in the development of protocols, and that is the use of frame relay technologies. Because frame relay can be implemented over a number of different media and standards (such as ISDN), the method has gained a lot of press over the last few years. In fact, frame relay is being touted in certain situations as a strong implementation method for IP (see Chapter 8 for more details on frame relay).

Bandwidth: Current Cost Problems

Although ISDN provides a number of options and potentially provides for a large boost in the bandwidth available to individual residences (through BRI ISDN), there is some concern about the cost of bandwidth versus some of the other connectivity options. The potential problem stems from three main reasons, as follows:

❀ ISDN is not very widely supported.

❀ Future options currently being examined have greater bandwidth potential.

❀ ISDN costs are often tariffed on a per-call basis.

At the heart of the main problem with ISDN is the lack of widespread utilization by ISPs for Internet connectivity. As a result, the cost for ISDN service is often greater per unit of bandwidth than other, better established methods of connectivity. Although this may change, ISDN is also being forced to contend with other potential connectivity methods that can provide even greater bandwidth for less cost than that delivered by ISDN. For example, Chapter 9 discusses a new technique used over standard twisted-pair wires called ADSL (*Asynchronous Digital Subscriber Line*) that can provide much greater bandwidth to end users. Yet another example is the introduction of cable modems to provide Internet connectivity. Although both of these methods have potential problems for use as WWW site connections, the end user can greatly benefit from these technologies.

As a result, the benefits of utilizing ISDN for end user access are lessened. After all, these new technologies have the potential to provide higher throughput for lower costs. Because the price of ISDN will only fall through increase in utilization, these developments have the potential to keep ISDN costs higher than necessary. To compound the problem, the tariff structure for ISDN in most areas is based on a per-use basis, either by calls or traffic. As a result, the connection charges for ISDN can be prohibitive, and the costs are hard to budget.

Long-Term Viability: Portability and Bandwidth

Given the problems of ISDN, including the limitations of the bandwidth available from the copper wires currently used, some concerns exist about the long-term viability of ISDN for Internet connectivity. If you choose ISDN as your connection method, you must consider two main issues as possible problems:

❀ Portability of service

❀ Potential problem of bandwidth usage

Portability of Service

Currently, the equipment required for ISDN service is a manager's worst nightmare. Because of the incompatibilities between switches manufactured by the various switch companies, the equipment used by each client must be specific to the switching implementation used by your local telephone company. Stemming from this requirement and the lack of utilization of ISDN by ISPs, two potential problems exist with the portability of ISDN services, as follows:

❀ Equipment portability across North America (and the world)

❀ Potential lack of ISP choices available in any one area

Equipment (Un)Portability

One of the main problems with ISDN service in North America and Europe (the two main areas of ISDN service) is the capability to utilize equipment in a variety of areas. As mentioned earlier, the North American market has the main problem of switch incompatibilities in various areas. The way in which TEs communicate with the Central Office therefore depends on the type of switch implemented.

Currently in North America, two main call setup dialogues are used, depending on which of the following two switches are being used:

❀ ATT 5ESS

❀ Northern Telecomm DMS100

Some equipment has been designed to work with either of these switches, but a lot still interoperates with only one specific switch. Consequently, a manager who may need to move ISDN equipment between sites, or one who maintains a number of sites, should look carefully at the equipment chosen to ensure that the equipment will work with both switches.

The problem with interoperability between North America and Europe exists because of a number of factors. The limiting factors include the following:

❀ **Telephone voice encoding:** The United States and Japan use one method for encoding analog voice into a digital signal (mu-law), whereas the rest of the world uses a different method (A-law). The problem generated by this issue can be resolved via equipment that allows selection of encoding methods.

❀ **Differences in requested services, the services offered by central offices, and the method of implementation:** The solution to this problem is based on correctly researching what services are offered in the area where you have an office, and ensuring that your equipment implements the service the same as the Central Office.

❉ **Regulatory controls:** Each country requires equipment to pass a number of tests on safety and reliability before approval for use in a specific country. This very costly procedure often discourages vendors from manufacturing a product for worldwide distribution, although a number of vendors do provide global usability.

❉ **User NT1s versus the telephone company's NT1:** One of the main differences between North America and Europe is that, in Europe, the telephone company provides the NT1 device, whereas in North America, the NT1 is supplied by the user. As a result, in North America, the NT1 and TA are often provided as a single unit. Because the telephone company provides the NT1 in Europe, the integrated equipment from North America cannot be used.

Choice of Providers

The issue of equipment portability can be an important issue for larger companies with a number of offices worldwide, but for most WWW site managers, the real portability issue stems from the capability to switch ISPs in your area. The basic tenet of competitive pricing is based on the presence of competition in one area.

If your area has only one ISP that offers ISDN service, then you will be stuck with this provider for as long as you utilize ISDN service. Given the cost of equipment and the need to set up your site, the fact that you may not have other options can be difficult.

Because of the lack of providers offering ISDN, it is recommended that you examine the number of ISPs offering ISDN as one of the evaluation criteria of whether or not to use this connectivity option. If a number of options are not available, you are often better off going with an older version of technology, or, at the very least, protecting yourself through a longer term contract (although the prices will likely fall over time).

>
> **Tip**
>
> Due to the benefits of having a larger bandwidth connection from their provider, most ISPs are eager to have a number of stable, long-term, high-bandwidth clients. These clients enable the ISPs to benefit from lower overall bandwidth costs by the purchase of more bandwidth. You should therefore be able to negotiate a better deal by offering a longer contract. A key issue to mention to the ISP is the reliability of revenue under long-term contracts.

Bandwidth Fluctuations

The main issue with using ISDN BRI for a WWW connectivity option is the potential problems that ISDN services can cause for the bandwidth availability for a WWW site. Remember that one of the main benefits of ISDN is the capability to receive a mixture of information via the ISDN lines. This is accomplished through signaling over the D channel. As a result, one BRI ISDN is able to allocate 128 Kbps for Internet connectivity for the majority of the time. Only when a request for a telephone or fax line comes into the NT1 will one of the 64Kbps B channels be utilized. Unfortunately, the on-the-fly utilization of bandwidth may cause problems for your WWW site. If the site has been designed around the higher 128Kbps bandwidth, the loss of 64 Kbps to voice or fax communication could result in unacceptable performance lags. If you plan to utilize the ISDN potential benefits through bandwidth reallocation, then you must make sure of your actual bandwidth needs, including voice and fax requirements.

Determining Hardware Requirements

To take advantage of the benefits of ISDN service, you must first acquire a couple of pieces of equipment. The required NT1s (in North America), terminal adapters, and networking devices will provide an ISDN connection to your WWW site. Because the devices have to work properly with the telephone company and your ISP, the process for equipment selection should involve both companies. Before discussing the consultation process, this section first looks at some options for ISDN equipment, and then provides some choices for each solution.

NT1s, Terminal Adapters (TAs), and Networking Devices

All of the ISDN interfaces from the NT1 to TAs to networking devices (ISDN-aware or not) can provide a number of different options for Internet connectivity. Because the equipment chosen for your ISDN connection will affect the ease of implementation and benefits that you gain from your connection, it is important to carefully examine some options before making a choice. Two important routes should be considered due to the flexibility and cost effectiveness.

Flexibility and Your Future

One possible solution for equipment problems is to choose a solution that not only provides the necessary ISDN interface, but also provides your network or site with more functionality and expandability. For example, if your ISDN solution is also being used to provide your internal office with Internet access, your ISDN interface can be a bridge from your BRI ISDN interface and your local Ethernet. Even more important, you should carefully examine the options available for future uses of this equipment. Some ISDN equipment includes support for most switch configurations (important if your connection site moves) and, for future expandability, some equipment supports a number of other connectivity interfaces (such as T1 and 56 Kbps). These added interfaces will provide you with options for upgrades and downgrades to your required connection. The main drawback with this type of equipment solution is that the cost of this equipment ranges from $1,200 to $2,700.

Cost Effectiveness and Affordability

Having a number of options and upgrade paths open to you can be useful, but the cost of these options also is a major concern. If your WWW site is the only machine needing access to the Internet via ISDN, or cost is the most critical factor, a number of options of cards for personal computers exist that may provide a more cost-effective connection to the ISDN interface. Because these cards generally act as S/T devices, you will likely be required to also buy a separate

NT1 device. Even so, this solution can provide you with access to your ISDN connection for a total cost as low as $650.

Telephone Company Equipment

No matter what solution for equipment you decide to pursue (long-term viability versus cost control), one source for your equipment that can remove many problems is your local telephone provider. The company providing ISDN service to you can suggest the type of equipment, as well as the companies that make reliable equipment, recommended for their connections. The ISDN provider may even provide NT1 equipment on a rental or lease basis. Although the prices charged for renting or leasing may be slightly higher than retail, you will at least know that the equipment works well with your provider's switching.

Note

Although the previous section discussed the telephone company as your ISDN provider, you should keep in mind that the discussion concerned the telephone company providing the access required only at a local loop level. You must also add access to the Internet provided through your ISP. Internet access (or bandwidth) may or may not be provided by your ISDN local loop provider—your telephone company.

ISP Equipment

Although your local loop ISDN provider is an excellent source of ISDN equipment for your connection, your ISP should also be consulted in setting up the equipment. In many cases, your ISP will be uniquely situated to provide you with technical and purchasing advice. By virtue of offering ISDN to customers, the ISP will have experience with the local loop provider, equipment suppliers, and even local consultants who could help with the installation.

Evaluating Costs

Having made your way this far through this chapter, you should now understand some of the benefits, potential problems and limitations, and equipment required to become an ISP. One of the most important aspects (from a business point of view) of evaluating ISDN as a connectivity option is the cost element. In the case of ISDN, costs bring about some very critical issues that are not resolved within the industry. As a result, the cost for ISDN tends to fluctuate as demand and conditions change. As the industry settles down, we can hope that a more definitive cost structure of ISDN service can be done. Until that time, however, managers should look at four main issues in evaluating ISDN connectivity:

- Telephone local loop charges

- ISP bandwidth charges

- Service installation charges

- Hardware costs

Local Loop Charges

The most important portion of the cost equation for ISDN connectivity options is the local loop costs. Because ISDN loop charges are controlled by a tariff process, the actual price charged depends on the current rate structure of your provider. Most of the regional Bell and provincial telephone companies are now offering ISDN services in one form or another, but, unfortunately, there does not appear to be any standard rate system. Even so, two main types of rate structures have developed:

- Basic rate plus usage

- Flat rate

Basic Rate Plus Usage

One rate structure that you may encounter is the basic rate plus usage charges. For a manager looking for a connectivity option for a WWW site, this type of rate structure is generally not advantageous. The basic principle is that the local loop provider charges a small flat rate ($15 to $30 per month) for ISDN access. On top of this fee, the provider charges a usage fee based on a number of criteria, such as the following:

- ❋ **The Number of calls** (generally about $0.06 cents per call). Providers appear to be leaning away from this policy, however, because of the frequent use of ISDN for dedicated services, which eliminates the number of calls.

- ❋ **The length of time that the channel has been open.** Needless to say, a manager looking to use ISDN for *dedicated* service will find this tariff method extremely expensive. A number of discussions on the USENET discussion groups have recently debated the issue of time-metered ISDN lines, and the rates bandied about are not nice—for example, the rate of $0.005 per minute is one number discussed. If this were to be used for a dedicated ISDN connection (required if you are trying to host a WWW site), the total monthly cost would not be worthwhile:

  60min × 24hr × 30 days × $0.005 = $216.00 per month

  Given the costs associated for 56Kbps digital lines and fractional T1 lines, this total seems quite excessive.

Flat Rate

Because the main solutions for ISDN metering do not appear to favor usage for dedicated Internet connectivity, the second rate structure should be more interesting to managers looking for connectivity. Flat rate structure is based on a principle of the telephone companies oversubscribing their bandwidth within the general usage patterns of the subscribers. So, for example, if the ISDN users generally are active on their lines for 20 percent of the time, the telephone company will base the flat rate on cost recovery (and some profit margin) at a slightly higher utilization. This cost will include long-run infrastructure upgrading and capital costs.

Generally, the ISDN tariffs for flat rate providers have been in flux because of changing usage patterns, but currently fluctuate between $60 and $125 per month and up. Several telephone companies have indicated a desire to increase the cost of the ISDN flat rate services. A fairly large backlash exists against such a move, however, so the end result is not yet known.

Tip

Careful attention should be paid to what sort of ISDN service you are purchasing from your local loop provider. In some cases, telephone companies have usage policies that prevent the use of ISDN lines for dedicated purposes. The policies are also reflected in the industry usage estimates. For example, the figure of 20 percent utilization is not just a number, but the actual figure quoted from a local provider. The provider allowed utilization of only 20 percent, and use beyond this point was either cut off or billed.

Bandwidth Charges

Besides the charges for local loop access from your site and your ISP, you will also be charged a fee for the amount of bandwidth utilized. Although some ISPs will require a payment of the local loop charges incurred on-site, in most instances, the fee is simply incorporated into the monthly fees. The billing policies are generally based on one of two methods, as follows:

- Base fee and usage

- Flat rate

Base Fee and Usage

A now-familiar billing policy, the base fee and usage option is sometimes offered for ISDN connections. Generally, the amount of the base fee covers the fixed costs of the ISDN connection (ISDN local loop charges and a capital cost recovery charge) and a small amount of bandwidth per month. Additional bandwidth will be provided at a rate that exceeds the price per unit that the ISP pays to its provider. The margin on bandwidth allows the ISP to maintain a certain level of productivity; consequently, the cost for bandwidth usage will reflect your ISP's place within the bandwidth hierarchy.

Tip

If you expect that your site will come close to more than 50 percent utilization of the bandwidth (remembering that 100 percent utilization, although theoretically possible, is not practically obtainable; in general, a rate of 65 to 85 percent utilization is achievable), then you should consider a flat rate policy, rather than the base fee and usage policy. Usage charges will likely cost more than the flat rate solution.

Flat Rate

Generally, the more popular billing policy followed by ISPs, the flat rate policy simply provides a set amount of bandwidth for a flat monthly fee. Because the ISP will generally oversubscribe its available bandwidth, the flat rate option will be priced lower than a similar bandwidth obtained via the usage policy.

The lower rate is due to the ISP's expectation that even though it sells you 128-Kbps bandwidth (for example), you will utilize less than x percent of the available bandwidth. If your site requires a large amount of bandwidth on a consistent basis, you will most likely be able to achieve greater cost effectiveness through a flat rate policy.

Setup Charges

Besides the monthly usage charges for local loop service and bandwidth from an ISP, using ISDN for WWW connectivity will also result in a number of setup charges. In most cases, the charges will be divided into two main categories, as follows:

- ❀ Charges levied by the providers

- ❀ Charges due to installation and configuration of equipment at your site

Provider-Based Setup Charges

In most cases, both of your providers will charge you a setup fee for ISDN service being activated for your site. In the case of the local loop provider, the charge will be for the following items:

❀ Configuring switches

❀ Allocating a Service Profile ID (SPID) to your devices

❀ Pulling line to your site (assuming this had not been done previously)

Most local loop providers also provide the option of supplied equipment, and installing this equipment will generally result in further charges. The installation charges for the local loop provider will generally be in the range of $100 to $120.

In addition to the local loop installation charge, you will likely be charged an installation fee by your ISP. Not only will this charge generally offset the local loop installation at the ISP site (unless you are responsible for installation on both ends), but the charge should also provide such basic services as setting up routing and some level of technical support during the installation process.

Installation and Configuration Charges

Besides the installation charges levied by your providers, your choice of ISDN for WWW connectivity will necessitate costs for the personnel to set up and configure the hardware based at your site. Depending on the type of equipment purchased for your connection and the level of expertise you have in-house, your connection may or may not be possible without outside help.

Obviously, purchasing technical assistance via a consultant carries a fiscal cost, but over the long run, the price may be worth it because of savings gained as a result of staff time. You should be very careful to assess your in-house expertise, because the equipment configuration is the foundation of your connectivity.

Hardware Costs

As previously discussed, the purchasing of ISDN hardware can be made from a local loop provider, ISP, or directly from an ISDN equipment manufacturer.

Although the manufacturer will generally provide the best price point, your providers may also be willing to assist in the installation process if equipment has been purchased from them. All of these factors have an impact in your costs for ISDN equipment, as does the type of connection that you require.

In the case of a complete networking device such as an ISDN to Ethernet bridge, the costs of such equipment can run from $1,200 to $2,500 and even higher. You should therefore carefully assess what sort of connectivity options you require or will require in the near future. Although expandability can be beneficial, you must also be careful not to overbuy. For a simpler connection method, such as a terminal adapter card for a PC, you should be able to find prices in the $300 to $700 range. In most cases, you will also be required to purchase an NT1 for approximately $200 to $400 (although a number of integrated devices do exist).

If you are interested in pricing equipment from the manufacturers directly, you will find that a number of companies exist and the prices can vary greatly. Make sure to define your needs rigorously before attempting to contact manufacturers, because the price will vary according to model. The following is a short list of some ISDN equipment manufacturers:

1. Adtran, Inc.
   901 Explorer Boulevard
   Huntsville, AL 35806–2807
   205–971–8000

2. Ascend Communications, Inc.
   1275 Harbor Bay Parkway
   Alameda, CA 94502
   800–272–3634; 510–769–6001

3. Bell Atlantic Teleproducts
   West Building, Suite 150
   50 East Swedesford Road
   Frazer, PA 19355
   800–221–0845; 215–695–2300

4. Cisco Systems, Inc.
   170 West Tasman Drive
   San Jose, CA 95134-1706
   408-526-4000
   800-553-NETS (6387)
   408-526-4100 fax

5. Combinet, Inc.
   333 West El Camino Real
   Sunnyvale, CA 94087
   800-967-6651; 408-522-9020

6. DigiBoard
   6400 Flying Cloud Drive
   Eden Prairie, MN 55344-3322
   800-344-4273; 612-943-9020

7. Extension Technology Corporation
   30 Hollis Street
   Framingham, MA 01701–8616
   800-856-2672; 508-872-7748

8. Gandalf Systems Corporation
   9 North Olney Avenue
   Cherry Hill Industrial Center–9
   Cherry Hill, NY 08003–1688
   800-426-3253; 609-424-9400

9. Hayes Microcomputer Products, Inc.
   5835 Peachtree Corners
   E Norcross, GA 30092–3405
   800-964-2937; 404-840-9200

10. Intel Corporation
    5200 NE Elam Young Parkway
    Hillsboro, OR 97124–6497
    800-538-3373; 503-629-7354

11. Motorola Inc.
    5000 Bradford Drive
    Huntsville, AL 35805–1993
    800-451-2369; 205-430-8000

12. Tone Commander Systems
    11609 49th Place West
    Mukilteo, WA 98275
    800-524-0024; 206-349-1000

Understanding Setup Requirements

Regardless of the costs of ISDN, you must meet a number of requirements before ISDN service can be set up at your site. Fulfilling these requirements will establish the basic structures needed to successfully implement ISDN for WWW connectivity. Although this is in no way a comprehensive list, you should pay special attention to the following three requirements before proceeding with ISDN implementation:

❀ Checking the local loop availability

❀ Assessing and choosing an ISP

❀ Obtaining sufficient technical resource people in networking and systems

Checking the Local Loop Availability

Of all the requirements for ISDN service, the most unforgiving process is the verification of the local loop availability at your site. Although the telephone company in your city or area of the city may provide ISDN service, this does not guarantee that the service will be available at your particular location. Because ISDN local loops are limited to 18,000 feet from a central office, the service is not always available.

To determine availability, you should be able to place a simple call to your telephone company, asking it to check your site for ISDN local loop availability.

Assuming that your area has been wired for ISDN, the company will check that the local loop length is short enough for ISDN. In general, it should take no more than 24 hours for the telephone company to inform you of the availability, and the process should cost you nothing.

A Note from the Author

The following section comes from personal experience. Not long ago, our company decided to look at ISDN as a method of providing a mid-level of bandwidth to our office. Although ISDN was available in our area, the local loop between our site and the Central Office would have exceeded the acceptable limits for ISDN service. As a result, we were not able to use ISDN as our connectivity solution.

Picking a Provider

As with all connectivity methods for WWW sites, the choice of an Internet Service Provider is one of the most critical choices that you can make as a manager. Because ISDN services are not offered by as many providers as the mainstream technologies, the choice of providers will often be limited. Although this may simplify your evaluation process, the lack of options makes the final choice even more important, because switching providers may be difficult or impossible. The rules developed for assessing all service providers still apply, but the use of ISDN has a number of special considerations:

- ※ Technical knowledge of ISDN

- ※ Protocols supported

- ※ Options for upgrades

Technical Knowledge of ISDN

The most important factor in choosing an ISP for your ISDN connectivity is the quality of technical staff on which the provider will be relying to maintain the other end of your ISDN link. Because ISDN can be difficult to understand, let alone maintain, the technical staff should be top-notch professionals. No test will positively identify the quality of the staff, but your provider should be willing to discuss the experience and qualifications of its staff. Be leery of an ISP that cannot even understand what you have learned from this chapter!

Protocols Supported

Given that an ISP has sufficient knowledge of ISDN to convince you that its staff is at least reasonably proficient, you should still try to choose a provider that offers a number of different implementations for IP encapsulation on the ISDN link. Because both PPP and frame relay are supported by most ISDN-capable ISPs, this criterion may not be an issue. As Chapter 8 details, frame relay can have a number of benefits for communications in certain situations, and you may want the option, if not now, then at a later date.

Upgrade Options

Although a single BRI interface can provide you with sufficient bandwidth for your current WWW site connectivity needs, you may need greater connectivity in the future. You should therefore pay close attention to the options available through your potential ISP. Because it is far easier to simply change connectivity methods while maintaining the same ISP than it is to switch ISPs, the provision of options (such as T1 connections, PRI ISDN support, and a proactive approach to emerging technologies) becomes even more important.

A Note from the Author

Whenever possible, try to avoid moving your site from one service provider to another. Because IP addressing and routing schemes may require that you re-address your hosts after a move, such a change can result in a significant cost on your part. Moreover, the move will have to be propagated throughout the Internet in order for the new routing to take effect. We actually have had the misfortune of experiencing the problems of such a change when our original service provider changed providers. As a result, our site was not available for 24 to 48 hours, and for some parts of the Internet for nearly a week. Needless to say, our clients and customers were not impressed, and the interruption could have proved costly.

Knowledge of Systems and Networking

Whereas checking the local loop and choosing an ISP for ISDN service are major concerns, you should also pay attention to the technical knowledge that is required to maintain any connectivity, and ISDN in particular. As with all Internet connectivity solutions, special attention should be paid to making sure that you at least have access to a networking (TCP/IP) expert and a system administrator who is knowledgeable about your particular needs and security concerns.

Beyond the basic needs of connectivity personnel, you must also deal with the specific technical problems with ISDN. To properly solve the unique problems of ISDN, you should have personnel who intimately understand the process behind ISDN. Also, because of the regional differences in implementation, the personnel should have experience installing and maintaining ISDN service in your area. If the type of personnel needed is not available, then you should at least try to find someone with experience with some method of digital connectivity solutions (56 Kbps or T1 experience may help).

Summary

Although ISDN provides a marked increase of bandwidth available to a WWW site at a relatively cost-effective price, a need still exists for even greater levels of bandwidth. If you want your WWW site to maintain a high graphic or time-based media content, then you may require bandwidth in an order of magnitude larger than the BRI ISDN offers. PRI ISDN may provide a solution, but the older digital services of T1 and T3 speeds can often provide flexible bandwidths at a low cost. The next chapter discusses some of the pros and cons of such connectivity options.

Checklist

The following are concerns that should be addressed at the conclusion of the chapter.

☑ ISDN service available?

☑ Costs of the service:

Local loop: Basic charge and usage? Dedicated?

Bandwidth: Basic charge and usage? Dedicated?

Provider setup costs?

Installation and configuration costs?

☑ ISDN equipment provision:

ISP?

Telephone company?

Purchase?

☑ Local loop length:

☑ Cost to extend local loop (if required)?

☑ ISP choice:

Knowledge of ISDN?

Upgrade path available?

Setup support available?

Bandwidth available from ISP?

Protocol used for link?

7

Entering the Global Arena: A T1/T3 Leased Line

So far, this book has detailed two digital connections that can be used for Internet connectivity: the older 56Kbps digital leased line and the newer ISDN service. This chapter details digital telephony's high bandwidth solutions for Internet connectivity: T1 and T3 access. As with the 56Kbps solution, the T1 and T3 solutions are based on the older technology of digital telephony.

This chapter starts with a short review of the history of digital telephony (detailed in Chapter 5), then reviews the classification hierarchy of digital telephony. Then it briefly details the technical background for digital leased lines, including the physical plant, multiplexing, and the newer technology for really high bandwidth connectivity. After discussing the technology behind T1 connectivity, many issues surrounding the availability of service and possible limitations is examined, including the local versus national debate, the impact of distance on costs, the problems with downstream bandwidth utilization, and the long-term viability of digital telephony connection methods through copper wire in the emerging light of fiber-optic connectivity options. The chapter ends with a discussion of some of the basic requirements for the use of T1 connectivity for Internet access, including a basic discussion of the hardware requirements, costs associated with the solution, and some other setup requirements. Special attention is paid to the possible solutions for shared or metered T1 access, as well as the leasing (via ISPs or Long Distance Carriers) of hardware requirements.

You will be better able to assess T1 connectivity for your site after reading this chapter. Not only will the technology used in connectivity be clearer, but you will have a good understanding of the requirements of this option. Finally, you will be better able to assess the overall benefit of T1 connectivity, including the potential limitations and some of the more unique implementation regimes that exist.

What are T1/T3 Leased Lines?

T1 and T3 leased lines are classifications of the North American standard for digital voice communications. In terms of Internet connectivity, the T1 lines represent the backbones of most commercial ISPs, and the T3 lines represent major backbones between the major long distance carriers. The following sections look at the classification of service and the technology used for utilization of these digital communication methods.

A Note from the Author

As was mentioned in Chapter 5, the use of the Tx hierarchy of digital telephone communications began in the early 1960s, and by the end of that decade, the majority of the long distance trunk lines had been converted from the old analog system to the newer digital trunks. As a result of the conversion to the digital system, a new classification of information was established.

A more detailed historical description of the history of the digital telephone system and the analog system that had been utilized prior to conversion can be found in Chapter 5. Because the historical change is the same for 56Kbps solutions, as well as the Tx hierarchy, these details were omitted in order to conserve space.

Classification of Tx Leased Lines

The digital telephone system implemented by AT&T in the 1960s is referred to as the *Tx Hierarchy* (see fig. 7.1). For telephone carriers, the hierarchy can be divided into four distinct levels: T1, T2, T3, and T4. Each level represents both a multiple of the basic voice channel (64 Kbps) and of the previous layer.

For example, a T1 represents 24 voice channels (1.544 Mbps), and a T2 represents either 96 voice channels or 4 T1s (6.312 Mbps). A T3 is 672 voice channels or 7 T2s or 28 T1s (44.736 Mbps). Finally, a T4 is 4,032 voice channels or 6 T3s or 42 T2s or 168 T1s (274.176 Mbps). In terms of Internet connectivity, only two of the channels are traditionally used, T1 and T3. As well, outside the hierarchy, but related to it, is a common process of using fractional T1s for connectivity (or fractions of one T1).

T1 Classification

The T1 classification is a telephone classification that represents 24 multiplexed digital voice channels over one channel bank. Because each voice communication channel represents 64 Kbps of data, the total data rate supported by this procedure is 1.544 Mbps (note that the actual data usage for a voice channel is 56 Kbps, but that 8 Kbps is used to ensure that signal is properly framed). In the case of Internet communication, the channel bank is actually not divided into separate channels unless the line is being used for multiple purposes, such as mixing voice and data.

Figure 7.1

Tx hierarchy.

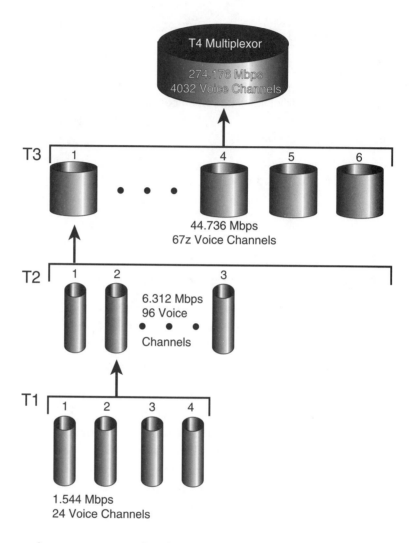

Given the current data uses associated with the Internet and WWW sites, the T1 carrier is actually a standard level of bandwidth for an ISP. Because the channel is symmetrical in bandwidth uses, the ISPs need to maintain a sufficient amount of bandwidth to deliver the information from their WWW sites to the rest of the Internet and to route the information requested by their individual users from the rest of the Internet. This requirement, and the data flows currently expressed by their users, means the T1 carrier generally provides sufficient bandwidth for a large number of dial-up users (as many as 1,000 dial-up lines per T1).

Note

Although a T1 carrier represents a tremendous amount of data in terms of the written word (about 40 pages of text per second), the changing nature of the Internet is putting pressure on this service as the basis of ISP connectivity. As more and more symmetrical-use applications are developed by end users (such as voice or video conferencing via the Internet), the data flows needed to support this level of activity will skyrocket.

The move to cable or fiber optics for user connections will only hasten the demise of the T1 as the standard. After all, if a user can demand 500 Kbps at any one time, the amount of bandwidth needed to support these data rates (assuming applications continue to rely on higher data rates) will rapidly exceed T1 levels. The key will be for ISPs to manage their conversion from the older Tx hierarchy to either the newer ISDN or fiber-based high-bandwidth solutions (see SONET later in this section). As the ISPs make these changes, the price of upstream bandwidth may become cheaper because downstream bandwidth becomes the limiting factor.

T3 Classification

The T3 classification is a telephone classification that represents 672 multiplexed digital voice channels over one channel bank. Because each voice communication channel represents 64 Kbps of data, the total data rate supported by this procedure is 44.736 Mbps. Because of the high level of bandwidth that is available under the T3 classification, the current use of a T3 channel is for the backbone infrastructure of the Internet. The major long distance carriers interconnect via a T3 channel (or multiple where needed), and only humongous WWW sites and organizations currently require T3 bandwidth.

Partial T1 Classifications

Because most ISPs have only a T1 (or perhaps multiple T1s for redundancy) of bandwidth, the purchase of a leased T1 from an ISP is not generally available (for T1 or greater, you are generally required to go through the long distance carriers). Still, there exists a significant number of organizations that have need for greater bandwidth than a dedicated 56 Kbps, but less than T1 bandwidth. The result has been the offering of a number of differential rates for partial T1s. Here an ISP leases part of their T1 as a dedicated connection. The result is that a number of partial T1 categories have developed in each area. No matter what area, the partial T1 will always be a multiple of 64 Kbps (one voice channel), so 128 Kbps, 256 Kbps, 512 Kbps, and so on.

Technical Background of Tx Leased Lines

In general, the technical functioning of the Tx hierarchy of leased lines is similar to the technical background of the dedicated 56 Kbps and ISDN offerings. Although some of the details were covered in Chapters 5 and 6, this section discusses a couple of technical issues that are specific to the Tx hierarchy (one section on multiplexing will be a partial review). A brief look is then taken at one of the possible future digital options for really high-speed connections: SONET.

Physical Plant of Tx Leased Lines

The first technological issue specific to the Tx hierarchy—or more precisely that only becomes an issue with the Tx hierarchy—is that of the physical plant. In terms of digital telephony, the physical plant of the structure revolves around the two major levels of service applicable to the Internet connectivity: T1 and T3.

T1 Physical Plant

Actually, the physical plant for all carriers up to T2 is the twisted pair copper wires that are available to all areas. These wires provide the bandwidth required for the T1 and T2 carrier channels. Because the bandwidth available on a single pair is not enough to carry a T2, multiple twisted pairs are used to provide the higher bandwidth needed to carry the data rates associated with the T2 channels.

T3+ Physical Plant

Although the data rates of the T1 and T2 carrier channels are low enough to be carried over the twisted pair infrastructure, the high data rates associated with the T3 and T4 carrier channels require that the medium provide greater bandwidth. As a result, T3 and T4 channels are usually carried over either coaxial or fiber-optic cables. The effective data rate of the actual signal is controlled by the multiplexor that is used on each channel.

Multiplexing and Tx Leased Lines

As was discussed in Chapters 5 and 6, the digital telephony system relies on Time Division Multiplexing to allow the allocation of channels on the different cabling media. In the case of a T1 multiplexor, recall that each source is sampled 8,000 times per second, and the frames of (24 samples × 8 bits + one framing bit) bits are taken during each sample. As a result, 1.544 Mbps is sent down the channel every second. In the case of the higher data rate channels, the multiplexor is able to sample more sources during each sample (of the 8,000 samples per second), and consequently a larger amount of data is able to be sent down the channel.

Note

It is useful here to clarify the terms bandwidth and data rate. In strict sense of the word, *bandwidth* refers to the amount of frequency that a particular media is able to carry. As such, bandwidth is always measured in terms of *hertz* (or kilo-, mega-, or gigahertz). On the other hand, the data rate (or effective data rate) is the amount of information that can be transmitted over a particular medium given the use of a particular technology.

The relationship between bandwidth and effective data rate is somewhat ambiguous because any one implementation of data transmission does not necessarily utilize the full bandwidth in any particular medium. Generally speaking, the effective data rate is governed by the physical limitations of the media, such as signal-to-noise ratio and attenuation. As the signal-to-noise ratio increases, the effective data rate decreases. As a result, media that is susceptible to a high noise (such as copper wires) has a much lower maximum effective data rate (as well as bandwidth), whereas media that does not suffer these problems will be able to carry greater data rates (such as optical cabling).

High Bandwidth Technology: Synchronous Optical Network (SONET)

Although the rates supported by the Tx hierarchy are incredibly high in terms of Internet access requirements at the current times, the increase in video and voice applications are quickly changing the needs. Given the growth rates that are being experienced, higher bandwidths may be required along the Internet backbones in the next few years. By the looks of it, the use of fiber-optic cable and a new international standard, Synchronous Optical Network (SONET), will provide the added bandwidth for higher data rates.

SONET, like the T3 and T4 digital services, is based on the use of fiber-optic cables for transmission. Unlike the Tx hierarchy, the SONET project relies on an asynchronous transfer mode (ATM—see Chapter 9, "ADSL and B-ISDN/ATM," for details) for the cell relay procedure rather than the frames used in the Tx methods. Because the photons of fiber-optics travel at much higher frequencies than the electricity of the electrical transmission methods, the data rates are considerably higher (see table 7.1).

Synchronous Digital Hierarchy
Table 7.1

Data Rate (Mbps)	Synchronous Optical Carrier Level Designation	Transport Signal Designation	CCIT Designation
51.84	OC-1	STS-1	-
155.52	OC-3	STS-3	STM-1
622.08	OC-12	STS-12	STM-4
1244.16	OC-24	STS-24	STM-8
2488.32	OC-48	STS-48	STM-16

Availability and Limitations of Tx Leased Connections

Given the Tx hierarchy is well-established and standardized across North America (a different system is used internationally), the overall availability is good. Even so, this section discusses the overall availability issues with the Tx hierarchy that surround the local/ISP versus long distance carrier debate. Once the benefits of each solution are examined, a number of limitations or possible concerns of the Tx connectivity option are examined.

Issues discussed include the following:

- The effect of the distance on the overall cost of leased lines and the relationship of decreasing marginal costs for higher data rates.

- The potential downstream bandwidth wastage, including some possible utilization methods.

- The long-term viability of the Tx hierarchy and the impact that emerging technologies will have on the technology in the future.

Local versus National Providers

The main issue in the availability of Tx connectivity is not the availability, considering Tx service is available in most areas, but the "who" of provision. Because the channels being leased are of a size equal to or larger than those used by local ISPs, the option of using a long distance carrier must be examined. Even so, the possible benefits of a local provider in terms of flexibility must be considered, as well. After discussing the possible cost rationales behind a long distance provider, the bandwidth food chain analogy for Internet connectivity is briefly refreshed to remind you of its impact on price.

Local Provider Flexibility

Be concerned regarding the use of a local ISP for the supply of higher bandwidth leased lines (T1+). The concern is that as a user of a large portion of the ISP's bandwidth, you may be paying a profit margin that is unnecessarily high in light of the option of going to a national provider, just as the ISP does. With this in mind, there are at least two good reasons for using a local ISP for higher bandwidth connectivity: pricing flexibility and the local support issue.

Pricing Flexibility

The first potential benefit for using a local provider for higher Tx bandwidth is the possible use of flexible pricing regimes that a local provider might offer. In particular, a local provider is more likely to offer a pricing structure based on a metered T1. Under this concept, the client (you) pays a flat monthly fee approximately equal to the cost of the local loop, plus a base amount of bandwidth. Additional bandwidth is charged at a slightly marked up rate as it is used. The result is that the ISP is able to provide a potentially lower cost level of bandwidth than a standard leased Tx connection.

TIP

It is possible that a fractional T1 could provide you with exactly the amount of bandwidth needed, but metered T1 is generally a better and more cost-effective option than fractional T1 bandwidth.

Note

Obviously this solution only works to your advantage if you use less than the full level of bandwidth available. As a result, you are able to save some money without leaving yourself open to the network lags that can result from a lower level of bandwidth, because your connection can theoretically provide the world with T1 access to your site at any time. However, because it is not accessed at all times at full capacity, you are able to save on the difference (minus the profit taking by the local ISP).

Local Support

Although the use of a Tx connection for Internet connectivity is not a simple procedure, it is likely that any site that requires such connectivity will have the personnel to support it. If this is not the case, the use of a local ISP may provide you with additional support in the event of problems. Because the local service providers often offer complete packages, including hardware, connectivity, and support, you might be able to reduce the overall technical requirements of your staff. The reduction in required personnel can save you money, and at the same time the ISPs will generally provide support for their equipment.

Long Distance Cost Rationales

Although local ISPs hold potential benefits for Tx connectivity providers, the crux of the issue with the long distance carriers is the cost levels. In most cases, your local ISP will be purchasing their bandwidth from a long distance carrier. As a result, the ISP will either charge more for a similar connection than the long distance carriers, or they will oversubscribe their bandwidth to a greater level. Either way, there exists a potential that you can gain either some cost or performance benefits by leasing your bandwidth directly from the long distance carrier yourself.

Explanation of the Bandwidth "Food Chain"

The previous discussion regarding the cost benefits that the long distance carriers can provide leads nicely into a re-illustration of the bandwidth food chain first discussed in Chapter 2. As you will recall, the Internet is actually a hierarchy of bandwidth connected together, with each level of the hierarchy either reselling the bandwidth at a higher rate, or oversubscribing the bandwidth to a slightly larger degree.

The costing mechanisms of leased telephone lines (the basis of the communications network that carries most of the Internet traffic) is that each higher level of bandwidth provides certain cost benefits over the lower levels. As a result, a provider that purchases a T3 connection from a long distance carrier (who own most of the backbones making up the Internet backbone) can then resell the T3 and make a profit. Though a T3 might cost $26,000 per month, the provider can resell the 28 T1s for $3,000 per T1. The result is a profit margin of approximately $50,000! Of course, the actual margin is actually considerably lower, given the need for additional technical support and hardware.

The degree to which price margins carry down the chain until the base dedicated connection is reached is significant (generally a dedicated 28.8 connection at this time). Because of the money you can save by purchasing a large level of bandwidth from a long distance carrier, you might consider sharing a larger connection in a cooperative manner in order to reduce costs.

Note

When considering a sharing arrangement with another party, look at the bandwidth use patterns of your potential partner(s). Obviously, if you can find a partner with complementary patterns, you both will benefit. For example, if you are hosting a large Web site but have little need for downstream bandwidth, you might consider a partner who is using a lot of downstream bandwidth. In many ways, most service providers are doing this when they sell user accounts and Web space (or server parks). Each client has different use patterns, and, as a result, the ISP is able to provide for both with less bandwidth than if each acquired the required amount separately.

Distance from the POP and Costs

As with all leased lines, the cost of the local loop to the ISP or long distance carrier's Point of Presence (POP) has a large impact on the costs of the service. Luckily, the majority of the leased lines only have to travel a few miles to get to the ISP or national provider's POP. In general, the cost of a T1 leased line is based on a flat rate plus x times the number of miles traveled. As a result, the most cost-effective solution might be local or the closest point of presence. For example, if the cheapest bandwidth in your area is 40 miles from your office, and a closer provider is only slightly more expensive (a couple of hundred dollars), then the overall cost of using the cheapest provider might be more expensive.

In cases when your site is located in a remote area, the distance factor for the leased lines can play a large role in the overall cost of the solution. As a basic rule of thumb, a leased line may become comparable to a satellite or microwave connection in terms of costs when the overall distance exceeds 500 miles. Although the satellite solutions have other potential problems, you should consider them in the event that your site is far away from the nearest POP.

Utilizing Wasted Downstream Bandwidth

One of the most overlooked limitations of any symmetrical leased line for the purposes of WWW site connectivity is possibly the potential waste of the downstream bandwidth. As has been mentioned previously, the leased connections provide fully symmetrical bandwidth, so in the case of a T1, 1.544 Mbps can be transferred in each direction. As a result, there exists the potential that the bandwidth might not be fully utilized in the downstream direction (the reasons are detailed shortly). In order to better discuss the possible underutilization and solution, this section examines the nature of WWW communications, then examines three options for increasing the utilization of the bandwidth.

Bandwidth Use Patterns

As was discussed previously, the Web is an excellent mechanism for the distribution of information, either in text form, or more and more as graphics, sound, and video. But, as a result of the nature of the Web, the usage of bandwidth of a WWW site is actually very asymmetrical. Each site has a large volume of data that is sent out to clients after receiving a small amount of data in the form of a request. As this scenario is replayed a number of times over, the end result is that an asymmetrical pattern solidifies. Because the newer WWW applications increase the data size of the delivered files, this utilization of the Internet will increase in the future.

If you're looking for connectivity for the sole purpose of providing WWW information to the Internet community, the result will be a very lopsided bandwidth pattern. Because most leased line sites also supply some measure of local network access services, the flow can be somewhat equalized as the users draw information into the internal network. Unfortunately, the needs of large or popular WWW sites are most likely greater than the needs of most internal networks. As the bandwidth requirements increase and the leased lines increase to T1 or T3 levels, an increasing amount of downstream bandwidth is underutilized.

Possible Utilization of Downstream Bandwidth

Given the potential for the underutilization of downstream bandwidth, consider the potential utilization regimes that might correct the problem. This section discusses three regimes that will correct the problem, examining the benefits and potential problems of the following:

- ⚛ Shared Txs

- ⚛ Leasing only upstream bandwidth from a provider

- ⚛ Selling the downstream bandwidth to users

Sharing Txs

The first possible solution to not utilizing the full downstream bandwidth is to find a partner with whom to share the bandwidth. In this case, you will want to make sure the partner is using the connection in ways that complement rather than compete with your use. A good example is a remote office that needs to access the main office via the Internet to consistently download information. As long as the flow of data is more into the partner's network, as opposed to out of the network, a shared resource will provide benefit.

Note

Even if a company does not have complementary bandwidth requirements to yours, a shared utilization of a Tx connection can still provide benefit. For example, the sharing of the bandwidth can allow you both to realize a lower price per bit rate than two lower bandwidth levels would allow. Please recall the economy of scale discussion in detail earlier in this chapter (specifically, the section explaining the Bandwidth "Food Chain").

Leasing Agreements for Upstream Bandwidth

Given the pursuit of some ISPs for a mainly user-type clientele, it is possibile that an ISP in your area has extra upstream bandwidth available. In this case, the ISP might be willing to provide you with an asymmetrical allotment of bandwidth in some metered Tx scenario. Perhaps the metered Tx provides you a set amount of bandwidth upstream (T1 levels, for instance) and a lower amount of downstream bandwidth (128 Kbps). As a result of these asymmetries of the connection, the provider is willing to charge a lower monthly rate. Of course, there will definitely be a charge associated with exceeding your downstream allotment of bandwidth!

Selling the Downstream Bandwidth to Users

The final potential solution to the problem of underutilized downstream bandwidth is to sell the bandwidth to users. A variation of sharing the bandwidth, this solution is more intensive because it targets not one big user, but many users whose general usage patterns complement your own. As a result, the bandwidth utilization by your site will be more symmetrical. Obviously, a major drawback of this solution is that you will have to sign up a number of clients and supply the appropriate services to them, so this solution could interfere in the operations of your real business—whatever it may be.

Warning

Currently there exists little or no profit in the dial-up user market for Internet services. This might sound like blasphemy in an Internet connectivity guide, but the truth of the matter is that although experiencing very large growth rates in number of users, most ISPs are also experiencing increasing losses. As a result of competition with cable and telephone companies, this could become even worse. Although the dial-up market might provide a method of recouping some of your connection costs, the likelihood of providing a profit for the connection is unlikely.

Long-Term Viability versus Emerging Technologies

The final concern about the Tx hierarchy and the leased lines based on it is the long-term viability of these services. Telephone companies are already moving to implement commercial services using the SONET standard. As a result, there may exist a price-to-bandwidth benefit for the really high-bandwidth users. In addition, as this technology is implemented, the costs-to-bandwidth benefits that it provides to the telephone (or cable) companies will be passed on to the ISPs and, in turn, to you (assuming the competitive market is actually competitive and reacting well to increases in the supply of bandwidth). Depending on the position that you occupy in the bandwidth food chain, you may be better off examining the newer technology of fiber-optics and SONET. (See Chapter 9 for a discussion of the benefits.)

Hardware Requirements

As with the previously described leased line solutions, the Tx connectivity options are very hardware-intensive. As a result, the solution can become very costly, although some alternatives are available (see the "Costs" section later in this chapter). In terms of the hardware required for a Tx connection, there are three main pieces of hardware that you need to have:

❋ A CSU/DSU

❋ A router

❋ A server

CSU/DSU

As was discussed in Chapter 5, the CSU/DSU is the channel service unit and the data service unit. In the case of Tx connectivity, it is quite common for the data service unit to be integrated into the router for your network. As a result, the majority of solutions will only require the less expensive channel service unit from the local loop provider.

Routers

As with any connectivity option, one of the most important issues is the functionality of routing, or correctly forwarding and accepting datagrams from and for your network. Consequently, the router becomes one of the most important pieces of hardware that your network will have. Possible options that you might want your router to have are the following:

❋ A basic IP router

❋ One with an integrated DSU

❋ Multiple protocol routers

❋ Routers that perform firewall functions

IP Routers

For a router to meet the needs of the Tx connectivity, the hardware, at the very least, must perform some basic functions. For starters, the router must have two interfaces, one for the leased line connection, the second for the attachment to the local host or network. Generally, the IP routers will provide one of two interfaces for the leased line, depending on whether the router includes a DSU. In this case, the V.35 interface is used. As for the local network connectivity, the routers are usually configured with ethernet interfaces, although routers do exist for Token-Ring networks.

Built-In DSUs

One of the options generally included in routers is DSU functionality. Because the DSU is the more expensive piece of telephone hardware, and because adding DSU functionality to the router is often more cost effective than a separate unit, including it is becoming a common practice. The result is reducing telephone hardware needs to the less costly channel service unit.

Hybrid Multiple Protocol Routers

The second possible option that can be combined with an IP router is function-ality for the support of another networking protocol, such as DECnet or IPX. As a result, the router is able to take packets from these other networking protocols and encapsulate the information for transport across the leased lines. The result is a router that not only supports Internet access and routing, but allows your internal network to operate across the Internet and to connect to other network sites with the same configuration (such as satellite offices connecting to the corporate network via IPX). The major concern with this solution is the fact that the multiprotocol routers have generally not been standardized, and, as a result, little or no interoperability is available across brands.

Routers and Firewalls

The third, and final, option in terms of routers is the inclusion of functionality for firewall services. In general, the inclusion of at least some basic packet filtering services are included in most routers. The result will be a hardware device that can allow or disallow traffic according to the rules established by the network administrator (see Chapter 3 for more about firewalls and the use of routers for security enhancement).

Servers

The third important piece of hardware of the Tx connectivity options is the WWW server. Obviously, a server is required for most of the connectivity options (actually all options have a server, whether or not you own it), but it is mentioned here for two reasons: routing and increased quality.

First of all, the server is mentioned because under the higher traffic options of the Tx hierarchy (except perhaps partial T1 connectivity), a server is no longer very effective in acting as a router for the connection. This is due to the fact that the high data rates require the speed of a hardware router in order to utilize the bandwidth effectively (software cannot keep up).

The second reason for specifically discussing the server here is to emphasize the fact that the Tx hierarchy is providing much higher levels of bandwidth than dedicated 28.8 SLIP/PPP, dedicated 56 Kbps, and ISDN. Because the bandwidth is higher, it is likely the requirements for the server will also be higher. Be careful to monitor your server to ensure that the hardware is not limiting the overall speed of your WWW site. Possible bottlenecks include processor speed, disk accesses, ethernet connectivity, and RAM. Of all the possible problems, the single greatest performance gain can usually be made by increasing your RAM.

Costs for Tx Connectivity

Although Tx connectivity provides a high level of connectivity versus the other options, the cost of this bandwidth is quite high in absolute terms. This section discusses the potential costs of solutions in terms of the initial costs and ongoing costs. The section concludes with a discussion of the possible benefits and difficulties associated with the alternative costing mechanism of a shared T1.

Initial Costs

The initial cost of the Tx connectivity solution breaks down into two components: hardware and installation. In each area, the following sections discuss the
costs associated with both the T1 and T3 connectivity options. In the case of
hardware, the section also discusses the alternative payment option that some
ISPs offer on leased hardware (thus lowering startup costs).

Initial Hardware Costs

The most costly portion of the hardware is the router. Although the CSU/DSU
can run as much as a few hundred to a thousand dollars, the cost of a Tx router
can run upwards of $120,000 dollars. In the case of T3 connectivity, the higher
end price will likely apply, though the router cost could be as low as $6,000 for
T1 (or fractional T1) connectivity.

Because of the expense of the routers, as well as the initial installation of the Tx
line and setup of the Internet access, a number of service providers offer options
where the router is actually their property, and you rent it from them. Although
this will definitely decrease the startup costs, there potentially is the additional
benefit of not being responsible for the maintenance and repair of the router
(although you will be paying for these services in the long run). As a result, the
length of downtime may be minimized if the ISP is willing to provide replacement routers in the event of a failure. This also spares you from the stress of
dealing with the problems directly.

Installation

Along with the hardware costs of the Tx connection, you are also going to pay
considerable setup or installation fees for the local loop installation and the ISP
routing and port configuration. In the case of T1, installation fees can run from
$1,500 to $4,000. On top of this, you will have to pay the ISP a service setup fee
of approximately $2,000.

Ongoing Costs

The ongoing costs of the Tx connectivity options are also very high, although the price per bit drops as you buy higher up the bandwidth chain. The ongoing costs can be broken down into two main components of service:

- ❋ The local loop

- ❋ Internet access

Leased Local Loop

The leased local loop is a requirement no matter where you get your actual Internet access from. In any case, the local loop is required between your site and either the ISP or the long distance carrier's POP. In either case, you will be charged a flat rate, plus a portion per mile of service. Prices can vary widely depending on your local telephone company, but the range appears to be between $300 and $500 for the flat rate, and $25 to $50 dollars per mile.

Internet Access

The second component of the ongoing costs in the Tx connectivity solution is the actual access to the Internet (or the backbone infrastructure that makes up the backbone of the Internet). For this service, you have one of two options, both in terms of the billing structure and the provider. Both of these choices, listed here, will affect the other decision in terms of feasibility and costs.

- ❋ Flat rate versus metered billing

- ❋ ISPs versus long distance carrier services

Flat Rate versus Metered

One of the first choices you will have to make in regards to the ongoing costs is whether to go for a flat rate or metered payment structure. Under a flat rate structure, you will be looking at $3,000 to $4,500 for a T1 connection (a T3 will cost approximately $25,000). One other possible option is to have a metered payment schedule, under which you are charged a basic rate ($1,000 to $1,500 for T1) that covers your connectivity to the ISP and allows you a basic amount of bandwidth (1 GB of throughput is common). For throughput over and above the base rate, you will be charged a rate per GB. This rate will naturally be greater per GB than the dedicated flat rate connection (a profit margin for the ISP will be added).

The benefit of the metered solution is that you may end up saving money if your usage is under the break-even amount (that is, the point where the meter charges are less than a flat rate charge). Unfortunately, this option could end up costing you more if the usage is actually higher than the break-even point. As a result, unless you are very sure of your usage, you should be cautious of this solution (see Chapter 1, "Bandwidth and Internet Connectivity").

ISPs versus Long Distance Carriers

The second choice concerning your ongoing costs is whether to go with an ISP or a long distance carrier. In the case of the ISP, you will generally be paying a higher rate for equivalent bandwidth in comparison to the long distance carriers (unless the POP for the carriers is considerably further away than the ISPs site).

Even with the price premium, the ISP may be a better solution anyway because the ISP might be more willing to provide services or options that the long distance carriers won't. Most long distance carriers, for example, will not provide metered T1 service, but ISPs likely will. As well, ISPs, being based locally, might be more able to provide added technical support for your connection.

"Shared" T1: A Dream Come True

Before closing this discussion on costs, it is worthwhile to look at an option for bandwidth leasing that might provide a cost effective solution: shared T1 (or Tx). In this solution, you and another party (or parties) agree to lease a T1 connection and share the total bandwidth among your sites (or offices). As a result, you may be able to gain considerable savings by moving up the bandwidth food chain. In considering this option, there are two key issues that you have to examine:

❋ The need for tracking use

❋ The physical location requirements

Cooperative Moving Up the Food Chain

One of the key benefits of the shared T1 is the potential economies of scale that this solution provides for both parties. An examination of bandwidth costs quickly shows that the bandwidth cost for half a T1 are closer to 65 percent of the costs of a full T1. As a result, your companies would be able to save approximately $450 per month each in sharing the T1.

As well, given the overall higher bandwidth, you will both be provided with better quality service because at any one time you have access to the entire T1 (assuming the other is not using any access at that time). In the cases where a complementary usage pattern exists, the overall benefit could be even greater.

Metering Requirement

One of the two main concerns with the shared T1 solution is the need to provide some tracking mechanisms for its usage. If, for example, your site used only 40 percent of the T1 one month and your partner used 60 percent, there has to be some way to track this so the appropriate costs can be charged to each participant. As a result, the overall budget stability of this solution is only slightly less than the exclusive flat rate solution (though it is better than a metered T1 from a service provider).

Physical Location Requirements

The second major concern with the shared T1 solution is the problem that the participants need to be in generally the same physical location (the ability to be connected via LAN on local cabling). Obviously, being located in the same office building would be ideal. This requirement stems from the fact that dedicated local loop lines are very expensive, and if an additional loop between the two parties were required, then the overall costs could be greater (or at least the savings would be reduced).

Setup Requirements

The setup requirements for the actual setup of a Tx connectivity solution are actually beyond the scope of this chapter, but the following basic issues should be examined:

❋ Routing

❋ Selecting an ISP or carrier

❋ Measuring the local loop

Routing

One of the first items that you should examine is the registration of a domain name and the setting up of routing for your connection. Because the ISP or carrier that you choose will likely act as one or both of your name servers, this issue cannot be dealt with until a provider is chosen. Even so, the registration of a domain name and preparation for setting up routing should be accomplished so that after connectivity is achieved, the routing falls into place quickly.

Selecting an ISP or Carrier

The second issue you should deal with in preparing for a Tx connection is the selection of an ISP or carrier for the service. Because the provider chosen affects the services available and possibly the cost, make sure that you have chosen a provider based on the best quality service at the most cost effective price. While choosing a provider, be careful that the issues of flexibility and service are in the forefront of your concerns.

Measuring the Local Loop

Finally, after you have chosen a provider, you must order your local loop and have the distance measured, which is done by the local telephone provider. Given the impact the local loop length can have on the cost of the solution, you at least need to get a good estimate to better weigh each option.

Summary

Tx connectivity provides the backbone services for both the majority of the major WWW sites and for the Internet itself. As a result, the hardware, service, and support for these solutions has been well developed. As for price-to-performance, the leased line solutions offer one of the best. Still, there are a number of developments that are gradually putting pressure on the long-term viability and cost effectiveness of these connectivity options. You will look at some of these solutions in Chapter 9.

Now that the major mainstream connectivity options have been examined, Chapter 8 looks at some more cutting-edge technology: cable and satellite connectivity. Actually, when it comes to these two connectivity methods, cutting-edge may actually be bleeding-edge...

Checklist

The following are concerns that should be addressed at the conclusion of the chapter.

☑ Bandwidth needed (from Chapter 2)?

☑ Local versus National Provider:

   Local pricing flexibility?

   Local support benefit?

   National provider price benefits?

   Distance to local Point of Presence:

☑ Possibility of sharing a Tx?

☑ Underutilized downstream bandwidth:

   Sell to users?

   Local dialup provider option?

☑ Router:

   ISP provided or purchase?

   Firewall needed?

   Multiprotocol router needed?

☑ CSU/DSU purchased?

☑ Server brought?

☑ Routing in place?

☑ Addresses available?

☑ Costs for bandwidth

Flat rate?

Metered?

8

Frame Relay

The increasing capabilities of computers and the new ways of connecting them together are creating new types of network topologies and new network traffic patterns. Traditional hierarchical terminal-to-host architectures were easily handled by star or tree networking topologies that no longer meet the standards of today's networking environments that demand new connectivity and bandwidth requirements. Not only are higher levels of bandwidth in demand by today's and tomorrow's network environments, but the efficient use of the bandwidth is being examined closely.

In this chapter, we will examine frame relay—a technology that has had a significant impact on the data network strategies of many individuals and corporations. As we will see, frame relay is a technology conceived in the 1980s in response to developing network requirements that are currently in place. Frame relay continues to enjoy wide deployment and growth today, and may in fact be the most commonly deployed wide area network (WAN) technology in today's world.

Frame Relay

Frame relay is a packet switching protocol based on standards defined by the American National Standards Institute (ANSI) and the International Telecommunications Union-Telecom Sector or ITU-T (formerly the CCITT). The primary thrust of these standards is the definition of a network access connection between a network and an end-station device such as a multi-protocol LAN router, frame relay access device (FRAD) or other piece of data terminal equipment (DTE). In this case, the network is typically the wide area communications network of a service provider and the end-station device would likely reside at a customer's premises.

One of the significant benefits of frame relay is its nearly global support for current network protocols such as TCP/IP, Novell's IPX, Apple Computer's AppleTalk, Digital Equipment Corporation's DecNet, OSI, and many others. The only requirement is that the specified network layer protocol has the capability to internetwork with Link Access Protocols for D channels (LAPD) as the layer two protocol. LAPD is a link-layer protocol that provides error-free communication between the physical layer and higher protocol layers such as TCP/IP. This capability is inherent in the majority of network layer protocols today and even those under development.

To properly understand frame relay, it is beneficial to examine it first from a historical perspective. This will discuss the issues that necessitated the development of a new protocol such as frame relay, the process of its definition and development, and a sense of the future of this protocol.

Frame Relay: A Historical Perspective

Frame relay began as an effort by several organizations to provide a better solution to the wide area networking requirements of the 1980s than what was possible using technologies of the time such as X.25. One of the primary objectives was simplification. This is evident in several aspects of the frame relay protocol.

First, due to rapidly improving quality of communications media and equipment, the notion was to develop a new protocol that would not require the robustness and resiliency of X.25. Earlier WAN protocols such as X.25 relied on analog transmission systems and copper media, which were predominant at the time. These links are much less reliable than the fiber media/digital transmission links available today. Fiber media/digital transmission links enable link-layer protocols to forego time-consuming error correction algorithms, which can be performed at higher protocol layers. This results in greater performance and efficiency without sacrificing data integrity. Frame relay is designed with this approach in mind. As you will see later during the examination of its frame structure, frame relay includes a cyclic redundancy check (CRC) algorithm for detecting and discarding corrupted bits; however, it does not include any protocol mechanisms for correcting bad data. Correction of bad data is handled by higher-layer protocols such as TCP (Transmission Control Protocol). Protocols such as TCP have the capability to sequence packets, detect corrupted or missing packets upon receipt by a destination device, and retransmit those specific packets.

Another difference between frame relay and X.25 is the absence of explicit, per-virtual-circuit flow control in frame relay. Now that many upper-layer protocols are effectively executing their own flow control algorithms, the need for this functionality at the link layer has diminished. Instead, very simple congestion notification mechanisms are provided to enable a network to inform a user device that the network resources are close to a congested state. This notification alerts higher-layer protocols that flow control may be needed. These mechanisms will be examined in detail later in this chapter.

Finally, an effort was implemented to use existing technologies and protocols for frame relay's foundation, rather than "starting from scratch." Frame relay is based on the Link Access Protocol for D-channel (LAPD) variant of the

High-level Data Link control frame format. High-level Data Link Control (HDLC) is a commonly implemented ISO standard bit-oriented, link-layer protocol that defines an encapsulation method of data on synchronous serial data links. This basis facilitated the implementation of frame relay with the existing technology of the time due to the well-documented and refined nature of these two protocols.

Frame Relay Standardization

The standardization process for frame relay began in 1984 with submissions to the U.S. Standards Committees. Success in early deployments in the late 1980s coupled with favorable views from the press fueled the momentum for the further development and deployment of frame relay. In 1988, the initial version of the frame relay protocol was approved by the ANSI committee and documented in ANSI T1.606 and ANSI T1.602. The final revision to these documents was completed in 1990 and documented in ANSI T1.617 and ANSI T1.618.

Note

The American National Standards Institute is the official U.S. agency responsible for American telecommunications standards.

A lack of consensus on the deployment and management strategies for frame relay networks limited its initial momentum. Various vendors were proceeding with implementations that could not guarantee interoperability or adequate functionality to meet the needs of current network environments.

In September 1990, a consortium of four vendors developed a management protocol known as the Local Management Interface, or LMI, to address the management of frame relay permanent virtual circuits. This initial consortium that consisted of representatives from Cisco Systems, Digital Equipment Corporation, StrataCom, and Northern Telecom is frequently referred to as the "gang of four."

The LMI proposal defined a new protocol and a series of messages based on Q.931, the signaling protocol used in ISDN. The focus of this protocol was to enable the configuration and maintenance of a network based on permanent virtual circuits (PVCs). This specification had several basic mandatory capabilities:

- ⚛ The capability of the network to notify the end-point user device of any active and present *Data Link Connection Identifiers* (DLCIs). DLCIs are identifiers of specific virtual connections between the end point and the carrier's network access point. These terms will be discussed in detail later in this chapter.

- ⚛ The capability of the network to notify the end-point user device of the removal or failure of any DLCIs.

- ⚛ The capability to provide real-time monitoring of the status of both physical and logical links between the carrier's network and the end-point user equipment.

This specification was proposed to ANSI to be adopted as a standard. This specification was revised and adopted as the Annex D to ANSI document T1.617. The other significant outcome of this standardization effort was the formation of the Frame Relay Forum, a multi-vendor organization dedicated to the development and enhancement of frame relay standards and technologies.

Frame Relay Fundamentals

Frame relay provides connection-oriented WAN connectivity between two end points. This means that data between these two end points travels over a fixed path. This is advantageous because the transmission is based on a connection-oriented protocol—frames are transmitted in sequential order to prevent possible duplicate or lost frames through the network.

At the heart of the frame relay protocol is the concept of a virtual circuit. This means that there may be multiple connections being transported across a single physical circuit as depicted in figure 8.1.

Figure 8.1
Virtual circuits and physical circuits.

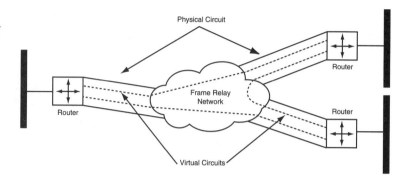

As we will discuss in detail later, these paths can be established in one of two ways:

- ✤ Permanent via permanent virtual circuits (PVCs)

- ✤ "Per Call" via switched virtual circuits (SVCs)

The underlying technology for establishing and monitoring SVCs is defined by the CCITT document Q.931, the same protocol used on today's ISDN networks; however, today's frame relay equipment typically only uses PVCs.

Note

As an interface between user and network equipment, frame relay provides a means for statistically multiplexing many logical data conversation or virtual circuits over a single physical transmission link as shown in figure 8.1. Statistical Time Division Multiplexing, or simply statistical multiplexing, is a bandwidth allocation scheme that forms the basis of packet, frame, and cell switching. It takes advantage of the bursty statistical nature of most data traffic.

As with Time Division Multiplexing (TDM), bandwidth is shared among multiple stations by dividing it into time slots to be allocated to individual stations. Unlike TDM, the allocation is not static in time—individual stations do not "own" time slots. When a station has data to send and the channel is idle, the station gets all the bandwidth. If the channel is not idle, the station must queue the data until the channel bandwidth is idle. As compared with time division multiplexing, statistical multiplexing results in reduced data emission time but adds potential queuing delay.

If the traffic is bursty and sound engineering design principles are used, the overall average transmission time should be less with statistical multiplexing than can be obtained with time division multiplexing.

Each virtual circuit or PVC has an identifying number called a Data Link Connection Identifier (DLCI) that only has local significance, meaning that it identifies the virtual circuit from the customer's DTE equipment to the point of access into the carrier's network. Therefore, the DLCI may be and often is a different value for the local and remote ends of the PVC as shown in figure 8.2.

Figure 8.2

Local significance of DLCIs.

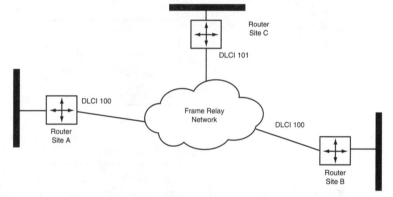

Routing tables in the frame relay switch use this local DLCI value to determine the destination path. Incoming DLCI values are read to determine the destination, and new DLCI values are recorded in the DLCI frame by all of the intervening frame relay switches along the PVC's path.

To properly understand the internal workings of frame relay and its implementation, it may be helpful to first examine the structure and components of the frame relay frame.

Frame Relay Frame Format

Like other synchronous protocols, frame relay's link access protocol uses "frames" to carry data across the access link. Frames are the basic data units between end-stations and the network. Frame relay uses a synchronous data transfer protocol at the link layer of the OSI model to carry data on the access link. The frame relay link access protocol is a subset of the ANSI T1.602 standard

(LAPD). These frames have a common structure containing a header, a data field, and a frame check sequence. Flags define the start and end of a frame.

As was mentioned earlier, one of the design goals of the frame relay protocols was simplification, particularly in light of the high level of complexity of other packet switching protocols such as X.25. As seen in figure 8.3, the frame relay frame is relatively simple and concise, comprised of only a handful of fields.

The frame relay "frame" consists of the following fields discussed in detail below: starting flag, control field, user data field, frame check sequence, and closing flag.

Figure 8.3

Frame format of frame relay.

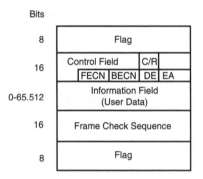

* The starting and closing flags are one byte fields containing the value of 01111110 used to designate the beginning or end of the frame relay frame. Frame relay uses the same value to designate the beginning and end of the frame. When the value 01111110 is detected by the endpoint device, it marks that the beginning of the frame and when it detects that value again it designates the end of the frame. Such a mechanism is necessary to identify the beginning and end of frame relay frames since they can vary in length.

* The control field is a 16-bit (2-octet) field that can be optionally extended to 3 or 4 octets. The control field contains the 10-bit Data Link Connection Identifier (DLCI) that defines the address. The control field also contains various control bits that define how the frame should be processed. These 10 bits permit over 1,000 virtual circuit addresses on every interface. In the unlikely event that 1,000 virtual circuits on an interface are not enough, extended addressing options allow for more circuits—about 268 million with two additional address octets. Special

management frames that have a unique DLCI address (typically 1023), may be passed between the network and the access device. These frames monitor the link status, indicating whether the link is active or inactive.

The control field also includes five additional subfields that provide the congestion management functions that are critical in the reliable transmission of data across a frame relay network.

- Command/Response (C/R) Indicator bit is a one-bit control bit that is not used and is ignored.

- Forward Explicit Congestion Notification (FECN) bit is a one-bit control bit that notifies the receiving user device that a node is experiencing congestion. If the value is set to 0, then no congestion is occurring within the network. When the FECN is set to 1, the user device is alerted that any new frames sent to the frame relay network on that PVC may encounter congestion.

- Backward Explicit Congestion Notification (BECN) bit is a one-bit control bit that notifies the sending user device that a node is experiencing congestion. If the value is set to 0, then no congestion is occurring within the network. When the BECN is set to 1, the user device is alerted that any new frames sent to the frame relay network on that PVC may encounter congestion.

- The Discard Eligibility (DE) bit is set by the end-point user device or DTE to tell the frame relay network that a frame has less priority than other frames and should be discarded before higher priority frames in the event of network congestion. This will be discussed in detail later in the section on congestion in frame relay networks.

- Extended Addressing (EA) bit is a one-bit control bit that allows addressing of two or more bytes. A value of 0 indicates that there is another byte in the address field. A value of 1 indicates that this is the final address byte.

- The information field is a variable length field containing the data being transmitted. Frame relay is capable of supporting multiple higher-level protocols by encapsulating the higher-level protocol inside the data field of the frame relay *frame*. Any type of information can be carried in this part of the frame. This allows the frame relay network to be transparent to these upper layer protocols, causing the network to look like a "private line" between two points. The information field (I-field) of the LAPD frame is of variable length. Although the theoretical maximum is 4,096 bytes (corresponding to the maximum integrity of the FCS), the actual maximums are vendor-specific.

❋ Located at the end of the frame just before the ending flag, the Frame Check Sequence (FCS) is a 16-bit field that checks the data in a frame to determine if it has been corrupted during transmission (most likely by line noise). Any frame received with an FCS indicating that an error is present is discarded by the network. The FCS covers all of the bits in a frame, from the first bit of the header to the last bit of the data field.

Circuit and Connection Characteristics

Now with an understanding of the fundamentals of frame relay and the structure of the frame, we will examine several key characteristics of the circuits and connections found in frame relay networks.

CIR

The committed information rate (CIR) defines the steady-state attainable data transmission rate between two specific frame relay end points that are connected by a PVC. This is an ensured minimum rate through the entire frame relay network via the specified PVC under normal operating conditions. For example, if a PVC has a committed information rate of 16 Kbps, then that PVC will be able to sustain a minimum data rate of 16 Kbps under normal conditions.

CIR values are determined when the PVC is provisioned or specified by the frame relay provider. The required sustained data rate is based on the actual throughput requirements of the data being transmitted. Typically this value is set at a rate appropriate to the sustained data throughput over a period of time. Data originating from multi-protocol LAN environments tends to be highly irregular, at times having little or no throughput requirements and then bursting to much higher levels as illustrated in figure 8.4.

Figure 8.4

*Data commun-
ications throughput
in a frame relay
network.*

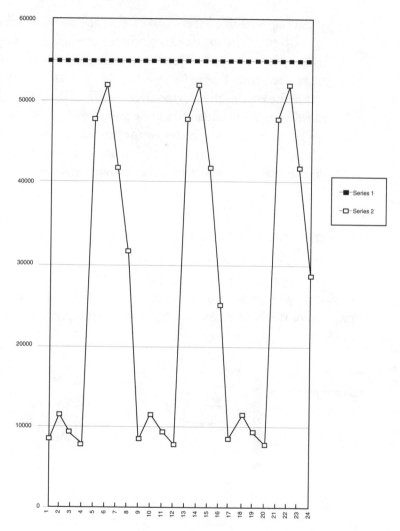

Ideally, the CIR for such a connection would be set to a value roughly equal to 16 Kbps. However, this brings up two questions:

✳ What about the throughput requirements during high bursts of traffic? This highlights one of the significant advantages to frame relay—the capability to allow traffic flows to burst to a level above the CIR up to a value specified by the frame relay provider (typically the port speed of the frame relay switch). This will be discussed in more detail in the next section on burst rates.

❀ What happens if it is determined that the provisioned CIR value is insufficient? CIR values can be changed when necessary by notifying the frame relay access provider. As we will discuss later in the section, "Cost Associated with Frame Relay," raising the CIR value will usually increase the cost of the service. The initial CIR value for a specific PVC should be determined after close analysis of the actual throughput requirements of the devices connecting to the frame relay network. This is a task that most frame relay providers can assist with and lend guidance to ensure the correct initial provisioning.

Port Rates and Bursting

One of the unique features of frame relay is the capability to burst above the CIR to the port speed for an extended period of time if the capacity in the frame relay service network is available. At the ingress point of a frame relay network, each physical port will be assigned a fixed maximum port rate as illustrated in figure 8.5.

Figure 8.5

Frame relay port access.

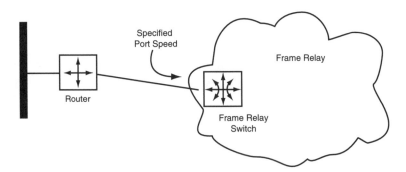

The majority of data communications traffic consists of high bursts of traffic followed by periods of lower or nonexistent data transmission as illustrated previously in figure 8.4. This has been one of the initial factors that caused many organizations to favor frame relay over traditional leased-line circuits. For example, if a connection between two sites is established via a 56Kbps leased-line connection, the actual line utilization and capacity might resemble the illustration in figure 8.4.

As you can see, the majority of the time there is a considerable disparity between the bandwidth that is being provisioned to and paid for by the consumer and the bandwidth that the network is actually using. This could be viewed as wasted bandwidth, wasted investment, or both because the consumer is paying for a full 56Kbps of bandwidth whether it is used or not.

On the contrary, frame relay makes more efficient use of the investment by allowing data rates to burst up the port speed of the frame relay connection. This value, specified by the frame relay provider, indicates the maximum data throughput for all of the PVCs being multiplexed across the physical circuit. So, while a given PVC might have a CIR of 32Kbps, it might be allowed to burst to 56Kbps during instances of high data transmission as depicted in figure 10.5. This makes more efficient use of bandwidth and significantly better use of the investment in the circuit. The costs associated with this PVC (the components of which will be discussed later in this chapter) more closely reflect the sustained throughput requirements and reduce the level of wasted bandwidth and financial investment.

Congestion Avoidance and Handling Mechanisms

Network resources such as access circuits and inter-nodal trunks are shared statistically or multiplexed in frame relay. It may be beneficial to refer to the note explaining statistical multiplexing earlier in this chapter. It is through resource sharing that frame relay provides users with high performance at lower cost when compared with traditional technologies such as X.25 and TDM. Since the sharing is statistical, sometimes the network can be congested when the traffic load to a resource exceeds its capacity. The network requires a method to protect itself in peak traffic overload situations and still maintain an acceptable level of performance.

This functionality is defined as *congestion control*. Congestion can occur as a result of increases in the overall traffic to the network or because of failures of network elements such as nodes and circuits. Congestion control is more critical in frame relay because there is no mandatory link layer flow control between an end-station and the network—one of the simplified aspects of frame relay. In a congestion situation, the frame relay network may be forced to discard frames.

Tip

The best way to handle congestion is to avoid it: by the use of reliable network elements, sound engineering design of the network, and cooperation between the network and end-stations.

Fortunately, the ANSI T1S1 Frame Relay Standard defines implicit and explicit mechanisms to alleviate network congestion when it is required. In implicit congestion control, the end-stations, upon recognizing degraded network performance, reduce their load to the network. In explicit congestion control, the network will transmit explicit signals that indicate network congestion to the end-stations. Here, we will examine two common explicit methods of indicating congestion to the DTE equipment attached to a frame relay network.

Forward Explicit Congestion Notification

Forward Explicit Congestion Notification (FECN) is a method of congestion control in which the FECN bit is set in a frame that is traveling to the destination end point.

FECN's purpose is to alert the destination end point that the network is experiencing congestion at some location on the PVC. FECN is often not used in frame relay networks for two reasons. First, the destination device that receives the congestion notification via the FECN bit is not the source of the traffic and therefore not the source of the congestion. Second, the frame relay protocol does not specify what the destination end point should do upon seeing the FECN bit set. For these reasons, the use of Backward Explicit Congestion Notification is often far more useful and more commonly implemented.

Backward Explicit Congestion Notification

Backward Explicit Congestion Notification (BECN) is a method of congestion notification in which the BECN bit is set on a return frame to indicate to the transmission source that congestion exists on the network in the opposite direction at some point in the PVC.

The purpose of this is to indicate to the source device that some point of the network is experiencing congestion and that it should modify its transmission rate to the network.

Discard Eligibility

In many networks, there may be some traffic considered to be noncritical and discardable in the event of frame relay network congestion. The purpose of this distinction is to allow critical traffic to reach its destination even if the network is overloaded. Traffic that is not critical can be identified by setting the Discard Eligibility (DE) bit in the frame relay header. Any data that is discarded relies on higher layer protocols, such as the Transmission Control Protocol (TCP) to retransmit any discarded frames. The DE bit is typically handled by the access device, commonly a router. The decision of marking or not marking traffic as discardable is the responsibility of the network administrator. For example, consider the network depicted in figure 8.6.

Figure 8.6

Discard eligibility in a frame relay network.

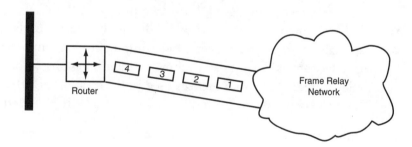

If data exists that needs to be transmitted from network A to network B, it might be broken down into two categories; data based on protocols with reliable retransmission capabilities, and data based on protocols with little or no retransmission capabilities. For example, if an FTP-based file transfer is taking place, it might seem appropriate to discard these packets during periods of network congestion. A TCP-based protocol, FTP provides for sequencing and retransmission of any lost packets. So, if the receiving device receives packets #1, #2, and #4, it would be able to request that packet #4 be retransmitted. Upon receiving all of the packets, the receiving station would then assemble them into the original datagram and deliver it to the higher-level protocols and applications. Given this example, it might be appropriate to allow the router A to mark FTP packets as being discardable. However, if router A is also transferring packets based on protocols with poor or nonexistent sequencing and retransmission capabilities, discarding packets could cause severe complications, consequently marking data as discardable without the option of retransmission.

Frame Relay Network Components

Frame relay networks are made up of frame relay access equipment, frame relay switching equipment, and public frame relay services.

Frame relay access equipment is the customer premises equipment (CPE) that uses frame relay to send information across the WAN. Access equipment may consist of bridges, routers, hosts, packet switches, or any other similar devices. In general, the same frame relay access equipment may be used either with private network frame relay switching equipment or with frame relay services.

Frame relay switching equipment consists of devices responsible for transporting the frame relay compliant information offered by the access equipment. Switching equipment may consist of T1/E1 multiplexers, packet switches, or any specialized frame relay switching equipment that implements the standard interface and is capable of switching and routing information received in frame-relay format. This equipment is used in the creation of either private or public frame relay networks (both of which possess identical underlying technology).

Public service providers (carriers) offer frame relay services by deploying frame relay switching equipment. Both frame relay access equipment and private frame relay switching equipment may be connected to services provided by a carrier. The service provider maintains access to the network via the standard frame relay interface and charges for the use of the service.

Frame Relay Access

Access to the frame relay service involves three elements: customer premises equipment (CPE), a transmission facility, and the network itself. The CPE may be any of the types of access equipment, such as frame relay compliant routers, or even private network switches with frame relay compliant interfaces.

The transmission or access facility must be appropriate for the speed involved— generally a 56/64 Kbps or T1/E1 link. When fractional T1/E1 service is desired, a full T1/E1 is still generally used for access. However, depending on the carrier offering, the unused portion of the T1/E1 may, in some cases, be used for transporting other traffic, such as voice. A standard CSU/DSU is used in conjunction with the 56/64Kbps or T1/E1 service.

At the network interface level, the carrier will be responsible for terminating the circuit appropriately. The carrier is also responsible for transporting the information to the appropriate transmission facility at the other end of the virtual circuit.

The transmission facilities at the two ends of the circuit may be of different speeds. This allows the users to mix and match so the speed matches the actual aggregate traffic needs at each site.

Carriers generally offer several options for buying the services. One option is to buy a given amount of service as if the service were a dedicated facility. This has the advantage of fixed pricing (no surprises) and straightforward comparison with dedicated bandwidth alternatives. Buying service by the frame or megabyte transmitted is also an option. This has the advantage of paying only for actual information transmitted; however, it is more difficult to predict the exact usage and subsequent cost.

Unlike most dedicated facilities, the services are often priced on a simplex basis within the network. This can be a major advantage when the application has a large amount of information in one direction and a small amount in the other.

Costs Associated with Frame Relay

One of the primary attractions of frame relay is that in many situations it may be less expensive than WAN connectivity solutions such as 56Kbps or T1 circuits. In part, this is due to equipment requirements often being considerably less demanding than requirements of leased-line networks.

Consider a network comprised of a central corporate facility and three remote satellite offices. In a 56Kbps leased-line environment (such as the one depicted in figure 8.7), if the corporate facility needs to maintain WAN communications with all three of the satellite offices, each connection to the respective satellite office would require an individual, physical connection.

Figure 8.7

Leased-line 56Kbps connectivity.

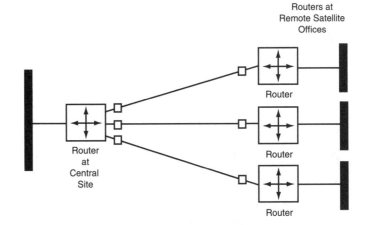

However, if frame relay is used for WAN connectivity, only one physical connection at the central corporate facility would be required. Connectivity to each of the remote satellite offices would be provided by establishing a PVC to each of those respective locations as illustrated in figure 8.8.

Figure 8.8

Frame relay connectivity.

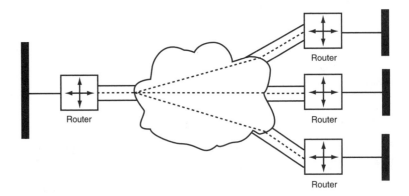

Furthermore, if direct connections were required between any of the remote satellite offices, PVCs between the appropriate sites could be provided without the need for additional physical ports or hardware. As you can see, frame relay can often present significant cost savings in network equipment hardware costs alone.

Often, the most significant savings presented by frame relay are in connectivity costs. These costs include a number of variables not offered in leased-line pricing such as 56Kbps circuits. For example, a 56Kbps circuit between a central corporate office and a remote satellite office might cost $250 per month. The cost for the same connectivity using frame relay could include several factors, two components of which are known as local port and CIR provisioning. Let's look at these factors in detail.

Local Port Cost Factor

The local port cost includes the cost for the local connection from the customer premises to the point of access into the frame relay provider's network. At this point of access, the customer's circuits terminate into a physical port on a frame relay switch as shown earlier in figure 8.5.

This port will be configured with a specific maximum data rate such as 56 Kbps, 384 Kbps, or perhaps even 512 Kbps. Obviously, a higher port rate is provided at a higher cost. The significance of this port rate is that it represents the highest burst capacity of the frame relay connection. For example, if your frame relay circuits are terminated into a port with a port rate of 384 Kbps, your maximum burst rate is 384 Kbps. This represents the maximum burst rate for all of the PVCs that are being transmitted across that single physical circuit.

CIR Provisioning Cost Factor

The other factor that determines frame relay pricing is CIR provisioning. As discussed earlier, CIR is the maximum guaranteed data rate for a given PVC throughout the frame relay network. For example, the connection between site A and site B in figure 8.2 might be granted a CIR of 16 Kbps. This means that the frame relay provider guarantees at least 16 Kbps average bandwidth between site A and site B to the customer. Provisioning a higher CIR results in a higher cost. The CIR requirements can be established by analyzing traffic flows and data throughput requirements to determine that the minimum level of throughput is sufficient. Remember, CIR is the guaranteed minimum—traffic will generally be able to exceed that level of commitment up to the burst capability of the connection.

One of the commonly used, and at times controversial, options with frame relay is the concept of 0 K CIR or a CIR of 0Kbps. This means that the provider is not providing any bandwidth guarantees through the network. At first, this may sound like a foolish notion, but it does at least merit some consideration. Proceed with an open mind. Many of the frame relay provider networks have been designed to sustain throughput requirements that exceed current requirements. Therefore, there may be little if any likelihood of inadequate bandwidth through the carrier's network.

Note

One might consider the analogy of a carpool express lane on a city expressway. Using the carpool express lane costs $1. If the expressway has eight lanes and very few cars traveling, traffic may flow at the same rate in the normal lanes as in the carpool express lanes. Therefore, there is no received benefit for paying the $1 and using the carpool lane. However, if traffic becomes congested, paying the $1 to use the express lane, which continues to flow at 55 miles per hour, may in fact be a good decision.

The same could be said for 0 K CIR. If the provider's network is lightly utilized, there may be little if any detectable difference between provisioning for 0 K CIR and 32 K CIR for example.

Other Cost Factors

There will often be other factors present in pricing factors for frame relay circuits. These often depend on the unique capabilities of the provider and often vary between frame relay providers.

Provisioning and pricing frame relay options requires an understanding of the actual throughput requirements of the WAN. Frame relay is similar to any other sort of network connectivity—if the bandwidth requirements of the applications and devices involved exceed the capacity of the network, performance and integrity issues can arise. A clear understanding of the requirements can help ensure that the appropriate network is deployed.

Summary

A major reason for the high level of interest regarding frame relay is that it is a technology that has been developed in response to a clear market need. With the proliferation of powerful end-point devices (such as PCs and workstations) operating with intelligent protocols (such as TCP/IP, XNS, and DECnet), users are seeking WAN communication methods that offer higher throughput and more cost-effective use of digital transmission lines. With that need in mind, frame relay has been rapidly developed and standardized to have the exact combination of characteristics needed by today's corporate networks.

Frame relay offers three primary benefits to the network:

❈ Reduced Internetworking Costs.

When using a private frame relay network, statistically multiplexed traffic from multiple sources over private backbone networks can reduce the number of circuits and corresponding cost of bandwidth in the wide area. Public frame relay services almost universally save money when compared to the equivalent service provided by dedicated leased lines. Since frame relay provides multiple logical connections within a single physical connection, access costs are also reduced. Equipment costs may be lowered by reducing the number of port connections required to access the network. For remote access devices, access line charges can be lowered by reducing the number of physical circuits needed to reach the networks.

❈ Increased Performance with Reduced Network Complexity.

By reducing the amount of processing (as compared to X.25) and by efficiently utilizing high-speed digital transmission lines, frame relay can improve performance and response time of applications. Frame relay reduces the complexity of the physical network without disrupting higher-level network functions. In fact, as discussed earlier, it actually utilizes the existence of these higher layer protocols to its advantage. It provides a common network transport for multiple traffic types while maintaining transparency to higher layer protocols unique to the individual traffic types. The frames contain addressing information that enables the network to route them to the proper destination.

❋ Increased Interoperability via International Standards.

Frame relay's simplified link layer protocol can be implemented over existing technology. Access devices often require only software changes or simple hardware modifications to support the interface standard. Existing packet switching equipment and T1/E1 multiplexers often can be upgraded to support frame relay over existing backbone networks. Frame relay is an accepted interface standard that vendors and service providers are adhering to and implementing. Most areas of the frame relay standards are well-defined and have been approved by ANSI and the ITU/TSS (formerly known as CCITT). There is exceptionally good agreement between the various standards. Furthermore, most equipment vendors and service providers have pledged their support for frame relay development and standards. The simplicity of the frame relay protocol accommodates quick and easy interoperability testing procedures between devices from different vendors. This interoperability testing is currently in progress among vendors as well as certification processes for carriers providing frame relay services.

Frame relay is a simplified form of packet-mode switching, optimized for transporting today's protocol-oriented data. The result of this simplification is that frame relay offers higher throughput, and still retains the bandwidth and equipment efficiencies that come from having multiple virtual circuits share a single port and transmission facility.

While new technologies such as ADSL and ATM are arriving and attracting attention in today's market, it is very likely that frame relay will continue to flourish and serve the WAN communication needs of many organizations in the future.

Checklist

This chapter should familiarize the reader with the following concepts:

☑ The origins and historical development of the frame relay protocol;

☑ The internal detail of frame relay and the capabilities that it offers to the networks of today;

☑ Some of the factors that can help a network administrator or manager determine if frame relay is the correct technology for their respective environment;

☑ A subset of the factors that determine the costs associated with frame relay and some tools to determine how to properly implement a frame relay network.

Frame relay has clearly had a significant impact on the wide area networking environments we find today. Its impact will surely continue to be felt in the years to come.

Emerging Technologies: ADSL & B-ISDN/ATM

With all of the available technologies for Internet connectivity, there still exists a potential need for even higher levels of bandwidth. As mentioned in Chapter 6, "Integrated Services Digital Network (ISDN) Connection," one such possible technology is Broadband ISDN or B-ISDN. Generally conceived for the backbone or very high bandwidth links, B-ISDN is commonly implemented on fiber-optic connections along with a switching protocol called Asynchronous Transfer Mode (ATM). There also exists an implementation of B-ISDN and ATM for desktop LANs over twisted-pair cabling. A second possible solution is that of Asymmetric Digital Subscriber Line (ADSL). ADSL is a technology still very much in its infancy aimed primarily at providing high bandwidth services within a reasonable geographical proximity. While still relatively new, these technologies may potentially revolutionize data and multimedia communications over the course of the next decade.

Unlike the previous chapters of this book, this chapter will not look at the costs and setup requirements of these two emerging technologies. The change in format is a result of the overall limited implementation of these two solutions. In reality, talking of costs and setup does not make sense when the technology is not globally available for Internet connectivity. Instead, this chapter will attempt to provide you with a general overview of the potential of the two higher bandwidth possibilities.

This overview will include two sections: technical background, and the availability and limitations of each technology. The technical background section will begin with ADSL, including what ADSL offers clients and how it works. From there, this chapter will address how B-ISDN and ATM work, starting with an examination of the architecture of B-ISDN. From this discussion, we will turn to ATM and the workings and benefits of this switching technology. Finally, the technology section will look at B-ISDN and ATM implementation in the form of SONET.

The "Availability and Limitations" section will look at the issues regarding ADSL availability and the slow implementation of such technology. After discussing the availability problem, this section will look ADSL's potential limitations for the provision of Internet connectivity caused by the limited length of local loop. This section will then turn to B-ISDN and its impact on the future of ISDN. Next, this section will look at a major concern with ATM: high overhead. In spite of ATM's higher overhead than other potential solutions, ATM still provides a robust switching technology for high-speed connectivity or for applications (such as video or sound) that are sensitive to latency. Finally, this section will look at a current implementation of ATM and B-ISDN, that of desktop ATM over twisted-pair cabling.

Again, you should regard this chapter as a look into the future of Internet connectivity. Neither of these solutions provide a viable solution (in our opinion) for current Internet connectivity. As such, they can only be viewed in terms of potential for future connectivity.

Technical Background

In order to properly examine the two technologies in terms of their future benefits to Internet connectivity, it is useful to discuss the technical foundation of each of these possible solutions. This chapter will first address the potential of ADSL and briefly touch on its working technology. This section continues with B-ISDN and ATM, discussing the B-ISDN architecture, the basis of ATM switching, and how this method works. Finally, this section will briefly look at SONET—a current implementation of these technologies.

Asymmetric Digital Subscriber Line

It is not surprising that a technology that can potentially provide greater bandwidth using the existing copper line infrastructure is sought after when you think about the demands the WWW has created. The following discussion will examine what ADSL offers and why the technology is touted as a possible solution for future bandwidth needs.

What ADSL Offers

Asymmetric Digital Subscriber Line (ADSL) is a new codec technology that takes advantage of the thousands, if not millions, of existing twisted-pair telephone lines. Its primary benefit is the potential for much higher throughput capabilities than are globally available over this infrastructure. Some of the other benefits of ADSL are as follows:

- ADSL provides multiple communications paths:

- ADSL transmits at rates greater than 6Mbps to a destination end-point device. This is a unidirectional transmission.

- ADSL provides for up to a 640Kbps bidirectional transmission over the same pair of twisted-pair cabling.

- ADSL provides support for existing telephone communications.

Due to bandwidth limitations and currently implemented hardware (modems), this infrastructure has been predominantly limited to applications such as voice, text, and low-resolution graphics. ADSL promises to exploit this existing physical infrastructure to provide a platform suitable for applications such as multimedia, high-resolution full-motion video, online movies, corporate LAN access, and Internet access to everyone's home.

ADSL will surely play a major role in the networking industry over the next decade. While new cabling infrastructures are being deployed throughout the world to support these high bandwidth applications, it will take years to reach all of the end users of these technologies.

A Note from the Author

I have some concern over the potential of ADSL to meet the bandwidth needs of the future. Because the bidirectional transmission is limited to 640Kbps, I wonder whether the technology will be sufficient to meet the needs of individuals who are using the Internet as a distribution mechanism for sound and video applications. As more areas are wired with fiber or fiber-coax, this technology will become less useful and cost-effective. As a result, I am somewhat doubtful that this solution will be implemented on a wide scale.

How ADSL Works

An ADSL connection comprises a pair of ADSL modems at each end of a twisted-pair telephone line. The ADSL modem provides three different communication channels:

* A high-speed communications channel, capable of transmission speeds as high as 6.1Mbps. This channel is unidirectional, meaning that the transmission is to the end-point device only. This channel will likely be used for applications such as multimedia communications, on-demand video services, or perhaps accessing remote CD-ROM archives. For example, a video stream such as a movie could be transmitted on this channel for viewing on a computer monitor.

* A medium-speed duplex channel providing bidirectional communications, typically at a rate between 16Kbps and 64Kbps.

* A low-speed POTS (Plain Old Telephone Service) channel to provide traditional telephone communications.

The actual transmission speeds supported by the high- and medium-speed channels depend largely on the type of wire being used and the distance between the ADSL modems. Table 10.1 lists current guidelines for the high transmission speeds of various cabling types, based on the distances between ADSL modems.

Table 10.1

Data Rate	Distance
1.544Mbps	up to 18,000 ft.
2.048Mbps	up to 16,000 ft.
6.312Mbps	up to 12,000 ft.
8.448Mbps	up to 9,000 ft.

ADSL High-Speed Channel Capabilities

Generally speaking, the distances handled by ADSL technologies will provide support for at least 90 percent of the target market sites because they are predominately within these distance ranges from a phone carrier's premises. For environments that exceed these distance capabilities, fiber-optic cabling can be used to achieve connectivity.

Broadband ISDN and ATM

Broadband ISDN is the extension of the ISDN standard to include even higher levels of bandwidth. The following three sections discuss the architecture of B-ISDN, the technology of ATM switching, and SONET—a current implementation of B-ISDN and ATM.

Broadband ISDN Architecture

The original ISDN structure put in place by ITU-T was based on the data rates supported by twisted-pair wiring existing in most areas. With a maximum data rate of 2Mbps for ISDN, the protocol was appropriate for the transmission medium. As the telephone and service providers began installing fiber-optic networks to replace copper wiring, it soon became obvious that the current ISDN standard would not provide support for high enough data rates.

B-ISDN was first developed in draft form in 1990 by the ITU-T in an effort to prevent the proprietary high bandwidth transmission methods from being employed. These higher bandwidth transmission rates are based on the need to support high-resolution video. As a result, three types of transmission service are supported by B-ISDN:

* full duplex 155.52Mbps service

* asymmetrical service, providing upstream data of 155.52 Mbps and downstream bandwidth of 622.08 Mbps

* the highest capacity service is a full-duplex 622.08 Mbps service

As well as supporting the new transmission services, B-ISDN is also backwards compatible with the 64Kbps services of the original ISDN (now referred to as narrowband ISDN). In addition, B-ISDN must also support the circuit and packet switching of narrowband ISDN. As a result, the newer implementations of B-ISDN will not cause the investment in equipment to be lost. The higher-speed transmissions are expected (recommended by the ITU-T) to be supported by asynchronous transfer mode (ATM).

ATM Transmission and Switching

Because of the high-speed connectivity that is possible under B-ISDN service (especially via the fiber-optic networks being put into place), a high-speed switching method is required—ATM. ATM is a cell relay-based switching protocol. The next section will discuss some basics of ATM functionality before detailing some of the benefits of using ATM with B-ISDN services. Finally, this section will look at SONET—an implementation of B-ISDN and ATM.

How ATM Works

ATM is a switching protocol that developed out of the need for a high-speed switching technology. Like frame relay, ATM assumes that the physical medium being transmitted over is of a high enough quality that the error correction built into other transmission protocols (such as X.25) is not required. In addition, the ATM protocol uses fixed sized cells for data transmission in contrast to frame relay, which enables a variable frame size. The ATM cells are 53 bytes long, with 5 bytes used as overhead for the protocol.

ATM is able to provide switching capabilities for high-speed links based on what sets it apart from frame relay and X.25:

⊛ all signal and control is done via a separate control channel, thus eliminating this information from the data packets

⊛ the fixed length cells can be generated, switched, and received faster

As a result of these distinctions, ATM is a much faster switching protocol than either frame relay or its predecessor, X.25. The simple nature of ATM in the hardware-implemented switching can take advantage of the overall higher levels of bandwidth available from B-ISDN or optical transmission (see SONET later in this chapter).

The Benefits of ATM

One of the main benefits of ATM is its support for virtual circuits as opposed to dedicated physical circuits. As a result, unlike traditional dedicated links (such as T1 connections), B-ISDN and ATM are able to provide bandwidth on demand. For example, suppose your site normally needs a T3 size connection to support all WWW transfers. At peak times, the bandwidth demand jumps to two T3s. Obviously, due to the fluctuating need for additional bandwidth, it is generally not cost effective to provide additional bandwidth permanently. As a result of bandwidth demands, the connections of all users will slow down as congestion builds.

Under ATM, the bandwidth needs of a system can be dynamically met. In the previous example, the additional bandwidth required causes congestion and subsequent connectivity performance reduction. ATM's virtual circuits enable the allocation of additional bandwidth to a link as required, consequently reducing or eliminating congestion and performance lags.

A Note from the Author

Just thinking about the potential benefits of ATM's virtual circuits to everyday users raises an interesting benefit. Under an ATM switched system, oversubscription policies of ISPs could possibly be eliminated (or at least the potential harmful effects could be). Because additional bandwidth will be added as required, the virtual circuits will prevent the ISP from overselling their bandwidth for a larger profit. We look forward to that day!

The second major benefit of the ATM system is the capability of ATM to scale upward to the higher data rate speeds of B-ISDN and optical cabling. This scalability is a result of the simplicity of the protocol and the cells used by ATM. Scalability combined with contained control functionality over a separate channel enables ATM to relay cells quickly.

Implementation: SONET

The telephone systems have over the past few years been developing a transmission capacity utilizing a structure based on 51.84Mbps multiples. This system, the synchronous optical network (SONET), has since been extended to include up to 6.448 Gbps. The implementation of cell relay (ATM) over the SONET system is the B-ISDN service in place today.

While B-ISDN and ATM can be implemented over other media than optical cabling, the high bandwidth availability on fiber-optic cabling makes it well suited for this use. Lower levels of connectivity are not as well suited to these solutions because of the negligible need for a fast switching technology and because of the potential overhead problem with ATM.

Availability and Limitations

Obviously, because ADSL, ATM, and B-ISDN are considered *emerging* technologies, it is not surprising that they are not generally available. Beyond this fact, these technologies also have a few limitations. In the case of ADSL, the limits of the speed of the connection versus the distance of the connection could prove to be a major problem. For B-ISDN and ATM, the potential problem for Internet connectivity is the high overhead of this cell relay technology. For a more practical application of B-ISDN and ATM, refer to the last section in this chapter entitled "ATM and B-ISDN on the Desktop."

ADSL: Slow in Coming

ADSL products are currently under development and production by several organizations such as Westell of Chicago, Illinois, Amati of San Jose, California, and Aware of Bedford, Massachusetts. In 1994, an organization called the ADSL forum was organized to promote the concepts, standards, and technologies of ADSL. The ADSL forum also seeks to expedite the development of new protocols and interfaces for the ADSL environment. The ADSL forum currently comprises more than 60 members, representing service providers, equipment manufacturers, and semiconductor companies worldwide. The ADSL forum maintains a World Wide Web site at:

```
http://www.sbexpos.com/sbexpos/associations/adsl/index.html
```

Note

The American National Standards Institute (ANSI) working group T1 E1.4 recently approved ADSL standard transmission rates at speeds up to 6.1Mbps. This standard is defined in document T1.413.

Currently, ADSL modems have been tested successfully with a number of telephone companies and hundreds of ADSL lines have been installed under test conditions in both North America and Europe. For example, in the spring of 1996, two prominent service providers, GTE Telephone Operations and US West have announced extensive ADSL trials. GTE Telephone Operation's trials are being conducted in Irving, Texas and US West is conducting trials in Denver, Colorado and Minneapolis, Minnesota. Currently these installations are market trials to refine the technologies and services made possible with ADSL.

Distance Limitations to ADSL

One potential limitation of the ADSL solution is the falling bandwidth capabilities versus the length of the local loop. This problem stems from the overall technological limitations of the copper line infrastructure. As the signal travels farther over the line a greater degree of signal degradation takes place, therefore limiting the amount of bandwidth available.

Since not all connections to a telephone company are available at the highest rates, this solution may not provide the necessary higher levels of bandwidth required for future applications. As a result, your location within a service area will affect the quality of your connection. Again, as with ISDN service, if your office is outside the maximum distance, then the service will not be available at all!

B-ISDN: The Future of ISDN

While ISDN has been developed for more than 20 years, B-ISDN has only been in development as a standard for eight years, with serious development on the standard only starting in 1990. As a result of the slowness in telephone and cable companies to take the fiber infrastructure to the doorstep, B-ISDN and ATM are seeing very limited availability. Even so, more services will continue to be offered as the level of connectivity, in terms of infrastructure, increases.

While B-ISDN was conceived with fiber optics in mind, the services are not limited to fiber-optic connectivity. Unfortunately, the use of B-ISDN services and ATM over slower links does not make a whole lot of sense because of ATM's inefficiency as a result of overhead.

ATM: Limitations

There are two main potential problems with ATM: the high overhead with ATM cells and the potential conflict between ATM cell size and IP datagram size. This section explains these potential problems, examining their impact on potential ATM implementations, and concludes with a final discussion of why ATM is used regardless of these potential limitations.

The High Overhead

As you will remember from the brief technical discussion of how ATM works, ATM cells are exactly 53 bytes long, with 5 of these bytes being used by the protocol and 48 bytes being used to carry the data. This means that ATM has an overhead of slightly more than 9 percent, which can easily expand to 13 percent with the consistent need to send cells on a regular basis. In comparison to other protocols, ATM's overhead is quite large.

For example, in frame relay, the average frame length is 128 bytes, with four bytes devoted to address and control information. As a result, the average overhead of the frame relay protocol is closer to 3 percent—three to four times as efficient as the ATM method. Given the inefficiency of the ATM protocol, it is amazing that the solution is used at all. Even more amazing is the use of ATM for IP-based data transmission.

ATM and IP: Well Suited?

The second major problem with using ATM for Internet connectivity is that ATM cell size and IP datagram size are not well suited for each other. As you will recall from Chapter 3, IP datagrams are generally between 500 and 1,500 octets (or bytes). Obviously, ATM is required to break each datagram into a high number of cells to send the cells out over the network.

Now imagine that one of the 1,500 or so cells for one datagram was lost (or discarded as a result of congestion). As a result, the datagram cannot be reconstructed at the end point of the network transmission. When the receiving host discovers that the datagram is missing, it must request that the information be resent. Given the high number of cells per datagram, the chance of these problems creating even greater inefficiency is considerable.

Why ATM?: Switching and Latency

Given the potential problems of ATM overhead and IP inefficiency, one might wonder why ATM should be implemented at all. The answer comes from the need for faster switching for high-speed networks, and the benefits that ATM provides in terms of latency.

Latency is the delay it takes one cell (or packet or datagram) to travel between the two hosts (sending and receiving hosts). Because larger packets are delayed longer than smaller ones, the small size of the ATM cells decreases the effective latency for ATM cells. As a result, especially in terms of congested networks or switches, ATM cells provide a large advantage in terms of speed between two hosts.

ATM and B-ISDN on the Desktop

One possible implementation of ATM and B-ISDN is realized in an interesting development by IBM (among others) of a B-ISDN/ATM solution that can be implemented over twisted-pair copper wires for LANs. The result is a LAN that supports 52+ Mbps connections using ATM for transmission.

The benefits of this solution are twofold. First, the solution provides a LAN-based implementation that can be extended to a WAN as the technology is implemented at the local and national levels. With Ethernet transmission methods, the connection to WANs requires a further protocol and more overhead. The second benefit is actually one for the entire industry—increased market for ATM products. As more ATM products are developed for LANs, the technology for chips behind ATM switches will become cheaper and as a result, the implementation of B-ISDN at the WAN level might be accelerated.

Summary

While the current technologies for dedicated connections can provide a sufficient degree of bandwidth for WWW sites, there exists the potential that applications being developed at this time (such as video broadcasting and conferencing via the Internet) will increase the overall bandwidth requirements for any one site. In addition, the uses of bandwidth can have some severe peaks and valleys. Increasing bandwidth on a permanent basis is not always cost-effective. The two technologies presented in this chapter provide possible solutions to some, if not all of these problems.

ADSL has the potential to provide greater utilization of the existing infrastructure for higher-speed links. Unfortunately, the links operate at a slower speed than may be required in the upstream direction. In addition, the downstream bandwidth is likely to be underutilized, unless there is some method of bandwidth sharing between high downstream and low upstream users. As a result of these possible limitations, ADSL is an intermediate solution for the bandwidth dilemma. A more permanent solution may be the second technology discussed in this chapter—B-ISDN and ATM.

Broadband ISDN and ATM provide an excellent potential growth path for the issues of bandwidth and technologically superior switching and bandwidth allocation. Because of the potential to support 622.08Mbps of bandwidth, B-ISDN possesses the necessary levels of bandwidth to properly provide a future development path. Unfortunately, these levels of bandwidth are generally only available via the fiber-optic networks that are only now being installed.

No matter what solutions are implemented in the future to provide higher levels of bandwidth, the result will be greater support for applications that depend on these resources.

Checklist

The following are concerns that should be addressed at the conclusion of the chapter.

ADSL

☑ Distance between modems?

☑ Physical wiring/cabling used?

☑ Bandwidth demands?

☑ Overhead entailed?

B-ISDN/ATM

☑ Transmission services supported?

☑ Physical wiring/cabling used?

☑ Bandwidth demands?

☑ Overhead entailed?

☑ High-speed network in place?

10

Cable and Satellite: User Connectivity?

Over the last year and a half, a great deal of media attention and industry speculation has been focused on the cable and satellite companies entering into the Internet connectivity field. Prominent cable companies in the United States and Canada have been running pilot projects to test the usage and interest into cable-based Internet access. Satellite companies have been rolling out satellite-based Internet access using the small "Direct TV"-style dishes. All of this activity begs the question: "What does all of this mean to the ISP manager in terms of connectivity options?"

In short, most of this hype means nothing in terms of Internet connectivity for a WWW site. As this chapter will detail, these two methods are too nascent, and are user- rather than provider-oriented. As a result, the services are either generally not available, do not provide the quality of service required, or are not cost-effective. While the future may provide a larger place in the Internet provider community for these technologies, currently neither are viable WWW site connectivity options.

What is "User Connectivity"?

Before detailing the reasons why the cable and satellite options are not more than novelties in terms of server connectivity, two critical concepts related to Internet connectivity and WWW activities must be explained. These two critical concepts are the client/server architecture of the WWW and bandwidth requirements that result from this architecture. This section will provide a better understanding of the client/server operation concepts and the resulting impact that this structure has on bandwidth requirements (in terms of client versus server requirements). At the end of this section, you will better understand the client/server architecture's practical impact on connectivity.

Client versus Server Roles

Most of the functionality and information of Internet WWW sites is controlled by the WWW server (or httpd). Information is stored on the server and requested by the clients. Requests are small packets of information that specify the particular file(s) required by each client. Because the clients can be from around the world, the server simply passes all information requested to the networking and routing protocols (TCP/IP). All of the requested information is passed through the server's Internet connection and then routed to the appropriate clients.

On the client side, requests for information are sent out over the Internet connection, and then the client waits to receive the requested information from the server. In the case of WWW requests, the browser generally allows the user to use a point-and-click interface to request information.

Bandwidth Rules All

The previous description of the client/server exchange of information in a WWW transaction may leave you a little confused, and asking "What does this have to do with my WWW connectivity?" The answer is that the client/server architecture of WWW operations dictates the amount of information that will be traveling in either direction of the request.

Let us take, for example, a simple request by a client for one page of information from a WWW server (see fig. 10.1). The client program on your machine makes a request to a WWW server based on your input (clicking on a hyperlink or typing in a URL). The request is sent via your Internet connectivity (downstream bandwidth is used). The server containing the desired information receives the request (*upstream* bandwidth used) and sends the information back to you (*downstream* bandwidth used). Your client program then receives the information by means of your Internet connection (*upstream* bandwidth used).

Figure 10.1

Client Request bandwidth usage.

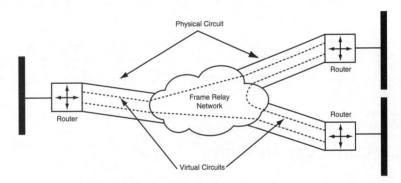

This analysis shows us the type of information flows that WWW operations create. Small request packets come into a WWW server and larger information packets travel out from a WWW server. Multiply this whole scenario by a large number of requests, and the net (pun intended) effect is that the *downstream* bandwidth requirements of a WWW server are generally much larger than the *upstream* bandwidth requirements.

Note

The previous analysis of the data flows of a WWW site, while simplistic, also details the main reason that ISPs usually host WWW sites on their Internet servers. Since the numerous dialup accounts produce a greater flow of information into the ISP than out of the ISP, the addition of WWW sites only creates a slightly larger degree of bandwidth required, if matched to the excess bandwidth available for out traveling data. As a result, the ISP can better utilize its available bandwidth through the inclusion of WWW sites on its server. Your site can gain the same benefit by using a WWW connection to support other data flows, such as office use.

Technical Background

Now that this chapter has established the data flows behind the client/server model of WWW traffic, it will detail the technology behind the two "user" connectivity methods. This section provides an overview of the technology behind the cable and satellite connectivity methods in order to prepare the groundwork for the discussion of the limitations of the cable and satellite options for WWW connectivity.

Cable Connectivity

The first of the two connectivity methods to be described is cable Internet connectivity. In order to better understand how this connectivity option has been implemented, this section will discuss the following topics:

* cable topology

* the current fiber-to-the-neighborhood approach

* the one-way communications method

* the two-way communications method

Coaxial Cable Topology

Because the Internet connectivity based on cable utilizes the existing infrastructure (with possible switch and cable upgrades), knowledge of the basic topology of the cable system is important in order to understand how the Internet access has been made available. The cable system starts at a point in each community (or portion of a community)that is referred to as the *head end*. The head end is the originating point for that community's cable signals, and collects the over-the-air and the satellite broadcasts of signals.

From the head end, the signals are carried on coaxial cable throughout the community. For TV signals, each signal is allocated 6 MHz of bandwidth on the coaxial cable through the use of frequency division multiplexing. This method allows multiple channels to be carried over one coaxial cable (one signal at 0-6 MHz, the next at 6-12 MHz, etc.), and as a result, this transmission method is referred to as the *broadband* method (as opposed to the *baseband* method, which uses the whole available bandwidth for each signal).

Note

Frequency division multiplexing is a method of dividing a large bandwidth cable into smaller logical cables. Because each coaxial cable can carry a large number of 6MHz channels, and since 6 MHz is all that is needed to carry one TV signal, frequency division multiplexing is used to allow multiple channels to be sent down each coaxial cable. In contrast, *time division multiplexing* (discussed in Chapter 6) provides the same functionality for baseband cabling systems.

As figure 10.2 illustrates, the cable is split in order to provide complete coverage over a community. Each time the cable is split, the signal is also split (and generally amplified). As a result, the entire signal is reproduced on each cable after each split. This allows for further resplitting in order to cover new areas. The resulting physical infrastructure is the tree-and-branch topology that is illustrated in figure 10.2.

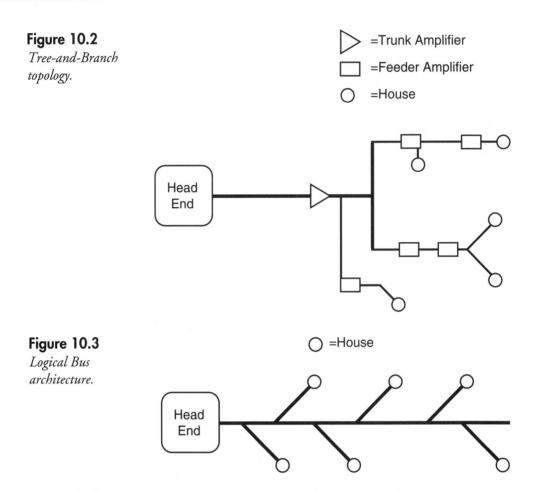

Figure 10.2
Tree-and-Branch topology.

▷ =Trunk Amplifier

☐ =Feeder Amplifier

○ =House

Head End

Figure 10.3
Logical Bus architecture.

○ =House

Head End

Even though the physical infrastructure of the cable system represents the tree-and-branch topology, the logical architecture is that of a bus architecture (see fig. 10.3). This is the result of the continuation of the entire signal to every subscriber; in other words, the signal continues to each house even when the TV is not on. In order to select the appropriate signal, the TV company uses a tuner to select the correct frequency (similar to the frequency selection on radios).

Note

A bus architecture is an architecture that has one "trunk" and with only one depth of branches. If the physical tree-and-branch architecture was stretched out, because of the repeaters the practical result is that of a bus architecture.

Note

In many ways, the cable architecture is similar to the Ethernet system that is used in many LANs today. Just as with the cable system, Ethernet LANs send all of the information to all hosts on the network at all times. In turn, the correct host (based on the Ethernet address—each Ethernet card has a unique address coded into the device) gathers all of the Ethernet packages addressed to it.

Fiber-to-the-Neighborhood Approach

Although the coaxial branch-and-tree topology is the established architecture of the cable company, over the past few years, the system has been modified because of advances in fiber-optic transmission technology. As a result of these developments, the cable companies are transforming the branch-and-tree topology to a new *hybrid fiber-and-coax* (HFC) system, where fiber is run out to the neighborhoods, and then coaxial cable is used for the connection to each door.

The transformation to the HFC system is due to the following benefits of the new fiber-optic technology:

❋ Fiber optics have a much wider range of frequencies than the coaxial method, and as a result are able to transmit a great deal more information than is possible over coax.

❋ Because of the nature of the transmission medium (light instead of electricity), the fiber-optic system is less prone to interference. As a result, the signal can be carried much farther without the need for amplification.

❀ Fiber is not taken right to the door. Because the laser transmitter and receiver need to utilize the fiber-optic cable, the technology is very expensive and prevents straight to the doorstep delivery.

As a result of the improvements that fiber optics represent in terms of the bandwidth and distance the signal can be carried, the cable companies have an incentive to convert their structures to fiber optics. Unfortunately, because of the high costs of the laser transmitters and receivers, many companies are not willing to install fiber-optic cable right to the individual subscribers. The development of the HFC system, in a configuration referred to as the Fiber-To-The-Neighborhood (FTTN) architecture was implemented to combat this unwillingness (see fig. 10.4).

Note

A number of authors, including Nicholas Negroponte, Professor of Media Technology at MIT, have argued that the Hybrid Fiber and Coax architecture is fatally flawed when it comes to Internet-based communications (see the "Availability and Limitations" section of this chapter for a more in-depth discussion of this argument). The only logical architecture—according to the communications experts (as opposed to the cable and telephone companies' financial experts) is to take fiber to the doorstep (http://www.hotwired.com/wired/3.10/departments/negroponte.html, "2020: The Fiber-Coax Legacy," *Wired* magazine, 3.10).

The FTTN architecture is based on the concept that the cable company takes fiber optics into an area of a couple hundred houses. From the end of the fiber-optic line, the signal is patched into a coaxial system that serves the couple hundred individual establishments.

As a result of this system, long lines of coax are replaced with the fiber-optic trunks, while the shorter local loops (for lack of a better term) remain coax. As a result, the number of amplifiers that are required for any single area is greatly reduced. Moreover, the overall bandwidth available to an area and the quality of the signal is improved, and even the number of amplifier failures is lessened.

Figure 10.4
FTTN architecture.

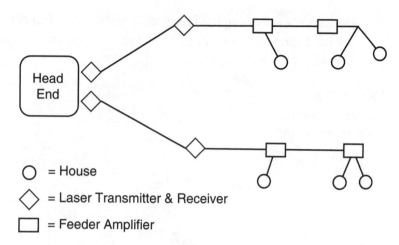

○ = House

◇ = Laser Transmitter & Receiver

☐ = Feeder Amplifier

As well as increasing the overall quality and cost effectiveness of the cable infrastructure, the FTTN architecture allows the infrastructure to be used for two-way communications. However, until the infrastructure is in a geographical area, the high noise ratio on the cable lines effectively prevents the infrastructure's use for two-way transmission. Because of this situation, many cable companies have developed an interim process that allows their infrastructure to be used for Internet connectivity: a one-way communications architecture.

One-Way Communications

The key to the one-way cable Internet solution is the concept of asymmetrical communications. Under this methodology, the cable company provides a connection that has high downstream (coming into your site) bandwidth, while low upstream bandwidth is provided by a connection to a local ISP.

As figure 10.5 illustrates, the cable company maintains a connection to the Internet (generally through a high-speed leased line), and traffic to and from the Internet is handled through a standard router. Traffic from the Internet is passed from the IP router to a hybrid router that determines to which cable head end the information should be passed. As a result, duplicate traffic is not required to be carried by all of the cable systems. After the traffic is passed from the head end along the local cable trunk, a device (called the *remote link adapter*—see the following Note) collects the information destined for that particular site. The security of the information passing along the cable infrastructure is maintained through the use of Digital Encryption Standard (DES) encryption (handled by the hardware) so that no one else on the cable system can intercept information intended for you.

Figure 10.5

Asymmetrical cable Internet connectivity.

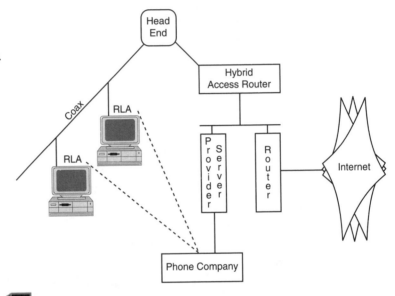

> **Note**
>
> The *remote link adapter* (RLA) is actually a form of networking device. On one interface is a coaxial interface similar to that on your TV. The device acts as an RF modem (because the signal from the cable company is an analog signal) and demodulates the signal before passing it to a networking interface (generally an Ethernet interface). As well, the RLA has another interface for the upstream connection. This interface can be anything from a modem communications jack (for SLIP or PPP) to an ISDN interface.

In this setup, upstream communications are handled over a link from your RLA and an ISP. As a result, the speed of access upstream is quite limited. The speed of the throughput of the downstream flow, moreover, is highly dependent on the upstream link. The faster the upstream link, the faster the downstream link. Some experts suggest that the downstream link more than doubles if the upstream link is upgraded from a standard 28.8 connection to an ISDN connection.

Two-Way Communications

The two-way cable communication is based on the principle of symmetrical or duplexed communication. As the cable companies upgrade their plant facilities to HFC systems, two-way capabilities can be added. In general, three main changes are required for the current cable system to be able to support two-way transmission of data:

⁂ Spectrum must be allocated for upstream data

⁂ Amplifiers must be upgraded

⁂ Some method of multiplexing of upstream data must be implemented

Spectrum Allocation

The first step in making the cable infrastructure two-way transmission-capable is to allocate the appropriate spectrum to the upstream data (see fig. 10.6). In general, the upstream data is allocated the 5 to 42 MHz frequency range. This frequency provides the bandwidth equivalent of about four channels of space (by channels, we mean TV channels—or the equivalent of approximately four T1 leased lines).

Figure 10.6

Cable transmission frequency spectrum map.

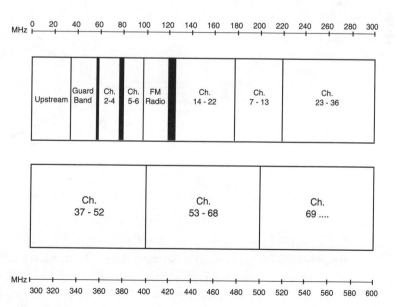

Two-Way Amplifiers

The second technological change that is required for the cable infrastructure to be converted to a symmetrical Internet connectivity is the replacement of current amplifiers with ones that are able to separate the upstream and downstream data and amplify the data appropriately. Mainly, these amplifiers must ensure that the upstream and downstream data is applied into the correct frequency range so as to avoid data loss. Because these amplifiers are expensive, cable companies are not generally replacing current amplifiers, but rather are only adding this capability to amplifiers that are being put into place when the lines are being upgraded to the fiber-coax hybrid cabling.

Upstream Multiplexing

As well as making the required hardware changes of new amplifiers, the cable company must also implement a method of multiplexing the multiple upstream data sources onto the coaxial cable. Because the method chosen affects over-all efficiency, a number of methods are being considered, depending on the type of applications that are expected over the link. The result is that the cable company may implement time division, or frequency division of carrier-sense multiplexing.

Figure 10.7

Sharing a cable infrastructure.

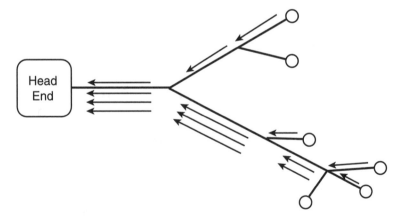

As figure 10.7 shows, multiple users' upstream data has to be multiplexed into the allocated frequencies for upstream data. The need to multiplex the data stems from the fact that each server is trying to place a different signal onto the network (as opposed to downstream traffic, which is broadcast to all nodes). The result is that the limited upstream data has to be shared by the number of nodes that are on the network. Consequently, the bandwidth available to any one node is limited by the activity of the other nodes.

Satellite Connectivity

Satellite connectivity for Internet access is similar to one-way cable Internet connectivity in that the transmission method relies on the backlink of a land connection for its upstream connectivity. Before discussing the technological background of the satellite backlink, this section first discusses the main determining fact of satellite communications: frequency.

Note

Two-way satellite communication has been ignored in this chapter because of the much higher costs that the satellite connectivity option represents in terms of short-distance hops. Because Internet connectivity for a WWW site is based on the use of the Internet for long-distance data transmissions (unlike a dedicated link between two offices via a private network that may cover long distances), this book ignores the price-to-cost benefits that the satellite link provides over long distances. Obviously, if your site is remote or removed from a source of Internet connectivity then the two-way satellite solution may become more cost effective for your organization. In general the distance must be greater than 500 miles before the satellite communication method is even comparable with the costs of similar bandwidth-leased lines (such as 56 Kbps or T1 dedicated lines).

Satellite Bandwidth: Frequency Communications

The main possible benefit of the use of satellite for Internet connectivity is the large level of bandwidth that the satellite-based solution provides (downstream only—see the next subsection). This high level of bandwidth is the result of the high frequency at which the satellite communications take place.

Any broadcast method using *radio frequency* (RF) in the United States is governed by the *Federal Communications Commission* (FCC) The equivalent in Canada is the *Canadian Radio and Television Commission* or CRTC. Under the

FCC's current designations, satellite communication takes place at the 3 to 30+ GHz frequency. As a result, an immense amount of bandwidth is available to send information through the satellites. (Remember that 4 KHz is enough bandwidth for voice communication, and 6 MHz is needed per television channel).

A Note from the Author

With the likelihood that the fiber-optics infrastructure will be put into place to the doorstep, there exists an interesting switch that might occur. According to some industry experts, the amount of bandwidth available as a result of fiber optics to the door will far and away exceed the amount of bandwidth available for use by RF broadcasting. As a result, broadcasting and connectivity issues will likely be placed on the land-based connections, while the limited RF broadcasting and wireless communications will be reserved for the use of mobile data requirements.

Unfortunately, satellite communication is very capital-intensive. Not only do you need a satellite (or at least access to one), a receiver/transmitter must be installed on your site. Because the size of the transmitter/receiver impacts the efficiency of the communications link, the use of a satellite for two-way communications requires a very large and expensive ($10,000 and up) satellite dish. Since the hardware for two-way communications is prohibitive for the use of satellites for Internet access (as much as $100,000), a new method of communication that utilizes a land link for upstream bandwidth has been developed.

Upstream Data through Land Connection

Like the one-way cable modem solution, the satellite solution provides a large downstream bandwidth (400 Kbps) and no upstream bandwidth (see fig. 10.8). The result is the system functions on a land link for its upstream requests. For example, the selection request for an FTP transfer travels by means of a land connection (SLIP, PPP, ISDN, etc.) to a network operations center for the satellite service provider. From there the request is proxied to the source of the information. As a result, the information requested is returned to the network operations center. From the network operations center, the information is uploaded by way of an uplink antenna to a satellite, which then transmits the information to the small (2 foot) dish attached to the computer of the original requester.

Figure 10.8

Satellite Internet connectivity.

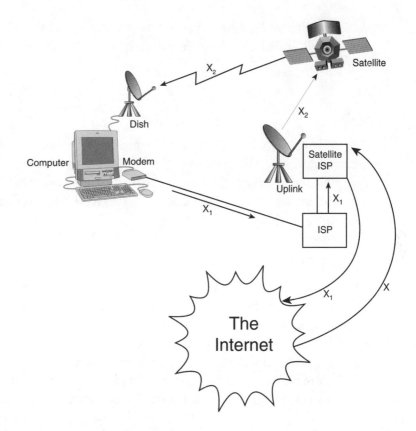

Availability and Limitations

Now that a brief technological explanation of the cable and satellite connectivity options has been presented, the two options can be examined in terms of their availability and limitations. After reading this section you should be fully aware of the availability problems and limitations of both the cable and satellite solutions.

Availability: Now and the Future

In terms of the current availability of these two options, the options are very different. For example, as will be discussed, the cable option is really only in the emerging stage in terms of one-way communications, and even more so in two-way communications. In contrast, the satellite solution is offered by a number of companies, and can be utilized at this time in most areas. This section details the overall availability of each method, including the two versions of both solutions.

Cable

The cable connectivity option is only starting to become available, and most of the availability is on the basis of trial subscriptions over a limited pilot area. There are, moreover, considerable differences between the availability of one-way and two-way cable Internet access, and these two methods also face different future availability horizons.

One-Way Communication

One-way cable connectivity is currently being rolled out by a number of cable companies across the continent. In some geographical areas this solution is still in test mode, and unless the cable companies offer this functionality to ISPs or provide Internet access themselves, the growth rate will be slow. Working against this connectivity method is the fact that it is often viewed as simply an interim step before two-way connectivity is offered. Even so, a number of products are becoming available, and the option is offered commercially in some areas. Since little or no upgrades are needed to the infrastructure in order to provide this service, the cable companies might start rolling out this service as the Internet continues to grow. The one-way cable option could be implemented in 98 percent of all homes in North America with commercial products such as Hybrid Networks' Hybrid Access System (HAS) IN channel service, Zenith's Communication Products HOMEWorks, Motorola's CyberSURFER, Intel's CablePort Adapter, and Time Warner Cable in Elmira New York (commercial trial).

Note

Given that the upstream bandwidth of this solution is limited to the amount of the traditional ISP connection, this solution makes little sense for a WWW site, since the majority of bandwidth use will be the result of upstream traffic. Even so, the implementation of this solution can have a severe impact on a WWW site and the connectivity needed to provide for that site. If implemented in an area of a site that contains locally relevant material, for instance, the increased bandwidth availability might result in a large increase in the amount of traffic that is requested off your site. After all, people are a lot more likely to surf deeper into your site if they think, because of the potentially high level of bandwidth available, that the time to download the information is going to be very short.

Two-Way Communication

If the timetable for one-way connectivity by means of cable can be seen as spotty at best, then the two-way connectivity via cable has to be seen as non-existent. Because of the hardware upgrades needed to support two-way communication via the cable infrastructure, the two-way connectivity has the added limitation of usable infrastructure. In the United States, the estimate of the infrastructure that has been upgraded to a level usable for two-way communication is currently between 16 and 25 percent (depending whether you are talking to the cable companies or not). The overall utilization is only expected to be near completion by the year 2000, and even then only the HFC discussed earlier will be implemented.

Besides the infrastructure limitations, the technology for implementing two-way connectivity at the client level is only now being developed. Although a number of proprietary cable modems have been developed, no standard for cable modems currently exists, and as a result, most modems are not interoperable with one another. Even though the cable companies have recently announced a plan to develop a standard for the specification of data transfers via cable, the planned end of April, 1996 standardization date is seen by some as unachievable. In fact, if the standard has to be approved by the ITU-T in order to establish an international standard, it is not likely that a true standard will develop for a couple of years.

Finally, even where infrastructures have been upgraded, cable companies are not necessarily offering two-way connectivity to the Internet. This situation may be as a result of cable companies not seeing a market (or at least not realizing the market potential), or because of a desire to pursue other options, such as video on demand, for this expanded infrastructure.

A Note from the Author

A prime example of a company not offering Internet connectivity in an area with upgraded infrastructure is right in my own neighborhood. A couple of months ago, the local cable company upgraded the infrastructure in our area to fiber optics and coax (I know this because for a couple of days my cable was out). Even so, the cable provider is not currently offering Internet services. Instead, the cable company is running a trial access period in another part of the country. If the trial goes well, then the local service in my area should be available in three to six months.

Satellite

Unlike the cable connection option, satellite connections have been around for a number of years. Even so, the newer one-way satellite connectivity options are only just becoming available, and are only being offered by a handful of companies. It is of course useful to keep in mind that satellite connections are inherently available in most areas on the North American continent (or anywhere else that satellite coverage exists—which is most of the world), because the connection is beamed from one point to another. The question remains, of course, whether or not any external links are available to these systems.

Downlink Satellite

In the case of the downlink satellite solution, where only downstream information is transmitted by the satellite, the technological rollout is relatively recent. Originally pursued for military purposes, the small-dish satellite reception units have only recently been converted into civilian applications, including TV and Internet access.

In terms of Internet access, there are very few service providers who are currently offering support for the one-way satellite communications. What is needed is a network operations center with the uplink satellite. Because uplink satellites are expensive, and because the cost of transmitting data can be prohibitive, the growth of companies supporting the system is low. Even so, since the satellite link can be offered to areas remotely (in other words, the network operations center need not be local to the client), this solution can be available in most areas. The limitation is that the companies offering service must have installation and sales people available in the area.

Two-Way Satellite

While the one-way satellite has been available for only a short period of time, the use of two-way satellites for linking remote corporate sites to a central office is well established. Unfortunately, this does not solve your Internet connectivity issues directly. While the satellite link between two offices allows communications between two sites, it does not necessarily allow communications with the Internet.

Communications with the Internet via two-way satellite requires some other method of connection to the Internet. For example, two offices connected by a two-way satellite connection can only pass information back and forth. Only if a link via a leased line, cable, etc., is added will traffic be able to travel to the rest of the Internet. As a result, two-way satellite connectivity can only be seen as part of the solution.

One method of alleviating the need for external Internet links is to have the satellite connection terminate at an ISP. Unfortunately, few ISPs are willing or able to accommodate a satellite connection. As a result, the availability of satellite connectivity is either expensive or very limited.

Bandwidth Limitations

Both cable and satellite connectivity solutions have some major bandwidth limitations in terms of the effective bandwidth that the solutions provide for WWW sites. In both solutions (barring the two-way satellite solution, which has little cost effectiveness in comparison to other land-based solutions), there exist a number of major limitations in terms of bandwidth. The following section outlines the basic difficulty with both solutions: greater downstream than upstream bandwidth. After an explanation of the problems associated with this scenario, this section will conclude by discussing a couple of additional bandwidth-related problems that can occur in the case of the newer two-way cable solutions:

- ❈ Shared bus

- ❈ Use restrictions on cable access

Coming Down is Always Easier than Going Up

As was mentioned at the beginning of this chapter, cable and satellite connectivity are solutions that favor the user over the provider because of the disparity between the downstream and upstream bandwidth. Given that WWW sites create data flows that are mainly upstream in nature, the upstream data is by far the more important consideration in terms of supporting a WWW site.

In the case of the satellite connectivity solutions currently being offered (not including private two-way satellite solutions), upstream bandwidth is limited to the overall bandwidth provided by a land-based connection. If the connection is an ISDN one, the solution will have 128 Kbps of upstream bandwidth, while a dedicated SLIP or PPP connection will provide 28.8 Kbps upstream bandwidth. In either case, satellite connectivity provides little or no benefit for the WWW connectivity solution as all WWW connectivity (upstream bandwidth) is provided by your traditional link.

While the satellite solution would provide more than adequate downstream bandwidth for your WWW site (such as requests to your site for information), the upstream bandwidth needed for the WWW site is based on more costly and smaller traditional links. In the event that the links are simultaneously used for the internal network Internet access as well as a WWW site, the total costs of satellite and traditional connectivity will likely be more costly than the traditional dedicated connectivity (such as fractional T1). Finally, the use of traditional dedicated connections also provides a more robust downstream bandwidth for the internal networks if the link required is greater than satellite connectivity (and without the latency effect of satellite communications). In the case of cable connectivity, the bandwidth issues are a little less clear-cut. For one-way cable connections, the same difficulties experienced with a satellite connection are also present. As a result, one-way cable connections are not suited for WWW connectivity. This leaves the possible option of utilizing a two-way cable connection for WWW site connectivity. While this solution provides a better option than the previous two, there exists two other bandwidth limitations that limit the functionality of the two-way cable connection for WWW sites.

Cable and Shared Bus

The first major limitation system is a result of the HFC system that is currently being put into place for two-way cable solutions. As a result of this system, a number of users (between 200 and 1,000 per cable subsystem) are required to share the bandwidth available in each area. Because the cable system is laid out in a logical bus architecture, any increase in the number of users directly impacts the amount of bandwidth available to other users. Given a total available bandwidth of approximately 6 Mbps, if each user were to use the same amount of upstream bandwidth, each site would have between 6 and 30 Kbps for upstream traffic. In terms of users, this amount of upstream bandwidth is sufficient, but in terms of a WWW server of any size, this bandwidth would not be sufficient for more than a small site.

Tip

As a cost-conscious manager, you may be tempted to use a cable connection for your WWW site, in hopes of utilizing upstream bandwidth that is going to "waste" on the cable system. After all, if most of the connections on a cable system are simple users, then the upstream bandwidth may be underutilized.

While this may be the case, it is more likely that the users will quickly begin to use the cable connectivity to facilitate applications that use both upstream and downstream bandwidth. This could be as simple as using an audio conferencing system for two-way communication via the Internet, or as complex as setting up a personnel WWW site. Although these uses can afford to have some degradation of service, a commercial or professional WWW site that experiences severe brownouts will not meet the objectives of attracting clients.

Use Restrictions and Cable

Other than the inherent bandwidth limitations discussed previously, the cable connectivity solution might also have an imposed limitation by the cable company. In a number of trials that have been performed, the cable company has either limited the amount of upstream bandwidth (at the user end), or at the very least has had use policies that discourage or forbid the use of cable connectivity for WWW sites. Obviously, the cable company is targeting end users with its current solutions (this is after all where the cable companies' strength lies), and as a result, the companies are making it less attractive for companies that want to use cable for WWW site connectivity.

Note

Obviously, in the long run the cable companies will be looking into providing even higher bandwidth to each and every residence or office. With the move to a completely fiber infrastructure, the companies will be able to provide bandwidth at levels that support full two-way services to all customers in any area. Unfortunately, because the costs for a completely fiber solution are approximately $400 per location higher than the hybrid solution, it looks as if the completely fiber solution is a number of years away.

Technical Limitations

As well as the bandwidth limitations that are common to both the satellite and the cable systems, there are also a couple of technical limitations of which you should be aware. In the case of cable solutions, there is the issue of limited Internet connectivity on the part of the cable company, and for satellite solutions, the issue is latency and lag time with satellite communications.

Cable Connectivity and Other Things

With either of the cable connectivity solutions, the current trend is for the cable company to purchase access to the Internet infrastructure and to provide Internet access to all of its clients. This is very different from the local loop role that the local telephone companies generally play. In the case of the telephone companies, the local loop is simply a means for your data to be transported to an ISP that has a connection to the Internet (actually, a connection to a long-distance carrier who provides access to the communications backbones). In the case of cable, the local loop and Internet connectivity have been combined.

Unfortunately, this approach by the cable company might result in you being forced to have lower bandwidth available than desired. Because few ISPs support (or will likely support in the future) cable connectivity, the result is that you are only able to use the basic cable offerings. At this time, most cable companies are unwilling (or unable) to offer dedicated services with guarantees on bandwidth. Because you are not able to opt for an ISP and use cable simply as a backbone, the solution provides fewer options than more traditional solutions.

Satellite and Latency

Although cable solutions have the difficulty of a minimal option for upstream bandwidth (depending on the cable company's offering), the satellite solutions avoid this problem by providing no upstream bandwidth! Unfortunately, even the downstream bandwidth that the satellite connection provides can be hindered by the latency of satellite connections. Since a satellite has a delay time for information to bounce off the satellite and down to your site, the requests made through a land connection may not immediately provide a response. Since any packet retries, etc., will require even more transmissions, the upstream link becomes even more important. As a result of the latency effect of satellites, the downstream bandwidth might appear inconsistent in speed.

Hardware

Even though both of the solutions discussed in this chapter do not (in our opinion) provide sufficient connectivity to support a WWW site, the next section details the hardware associated with each solution. This information enables you to better understand how each solution is implemented, despite whether cable or satellite is being considered.

Cable

Choosing hardware for cable solutions presents an interesting problem for a manager looking for Internet connectivity. The hardware is dependent on the choice between one- and two-way connectivity (although the hardware for each is related). In the case of one-way communication, remote link adapters are used, while in the case of two-way communication, a cable modem is used.

Note

In all cases requiring cable Internet hardware, no standard exists for the equipment that is currently available. As a result, each cable company implements its tests based on the proprietary equipment that it has selected. Although the cable companies appear to be moving toward a standard (according to cable companies, by April of this year), the

> current situation means that equipment for one cable company may not work in another cable company area. Since cable companies are generally smaller than the regional telephone companies, this non-interoperability may cause some serious problems.

Remote Link Adapter

As discussed before, a remote link adapter is a device that combines three functional tasks. First, the adapter acts as a cable demodulator (as opposed to a MOdulator/DEModulator or MODEM) for the information that is received by means of the cable coax. Second, the adapter has an interface for the local network or PC connection. In most cases, this is an Ethernet adapter or port, so that the adapter can be a separate node on the internal network. Third, the adapter has an interface for the upstream link to the Internet. This connection could be a simple modem interface, or an ISDN terminal adapter. The cost of a remote link adapter runs around $500, but a cable company will usually rent it for $8–$10 on a monthly basis.

Cable Modems

Although one-way cable solutions require a complex remote link adapter, the two-way cable solutions provide a more simplified solution for hardware. In the case of two-way connections, the hardware required is a cable modem. This device takes the signal from the cable signal, de-encrypts the information (remember the DES encryption used because of cable's broadcast nature), demodulates the information into a digital signal, and then passes the information to a computer interface (either serial or more likely Ethernet—because of the need for the LAN connection to be able to handle the higher speeds of cable connections). As well, the cable modem takes information from the computer or computer network and routes this information over the coax (after modulating the digital information back into the required analog signal).

Satellite

The hardware needed for the satellite connectivity options is considerably different from the cable hardware previously described. In the case of satellite connectivity, the hardware consists of two elements: a satellite system (dish) and a LAN connectivity system (computer card and local link device).

Satellite Dish

For one-way satellite solutions, the hardware for the satellite dish is based on the small satellite dishes used for Direct TV. The dish (60 centimeters in diameter) is either wall-mounted or pole-mounted on your building. Because the signal received from the satellite is actually an RF signal, a simple coax cable is used to bring the information from the dish to your computer. From the coaxial cable, the information is passed to an adapter card in your computer.

LAN Connectivity

LAN connectivity for the satellite solution is based on a number of components. Possibly the most important component is the adapter card for your host. This card is a digital satellite receiver that takes the signal from the satellite dish and converts the signal (analog) into digital information that the computer can understand. The card is generally based on the ISA architecture.

The second component of the satellite connectivity hardware is the local serial link equipment. Simply equipment for the upstream connectivity, this serial link is generally a 28.8 modem that is either internal or external to the computer. If desired, connectivity could be provided any number of other ways, including through ISDN and dedicated lines. The equipment required would be specific to the connectivity solution chosen.

Costs

Although both of the solutions discussed in this chapter do not provide sufficient connectivity to support a WWW site, the next section details the costs associated with each solution. The information presented here enables you to better evaluate the costs of each solution, and make the price comparisons needed to properly assess the connectivity options.

Cable

Costs for cable connectivity options are based on a number of components. No matter what solution is chosen, you will have to have a connectivity option from your cable company. In the event that a one-way solution is chosen, you will also have to pay for a link from a local service provider, and finally, you will be required to pay for the hardware needed to implement the connectivity option.

Cable Provider

The first component of the cable connectivity solution's costs is the actual connectivity from the cable company. While currently very few companies offer this service, the companies that do offer service have very unique rate structures. Given that the speed of the connection is influenced by the cable company's connectivity to the Internet, and not your link to the cable company, most companies are currently offering service on an unlimited basis, with no bandwidth charges. Even more interesting, is the fact that the services have generally been priced in the $40 to $100 range.

Note

A number of reports examine the costs of supplying bandwidth by means of a variety of media. Sharon Eisner Gillett's report, in particular (http://farnsworth.mit.edu/Pubs/gillett_connecting_home/abstract.html), examined and compared the costs of ISDN to cable. This report concluded that the costs per cable subscriber were considerably (like an order of magnitude) less than the costs associated with ISDN based on hardware costs. This would explain the lower costs associated with cable delivery systems than telephony delivery mechanisms.

The real unknown quantity in the cable solution is the amount of Internet bandwidth purchased by the cable company for use in each area. Since the cable company can realize economies of scale (by purchasing larger bandwidth pipes in comparison to ISPs), this may result in a better quality of service over time. In fact, cable companies are working to connect the cable head ends together through high-speed links, thus providing a further backbone for Internet connectivity. If this trend continues, the national amalgamation of the cable companies will no longer rely on external Internet links, and bandwidth may improve. The final step to full service to clients will be the complete fiber network base.

Internet Service Provider

In the event that you choose a one-way cable solution, you will also be required to pay for a local Internet link from an ISP. What this link will cost you depends on the speed of the link chosen. Please refer to the various connectivity chapters to detail the total cost of the solution you chose, whether it be an SLIP- or a PPP-dedicated connection (Chapter 4), a dedicated 56Kbps line (Chapter 5), or an ISDN line (Chapter 6).

Hardware and Setup

Like the other costs, the costs for hardware and setup will depend on the type of solution chosen. In the case of one-way connectivity, the hardware for this solution can be as much as $1,000, all-inclusive. For the two-way modem communications, a number of companies offer products in the $300 to $500 range. In all cases of trials to date, the cable companies have provided a cable modem on a lease basis, so that the price of the modem is amortized over the life of the modem (similar to the way your cable TV converter is paid for today).

Satellite

The satellite connectivity method has a number of costs that you must take into consideration. Satellite connectivity costs include the following components:

- Local Internet connectivity
- Hardware
- Monthly satellite costs
- Satellite bandwidth costs

The combination of these costs, combined with its poor quality connection for WWW sites, makes this option non–cost-effective.

Local Connectivity

As with the one-way cable solution, the satellite connectivity option relies on an external link to the Internet for the upstream bandwidth. As a result, a WWW site using this solution is still required to use a local ISP for dedicated upstream bandwidth. No matter which solution is chosen, this represents a considerable expense for you (not to mention that the satellite connection provides *no* benefit for your WWW site in terms of connectivity for your clients).

Hardware and Setup

The second major drawback of the satellite connectivity solution is the high initial cost of the hardware. Although the price may continue to drop as more people utilize this solution, currently the hardware can cost as much as $1,400 for the entire hardware package, including dish, cables, and card. On top of this you are looking at approximately $300 for installation, and all of the hardware and setup costs of the local connectivity solution that you chose.

Monthly Costs

The monthly charges currently being used for satellite connectivity are actually quite reasonable, and vary depending on the level of bundled bandwidth that comes with basic access. For basic services, bandwidth can be as low as 30 MB per month, and the cost as low as $15 per month. For a more robust bundle of bandwidth (130 MB per month), the price is in the $55 per month range.

Bandwidth Charges

The final costs associated with the satellite connectivity solution—the costs that actually make this solution suspect even for the Internet users—are the bandwidth charges. Other than the bandwidth bundled with the basic services, the cost of bandwidth per GB of data can range from $600 per GB in off-peak hours, to $800 per GB in peak periods. Compared to the bandwidth charges of even the most expensive ISPs, this appears to be highway (or in this case *skyway*) robbery!

Setup Requirements

The setup requirements for either cable or satellite solutions are simple, since both solutions generally come with setup. In the case of cable connectivity, the setup service is provided when the cable company installs the equipment at your location. Installation is not required for satellite connectivity, but because of the complexity of the system, it is highly recommended depending on the specifics of your connectivity requirements. Over and above the basic setup requirements, the cable solution also has a further requirement—location—explained in the following section.

Cable Connectivity: The Right Area

By far the most important requirement for the cable connectivity solution is the location of your site. Because the solution, or at least the two-way solution, is only potentially available in a very small area, the location of your site is very restricted to be considered a solution. While the limited availability may not be a factor, you should only consider the solution if the availability of two-way communication is being offered in your area.

Summary

As has been demonstrated, the cable and satellite connectivity solutions fail to meet the requirements of most WWW sites. In both cases, the upstream bandwidth, most important to a WWW site, is severely limited. In the case of the satellite or one-way cable solutions, the upstream bandwidth is zero! In the case of the two-way cable system, the amount of users per cable bus can drastically affect bandwidth, and as a result the instability of the available bandwidth makes this a poor business solution.

Although these two emerging technologies are not currently providing any of the benefits needed for a WWW site, the cable solution might prove to be the long-term solution after a full fiber-optic infrastructure is in place. As the next chapter illustrates, there are also a number of other emerging technologies that not only provide better current prospects than cable and satellite, but also represent some of the most promising future trends.

Checklist

The following are concerns that should be addressed at the conclusion of the chapter.

Cable

☑ Available in area?

☑ FTTN or full fiber available in your area?

☑ Bidirectional cable available?

☑ Cable provider allows WWW site usage?

☑ Cost of basic cable Internet?

☑ Hardware costs?

Satellite

☑ Available in your area?

☑ Local ISP access available?

☑ Cost of bandwidth?

☑ Monthly cost of satellite?

☑ Hardware costs?

Does either solution meet your bandwidth needs?

Renting a Home for Your HTML

Although the information presented in the past seven chapters provides you with a number of different connectivity options, all of the options are based on the principle of creating a dedicated link to your site and host. From your WWW server, you will be able to provide information and services to the world. For some organizations, dedicated connections provide excellent Internet connectivity; for others, the dedicated connections create more problems than they solve.

In the case of organizations looking for a simple and cost-effective connectivity option, a number of solutions exist that do not require the degree of technical expertise of the dedicated solutions. This chapter examines the first of two possible methods, renting space on a commercial WWW provider's server, while the second method, a Server Park, will be discussed in Chapter 12 , "Server Park: Cost-Effective High Bandwidth Access."

To better understand the benefits and limitations of renting WWW space, this chapter first details what HTML is and how HTML works. After discussing the history and technological background of HTML, this chapter examines three rental paradigms:

- Simple pages

- Bulk space

- Virtual servers

Each paradigm is examined for availability, cost, benefits and limitations, and the setup requirements. At the end of this chapter, you should be able to determine whether renting space will fulfill your needs, and what the potential problems are with this solution.

Understanding HTML and How It Works

HyperText Markup Language (HTML) is the basis on which the World Wide Web is founded. Like all markup languages, HTML provides a set of characteristics that can be applied to the information being processed. These characteristics, called *tags*, together make up the HTML standard. This section examines the history of HTML and the predecessor of HTML, *Standard General Markup Language* (SGML).

After providing a brief history of the markup languages, a short explanation of the various HTML standards is provided, including the current standard, proposed amendments, and the current extensions. From the markup languages, this section turns to the actual server used for WWW sites, the httpd. Finally, a brief technical background on the various aspects of WWW sites is presented.

The History of HTML and Its Big Brother, SGML

As mentioned in Chapter 1, "Bandwidth and Internet Connectivity," the CERN Institute, working from the idea of hypertext as developed by Ted Nelson of Stanford Research Institute (SRI) in the 1960s, developed an implementation of a markup language that was to be named HyperText Markup Language (HTML). The concept behind this language was to provide a mechanism for organizing data and information for collaboration between physicists.

It is not generally realized that HTML is a derivative of SGML, and how the HTML standard developed is based on the original SGML methodology. To better understand the HTML that is used for WWW sites today, this section first discusses SGML, and then the evolution of HTML, and concludes with a brief discussion of the expansion of the World Wide Web.

Standard General Markup Language

Standard General Markup Language, or SGML, is a international standard used to describe marked-up electronic text. The term *markup* stems from the traditional printing methods where annotations and other marks were inserted into the text of documents to inform printers or typists how the document was to be formatted. As document management became computerized, markups came to include special codes used to dictate formatting and other printing information.

Although SGML is indeed a markup language, it is also a *metalanguage*—a language that can be used to define other languages. By using SGML to define markup languages, language composers can gain the benefits of an internationally defined system. It was with the benefits of SGML in mind that the Internet community turned to SGML for the basis of HTML 2.0 standard. But the discussion of the HTML 2.0 standard is a bit premature without some overview of the evolution of the HTML standard.

The Evolution of HTML

In the original specification, HTML provided for a simple set of tags that allowed for basic text and links. Because the original browsers were designed for text-only viewing, the HTML specification did not provide large amounts of support for fancy layout, columns, or graphics (other than a basic image as a link). Also, the specification was not based on SGML, and in fact had not gone through the standards process. The system of HTML in place worked for a few years with the limited use that HTML and WWW sites were seeing. This all changed as the WWW began to grow at an enormous rate.

The change in the HTML growth came with the development of a graphical WWW browser (a client program that allows the user to view the HTML in a standard manner). In 1992, Marc Andreessen was working on an information collaboration project for NCSA. Aware of the project developed by CERN, Andreessen worked to develop a Web Browser that used the same specification, but allowed the use of a graphical interface for use with GUI systems. This first graphical browser included the capability to view text and graphics, as well as to launch other programs for the utilization of sound and high-resolution graphics (*helper applications* as they have become known).

As a result of the increase in use that the graphical browsers created (including the new browser created by Marc Andreessen's private company, Netscape), the WWW flourished. As more and more people began using WWW sites to exchange information, the HTML standard began to feel strains. Because the markup language was designed only to provide simple text processing information that was independent of the systems used to view documents, the HTML specification was limited in what it could do. As clients demanded greater versatility from the standard, the browser companies began to extend the original specification to include graphics support, control over text, and layout options.

In 1994, in response to the standard quickly become "polluted" with nonstandard elements, the HTML Working Group was organized. The Group, which includes representation from the major browser companies, is attempting to standardize HTML 2.0 based on a formal document type definition (DTD) of SGML. Level 1 of HTML is now defined as the original standard provided by Tim Berners-Lee. Although HTML 2.0 is generally supported by all browsers, at the time of this writing, it has not been officially declared. That declaration is expected shortly.

The Expanding Web

With the standardization of HTML into an SGML DTD, the WWW quickly expanded to include the new functionality such as support for video, graphics, layout control, greater scripting and forms. The Web's capability to publish and make information available worldwide, with formatting familiar to standard publishing at very little cost, has caught the attention of users and businesses. The Web's potential for graphics, sound, and video methods of portraying information created an explosion of users and providers.

Simultaneously, Web browsers have continued to develop and progress, including more and more features (the current most-used browser is Netscape by Netscape, Inc.). Today, some of the most exciting developments for the WWW include VRML (Virtual Reality Modeling Language), Java (a scripting/programming tool that allows applications to be embedded in HTML code), and narrow-casting audio and video.

The HTML Standard

Although browsers continue to evolve and new features continue to be added, the only way to ensure that all browsers can correctly interpret your pages is to use only the standard features of HTML. Unfortunately, most of the exciting features, such as forms, MIME types, fonts, and layout control are not yet part of the standard. Currently, only HTML 1.0 has been standardized, although 2.0 is the de facto standard used by all Web browsers. This next section will briefly describe the main functionality of each of the standards, and their current status.

Standard HTML 1.0

HTML 1.0 is the original specification designed by Tim Berners-Lee for the CERN organization. Because the standard was not designed around an SGML DTD, the 1.0 standard lacks the extendibility and robust structure that SGML can provide in even the most poorly designed WWW documents. For more on HTML 1.0, visit **http://www.w3.org/hypertext/WWW/MarkUp.archive/ html-spec.txt**. Although modified greatly by individual users over the years, the base standard provided only the rudimentary level of text handling (headers, preformatted text, simple structure, and so on). Given the trend toward a broken version of this standard, the HTML Working Group is working to replace the standard with an updated HTML 2.0.

Defacto HTML 2.0

Although HTML 2.0 has not yet been formally declared a standard, almost all browsers now support the current draft standard that has been made available (**http://www.w3.org/hypertext/WWW/MarkUp/html-spec/**). The widespread support is due to the advanced features for which the 2.0 standard provides, such as images, logical styles, forms, and lists. As a result of these functions, HTML authors are better able to format their documents to look like the printed documents with which we are all so familiar. Add to this the hypertext functionality of HTML, and the WWW has developed into a strong tool for organizing and presenting information.

Proposed HTML 3.0

The next major revision of HTML is designated HTML 3.0, and is currently being drafted by the working group (**http://www.w3.org/hypertext/WWW/MarkUp/html3/html3.txt**). Although the standard is not yet set, a number of the provisions of the proposed standard have already been implemented by some of the browsers.

Some of the major changes that HTML 3.0 will bring are the inclusion of tables, improved graphics capabilities (including the capability to position the graphics relative to the page), expanded character sets, and increased control over the presentation of the information.

Some browsers have already moved beyond even these improvements; see the next section for standard extensions beyond what is proposed under HTML 3.0.

Extensions to the Standard

Although the move to standardize HTML via SGML is intended to prevent the balkanization (the breaking up) of the standard into proprietary electronic publishing formats, the move has failed in many respects. This is due to the fact that the demands of consumers are increasing faster than the standards organization. As a result, increasing market forces are encouraging individual browser companies to add their own proprietary extensions.

Possibly, the chief culprit of extensions is Netscape. Whether the extensions are the inclusion of tables (proposed under 3.0) or the addition of frames (to allow greater control over layout and allow users to view information in a much more understandable and easy format), Netscape has not hesitated to add the features that it perceives to be desired. If the process continues, the standards body may be faced with a growing user base that accepts the Netscape extensions as a de facto standard.

A Note from the Author

In general, adherence to standards is the only guarantee that the information presented via the WWW does not become fragmented. Poorly implemented extensions can result in the page being unreadable by any browser not compatible by the extensions. Moreover, the use of extensions by Netscape has opened the door for other companies to create their own proprietary WWW languages. An example of this possibility was Microsoft's release of their browser, the "Internet Explorer," with new extensions. Luckily for the Internet, the new Microsoft "standard" has not been widely accepted.

To maintain compatability across the entire Internet, we recommend that you use only the latest standard in developing your WWW site. Although 2.0 is not final, the draft is set enough for the standard to be reasonably stable. As for extensions or 3.0 elements, you should avoid these elements unless absolutely required. Even then, make sure that you fully understand how each element should be implemented. Well-implemented elements should not render your page unreadable by older browsers.

httpd Servers

Like most services available via the Internet, WWW services are controlled by a daemon. The httpd, or HyperText Transport Protocol daemon, controls access to your WWW documents. To illustrate the nature of the daemon, this section first looks at what an httpd server is, and then details a couple of the more popular httpd servers. By understanding some of the technical details of the httpd, you will be better prepared to understand what a rental site can and should provide.

What is an httpd Server?

Web browsers, ftp, and telnet programs are often referred to as *client* programs. To retrieve information from the Internet, client programs interact with other pieces of software known generically as *servers*. In UNIX, servers belong to a set of programs known as *daemons*. The UNIX convention is to name such programs with a trailing *d* to indicate that they are daemons. So, ftp talks to a server called ftpd, telnet corresponds with telnetd, and Web browsers are served by HTTP servers, or httpd.

Servers Available

httpd servers are available on almost every platform imaginable, from a variety of UNIX systems to Windows to Macintosh. Because the majority of Internet sites are based on one version of UNIX or another, this section concentrates on the two main httpd servers used on UNIX systems:

* NCSA httpd

* CERN httpd

NCSA httpd

The *National Center for Supercomputing Applications* (NCSA) has long been providing applications for use on the Internet free of charge. The NCSA httpd is one such product, and is available for most UNIX-based operating systems. The server provides all of the basic httpd functions, including both global and per-directory security access control. To install the server, often you must download and compile (the source code is downloaded and then used to create a binary image) the server on your host machine. NCSA provides one of the most popular WWW servers in the world.

CERN httpd Servers

The CERN httpd server is a derivative of the original server used by Tim Berners-Lee for the CERN WWW project. Not only has the server survived and adapted, but simultaneously has developed into a robust method of managing your

WWW site. Like the NCSA server, the CERN server is available for most UNIX flavors. Moreover, the CERN server provides some excellent functionality for searches and CGI scripts (see the detailed discussion later in this chapter). The CERN Server can perform simple firewall services by acting as a proxy for WWW, ftp, news, and wais services. CERN also can act as a wais gateway, although the more services offered, the greater amount of hardware resources that will be required.

The Technical Background of HTML

Now that you have looked at the language of the WWW (HTML), and the server for the WWW (httpd), it is time for more in-depth look at the technical workings of the WWW. In general, the WWW site is a collection of three main elements:

※ httpd and HTML

※ CGI scripts

※ Interactive applications

In this section, a brief discussion about how the httpd server works is presented, as well as a discussion on the use of CGI scripts. Finally, a glance at the most interesting WWW services, interactive applications, are examined.

How Do httpd Servers Work?

An HTTP server takes requests from Web clients, such as Web browsers, and fulfills them. It essentially serves HTML documents to the Web browser. A server does this by understanding HTTP, (HyperText Transfer Protocol). HTTP defines the syntax that a browser uses to request a Web page, as well as the syntax that a Web daemon must understand and fulfill. HTTP, the "language" of the Web, is defined to ride on top of TCP/IP, the "language" of the Internet. So, basically, a Web server's life cycle consists of waiting for requests for Web pages, reading the requested information from its file system (or database), formatting it into a proper HTTP response, and finally sending the response to the Web client. At this point, it begins listening for another request, and the cycle continues. Sophisticated HTTP servers can answer multiple requests simultaneously, allowing quicker or equitable response time to more client programs.

CGI Scripting

The Common Gateway Interface (CGI) is the current application programming interface (API) for servers to communicate with scripts or programs. CGI promotes dynamic WWW pages—an eye-opening contrast to plain, old static WWW pages. CGI scripts can be written in a number of different languages, but the most common are PERL and C. Both languages provide a different set of functionality tools, and each are better suited for different tasks. JavaScript is a newer scripting language specifically designed for WWW scripting of applets (small applications) that can be delivered via the WWW.

A Note from the Author

Dynamic pages are pages that have a greater level of interactivity for the users. For example, a static page would have a graphic, while a more interactive or dynamic page could have the same graphic as an animated figure.

Scripting is one of the most exciting methods of increasing the functionality of your WWW pages. Even so, scripting can be very difficult to correctly implement, and in most cases, the scripts can provide security holes for the WWW server. For example, a script could write information from another file to your hard disk, enabling an unscrupulous person to overrun your hard disk, causing your system to crash. As a result, most site administrators require that any scripts either be done by in-house programmers, or be proofed by the system's administrator prior to installation.

Interactive Applications

As mentioned in the previous section, CGI scripting can provide a method of dynamically creating WWW pages. The dynamic aspect of CGI scripts and the subsequent interactive nature of it makes it an exciting proposal for the WWW. Although basic scripts can provide some degree of interaction with the users, true interactive applications often rely on other programs in conjunction with scripts to interface with WWW browsers.

For example, one of the most dynamic areas on the WWW is the provision of up-to-date data via WWW-searchable databases. In this case, the power of database engines is tapped via a series of CGI scripts that link the WWW forms to the database. Query forms provide the user with a method of defining searches, and the results are returned in HTML format for browser viewing. Data can be updated in the database on a regular basis (often via other WWW forms) to provide an up-to-date information source.

A Note from the Author

Databases provide a mechanism for controlling access to the information, whereas the WWW pages provide the front-end for the client. In this type of application, the validity of the data becomes the key issue. Because data often is taken from other sources and then passed onto the WWW databases (most companies provide only subsets of larger databases, and therefore are not willing to allow public access to internal databases), the most difficult task is data maintenance. In a number of cases in which we have been involved, we have been able to use Internet tools to facilitate and automate the maintenance process. For example, we have utilized e-mail files (sent from the internal database coordinator) and created automatic methods of parsing the information out of these files. Although the setup of these systems is generally difficult, the result is a large savings in time and resources.

Using a Simple Home Page

Now that you are familiar with the technical background and functionality of WWW sites, it is time to look at the various space rental options that are available. The first option to examine is the basic home page. This section examines the availability, costs, benefits, limitations, and setup requirements of this solution. You should then be able to determine whether the simple home page will meet your needs, and if so, how to go about arranging rental space for it.

Availability

Simple home page services are widely available from most ISPs and a number of other consulting companies. The quality of the services offered varies according to the company chosen, but in general, renting space for a home page includes the technical expertise in addition to the storage space. The ISP or WWW consulting company will provide HTML markup and graphics services, and will store your page for a set period of time (generally one year at a time).

Although the basic services include the HTML markup of your information, and possibly the scanning of one picture, higher level functionality is available at extra cost. For example, to include imagemaps or forms, you will be required to pay the creation fees by the WWW company. Extra pages will increase the yearly fee charged for the WWW page(s).

Finally, basic home pages have recently seen an increase in price levels through the inclusion of references to your page in a virtual mall setting. Under these programs, a larger commercial provider creates a "mall" of WWW sites. Because of the larger number of services available in each virtual mall, traffic increases. As a result, the ISP can charge higher prices for the inclusion of your site in the mall directory.

Costs

Speaking of prices, one of the most fluid aspects of WWW site rental is the cost for each page. Generally, the prices for hosting WWW home pages are considerably higher than the costs associated with renting space on a WWW server. The higher prices are justified (by the companies charging them) by including bundled services with the home pages. For example, a WWW consulting company may include the setup and four changes per year in its price for a WWW page. By supplying all of the technical requirements for the client, and possibly including advertising functions (such as page registration in online search engines), the consulting company is able to charge more for the service. What it all boils down to is basically this: Hosting is more service-oriented, with the company providing markup and maintenance services. Renting space is simply paying for disk space and bandwidth from a provider, the rest is self service. An ISP provides Internet access in whatever form, and may offer both markup and maintenance services. A consulting company offering home pages is technically an ISP, but generally does not offer services other than home page rental.

Warning

When purchasing a home page, be very careful to investigate what the rental includes. Most companies limit the amount of bandwidth (that is, hits) that any one page can have during a month. If your page is extremely popular, the company reserves the right to terminate your site's access. As a result of this clause, you may find yourself with an interruption in service or being forced to pay higher rates.

Finally, the cost of the WWW page will likely be a flat rate for a period of time. Prices can range greatly (from $30 per year to thousands per year) depending on the services provided with the home page. For a yearly rental of space for one simple page (including setup and four changes), you should expect to pay between $50 and $100 per year. Anything greater should cause you to ask some very pointed questions about the rates.

Potential Benefits and Limitations

As with all connectivityoptions, simple home page rental has a number of benefits and limitations. As a result of these benefits and limitations, this option is better suited to certain clients and situations. To understand whether the home page connectivity solution will meet your needs, you need to first understand the benefits and limitations of the following:

- Simplicity of implementation

- Access to changes for your site

- Limitations for site size

Simplicity of Implementation

The main benefit of a home page rental is the simplicity of the solution. Depending on your service provider, you may be able to create a home page with little or no knowledge of HTML and WWW site administration. For that reason, the home page solution is best suited for smaller companies or individuals who do not have the technical expertise or inclination to manage the markup functions of their WWW site.

Access for Site Changes

The simplicity of the home page approach to WWW connectivity is also one of its main drawbacks. Because the service provider provides the markup services for a WWW page, the company generally does not allow the client access to the home page for changes. All changes must therefore go through the service provider. In most cases, this is not a problem because providers allow a limited number of changes per year (quarterly changes is a common approach). For a site that changes rapidly, or one for which rapid development and growth is expected, the home page solution will limit your options and may even cost you more than the convenience is worth.

Size Limitations

The second main limitation of the home page solution is related to your site's growth potential. Because most home page agreements are based on the number of pages that you have on a site (a page is normally limited to one page of text and graphics with a maximum of one medium graphic per page), the growth of your site can quickly increase the costs of the solution beyond a sustainable level. For example, a site with thirty pages of information could easily result in $3,000 per year or $250 per month. At this price, you could easily subcontract maintenance for your site while renting bulk space to host the service. The result would be greater control at a lesser cost.

Setup Requirements

Given the benefits and limitations of the home page solution to Internet connectivity, it is not surprising that the setup requirements are not difficult or extensive. The requirements are limited to two main points: choosing a provider and gathering the information and graphics that you wish to include on your site.

Choosing a Provider

The first step, after deciding that you would like to rent space for your organization's WWW home page, is to choose a provider. Although lists such as the ones available online (or in the appendix of this book) can provide you with a good starting point for finding providers in your area, this information can be augmented through a perusal of trade newspapers in your area (such as *The Computer Paper* or *Internet News*, two free newspaper-style publications in Vancouver, Canada).

In choosing a provider, you should make sure that the flexibility and services that are offered are what you need and want. Make sure that you do not pay more money for services than are required. For example, if you are interested only in providing online information for sales associates to peruse around the country, then services such as promotion or advertising may not be worthwhile. Because your site will primarily be used as a tool for your associates, search engine registration and WWW mall locations are not essential services for your organization.

Providing Information and Graphics

After choosing your provider, the final major task of putting up a home page is the provision of the information and graphics to your ISP. Like any form of publication, the design and layout of the information can affect the reception of your site. In WWW sites, simplicity and small size (in terms of file sizes, not page sizes) are virtues. The painful experience of downloading a large graphic-filled page will attest to these virtues. Five minutes for dubious information is not going to make you want to come back to the site anytime soon.

Remember also that the home page will likely be seen by people from all around the world. With this international exposure, you should be certain to include your full address and telephone area code on your site. Failure to acknowledge your location in the global Internet world can have some unusual consequences. For example, a company with a similar name may provide services in another country. Without an identification of your country on your organization's WWW page, you may end up receiving e-mail complaining about the other company's services. Because considerable overlap in naming occurs across international boundaries, this problem may snowball as the Internet continues to grow.

Evaluating the Pros and Cons of Rented Space

After collecting your information, perhaps you realize that your site will be quite large, or that the information will require monthly or weekly updates. Obviously, the home page solution is not optimal for your scenario. Perhaps you have a good working knowledge of HTML, but do not have the hardware or system administration skills to successfully manage an Internet server. In these cases, rental of bulk WWW space may be the best solution for you. This section discusses the availability, costs, potential benefits and limitations, and setup requirements of a bulk rental site. At the end of this section, you should be able to evaluate the rental site to see whether the solution will fully meet your needs. If the rental site does not meet your needs, the section sets the stage for the discussion of the final space rental solution—virtual servers.

Availability

The availability of bulk space on WWW servers is somewhat sporadic. Although the service has a number of benefits in terms of your control over your site, the providers are less interested in providing this solution because of the lower value-added basis of the product. Even so, the benefits of the Internet itself actually comes into play, as the market becomes internationalized. Through a simple set of procedures, you can easily manage a site anywhere in the world. The benefits and drawbacks of using local versus remote providers will be discussed in the sections that follow.

Local Providers

Even though WWW space can be managed remotely, a number of benefits exist in locating your site locally. First, you are more likely to be able to verify the company's existence and reliability through a visit to its offices. Also, the extra benefits of local access may result in access to technical resources. Finally, no matter how much the world of commerce and business changes, the fact remains that most people are more comfortable dealing with people in person. If a problem with your site should arise, a local provider allows you the opportunity to conveniently meet to solve the problem (in a cost-effective way).

WWW Space: An International Market

Regardless of the benefits of local provision of WWW space, the international marketplace is a valuable resource for WWW space. Companies around the globe offer WWW site storage services. In some cases, this service is cheaper than service in your area. In other cases, the site provides better access from the Internet to your site. Whatever the situation may be, a simple local Internet dial-up connection allows you universal access to your site, whether it is down the road or around the world. The main drawback with rented space on a nonlocal server is the lack of direct access to the providers. Even telephone conversations required to clear up issues can become costly. Still, if you are comfortable in dealing with clients and suppliers from remote locations, the combination of telnet sessions and e-mail can provide you with excellent WWW service (including access to services such as custom programming or searching tools).

Cost

Unlike basic home page rentals, WWW space rental includes a number of components that may affect the final cost:

- ❈ Space required

- ❈ Bandwidth used

- ❈ Dial-up access

- ❈ Any "extras"

Space Required

The amount of space that your WWW site requires should only marginally affect your WWW rental price. This might seem confusing, given that disk space appears to be the basis for this connectivity method; however, the low cost of hard disk space is the reason for the low impact of space. In most cases, WWW space companies charge a flat rate per month for the space and the base management of the service. Fees can range from $10 to $150 for 10 MB of space. The actual cost depends on the amount of provided support, the space rented (bulk space is cheaper), and the quality of the server on which your site will reside.

Bandwidth

Space on the server will only marginally affect your total cost. The bulk of the cost is derived from the bandwidth charges. Although most sites (you mean WWW space companies?) will allow a base amount of throughput per month, any extra will result in higher charges. For example, the site may be allowed 100 MB of throughput per month with extra throughput ranging from as high as $100 per 100 MB, to as low as $2.50 per 100 MB. A more reasonable range is $5–$10 per 100 MB of throughput. Obviously, if your site is large and experiences heavy traffic, you will incur a large bandwidth cost. When you reach a high level of traffic, you may want to re-examine your decision for rental to see whether the traffic warrants the cost of a dedicated link.

A Note from the Author

Because the bandwidth used by the WWW site is billed at a higher rate than the ISP pays its access provider, a certain level of usage exists that makes the dedicated link actually cheaper in hard costs than a rented site. This point generally refers only to the hard costs (direct external costs versus the cost associated with the use of human resources of your staff), because the costs of connection maintenance are harder to estimate. Still, the benefits of having direct control over a site may outweigh the costs of maintenance. At this point, a dedicated connection becomes worthwhile.

Dial-up Access

The third component of your rented space cost is the link between the site and your office. Because the link serves primarily as a means to update the site on an as-needed basis, simple SLIP or PPP dial-up access should suffice as your connectivity method. As a result, the most you should pay for this access in most areas is $25 per month. As well, a number of service providers will include the local link in the base cost for site storage.

"Extras"

As with any of the rental options, the extras are a source for high cost. From CGI scripting to the provision of advertising links for your site, the extras can provide your site with the edge to make it a premium site. Of course, all the little extras also cost extra. Rates for custom programming can range from as low as $50 per hour up to $200 per hour. In some cases, the lower rates are a result of inexperience, and the extra time required by the inexperienced will result in higher costs. On the other hand, it is our opinion that the $200 rates better provide everything you need, and then some, to be justifiable!

Tip

If your provider is charging you $200 per hour, I recommend that you take some extra time to look around for another provider, or at least a consultant to do your work. In fact, we are more than willing to help you out, and I can guarantee that we will not charge you $200 per hour (at least not in this century)! Our e-mail addresses are in the author biography of this book if you have any questions.

Potential Benefits and Limitations

Once again, like the rental of home page(s), the rental of WWW space has a number of benefits, and some corresponding limitations. As with most connectivity options, the limitations are a result of the benefits. The main benefits include the access that this solution provides in terms of the following:

❀ Higher bandwidth

❀ File access

In exchange, you must deal with the following limitations:

❀ Potential image issues

❀ Scripting difficulties

❀ Discretionary availability of utilities on the remote server

Low Cost with High Bandwidth

Possibly the greatest benefit of a rented WWW site, as with any rental solution, is that your files are available to the rest of the Internet at a higher bandwidth rate than would be possible with a dedicated connection at the same price. Although the WWW site may cost you $150.00 to $200.00 per month, the world accesses your files at T1 speeds—a far cry from the dedicated 28.8 Kbps solution that you could afford for that rate.

Access to Files

The second benefit that a rented WWW space can provide is greater access to your WWW files when compared to the access provided by the standard home page solution. Because you are responsible for the HTML markup of your files, the solution allows you to change your pages at will, without an increase in cost that may result from a standard home page setup by your provider. Furthermore, you can divide your space to your specifications, sparing the cost resulting from extra pages as long as the total space used is within your allotted amount.

Image

The first limitation of this particular solution is a result of the solution's more robust possibilities. As your site grows and experiences heavier traffic, the scenarios resulting from a rented site solution may no longer be considered a solution. Because most providers will only set up a directory below the user level of directories, the URL for your company will not reflect your organization. For example, your URL could be

http://www.global-village.net/sites/your_company

Needless to say, the benefits of a more straightforward URL can be numerous, including name recognition and typability, such as

http://www.your_company.com

Scripting

The second problematic aspect of a rented WWW site is the use of scripts. Because the site resides on a another organization's server, most systems administrators are cautious about allowing users to install scripts. Because scripts can provide security hazards (such as potential disk overruns) for a site, administrators will require that scripts be approved prior to installation. Although this problem is present in all rental solutions, it increases as your site becomes larger. Scripts can be useful for providing a better level of interactivity for your clients, including search engines, clickable images, and the collection of information via forms.

Availability of Utilities

The final limitation covered here is the availability of utilities on the server. Because the maintenance of the WWW site will be your responsibility, the online utilities available become important. Utilities for searching, file editing, and image manipulation are often needed for WWW site maintenance. If the server does not make these utilities available, then your work can be hindered.

A Note from the Author

Do not assume that, just because your service provider offers commercial service, the appropriate utilities will be available for your use. For example, a server on which our company was maintaining a site did not have installed emacs (an editing program for UNIX systems) or PERL. Because both of these utilities are often needed in the maintenance of WWW sites, we were limited by the amount and type of work that was possible.

Setup Requirements

Other than the requirements already identified under the simple home page solution, rented WWW space also has two additional requirements. The first is a dial-up account with an ISP. This account can be with the WWW space provider, but is not required to be. In any case, the account should provide full shell access because you will be required to manage the files on the remote WWW server via a telnet session.

Along with a dial-up account, you will need a WWW site manager who is knowledgeable of basic UNIX utilities (telnet, ftp, and file editing) and HTML. HTML can be fairly easy to learn, but proper use requires a fair level of mastery—poorly written HTML code can result in a site that does not appear as intended.

Understanding the Virtual Server

The final version of rented WWW space is the virtual server. In reality, a virtual server is simply an extension of the rented WWW space model that includes a domain name to associate with your site. This section briefly examines the availability, cost, benefits and limitations, and setup requirements.

Availability

In general, virtual servers are less likely to be available in any areas other than simple home page or WWW space rental. The lack of availability is often a result of two main issues:

- The need for individually registered domain names

- The technical requirements for setup on the service provider's host

Domain Names

The first limitation of availability is not so much an availability issue as one of usability. Because the number of domain names is limited, the availability of names that relate to your organization may consequently be limited as well. The domain is the key to the image benefits that this connectivity method provides, so the lack of a suitable domain name can make this a nonviable solution. If the domain issue is not a concern for your site, either because the domain exists or name recognition is not critical to your site, then the main aspect of availability becomes the technical requirements for virtual domain setup on the server side.

An important capability of interest to Web providers is the concept of a virtual server, or virtual domain. This allows a single computer to serve Web pages for multiple domains transparently. This makes every domain appear to be completely independent of the others, a feature desired by many Web customers. Having your own domain has come to be a sort of status symbol on today's Internet. For this reason, a virtual domain is sometimes disparagingly referred to as a *vanity domain.*

Technical Requirements to Set Up a Virtual Server

To enable a single system to appear to be many, operating system support is needed that can associate a single network device with multiple IP addresses. This capability is known as IP aliasing. At this time, it is widely available on various forms of UNIX, although on some occasions it is given a different name. Also, the system administrator may be required to apply a patch—used to repair or upgrade current software without replacing the software completely (or other additional software)—to the operating system. On some forms of UNIX, IP aliasing is not currently available, and requires more subtle trickery through such methods as associating the extra addresses with unused network drivers.

The difficulties sometimes associated with setting up virtual servers require a competent UNIX system administrator. The administrator should be able to set up a machine to use virtual domain technology by reading available documentation. A good place to start source of information on setting up virtual domains is **http://www.thesphere.com/~dlp/TwoServers/**, which goes into some depth on how to do this for various platforms. Usually, it is only necessary to read the operating system documentation and the documentation for your HTTP daemon.

Because of the somewhat more difficult technical problems sometimes associated with the use of virtual domains, the technical requirements could be an accessibility limitation. This is due to the possibility that the systems administrator is not familiar with the process. Some ISPs may not offer the virtual domain option to avoid problems resulting from an administrator's unfamiliarity with it.

Costs

Like the space rental solution, the virtual server has a number of costs that must be borne out. Just like the other two space rental solutions, the virtual server solution charges for the "extras" provided by the service provider in the areas of advertising, promotion, and scripting. Also, the virtual server solution requires a local link, just as the rented WWW space solution does. Above and beyond these costs are charges for the following:

❀ Domain registration

❀ Hard disk and RAM space

❀ Bandwidth

Domain Registration

Domain registration takes place with InterNIC Internet registration services. As a result of the recent changes, domain name registrations cost $100 for the first two years and $50 per year thereafter. Beyond this InterNIC fee, your provider may charge an additional fee for processing your domain name and setting up the technical details of the domain (including routing).

Space: Disk and RAM

As a result of the need to map your domain name to your files on their server, the service provider will charge you a larger fee for the base virtual server rate than for the rented WWW space solution. These additional costs are a result of the extra effort required to set up, maintain, and run the virtual server. Because the server requires a process to be running to alias the IP addresses of the site to your domain name, the result is a greater use of server processing and RAM. Generally, the charge for a virtual server will be slightly larger than a similarly sized WWW rental site.

Bandwidth

As with the rented WWW space solution previously discussed, a virtual server requires you to pay for your site's bandwidth usage. Although the rates and usage may not vary greatly, developing a complete site may appear as a more natural solution for a virtual domain. Be cautious of higher bandwidth rates associated with the more permanent appearance of a virtual server.

Potential Benefits and Limitations

Because the virtual server solution simply adds a domain name and appearance of a server for your site, the benefits and limitations are very similar to that of the rented WWW site solution. Even so, the virtual server solution provides one key advantage in image management, and raises even more pointedly the trade-off between control over your server and the costs.

The Image

The key benefit of a virtual server over rental space on a WWW server is the presentation of your site as an integrated entity. The domain name used will (or should) reflect some of your corporate image, resulting in a more professional image that clients will take note of. From their point of view, there is no difference between your site running as a virtual server on a machine behind a T1, and you having your server on a dedicated machine in your office connected by a T1 (although the actual bandwidth available for your site may be limited by the service provider's overall usage).

Control versus Cost

Because a virtual server provides most of the services that a dedicated machine and connection can provide, the solution challenges the need for dedicated connections for WWW site connectivity. Obviously, the solution does not provide any significant connectivity spin-offs for your internal network, but the WWW connectivity is as good, if not better than that provided by a dedicated connection. The question of whether to have a dedicated connection versus a virtual server boils down to the control issue.

Because a virtual server is running on a service provider's host, the provider has control over what processes and scripts you are allowed to run. As a result, the virtual server solution limits the amount of control that you can have over your site. If you are interested in exploring the benefits of some of the more exciting WWW capabilities, the lack of control and the need to confirm installation of scripts will limit your options. At the very least, these restrictions may increase the time needed to implement unique features on your WWW site.

Setup Requirements

Other than the basic requirements common with the rented WWW space solution, the virtual server also has the requirements of registering a domain name with InterNIC. This can be as simple as providing the information to your service provider; however, you may also be required to fill out the forms and submit them to InterNIC yourself.

Summary

In conclusion, the rental of WWW space can provide an excellent mechanism for bringing your WWW information to the rest of the Internet, whether it is provided through a simple home page, bulk WWW space on a commercial server, or a virtual server. Unfortunately, the high degree of bandwidth versus cost comes at a price—control and access to your WWW site. As a result of these limitations, you may not be able to develop your site as rapidly as you wish. In response to the control issue, you can connect your site via a dedicated link. This, unfortunately, costs a great deal of money to provide at the same level of bandwidth as the other options. A possible solution to this control versus cost dilemma is a server park, which is discussed in the next chapter.

Checklist

Does the ISP offer home page, rented space, and virtual servers? The following are concerns that should be addressed at the conclusion of the chapter.

Home Page

☑ Size of site?

☑ Rules for changes?

☑ Costs for a month:

☑ Is your technological knowledge limited?

☑ Do you require internal network access to Internet?

Rented Space

- ☑ What level of bandwidth is available from ISP?

- ☑ Use a local provider or international provider?

- ☑ How much space is required?

- ☑ Dialup link in place?

- ☑ Are you going to require a large amount of scripting?

- ☑ Are all the necessary utilities available on server?

- ☑ Does the WWW site provide appropriate image?

- ☑ Cost for a month:

Virtual Server

- ☑ Domain name registered?

- ☑ Is virtual server solution supported?

- ☑ How much space required?

- ☑ Extra processes required?

- ☑ Image needed?

- ☑ Control of server available?

Server Park: Cost-Effective High Bandwidth Access?

The previous chapter detailed a number of different methods of gaining access for your WWW site through renting space on a commercial server. In all cases, to one degree or another, the benefits of a rented site were shown to be offset by the lack of control that you have over these sites. Although rented space can provide good external access to your WWW site, this solution limits the benefits of access for your internal network. Also, the fact that the server is run by a commercial provider is likely to curtail the amount of access and freedom you have with that site.

One possible alternative to either rented space or dedicated connections is a hybrid connectivity solution called a server park. This chapter starts by explaining what a server park is, including the concepts behind the idea and the technical background of the solution. The chapter then examines the availability, costs, benefits and limitations, and setup requirements. When you have finished with this chapter, you will be able to identify the key uses for the server park connectivity option, and you will be able to better evaluate the option for your connectivity needs.

What is a Server Park?

As previously mentioned, a server park is a place that enables you to connect a computer to an ISP's LAN, which in turn has access to the Internet. Because LAN connectivity methods provide more-than adequate throughput in comparison to the Internet connectivity methods (Ethernet has a 10Mbps connectivity as opposed to a T1 with 1.544Mbps connectivity), your server has the connectivity equivalent of being directly attached to the T1.

A Note from the Author

The name for this connectivity option is derived from the trailer park concept in housing. Instead of owning the land that your house is built on, you can move a (relatively) portable house into a complex designed for such houses. In the case of a server park, you move a server that you own onto the LAN of your ISP in order to gain access to the ISP's Internet connectivity.

Before assessing this solution in terms of availability and costs, this section first provides some background information on the server park idea. This information includes a brief discussion on the concept behind the server park solution and the technical background of this solution.

The Concept Behind a Server Park

The server park solution combines the bandwidth benefits of rented WWW space with the control of owning the server and with maintenance through a dedicated link. This section examines two main concepts behind the server park:

⚛ High bandwidth external access

⚛ Client control over the server

High Bandwidth External Access

One of the main functional components of the server park connectivity option is that WWW access is based on the connectivity of your commercial provider rather than on the link you use to connect your internal office. Because the main problem with dedicated links is that the costs of such links are very high at lower levels and only at the higher bandwidth levels are economies of scale realized, this solution can provide more cost effective bandwidth (see Chapters 4–7 for discussion of traditional dedicated links). This truism enables large ISPs to provide service more cost effectively than smaller provider links.

The server park concept enables you to have a WWW server accessible to the Internet at data rates higher than comparable cost-dedicated links. The main problem of low-speed links is that fluctuating usage causes spikes in bandwidth requirements. Only if your usage is a small component of the overall bandwidth usage will these spikes be absorbed without severe degradation of service.

Customer Control Over a Server

The previous section describes one benefit of server parks, but high bandwidth external access is also present in all of the WWW space rental solutions. The difference between the server park and space rental solution is the added benefit that a server park provides in terms of control over the WWW site.

One of the main difficulties with all rental solutions is the lack of access and control that these solutions provide. Because the server park host is a machine that you own and operate (remotely), you can alter the services and utilities on the server at your option. This flexibility enables you to react to market changes and experiment with new technologies as they become available.

Technical Background for a Server Park

Now that the concept behind a server park has been explained, some discussion of the technical implementation of this connectivity option is in order. To better understand the server park option, two main concepts must be explained:

- ❀ LAN backbone connectivity

- ❀ The low-speed management link

LAN Backbone Connectivity

The server park is connected to the Internet through the LAN connection between the server and the IPS. Specifically, your server is added to the LAN of your ISP (needless to say, your ISP must have a LAN to support this option) by means of a high-speed connectivity option. Depending on the technology implemented by your ISP, this link will be an Ethernet (10 Mbps or 100 Mbps) or token ring network connection.

At this point, the ISP will provide you with an IP address for its network. The address enables datagrams bearing that specific address to be correctly identified with your host (routing must be set up to identify your host as part of the ISP's subnet, but most ISPs will set that up for you). After your domain name has been associated with that address, the server will be accessible by the outside world at the rate of the ISP's connectivity (generally, this is the minimum of one T1 connection).

Low-Speed Management Link

A low-speed management link from your office to the ISP can be added to the LAN connectivity of your server. This connection allows dedicated access to your server for the purposes of managing your WWW site. Simultaneously, the link can provide a low-cost connectivity option for your internal Internet access requirements.

The low-speed link can be set up in a number of different ways, but by far the most cost-effective involves a modem at either end of the link, and a host computer at your office. One modem is connected to the server in the server park (the serial interface must be configured as an IP address from a separate network or subnet than is used for the LAN interface (Ethernet)), and the other modem is connected to the internal office host. A standard telephone link is provided between the two modems (the speed of which should be 28.8 Kbps if you plan to support anything more than electronic mail over the link).

The internal host must have two IP subnet addresses, one for the serial link (the same subnet as the server's serial IP address) and one for the internal network interface. With the proper configuration of the two serial connections—the server park server and the internal host—e-mail can be routed to the desk of each individual user, and access to other Internet services (WWW, ftp, news, and so on) can be provided at the desktop.

Availability

Generally, the availability of server parks is somewhat low. Given the potential benefits of the server park solution, why have the number of server park facilities not increased? The low level of availability stems from three main factors:

❀ Only local ISPs can provide service

❀ The security risks of a server park solution

❀ The amount of resources required by the ISP to support server parks

Necessity of Having a Local Provider

The first limiting factor in the provision of server park service is that the server park be in the local geographical area of your operations. Because your local area does not have as great of a choice of providers as the entire continent (or world) can provide, this requirement limits your choices. This local provider requirement stems from two main issues:

❀ The physical setup of the server

❀ Access required for the continued maintenance of the server

Physical Access Requirements: Setup

Although most server configuration and setup can be done before taking the server to the ISP's site, it is inevitable that some setup will be required at the ISP's site. This requirement stems from the fact that your server must be installed on the ISP's LAN and configured to communicate effectively between the LAN and the serial interfaces.

It is recommended that your server park be easily accessible in terms of physical distance. Even if the server installation initially requires only a small amount of time, having the site too far away from your office is not practical because unforeseen problems can result in additional trips to the site.

A Note from the Author

Trust us when we say that unforeseen problems can and likely will arise. When we were setting up our server in a server park, we did the majority of the configuration in our office, and did not take the server to the ISP site until our staff had the networking (including the local link) properly configured.

Our plan was to accomplish the remainder of the service configuration (including the WWW daemon configuration) by means of the local link. Unfortunately, when we arrived at the local site, the server would not even turn on! After a couple hours of removing devices and checking all components, we took the server back to our office. Only later did we discover the cause of our problems—that the server's processor was not firmly attached to the motherboard!

Access Requirements: Maintenance

Understanding that the unforeseen can happen, the second reason for having local access to your server is because it will need ongoing maintenance. Even if you never have a piece of hardware fail (and if this is the case, please let me know what hardware you use), you will undoubtedly need to have access to the server for the purposes of upgrading and maintaining your WWW site. Although the nature of the Internet makes telnet access possible from anywhere in the world, the amount of access required may result in the necessity of a dedicated connection.

Because a server park allows the possibility of a dedicated link right off the server (for little or no additional cost), a need exists to be able to establish a connection directly to the server. Dedicated connection costs for local loop access increases with the distance over which the link must be maintained, so you are generally better off having a local provider.

Security Concerns Limit Availability

The second concern that limits the availability of server park connectivity options is one that both you and the ISP will have—concern over security. You, the client, will at the very least desire access to your server for the purposes of emergency maintenance. Because failure could occur at any time (and because down time is devastating to a site's viability), you will inevitably require an agreement for after-hours access to the server.

This access, critical to the maintenance of the server, represents a security risk for the ISP. Unless your server is in a separate complex behind lock and key, you will need to either have direct access to the ISP's site or be able to call an ISP technician for access. In either case, the access will cause concern for most ISPs, because their servers are also their livelihood.

A second option is for you to allow the ISP the necessary information about your server so that the ISP can perform any on-site maintenance that is required. Obviously, this represents a security risk to your system because access would have to be at the root or superuser level. If information on the server is sensitive in any way, allowing the ISP access may present a problem. Doing so will likely also increase the overall cost of your connectivity solution.

ISP Resource Limitations

The third limiting factor to the availability of server park service is the large resource requirements that server parks place on ISPs. The resource limitations force the ISPs that wish to offer the server park option to either increase their resources or lower the quality of their service. The three main factors are as follows:

❀ The bandwidth required by ISPs

❀ The need for an internal network

❀ The need for physical space for equipment

Bandwidth Usage

Because the ISP cannot control the types and amount of information provided by the server park, the ISP is less able to plan for the amount of bandwidth required to maintain an adequate service level for all its customers. Given the congestion problems that can occur on most networks, the ISP must be very careful not to allow too many servers into a server park. For example, let's assume that the ISP has five servers in a server park, each using one GB of bandwidth in the first month of service. If bandwidth usage increases to 3 GB in the second month of service, the provider's service level will decrease. If the server park option is allowed, the ISP must monitor usage, and may require a minimum bandwidth purchase each month to offset the increase in the bandwidth required for the entire network.

Internal Network Required

A very basic but not always present feature that is required for server park service is an internal network at the ISP's site. Without a high-speed network available for your server to park on, the entire scenario becomes unfeasible. Although single connections to the ISP server can be used, this type of solution can result in bottlenecks of information if the ISP host cannot keep up with routing requests.

Note

Given the relative ease in which an Internet server can be set up, a number of smaller ISPs exist that do not require an internal network. After all, if you have only one computer, you do not need a network! You should be very careful about using a provider that does not have the resources available to manage a server park. Because of the added

> configuration difficulties that the server park solution creates, you are better off using a provider that understands the technical management of this solution.

Server Hardware Space Required

Physical park space is the third resource requirement for service providers that may limit the number of ISPs that can provide the server park solution. Because servers should be housed in a secure and climate-controlled area, the provider needs a suitable area for each server (including access areas for the systems administrators of the servers). As well as being secure from theft, the servers should be on a consistent power supply, with an Uninterruptable Power Supply (UPS) backup system if possible.

Costs

Because of the limited number of providers who offer the server park solution, and the limited number of spaces available for each provider, the costs for a server park are not well established. To best estimate your costs, you should compare a collection of similar services and find an aggregate total. Breaking the costs down into the initial costs and the ongoing costs is useful.

Initial Costs

Unlike the WWW space rental solutions, the server park solution has two major initial costs:

- ❋ Purchasing a server

- ❋ Setting up a server

Because both cost issues need to be addressed up front, the server park solution is both a more permanent and a more risky solution. If you are not certain that your WWW site will be an ongoing part of your information distribution solution, then the investments required may not be worthwhile. Still, as is shown by the following discussion of the two major cost items—purchasing and setting up the server—some of the risk can be alleviated by proper planning.

Purchasing the Server

By far the largest component of the initial costs of a server park is the purchase of the server. Because your server needs are determined by the functionality of your WWW site, advice here on a particular brand name of hardware or software is pointless. Still, you may want to consider what you will do with the server should you decide to shut down your WWW server some time in the future. If your office uses Intel PCs, then you may want to consider one of the many server solutions available for that hardware platform. On the other hand, server workstation class companies (Sun, HP, DEC, and so on) offer excellent integrated WWW server packages. The solution from Sun is embodied in a number of configured systems that include all of the software needed to setup a WWW server. As well, the support packaged with the systems can make the difference between a sucessful site and one that fails.

Setting Up the Server

Although the functionality of your WWW site and your preferences will largely determine your hardware needs, in most cases, the operating system that you choose will determine the time and cost required for your server setup. With some commercially integrated products, the setup is relatively simple, and your system administrator may be able to work it out without professional help. On the other hand, freeware or shareware operating systems may require greater setup time, but save money in purchase costs. No one solution provides the best option for all situations. If your organization is unable to provide the technical expertise needed for the setup of the more difficult (less polished) solutions, then a packaged solution (such as that from Sun or Hewlett-Packard) may be worth the money.

A Note from the Author

The process of setting up an Internet server for a server park can be very difficult. For example, setting up a server using Intel hardware and a freeware operating system (such as Linux or FreeBSD) requires a vast knowledge of UNIX operating systems and the hardware being used (especially modems). In one installation in which we were involved, the whole process took more than twenty hours of technical time!

Ongoing Costs

After your server is installed, you will also have to pay a number of ongoing costs for the connectivity solution. Three components of monthly cost determine the overall monthly cost of the solution:

⬡ Monthly site fee

⬡ Charges for bandwidth usage

⬡ Charges for your local link

Whatever the total costs of the server park solution might be, you should ensure that a large enough dedicated link designed to meet your needs is not less expensive than the total costs associated for the server park solution. If a sufficiently large dedicated link is less than the server park option, then your site can be connected to the Internet in a more cost effective manner via the dedicated link.

Monthly Site Fee

Monthly site fees are the means that most ISPs use to limit their exposure to over-usage of bandwidth. By charging a monthly fee, the ISP can guarantee a certain amount of revenue. As a result of this revenue, the ISP can provide the services and bandwidth needed to buffer its network in the event that your server uses a lot of bandwidth. (The next section on bandwidth discusses a deterrent to using vast amounts of bandwidth.)

Because the purpose of the site fee is to guarantee revenue for the ISP, the breakdown for the fee's components will likely be based on the following items:

1. The ISP will likely charge you for the network node that your server will occupy on the internal LAN.

2. The ISP will charge you for a set amount of server bandwidth that it provides each month.

3. The ISP will charge you for physical space and resources (such as power) used by the server.

Also, some ISPs may include an access fee to cover the staff time required to monitor your access to the server.

No matter how the site fee is broken down, ultimately you will be charged a base monthly fee for your server. If the ISP is willing to allow access during office hours and emergency access for after hours, as well as provide you with 2 GB of throughput (a conservative usage level on a dedicated 28.8 link—the lowest cost dedicated link), then you should expect to pay from $300 to $500, depending on the costs of dedicated links in your area.

Note

Because a server park offers a minimum of a dedicated link to your internal office that is equal to the level of a dedicated 28.8Kbps connection, it is not unreasonable to expect the server park option to be at least as expensive as the dedicated 28.8Kbps connection. As well, the fee will likely be more because of the extra benefit (other than bandwidth) of T1 or better access for your WWW site. The other fees for bandwidth and local link will simply be the cost recovered by the ISP.

Bandwidth Usage

Beyond the bandwidth supplied with your site fee, you will be charged a bandwidth fee for bandwidth used beyond what is originally allocated to your site. Although the service provider will undoubtedly charge you a rate near to the rate charged to dedicated links and virtual servers, you should keep in mind that the cost for a dedicated T1 can be as low as $3,200 per month. Add to that a technician to manage the server and link—say, $4,000 per month—and you are looking at a cost level of $7,000 to $8,000 per month. If a provider charges $80 per GB, then using more than 100 GB per month on average would be your break-even point. If your site is going to use any more bandwidth, you should reconsider the server park solution.

Local Link

Even though your ISP should not charge you anything for the local dedicated link because you are providing the modem and are paying for any bandwidth used, you will be responsible for the local telephone loop. Your connection will be based on modem connections, so a regular telephone should be sufficient. Just remember that you will be required to pay for two telephone lines, one at either end of your local loop.

Hardware Requirements

Although the hardware required for the server park solution is not too different from the hardware required for any WWW server, a few specific requirements for server park solutions do exist. To better understand the needed hardware, this section discusses the three main issues with server park requirements:

❋ ISP site requirements

❋ Server issues

❋ The site-to-office link hardware

This section does not recommend specific hardware (due to various service provider constraints), but instead puts forth some of the critical issues surrounding hardware for this connectivity option.

Site-Specific Requirements

The first major hardware issue that you should resolve prior to choosing an ISP is that of site-specific requirements. These requirements fall into two main categories:

❋ Requirements for technical reasons

❋ Requirements for administrative reasons

In the first case, the requirements are situation-oriented and are limitations that cannot be changed. The second set of requirements are human preferences and can be changed if the need evolves.

Technical Requirements for Site Hardware

This category of requirements generally is the result of the type of networking solution required to connect your server to the internal LAN. If the ISP uses a twisted-pair Ethernet network, then your server must also support this type of network (although this does not prevent you from supporting multiple networking methods in addition to your ISP's networking system). In addition, your operating system must be able to support the type of IP networking that the ISP requires for correctly routing your IP datagrams. If your operating system does not support multihomed IP addressing, then using the server with an administrative serial link is not possible.

Because your technical requirements are dependent on the technology previously implemented by the ISP (in the case of networking) or the requirements of the connectivity solution (in the case of a multihomed operating system), being constrained by these requirements is acceptable. Even so, you may want to shop around for the ISP that best matches your hardware capabilities (or desires).

A Note from the Author

For example, when we were looking for a place to park our server, one of the local ISP options required any server park server to be a Sun system. Because the hardware we used was not a Sun, and we did not want to purchase a new server, we shopped around and eventually found an ISP who would accept our Linux-based server.

Administrative Requirements for Site Hardware

Although technical requirements for site hardware are generally acceptable and unavoidable (without changing ISPs), administrative requirements are generally unnecessary and should be frowned upon. Administrative requirements are generally hardware requirements imposed by an ISP in the name of operational efficiency. For example, the ISP may require that all servers be Sun machines running Solaris. The reason generally given is that the systems administrators of the ISP are familiar with these systems and, in the event of a failure, they would be able to assist.

This reasoning may be true but it is not necessarily valid. After all, the advantage of a server park is that it allows you to control your own server. If you are comfortable with an Intel machine running Linux, then you should be allowed to install that server. Forcing you to adapt to the capabilities of the ISP defeats the purpose, and may end up costing considerable amounts for support. Even though you should happily accept suggestions from your ISP, the final decision should always be in your hands unless technology, not people, requires otherwise.

A Note from the Author

When we were examining ISPs in our area for a server park solution, we came across a provider that required specific hardware for servers. Although the ISP claimed that the benefits of specific hardware were worth the hassle, we found not only that the required hardware was expensive in terms of price to performance, but that the maintenance of this hardware would require staff retooling or outside contract. Needless to say, we shopped around for another provider and found one that understood the meaning of service in Internet Service Provider!

Servers

Obviously, given the solution's name, the server for the server park solution is a key piece of hardware. When looking for a server, you should pay careful attention to three main areas:

- Networking hardware
- Processing power
- Storage capability (both RAM and drives)

Networking Hardware

Because of your need to connect your server to the ISP's backbone, you must make sure that you purchase a networking interface that matches. The task is not as simple as choosing any card that matches the interface. You must also ensure that your card will work with the chosen operating system. In addition, some care should be paid to the quality of your card. Because the networking card will be responsible for conveying the information from your server to the Internet link, the speed at which your card can accomplish this task is very important. Generally, the card should be of a higher quality (32-bit on a fast bus interface) than common networking devices (Global Village Consulting uses an Intel Ether Express Pro, although a number of other good cards are available).

Processing Capability

Although the networking interface controls how quickly information travels down the networking pipe to the Internet interface, the processing power of your computer determines how well your WWW server handles the internal network's routing requests. Even so, a 386 25 Mz can run a WWW server; the issue is one of processor speed. Processor speed is based on the complexity of your site—the more complex the site, the faster processor required. Generally speaking, unless the server is running a huge WWW site with a number of processor-intense functions, then the server need not be too robust (a Pentium 100 Mz or equivalent will suffice).

RAM, More RAM, and Drives

Even though the processor speed is not the critical component of your system, your server's RAM makes all the difference in the world. Because UNIX systems rely heavily on *swap space* (drive space used as virtual memory), it is very difficult to actually run out of memory (used for processing WWW requests, buffering search results, or running processes for clients). Unfortunately, drive space is about 1,000 times slower than RAM, so if your server is forced to use swap space rather than RAM, the process will slow down horribly. As a result, the more RAM your server has, the better (within reason, although we have seen a number of servers requiring more than of 100 MB of RAM). A simple server should be able to function on as little as 32 MB of RAM.

You should try to ensure the expandability of your drives because online files can grow rapidly. You should also consider investing in a Redundant Array of Inexpensive Disks (RAID) drive system if the WWW server is a critical system in your organization. The advantages of a RAID drive system are that if one of the drives fails, you are able to take the broken drive out and replace it without shutting down the system. To be even more secure in the knowledge of your data's integrity, the system can be "hot" swapped—allowing the replacement of drives on-the-fly. A reliable backup device should also be added to any system.

Site-to-Office Connection

The final hardware requirement for the server park connectivity solution is that which is required for the server site-to-office link. Because this link provides only a server management tool and staff access to Internet resources, the link is not as critical as most dedicated links and you may wish to examine the possibility of using two modems (one at either location) for connectivity, rather than a router(s).

Although routers provide a more transparent link between the two sites, with a little effort and configuration, most hosts can supply similar functions. If your internal network hosts are unable to provide routing functionality, then a router on that side of the link can be substituted for the modem. No matter what solution is chosen, you should make sure that the link is automatically reestablished in the event that the line is dropped. Link re-establishment can be performed by a simple re-dial script on either the host or router.

Tip

Because your server in the server park is designed to be accessed by the rest of the Internet, you may want to make the internal host or router responsible for the re-dial attempts. This setup allows you to disable the modem or router's call-answering functionality, thus eliminating a potential security risk (spoofing) for your internal network.

Benefits and Limitations

Of all of the connectivity options presented in this book, the server park solution provides the greatest degree of benefits for the costs associated. Although the server park is not the best option in all situations, you should take a serious look at this option as a comparison point for your connectivity solution. After detailing the potential benefits of the server park, this section presents some of the possible concerns about this solution.

Benefits

As mentioned previously, the server park connectivity option provides a robust solution that effectively meets a number of the major requirements for WWW Internet connectivity. The main issues that can be addressed by the server park solution are as follows:

- ❋ The control over services

- ❋ Access to high bandwidth for the external clients

- ❋ Added benefits for the internal network

Greater Control Over the Server

One of the most important benefits of the server park solution, and the benefit that sets this option apart from the rental options discussed in the last chapter, is the degree of control that the server park option allows. Because the server in question belongs to your organization and is solely within your control, you can change and add services to the server as needed. Having this flexibility enables you to add files, modify files, increase functionality through added services, and provide access.

Although access to the server (in a physical sense) may be more restrictive than in a dedicated connection solution, the practical result may be similar. This similarity hinges on the fact that most of the configuration and alteration of the service can be done remotely by means of a telnet session.

A Note from the Author

To illustrate the possibility of remote management of a WWW server, you need look only as far as our company. One significant part of our business is managing Internet servers for clients. This service is performed by our technical staff without ever physically traveling to the location. Although managing the servers over a relatively slow (28.8 Kbps) link may slow the process, the text-based command functions limit the amount of data that needs to be transferred.

High Bandwidth versus Cost

Although the server park allows access similar to that of the dedicated connectivity options discussed previously, the server park option avoids one of the main problems with dedicated connection solution: the high cost of bandwidth. In the case of the server park, the potential bandwidth of your WWW site is limited only by the bandwidth that the ISP has available. Because this should be no less than T1 levels, you can provide your site to the world at T1 speeds for much less than T1 costs. The server park solution, therefore, can provide you with higher bandwidth than otherwise affordable, especially if your overall usage is relatively low.

Link to Internal Network

The third and final major benefit that results from the server park solution is its spin-off benefits for your internal network as a result of its dedicated management link. Even though the speed of the link is limited to 28.8 Kbps (although you may wish to increase this speed, if available, through an ISDN or dedicated 56Kbps connection from the telephone company), you can provide full Internet access to your entire network. If, instead, you have a network that is too large to support full interactive Internet services, you can at least provide e-mail services to all staff with no additional costs.

Limitations

Although the server park solution addresses a number of the requirements for WWW site connectivity, you should keep in mind a few areas of concern, including:

- ❋ Physical access restrictions to your server

- ❋ Potentially high bandwidth costs

- ❋ Limited size of the site-to-office connection

Physical Access to Your Server

The first concern that you should consider when looking at the server park solution for your connectivity is the limitation of physical access to your server. Because the degree of restriction will depend on your relationship with your service provider, this restriction may not prove to be a problem. Obviously, if you have a key to the site and full 24-hour access, the restriction does not concern you.

A Note from the Author

Obviously, most service providers will not allow you full access to the server park site. Traditionally, the access will be restricted to the office hours for emergency and emergency access for a fee after hours. Although this policy is understandable on the part of the ISPs, you do not necessarily need to accept these restrictions. If you can develop a decent degree of trust and communication with your ISP, you should be able to work out a better scenario. For example, in our situation, we have unlimited daytime access to the server and emergency 24-hour access free of charge.

Bandwidth Costs

The second major concern that you should examine is bandwidth costs at the server park. Given that you can increase the services available through your server at your discretion, you should pay close attention to the effect that these services will have on your bandwidth usage. If your server will consistently be using considerable bandwidth, you may be better off with a large dedicated link to your office. The possibility of this scenario arising brings about the final possible concern: the site-to-office connection.

Limited Site-to-Office Connection

To maintain the cost effectiveness of the server park solution, your link will most likely be limited to a 28.8Kbps serial connection. As a result, the link may not be able to fully supply your office with the access you require. Although a 28.8 Kbps link can possibly support 10 to 20 individuals with moderate use, larger networks will not be able to maintain full access over such a link. If internal access is a major concern for your organization, then the server park solution may not meet your requirements.

Setup Requirements

Because the server park option requires the same setup and maintenance of a WWW server as does the dedicated connection option, the setup requirements for the two solutions are very similar. Both options require you to install and configure the required software on your server, including DNS, WWW servers, ftp, and any custom scripts. As well, your connectivity will depend on the reliability of your systems because access to your server may be limited. As a result, the issue of maintenance takes an even greater role. Two key issues should be addressed before selecting the server park as your connectivity option:

⚛ Do you have personnel with systems and networking administration experience?

⚛ Do your personnel have good working knowledge of routing, subnetting, maintenance, and backups?

Personnel

One of the most important setup requirements of the server park solution is quality personnel. Because your WWW site will depend on the maintenance and setup of your server, having quality personnel on hand is as critical for the server park option as it is to the dedicated connection option. In addition, your personnel should have experience with LAN administration and networking in order to connect your server up to the ISP's LAN and to provide the serial link to your office.

Knowledge

When choosing your personnel, you should pay special attention to their abilities to deal with routing and subnetting issues, hardware maintenance, and backup procedures. Because the WWW server will need to be multihomed to provide the necessary connectivity, including the local link and LAN connectivity, your personnel should be familiar with IP addressing needs and subnetting. To ensure that all e-mail and datagrams are correctly forwarded to and from the internal network, a good knowledge of routing is also useful.

The second main area of knowledge useful in this solution is that of hardware maintenance and data backup procedures. Because the quality of your WWW services depends on the reliability of your server, your personnel should be cognizant of potential hardware failures and have appropriate plans in place in case of failure. In the case of drive failure, the proper use of backup procedures will ensure data recovery and minimize the amount of site downtime.

Summary

After reading this book, you should be in a better position to correctly identify your need in terms of Internet connectivity. Although the possible options and costs will vary according to your local area, you will understand, at the very least, some of the general benefits and problems of each possible solution. In the end, no one solution provides a perfect solution for every situation.

Even so, I believe that the server park solution is often overlooked as a connectivity option. I have found that this option combines a number of the best characteristics of dedicated connection and rented WWW space. The result is a robust solution that may provide a good medium-level connectivity option for most organizations.

A Note from the Author

We hope that you have learned enough to make the decisions necessary to put your site online. If you have any comments or suggestions, please feel free to contact the authors via e-mail. Until we meet on the Net, may your connection be strong and the surfing good.

Leon Salvail—lsalvail@global-village.net

Steve Besler—skb@global-village.net

Sacha Mallais—sacha@global-village.net

The Partners of Global Village Consulting—http://www.global-village.net

Checklist

The following are concerns that should be addressed at the conclusion of the chapter.

☑ Is the server park option available?

☑ What is the connectivity of the ISP?

☑ Do you need the control over your site?

☑ What level of access to your server is provided?

☑ Is the bandwidth cost equivalent to rented space solution?

☑ Do you have the hardware available?

☑ Do you have the personnel to maintain the server?

☑ Routing available from ISP?

☑ Addressing in place?

☑ Domain name registered?

☑ Local link option available?

Introduction

As anyone who has used the Internet can tell you, the information available is outstanding, but at the same time the fluidity of the data can cause some problems in keeping yourself up-to-date. In the case of finding an ISP, the following listings are as up-to-date as we can possibly manage in this book, but at the same time, you should only use them as a rough guide—a starting point.

Information about the ISP List

The information provided in this book was generously provided by Paul Celestin of:

Celestin Company, Inc.

5652 NE Meadow Road

Kingston, WA 98346-9505

Phone: 360 297 8091

Fax: 360 297 8092

Email: info@celestin.com

For more information regarding Celestin Company, please visit their Web site at:

http://www.celestin.com/

Up-to-Date Text Listing

An up-to-date text version of Providers of Commercial Internet Access (POCIA) Directory can be obtained at:

```
ftp://ftp.celestin.com/biz/celestin/pocia/pocia.txt
```

You may also retrieve the latest copy (as well as additional information on Celestin Company and its products) using email. For information on how this works, send a blank message to:

```
info@celestin.com
```

If you have Web access, try **http://www.celestin.com/pocia/** for the hypertext version of this list, which includes addresses, telephone numbers, fax numbers, email addresses, and pricing.

Celestin Company Caveat

Copyright 1994–1996 by Celestin Company, Inc. All rights reserved worldwide. The information in the text directory is provided as-is and without any express or implied warranties, including, without limitation, the implied warranties of merchantability and fitness for a particular purpose. You may use the information in the text directory for noncommercial purposes only. Contact Celestin Company if you want to use the text directory for a commercial purpose. For example, if you would like to post the text file on a public BBS, you may do so. However, if you would like to reproduce the text file (in whole or in part) in a newsletter, book, article, or other commercial media, please contact the author:

```
Email: gvc@cafe.net
```

All the information in this directory was supplied to Celestin Company directly by the service providers and is subject to change without notice. Celestin Company does not endorse any of the providers in this directory. If you do not see a provider listed for your area, please do not ask us about it, because we only know about providers in this directory. This directory is brought to you as a public service. Celestin Company does not receive any compensation from the providers listed here. Since Internet service providers come and go, and frequently change their offers, we strongly urge you to contact them for additional information and/or restrictions.

Some Additional Information

The listings of Internet service providers in the U.S. and Canada are sorted by area code. Information provided includes the service provider's name, address, voice phone number, fax phone number, Web site URL, email address, and the levels of connectivity offered by this provider.

Free Service Providers

For the cost of a long distance phone call, you can dial any of these Internet providers and give the Internet a try.

Internet Providers		
Organization	Modem Number	Email Address
Free.org (Shell, SLIP, PPP)	715 743 1600	info@free.org
Free.I.Net (must dial via AT&T)	801 471 2266	info@free.i.net
SLIPNET (Shell, SLIP, PPP)	217 792 2777	info@slip.net

Listing of ISPs

AGIS (Apex Global Information Services)
22015 West Outer Drive
Dearborn, MI 48124 USA
Phone: 313 730 1130
Fax: 313 563 6119
Email: info@agis.net
Levels of Connectivity
Supported: T1

ANS
1875 Campus Commons
Drive, Suite 220
Reston, VA 22091-1552 USA
Phone: 800 456 8267 or 703
758 7700
Fax: 703 758 7717
Email: info@ans.net
Web site: http://www.ans.net
Levels of Connectivity
Supported: SLIP, PPP

BBN Planet
150 Cambridgepark Drive,
Cambridge, MA 02140 USA
Phone: 617 873 2905
Fax: 617 873 3599
Email: info@bbnplanet.com
Web site: http://
www.bbnplanet.com.
Levels of Connectivity
Supported: 56kb, T1

Concentric Research Corporation
400 41st Street
Bay City, MI 48708 USA
Phone: 800 745 2747
Fax: 517 895 0529
Email: info@cris.com
Web site: http://www.cris.com
Levels of Connectivity
Supported: Shell, SLIP,
56kb, T1

CRL Network Services
One Kearny Street, Suite 1450
San Francisco, CA 94108 USA
Phone: 415 837 5300
Fax: 415 392 9000
Email: sales@crl.com
Web site: http://www.crl.com
Levels of Connectivity
Supported: Shell, PPP, SLIP,
UUCP, 56kb, T1

DataXchange Network, Inc
P.O. Box 5272
Clearwater, FL 34618 USA
Phone: 800 863 1550
Fax: 703 903 7413
Email: info@dx.net
Levels of Connectivity
Supported: 56kb, T1

Delphi Internet Services Corporation

1030 Massachusetts Avenue,
Cambridge, MA 02138 USA

Phone: 800 695 4005

Fax: 617 491 6642

Email: info@delphi.com

Web site: http://
www.delphi.com

Levels of Connectivity
Supported: Shell

EarthLink Network, Inc.

3171 Los Feliz Blvd., Suite 203
Los Angeles, CA 90039 USA

Phone: 213 644 9500

Fax: 213 644 9510

Email: info@earthlink.net

Web site: http://
www.earthlink.net

Levels of Connectivity
Supported: SLIP, PPP, ISDN,
56kb, T1

Exodus Communications, Inc.

948 Benecia Avenue,
Sunnyvale, CA 94086 USA

Phone: 408 522 8450

Fax: 408 736 6843

Email: info@exodus.net

Web site: http://
www.exodus.net

4GL Corporation

12314 Rocky Knoll Drive
P. O. Box 820486
Houston, TX 77282-0486 USA

Phone: 713 589 8077

Email: mailto:info@4gl.com

Web site: http://www.4gl.com

Levels of Connectivity
Supported: PPP, ISDN,
56kb, T1

Global Connect, Inc.

497 Queens Creek Road
Williamsburg, VA 23185

Phone: 804 229 4484

Fax: 804 229 6557

Levels of Connectivity
Supported: SLIP, PPP, UUCP

Global Enterprise Services, Inc. (The JvNCnet)

3 Independence Way
Princeton, NJ 08540 USA

Phone: 1-800-35-TIGER

Fax: 1-609-897-7310

Email: market@jvnc.net

Web site: http://www-
ges.jvnc.net

Levels of Connectivity Supported: SLIP, ISDN, 56kb, T1

Information Access Technologies, Inc.

HoloNet Internet Service
2115 Milvia Street, 4th Floor
Berkeley, CA 94704-1112 USA

Phone: 510 704 0160

Fax: 510 704 8019

Email: info@holonet.net

Web site: http://
www.holonet.net

Levels of Connectivity
Supported: Shell, SLIP, PPP,
UUCP, ISDN, 56kb, T1

Institute for Global Communications

18 DeBoom St.
San Francisco, CA 94107 USA

Phone: 415 442 0220

Fax: 415 546 1794

Email: igc-info@igc.apc.org

Web site: http://
www.igc.apc.org

Levels of Connectivity
Supported: PPP, SLIP, UUCP

Liberty Information Network

446 S Anaheim Hills Road,
Suite 102
Anaheim, CA 92807 USA

Phone: 800 218 5157 or 714
996 9999

Fax: 714 961 8700 Attn: ISP
INFO

Email: info@liberty.com

Web site: http://
www.liberty.com

MIDnet

201 North Eighth Street
Suite 421
Lincoln, NE 68508 USA

Phone: 800 682 5550

Fax: 402 472 0240

Email: info@mid.net

Web site: http://www.mid.net

Levels of Connectivity
Supported: 56kb, T1

Moran Communications
1576 Sweet Home Road
Amherst, NY 14228 USA
Phone: 716 639 1254
Fax: 716 636 3630
Email: info@moran.com
Web site: http://
www.moran.com
Levels of Connectivity
Supported: PPP, UUCP, ISDN,
56kb, T1

NETCOM On-Line Commu-nications Services, Inc.
3031 Tisch Way
San Jose, CA 95128 USA
Phone: 800 353 6600 or 408
983 5950
Fax: 408 241 9145
Email: info@netcom.com
Web site: http://
www.netcom.com
Levels of Connectivity
Supported: Shell, Direct,
56kb, T1

Network 99, Inc.
Phone: 703 442 7353
East Coast
602 780 7533 West Coast
800 NET 99IP
Levels of Connectivity
Supported: T1

Netrex, Inc
3000 Town Center
Suite 1100
Southfield, MI 48075 USA
Phone: 800 3 NETREX
Fax: 810 352 2375
Email: info@netrex.com
Web site: http://
www.netrex.com
Levels of Connectivity
Supported: ISDN, 56kb, T1

Performance Systems International
510 Huntmar Park Drive
Herndon, VA 22070
Phone: 800 827 7482
Fax   703 904 1207
Levels of Connectivity
Supported: PPP, UUCP

Portal Information Network
20863 Stevens Creek Blvd.
Suite 200
Cupertino, CA 95014 USA
Phone: 408 973 9111
Fax: 408 725 1580
Email: info@portal.com
Web site: http://
www.portal.com
Levels of Connectivity Sup-
ported: Shell, SLIP, PPP,
UUCP

SprintLink
VARESA0115
12502 Sunrise Valley Dr.
Reston, VA 22096 USA
Phone: 703 827 7240 or 800
817 7755
Email: info@sprint.net
Web site: http://
www.sprintlink.net
Levels of Connectivity Sup-
ported: SLIP, PPP, UUCP,
ISDN, 56kb, T1

Structured Network Systems, Inc.
15635 SE 114th Ave.
Suite 201
Clackamas, OR 97015 USA
Phone: 800 881 0962
Fax: 503 656 3235
Email: sales@structured.net
Web site: http://
www.structured.net
Levels of Connectivity Sup-
ported: 56kb, T1

The ThoughtPort Authority Inc.
2000 E. Broadway
Suite 242
Columbia, MO 65201 USA
Phone: 800 ISP 6870
Fax: 314 474 4122
Email: info@thoughtport.com
Web site: http://
www.thoughtport.com
Levels of Connectivity Sup-
ported: SLIP, PPP, ISDN,
56kb, T1

WareNet

26081 Merit Circle #116
Laguna Hills, CA 92653 USA
Phone: 714 348 3295
Fax: 714 348 8665
Email: info@ware.net
Web site: http://www.ware.net
Levels of Connectivity Supported: Shell, SLIP, PPP, ISDN, 56kb, T1

Zocalo Engineering

2355 Virginia Street
Berkeley, CA 94709-1315 USA
Phone: 510 540 8000
Fax: 510 548 1891
Email: info@zocalo.net
Web site: http://
www.zocalo.net/frompocia.html
Levels of Connectivity Supported: Shell, SLIP, PPP, 56kb, 128kb, 384kb, T1

Freenets

Free.Org, USA

Levels of Connectivity Supported: Shell, SLIP, PPP
Email: info@free.org
Web site: http://
www.free.org/

Free.I.Net

Levels of Connectivity Supported: Shell, SLIP, PPP

SLIPNET

25 Stillman Street, #200
San Francisco, CA 94107
Phone: 415 281 3132
Fax: 415 281 4498
Levels of Connectivity Supported: Shell, SLIP, PPP

ISPs for Area Code 201

Carroll-Net, Inc.

162 Elm Ave.
Bogota, NJ 07603 USA
Phone: 201 488 1332
Email: info@carroll.com
Web site: http://
www.carroll.com
Levels of Connectivity Supported: Shell, SLIP, PPP

Crystal Palace Networking, Inc.

287 Newton-Sparta Road
Newton, NJ 07871 USA
Phone: 201 300 0881
Fax: 201 300 0691
Email:
info@crystal.palace.net
Web site: http://
www.palace.net
Levels of Connectivity Supported: Shell, PPP

Digital Express Group, Inc.

6006 Greenbelt Road
Suite 228
Greenbelt, MD 20770 USA
Phone: 301 847 5000 or 301 847 5050
Fax: 301 847 5215
Email: info@digex.net
Web site: http://
www.digex.net
Levels of Connectivity Supported: Shell, SLIP, PPP, 56kb, T1

Eclipse Internet Access

P.O. Box 512
Plainfield, NJ 07061 USA
Phone: 800 483 1223
Fax: 908 755 6379
Email: info@eclipse.net
Web site: http://
www.eclipse.net
Levels of Connectivity Supported: PPP, 56kb, T1

Galaxy Networks

8 Fox Hollow Road
Ramsey, NJ 07446 USA
Phone: 201 825 2310
Fax: 201 825 2356
Email: info@galaxy.net
Web site: http://
www.galaxy.net
Levels of Connectivity Supported: Shell, SLIP, PPP, UUCP, 56kb, T1

GBN InternetAccess

83A Burlews Court
Hackensack, NJ 07601 USA
Phone: 201 343 6427
Fax: 201 343 6110
Email: gbninfo@gbn.net
Web site: http://www.gbn.net
Levels of Connectivity Supported: Shell, SLIP, PPP, UUCP, ISDN, 56kb, T1

I-2000 Inc.

416 Main Street
Metuchen, NJ 08840 USA
Phone: 800 464 3820
Fax: 908 906 2396
Email: info@i-2000.com
Web site: http://www.
i-2000.com
Levels of Connectivity Supported: SLIP, PPP, 56kb, T1

INTAC Access Corporation

256 Broad Avenue

Palisades Park, NJ 07650 USA

Phone: 800 50 INTAC

Fax: 201 944 1434

Email: info@intac.com

Web site: http://
www.intac.com

Levels of Connectivity Supported: Shell, SLIP, PPP, UUCP, ISDN, 56kb, T1

Interactive Networks, Inc.

250 East 17th Street

Paterson, NJ 07524 USA

Phone: 201 881 1878 or 1 800 561 1878

Fax: 201 881 1788

Email: info@interactive.net

Web site: http://
www.interacitve.net

Levels of Connectivity Supported: Shell, SLIP, PPP, UUCP, ISDN, 56kb, T1

Intercall, Inc

33 Route 17 South

Rutherford, NJ 07073 USA

Phone: 800 758 7329

Fax: 201 939 2507

Email: sales@intercall.com

Web site: http://
www.intercall.com

Levels of Connectivity Supported: SLIP, PPP

InterCom Online

1412 Avenue M, Suite 2428

Brooklyn, NY 11230

Phone: 212 714 7183

Levels of Connectivity Supported: Shell

The Internet Connection Corp.

906 Summit Ave.

Jersey City, NJ 07302 USA

Phone: 201 435 4414

Fax: 201 451 7240

Email: info@cnct.com

Web site: http://cnct.com

Levels of Connectivity Supported: Shell, SLIP, PPP, UUCP, 56kb

Internet Online Services

294 State Street

Hackensack, NJ 07601

Phone: 201 928 1000 x226

Fax: 201 928 1057

Levels of Connectivity Supported: Shell, SLIP, PPP

Lightning Internet Services, LLC

327C Sagamore Avenue

Mineola, NY 11501 USA

Phone: 516 248 8400

Fax: 516 248 8897

Email: sales@lightning.net

Web site: http://
www.lightning.net

Levels of Connectivity Supported: ISDN, 56kb, T1

Mordor International BBS

Jersey City, New Jersey

Fax: 201 433 4222

Levels of Connectivity Supported: Shell

New York Net

Hollis Hills, NY 11427-1416

Phone: 718 776 6811

Fax: 718 217 9407

Levels of Connectivity Supported: SLIP, PPP, 56kb, T1

NIC - Neighborhood Internet Connection

637 Wyckoff Ave #294

Wyckoff, NJ 07481 USA

Phone: 201 934 1445

Fax: 201 934 1445

Email: info@nic.com

Web site: http://www.nic.com

Levels of Connectivity Supported: Shell, SLIP, PPP, UUCP, 56kb

Openix - Open Internet Exchange

25 Green Village Rd

Madison, NJ 07940 USA

Phone: 201 443 0400

Fax: 201 377 0418

Email: info@openix.com

Web site: http://
www.openix.com

Levels of Connectivity Supported: Shell, SLIP, PPP, UUCP, 56kb, T1

Planet Access Networks

7 Waterloo Rd
Suite 202
Stanhope, NJ 07874 USA
Phone: 201 691 4704
Fax: 201 691 7588
Email: info@planet.net
Web site: http://
www.planet.net
Levels of Connectivity Supported: Shell, SLIP, PPP,
UUCP, ISDN, 56kb, T1

ZONE One Network Exchange

304 Hudson Street
New York, NY 10013 USA
Phone: 212 824 4000
Fax: 212 824 4009
Email: info@zone.net
Web site: http://www.zone.net
Levels of Connectivity Supported: Shell, SLIP, PPP,
UUCP, ISDN, 56kb, T1

ISPs for Area Code 202

American Information Network

P.O. Box 2083
Columbia, MD 21045 USA
Phone: 410 855 2353
Fax: 410 715 6808
Email: info@ai.net
Web site: http://www.ai.net
Levels of Connectivity Supported: Shell, SLIP, PPP,
UUCP, ISDN, 56kb, T1

ARInternet Corporation

8201 Corporate Drive
Suite 1100
Landover, MD 20785 USA
Phone: 301 459 7171
Fax: 301 459 7174
Email: info@ari.net
Web site: http://www.ari.net
Levels of Connectivity Supported: Shell, SLIP, PPP, ISDN,
56kb, T1, Web Hosting

CAPCON Library Network

1320 - 19th Street, NW, Suite 400
Washington, DC 20036 USA
Phone: 202 331 5771
Fax: 202 797 7719
Email: info@capcon.net
Levels of Connectivity Supported: SLIP, PPP

Charm.Net

2228 E. Lombard Street
Baltimore, MD 21231 USA
Phone: 410 558 3900
Fax: 410 558 3901
Email: info@charm.net
Web site: http://
www.charm.net
Levels of Connectivity Supported: Shell, SLIP, PPP

Cyber Services, Inc.

8027 Leesburg Pike
Suite 317
Vienna, VA 22182 USA
Phone: 703 749 9590
Fax: 703 749 9598
Email: info@cs.com
Web site: http://www.cs.com
Levels of Connectivity Supported: Shell, SLIP, PPP,
UUCP, ISDN, 56kb, T1

Digital Express Group, Inc.

6006 Greenbelt Road
Suite 228
Greenbelt, MD 20770 USA
Phone: 301 847 5000 or 301 847 5050
Fax: 301 847 5215
Email: info@digex.net
Web site: http://
www.digex.net
Levels of Connectivity Supported: Shell, SLIP, PPP, 56kb,
T1

Genuine Computing Resources

5429 Mapledale Plaza,
Suite 122
Woodbridge, VA 22193
Phone: 703 878 4680
Fax: 703 878 4220
Levels of Connectivity Supported: Shell, SLIP, PPP,
UUCP

I-Link Ltd
1 Chisholm Trail
Round Rock, TX 78681 USA
Phone: 800 ILINK 99
Fax: 512 244 9681
Email: info@i-link.net
Web site: http://www.
i-link.net
Levels of Connectivity Supported: PPP, ISDN, 56kb, T1

Internet Online, Inc.
Phone: 301 652 6100
Fax: 202 301 703
Email: info@intr.net
Web site: http://www.intr.net
Levels of Connectivity Supported: Shell, SLIP, PPP, 56kb, T1

Interpath
P.O. Box 12800
Raleigh, NC 27605 USA
Phone: 800 849 6305
Fax: 919 890 6319
Email: info@interpath.net
Web site: http://
www.interpath.net
Levels of Connectivity Supported: Shell, SLIP, PPP, UUCP

KIVEX, Inc.
3 Bethesda Metro Center
Suite B-001
Bethesda, MD 80214 USA
Phone: 800 47 KIVEX
Fax: 301 215 5991
Email: info@kivex.com
Web site: http://
www.kivex.com
Levels of Connectivity Supported: Shell, SLIP, PPP, ISDN, 56k, T1, Web Hosting

LaserNet
11200 Waples Mill Road
Suite 210
Fairfax, VA 22020
Phone: 703 591 4232
Fax: 703 591 7164
Email: info@laser.net
Web site: http://
www.laser.net
Levels of Connectivity Supported: Shell, SLIP, PPP, 56kb, T1

Quantum Networking Solutions, Inc.
2022 Cliff Drive, Suite 121
Santa Barbara, CA 93109
Phone: 805 538 2028 or 703 878 4680
Fax: 805 563 9147 or 703 878 4220
Levels of Connectivity Supported: Shell, SLIP, PPP, UUCP

RadixNet Internet Services
6230 Oxon Hill Road
Oxon Hill, MD 20745 USA
Phone: 301 567 9831
Fax: 301 839 0836
Email: info@radix.net
Web site: http://
www.radix.net
Levels of Connectivity Supported: Shell, SLIP, PPP, 56kb, T1

Smartnet Internet Services, LLC
8562A Laureldale Drive
Laurel, MD 20724 USA
Phone: 301 470 3400 or 410 792 4555
Fax: 410 792 4571
Email: info@smart.net
Web site: http://
www.smart.net
Levels of Connectivity Supported: PPP, 56kb, T1, Web Hosting

SONNETS, Inc.
13904 Stonefield Lane
Clifton, VA 22024 USA
Phone: 703 502 8589
Fax: 703 502 8564
Email: office@sonnets.net
Web site: http://
www.sonnets.net
Levels of Connectivity Supported: Shell, SLIP, PPP, 56kb, T1, Web Hosting

UltraPlex Information Providers
P.O. Box 626
Laurel, MD 20725-0626 USA
Phone: 301 598 6UPX or 410 880 4604
Email: info@upx.net
Web site: http://www.upx.net
Levels of Connectivity Supported: Shell, PPP, UUCP, ISDN, 56kb

Universal Telecomm Corporation

3008 Franklin Corner Lane
Herndon, VA 22071 USA
Phone: 703 758 0550
Fax: 703 758 0549
Email: root@utc.net
Web site: http://www.utc.net
Levels of Connectivity Supported: SLIP, PPP, T1

US Net, Inc.

3316 Kilkenny Street
Silver Spring, MD 20904
Phone: 301 572 5926
Fax: 301 572 5201
Levels of Connectivity Supported: Shell, SLIP, PPP, UUCP

World Web Limited

Phone: 703 518 5005
Fax: 703 838 2002
Email: info@worldweb.net
Web site: http://www.worldweb.net
Levels of Connectivity Supported: PPP, ISDN, 56kb, T1

Xpress Internet Services

18825 Birdseye Drive
Germantown, MD 20874 USA
Phone: 301 601 5050
Fax: 301 601 5055
Email: info@xis.com
Web site: http://www.xis.com
Levels of Connectivity Supported: SLIP, PPP

ISPs for Area Code 203

Computerized Horizons

2490 Black Rock Tpke. #309
Fairfield, CT 06432-2404 USA
Phone: 203 335 7431
Fax: 203 335 3007
Email: info@fcc.com
Web site: http://www.fcc.com
Levels of Connectivity Supported: Shell, SLIP

Continuum Communications, Inc.

P.O. Box 39
Norwich, CT 06360 USA
Phone: 203 885 3576
Email: gph@q.continuum.net
Web site: http://www.continuum.net
Levels of Connectivity Supported: Shell, SLIP, PPP

Connix: The Connecticut Internet Exchange

6 Way Road, Suite 33
Middlefield, CT 06455 USA
Phone: 860 349 7059
Fax: 860 349 7058
Email: office@connix.com
Web site: http://www.connix.com
Levels of Connectivity Supported: Shell, SLIP, PPP, UUCP, ISDN, 56kb, T1

Futuris Networks, Inc.

500 Summer Street, Suite 303
Stamford, CT 06901
Phone: 203 359 8868
Levels of Connectivity Supported: Shell, SLIP

I-2000 Inc.

416 Main Street
Metuchen, NJ 08840 USA
Phone: 800 464 3820
Fax: 908 906 2396
Email: info@i-2000.com
Web site: http://www.i-2000.com
Levels of Connectivity Supported: SLIP, PPP, ISDN, 56kb, T1

imagine.com

92 Weston Street
Suite #12
Hartford, CT 06120 USA
Phone: 860 527 9245
Fax: 860 293 0762
Email: Postmaster@imagine.com
Web site: http://www.imagine.com
Levels of Connectivity Supported: SLIP, PPP, ISDN, 56kb, T1

Internet84, LLC

36 Tamarack Avenue, #126
Danbury, CT 06811 USA
Phone: 203 830 2122
Fax: 203 830 2123
Email: staff@i84.net
Web site: http://www.i84.net
Levels of Connectivity Supported: Shell, SLIP, PPP, ISDN, 56kb, T1, Web Hosting

Lightning Internet Services, LLC

327C Sagamore Avenue

Mineola, NY 11501 USA

Phone: 516 248 8400

Fax: 516 248 8897

Email: sales@lightning.net

Web site: http://www.lightning.net

Levels of Connectivity Supported: ISDN, 56kb, T1

MCIX, Inc.

5 Roosevelt Ave

Mystic, CT 06355 USA

Phone: 860 572 8720

Fax: 860 572 8720

Email: info@mcix.com

Web site: http://www.mcix.com

Levels of Connectivity Supported: Shell, SLIP, PPP, UUCP, ISDN, 56kb, T1

Mindport Internet Services, Inc.

P.O. Box 208

Norwich, CT 06360 USA

Phone: 860 892 2081

Fax: 860 892 2084

Email: staff@mindport.net

Web site: http://www.mindport.net

Levels of Connectivity Supported: Shell, SLIP, PPP, UUCP, ISDN, 56kb, T1

NETPLEX

32 Lorraine Street

Hartford, CT 06105 USA

Phone: 203 233 1111

Fax: 203 232 2221

Email: info@ntplx.net

Web site: http://www.ntplx.net

Levels of Connectivity Supported: Shell, SLIP, PPP, UUCP, 56kb, T1

North American Internet Company

835 North Mountain Road

Newington, CT 06111 USA

Phone: 800 952 INET

Fax: 203 953 5635

Email: info@nai.net

Web site: http://www.nai.net

Levels of Connectivity Supported: Shell, SLIP, PPP, 56kb, T1

Paradigm Communications, Inc.

416 Highland Avenue

P. O. Box 1334

Cheshire, CT 06410-1334 USA

Phone: 203 250 7397

Fax: 203 250 2250

Email: info@pcnet.com

Web site: http://www.pcnet.com

Levels of Connectivity Supported: PPP, UUCP, ISDN, 56kb, T1

ZONE One Network Exchange

304 Hudson Street

New York, NY 10013 USA

Phone: 212 824 4000

Fax: 212 824 4009

Email: info@zone.net

Web site: http://www.zone.net

Levels of Connectivity Supported: Shell, SLIP, PPP, UUCP, ISDN, 56kb, T1

ISPs for Area Code 204

Cycor Communications Incorporated

P.O. Box 454

Prince Edward Island, C1A 7K7 Canada

Email: signup@cycor.ca

Web site: http://www.cycor.ca

Levels of Connectivity Supported: SLIP, PPP, ISDN, 56kb, T1

Gate West Communications

P.O. Box 64007

525 London St.

Winnipeg, MB R2K 2Z0 Canada

Phone: 204 663 2931

Fax: 204 667 1379

Email: info@gatewest.net

Web site: http://www.gatewest.net

Levels of Connectivity Supported: Shell, PPP, UUCP, ISDN, 56kb, T1

ISPs for Area Code 205

AIRnet Internet Services, Inc. (AIRnet.net)
1226 Cave Spring Road
Owens Cross Roads, AL 35763 USA
Phone: 800 247 6388 [1-800-AIRnet-8]
Fax: Call for access
Email: efelton@AIRnet.net
Web site: http://www.AIRnet.net
Levels of Connectivity Supported: Telnet, Shell, SLIP, PPP, UUCP, ISDN, 56kb, T1

Community Internet Connect, Inc.
120 Suffolk Drive
Madison, AL 35758 USA
Phone: 205 722 0199
Fax: 205 722 0199 (initiate voice)
Email: info@cici.com
Web site: http://www.cici.com/homepage.html
Levels of Connectivity Supported: Shell, SLIP, PPP

HiWAAY Information Services
1000 Monte Sano Blvd
P O Box 2555
Huntsville, AL 35804 USA
Phone: 205 533 3131
Fax: 205 533 6616
Email: info@HiWAAY.net
Web site: http://www.HiWAAY.net
Levels of Connectivity Supported: Shell, SLIP, PPP, ISDN, 56kb, T1

Hub City Area Access
110 Fox Run Drive
Hattiesburg, MS 39401 USA
Phone: 601 268 6156
Fax: 601 268 3799
Email: info@hub1.hubcity.com
Web site: http://hub1.hubcity.com
Levels of Connectivity Supported: Shell, SLIP, PPP, UUCP, 56kb, T1

interQuest
799 James Record Rd.
Huntsville, AL 35824 USA
Phone: 205 464 8280
Fax: 205 461 8538
Email: info@iquest.com
Web site: http://www.iquest.com
Levels of Connectivity Supported: Shell, SLIP, PPP, UUCP, ISDN, 56kb

MindSpring Enterprises, Inc.
1430 West Peachtree St NW, Suite 400
Atlanta, GA 30309 USA
Phone: 800 719 4332
Fax: 404 815 8805
Email: info@mindspring.com
Web site: http://www.mindspring.com
Levels of Connectivity Supported: SLIP, PPP, UUCP, ISDN, 56kb

Renaissance Internet Services
3405 Triana Blvd.
Huntsville, AL 35805 USA
Phone: 205 535 2113
Fax: 205 535 2110
Email: info@ro.com
Web site: http://www.ro.com
Levels of Connectivity Supported: Shell, PPP, ISDN, 56kb, T1

Scott Network Services, Inc.
P. O. Box 361353
Birmingham, AL 35236 USA
Phone: 205 987 5889
Email: info@scott.net
Web site: http://www.scott.net
Levels of Connectivity Supported: Shell, SLIP, PPP, UUCP, ISDN, 56kb

ISPs for Area Code 206

Blarg! Online Services
2508 5th Avenue, Suite 125
Seattle, WA 98121 USA
Phone: 206 782 6578
Fax: 206 706 0618
Email: info@blarg.net
Web site: http://www.blarg.net
Levels of Connectivity Supported: Shell, SLIP, PPP, ISDN, 56kb, T1

Cyberspace

300 Queene Anne Avenue N, #396

Seattle, WA 98109-4599 USA

Phone: 206 281 5397

Fax: 206 281 0421

Email: info@cyberspace.com

Web site: http://www.cyberspace.com

Levels of Connectivity Supported: Shell, SLIP, PPP

Digital Forest

19020 NE 84th

Redmond, WA 98053 USA

Phone: 206 836 4272

Fax: 206 836 3409

Email: info@forest.net

Web site: http://www.forest.net

Dial-up via Apple Remote Access

Eskimo North

P.O. Box 55816

Seattle, WA 98155

Phone: 206 367 7457

Levels of Connectivity Supported: Shell, SLIP

I-Link Ltd

1 Chisholm Trail

Round Rock, TX 78681 USA

Phone: 800 ILINK 99

Fax: 512 244 9681

Email: info@i-link.net

Web site: http://www.i-link.net

Levels of Connectivity Supported: PPP, ISDN, 56kb, T1

InEx Net

23632 HWY 99 #F-346

Edmonds, WA 98026 USA

Phone: 206 670 1131

Email: info@inex.com

Web site: http://www.inex.com

Levels of Connectivity Supported: Shell, SLIP, PPP, UUCP, 56kb

Interconnected Associates Inc. (IXA)

300 E. Pike Street, Suite 2001

Seattle, WA 98122 USA

Phone: 206 622 7337

Fax: 206 621 0567

Email: mike@ixa.com

Web site: http://www.ixa.com

Levels of Connectivity Supported: 56kb, T1

Internet Express

1155 Kelly Johnson Blvd, Ste 400

Colorado Springs, CO 80920-3959 USA

Phone: 800 592 1240

Fax: 719 592 1201

Email: service@usa.net

Web site: http://www.usa.net

Levels of Connectivity Supported: Shell, SLIP, PPP, UUCP, 56kb, T1

ISOMEDIA.COM

2441 - 152nd Avenue NE

Redmond, WA 98052 USA

Phone: 206 881 8769

Fax: 206 869 9437

Email: info@isomedia.com

Web site: http://www.isomedia.com

Levels of Connectivity Supported: PPP

Olympic Computing Solutions

P.O. Box 45285

Seattle, WA 98145 USA

Phone: 206 989 6698

Fax: 206 547 7445

Email: ocs@oz.net

Web site: http://sensemedia.net

Levels of Connectivity Supported: SLIP, PPP

Oregon Information Technology Centeres, Inc.

dba @harborside

15711 Hwy 101

Brookings, OR 97415 USA

Phone: 503 469 6699

Fax: 503 469 9163

Email: hmaster@harborside.com

Web site: http://www.harborside.com

Levels of Connectivity Supported: Shell, SLIP, PPP

Northwest Nexus, Inc.

P.O. Box 40597

Bellevue, WA 98015-4597

Phone: 206 455 3505

Fax: 206 455 4672

Levels of Connectivity Supported: Shell, SLIP, PPP, UUCP

NorthWestNet

15400 S.E. 30th Place, Suite 202

Bellevue, WA 98007 USA

Phone: 206 562 3000

Fax: 206 562 4822

Email: info@nwnet.net

Web site: http://www.nwnet.net

Levels of Connectivity Supported: T1

Pacific Rim Network, Inc.

P.O. Box 5006

Bellingham, WA 98227 USA

Phone: 360 650 0442 x 11

Fax: 360 738 8315

Email: info@pacificrim.net

Web site: http://www.pacificrim.net

Levels of Connectivity Supported: PPP, ISDN, 56kb, 128kb, T1

Seanet Online Services

Columbia Seafirst Center

701 Fifth Avenue, Suite 6801

Seattle, WA 98104

Phone: 206 343 7828

Fax: 206 628 0722

Levels of Connectivity Supported: Shell, SLIP, PPP, UUCP

SenseMedia

P.O. Box 228

Felton, CA 95018 USA

Phone: 408 335 9400

Email: info@sensemedia.net

Web site: http://sensemedia.net

Levels of Connectivity Supported: SLIP, PPP

Structured Network Systems, Inc.

15635 SE 114th Ave., Suite 201

Clackamas, OR 97015 USA

Phone: 800 881 0962

Fax: 503 656 3235

Email: sales@structured.net

Web site: http://www.structured.net

Levels of Connectivity Supported: 56kb, T1

Teleport, Inc.

319 SW Washington, Suite 604

Portland, OR 97204 USA

Phone: 503 223 4245

Fax: 503 223 4372

Email: info@teleport.com

Web site: http://www.teleport.com

Transport Logic

13500 SW Pacific Hwy, #513

Portland, OR 97223 USA

Phone: 503 243 1940

Email: info@transport.com

Web site: http://www.transport.com

Levels of Connectivity Supported: Shell, SLIP, PPP, ISDN, 56kb, T1

WLN

P.O. Box 3888

Lacey, WA 98503-0888 USA

Phone: 800 342 5956 or 360 923 4000

Fax: 360 923 4009

Email: info@wln.com

Levels of Connectivity Supported: Shell, SLIP, PPP

ISPs for Area Code 207

Agate Internet

31 Central Street, Suite 312

Bangor, ME 04401 USA

Phone: 207 947 8248

Fax: 207 947 4432

Email: info@agate.net

Web site: http://www.agate.net

Levels of Connectivity Supported: SLIP, PPP, 56kb, T1

Internet Maine

449 Forest Avenue, Suite 11

Portland, ME 04101 USA

Phone: 207 780 0416

Email: info@mainelink.net

Web site: http://www.mainelink.net

Levels of Connectivity Supported: Shell, SLIP, PPP, UUCP

MaineStreet Communications

208 Portland Rd.

ME, 04039 USA

Phone: 207 657 5235

Email: rainmaker@maine.com

Web site: http://www.maine.com

Levels of Connectivity Supported: Shell, SLIP, UUCP, ISDN, 56kb

Midcoast Internet Solutions

HC 32 Box 291
Owls Head, ME 04854   USA
Phone: 207 594 8277
Email: accounts@midcoast.com
Web site: http://
www.midcoast.com
Levels of Connectivity Supported: Shell, PPP, 56kb

MV Communications, Inc.

P.O. Box 4963
Manchester, NH 03108-4963
USA
Phone: 603 429 2223
Fax: 603 424 0386
Email: info@mv.mv.com
Web site: http://www.mv.com
Levels of Connectivity Supported: Shell, SLIP, PPP,
UUCP, 56kb, T1

Northern Lights Internet Services

P.O. Box 1961
Portland, ME 04104 USA
Phone: 207 773 4941
Email: jkilday@nlbbs.com
Web site: http://
www.nlbbs.com
Levels of Connectivity Supported: Shell, SLIP, PPP,
UUCP, 56kb

ISPs for Area Code 208

Micron Internet Services

8000 S Federal Way
P.O. Box 6
Boise, ID 83707-0006 USA
Phone: 208 368 5400
Fax: 208 368 5640
Email: sales@micron.net
Web site: http://
www.micron.net
Levels of Connectivity Supported: SLIP, PPP, 56kb, T1

Minnesota Regional Network

511 - 11th Avenue South,
Box 212
Minneapolis, MN 55415
Phone: 612 342 2570
Levels of Connectivity Supported: Shell, SLIP, UUCP

NICOH Net

200 S. Main, Suite O
Pocatello, ID 83204
Phone: 208 233 5802
Fax: 208 233 5911
Levels of Connectivity Supported: Shell, SLIP, PPP,
UUCP

NorthWestNet

15400 S.E. 30th Place, Suite 202
Bellevue, WA 98007 USA
Phone: 206 562 3000
Fax: 206 562 4822
Email: info@nwnet.net
Web site: http://
www.nwnet.net
Levels of Connectivity Supported: T1

Primenet

2320 W. Peoria Avenue,
Suite A103
Phoenix, AZ 85029 USA
Phone: 602 870 1010 or 800 4
NET FUN
Fax: 602 870 1010
Email: info@primenet.com
Web site: http://
www.primenet.com
Levels of Connectivity Supported: Shell, SLIP, PPP,
UUCP

SRVnet

Phone: 208 524 6237
Email: nlp@srv.net
Web site: http://www.srv.net
Levels of Connectivity Supported: Shell, SLIP, PPP,
UUCP, ISDN, 56kb, T1

Structured Network Systems, Inc.

15635 SE 114th Ave., Suite 201
Clackamas, OR 97015 USA
Phone: 800 881 0962
Fax: 503 656 3235
Email: sales@structured.net
Web site: http://
www.structured.net
Levels of Connectivity Supported: 56kb, T1

Transport Logic

13500 SW Pacific Hwy #513
Portland, OR 97223 USA
Phone: 503 243 1940
Email: info@transport.com
Web site: http://
www.transport.com
Levels of Connectivity Supported: Shell, SLIP, PPP, ISDN,
56kb, T1

ISPs for Area Code 209

The Computer Depot
27A Main St.
Jackson, CA 95642 USA
Phone: 209 223 5043
Fax: 209 223 5046
Email: admin@cdepot.net
Web site: http://
www.cdepot.net
Levels of Connectivity Supported: Shell, SLIP, PPP,
ISDN, 56kb, T1

Cybergate Information Services
P.O. Box 25758
Fresno, CA 93729 USA
Phone: 209 486 4283
Fax: 209 275 2767
Email: cis@cybergate.com
Levels of Connectivity Supported: Shell

Infonet Communications, Inc.
2109 W. Bullard, Ste. 145
Fresno, CA 93711 USA
Phone: 209 446 2360
Fax: 209 438 8064
Email: mikeb@icinet.net
Web site: http://
www.icinet.net
Levels of Connectivity Supported: PPP, UUCP, ISDN,
56kb, T1

InReach Internet Communications
P.O. Box 470425
San Francisco, CA 94147 USA
Phone: 800 4 INREACH
Fax: 800 399 7499
Email: info@inreach.com
Web site: http://
www.inreach.com
Levels of Connectivity Supported: PPP, UUCP, ISDN

InterNex Tiara
2302 Walsh Ave
Santa Clara, CA 95051 USA
Phone: 408 496 5466
Fax: 408 496 5485
Email: info@internex.net
Web site: http://
www.internex.net
Levels of Connectivity Supported: SLIP, PPP, ISDN,
56kb, T1, Frame Relay, Web Services

Primenet
2320 W. Peoria Avenue, Suite A103
Phoenix, AZ 85029 USA
Phone: 602 870 1010 or 800 4 NET FUN
Fax: 602 870 1010
Email: info@primenet.com
Web site: http://
www.primenet.com
Levels of Connectivity Supported: Shell, SLIP, PPP,
UUCP

ValleyNet Communications
2300 Tulare, Suite 100
Fresno, CA 93721-2226 USA
Phone: 800 426 8638 or 209 486 8638
Fax: 209 495 4940
Email: info@valleynet.com
Web site: http://
www.valleynet.com
Levels of Connectivity Supported: Shell, SLIP, PPP,
UUCP, ISDN, 56kb, T1, Web Hosting

West Coast Online
6050 Commerce Blvd., Suite 210
Rohnert Park, CA 94928 USA
Phone: 707 586 3060
Fax: 707 586 5254
Email: info@calon.com
Web site: http://
www.calon.com
Levels of Connectivity Supported: Shell, SLIP, PPP,
UUCP

ISPs for Area Code 210

Connect International Inc.
45 N.E. Loop 410, Suite 180
San Antonio, TX 78216 USA
Phone: 210 341 2599
Fax: 210 341 6725
Email: info@connecti.com
Web site: http://
www.connecti.com
Levels of Connectivity Supported: Shell, PPP, UUCP,
ISDN, 56kb, T1

Delta Design and Development Inc.

6448 Hwy. 290 East, Suite F108
Austin, TX 78723 USA
Phone: 800 763 8265
Fax: 512 467 8462
Email: sales@deltaweb.com
Web site: http://www.deltaweb.com
Levels of Connectivity Supported: PPP, ISDN, 56kb, T1

The Eden Matrix

101 W. 6th Street, Suite 210
Austin, TX 78701 USA
Phone: 512 478 9900
Fax: 512 478 9934
Email: info@eden.com
Web site: http://www.eden.com
Levels of Connectivity Supported: Shell, SLIP, PPP, ISDN, T1

I-Link Ltd

1 Chisholm Trail
Round Rock, TX 78681 USA
Phone: 800 ILINK 99
Fax: 512 244 9681
Email: info@i-link.net
Web site: www.i-link.net
Levels of Connectivity Supported: PPP, ISDN, 56kb, T1

Phoenix DataNet, Inc.

17100 El Camino Real
Houston, TX 77058 USA
Phone: 713 486 8337
Fax: 713 486 7464
Email: info@phoenix.net
Web site: http://www.phoenix.net
Levels of Connectivity Supported: Shell, SLIP, PPP, ISDN, 56kb, T1

ISPs for Area Code 212

Advanced Standards, Inc advn.com

19 W 44 St., Suite 615
New York, NY 10036 USA
Phone: 212 302 3366
Email: kolian@advn.com
Levels of Connectivity Supported: Shell, PPP, UUCP, 56kb

Alternet (UUNET Technologies, Inc.)

3110 Fairview Park Drive, Suite 570
Falls Church, VA 22042
Phone: 703 204 8000
Fax: 703 204 8001
Email: info@alter.net
Levels of Connectivity Supported: SLIP, PPP

Blythe Systems

39 West 14th Street, #206
New York, NY 10011 USA
Phone: 212 226 7171
Fax: 212 274 8712
Email: infodesk@blythe.org
Levels of Connectivity Supported: Shell

BrainLINK

87-90 118 St
Richmond Hill, NY 11418 USA
Phone: 718 805 6559
Fax: 718 805 6564
Email: info@beast.brainlink.com
Web site: http://www.brainlink.com
Levels of Connectivity Supported: Shell

bway.net / Outernet, Inc.

626 Broadway, Suite 3A
New York, NY 10012 USA
Phone: 212 982 9800
Fax: 212 982 5499
Email: info@bway.net
Web site: http://www.bway.net
Levels of Connectivity Supported: Shell, SLIP, PPP, UUCP, ISDN, 56kb, T1, Web Hosting

Calyx Internet Access

271 East 10th Street, Suite 100
New York, NY 10009 USA
Phone: 212 475 5051
Fax: 212 475 5051
Email: info@calyx.net
Web site: http://
www.calyx.net
Levels of Connectivity Supported: Shell, SLIP, PPP,
UUCP, 56kb, T1

Creative Data Consultants (SILLY.COM)

Bayside, NY 11364 USA
Phone: 718 229 0489 x23
Fax: 718 229 7096
Email: info@silly.com
Web site: http://
www.silly.com
Levels of Connectivity Supported: Shell, SLIP, PPP,
UUCP

Digital Express Group, Inc.

6006 Greenbelt Road, Suite 228
Greenbelt, MD 20770 USA
Phone: 301 847 5000 or 301
847 5050
Fax: 301 847 5215
Email: http://www.silly.com
Web site: http://
www.digex.net
Levels of Connectivity Supported: Shell, SLIP, PPP,
56kb, T1

Echo Communications Group

97 Perry Street, Suite 13
New York, NY 10014
Phone: 212 255 3839
Fax: 212 255 9440
Levels of Connectivity Supported: Shell, SLIP, PPP
Modem: 212 989 3286

escape.com - Kazan Corp

16 East 55th Street, 5th Floor
New York, NY 10022
Phone: 212 888 8780
Fax: 212 832 0344
Levels of Connectivity Supported: Shell, SLIP, PPP,
UUCP

I-2000 Inc.

416 Main Street
Metuchen, NJ 08840 USA
Phone: 800 464 3820
Fax: 908 906 2396
Email: info@i-2000.com
Web site: http://www.i-
2000.com
Levels of Connectivity Supported: SLIP, PPP, 56kb T1

I-Link Ltd

1 Chisholm Trail
Round Rock, TX 78681 USA
Phone: 800 ILINK 99
Fax: 512 244 9681
Email: info@i-link.net
Web site: http://www.i-
link.net
Levels of Connectivity Supported: PPP, ISDN, 56kb, T1

Ingress Communications Inc.

538 - 2nd Avenue
New York, NY 10016
Phone: 212 679 2838
Fax: 212 213 0736
Levels of Connectivity Supported: Shell, SLIP, PPP,
UUCP

INTAC Access Corporation

256 Broad Avenue
Palisades Park, NJ 07650 USA
Phone: 800 50 INTAC
Fax: 201 944 1434
Email: info@intac.com
Web site: http://
www.intac.com
Levels of Connectivity Supported: Shell, SLIP, PPP,
UUCP, ISDN, 56kb, T1

Intellitech Walrus

90 John Street, 27th Fl.
New York, NY 10038 USA
Phone: 212 406 5000
Email: info@walrus.com
Web site: http://
www.walrus.com
Levels of Connectivity Supported: Shell, SLIP, PPP,
UUCP, ISDN, 56kb, T1

Interactive Networks, Inc.

250 East 17th Street
Paterson, NJ 07524 USA
Phone: 201 881 1878 or 1 800
561 1878
Fax: 201 881 1788
Email: info@interactive.net
Web site: http://
www.interacitve.net
Levels of Connectivity Supported: Shell, SLIP, PPP,
UUCP, ISDN, 56kb, T1

Intercall, Inc
33 Route 17 South
Rutherford, NJ 07073
Phone: 800 758 7329
Fax: 201 939 2507
Email: sales@intercall.com
Web site: http://
www.intercall.com
Levels of Connectivity Supported: SLIP, PPP

InterCom Online
1412 Avenue M, Suite 2428
Brooklyn, NY 11230
Phone: 212 714 7183
Levels of Connectivity Supported: Shell

The Internet Connection Corp.
906 Summit Ave.
Jersey City, NJ 07302 USA
Phone: 201 435 4414
Fax: 201 451 7240
Email: info@cnct.com
Web site: http://cnct.com
Levels of Connectivity Supported: Shell, SLIP, PPP, UUCP, 56kb

Internet Online Services
294 State Street
Hackensack, NJ 07601
Phone: 201 928 1000 x226
Fax: 201 928 1057
Levels of Connectivity Supported: Shell, SLIP, PPP

Internet QuickLink Corp.
415 West 57th Street, Suite 1D
New York, NY 10019 USA
Phone: 212 307 1669
Fax: 212 586 1303
Email: info@quicklink.com
Web site: http://
www.quicklink.com
Levels of Connectivity Supported: Shell, SLIP, PPP, ISDN, 56kb, T1

Interport Communications Corp.
1133 Broadway Avenue
New York, NY 10010
Phone: 212 989 1128
Levels of Connectivity Supported: Shell, SLIP, PPP

Lightning Internet Services, LLC
327C Sagamore Avenue
Mineola, NY 11501 USA
Phone: 516 248 8400
Fax: 516 248 8897
Email: sales@lightning.net
Web site: http://
www.lightning.net
Levels of Connectivity Supported: ISDN, 56kb, T1

Long Island Internet HeadQuarters
506 Route 110
Melville, NY 11747 USA
Phone: 516 439 7800
Fax: 516 439 7321
Email: support@pb.net
Web site: http://www.pb.net
Levels of Connectivity Supported: Shell, SLIP, PPP, UUCP, ISDN, 56kb, T1

Mordor International BBS
Jersey City, New Jersey
Fax: 201 433 4222
Levels of Connectivity Supported: Shell

Mnematics, Incorporated
P.O. Box 19
Sparkill, NY 10976-0019 USA
Phone: 914 359 4546
Fax: 914 359 0361
Email: service@mne.com
Web site: http://www.mne.com
Levels of Connectivity Supported: Shell, Slip, UUCP

New World Data
253-17 80th Ave. Suite 2B
Floral Park, NY 11004 USA
Phone: 718 962 1725
Fax: 718 962 1708
Email: dmk@nwdc.com
Web site: http://
www.nwdc.com/
Levels of Connectivity Supported: Shell, Slip, PPP, UUCP, ISDN, 56kb, T1

New York Net
82-04 - 218th Street
Hollis Hills, NY 11427-1416
voice 718 776 6811
fax 718 217 9407
Levels of Connectivity Supported: Slip, PPP, 56kb, T1

NY WEBB, Inc.
1133 Broadway, Rm 1226
New York, NY 10010 USA
Phone: 800 458 4660
Fax: 212 691 660
Email: `wayne@webb.com`
Web site: `http://www.webb.com`
Levels of Connectivity Supported: Shell, SLIP, PPP, UUCP

NYSERNet
200 Elwood Davis Road
Liverpool, NY 13088-6147 USA
Phone: 800 493 4367
Fax: 315 453 3052
Email: `sales@nysernet.org`
Web site: `http://nysernet.org`
Levels of Connectivity Supported: Shell, 56kb, T1

Panix (Public Access uNIX)
New York, NY USA
Phone: 212 741 4400
Fax: 212 741 5311
Email: `info@panix.com`
Web site: `http://www.panix.com`
Levels of Connectivity Supported: Shell, SLIP, PPP

Phantom Access Technologies, Inc. / MindVox
1133 Broadway, Suite 1126
New York, NY 10010 USA
Phone: 212 843 5529
Fax: 212 843 5531
Email: `info@phantom.com`
Web site: `http://www.phantom.com`
Levels of Connectivity Supported: Shell, SLIP, PPP

Pipeline New York
150 Broadway, Suite 610
New York, NY 10038 USA
Phone: 212 267 3636
Fax: 212 267 4380
Email: `mailto:info@pipeline.com`
Web site: `http://www.pipeline.com`
Levels of Connectivity Supported: Shell

Real Life Pictures RealNet
58 W36th Street, 2nd Floor
New York, NY 10018 USA
Phone: 212 366 4434
Email: `reallife@walrus.com`
Web site: `http://www.reallife.com`
Levels of Connectivity Supported: Shell, SLIP, PPP, ISDN, 56kb, 384b, T1

Spacelab.Net
60 Spring Street, Suite 1208
New York, NY 10012 USA
Phone: 212 966 8844
Fax: 212 966 9873
Email: `mike@mxol.com`
Levels of Connectivity Supported: Shell, SLIP, PPP, ISDN, 56kb, T1

The ThoughtPort Authority Inc.
2000 E. Broadway, Suite 242
Columbia, MO 65201 USA
Phone: 800 ISP 6870
Fax: 314 474 4122
Email: `info@thoughtport.com`
Web site: `http://www.thoughtport.com`
Levels of Connectivity Supported: SLIP, PPP, ISDN, 56kb, T1

ThoughtPort of New York City
95 Horatio Street, Suite 401
New York, NY 10014-1530 USA
Phone: 212 645 7970
Fax: 212 924 4360
Email: `info@precipice.com`
Web site: `http://www.precipice.com`
Levels of Connectivity Supported: SLIP, PPP, UUCP, ISDN, T1

tunanet/InfoHouse
151 1st Ave #34
NYC. NY 10009 USA
Phone: 212 229 8224
Fax: 212 228 7051
Email: `info@tunanet.com`
Web site: `http://www.tunanet.com`
Levels of Connectivity Supported: PPP, UUCP, ISDN

ZONE One Network Exchange
304 Hudson Street
New York, NY 10013 USA
Phone: 212 824 4000
Fax: 212 824 4009
Email: info@zone.net
Web site: http://www.zone.net
Levels of Connectivity Supported: Shell, SLIP, PPP, UUCP, ISDN, 56kb, T1

ISPs for Area Code 213

ArtNetwork
844 S. Robertson
Los Angeles, CA 90035 USA
Phone: 800 395 0692
Fax: 310 652 7114
Email: info@artnet.net
Web site: http://www.artnet.net
Levels of Connectivity Supported: Shell, SLIP, PPP, UUCP, ISDN, 56kb, T1

BeachNet Internet Access
BeachNet, Inc.
Marina Del Rey, CA 90292 USA
Phone: 310 823 3308
Fax: 310 823 1390
Email: info@beachnet.com
Web site: http://www.beachnet.com
Levels of Connectivity Supported: SLIP, PPP, T1

Cogent Software, Inc.
221 E. Walnut St., Suite 215
Pasadena, CA 91101 USA
Phone: 818 585 2788
Fax: 818 585 2785
Email: info@cogsoft.com
Web site: http://www.cogsoft.com
Levels of Connectivity Supported: Shell, PPP, ISDN, 56kb, T1

Cyberverse Online
2221 Rosecrans Avenue, Suite 130
El Segundo, CA 90245 USA
Phone: 310 643 3783
Fax: 310 643 6137
Email: info@cyberverse.com
Web site: http://www.cyberverse.com
Levels of Connectivity Supported: Shell, SLIP, PPP

Delta Internet Services
731 E. Ball Rd., Suite 204
Anaheim, CA 92805 USA
Phone: 714 778 0370
Fax: 714 778 1064
Email: info@delta.net
Web site: http://www.delta.net
Levels of Connectivity Supported: Shell, SLIP, PPP, UUCP, ISDN, 56kb, T1

DigiLink Network Services
4429 W. 169th Street
Lawndale, CA 90260-3252
voice 310 542 7421
Web site: http://www.dfw.net
Levels of Connectivity Supported: ISDN

DirectNet
3333 Wilshire BLvd., Suite 607
Los Angeles, CA 90010
Phone: 213 383 3144
Fax: 213 383 8038
Levels of Connectivity Supported: Shell, PPP, ISDN

Electriciti
2271 India Street, Suite C
San Diego, CA 92101
Phone: 619 338 9000
Fax: 619 687 3879
Levels of Connectivity Supported: SLIP, PPP, UUCP

Exodus Communications, Inc.
948 Benecia Avenue
Sunnyvale, CA 94086 USA
Phone: 408 522 8450
Fax: 408 736 6843
Email: info@exodus.net
Web site: http://www.exodus.net
Levels of Connectivity Supported: ISDN, 56kb, T1

Flamingo Communications Inc.

19401 So. Vermont Ave., Suite D-104
Torrance, CA 90502 USA
Phone: 310 532 3533
Fax: 310 532 3622
Email: sales@fcom.com
Web site: http://www.fcom.com
Levels of Connectivity Supported: Shell, SLIP, PPP

I-Link Ltd

1 Chisholm Trail
Round Rock, TX 78681 USA
Phone: 800 ILINK 99
Fax: 512 244 9681
Email: info@i-link.net
Web site: http://www.i-link.net
Levels of Connectivity Supported: PPP, ISDN, 56kb, T1

Instant Internet Corporation (InstaNet)

21010 Devonshire St.
Chatsworth, CA. 91311 USA
Phone: 818 772 0097
Fax: 818 772 9941
Email: charlyg@instanet.com
Web site: http://www.instanet.com
Levels of Connectivity Supported: PPP, UUCP, ISDN, 56kb

InterWorld Communications, Inc.

222 N. Sepulveda Blvd., Suite 1560
El Segundo, CA 90245 USA
Phone: 310 726 0500
Fax: 310 726 0559
Email: sales@interworld.net
Web site: http://www.interworld.net
Levels of Connectivity Supported: SLIP, PPP, UUCP, ISDN, 56kb, T1, Web Hosting

KAIWAN Internet

12550 Brookhurst Street, Suite H
Garden Grove, CA 92640 USA
Phone: 714 638 2139
Fax: 714 638 0455
Email: info@kaiwan.com
Web site: http://www.kaiwan.com
Levels of Connectivity Supported: Shell, SLIP, PPP, UUCP, 56kb, T1

KTB Internet Online

P.O. Box 3121
Glendale, CA 91221 USA
Phone: 818 240 6600
Fax: 818 240 6600
Email: info@ktb.net
Web site: http://www.ktb.net
Levels of Connectivity Supported: Shell, SLIP, PPP, UUCP, ISDN, 56kb, T1

Liberty Information Network

446 S Anaheim Hills Road, Suite 102
Anaheim, CA 92807 USA
Phone: 800 218 5157 or 714 996 9999
Fax: 714 961 8700 Attn: ISP INFO
Email: info@liberty.com
Web site: http://www.liberty.com
Levels of Connectivity Supported: Shell, SLIP, PPP, UUCP, ISDN, 56kb, T1

The Loop Internet Switch Co.

6611 Santa Monica Blvd.
Los Angeles, CA 90038 USA
Phone: 213 465 1311
Fax: 213 469 2193
Email: info@loop.com
Web site: http://www.loop.com/rates.html
Levels of Connectivity Supported: SLIP, PPP

Leonardo Internet

927 6th Street
Santa Monica, CA 90403 USA
Phone: 310 395 5500
Fax: 310 395 9924
Email: jimp@leonardo.net
Web site: http://leonardo.net
Levels of Connectivity Supported: Shell, PPP, 56kb, T1

Network Intensive

8001 Irvine Center Drive, Suite #1130

Irvine, CA 92718 USA

Phone: 714 450 8400

Fax: 714 450 8410

Email: info@ni.net

Web site: http://www.ni.net

Levels of Connectivity Supported: Shell, SLIP, PPP, UUCP, ISDN, 56kb, T1

Online-LA

8671 Wilshire Blvd.

Beverly Hills, CA 90211 USA

Phone: 310 967 8000

Fax: 310 358 5610

Email: mailto:sales@online-la.com

Web site: http://www.online-la.com

Levels of Connectivity Supported: PP, ISDN, 56kb, T1

OutWest Network Services Inc.

440 Western Avenue, Suite 101

Glendale, CA 91201 USA

Phone: 818 545 1996

Email: info@outwest.net

Web site: http://outwest.net/

Levels of Connectivity Supported: Shell, SLIP, PPP, UUCP, 56kb, T1

Primenet

2320 W. Peoria Avenue, Suite A103

Phoenix, AZ 85029 USA

Phone: 602 870 1010 or 800 4 NET FUN

Fax: 602 870 1010

Email: info@primenet.com

Web site: http://www.primenet.com

Levels of Connectivity Supported: Shell, SLIP, PPP, UUCP

QuickCom Internet Communcations

5724 W. Third St. Ste.# 507

Los Angeles, CA 90036 USA

Phone: 213 634 7735

Fax: 213 634 7722

Email: info@quickcom.net

Web site: http://www.quickcom.net

Levels of Connectivity Supported: PPP, ISDN, 56kb. T1

SoftAware

4676 Admiralty Way, Suite 410

Marina del Rey, CA 90292 USA

Phone: 310 305 0275

Email: info@softaware.com

Web site: http://www.softaware.com

Levels of Connectivity Supported: T1

Saigon Enterprises

P.O. Box 3121

Glendale, CA 91221-0121 USA

Phone: 818 246 0689

Fax: 818 240 6600

Email: info@saigon.net

Web site: http://www.saigon.net

Levels of Connectivity Supported: Shell, SLIP, PPP, UUCP, ISDN, 56kb, T1

ViaNet Communications

800 El Camino Real West, Suite 180

Mountain View, CA 94040

Phone: 415 903 2242

Fax: 415 903 2241

Levels of Connectivity Supported: Shell, SLIP, PPP, UUCP

ISPs for Area Code 214

Alternet (UUNET Technologies, Inc.)

3110 Fairview Park Drive, Suite 570

Falls Church, VA 22042

Phone: 703 204 8000

Fax: 703 204 8001

Email: info@alter.net

Web site: info@alter.net

Levels of Connectivity Supported: SLIP, PPP

ANET (American Internet)

2225 E. Randol Mill Rd, Suite 209

Arlington, TX 76011 USA

Phone: 800 776 8894

Fax: 817 633 4816

Email: sales@anet-dfw.com

Web site: http://www.anet-dfw.com

Levels of Connectivity Supported: Shell, PPP, ISDN, 56kb, T1

CompuTek

1005 Business Parkway

Richardson, TX 75081 USA

Phone: 214 994 0190

Fax: 214 994 0350

Email: info@computek.net

Web site: http://www.computek.net

Levels of Connectivity Supported: SLIP, PPP, ISDN, 56kb, T1

Connection Technologies - ConnectNet

14651 Dallas Parkway, Suite 424

Dallas, TX 75240 USA

Phone: 214 490 7100

Fax: 214 490 7108

Email: sales@connect.net

Web site: http://www.connect.net

Levels of Connectivity Supported: SLIP, PPP, UUCP, ISDN, 56kb, T1

Delta Design and Development Inc.

6448 Hwy. 290 East, Suite F108

Austin, TX 78723 USA

Phone: 800 763 8265

Fax: 512 467 8462

Email: sales@deltaweb.com

Web site: http://www.deltaweb.com

Levels of Connectivity Supported: PPP, ISDN, 56kb, T1

DFW Internet Services, Inc.

204 East Belknap, Suite 200

Ft. Worth, TX 76103 USA

Phone: 817 332 5116 or Metro 817 429 3520

Fax: 817 870 1501

Email: info@dfw.net

Web site: http://www.dfw.net

Levels of Connectivity Supported: Shell, SLIP, PPP, UUCP, ISDN, 56kb, T1

I-Link Ltd

1 Chisholm Trail

Round Rock, TX 78681 USA

Phone: 800 ILINK 99

Fax: 512 244 9681

Email: info@i-link.net

Web site: http://www.i-link.net

Levels of Connectivity Supported: PPP, ISDN, 56kb, T1

OnRamp Technologies, Inc.

1950 Stemmons Freeway, Suite 5061

Dallas, TX 75207 USA

Phone: 214 672 7267

Fax: 214 713 5400

Email: info@onramp.net

Web site: http://www.onramp.net

Levels of Connectivity Supported: SLIP, PPP, UUCP, ISDN, 56kb, T1

PICnet

12801 North Central Expressway, Suite 1518

Dallas, TX 75243 USA

Phone: 214 789 0456

Fax: 214 789 0460

Email: info@pic.net

Web site: http://www.pic.net

Levels of Connectivity Supported: SLIP, PPP, 56kb, T1

Texas Metronet, Inc.

860 Kinwest Pkwy, Suite 179

Irving, TX 75063-3440

Phone: 214 705 2900

Fax: 214 401 2802

Levels of Connectivity Supported: Shell, SLIP, PPP, UUCP

ISPs for Area Code 215

Cheap Net

P.O. Box 22

Yorklyn, DE 19736 USA

Phone: 302 993 8420

Fax: 302 993 8419

Email: sammy@ravenet.com

Levels of Connectivity Supported: Shell

Digital Express Group, Inc.
6006 Greenbelt Road, Suite 228
Greenbelt, MD 20770 USA
Phone: 301 847 5000 or 301
847 5050
Fax: 301 847 5215
Email: info@digex.net
Web site: http://
www.digex.net
Levels of Connectivity Supported: Shell, SLIP, PPP,
56kb, T1

epix
100 Lake Street
Dallas, PA 18612 USA
Phone: 800 374 9669
Fax: 717 675 5711
Email: karndt@epix.net
Web site: http://www.epix.net
Levels of Connectivity Supported: SLIP, PPP, ISDN,
56kb, T1

FishNet (Prometheus Information Corp.)
1006 West Ninth Ave
King Of Prussia, PA 10406
USA
Phone: 610 337 9994
Fax: 610 337 9918
Email: info@pond.com
Web site: http://www.pond.com
Levels of Connectivity Supported: Shell, SLIP, PPP

GlobalQUEST, Inc.
P.O. Box 443
Malvern, PA 19355-0443 USA
Phone: 610 696 8111
Fax: 610 696 8575
Email: info@globalquest.net
Web site: http://
www.globalquest.net
Levels of Connectivity Supported: PPP, UUCP, 56kb, T1

I-2000 Inc.
416 Main Street
Metuchen, NJ 08840 USA
Phone: 800 464 3820
Fax: 908 906 2396
Email: info@i-2000.com
Web site: http://www.
i-2000.com
Levels of Connectivity Supported: SLIP, PPP, ISDN,
56kb, T1

Internet Tidal Wave
1444 Hamilton Street, Suite
500
Allentown, PA 18102-4266
USA
Phone: 610 770 6187
Fax: 610 770 6186
Email: info@itw.com
Web site: http://www.itw.com
Levels of Connectivity Supported: Shell, SLIP, PPP, ISDN,
56kb, T1

InterNetworking Technologies
P.O. Box 852
Milford, DE 19963 USA
Phone: 302 398 4369
Email: itnt.com@itnt.com
Web site: http://www.itnt.com
Levels of Connectivity Supported: Shell, SLIP, PPP, ISDN,
56kb

The Magnetic Page
P. O. Box 1787
Wilmington, DE 19899 USA
Phone: 302 651 9753
Fax: 302 426 9731
Email: info@magpage.com
Web site: http://
www.magpage.com
Levels of Connectivity Supported: Shell, SLIP, PPP,
UUCP, ISDN, 56kb, T1

Microserve Information Systems
222 Temperance Hill
Plymouth, PA 18651 USA
Phone: 800 380 INET or 717
821 5964
Fax: 717 779 5490
Email: info@microserve.ne
Web site: http://
www.microserve.net
Levels of Connectivity Supported: Shell, PPP, UUCP

Net Access
P.O. Box 502
Glenside, PA 19117 USA
Phone: 215 576 8669
Email: support@netaxs.com
Web site: http://
www.netaxs.com
Levels of Connectivity Supported: Shell, SLIP, PPP, UUCP, ISDN, 56kb, T1

NetReach, Incorporated
41 St. James Place
Ardmore, PA 19003 USA
Phone: 215 283 2300
Fax: 215 642 0453
Email: info@netreach.net
Web site: http://
www.netreach.net
Levels of Connectivity Supported: Shell, SLIP, PPP, UUCP, ISDN, 56kb, T1

Network Analysis Group
7540 Windsor Drive, Suite 90
Allentown, PA 7540 USA
Phone: 800 624 9240
Fax: 800 607 9548
Email: nag@good.freedom.net
Web site: http://
webmart.freedom.net
Levels of Connectivity Supported: 56kb, T1

OpNet
901 Glenbrook Av
Bryn Mawr, PA 19010 USA
Phone: 610 520 2880
Fax: 610 520 2881
Email: info@op.net
Web site: http://www.op.net
Levels of Connectivity Supported: Shell, SLIP, PPP, UUCP, 56kb, T1

RaveNet Systems Inc
P.O. Box 22
Yorklyn, DE 19736 USA
Phone: 302 993 8420
Fax: 302 993 8419
Email: waltemus@ravenet.com
Web site: http://
www.ravenet.com
Levels of Connectivity Supported: PPP, UUCP, ISDN, 56kb, T1

VivaNET, Inc.
1555 East Henrietta Road
Rochester, NY 14623 USA
Phone: 800 836 UNIX
Fax: 716 272 7627
Email: info@vivanet.com
Web site: http://
www.vivanet.com
Levels of Connectivity Supported: Shell, SLIP, PPP, UUCP, ISDN, 56kb, T1

VoiceNet
17 Richard Rd.
Ivyland, PA 18974 USA
Phone: 800 835 5710
Fax: 215 674 9662
Email: info@voicenet.com
Web site: http://
www.voicenet.com
Levels of Connectivity Supported: Shell, SLIP, PPP, UUCP, ISDN, 56kb, T1

You Tools Corporation / FASTNET
Two Courtney Place - Suite 140
3864 Courtney Street
Bethlehem, PA 18017 USA
Phone: 610 954 5910
Fax: 610 954 5925
Email: info@fast.net
Web site: http://
www.youtools.com
Levels of Connectivity Supported: SLIP, PPP, UUCP, ISDN, 56kb, T1

ISPs for Area Code 216

APK Net, Ltd
1621 Euclid Ave, Suite 1216
Cleveland, OH 44115 USA
Phone: 216 481 9428
Fax: 216 481 9425
Email: support@apk.net
Web site: http://www.apk.net
Levels of Connectivity Supported: Shell, SLIP. PPP, UUCP, ISDN, 56kb, T1

Branch Information Services

2901 Hubbard

Ann Arbor, MI 48105 USA

Phone: 313 741 4442

Fax: 313 995 1931

Email: branch-info@branch.com

Web site: http://branch.com

Levels of Connectivity Supported: SLIP, PPP, ISDN, 56kb, T1

CanNet Internet Services

P.O. Box 0115

Canton, OH 44707 USA

Phone: 216 484 2260

Fax: 216 484 0508

Email: info@cannet.com

Web site: http://www.cannet.com

Levels of Connectivity Supported: Shell, SLIP, PPP, UUCP, 56kb, T1

CommercePark Interactive, Ltd.

1228 Euclid Avenue, Suite #370

Cleveland, OH 44115 USA

Phone: 216 523 2240

Fax: 216 523 8338

Email: info@commercepark.com

Web site: http://www.commercepark.com

Levels of Connectivity Supported: SLIP, PPP, ISDN, 56kb, T1

ExchangeNet

25931 Euclid Ave. #145

OH 44132 USA

Email: info@en.com

Web site: http://www.en.com

Levels of Connectivity Supported: Shell, SLIP, PPP, UUCP, ISDN, 56kb, T1

Gateway to Internet Services

P.O. Box 271

Cuyahoga Falls, OH 44222-0271 USA

Phone: 216 656 5511 (Cleveland) 216 342 3922 (Akron)

Fax: 216 656 5440 (Cleveland) 216 929 2756 (Akron)

Email: sales@gwis.com

Web site: http://www.gwis.com

Levels of Connectivity Supported: Shell, SLIP, PPP, UUCP, ISDN, 56kb, T1

OARnet

2455 North Star Road

Columbus, OH 43221 USA

Phone: 614 728 8100 or 800 627 8101

Fax: 614 728 8110

Email: info@oar.net

Web site: http://www.oar.net

Levels of Connectivity Supported: Shell, SLIP, PPP

Multiverse, Inc.

1965 E 6th St., Suite 610

Cleveland, OH 44114 USA

Phone: 216 344 3080

Fax: 216 479 7624

Email: noc@multiverse.net

Web site: http://mvwww.multiverse.com

Levels of Connectivity Supported: Shell, SLIP, PPP, UUCP, ISDN, 56kb, T1

New Age Consulting Service

6206 Timberlane Drive

Independence, OH 44131 USA

Phone: 216 524 3162

Fax: 216 524 8388

Email: damin@nacs.net

Levels of Connectivity Supported: Shell, SLIP, PPP, UUCP

ISPs for Area Code 217

Allied Access Inc.

1002 Walnut Street

Murphysboro, IL 62966 USA

Phone: 618 684 2255 or 800 INETDOM

Fax: 618 684 5907

Email: sales@intrnet.net

Web site: http://www.intrnet.net

Levels of Connectivity Supported: Shell, SLIP, PPP

Net66

502 East John Street, Suite 1B

Champaign, IL 61820 USA

Phone: 217 328 0066

Fax: 217 344 6727

Email: sales@net66.com

Web site: http://
www.net66.com

Levels of Connectivity Supported: Shell, PPP, UUCP, ISDN

Shouting Ground Technologies, Inc.

P.O. Box 5039 Station A

Champaign, IL 61820 USA

Phone: 217 351 7921

Fax: 217 351 7922

Email: admin@shout.net

Web site: http://
www.shout.net

Levels of Connectivity Supported: Shell, SLIP, PPP, ISDN, 56kb, T1

ISPs for Area Code 218

Minnesota OnLine

23 Empire Drive, Suite 152

Saint Paul, MN 55103-1857

USA

Phone: 612 225 1110

Fax: 612 225 1424

Email: info@mn.state.net

Web site: http://
www.state.net

Levels of Connectivity Supported: SLIP, PPP, UUCP, ISDN, 56kb, T1

Protocol Communications, Inc.

6280 Highway 65 NE,

Suite 401

Minneapolis, MN 55432-5136

USA

Phone: 612 541 9900

Fax: 612 541 1586

Email: info@protocom.com

Web site: http://
www.protocom.com

Levels of Connectivity Supported: Shell, SLIP, PPP, UUCP, ISDN, 56kb, T1

Red River Net

P.O. Box 388

Fargo, ND 58107

Phone 701 232 2227

Levels of Connectivity Supported: Shell, SLIP

ISPs for Area Code 219

Custom Logic Systems

Post Office Box 163

Mishawaka, IN 46546-0163

USA

Phone: 219 255 5201

Fax: 219 255 5848

Email: info@cl-sys.com

Web site: http://www.
cl-sys.com

Levels of Connectivity Supported: PPP, UUCP

Wink Communications Group, Inc.

2500 W Higgins Rd, Suite 480

Hoffman Estates, IL 60195

USA

Phone: 708 310 9465

Fax: 708 310 3477

Email: sales@winkcomm.com

Web site: http://
www.winkcomm.com

Levels of Connectivity Supported: ISDN, 56kb, T1

ISPs for Area Code 301

ABSnet Internet Services

200 East Lexington Street, Suite 1602

Baltimore, MD 21202 USA

Phone: 410 361 8160

Fax: 410 361 8162

Email: info@abs.net

Web site: http://www.abs.net

Levels of Connectivity Supported: Shell, SLIP, PPP, UUCP, ISDN, 56kb, T1

American Information Network

P.O. Box 2083

Columbia, MD 21045 USA

Phone: 410 855 2353

Fax: 410 715 6808

Email: info@ai.net

Web site: http://www.ai.net

Levels of Connectivity Supported: Shell, SLIP, PPP, UUCP, ISDN, 56kb, T1

ARInternet Corporation

8201 Corporate Drive, Suite 1100

Landover, MD 20785 USA

Phone: 301 459 7171

Fax: 301 459 7174

Email: info@ari.net

Web site: http://www.ari.net

Levels of Connectivity Supported: Shell, SLIP, PPP, ISDN, 56kb, T1, Web Hosting

CAPCON Library Network

1320 - 19th Street, NW, Suite 400

Washington, DC 20036 USA

Phone: 202 331 5771

Fax: 202 797 7719

Email: mailto:info@capcon.net

Levels of Connectivity Supported: SLIP, PPP

Charm.Net

2228 E. Lombard Street

Baltimore, MD 21231 USA

Phone: 410 558 3900

Fax: 410 558 3901

Email: info@charm.net

Web site: http://www.charm.net

Levels of Connectivity Supported: Shell, SLIP, PPP

Clark Internet Services, Inc. ClarkNet

10600 Route 108

Ellicott City, MD 21042 USA

Phone: 410 995 0691

Fax: 410 730 9765

Email: info@clark.net

Web site: http://www.clark.net

Levels of Connectivity Supported: Shell, SLIP, PPP, UUCP

Cyber Services, Inc.

8027 Leesburg Pike, Suite 317

Vienna, VA 22182 USA

Phone: 703 749 9590

Fax: 703 749 9598

Email: info@cs.com

Web site: http://www.cs.com

Levels of Connectivity Supported: Shell, SLIP, PPP, UUCP, ISDN, 56kb, T1

Digital Express Group, Inc.

6006 Greenbelt Road, Suite 228

Greenbelt, MD 20770 USA

Phone: 301 847 5000 or 301 847 5050

Fax: 301 847 5215

Email: info@digex.net

Web site: http://www.digex.net

Levels of Connectivity Supported: Shell, SLIP, PPP, 56kb, T1

FredNet

P.O. Box 3966

Frederick, Md. 21705-3966 USA

Phone: 301 631 5300

Fax: 301 698 1260

Email: info@fred.net

Web site: http://www.fred.net

Levels of Connectivity Supported: Shell, SLIP, PPP, UUCP, ISDN, 56kb, T1

Genuine Computing Resources

5429 Mapledale Plaza, Suite 122

Woodbridge, VA 22193

Phone: 703 878 4680

Fax: 703 878 4220

Levels of Connectivity Supported: Shell, SLIP, PPP, UUCP

Internet Online, Inc.

4925 St. Elmo Avenue

MD, 20814 USA

Phone: 301 652 6100

Fax: 202 301 703

Email: info@intr.net

Web site: http://www.intr.net

Levels of Connectivity Supported: Shell, Slip, PPP, 56kb, T1

KIVEX, Inc.
3 Bethesda Metro Center,
Suite B-001
Bethesda, MD 80214 USA
Phone: 800 47 KIVEX
Fax: 301 215 5991
Email: info@kivex.com
Web site: http://
www.kivex.com
Levels of Connectivity Supported: Shell, SLIP, PPP, ISDN, 56kb, T1

Kompleat Internet Services LLC
7605 Ridge Rd
Frederick, MD 21702 USA
Phone: 301 293 4333
Fax: 301 293 4332
Email: netadmin@kis.net
Web site: http://www.kis.net
Levels of Connectivity Supported: SLIP, PPP, UUCP, ISDN, 56kb, T1

LaserNet
11200 Waples Mill Road,
Suite 210
Fairfax, VA 22020 USA
Phone: 703 591 4232
Fax: 703 591 7164
Email: info@laser.net
Web site: http://
www.laser.net
Levels of Connectivity Supported: Shell, SLIP, PPP, 56kb, T1

Quantum Networking Solutions, Inc.
2022 Cliff Drive, Suite 121
Santa Barbara, CA 93109
Phone: 805 538 2028 or 703 878 4680
Fax: 805 563 9147 or 703 878 4220
Levels of Connectivity Supported: Shell, SLIP, PPP, UUCP

RadixNet Internet Services
6230 Oxon Hill Road
Oxon Hill, MD 20745 USA
Phone: 301 567 9831
Fax: 301 839 0836
Email: info@radix.net
Web site: http://
www.radix.net
Levels of Connectivity Supported: Shell, SLIP, PPP, 56kb, T1

Smartnet Internet Services, LLC
8562A Laureldale Drive
Laurel, MD 20724 USA
Phone: 301 470 3400 or 410 792 4555
Fax: 410 792 4571
Email: info@smart.net
Web site: http://
www.smart.net
Levels of Connectivity Supported: PPP, 56kb, T1

SONNETS, Inc.
13904 Stonefield Lane
Clifton, VA 22024 USA
Phone: 703 502 8589
Fax: 703 502 8564
Email: office@sonnets.net
Web site: http://
www.sonnets.net
Levels of Connectivity Supported: Shell, SLIP, PPP, 56kb, T1

SURAnet
8400 Baltimore Boulevard
College Park, MD 20740
Phone: 301 982 4600
Fax: 301 982 4605
Levels of Connectivity Supported: SLIP, PPP

UltraPlex Information Providers
P.O.Box 626
Laurel, MD 20725-0626 USA
Phone: 301 598 6UPX or 410 880 4604
Email: info@upx.net
Web site: http://www.upx.net
Levels of Connectivity Supported: Shell, PPP, UUCP, ISDN, 56kb

Universal Telecomm Corporation
3008, Franklin Corner Lane
Herndon, VA 22071 USA
Phone: 703 758 0550
Fax: 703 758 0549
Email: root@utc.net
Web site: http://www.utc.net
Levels of Connectivity Supported: SLIP, PPP, T1

US Net, Inc.
3316 Kilkenny Street
Silver Spring, MD 20904
Phone: 301 572 5926
Fax: 301 572 5201
Levels of Connectivity Supported: Shell, SLIP, PPP, UUCP

World Web Limited
906 King Street
VA, 22314 USA
Phone: 703 838 2000
Fax: 703 518 5005
Email: info@worldweb.net
Web site: http://www.worldweb.net
Levels of Connectivity Supported: PPP, ISDN, 56kb, T1

Xpress Internet Services
18825 Birdseye Drive
Germantown, MD 20874 USA
Phone: 301 601 5050
Fax: 301 601 5055
Email: info@xis.com
Web site: http://xis.com
Levels of Connectivity Supported: SLIP, PPP

ISPs for Area Code 302

Cheap Net
P.O. Box 22
Yorklyn, DE 19736 USA
Phone: 302 993 8420
Fax: 302 993 8419
Email: sammy@ravenet.com
Levels of Connectivity Supported: Shell

Delaware Common Access Network (DCANet)
1204 West Street
Wilmington, DE 19801-1026
USA
Phone: 302 654 1019
Fax: 302 426 1568
Email: info@dca.net
Web site: http://www.dca.net
Levels of Connectivity Supported: Shell, SLIP, PPP, UUCP, ISDN, 56kb, T1

First State Web, Inc.
652 Woodview Drive
Hockessin, DE 19707-9665
USA
Phone: 302 234 0721
Fax: 302 239 8056
Email: info@wittnet.com
Web site: http://www.wittnet.com
Levels of Connectivity Supported: Shell, SLIP, PPP, ISDN, 56kb

InterNetworking Technologies
P.O. Box 852
Milford, DE 19963 USA
Phone: 302 398 4369
Email: itnt.com@itnt.com
Web site: http://www.itnt.com
Levels of Connectivity Supported: Shell, SLIP, PPP, ISDN, 56kb

The Magnetic Page
P. O. Box 1787
Wilmington, DE 19899 USA
Phone: 302 651 9753
Fax: 302 426 9731
Email: info@magpage.com
Web site: http://www.magpage.com
Levels of Connectivity Supported: Shell, SLIP, PPP, UUCP, ISDN, 56kb, T1

RaveNet Systems Inc
P.O. Box 22
Yorklyn, DE 19736 USA
Phone: 302 993 8420
Fax: 302 993 8419
Email: waltemus@ravenet.com
Web site: http://www.ravenet.com
Levels of Connectivity Supported: PPP, UUCP, ISDN, 56kb, T1

SSNet, Inc.
1254 Lorewood Grove Road
Middletown, DE 19709
Phone: 302 378 1386
Fax: 302 378 3871
Levels of Connectivity Supported: Shell, SLIP, PPP, UUCP

ISPs for Area Code 303

ABWAM, Inc.
8601 F-5 W. Cross Dr. #304
Littleton, CO 80123 USA
Phone: 303 730 6050
Email: info@entertain.com
Web site: http://
www.entertain.com
Levels of Connectivity Supported: Shell, SLIP, PPP, UUCP, ISDN, 56kb, T1

Colorado SuperNet, Inc.
999 - 18th Street, Suite 2640
Denver, CO 80202 USA
Phone: 303 296 8202
Fax: 303 296 8224
Email: http://
www.entertain.com
Web site: http://www.csn.net
Levels of Connectivity Supported: Shell, SLIP, PPP, UUCP, ISDN, 56kb, T1

CSDC, Inc.
2525 Arapahoe Suite E4-447
Boulder, CO 80302 USA
Phone: 303 665 8053
Fax: 303 443 0808
Email: support@ares.csd.net
Web site: http://www.csd.net
Levels of Connectivity Supported: Shell, SLIP, PPP, ISDN, 56kb, T1

The Denver Exchange, Inc. - TDE Internet
P.O. Box 11271
Denver, CO 80211-0271 USA
Phone: 303 455 4252
Fax: 303 964 9024
Email: info@tde.com
Web site: http://www.tde.com
Levels of Connectivity Supported: SLIP, PPP, ISDN, 56kb

ENVISIONET, Inc.
7400 East Arapahoe Road, Suite 202
Englewood, CO 80112 USA
Phone: 303 770 2408
Fax: 303 770 2239
Email: info@envisionet.net
Web site: http://
www.envisionet.net
Levels of Connectivity Supported: SLIP, PPP

EZLink Internet Access
1304 Westward Drive
Fort Collins, CO 80521 USA
Phone: 970 482 0807
Fax: 970 224 1933
Email: ezadmin@ezlink.com
Web site: http://
www.ezlink.com
Levels of Connectivity Supported: Shell, SLIP, PPP, UUCP

I-Link Ltd
1 Chisholm Trail
Round Rock, TX 78681 USA
Phone: 800 ILINK 99
Fax: 512 244 9681
Email: info@i-link.net
Web site: http://www.i-link.net
Levels of Connectivity Supported: PPP, ISDN, 56kb, T1

Indra's Net, Inc.
P.O. Box 7547
Boulder, CO 80306 USA
Phone: 303 546 9151
Fax: 303 546 6220
Email: info@indra.com
Web site: http://
www.indra.com
Levels of Connectivity Supported: Shell, SLIP, PPP, UUCP

Internet Express
1155 Kelly Johnson Blvd, Suite 400
Colorado Springs, CO 80920-3959 USA
Phone: 800 592 1240
Fax: 719 592 1201
Email: service@usa.net
Web site: http://www.usa.net
Levels of Connectivity Supported: Shell, SLIP, PPP, UUCP, 56kb, T1

NETConnect
P.O. Box 3425
Cedar City, UT 84720 USA
Phone: 800 689 8001
Fax: 801 865 7079
Email: office@tcd.net
Web site: http://www.tcd.net
Levels of Connectivity Supported: SLIP, PPP, UUCP, 56kb, T1

NetWay 2001, Inc.
26 W. Dry Creek Circle, Suite 600
Littleton, CO 80120 USA
Phone: 303 794 1000
Fax: 303 798 5110
Email: info@netway.net
Web site: http://www.netway.net
Levels of Connectivity Supported: Shell, SLIP, PPP, UUCP, ISDN, 56kb, T1

New Mexico Technet, Inc.
4100 Osuna NE, Suite 103
Albuquerque, NM 87109
Phone: 505 345 6555
Fax: 505 345 6559
Levels of Connectivity Supported: Shell, SLIP, PPP

Online Network Enterprises, Inc.
4888 Pearl East Circle, Suite 101
Boulder, CO 80301 USA
Phone: 303 444 2522
Fax: 303 444 2797
Email: info@netONE.com
Web site: http://www.netONE.com
Levels of Connectivity Supported: PPP, ISDN, 56kb, T1

Rocky Mountain Internet
2860 S. Circle Drive, Suite 2202
Colorado Springs, CO 80906 USA
Phone: 800 900 7644
Fax: 719 576 0301
Email: info@rmii.com
Web site: http://www.rmii.com
Levels of Connectivity Supported: Shell, SLIP, PPP, UUCP

Shaman Exchange, Inc.
Denver Area Super Highway (DASH)
12708 Foxton Rd.
Foxton, CO 80441 USA
Phone: 303 674 9784
Email: info@dash.com
Web site: http://www.dash.com
Levels of Connectivity Supported: Shell, SLIP

Stonehenge Internet Communications
9244 South Weeping Willow
Highlands Ranch, CO 80126 USA
Phone: 800 RUN INET
Fax: 303 470 8671
Email: info@henge.com
Levels of Connectivity Supported: Shell, SLIP, PPP, UUCP, ISDN, 56kb, T1

Tesser
1920 13th Street, Suite C
Boulder, CO 80302 USA
Phone: 303 442 9033
Fax: 303 449 0170
Email: info@tesser.com
Web site: http://www.tesser.com
Levels of Connectivity Supported: UUCP

ISPs for Area Code 304

RAM Technologies Inc.
P.O. Box 1760
2025 13th Street
Ashland, KY 41105-1760 USA
Phone: 800 950 1726
Fax: 606 329 9203
Email: info@ramlink.net
Web site: http://www.ramlink.net
Levels of Connectivity Supported: Shell, SLIP, PPP, 56kb, T1

ISPs for Area Code 305

Acquired Knowledge Systems, Inc.
817 SW 8 Terrace
Fort Lauderdale, FL 33315 USA
Phone: 954 525 2574
Fax: 954 462 2329
Email: info@aksi.net
Web site: http://www.aksi.net
Levels of Connectivity Supported: Shell, SLIP, PPP, ISDN

CyberGate, Inc.
662 South Military Trail
Deerfield Beach, FL 33442 USA
Phone: 305 428 4283
Fax: 305 428 7977
Email: sales@gate.net
Web site: http://www.gate.net
Levels of Connectivity Supported: Shell, SLIP, PPP, UUCP

Electronic Link
P.O. Box 562105
Miami, FL 33256-2105 USA
Phone: 305 378 1128
Fax: 305 378 1072
Email: info@elink.net
Web site: http://www.elink.net
Levels of Connectivity Supported: Shell, SLIP, PPP, UUCP, ISDN, 56kb, T1

The EmiNet Domain
1325 S. Congress Ave, Suite 241
Boynton Beach, FL 33426 USA
Phone: 407 731 0222
Fax: 407 731 2521
Email: info@emi.net
Web site: http://www.emi.net
Levels of Connectivity Supported: Shell, SLIP, PPP, UUCP, ISDN, 56kb, T1

Magg Information Services, Inc.
7950 South Military Trail, Suite 202
Lake Worth, FL 33463 USA
Phone: 407 642 9841
Fax: 407 642 8115
Email: help@magg.net
Web site: http://www.magg.net
Levels of Connectivity Supported: Shell, SLIP, PPP, ISDN, 56kb, T1

Netpoint Communications, Inc.
11077 Biscayne Blvd., Suite 304
Miami, FL 33161 USA
Phone: 305 891 1955
Fax: 305 891 2110
Email: info@netpoint.net
Web site: http://www.netpoint.net
Levels of Connectivity Supported: SLIP, PPP, ISDN, 56kb, T1

NetMiami Internet Corporation
P.O. Box 1701
Miami, FL 33265-1707 USA
Phone: 305 554 4463
Fax: 305 554 0222
Email: picard@netmiami.com
Levels of Connectivity Supported: Shell, SLIP, PPP

ICANECT
1020 NW 163 Drive
Miami, FL 33139 USA
Phone: 305 621 9200
Fax: 305 621 2227
Email: sales@icanect.net
Web site: http://www.icanect.net
Levels of Connectivity Supported: Shell, SLIP, PPP, ISDN, 56kb, T1

InteleCom Data Systems, Inc.
East Greenwich, RI USA
Phone: 401 885 6855
Email: info@ids.net
Web site: http://www.ids.net
Levels of Connectivity Supported: Shell, SLIP, PPP, UUCP

Internet Providers of Florida, Inc

Capital Bank Plaza

10700 Kendall Dr, Suite 204

Miami, Fl 33176 USA

Phone: 305 273 7978

Fax: 305 273 1887

Email: office@ipof.fla.net

Web site: http://www.fla.net

Levels of Connectivity Supported: SLIP, PPP, UUCP, 56kb, T1

Internet World Information Network

Road, Suite 169

FL 33139

Phone: 305 535 3090 or 305 535 3080

Phone: 305 672 2222

Fax: 305 535 3080

Email: webmaster@winnet.net

Web site: http://winnet.net

Levels of Connectivity Supported: Shell, SLIP, PPP, UUCP, ISDN, 56kb

Paradise Communications, Inc.

1000 Circle 75 Pkwy, Suite 120

Atlanta, GA 30339 USA

Phone: 404 980 0078

Fax: 404 984 1796

Email: info@paradise.net

Web site: http://www.paradise.net

Levels of Connectivity Supported: Shell, SLIP, PPP, UUCP, ISDN, 56kb, T1

PSS InterNet Services

2455 West International Speedway Blvd ,Suite #807

Daytona Beach, FL 32114 USA

Phone: 800 463 8499

Fax: 904 253 1006

Email: mailto:support@america.com

Web site: http://www.america.com

Levels of Connectivity Supported: Shell, SLIP, PPP

Safari Internet

1137 North Federal Highway

Ft Lauderdale, FL 33304 USA

Phone: 954 537 9550

Fax: 954 537 7959

Email: sales@safari.net

Web site: http://www.safari.net

Levels of Connectivity Supported: Shell, SLIP, PPP, ISDN, 56kb, T1

SatelNet Communications, Inc.

3921 SW 47 Ave,Suite 1011

Davie, FL 33314 USA

Phone: 305 321 5660

Fax: 305 321 6208

Email: info@satelnet.org

Web site: http://www.satelnet.org

Levels of Connectivity Supported: Shell, SLIP, PPP, UUCP, ISDN, 56kb, T1

Shadow Information Services, Inc.

2000 Nw 88 Court

Miami, FL 33172 USA

Phone: 305 594 2450

Fax: 305 599 1140

Email: admin@shadow.net

Web site: http://www.shadow.net

Levels of Connectivity Supported: SLIP, PPP, Shell

WebIMAGE, Inc an internet presence provider

1900 S.Harbor City Blvd, Suite 328

Melbourne, FL 32901 USA

Phone: 407 723 0001

Email: info@webimage.com

Web site: http://www.webimage.com

Levels of Connectivity Supported: 56kb, T1

Zimmerman Communications

1061 SW 75 Ave

Plantation, FL 33317 USA

Phone: 954 584 0199

Fax: 954 584 0199

Email: bob@zim.com

Web site: http://www.zim.com

Levels of Connectivity Supported: PPP, ISDN, 56kb

ISPs for Area Code 306

Cycor Communications Incorporated
P.O. Box 454
Charlottetown, Prince Edward Island C1A 7K7, Canada
Phone: 800 282 9267 and 902 892 7354
Fax: 902 629 2456
Email: signup@cycor.ca
Web site: http://www.cycor.ca
Levels of Connectivity Supported: SLIP, PPP, ISDN, 56kb, T1

ISPs for Area Code 307

CoffeyNet
142 South Center St.
Casper, WY 82601 USA
Phone: 307 234 5443
Fax: 307 234 5446
Email: web@coffey.com
Web site: http://www.coffey.com
Levels of Connectivity Supported: Shell, SLIP, PPP, 56kb, T1

NETConnect
P.O. Box 3425
Cedar City, UT 84720 USA
Phone: 800 689 8001
Fax: 801 865 7079
Email: office@tcd.net
Web site: http://www.tcd.net
Levels of Connectivity Supported: SLIP, PPP, UUCP, 56kb, T1

wyoming.com
312 S. 4th Street
Lander, WY 82520 USA
Phone: 307 332 3030 (800) WYO-I-NET
Fax: 307-332-5720
Email: info@wyoming.com
Web site: http://www.wyoming.com
Levels of Connectivity Supported: SLIP

ISPs for Area Code 308

Synergy Communications, Inc.
1941 South 42nd Street
Omaha, NE 68105 USA
Phone: 800 345 9669
Fax: 402 346 0208
Email: info@synergy.net
Levels of Connectivity Supported: PPP

ISPs for Area Code 309

CICNet, Inc.
2901 Hubbard Drive
Ann Arbor, MI 48105 USA
Phone: 313 998 6103
Fax: 313 998 6105
Email: info@cic.net
Web site: http://www.cic.net
Levels of Connectivity Supported: Shell, SLIP, PPP, 56kb, T1

Driscoll Communications
107 Partridge Lane, Lower Level
Metamora, IL 61548 USA
Phone: 309 367 2006
Email: info@dris.com
Web site: http://www.dris.com
Levels of Connectivity Supported: SLIP, PPP, UUCP, ISDN, 56kb, T1

Interactive Communications & Explorations (ICEnet)
607B South Main #161
Normal, IL 61761 USA
Phone: 309 454 4638
Email: icenet@ice.net
Web site: http://www.ice.net
Levels of Connectivity Supported: Shell, SLIP, PPP, UUCP, ISDN, 56kb, T1

ISPs for Area Code 310

ArtNetwork
844 S. Robertson
Los Angeles, CA 90035 USA
Phone: 800 395 0692
Fax: 310 652 7114
Email: info@artnet.net
Web site: http://www.artnet.net
Levels of Connectivity Supported: Shell, SLIP, PPP, UUCP, ISDN, 56kb, T1

BeachNet Internet Access

BeachNet, Inc.

Marina Del Rey, CA 90292
USA

Phone: 310 823 3308

Fax: 310 823 1390

Email: info@beachnet.com

Web site: http://
www.beachnet.com

Levels of Connectivity Supported: SLIP, PPP, T1

Business Access Technologies

3484 E. Orangethorpe

Anaheim, Ca. 92806 USA

Phone: 714 577 8978

Email: Techs@batech.com

Web site: http://batech.com

Levels of Connectivity Supported: Shell, PPP, 56kb

Cloverleaf Communications

7862 Yorkshire

Stanton, CA 90680 USA

Phone: 714 895 3075

Fax: 310 420 7255

Email:
mailto:sales@cloverleaf.com

Web site: http://
www.cloverleaf.com

Levels of Connectivity Supported: Shell, SLIP, PPP,
UUCP

Cogent Software, Inc.

221 E. Walnut St., Suite 215

Pasadena,CA 91101 USA

Phone: 818 585 2788

Fax: 818 585 2785

Email: info@cogsoft.com

Web site: http://
www.cogsoft.com

Levels of Connectivity Supported: Shell, PPP, ISDN,
56kb, T1

CruzNet

215 E. Orangethorpe Ave.
Suite 333

Fullerton, CA 92632 USA

Phone: 714 680 6600

Fax: 714 680 4241

Email: info@cruznet.net

Web site: http://
www.cruznet.net

Levels of Connectivity Supported: Shell, SLIP, PPP,
UUCP, ISDN, 56kb, T1

Cyberverse Online

2221 Rosecrans Avenue,
Suite 130

El Segundo, CA 90245 USA

Phone: 310 643 3783

Fax: 310 643 6137

Email: info@cyberverse.com

Web site: http://
www.cyberverse.com

Levels of Connectivity Supported: Shell, SLIP, PPP

Delta Internet Services

731 E. Ball Rd., Suite 204

Anaheim,CA 92805 USA

Phone: 714 778 0370

Fax: 714 778 1064

Email: info@delta.net

Web site: http://
www.delta.net

Levels of Connectivity Supported: Shell, SLIP, PPP,
UUCP, ISDN, 56kb, T1

DigiLink Network Services

4429 W. 169th Street

Lawndale, CA 90260-3252

Phone: 310 542 7421

Web site: http://www.dfw.net

Levels of Connectivity Supported: PPP

Exodus Communications, Inc.

948 Benecia Avenue

Sunnyvale, CA 94086 USA

Phone: 408 522 8450

Fax: 408 736 6843

Email: info@exodus.net

Web site: http://
www.exodus.net

Levels of Connectivity Supported: ISDN, 56kb, T1

Flamingo Communications Inc.

19401 So. Vermont Ave., Suite D-104

Torrance, CA 90502 USA

Phone: 310 532 3533

Fax: 310 532 3622

Email: sales@fcom.com

Web site: http://www.fcom.com

Levels of Connectivity Supported: Shell, SLIP, PPP

Instant Internet Corporation (InstaNet)

21010 Devonshire St.

Chatsworth, CA. 91311 USA

Phone: 818 772 0097

Fax: 818 772 9941

Email: charlyg@instanet.com

Web site: http://www.instanet.com

Levels of Connectivity Supported: PPP, UUPp, ISDN, 56kb

InterWorld Communications, Inc.

222 N. Sepulveda Blvd., Suite 1560

El Segundo, CA 90245 USA

Phone: 310 726 0500

Fax: 310 726 0559

Email: sales@interworld.net

Web site: http://www.interworld.net

Levels of Connectivity Supported: SLIP, PPP, UUCP, ISDN, 56kb, T1

KAIWAN Internet

12550 Brookhurst Street, Suite H

Garden Grove, CA 92640 USA

Phone: 714 638 2139

Fax: 714 638 0455

Email: info@kaiwan.com

Web site: http://www.kaiwan.com

Levels of Connectivity Supported: Shell, SLIP, PPP, UUCP, ISDN, 56kb

KTB Internet Online

P.O. Box 3121

Glendale, CA 91221 USA

Phone: 818 240 6600

Fax: 818 240 6600

Email: info@ktb.net

Web site: http://www.ktb.net

Levels of Connectivity Supported: Shell, SLIP, PPP, UUCP, ISDN, 56kb, T1

The Loop Internet Switch Co.

6611 Santa Monica Blvd.

Los Angeles, CA 90038 USA

Phone: 213 465 1311

Fax: 213 469 2193

Email: info@loop.com

Web site: http://www.loop.com/rates.html

Levels of Connectivity Supported: SLIP, PPP

Leonardo Internet

927 6th Street

Santa Monica, CA 90403 USA

Phone: 310 395 5500

Fax: 310 395 9924

Email: jimp@leonardo.net

Web site: http://leonardo.net

Levels of Connectivity Supported: Shell, PPP, ISDN, 56kb, T1

Liberty Information Network

446 S Anaheim Hills Road, Suite 102

Anaheim, CA 92807 USA

Phone: 800 218 5157 or 714 996 9999

Fax: 714 961 8700 Attn: ISP INFO

Email: info@liberty.com

Web site: http://www.liberty.com

Levels of Connectivity Supported: Shell, SLIP, PPP, UUCP, ISDN, 56kb, T1

Lightside, Inc.

101 N. Citrus, Suite #4A

Covina, CA 91723 USA

Phone: 818 858 9261

Fax: 818 858 8982

Email: Lightside@Lightside.Com

Web site: http://www.lightside.Net

Levels of Connectivity Supported: SLIP, PPP, 56kb, T1

Network Intensive

8001 Irvine Center Drive, Suite #1130

Irvine, CA 92718 USA

Phone: 714 450 8400

Fax: 714 450 8410

Email: info@ni.net

Web site: http://www.ni.net

Levels of Connectivity Supported: Shell, UUCP, SLIP, PPP, ISDN, 56kb, T1

Online-LA
8671 Wilshire Blvd.
Beverly Hills, CA 90211 USA
Phone: 310 967 8000
Fax: 310 358 5610
Email: sales@online-la.com
Web site: http://www.online-la.com
Levels of Connectivity Supported: PPP, ISDN, 56kb, T1

OutWest Network Services Inc.
440 Western Avenue, Suite 101
Glendale, CA 91201 USA
Phone: 818 545 1996
Email: info@outwest.net
Web site: http://outwest.net
Levels of Connectivity Supported: Shell, SLIP, PPP, UUCP, ISDN, 56kb, T1

QuickCom Internet Communcations
5724 W. Third St. Ste.# 507
Los Angeles, CA 90036 USA
Phone: 213 634 7735
Fax: 213 634 7722
Email: info@quickcom.net
Web site: http://www.quickcom.net
Levels of Connectivity Supported: PPP, ISDN, 56kb, T1

QuickNet, Inc.
7401 Seabluff Drive, Suite #110
Huntington Beach, CA 92648-2433 USA
Phone: 714 969 1091
Email: sales@quick.net
Web site: http://www.quick.net
Levels of Connectivity Supported: Shell, PPP, UUCP, ISDN, 56kb, T1

Saigon Enterprises
P.O. Box 3121
Glendale, CA 91221-0121 USA
Phone: 818 246 0689
Fax: 818 240 6600
Email: info@saigon.net
Web site: http://www.saigon.net
Levels of Connectivity Supported: Shell, SLIP, PPP, UUCP, ISDN, 56kb, T1

SoftAware
4676 Admiralty Way, Suite 410
Marina del Rey, CA 90292 USA
Phone: 310 305 0275
Email: info@softaware.com
Web site: http://www.softaware.com
Levels of Connectivity Supported: T1

ViaNet Communications
800 El Camino Real West, Suite 180
Mountain View, CA 94040
Phone: 415 903 2242
Fax: 415 903 2241
Levels of Connectivity Supported: Shell, SLIP, PPP, UUCP

ISPs for Area Code 312

American Information Systems, Inc.
911 North Plum Grove Road, Suite F
Schaumburg, IL 60173 USA
Phone: 708 413 8400
Fax: 708 413 8401
Email: info@ais.net
Web site: http://www.ais.net
Levels of Connectivity Supported: Shell, SLIP, PPP, UUCP

CICNet, Inc.
2901 Hubbard Drive
Ann Arbor, MI 48105 USA
Phone: 313 998 6103
Fax: 313 998 6105
Email: info@cic.net
Web site: http://www.cic.net
Levels of Connectivity Supported: Shell, SLIP, PPP, 56kb, T1

CIN.net (Computerese Information Network)
721 West Golf Road
Hoffman Estates, IL 60194 USA
Phone: 708 310 1188
Fax: 708 885 8308
Email: info@cin.net
Web site: http://www.cin.net
Levels of Connectivity Supported: Shell, SLIP, PPP, UUCP, ISDN, 56kb, T1

Compunet Technology Consultants

P.O. Box 880

Naperville, IL 60540 USA

Phone: 708 355 XNET

Fax: 708 355 UFAX

Email: webmaster@ms.com-punet.com

Web site: http://www.com-punet.com

Levels of Connectivity Supported: SLIP, PPP, ISDN, 56kb, T1

InterAccess Co.

3345 Commercial Ave.

Northbrook, IL 60062 USA

Phone: 708 498 2542

Fax: 708 498 3289

Email: info@interaccess.com

Web site: http://www.interaccess.com

Levels of Connectivity Supported: Shell, SLIP, PPP, UUCP, ISDN, 56kb, T1

Interactive Network Systems, Inc.

2316 West 108th Place

Chicago, Illinois 60643 USA

Phone: 312 881 3039

Fax: 312 881 3064

Email: info@insnet.com

Web site: http://www.insnet.com

Levels of Connectivity Supported: Shell, SLIP, PPP, ISDN, 56kb, T1

MCSNet

1300 W. Belmont, Suite 405

Chicago, IL 60657 USA

Phone: 312 803 6271

Fax: 312 803 6271

Email: info@mcs.net

Web site: http://www.mcs.net

Levels of Connectivity Supported: Shell, SLIP, UUCP

The Planet Group, Inc.

1608 Milwaukee Avenue, Suite 1200

Chicago, IL 60647 USA

Phone: 312 772 8333

Fax: 312 772 9214

Email: info@www.planet-group.com

Web site: http://www.planet-group.com

Levels of Connectivity Supported: Shell, SLIP, PPP, UUCP, ISDN, 56kb, T1

Ripco Communications, Inc.

3163 N. Clybourn Avenue

Chicago, IL 60618-6424

Phone 312 477 6210

Levels of Connectivity Supported: Shell, SLIP, PPP, UUCP

Tezcatlipoca, Inc.

Tezcat

1573-A N. Milwaukee, Suite 440

Chicago, IL 60622 USA

Phone: 312 850 0181

Fax: 312 850 0492

Email: info@tezcat.com

Web site: http://www.tezcat.com

Levels of Connectivity Supported: Shell, SLIP, PPP

The ThoughtPort Authority Inc.

2000 E. Broadway, Suite 242

Columbia, MO 65201 USA

Phone: 800 ISP 6870

Fax: 314 474 4122

Email: info@thoughtport.com

Web site: http://www.thoughtport.com

Levels of Connectivity Supported: SLIP, PPP, ISDN, 56kb, T1

VoiceNet

17 Richard Rd.

Ivyland, PA 18974 USA

Phone: 800 835 5710

Fax: 215 674 9662

Email: info@voicenet.com

Web site: http://www.voicenet.com

Levels of Connectivity Supported: Shell, SLIP, PPP, UUCP, ISDN, 56kb, T1

Wink Communications Group, Inc.

2500 W Higgins Rd, Suite 480
Hoffman Estates, IL 60195
USA
Phone: 708 310 9465
Fax: 708 310 3477
Email: sales@winkcomm.com
Web site: http://
www.winkcomm.com
Levels of Connectivity Supported: ISDN, 56kb, T1

WorldWide Access

20 North Wacker Drive, Suite
766
Chicago, IL 60606 USA
Phone: 312 803 9921
Fax: 312 803 9923
Email: info@wwa.com
Web site: http://www.wwa.com
Levels of Connectivity Supported: Shell, SLIP, PPP,
UUCP, ISDN, 56kb, T1

XNet Information Systems

3080 E. Ogden Ave Suite 202
Lisle, IL 60532 USA
Phone: 708 983 6064
Fax: 708 983 6879
Email: info@xnet.com
Web site: http://www.xnet.com
Levels of Connectivity Supported: Shell, SLIP, PPP,
UUCP, ISDN, 56kb, T1

VoiceNet

17 Richard Rd.
Ivyland, PA 18974 USA
Phone: 800 835 5710
Fax: 215 674 9662
Email: info@voicenet.com
Web site: http://
www.voicenet.com
Levels of Connectivity Supported: Shell, SLIP, PPP,
UUCP, ISDN, 56kb, T1

ISPs for Area Code 313

Branch Information Services

2901 Hubbard
Ann Arbor, MI 48105 USA
Phone: 313 741 4442
Fax: 313 995 1931
Email: branch-info@branch.com
Web site: http://branch.com
Levels of Connectivity Supported: SLIP, PPP, ISDN,
56kb, T1

CICNet, Inc.

2901 Hubbard Drive
Ann Arbor, MI 48105 USA
Phone: 313 998 6103
Fax: 313 998 6105
Email: info@cic.net
Web site: http://www.cic.net
Levels of Connectivity Supported: Shell, SLIP, PPP,
56kb, T1

Great Lakes Information Systems

P.O. Box 189216
Utica, Michigan 48318-9216
USA
Phone: 810 786 0454
Fax: 810 786 0325
Email: info@glis.net
Web site: http://www.glis.net
Levels of Connectivity Supported: PPP, UUCP, 56kb, T1

ICNET / Innovative Concepts

2901 Hubbard
Ann Arbor, MI 48105
Phone: 313 998 0090
Fax: 313 998 0816
Levels of Connectivity Supported: Shell, SLIP, PPP,
UUCP

Isthmus Corporation

2006 Hogback Rd.
Ann Arbor, MI 48105-9750
USA
Phone: 313 973 2100
Fax: 313 973 2117
Email: info@izzy.net
Web site: http://www.izzy.net
Levels of Connectivity Supported: Shell, SLIP, PPP,
UUCP

Michigan Internet Cooperative Association (MICA.net)

P.O. Box 40899
Redford, MI 48240 USA
Phone: 810 355 1438
Email: info@coop.mica.
Web site: http://www.mica.net
Levels of Connectivity Supported: SLIP, PPP, 56kb, T1

Mich.com, Inc.
21042 Laurelwood
Farmington, MI 48336 USA
Phone: 810 478 4300
Fax: 810 478 4302
Email: info@mich.com
Web site: http://www.mich.com
Levels of Connectivity Supported: Shell, SLIP, PPP, UUCP, 56kb, T1

Msen, Inc.
320 Miller Avenue
Ann Arbor, MI 48103
Phone: 313 998 4562
Fax: 313 998 4563
Levels of Connectivity Supported: Shell, SLIP, PPP, UUCP

RustNet, Inc.
6905 Telegraph Rd., Suite 315
Bloomfield Hills, MI 48301
USA
Phone: 810 642 2276
Fax: 810 642 3676
Email: info@rust.net
Web site: http://www.rust.net
Levels of Connectivity Supported: Shell, PPP, ISDN, 56kb, T1

Voyager Information Networks, Inc.
600 West St. Jospeh Hwy.,
Suite 20
Lansing, MI 48933 USA
Phone: 517 485 9068
Fax: 517 485 9074
Email: help@voyager.net
Web site: http://www.voyager.net
Levels of Connectivity Supported: PPP, ISDN, 56kb, T1

ISPs for Area Code 314

accessU.S. Inc.
P.O. Box 985
1500 Main Street
Mt. Vernon, IL 62864 USA
Phone: 800 638 6373
Fax: 618 244 9175
Email: info@accessus.net
Web site: http://www.accessus.net
Levels of Connectivity Supported: SLIP, PPP, ISDN, 56kb, T1

Allied Access Inc.
1002 Walnut Street
Murphysboro, IL 62966 USA
Phone: 618 684 2255 or 800 INETDOM
Fax: 618 684 5907
Email: sales@intrnet.net
Levels of Connectivity Supported: Shell, SLIP, PPP

Inlink
P.O. Box 410890
St. Louis, MO 63141-0890
USA
Phone: 314 432 0935
Fax: 314 432 2569
Email: support@inlink.com
Web site: http://www.inlink.com
Levels of Connectivity Supported: SLIP, PPP, ISDN

MVP-Net, Inc.
5494 Brown Road, Suite 109
Hazelwood, MO 63042 USA
Phone: 314 731 2252
Fax: 314 731 2260
Email: info@MO.NET
Web site: http://www.mo.net
Levels of Connectivity Supported: Shell, SLIP, PPP, UUCP, ISDN, 56kb, T1

NeoSoft, Inc.
3408 Magnum Road
Houston, TX 77092
Phone: 800 GET NEOSOFT or 713 684 5969
Fax: 713 684 5922
Levels of Connectivity Supported: Shell, SLIP, PPP, UUCP

Online Information Access Network

3 Sunset Hills Executive Park
Edwardsville, IL 62025 USA
Phone: 618 692 9813
Fax: 618 692 9874
Email: info@oia.net
Web site: http://www.oia.net
Levels of Connectivity Supported: Shell, SLIP

SOCKET Internet Services Corporation

607 East Jackson Street
Columbia, MO 65203 USA
Phone: 314 499 9131
Fax: 314 875 5812
Email: office@socketis.net
Web site: http://www.socketis.net
Levels of Connectivity Supported: SLIP, PPP, ISDN, 56kb

Tetranet Communications, Inc.

15444 Clayton Rd, Suite 325
P.O. Box 7012
Chesterfield, MO 63006-7012
USA
Phone: 314 256 4495
Fax: 314 256 9756
Email: info@tetranet.net
Web site: http://www.tetranet.net
Levels of Connectivity Supported: Shell, PPP, UUCP, ISDN, 56kb, T1

The ThoughtPort Authority Inc.

2000 E. Broadway, Suite 242
Columbia, MO 65201 USA
Phone: 800 ISP 6870
Fax: 314 474 4122
Email: info@thoughtport.com
Web site: http://www.thoughtport.com
Levels of Connectivity Supported: SLIP, PPP, ISDN, 56kb, T1

ISPs for Area Code 315

NYSERNet

200 Elwood Davis Road
Liverpool, NY 13088-6147
USA
Phone: 800 493 4367
Fax: 315 453 3052
Email: sales@nysernet.org
Web site: http://nysernet.org
Levels of Connectivity Supported: Shell, PPP, 56kb, T1

ServiceTech, Inc.

182 Monroe Ave
Rochester, NY 14607 USA
Phone: 716 263 3360
Fax: 716 423 1596
Email: info@servtech.com
Web site: http://www.servtech.com
Levels of Connectivity Supported: Shell, PPP, ISDN, 56kb, T1

Spectra.net

139 Grand Avenue
NY 13790
Phone: 607 798 7300
607 798 7771
607 770 0090
Fax: 607 717 315
Email: info@spectra.net
Web site: http://www.spectra.net
Levels of Connectivity Supported: Shell, SLIP, PPP, ISDN, 56kb, T1

Syracuse Internet

P.O. Box 89
Liverpool, NY 13088 USA
Phone: 315 233 1948
Fax: 315 453 5683
Email: info@vcomm.net
Web site: http://www.vcomm.net
Levels of Connectivity Supported: Shell, SLIP, PPP, UUCP, 56kp, T1

VivaNET, Inc.

1555 East Henrietta Road
Rochester, NY 14623 USA
Phone: 800 836 UNIX
Fax: 716 272 7627
Web site: http://www.vivanet.com
Levels of Connectivity Supported: Shell, SLIP, PPP, UUCP, ISDN, 56kb, T1

ISPs for Area Code 316

Elysian Fields, Inc.
200 N. Broadway, Suites 400 & 500
Wichita, KS 67202 USA
Phone: 316 267 2636
Fax: 316 267 5265
Email: info@elysian.net
Web site: http://www.elysian.net
Levels of Connectivity Supported: Shell, SLIP, PPP, UUCP, 56kb

Future Net, Inc.
8100 E 22nd St N, Bldg 2100
Suite 200B
Wichita, KS 67226 USA
Phone: 316 652 0070
Fax: 316 652 0339
Email: rgmann@fn.net
Web site: http://www.fn.net
Levels of Connectivity Supported: Shell, SLIP, ISDN, 56kb, T1

SouthWind Internet Access, Inc.
120 S. Market, Suite 330
Wichita, KS 67202
voice 316 263 7963
fax 316 267 3943
Levels of Connectivity Supported: Shell, SLIP, UUCP

ISPs for Area Code 317

HolliCom Internet Services
6810 West 400 South
Russiaville, IN 46979 USA
Phone: 317 883 4500
Fax: 317 883 7669
Email: cale@holli.com
Web site: http://www.holli.com
Levels of Connectivity Supported: Shell, SLIP, PPP, UUCP, ISDN, 56kb, T1

IQuest Internet, Inc.
2035 East 46th Street
Indianapolis, IN 46205 USA
Phone: 317 259 5050
Fax: 317 259 7289
Email: info@iquest.net
Web site: http://www.iquest.net
Levels of Connectivity Supported: Shell, SLIP, PPP, UUCP

Metropolitan Data Networks Limited
100 Executive Drive Suite F
Lafayette, IN 47905-4864 USA
Phone: 317 449 0539
Fax: 317 449 0638
Email: info@mdn.com
Web site: http://www.mdn.com
Levels of Connectivity Supported: SLIP, PPP, UUCP, T1

Net Direct
6251 N. Winthrop, Suite #5
Indianapolis, IN 46220 USA
Phone: 317 251 5252
Fax: 317 726 5239
Email: kat@inetdirect.net
Web site: http://www.inetdirect.net
Levels of Connectivity Supported: SLIP, PPP, UUCP, 56kb, T1

Sol Tec, Inc.
539 East 53rd Street
Indianapolis, IN 46220, USA
Phone: 317 920 1SOL or 800 SOL1TEC
Fax: 317 925 1765
Email: info@soltec.com
Web site: http://www.soltec.com

ISPs for Area Code 318

Linknet Internet Services
2230 S. MacArthur Drive, Suite 3
Alexandria, Louisiana 71301 USA
Phone: 318 442 5465
Fax: 318 449 4950
Email: rdalton@linknet.net
Web site: http://www.linknet.net
Levels of Connectivity Supported: Shell, PPP, 56kb

Net-Connect, Ltd.
1326 West Pinhook Rd,
Suite 100
Lafayette, LA 70503 USA
Phone: 318 234 4396
Fax: 318 232 5320
Email: services@net-
connect.net
Web site: http://www.
net-connect.net
Levels of Connectivity Sup-
ported: SLIP, PPP, 56kb, T1

ISPs for Area Code 319

Freese-Notis Weather.Net
2411 Grand Avenue
Des Moines, IA 50312 USA
Phone: 515 282 9310
Fax: 515 282 6832
Email: hfreese@weather.net
Web site: http://
www.weather.net
Levels of Connectivity Sup-
ported: PPP, 56kb, T1

ia.net
3417 Center Point Road N.E.
Cedar Rapids, IA 52402 USA
Phone: 319 393 1095
Fax: 319 378 1489
Email: info@ia.net
Web site: http://www.ia.net
Levels of Connectivity Sup-
ported: Shell, SLIP, PPP,
UUCP, 56kb, T1

INTERLINK L.C.
3459 270th Ave.
P.O. Box 967
Keokuk, IA 52632-0967 USA
Phone: 319 524 2895
Fax: 319 524 2946
Email: postmaster@interl.net
Web site: http://
www.interl.net
Levels of Connectivity Sup-
ported: Shell, PPP, ISDN,
56kb, T1

Iowa Network Services
4201 Corporate Drive
West Des Moines, IA 50265
USA
Phone: 800 546 6587
Fax: 515 830 0345
Email: service@netins.net
Web site: http://
www.netins.net
Levels of Connectivity Sup-
ported: Shell, SLIP, PPP,
UUCP, 56kb, T1, Web Hosting

ISPs for Area Code 334

Datasync Internet
P. O. Box 399
Ocean Springs, MS 39566-
0399 USA
Phone: 601 872 0001 or 601
452 0011 or 334 476 8155
Email: info@datasync.com
Web site: http://
www.datasync.com
Levels of Connectivity Sup-
ported: Shell, SLIP, PPP,
UUCP, 56kb, T1

**Gulf Coast Internet
Company**
41 North Jefferson Street
Rhodes Building, Suite 401
Pensacola, FL 32501 USA
Phone: 904 438 5700
Fax: 904 438 5750
Email: info@gulf.net
Web site: http://www.gulf.net
Levels of Connectivity Sup-
ported: Shell, SLIP, PPP,
UUCP, ISDN, 56kb, T1

OnLine Montgomery
5757-E Atlanta Highway
Montgomery, AL 36117 USA
Phone: 334 271 9576
Fax: 334 272 1771
Email: rverble@bbs.olm.com
Web site: http://www.olm.com
Levels of Connectivity Sup-
ported: Shell, SLIP

MindSpring Enterprises, Inc.
1430 West Peachtree St NW,
Suite 400
Atlanta, GA 30309 USA
Phone: 800 719 4332
Fax: 404 815 8805
Email: info@mindspring.com
Web site: info@mindspring.com
Levels of Connectivity Sup-
ported: SLIP, PPP, UUCP,
ISDN, 56kb

Scott Network Services, Inc.
P.O. Box 361353
Birmingham, AL 35236 USA
Phone: 205 987 5889
Email: info@scott.net
Web site: http://
www.scott.net
Levels of Connectivity Supported: Shell, SLIP, PPP,
UUCP, ISDN

WSNetwork Communications Services, Inc.
448 South Lawrence St.
Montgomery, AL 36104 USA
Phone: 334 263 5505 or 800
INET 750
Fax: 334 262 3522
Email: custserv@wsnet.com
Web site: http://
www.wsnet.com
Levels of Connectivity Supported: Shell, PPP, UUCP,
ISDN, 56kb, T1

ISPs for Area Code 360

The Bellingham Internet Cafe
206 W. Magnolia
Bellingham, WA 98225 USA
Phone: 360 650 0442
Fax: 360 738 8315
Email: tonys@inet-cafe.com
Web site: http://www.inet-cafe.com
Levels of Connectivity Supported: Shell, PPP, ISDN,
56kb, T1

Interconnected Associates Inc. (IXA)
300 E. Pike Street, Suite 2001
Seattle, WA 98122 USA
Phone: 206 622 7337
Fax: 206 621 0567
Email: mike@ixa.com
Web site: http://www.ixa.com
Levels of Connectivity Supported: 56kb, T1

NorthWest CommLink
511B N. Baker
Mt. Vernon, WA 98273
Phone: 360 336 0103
Levels of Connectivity Supported: Shell, SLIP, PPP

NorthWestNet
15400 S.E. 30th Place,
Suite 202
Bellevue, WA 98007 USA
Phone: 206 562 3000
Fax: 206 562 4822
Email: info@nwnet.net
Web site: http://
www.nwnet.net
Levels of Connectivity Supported: T1

Olympia Networking Services
120 N State, Suite 1021
Olympia, WA 98501-8212
USA
Phone: 360 753 3636
Fax: 360 357 6160
Email: info@olywa.net
Web site: http://
www.olywa.net
Levels of Connectivity Supported: SLIP, PPP, UUCP,
ISDN, 56kb, T1

Olympic Net
P.O. Box 945
Silverdale, WA 98383 USA
Phone: 360 692 0651
Fax: 360 692 1507
Email: info@olympic.net
Web site: http://
www.olympic.net
Levels of Connectivity Supported: Shell, SLIP, PPP

Olympus
537 Tyler Street
Port Townsend, WA 98368
USA
Phone: 360 385 0464
Email: info@olympus.net
Web site: http://
www.olympus.net
Levels of Connectivity Supported: PPP

Pacifier Computers (Pacifier Online Data Service)
1800 F. Street
Vancouver, WA 98663 USA
Phone: 360 693 2116
Fax: 360 254 3898
Email: info@pacifier.com
Web site: http://
www.pacifier.com
Levels of Connectivity Supported: Shell, SLIP, PPP,
UUCP

Pacific Rim Network, Inc.
P.O. Box 5006
Bellingham, WA 98227 USA
Phone: 360 650 0442 x 11
Fax: 360 738 8315
Email: info@pacificrim.net
Web site: http://
www.pacificrim.net
Levels of Connectivity Supported: PPP, ISDN, 56kb,
128kb, T1

Performa Services
East 500 Haskell Hill Road
Shelton, WA 98584 USA
Phone: 360 426 0738
Email: patrick@westsound.com
Web site: http://
www.westsound.com
Levels of Connectivity Supported: SLIP, PPP

Premier1 Internet Services
P.O. Box 1198
Sultan, WA 98294 USA
Phone: 360 793 3658
Fax: 360 793 3791
Email:
mailto:info@premier1.net
Web site: http://
www.premier1.net
Levels of Connectivity Supported: Shell, SLIP, PPP,
UUCP, 56kb

Skagit On-Line Services
P.O. Box 566
Burlington, WA 98233
Phone: 360 755 0190
Fax: 360 755 0956
Levels of Connectivity Supported: Shell, SLIP, PPP,
UUCP

Structured Network Systems, Inc.
15635 SE 114th Ave., Suite 201
Clackamas, OR 97015 USA
Phone: 800 881 0962
Fax: 503 656 3235
Email: sales@structured.net
Web site: http://
www.structured.net
Levels of Connectivity Supported: 56kb, T1

Teleport, Inc.
319 SW Washington, Suite 604
Portland, OR 97204 USA
Phone: 503 223 4245
Fax: 503 223 4372
Email: info@teleport.com
Web site: http://
www.teleport.com
Levels of Connectivity Supported: Shell, SLIP, PPP

Transport Logic
13500 SW Pacific Hwy #513
Portland, OR 97223 USA
Phone: 503 243 1940
Email: info@transport.com
Web site: http://
www.transport.com
Levels of Connectivity Supported: SLIP, PPP, ISDN,
56kb, T1

TSCNet Inc.
10049 Cleer Creek Blvd, Suite 103
P.O. Box 3686
Silverdale, WA 98383-3686
USA
Phone: 360 613 0708
Fax: 360 698 3563
Email: info@tscnet.com
Web site: http://
www.tscnet.com
Levels of Connectivity Supported: Shell, SLIP, PPP,
UUCP

Whidbey Connections, Inc.
P.O. Box 1048
302 N. Main Street
Coupeville, WA 98239-1048
Phone: 360 678 1070
Fax: 360 678 6129
Levels of Connectivity Supported: Shell, SLIP, PPP,
UUCP

WLN
P.O. Box 3888
Lacey, WA 98503-0888 USA
Phone: 800 342 5956 or 360
923 4000
Fax: 360 923 4009
Email: info@wln.com
Levels of Connectivity Supported: Shell, SLIP, PPP

ISPs for Area Code 401

brainiac services inc.
P.O. Box 5069
Greene, RI 02827 USA
Phone: 401 539 9050
Email: info@brainiac.com
Web site: http://
www.brainiac.com
Levels of Connectivity Supported: Shell, SLIP, PPP,
UUCP, ISDN, 56kb, T1

CompUtopia
205 Hallene Road, Unit A6
Warwick, RI 02886 USA
Phone: 401 732 5588
Fax: 401 732 5518
Email: allan@computopia.com
Web site: http://
www.computopia.com
Levels of Connectivity Supported: ISDN, 56kb, T1

InteleCom Data Systems, Inc.
East Greenwich, RI USA
Phone: 401 885 6855
Email: info@ids.net
Web site: http://www.ids.net
Levels of Connectivity Supported: Shell, SLIP, PPP,
UUCP

The Internet Connection, Inc.
Brookside Office Park
272 Chauncy St, Suite 6
Mansfield, MA 02048 USA
Phone: 508 261 0383
Fax: 508 730 1049
Email: info@ici.net
Web site: http://www.ici.net
Levels of Connectivity Supported: Shell, SLIP, PPP,
UUCP, ISDN, 56kb, T1

MCIX, Inc.
5 Roosevelt Ave
Mystic, CT 06355 USA
Phone: 860 572 8720
Fax: 860 572 8720
Email: info@mcix.com
Web site: http://www.mcix.com
Levels of Connectivity Supported: Shell, SLIP, PPP,
UUCP, ISDN, 56kb, T1

Plymouth Commercial Internet eXchange
190 Old Derby Street,
Suite #115
Hingham, MA 02043 USA
Phone: 617 741 5900
Fax: 617 741 5416
Email: info@pcix.com
Web site: http://www.pcix.com
Levels of Connectivity Supported: Shell, SLIP, PPP,
UUCP, ISDN, 56kb, T1

Saturn Internet Corporation
151 Pearl Street, 4th Floor
Boston, MA 02110 USA
Phone: 617 451 9121
Fax: 617 451 0358
Email: info@saturn.net
Web site: http://
www.saturn.net
Levels of Connectivity Supported: SLIP, PPP, 56kb, T1

ISPs for Area Code 402

Greater Omaha Public Access Unix Corporation
5062 So. 108th, Suite 345
Omaha, NE 68137 USA
Phone: 402 558 5030
Fax: 402 339 2327
Email: info@gonix.com
Web site: http://
www.gonix.com
Levels of Connectivity Supported: Shell, SLIP, PPP,
UUCP

Internet Nebraska
1719 N. Cotner Blvd.
Lincoln, NE 68505-5301
Phone: 402 434 8680
Levels of Connectivity Supported: Shell, SLIP, PPP,
UUCP

Iowa Network Services
4201 Corporate Drive
West Des Moines, IA 50265
USA
Phone: 800 546 6587
Fax: 515 830 0345
Email: service@netins.net
Web site: http://
www.netins.net
Levels of Connectivity Supported: Shell, SLIP, PPP,
UUCP, 56kb, T1, Web Hosting

The Online Pitstop
P.O. Box 1051
Bellevue, NE 68005 USA
Phone: 402 291 1542
Email: bob@top.net
Web site: http://www.top.net
Levels of Connectivity Supported: Shell, SLIP, ISDN

Pioneer Internet
504 4th Street
Sergeant Bluff, IA 51054
Phone: 712 271 0101
Fax: 712 943 4742
Email: info@pionet.net
Web site: http://
www.pionet.net
Levels of Connectivity Supported: PPP, 56kb, T1

ProLinx Communications, Inc.
P.O. Box 31185
Omaha, NE 68131-0185 USA
Phone: 402 551 3036
Email:
techsupport@nfinity.nfinity.com
Web site: http://
www.nfinity.com
Levels of Connectivity Supported: Shell, SLIP, PPP,
UUCP, ISDN, 56kb, T1

Synergy Communications, Inc.
1941 South 42nd Street
Omaha, NE 68105 USA
Phone: 800 345 9669
Fax: 402 346 0208
Email: info@synergy.net
Levels of Connectivity Supported: PPP

Zelcom International, Incorporated
2819 S. 125th Ave., Suite 256
Omaha, NE 68144 USA
Phone: 402 333 2441
Fax: 402 333 4583
Email: administration-
dept@zelcom.com
Web site: http://
www.zelcom.com/
Levels of Connectivity Supported: SLIP

ISPs for Area Code 403

AGT Limited
10020 100 Street
Edmonton, Alberta T5J 0N5
Canada
Phone: 800 608 1155
Fax: 800 218 2638
Email: info@agt.net
Web site: http://www.agt.net
Levels of Connectivity Supported: SLIP, PPP, ISDN,
56kb

Alberta SuperNet Inc.
Suite#325, 10909 Jasper Avenue
Alberta T5J 3L9 Canada
Phone: 403 424 0743
Email: info@supernet.ab.ca
Web site: http://
www.supernet.ab.ca
Levels of Connectivity Supported: Shell, SLIP, PPP,
UUCP, 56kb, T1

CCI Networks
4130 95th Street
Alberta T6E 6H5 CANADA
Phone: 403 450 9143
Email: info@ccinet.ab.ca
Web site: http://
www.ccinet.ab.ca
Levels of Connectivity Supported: SLIP, PPP, UUCP,
ISDN, 56kb

Cycor Communications Incorporated

P.O. Box 454

Prince Edward Island C1A 7K7 Canada

Email: signup@cycor.ca

Web site: http://www.cycor.ca

Levels of Connectivity Supported: SLIP, PPP, ISDN, 56kb, T1

Debug Computer Services

Box #53096

Marlborough Postal Outlet

Calgary, AB T2C 7P1 Canada

Phone: 403 248 5798

Levels of Connectivity Supported: Shell

TST Consulting

877 17 Street SW.

Medicine Hat, AB T1A 4X9 Canada

Phone: 403 529 1560

Fax: 403 526 1560

Email: sales@TST-MedHat.com

Web site: ="http://www.TST-MedHat.com

Levels of Connectivity Supported: Shell, PPP, ISDN, 56kb

UUNET Canada Inc.

1 Yonge Street, Suite 1400

Toronto, Ontario M5E 1J9 Canada

Phone: 416 368 6621

Fax: 416 368 1350

Levels of Connectivity Supported: SLIP, PPP, UUCP, ISDN, 56kb, T1

ISPs for Area Code 404

CyberNet Communications Corporation

3939 Roswell Rd, Suite B-2

Marietta, GA 30062 USA

Phone: 404 518 5711

Fax: 404 518 6404

Email: sfeingold@atlwin.com

Web site: http://www.atlwin.com

Levels of Connectivity Supported: SLIP, PPP, UUCP, ISDN, 56kb, T1

Digital Service Consultants Inc.

3688 Clearview Ave, Suite 211

Atlanta, GA 30340 USA

Phone: 770 455 9022

Fax: 770 455 7714

Email: info@dscga.com

Web site: http://www.dscga.com

Levels of Connectivity Supported: PPP, ISDN, 56kb, T1

First Internet Resources

7511 Chapman Highway

Knoxville, TN 37920 USA

Phone: 800 577 5969

Fax: 615 577 1505

Email: jcarter@1stresource.com

Web site: http://www.1stresource.com

Levels of Connectivity Supported: SLIP, PPP, UUCP, ISDN, 56kb, T1

I-Link Ltd

1 Chisholm Trail

Round Rock, TX 78681 USA

Phone: 800 ILINK 99

Fax: 512 244 9681

Email: info@i-link.net

Web site: http://www.i-link.net

Levels of Connectivity Supported: PPP, ISDN, 56kb, T1

Internet Atlanta

340 Knoll Ridge Court

Alpharetta, GA 30202

Phone: 404 410 9000

Fax: 404 410 9005

Email: info@atlanta.com

Web site: http://www.atlanta.com

Levels of Connectivity Supported: Shell, SLIP, PPP, UUCP

The INTERNET Connection, LLC
P.O. Box 670673
Marietta, GA 30066 USA
Phone: 404 419 6100
Fax: 404 919 1568
Email: info@is.net
Web site: http://
www.ticllc.net
Levels of Connectivity Supported: Shell, SLIP, PPP

MindSpring Enterprises, Inc.
1430 West Peachtree St NW,
Suite 400
Atlanta, GA 30309 USA
Phone: 800 719 4332
Fax: 404 815 8805
Email: info@mindspring.com
Web site: http://
www.mindspring.com
Levels of Connectivity Supported: SLIP, PPP, UUCP,
56kb

NetDepot Inc.
1310 Cumberland Court
Smyrna, GA 30080 USA
Phone: 770 434 5595
Fax: 770 953 6830
Email: info@netdepot.com
Web site: http://
www.netdepot.com
Levels of Connectivity Supported: SLIP, PPP, ISDN,
56kb, T1

Paradise Communications, Inc.
1000 Circle 75 Pkwy,
Suite 120
Atlanta, GA 30339 USA
Phone: 404 980 0078
Fax: 404 984 1796
Email: info@paradise.net
Web site: http://
www.paradise.net
Levels of Connectivity Supported: Shell, SLIP, PPP,
UUCP, ISDN, 56kb, T1

Random Access, Inc.
6160 Peachtree-Dunwoody Rd.,
#A-100
Atlanta, GA 30328 USA
Phone: 404 804 1190 or
800 910 1190
Fax: 404 804 4546
Email: sales@randomc.com
Web site: http://
www.randomc.com
Levels of Connectivity Supported: Shell, SLIP, PPP,
UUCP, ISDN, 56kb, T1

vividnet
2400 Herodian Way, Suite 170
Atlanta, GA 30080 USA
Phone: 770 933 0999
Fax: 770 951 1881
Email: webadmin@vivid.net
Web site: http://
www.vivid.net
Levels of Connectivity Supported: SLIP, PPP, ISDN,
56kb, T1

ISPs for Area Code 405

Internet Oklahoma
9500 Westgate, #120
Oklahoma City, OK 73162
Phone: 405 721 1580 or 918
583 1161
Fax: 405 721 4861 or 918 584
7222
Levels of Connectivity Supported: Shell, SLIP, PPP

Questar Network Services
5900 Mosteller Drive, 15th
Floor
Oklahoma City, OK 73112
Phone: 405 848 3228
Fax: 405 843 9434
Levels of Connectivity Supported: Shell, SLIP, PPP,
UUCP

ISPs for Area Code 406

CyberPort Montana
100 2nd. St. E., Suite 209
Whitefish, MT 59937 USA
Phone: 406 863 3221
Fax: 406 862 9159
Email: skippy@cyberport.net
Web site: http://
www.cyberport.net
Levels of Connectivity Supported: SLIP, 56kb

Internet Montana

2407 Montana Avenue
Billings, MT 59101 USA
Phone: 406 255 9699
Fax: 406 255 9699
Email: support@comp-unltd.com
Web site: http://www.comp-unltd.com
Levels of Connectivity Supported: SLIP, PPP, 56kb, T1

Montana Internet Cooperative

314 N. Last Chance Gulch
Helena, MT 59601 USA
Phone: 406 443 3347
Email: admin@mt.net
Web site: http://www.mt.net
Levels of Connectivity Supported: Shell, SLIP, PPP, UUCP, 56kb, T1

Montana Online

1801 S. 3rd W
Missoula, MT 59801
Phone: 406 721 4952
Fax: 406 721 4953
Levels of Connectivity Supported: Shell, SLIP, PPP

NorthWestNet

15400 S.E. 30th Place,
Suite 202
Bellevue, WA 98007 USA
Phone: 206 562 3000
Fax: 206 562 4822
Email: info@nwnet.net
Web site: http://www.nwnet.net
Levels of Connectivity Supported: T1

ISPs for Area Code 407

Acquired Knowledge Systems, Inc.

817 SW 8 Terrace
Fort Lauderdale, FL 33315
USA
Phone: 954 525 2574
Fax: 954 462 2329
Email: info@aksi.net
Web site: http://www.aksi.net
Levels of Connectivity Supported: Shell, SLIP, PPP, ISDN

CyberGate, Inc.

662 South Military Trail
Deerfield Beach, FL 33442
USA
Phone: 305 428 4283
Fax: 305 428 7977
Email: sales@gate.net
Web site: http://www.gate.net

The EmiNet Domain

1325 S. Congress Ave,
Suite 241
Boynton Beach, FL 33426
USA
Phone: 407 731 0222
Fax: 407 731 2521
Email: info@emi.net
Web site: http://www.emi.net
Levels of Connectivity Supported: Shell, SLIP, PPP, UUCP, ISDN, 56kb, T1

Florida Online

3815 N US 1, #59
Cocoa, FL 32926 USA
Phone: 407 635 8888
Fax: 407 635 9050
Email: info@digital.net
Web site: http://digital.net
Levels of Connectivity Supported: Shell, SLIP, PPP, UUCP

GS-Link Systems Inc.

One Purlieu Place, Suite 220
Winter Park, Florida 32792
USA
Phone: 407 671 8682
Fax: 407 671 4786
Email: info@gslink
Web site: http://www.gslink.net
Levels of Connectivity Supported: Shell, SLIP, PPP, ISDN, 56kb, T1

I-Link Ltd

1 Chisholm Trail
Round Rock, TX 78681 USA
Phone: 800 ILINK 99
Fax: 512 244 9681
Email: info@i-link.net
Web site: http://www.i-link.net

ICANECT
1020 NW 163 Drive
Miami, FL 33139 USA
Phone: 305 621 9200
Fax: 305 621 2227
Email: sales@icanect.net
Web site: http://
www.icanect.net
Levels of Connectivity Supported: Shell, SLIP, PPP,
ISDN, 56kb, T1, Web Hosting

**InteleCom Data Systems,
Inc.**
East Greenwich, RI USA
Phone: 401 885 6855
Email: info@ids.net
Web site: http://www.ids.net
Levels of Connectivity Supported: Shell, SLIP, PPP,
UUCP

**Internet Providers of Florida,
Inc**
Capital Bank Plaza
10700 Kendall Dr, Suite 204
Miami, Fl 33176 USA
Phone: 305 273 7978
Fax: 305 273 1887
Email: office@ipof.fla.net
Web site: http://www.fla.net
Levels of Connectivity Supported: SLIP, PPP, UUCP,
56kb, T1

InternetU
2060 Palm Bay Road NE, #3
Palm Bay, FL 32905 USA
Phone: 407 952 8487
Fax: 407 722 2863
Email: info@iu.net
Web site: http://iu.net
Levels of Connectivity Supported: Shell, SLIP, PPP,
UUCP

**Magg Information Services,
Inc.**
7950 South Military Trail,
Suite 202
Lake Worth, FL 33463 USA
Phone: 407 642 9841
Fax: 407 642 8115
Email: help@magg.net
Web site: http://www.magg.net
Levels of Connectivity Supported: Shell, SLIP, PPP,
ISDN, 56kb, T1

MagicNet, Inc.
10149 University Blvd.
Orlando, FL 32817 USA
Phone: 407 657 2202
Fax: 407 679 8562
Email: info@magicnet.net
Web site: http://
www.magicnet.net
Levels of Connectivity Supported: Shell, SLIP, PPP,
UUCP, 56kb, T1

**MetroLink Internet Services,
Inc.**
1901 S. Harbor City Blvd.,
Suite 600
Melbourne, FL 32901 USA
Phone: 407 726 6707
Fax: 407 726 8063
Email: jtaylor@metrolink.net
Web site: http://
www.metrolink.net
Levels of Connectivity Supported: Shell, SLIP, PPP,
UUCP, 56kb, T1

PSS InterNet Services
2455 West Int'l Speedway
Blvd., Suite #807
Daytona Beach, FL 32114
USA
Phone: 800 463 8499
Fax: 904 253 1006
Email: support@america.com
Web site: http://
www.america.com
Levels of Connectivity Supported: Shell, SLIP, PPP

Shadow Information Services, Inc.
2000 Nw 88 Court
Miami , FL 33172 USA
Phone: 305 594 2450
Fax: 305 599 1140
Email: admin@shadow.net
Web site: http://
www.shadow.net
Levels of Connectivity Supported: Shell, SLIP, PPP

WAM / NetRunner

123 NW 13th St., #214-12
Boca Raton, FL 33432 USA
Phone: 407 392 9422
Fax: 407 852 8756
Email: wam@wamsyst.com
Web site: http://
www.netrunner.net
Levels of Connectivity Sup-
ported: Shell, SLIP, PPP,
USDN, T1

WebIMAGE, Inc (an internet presence provider)

1900 S.Harbor City Blvd., Suite
328
Melbourne, FL 32901 USA
Phone: 407 723 0001
Email: info@webimage.com
Web site: http://
www.webimage.com
Levels of Connectivity Sup-
ported: 56kb, T1

ISPs for Area Code 408

A-Link Network Services, Inc.

298 South Sunnyvale Ave.,
Suite 102
Sunnyvale, CA 94086 USA
Phone: 408 720 6161
Fax: 408 720 6160
Email: info@alink.net
Web site: http://
www.alink.net
Levels of Connectivity Sup-
ported: PPP, UUCP, ISDN,
56kb, T1, Web Hosting

Aimnet Information Services

20410 Town Center Lane, Suite
290
Cupertino, CA 95014 USA
Phone: 408 257 0900
Fax: 408 257 5452
Email: info@aimnet.com
Web site: http://
www.aimnet.com
Levels of Connectivity Sup-
ported: Shell, SLIP, PPP,
UUCP

Alternet (UUNET Technologies, Inc.)

3110 Fairview Park Drive, Suite
570
Falls Church, VA 22042
Phone: 703 204 8000
Fax: 703 204 8001
Email: info@alter.net
Levels of Connectivity Sup-
ported: SLIP, PPP

Bay Area Internet Solutions

7246 Sharon Drive, Suite H
San Jose, CA 95129 USA
Phone: 408 447 8690
Fax: 408 447 8691
Email: info@bayarea.net
Web site: http://
www.bayarea.net
Levels of Connectivity Sup-
ported: Shell, SLIP, PPP,
UUCP, 56kb, T1

Brainstorm's Internet Power Connection

958 San Leandro Ave, Suite 300
Mountain View, CA 94043
USA
Phone: 415 ISDN-411 (473-
6411)
Fax: 415 988 2906
Email: info@brainstorm.net
Web site: http://
www.brainstorm.net
Levels of Connectivity Sup-
ported: SLIP, PPP, ISDN,
56kb, T1

BTR Communications

P.O. Box 4148
CA 94040
Email: support@btr.com
Levels of Connectivity Sup-
ported: Shell

Click.Net

204 Second Avenue, Suite 346
San Mateo, CA 94401 USA
Phone: 415 579 2535
Fax: 415 570 4807
Email: info@click.net
Web site: http://
www.clicknet.com
Levels of Connectivity Sup-
ported: PPP, ISDN

Cruzio

903 Pacific Avenue, Suite 204
Santa Cruz, CA 95060 USA
Phone: 408 423 1162
Email: office@cruzio.com
Web site: http://
www.cruzio.com
Levels of Connectivity Sup-
ported: Shell, SLIP, PPP

Direct Network Access
2039 Shattuck Avenue,
Suite 206
Berkeley, CA 94704 USA
Phone: 510 649 6110
Fax: 510 649 7130
Email: support@dnai.com
Web site: http://www.dnai.com
Levels of Connectivity Supported: PPP, ISDN, 56kb, T1

The Duck Pond Public Unix
2351 Sutter Avenue, #6
Santa Clara, CA 95059-6640
Fax: 408 249 9630
Levels of Connectivity Supported: Shell

Electriciti
2271 India Street, Suite C
San Diego, CA 92101
Phone: 619 338 9000
Fax: 619 687 3879
Levels of Connectivity Supported: SLIP, PPP, UUCP

Exodus Communications, Inc.
948 Benecia Avenue
Sunnyvale, CA 94086 USA
Phone: 408 522 8450
Fax: 408 736 6843
Email: info@exodus.net
Web site: http://www.exodus.net
Levels of Connectivity Supported: ISDN, 56kb, T1

GST Net
37682 Carriage Circle Common
Fremont, CA 94536 USA
Phone: 510 792 0768
Fax: 510 792 0768
Email: info@gst.net
Web site: http://www.gst.net
Levels of Connectivity Supported: PPP, ISDN, 56kb, T1

ICOnetworks
5617 Scotts Valley Drive
Scotts Valley, CA 95066 USA
Phone: 408 461 4638
Fax: 408 438 8390
Email: info@ico.net
Web site: http://www.ico.net
Levels of Connectivity Supported: SLIP, PPP, ISDN, 56kb, T1

Infoserv Connections
P.O. Box 419
Felton, CA 95018
Phone: 408 335 5600
Fax: 408 335 4250
Levels of Connectivity Supported: PPP, UUCP

Internet Avenue
1800 Wyatt Dr., Suite 15
Santa Clara, CA 95054 USA
Phone: 408 727 0777
Fax: 408 727 1719
Email: sales@ave.net
Web site: http://www.ave.net
Levels of Connectivity Supported: SLIP, PPP, UUCP, ISDN, 56kb, T1

InterNex Tiara
2302 Walsh Ave
Santa Clara, CA 95051 USA
Phone: 408 496 5466
Fax: 408 496 5485
Email: info@internex.net
Web site: http://www.internex.net
Levels of Connectivity Supported: SLIP, PPP, ISDN, 56kb, T1, Frame Relay, Web Services

ISP Networks
60 Federal Street, Suite 555
San Francisco, CA 94111 USA
Phone: 800 724 7100
Fax: 415 778 5101
Email: info@isp.net
Web site: http://www.isp.net
Levels of Connectivity Supported: SLIP, PPP, UUCP, ISDN, 56kb, T1, Web Hosting

Liberty Information Network
446 S Anaheim Hills Rd., Suite 102
Anaheim, CA 92807 USA
Phone: 800 218 5157 or 714 996 9999
Fax: 714 961 8700 Attn: ISP INFO
Email: info@liberty.com
Web site: http://www.liberty.com
Levels of Connectivity Supported: Shell, SLIP, PPP, UUCP, ISDN, 56kb, T1

meernet
P.O. Box 390804
Mountain View, CA 94039
USA
Phone: 415 428 7111
Email: info@meer.net
Web site: http://www.meer.net
Levels of Connectivity Supported: PPP, ISDN

Monterey Bay Internet
484 Lighthouse Ave., Suite 206
Monterey, CA 93940 USA
Phone: 408 642 6100
Fax: 408 642 6101
Email: info@mbay.net
Web site: http://www.mbay.net
Levels of Connectivity Supported: Shell, SLIP, PPP, ISDN, 56kb, T1

NetGate Communications
2175 De La Cruz Blvd.,
Suite 16
Santa Clara, CA 95050-3036
USA
Phone: 408 565 9601
Email: sales@netgate.net
Web site: http://www.netgate.net
Levels of Connectivity Supported: Shell, SLIP, PPP

Network Solutions
1000 Ames Ave., Suite C50
Milpitas, CA 95035 USA
Phone: 408 946 6895
Fax: 408 946 6899
Email: info@inow.com
Web site: http://www.inow.com
Levels of Connectivity Supported: Shell, PPP, UUCP, T1

QuakeNet
830 Wilmington Road
San Mateo, CA 94402 USA
Phone: 415 655 6607
Fax: 415 377 0635
Email: info@quake.net
Web site: http://www.quake.net
Levels of Connectivity Supported: SLIP, PPP

San Jose Co-op
4960 Almaden Expy
San Jose, CA 95118 USA
Phone: 408 978 3958
Fax: 408 448 8073
Email: sales@sj-coop.net
Web site: www.sj-coop.net
Levels of Connectivity Supported: Shell, PPP, UUCP, ISDN, 56kb

Scruz-Net
903 Pacific Avenue, #203A
Santa Cruz, CA 95060
Phone: 800 319 5555 or 408 457 5050
Fax: 408 457 1020
Levels of Connectivity Supported: SLIP, PPP, ISDN

SenseMedia
P.O.B. 228
Felton, CA 95018 USA
Phone: 408 335 9400
Email: info@sensemedia.net
Web site: http://sensemedia.net
Levels of Connectivity Supported: SLIP, PPP

South Valley Internet
P.O. Box 1246
San Martin, CA 95046-1246
USA
Phone: 408 683 4533
Fax: 408 683 4533
Email: info@garlic.com
Web site: http://www.garlic.com
Levels of Connectivity Supported: Shell, SLIP, PPP, UUCP, 56kb, T1

Silicon Valley Public Access Link (SV-PAL)
1777 Hamilton Ave.,
Suite 208A
San Jose, CA 95125 USA
Phone: 408 448 3071
Email: abem@svpal.org
Web site: http://www.svpal.org
Levels of Connectivity Supported: Dial-up

West Coast Online
6050 Commerce Blvd.,
Suite 210
Rohnert Park, CA 94928 USA
Phone: 707 586 3060
Fax: 707 586 5254
Email: info@calon.com
Web site: http://www.calon.com
Levels of Connectivity Supported: Shell, SLIP, PPP

zNET
777 South Pacific Coast
Highway, Suite 204
Solana Beach, CA 92075
Phone: 619 755 7772
Fax: 619 755 8149
Levels of Connectivity Supported: SLIP, PPP, UUCP

Zocalo Engineering
2355 Virginia Street
Berkeley, CA 94709-1315
USA
Phone: 510 540 8000
Fax: 510 548 1891
Email: info@zocalo.net
Web site: http://
www.zocalo.net
Levels of Connectivity Supported: Shell, SLIP, PPP, 56kb,
128kb, 384kb, T1

ISPs for Area Code 409

Brazos Information Highway Services
P.O. Box 10103
College Station, TX 77842
USA
Phone: 409 693 9336
Fax: 409 764 8198
Email: info@bihs.net
Web site: http://www.bihs.net
Levels of Connectivity Supported: PPP, 56kb, T1

CVTV - Internet
P.O. Box 610
La Grange, TX 78945 USA
Phone: 800 247 8885
Fax: 409 247 5127
Email: cyndyz@cvtv.net
Web site: http://www.cvtv.net

Cybercom Corporation
416 Tarrow
College Station, TX 77845
USA
Phone: 409 268 0771
Fax: 409 260 2652
Email: www@cy-net.net
Web site: http://www.cy-net.net
Levels of Connectivity Supported: Shell, SLIP, PPP,
UUCP, 56kb, T1

Delta Design and Development Inc.
6448 Hwy. 290 East, Suite F108
Austin, TX 78723 USA
Phone: 800 763 8265
Fax: 512 467 8462
Email: sales@deltaweb.com
Web site: http://www.deltaweb.com
Levels of Connectivity Supported: PPP, ISDN, 56kb, T1

Fayette Area Internet Services
135 W. Travis, Suite 2
La Grange, TX 78945 USA
Phone: 409 968 3999
Fax: 409 968 3225
Email: mcooper@fais.net
Web site: http://www.fais.net
Levels of Connectivity Supported: PPP, 56kb, T1

Internet Connect Services, Inc.
202 W. Goodwin
Victoria, TX 77901
Phone: 512 572 9987
Fax: 512 572 8193
Levels of Connectivity Supported: Shell, SLIP, PPP,
UUCP

PERnet Communications, Inc.
2300 Hwy 365, Suite 600
Nederland, TX 77627 USA
Phone: 409 729 4638
Fax: 409 727 3019
Email: info@mail.pernet.net
Web site: http://www.pernet.net
Levels of Connectivity Supported: Shell, SLIP, PPP,
56kb, T1

Phoenix DataNet, Inc.
17100 El Camino Real
Houston, TX 77058 USA
Phone: 713 486 8337
Fax: 713 486 7464
Email: info@phoenix.net
Web site: http://www.phoenix.net
Levels of Connectivity Supported: Shell, SLIP, PPP,
ISDN, 56kb, T1

ISPs for Area Code 410

ABSnet Internet Services

200 East Lexington Street,
Suite 1602
Baltimore, MD 21202 USA
Phone: 410 361 8160
Fax: 410 361 8162
Email: info@abs.net
Web site: http://www.abs.net
Levels of Connectivity Supported: Shell, SLIP, PPP,
UUCP, ISDN, 56kb T1

American Information Network

P.O. Box 2083
Columbia, MD 21045 USA
Phone: 410 855 2353
Fax: 410 715 6808
Email: info@ai.net
Web site: http://www.ai.net
Levels of Connectivity Supported: Shell, SLIP, PPP,
UUCP, ISDN, 56kb, T1

ARInternet Corporation

8201 Corporate Drive, Suite
1100
Landover, MD 20785 USA
Phone: 301 459 7171
Fax: 301 459 7174
Email: info@ari.net
Web site: http://www.ari.net
Levels of Connectivity Supported: Shell, SLIP, PPP,
ISDN, 56kb, T1, Web Hosting

BayServe Technologies, Inc.

P.O. Box 621
Pasadena, MD 21122 USA
Phone: 410 360 2216
Fax: 410 360 2216
Email: sales@bayserve.net
Web site: http://
www.bayserve.net
Levels of Connectivity Supported: Shell, SLIP, PPP,
UUCP, ISDN, 56kb, T1, Web
Hosting

CAPCON Library Network

1320 - 19th Street, NW,
Suite 400
Washington, DC 20036 USA
Phone: 202 331 5771
Fax: 202 797 7719
Email: info@capcon.net
Levels of Connectivity Supported: SLIP, PPP

Charm.Net

2228 E. Lombard Street
Baltimore, MD 21231 USA
Phone: 410 558 3900
Fax: 410 558 3901
Email: info@charm.net
Web site: http://
www.charm.net
Levels of Connectivity Supported: Shell, SLIP, PPP

Clark Internet Services, Inc. ClarkNet

10600 Route 108
Ellicott City, MD 21042 USA
Phone: 410 995 0691
Fax: 410 730 9765
Email: info@clark.net
Web site: http://
www.clark.net
Levels of Connectivity Supported: Shell, SLIP, PPP,
UUCP

Cyber Services, Inc.

8027 Leesburg Pike, Suite 317
Vienna, VA 22182 USA
Phone: 703 749 9590
Fax: 703 749 9598
Email: info@cs.com
Web site: http://www.cs.com
Levels of Connectivity Supported: Shell, SLIP, PPP,
UUCP, ISDN, 56kb, T1

Digital Express Group, Inc.

6006 Greenbelt Road, Suite 228
Greenbelt, MD 20770 USA
Phone: 301 847 5000 or
847 5050
Fax: 301 847 5215
Email: info@digex.net
Web site: http://
www.digex.net
Levels of Connectivity Supported: Shell, SLIP, PPP,
56kb, T1

jaguNET Access Services
10 Donn Court
Perry Hall, MD 21128-9600
USA
Phone: 410 931 3157
Fax: 410 931 3157 (call 1st)
Email: info@jagunet.com
Web site: http://
www.jaguNET.com
Levels of Connectivity Supported: SLIP, PPP, UUCP, ISDN, 56kb, T1

KIVEX, Inc.
3 Bethesda Metro Center, Suite B-001
Bethesda, MD 80214 USA
Phone: 800 47 KIVEX
Fax: 301 215 5991
Email: info@kivex.com
Web site: http://
www.kivex.com
Levels of Connectivity Supported: Shell, SLIP, PPP, ISDN, 56kb, T1, Web Hosting

Softaid Internet Services Inc.
8310 Guilford Rd.
Columbia, MD 21046 USA
Phone: 410 290 7763
Fax: 410 381 3253
Email: sales@softaid.net
Web site: http://
www.softaid.net
Levels of Connectivity Supported: Shell, SLIP, PPP, ISDN, 56kb, T1

Smartnet Internet Services, LLC
8562A Laureldale Drive
Laurel, MD 20724 USA
Phone: 301 470 3400 or 410 792 4555
Fax: 410 792 4571
Email: info@smart.net
Web site: http://
www.smart.net
Levels of Connectivity Supported: PPP, 56kb, T1, Web Hosting

UltraPlex Information Providers
P.O.Box 626
Laurel, MD 20725-0626 USA
Phone: 301 598 6UPX & 410 880 4604
Email: info@upx.net
Web site: http://www.upx.net
Levels of Connectivity Supported: Shell, PPP, UUCP, ISDN, 56kb

US Net, Inc.
3316 Kilkenny Street
Silver Spring, MD 20904
Phone: 301 572 5926
Fax: 301 572 5201
Levels of Connectivity Supported: Shell, SLIP, PPP, UUCP

ISPs for Area Code 412

CityNet, Inc.
1739 East Carson Street
Box 352
Pittsburgh, PA 15203 USA
Phone: 412 481 5406
Fax: 412 431 1315
Email: info@city-net.com
Web site: http://www.
city-net.com
Levels of Connectivity Supported: Shell, SLIP, PPP, UUCP, 56kb, T1

epix
100 Lake Street
Dallas, PA 18612 USA
Phone: 800 374 9669
Fax: 717 675 5711
Email: karndt@epix.net
Web site: http://www.epix.net
Levels of Connectivity Supported: SLIP, PPP, ISDN, 56kb, T1

Exodus Communications, Inc.
948 Benecia Avenue
Sunnyvale, CA 94086 USA
Phone: 408 522 8450
Fax: 408 736 6843
Email: info@exodus.net
Web site: http://
www.exodus.net
Levels of Connectivity Supported: ISDN, 56kb, T1

FYI Networks
110 Auman Lane
Valencia, PA 16059 USA
Phone: 412 898 2323
Fax: 412 898 2286
Email: info@fyi.net
Web site: http://www.fyi.net
Levels of Connectivity Supported: Shell, SLIP, PPP, UUCP, 56kb, T1

Pittsburgh OnLine Inc.
4516 Henry St., Suite 202
Pittsburgh, PA 15213 USA
Phone: 412 681 6130
Fax: 412 681 4384
Email: sales@pgh.net
Web site: http://www.pgh.net
Levels of Connectivity Supported: Shell, SLIP, PPP, UUCP, 56kb, T1

Stargate Industries, Inc.
P.O. Box 447
Library, PA 15129 USA
Phone: 412 942 4218
Fax: 412 942 5715
Email: info@sgi.net
Web site: http://www.sgi.net
Levels of Connectivity Supported: SLIP, PPP, ISDN

Telerama Public Access Internet
P.O. Box 60024
Pittsburgh, PA 15211
Phone: 412 481 3505
Fax: 412 481 8568
Levels of Connectivity Supported: Shell, SLIP, PPP

The ThoughtPort Authority Inc.
2000 E. Broadway, Suite 242
Columbia, MO 65201 USA
Phone: 800 ISP 6870
Fax: 314 474 4122
Email: info@thoughtport.com
Web site: http://www.thoughtport.com
Levels of Connectivity Supported: SLIP, PPP, ISDN, 56kb, T1

USA OnRamp
107 6th Street
10th Floor Fulton Buuilding
Pittsburgh, PA 15222 USA
Phone: 412 391 4382
Fax: 412 391 9848
Email: info@usaor.com
Web site: http://www.usaor.com
Levels of Connectivity Supported: SLIP, PPP, UUCP, 56kb, T1

Westmoreland Online Incorporated
P.O. Box 1504
Greensburg, PA 15601 USA
Phone: 412 830 4900
Fax: 412 830 8199
Email: sales@westol.com
Web site: http://www.westol.com
Levels of Connectivity Supported: Shell, PPP, 56kb, T1

ISPs for Area Code 413

Mallard Electronics, Inc.
59 Interstate Drive
P.O. Box 486
West Springfield, MA 01090-0486
Phone: 413 732 0214
Levels of Connectivity Supported: Shell, SLIP, UUCP

ShaysNet.COM
389 Adams Road
Greenfield, MA 01301-1361
Phone: 413 772 2923
Levels of Connectivity Supported: Shell, SLIP, UUCP

SoVerNet, Inc.
5 Rockingham Street
Bellows Falls, VT 05101 USA
Phone: 802 463 2111
Fax: 802 463 2110
Email: info@sover.net
Web site: http://www.sover.net
Levels of Connectivity Supported: Shell, SLIP, PPP, UUCP, ISDN, 56kb T1

the spa!, inc.
P.O. Box 2661
Springfield, MA 01101-2661 USA
Phone: 413 539 9818
Fax: 413 534 7058
Email: info@the-spa.com
Web site: http://www.the-spa.com
Levels of Connectivity Supported: Shell, SLIP, PPP, 56kb, T1

ISPs for Area Code 414

Excel.Net, Inc.
1832 North 20th Street
Sheboygan, WI 53081 USA
Phone: 414 452 0455
Fax: 414 458 7755
Email: manager@excel.net
Web site: http://
www.excel.net
Levels of Connectivity Supported: Shell, SLIP, PPP

Exec-PC
2105 South 170th St.
New Berlin, WI 53151 USA
Phone: 414 789 4200
Fax: 414 789 1946
Email: info@execpc.com
Web site: http://
www.execpc.com
Levels of Connectivity Supported: Shell, SLIP, PPP, ISDN

FullFeed Communications
Madison, WI 53704-2488
Phone: 608 246 4239
Levels of Connectivity Supported: Shell, SLIP, PPP, UUCP

Internet Access LLC
522 College St
Lake Mills, WI 53551 USA
Phone: 414 648 3837, 414 674 6833
Fax: 414 674 6876
Email: info@intaccess.com
Web site: http://
www.intaccess.com
Levels of Connectivity Supported: PPP, ISDN, 56kb, T1

MIX Communications
P. O. Box 17166
Milwaukee, WI 53217 USA
Phone: 414 351 1868
Fax: 414 351 5783
Email: info@mixcom.com
Web site: http://
www.mixcom.com
Levels of Connectivity Supported: Shell, SLIP, PPP, UUCP

NetNet, Inc.
1046 Grey Court
Green Bay, WI 54307 USA
Phone: 414 499 1339
Fax: 414 499 8001
Email: info@netnet.net
Web site: http://
www.netnet.net
Levels of Connectivity Supported: Shell, SLIP, PPP, UUCP, 56kb, T1

The Peoples Telephone Company
201 Stark Street
Randolph, WI 53956 USA
Phone: 414 326 3151
Fax: 414 326 4125
Email: info@peoples.net
Web site: http://
www.peoples.net
Levels of Connectivity Supported: Shell, SLIP, PPP, UUCP, 56kb, T1

TRC Access
240 Regency Court
Brookfield, WI 53045 USA
Phone: 414 827 9111
Fax: 414 827 9177
Email: info@trcaccess.net
Web site: http://
www.trcaccess.net
Levels of Connectivity Supported: Shell, PPP, 56kb T1

Wink Communications Group, Inc.
2500 W Higgins Rd., Suite 480
Hoffman Estates, IL 60195 USA
Phone: 708 310 9465
Fax: 708 310 3477
Email: sales@winkcomm.com
Web site: www.winkcomm.com
Levels of Connectivity Supported: ISDN, 56kb, T1

ISPs for Area Code 415

A-Link Network Services, Inc.
298 South Sunnyvale Ave., Suite 102
Sunnyvale, CA 94086 USA
Phone: 408 720 6161
Fax: 408 720 6160
Email: info@alink.net
Web site: http://
www.alink.net
Levels of Connectivity Supported: PPP, UUCP, ISDN, 56kb, T1

Aimnet Information Services

20410 Town Center Lane,
Suite 290
Cupertino, CA 95014 USA
Phone: 408 257 0900
Fax: 408 257 5452
Email: info@aimnet.com
Web site: http://
www.aimnet.com
Levels of Connectivity Supported: Shell, SLIP, PPP,
UUCP

Alternet (UUNET Technologies, Inc.)

3110 Fairview Park Drive,
Suite 570
Falls Church, VA 22042
Phone: 703 204 8000
Fax: 703 204 8001
Email: info@alter.net
Levels of Connectivity Supported: SLIP, PPP

APlatform

P.O. Box 805
CA, 94041
Phone: 415 941 2647 or 415
941 2647
Email: support@aplatform.com
Web site: http://
www.aplatform.com
Levels of Connectivity Supported: Shell, SLIP, PPP,
UUCP

Bay Area Internet Solutions

7246 Sharon Drive, Suite H
San Jose, CA 95129 USA
Phone: 408 447 8690
Fax: 408 447 8691
Email: info@bayarea.net
Web site: http://
www.bayarea.net
Levels of Connectivity Supported: Shell, SLIP, PPP,
UUCP, 56kb, T1

Beckemeyer Development

P.O. Box 21575
Oakland, CA 94610 USA
Phone: 510 530 9637
Fax: 510 530 0451
Email: info@bdt.com
Web site: http://www.bdt.com
Levels of Connectivity Supported: SLIP, PPP, UUCP,
ISDN, 56kb, T1

Brainstorm's Internet Power Connection

958 San Leandro Ave., Suite
300
Mountain View, CA 94043
USA
Phone: 415 ISDN-411 (473-
6411)
Fax: 415 988 2906
Email: info@brainstorm.net
Web site: http://
www.brainstorm.net
Levels of Connectivity Supported: SLIP, PPP, ISDN,
56kb, T1

BTR Communications

P.O. Box 4148
CA 94040
Email: support@btr.com
Levels of Connectivity Supported: Shell

Click.Net

204 Second Avenue, Suite 346
San Mateo, CA 94401 USA
Phone: 415 579 2535
Fax: 415 570 4807
Email: info@click.net
Web site: http://
www.clicknet.com
Levels of Connectivity Supported: PPP, ISDN

Community ConneXion - NEXUS-Berkeley

2801 Cherry Street, Suite 1
Berkeley, CA 94705 USA
Email: info@c2.org
Web site: http://www.c2.org
Levels of Connectivity Supported: Shell

Datatamers

P.O. Box 2467
Menlo Park, CA 94026-2467
USA
Phone: 415 364 7919
Fax: 415 364 7919
Email: info@datatamers.com
Web site: http://
www.datatamers.com
Levels of Connectivity Supported: Shell, PPP, 56kb

Direct Network Access

2039 Shattuck Avenue, Suite 206

Berkeley, CA 94704 USA

Phone: 510 649 6110

Fax: 510 649 7130

Email: support@dnai.com

Web site: http://www.dnai.com

Levels of Connectivity Supported: PPP, ISDN, 56kb, T1

emf.net

2039 Shattuck Ave., Suite 405

Berkeley, CA 94704 USA

Phone: 510 704 2929

Fax: 510 704 2910

Email: info@emf.net

Web site: http://www.emf.net

Levels of Connectivity Supported: SLIP, PPP, ISDN, 56kb, T1, Web Hosting

Exodus Communications, Inc.

948 Benecia Avenue

Sunnyvale, CA 94086 USA

Phone: 408 522 8450

Fax: 408 736 6843

Email: info@exodus.net

Web site: http://www.exodus.net

Levels of Connectivity Supported: ISDN, 56kb, T1

GST Net

37682 Carriage Circle Common

Fremont, CA 94536 USA

Phone: 510 792 0768

Fax: 510 792 0768

Email: info@gst.net

Web site: http://www.gst.net

Levels of Connectivity Supported: PPP, ISDN, 56kb, T1

I-Link Ltd

1 Chisholm Trail

Round Rock, TX 78681 USA

Phone: 800 ILINK 99

Fax: 512 244 9681

Email: info@i-link.net

Web site: http://www.i-link.net

Levels of Connectivity Supported: PP, ISDN, 56kb, T1

Idiom Consulting

2406 Roosevelt Ave

Berkeley, CA 94703 USA

Phone: 510 644 0441

Email: info@idiom.com

Web site: http://www.idiom.com

Levels of Connectivity Supported: Shell, SLIP, PPP

InReach Internet Communications

P.O. Box 470425

San Francisco, CA 94147 USA

Phone: 800 4 INREACH

Fax: 800 399 7499

Email: info@inreach.com

Web site: http://www.inreach.com

Levels of Connectivity Supported: PPP, UUCP, ISDN

InterNex Tiara

2302 Walsh Ave

Santa Clara, CA 95051 USA

Phone: 408 496 5466

Fax: 408 496 5485

Email: info@internex.net

Web site: http://www.internex.net

Levels of Connectivity Supported: SLIP, PPP, ISDN, 56kb, T1, Frame Relay, Web Services

ISP Networks

60 Federal Street, Suite 555

San Francisco, CA 94111 USA

Phone: 800 724 7100

Fax: 415 778 5101

Email: info@isp.net

Web site: http://www.isp.net

Levels of Connectivity Supported: SLIP, PPP, UUCP, ISDN, 56kb, T1, Web Hosting

LanMinds, Inc.

1442A Walnut Street, #431

Berkeley, CA 94709 USA

Phone: 510 843 6389

Fax: 510 843 6390

Email: info@lanminds.com

Web site: http://www.lanminds.com

Levels of Connectivity Supported: SLIP, PPP, UUCP, ISDN, 56kb

Liberty Information Network
446 S Anaheim Hills Rd.,
Suite 102
Anaheim, CA 92807 USA
Phone: 800 218 5157 or 714
996 9999
Fax: 714 961 8700
Attn: ISP INFO
Email: info@liberty.com
Web site: http://
www.liberty.com
Levels of Connectivity Supported: Shell, SLIP, PPP,
UUCP, ISDN, 56kb, T1

LineX Communications
P.O. Box 150531
San Rafael, CA 94915
Phone: 415 455 1650
Levels of Connectivity Supported: Shell, SLIP, PPP, 56kb,
128kb

meernet
P. O. Box 390804
Mountain View, CA 94039
USA
Phone: 415 428 7111
Email: info@meer.net
Web site: http://www.meer.net
Levels of Connectivity Supported: PPP, ISDN

MobiusNet
243 Vallejo Street
San Francisco, CA 94111 USA
Phone: 415 821 0600
Email: info@mobius.net
Web site: http://
www.mobius.net
Levels of Connectivity Supported: SLIP, PPP, ISDN, T1

NetGate Communications
2175 De La Cruz Blvd.,
Suite 16
Santa Clara, CA 95050-3036
USA
Phone: 408 565 9601
Email: :sales@netgate.net
Web site: http://
www.netgate.net
Levels of Connectivity Supported: Shell, SLIP, PPP

Network Solutions
1000 Ames Ave., Suite C50
Milpitas, CA 95035 USA
Phone: 408 946 6895
Fax: 408 946 6899
Email: info@inow.com
Web site: http://www.inow.com
Levels of Connectivity Supported: Shell, PPP, UUCP, T1

QuakeNet
830 Wilmington Road
San Mateo, CA 94402 USA
Phone: 415 655 6607
Fax: 415 377 0635
Email: info@quake.net
Web site: http://
www.quake.net
Levels of Connectivity Supported: SLIP, PPP, UUCP

**San Francisco Online
(Televolve, Inc.)**
221 14th Street
San Francisco, CA 94103 USA
Phone: 415 861 7712
Fax: 415 861 7562
Email: info@sfo.com
Web site: http://www.sfo.com
Levels of Connectivity Supported: Shell, SLIP, PPP,
UUCP, ISDN, 56kb, T1

Sirius
350 Townsend, Suite #425
San Francisco, CA 94107 USA
Phone: 415 284 4700
Fax: 415 284 4704
Email: info@sirius.com
Web site: http://
www.sirius.com
Levels of Connectivity Supported: SLIP, PPP, ISDN

SLIPNET
25 Stillman Street, #200
San Francisco, CA 94107
Phone: 415 281 3132
Fax: 415 281 4498
Levels of Connectivity Supported: Shell, SLIP, PPP

**Silicon Valley Public Access
Link (SV-PAL)**
1777 Hamilton Ave.,
Suite 208A
San Jose, CA 95125 USA
Phone: 408 448 3071
Email: abem@svpal.org
Web site: http://
www.svpal.org
Levels of Connectivity Supported: Dial-up

22 Solutions
1040 Fell, Suite 3
San Francisco, CA 94117 USA
Phone: 415 431 9903
Email: info@catch22.com
Web site: http://
www.catch22.com
Levels of Connectivity Supported: Shell, SLIP, PPP,
UUCP, ISDN, 56kb, T1

Ultima Tool
927 Hampshire Street
San Francisco, CA 94110 USA
Phone: 415 775 8960
Email: info@ultima.org
Web site: http://
www.ultima.org
Levels of Connectivity Supported: Shell, SLIP, PPP

Value Net Internetwork Services
2855 Mitchell Drive, Suite 105
Walnut Creek, CA 94598
USA
Phone: 510 943 5769
Fax: 510 943 1708
Email: info@value.net
Web site: http://
www.value.net
Levels of Connectivity Supported: Shell, SLIP, PPP,
ISDN, 56kb, T1

ViaNet Communications
800 El Camino Real West, Suite 180
Mountain View, CA 94040
Phone: 415 903 2242
Fax: 415 903 2241
Levels of Connectivity Supported: Shell, SLIP, PPP,
UUCP

The WELL
1750 Bridgeway Road
Sausalito, CA 94965-1900
Phone: 415 332 4335
Fax: 415 332 4927
Levels of Connectivity Supported: Shell

West Coast Online
6050 Commerce Blvd., Suite 210
Rohnert Park, CA 94928 USA
Phone: 707 586 3060
Fax: 707 586 5254
Email: info@calon.com
Web site: http://
www.calon.com
Levels of Connectivity Supported: Shell, SLIP, PPP,
UUCP

zNET
777 South Pacific Coast Highway, Suite 204
Solana Beach, CA 92075
Phone: 619 755 7772
Fax: 619 755 8149
Levels of Connectivity Supported: SLIP, PPP, UUCP

Zocalo Engineering
2355 Virginia Street
Berkeley, CA 94709-1315
USA
Phone: 510 540 8000
Fax: 510 548 1891
Email: info@zocalo.net
Web site: http://
www.zocalo.net
Levels of Connectivity Supported: Shell, SLIP, PPP, 56kb,
128kb, 384kb, T1

ISPs for Area Code 416

ComputerLink/Internet Direct
5415 Dundas Street #301
Etobicoke, ON M9B 1B5
Canada
Phone: 416 233 7150
Fax: 416 233 6970
Email: info@idirect.com
Web site: http://
www.idirect.com
Levels of Connectivity Supported: SLIP, PPP, UUCP,
ISDN, 56kb, T1

Cycor Communications Incorporated
P.O. Box 454
Prince Edward Island, C1A 7K7
Canada
Email: signup@cycor.ca
Web site: http://www.cycor.ca
Levels of Connectivity Supported: SLIP, PPP, ISDN,
56kb, T1

HookUp Communications
1075 North Service Road West,
Suite 207
Oakville, ON L6M 2G2
Canada
Phone: 905 847 8000
Fax: 905 847 8866
Levels of Connectivity Supported: Shell, SLIP, PPP,
UUCP

InterLog Internet Services
1235 Bay Street, Suite 400
Toronto, Ontario M5R 3K4
Canada
Phone: 416 975 2655
Fax: 416 532 5015
Levels of Connectivity Supported: Shell, SLIP, PPP

Internet Light and Power
2235 Sheppard Avenue East
Suite 905 (Atria II)
Toronto, Ontario M2J 5B5
Canada
Phone: 416 502 1512
Fax: 416 502 3333
Email: staff@ilap.com
Web site: http://www.ilap.com
Levels of Connectivity Supported: Shell, SLIP, PPP,
ISDN, 56kb

Internex Online, Inc.
1801 - 1 Yonge Street
Toronto, Ontario M5E 1W7
Canada
Phone: 416 363 8676
Levels of Connectivity Supported: Shell, SLIP, PPP

Magic Online Services International Inc.
260 Richmond Street West,
Suite 206
Toronto, Ontario M5V 1W5
CANADA
Phone: 416 591 6490
Fax: 416 591 6409
Email: info@magic.ca
Web site: http://www.magic.ca
Levels of Connectivity Supported: SLIP, PPP, UUCP,
ISDN

Neptune Internet Services
465 Davis Dr., Suite 404
Newmarket, Ontario L0G 1E0
Canada
Phone: 905 895 0898
Fax: 905 863 4679
Email: info@neptune.on.ca
Web site: http://www.neptune.on.ca
Levels of Connectivity Supported: Shell, SLIP, PPP,
UUCP, ISDN, 56kb, T1

UUNET Canada Inc.
1 Yonge Street, Suite 1400
Toronto, Ontario M5E 1J9
Canada
Phone: 416 368 6621
Fax: 416 368 1350
Levels of Connectivity Supported: SLIP, PPP, UUCP,
ISDN, 56kb, T1

ISPs for Area Code 417

DialNet (Digital Internet Access Link, Inc.)
300 South Jefferson, Suite #514
Springfield, MO 65806 USA
Phone: 417 873 DIAL (3425)
or 1-800 701 DIAL (3425)
Fax: 417 873 9420
Email: sales@dialnet.net
Web site: http://www.dialnet.net
Levels of Connectivity Supported: Shell, SLIP, PPP,
UUCP, 56kb, T1

Panther Creek Information Services
Route 1, Box 262
Fordland, MO 65652 USA
Phone: 417 767 2126
Fax: 417 767 2044
Email: info@pcis.net
Web site: http://www.pcis.net
Levels of Connectivity Supported: SLIP, PP, 56kb, T1

Woodtech Information Systems, Inc.
1736 E. Sunshine, Suite 509
Springfield, MO 65804 USA
Phone: 417 886 0234
Fax: 417 886 2170
Email: info@woodtech.com
Web site: http://www.woodtech.com
Levels of Connectivity Supported: Shell, SLIP, PPP,
UUCP, 56kb, T1

ISPs for Area Code 418

autoroute.net (System Technology Development Inc.)

1100 Begin Street, Suite 100
Montreal (St-Laurent), PQ
(Quebec), H4R 1X1 CANADA
Phone: 514 333 3145
Fax: 514 334 7671
Email: info@autoroute.net
Web site: http://
www.autoroute.net
Levels of Connectivity Supported: Shell, SLIP, PPP,
UUCP, ISDN, 56kb, T1

UUNET Canada Inc.

1 Yonge Street, Suite 1400
Toronto, Ontario M5E 1J9
Canada
Phone: 416 368 6621
Fax: 416 368 1350
Levels of Connectivity Supported: SLIP, PPP, UUCP,
ISDN, 56kb, T1

ISPs for Area Code 419

Branch Information Services

2901 Hubbard
Ann Arbor, MI 48105 USA
Phone: 313-741-4442
Fax: 313-995-1931
Email: branch-info@branch.com
Web site: http://branch.com
Levels of Connectivity Supported: SLIP, PPP, ISDN,
56kb, T1

GlassNet Communications, LTD.

4218 Airport Hwy.
Toledo, OH 43615-7009 USA
Phone: 419 382 6800
Fax: 419 381 9492
Email: info@glasscity.net
Web site: http://
www.glasscity.net
Levels of Connectivity Supported: PPP, 56kb, T1

OARnet

2455 North Star Road
Columbus, OH 43221 USA
Phone: 614 728 8100 or 800
627 8101
Fax: 614 728 8110
Email: info@oar.net
Web site: http://www.oar.net
Levels of Connectivity Supported: Shell, SLIP, PPP

Primenet

2320 W. Peoria Avenue,
Suite A103
Phoenix, AZ 85029 USA
Phone: 602 870 1010 or 800 4
NET FUN
Fax: 602 870 1010
Email: info@primenet.com
Web site: http://
www.primenet.com

ISPs for Area Code 423

accessU.S. Inc.

P.O. Box 985
1500 Main Street
Mt. Vernon, IL 62864 USA
Phone: 800 638 6373
Fax: 618 244 9175
Email: info@accessus.net
Web site: http://
www.accessus.net
Levels of Connectivity Supported: SLIP, PPP, ISDN,
56kb, T1

MindSpring Enterprises, Inc.

1430 West Peachtree St NW,
Suite 400
Atlanta, GA 30309 USA
Phone: 800 719 4332
Fax: 404 815 8805
Email: info@mindspring.com
Web site: http://
www.mindspring.com
Levels of Connectivity Supported: SLIP, PPP, UUCP,
ISDN, 56kb

Preferred Internet, Inc.

5925 Cochise Trail
Kingsport, TN 37664 USA
Phone: 615 323 1142
Fax: 615 323 6827
Email: info@preferred.com
Web site: http://
www.preferred.com
Levels of Connectivity Supported: Shell, SLIP, PPP,
UUCP, ISDN, 56kb, T1

Virtual Interactive Center
P.O. Box 31571
Knoxville, TN 37930 USA
Phone: 423 544 7902
Fax: 423 691 5131
Email: info@vic.com
Web site: http://www.vic.com
Levels of Connectivity Supported: Shell, SLIP, PPP, UUCP, ISDN, 56kb, T1

ISPs for Area Code 501

A2ZNET
141 East Highway 72, Suite 7
Collierville, TN 38017 USA
Phone: 901 854 1871
Fax: 901 854 1872
Email: webmaster@a2znet.com
Web site: http://www.a2znet.com
Levels of Connectivity Supported: Shell, SLIP, PPP, UUCP, ISDN, 56kb, T1

Aristotle Internet Access
323 Center Stree, Suite 810
Little Rock, AR 72201 USA
Phone: 501 374 4638
Fax: 501 376 1377
Email: info@aristotle.net
Web site: http://www.aristotle.net
Levels of Connectivity Supported: PPP

Cloverleaf Technologies
P.O. Box 6185
Texarkana, TX 75505-6185 USA
Phone: 903 832 1367
Email: helpdesk@clover.cleaf.com
Levels of Connectivity Supported: Shell, SLIP

IntelliNet ISP
523 South Louisiana, Suite 550
Little Rock, AR 72201 USA
Phone: 501 376 7676
Fax: 501 375 3063
Email: info@intellinet.com
Web site: http://www.intellinet.com
Levels of Connectivity Supported: Shell, SLIP, PPP, UUCP, 56kb

ISPs for Area Code 502

accessU.S. Inc.
P.O. Box 985
1500 Main Street
Mt. Vernon, IL 62864 USA
Phone: 800 638 6373
Fax: 618 244 9175
Email: info@accessus.net
Web site: http://www.accessus.net
Levels of Connectivity Supported: SLIP, PPP, ISDN, 56kb, T1

IgLou Internet Services
3315 Gilmore Industrial Blvd.
Louisville, KY 40213
Phone: 800 436 IGLOU
Fax: 502 968 0449
Levels of Connectivity Supported: Shell, SLIP, PPP, UUCP

Mikrotec Internet Services, Inc.
1001 Winchester Rd.
Lexington, KY 40505 USA
Phone: 606 225 1488
Fax: 606 225 5852
Email: info@mis.net
Web site: http://www.mis.net
Levels of Connectivity Supported: Shell, SLIP, PPP, UUCP, ISDN, 56kb, T1

ISPs for Area Code 503

Alternet (UUNET Technologies, Inc.)
3110 Fairview Park Drive, Suite 570
Falls Church, VA 22042
Phone: 703 204 8000
Fax: 703 204 8001
Email: info@alter.net
Levels of Connectivity Supported: SLIP, PPP

aracnet.com
3935 S.W. 114th Ave
Beaverton, OR 97005-2241
USA
Phone: 503 626 8696
Fax: 503 626 8675
Email: info@aracnet.com
Web site: http://
www.aracnet.com
Levels of Connectivity Supported: Shell, SLIP, PPP,
56kb, T1

aVastNet
P.O. Box 6
Canby, OR 97013 USA
Phone: 503 263 0912
Fax: 503 266 2015
Email: info@vastnet.com
Web site: http://
www.vastnet.com
Levels of Connectivity Supported: Shell, SLIP, PPP,
UUCP

Cascade Connection
2606 N.E. 10th Avenue
Portland, OR 97212 USA
Phone: 503 282 8303
Fax: 503 282 8303
Email: info@casconn.com
Web site: http://casconn.com
Levels of Connectivity Supported: PPP

Cenornet
P.O. Box 211
West Linn, OR 97068 USA
Phone: 503 557 9047
Email: info@cenornet.com
Web site: http://
www.cenornet.com
Levels of Connectivity Supported: PPP

Colossus Inc.
Box 146571
Chicago, IL 60614 USA
Phone: 312 528 1000 x19
Email:
colossus@romney.mtjeff.com
Web site: http://
romney.mtjeff.com/colossus/
Levels of Connectivity Supported: Shell, SLIP, PPP,
UUCP

Data Research Group, Inc.
1011 Valley River Way,
116B-158
Eugene, OR 97401 USA
Phone: 503 465 3282
Fax: 503 465 4968
Email: info@ordata.com
Levels of Connectivity Supported: Shell, SLIP, PPP

Europa
320 SW Stark Street, Suite 427
Portland, OR 97204
Phone: 503 222 9508
Fax: 503 796 9134
Levels of Connectivity Supported: Shell, SLIP, PPP,
UUCP

Gorge Networks
Hood River , OR 97031 USA
Phone: 503 386 8300
Email: postmaster@gorge.net
Web site: http://
www.gorge.net
Levels of Connectivity Supported: PPP

Hevanet Communications
625 SW 10th Avenue,
Suite 181B
Portland, OR 97205 USA
Phone: 503 228 3520
Fax: 503 274 4144
Email: info@hevanet.com
Web site: http://
www.hevanet.com
Levels of Connectivity Supported: Shell, SLIP

I-Link Ltd
1 Chisholm Trail
Round Rock, TX 78681 USA
Phone: 800 ILINK 99
Fax: 512 244 9681
Email: info@i-link.net
Web site: http://www.i-link.net
Levels of Connectivity Supported: PPP, IUSDN,
56kb, T1

Interconnected Associates Inc. (IXA)
300 E. Pike Street, Suite 2001
Seattle, WA 98122 USA
Phone: 206 622 7337
Fax: 206 621 0567
Email: mike@ixa.com
Web site: http://www.ixa.com
Levels of Connectivity Supported: 56kb, T1

Internet Communications

17390 SW Washington Ct
Beaverton, OR 97007 USA
Phone: 503 848 8139
Fax: 503 591 0488
Email: info@iccom.com
Web site: http://
www.iccom.com
Levels of Connectivity Supported: Shell, SLIP, PPP,
ISDN, 56kb, T1, Web Hosting

NorthWestNet

15400 S.E. 30th Place, Suite
202
Bellevue, WA 98007 USA
Phone: 206 562 3000
Fax: 206 562 4822
Email: info@nwnet.net
Web site: http://
www.nwnet.net
Levels of Connectivity Supported: T1

Open Door Networks, Inc.

110 S. Laurel Street
Ashland, OR 97520
Phone: 503 488 4127
Fax: 503 488 1708
Levels of Connectivity Supported: ARA

Oregon Information Technology Centeres, Inc.

dba @harborside
15711 Hwy 101
Brookings, OR 97415 USA
Phone: 503 469 6699
Fax: 503 469 9163
Email: hmaster@harborside.com
Web site: http://
www.harborside.com
Levels of Connectivity Supported: Shell, SLIP, PPP

Pacifier Computers (Pacifier Online Data Service)

1800 F. Street
Vancouver, WA 98663 USA
Phone: 360 693 2116
Fax: 360 254 3898
Email: info@pacifier.com
Web site: http://
www.pacifier.com
Levels of Connectivity Supported: Shell, SLIP, PPP,
UUCP

RainDrop Laboratories/ Agora

5627 SW 45th
Portland, OR 97221-3505
USA
Email: info@agora.rdrop.com
Web site: http://
www.rdrop.com
Levels of Connectivity Supported: Shell, SLIP

Structured Network Systems, Inc.

15635 SE 114th Ave., Suite 201
Clackamas, OR 97015 USA
Phone: 800 881 0962
Fax: 503 656 3235
Email: sales@structured.net
Web site: http://
www.structured.net
Levels of Connectivity Supported: 56kb, T1

Teleport, Inc.

319 SW Washington, Suite 604
Portland, OR 97204 USA
Phone: 503 223 4245
Fax: 503 223 4372
Email: info@teleport.com
Web site: http://
www.teleport.com
Levels of Connectivity Supported: Shell, SLIP, PPP

Transport Logic

13500 SW Pacific Hwy., #513
Portland, OR 97223 USA
Phone: 503 243 1940
Email: info@transport.com
Web site: http://
www.transport.com
Levels of Connectivity Supported: Shell, SLIP, PPP,
ISDN, 56kb, T1

WLN

P.O. Box 3888
Lacey, WA 98503-0888 USA
Phone: 800 342 5956 or 360
923 4000
Fax: 360 923 4009
Email: info@wln.com
Levels of Connectivity Supported: Shell, SLIP, PPP

ISPs for Area Code 504

AccessCom Internet Services
3221 Danny Pk.
Metairie, LA 70002 USA
Phone: 504 887 0022
Fax: 504 456 0995
Email: info@accesscom.net
Web site: http://
www.accesscom.net
Levels of Connectivity Supported: Shell, SLIP, PPP, UUCP, ISDN, 56kb, T1, Web Hosting

Communique Inc.

1515 Poydras Street, Suite 1305
New Orleans, LA 70112 USA
Phone: 504 527 6200
Fax: 504 257 6030
Email:
mailto:info@communique.net
Web site: http://
www.communique.net
Levels of Connectivity Supported: PPP, UUCP

Cyberlink

P.O. Box 190
Arabi, LA 70032-0190 USA
Phone: 504 277 4186
Fax: 504 277 4186
Email:cladmin@eayor.
cyberlink-no.com
Web site: http://
www.cyberlink-no.com
Levels of Connectivity Supported: Shell, PPP

Hollingsworth Information Services, Inc

10761 Perkins Road
Baton Rouge, LA 70810 USA
Phone: 504 769 2156
Fax: 504 769 1814
Email: :webmaster@rouge.net
Web site: http://rouge.net
Levels of Connectivity Supported: SLIP, PPP, ISDN

Hub City Area Access

110 Fox Run Drive
Hattiesburg, MS 39401 USA
Phone: 601 268 6156
Fax: 601 268 3799
Email: info@hub1.hubcity.com
Web site: http://
hub1.hubcity.com
Levels of Connectivity Supported: Shell, SLIP, PPP, UUCP, 56kb, T1

I-Link Ltd

1 Chisholm Trail
Round Rock, TX 78681 USA
Phone: 800 ILINK 99
Fax: 512 244 9681
Email: info@i-link.net
Web site: http://www.
i-link.net
Levels of Connectivity Supported: PPP, ISDN, 56kb, T1

InterSurf Online, Inc.

4608 Jones Creek Roak, Suite 220
Baton Rouge, LA 70817 USA
Phone: 504 755 0500
Fax: 504 755 0800
Email: info@intersurf.net
Web site: http://
www.intersurf.net
Levels of Connectivity Supported: Shell, SLIP, PPP, UUCP, ISDN, 56kb, T1

JAMNet Internet Services, Inc.

1031 Whitney Avenue, Suite A
Gretna, LA 70056 USA
Phone: 504 361 3492
Fax: 504 366 8400
Email: info@jis.net
Web site: http://www.jis.net
Levels of Connectivity Supported: PPP, ISDN, 56kb, T1

NeoSoft, Inc.

3408 Magnum Road
Houston, TX 77092
Phone: 800 GET NEOSOFT or 713 684 5969
Fax: 713 684 5922
Levels of Connectivity Supported: Shell, SLIP, PPP, UUCP

ISPs for Area Code 505

Computer Systems Consulting
P.O. Box 5178
Santa Fe, NM 87502-5178
USA
Phone: 505 984 0085
Fax: 505 984 0085
Email: info@spy.org
Web site: http://www.spy.org
Levels of Connectivity Supported: Shell, UUCP

Internet Direct, Inc.
1366 East Thomas Road, Suite 210
Phoenix, AZ 85014 USA
Phone: 1 800 TRY EMAIL
Fax: 602 274 8518
Email: info@direct.net
Web site: http://www.indirect.com
Levels of Connectivity Supported: Shell, SLIP, PPP, UUCP, 56kb, T1

Internet Express
1155 Kelly Johnson Blvd, Ste 400
Colorado Springs, CO 80920-3959 USA
Phone: 800-592-1240
Fax: 719-592-1201
Email: service@usa.net
Web site: http://www.usa.net
Levels of Connectivity Supported: Shell, SLIP, PPP, UUCP, 56kb, T1

Network Intensive
8001 Irvine Center Drive, Suite #1130
Irvine, CA 92718 USA
Phone: 714 450 8400
Fax: 714 450 8410
Email: info@ni.net
Web site: http://www.ni.net
Levels of Connectivity Supported: Shell, SLIP, PPP, UUCP, ISDN, 56kb, T1

New Mexico Internet Access
1619 Saunders SW
Albuquerque, NM 87105 USA
Phone: 505 877 0617
Email: info@nmia.com
Web site: http://www.nmia.com
Levels of Connectivity Supported: Shell, SLIP, PPP, UUCP, 56kb

New Mexico Technet, Inc.
4100 Osuna NE, Suite 103
Albuquerque, NM 87109
Phone: 505 345 6555
Fax: 505 345 6559
Levels of Connectivity Supported: Shell, SLIP, PPP

Southwest Cyberport
3240 C Juan Tabo NE
Albuquerque, NM 87111 USA
Phone: 505 293 5967
Fax: 505 271 5477
Email: info@swcp.com
Web site: http://www.swcp.com
Levels of Connectivity Supported: Shell, SLIP, PPP, UUCP, 56kb, T1

WhiteHorse Communications ,Inc.
5812 Cromo Dr., Suite 202
El Paso, TX 79912 USA
Phone: 915 584 6630
Fax: 915 585 2569
Email: info@whc.net
Web site: http://www.whc.net
Levels of Connectivity Supported: Shell, SLIP, PPP, 56kb, T1

Zynet Southwest
532 Jefferson Ne, Suite 208
Albuquerque, NM 87108 USA
Phone: 505 266 8511
Fax: 505 266 8943
Email: info@zynet.com
Web site: http://www.zynet.com
Levels of Connectivity Supported: Shell, SLIP, PPP

ISPs for Area Code 506

Agate Internet
31 Central Street, Suite 312
Bangor, ME 04401 USA
Phone: 207 947 8248
Fax: 207 947 4432
Email: info@agate.net
Web site: http://www.agate.net
Levels of Connectivity Supported: SLIP, PPP, 56kb, T1

Cycor Communications Incorporated

P.O. Box 454

Prince Edward Island, C1A 7K7

Canada

Email: :signup@cycor.ca

Web site: http://www.cycor.ca

Levels of Connectivity Supported: SLIP, PPP, ISDN, 56kb, T1

ISPs for Area Code 507

Desktop Media

1143 S. Broadway

Albert Lea, MN 56007 USA

Phone: 507 373 2155

Fax: 507 373 0060

Email: mailto:isp@dm.deskmedia.com

Web site: http://dm.deskmedia.com

Levels of Connectivity Supported: PPP, 56kb, T1

Internet Connections, Inc.

P.O. Box 205

Mankato, MN 56002-0205

Phone: 507 625 7320

Fax: 507 625 7320 (call ahead to fax)

Levels of Connectivity Supported: SLIP, PPP

Millennium Communications, Inc.

1300 Nicollet Mall, Suite 5083

Minneapolis, MN 55403

Phone: 612 338 5509

Fax: 507 282 8943

Levels of Connectivity Supported: Shell, SLIP, PPP, UUCP

Minnesota OnLine

23 Empire Drive, Suite 152

Saint Paul, MN 55103-1857

USA

Phone: 612 225 1110

Fax: 612 225 1424

Email: info@mn.state.net

Web site: http://www.state.net

Levels of Connectivity Supported: SLIP, PPP, UUCP, ISDN, 56kb, T1

Minnesota Regional Network

511 - 11th Avenue South, Box 212

Minneapolis, MN 55415

Phone: 612 342 2570

Levels of Connectivity Supported: SLIP, UUCP

Protocol Communications, Inc.

6280 Highway 65 NE, Suite 401

Minneapolis, MN 55432-5136

USA

Phone: 612 541 9900

Fax: 612 541 1586

Email: info@protocom.com

Web site: http://www.protocom.com

Levels of Connectivity Supported: Shell, SLIP, PPP, 56kb, T1

ISPs for Area Code 508

Argo Communications

129 North Main Street

Mansfield, MA 02048 USA

Phone: 508 261 6121

Fax: 508 261 0221

Email: info@argo.net

Web site: http://www.argo.net

Levels of Connectivity Supported: Shell, SLIP, PPP, UUCP, ISDN, 56kb, T1

Channel 1

1030 Massachusetts Ave

Cambridge, MA 02138 USA

Phone: 617 864 0100

Fax: 617 354 3100

Email: support@channel1.com

Web site: http://www.channel1.com

Levels of Connectivity Supported: Shell, SLIP, PPP, ISDN, T1

CompUtopia
205 Hallene Road, Unit A6
Warwick, RI 02886 USA
Phone: 401 732 5588
Fax: 401 732 5518
Email: allan@computopia.com
Web site: http://
www.computopia.com
Levels of Connectivity Supported: ISDN, 56kb, T1

The Destek Group, Inc.
21 Hinds Lane
Pelham, NH 03076-3013
Phone: 603 635 3857 or 508
363 2413
Fax: 508 363 2115
Levels of Connectivity Supported: Shell, SLIP, PPP, UUCP

Empire.Net, Inc.
127 Main Street, Suite 5
Nashua, NH 03060 USA
Phone: 603 889 1220
Fax: 603 889 0366
Email: info@empire.net
Web site: http://
www.empire.net
Levels of Connectivity Supported: Telnet, Shell, SLIP, PPP, UUCP, ISDN, 56kb, T1

FOURnet Information Network
P.O. Box 38
West Wareham, MA 02576-0038 USA
Phone: 508 291 2900 code 2954139
Email: info@four.net
Web site: http://www.four.net
Levels of Connectivity Supported: Shell, SLIP, Telnet, PPP, UUCP, Domain Hosting

The Internet Access Company
7 Railroad Avenue,
MA 01730
Levels of Connectivity Supported: Shell, SLIP, PPP

The Internet Connection, Inc.
Brookside Office Park
272 Chauncy St, Suite 6
Mansfield, MA 02048 USA
Phone: 508 261 0383
Fax: 508 730 1049
Email: info@ici.net
Web site: http://www.ici.net
Levels of Connectivity Supported: Shell, SLIP, PPP, UUCP, ISDN, 56kb, T1

intuitive information, inc.
P.O. Box 10
Ashburnham, MA 01430
Phone: 508 342 1100
Fax: 508 342 2075
Levels of Connectivity Supported: Shell, SLIP, PPP, UUCP

Kersur Technologies, Inc.
25 Lorraine Metcalf Drive
Wrentham, MA 02093 USA
Phone: 508 384 1404
Email: info@kersur.net
Web site: http://
www.kersur.net
Levels of Connectivity Supported: SLIP, PPP, UUCP

MV Communications, Inc.
P.O. Box 4963
Manchester, NH 03108-4963
USA
Phone: 603 429 2223
Fax: 603 424 0386
Email: info@mv.mv.com
Web site: http://www.mv.com
Levels of Connectivity Supported: Shell, SLIP, PPP, UUCP, 56kb, T1

PICTAC Personal Internet Connections To All Corners
P.O. Box 79567
No. Dartmouth, MA 02747-0988 USA
Phone: 508 999 1565
Email: sales@pictac.com
Web site: http://
www.pictac.com
Levels of Connectivity Supported: Shell, SLIP, PPP, UUCP

Pioneer Global Telecommunications, Inc.

811 Boylston Street

Boston, MA 02116 USA

Phone: 617 375 0200

Fax: 617 375 0201

Email: info@pn.com

Web site: http://www.pn.com

Levels of Connectivity Supported: SLIP, PPP, UUCP,ISDN, 56kb, T1

Plymouth Commercial Internet eXchange

190 Old Derby Street, Suite 115

Hingham, MA 02043 USA

Phone: 617 741 5900

Fax: 617 741 5416

Email: info@pcix.com

Web site: http://www.pcix.com

Levels of Connectivity Supported: Shell, SLIP, PPP, UUCP, ISDN, 56kb, T1

Saturn Internet Corporation

151 Pearl Street, 4th Floor

Boston, MA 02110 USA

Phone: 617 451 9121

Fax: 617 451 0358

Email: info@saturn.net

Web site: http://www.saturn.net

Levels of Connectivity Supported: SLIP, PPP, 56kb, T1

Shore.Net

145 Munroe Street, Suite 405

Lynn, MA 01901 USA

Phone: 617 593 3110

Fax: 617 593 6858

Email: info@shore.net

Web site: http://www.shore.net

Levels of Connectivity Supported: Shell, SLIP, PPP, UUCP, ISDN, 56kb, T1

StarNet (Advanced Communication Systems, Inc.)

54 West Dane St.

Clemenzi Industrial Park

Beverly, MA 01915 USA

Phone: 508 922 8238 or 800 779 3309

Fax: 508 921 8456

Email: info@star.net

Web site: http://www.star.net

Levels of Connectivity Supported: SLIP, PPP, ISDN, 56kb, T1

TerraNet, Inc.

729 Boylston Street, Flr 5

Boston, MA 02116 USA

Phone: 617 450 9000

Fax: 617 450 9003

Email: info@terra.net

Web site: http://www.terra.net

Levels of Connectivity Supported: SLIP, PPP, ISDN, 56kb, T1

UltraNet Communications, Inc.

910 Boston Post Road, Suite 220

Marlborough, MA 01752 USA

Phone: 508 229 8400 or 800 763 8111

Fax: 508 229 2375

Email: info@ultranet.com

Web site: http://www.ultranet.com

Levels of Connectivity Supported: SLIP, PPP, ISDN, 56kb, T1

USAinternet, Inc.

99 Rosewood Drive, Mailstop 265

Danvers, MA 01923-1300 USA

Phone: 800 236 9737

Fax: 508 777 0180

Email: info@usa1.com

Web site: http://www.usa1.com

Levels of Connectivity Supported: SLIP, PPP, ISDN, 56kb, T1

The World

Software Tool & Die

1330 Beacon Street

Brookline, MA 02146 USA

Phone: 617 739 0202

Email: info@world.std.com

Web site: http://www.world.std.com

Levels of Connectivity Supported: Shell, SLIP

Wilder Systems, Inc.

400 W. Cummings Park, Suite 2350
Woburn, MA 01801
Phone: 617 933 8810
Fax: 617 933 8648
Levels of Connectivity Supported: Shell, SLIP, PPP

ISPs for Area Code 509

Cascade Connections, Inc.

P.O. Box 3929
Wenatchee, WA 98807 USA
Phone: 509 663 4259
Email: carrie@cascade.net
Web site: http://
www.cascade.net
Levels of Connectivity Supported: Shell, PPP

Interconnected Associates Inc. (IXA)

300 E. Pike Street, Suite 2001
Seattle, WA 98122 USA
Phone: 206 622 7337
Fax: 206 621 0567
Email: mike@ixa.com
Web site: http://www.ixa.com
Levels of Connectivity Supported: 56kb, T1

Internet On-Ramp, Inc.

915 W. 2nd Ave., Suite 1
Spokane, WA 99204 USA
Phone: 509 624 RAMP
Fax: 509 622 2866
Email: info@on-ramp.ior.com
Web site: http://www.ior.com
Levels of Connectivity Supported: Shell, SLIP, PPP, UUCP, ISDN, 56kb, T1

NorthWestNet

15400 S.E. 30th Place, Suite 202
Bellevue, WA 98007 USA
Phone: 206 562 3000
Fax: 206 562 4822
Email: info@nwnet.net
Web site: http://
www.nwnet.net
Levels of Connectivity Supported: T1

Structured Network Systems, Inc.

15635 SE 114th Ave., Suite 201
Clackamas, OR 97015 USA
Phone: 800 881 0962
Fax: 503 656 3235
Email: sales@structured.net
Web site: http://
www.structured.net
Levels of Connectivity Supported: 56kb, T1

Transport Logic

13500 SW Pacific Hwy, #513
Portland, OR 97223 USA
Phone: 503 243 1940
Email: info@transport.com
Web site: http://
www.transport.com
Levels of Connectivity Supported: Shell, SLIP, PPP, ISDN, 56kb, 1

WLN

P.O. Box 3888
Lacey, WA 98503-0888 USA
Phone: 800 342 5956 or 360 923 4000
Fax: 360 923 4009
Email: info@wln.com
Levels of Connectivity Supported: Shell, SLIP, PPP

ISPs for Area Code 510

A-Link Network Services, Inc.

298 South Sunnyvale Avenue, Suite 102
Sunnyvale, CA 94086 USA
Phone: 408 720 6161
Fax: 408 720 6160
Email: info@alink.net
Web site: http://
www.alink.net
Levels of Connectivity Supported: PPP, UUCP, ISDN, 56kb, T1, Web Hosting

Aimnet Information Services

20410 Town Center Lane, Suite 290
Cupertino, CA 95014 USA
Phone: 408 257 0900
Fax: 408 257 5452
Email: info@aimnet.com
Web site: http://
www.aimnet.com
Levels of Connectivity Supported: Shell, SLIP, PPP, UUCP

Alternet (UUNET Technologies, Inc.)
3110 Fairview Park Drive,
Suite 570
Falls Church, VA 22042
Phone: 703 204 8000
Fax: 703 204 8001
Email: info@alter.net
Levels of Connectivity Supported: SLIP, PPP

Beckemeyer Development
P.O. Box 21575
Oakland, CA 94610 USA
Phone: 510 530 9637
Fax: 510 530 0451
Email: info@bdt.com
Web site: http://www.bdt.com
Levels of Connectivity Supported: SLIP, PPP, UUCP,
ISDN, 56kb, T1

BTR Communications
P.O. Box 4148
CA 94040
Email: :support@btr.com
Levels of Connectivity Supported: Shell

Community ConneXion - NEXUS-Berkeley
2801 Cherry Street, Suite 1
Berkeley, CA 94705 USA
Email: info@c2.org
Web site: http://www.c2.org
Levels of Connectivity Supported: Shell

Direct Network Access
2039 Shattuck Avenue,
Suite 206
Berkeley, CA 94704 USA
Phone: 510 649 6110
Fax: 510 649 7130
Email: support@dnai.com
Web site: http://www.dnai.com
Levels of Connectivity Supported: PPP, ISDN, 56kb, T1

emf.net
2039 Shattuck Ave., Suite 405
Berkeley, CA 94704 USA
Phone: 510 704 2929
Fax: 510 704 2910
Email: info@emf.net
Web site: http://www.emf.net
Levels of Connectivity Supported: SLIP, PPP, ISDN,
56kb, T1, Web Hosting

Exodus Communications, Inc.
948 Benecia Avenue
Sunnyvale, CA 94086 USA
Phone: 408 522 8450
Fax: 408 736 6843
Email: info@exodus.net
Web site: http://www.exodus.net
Levels of Connectivity Supported: ISDN, 56kb, T1

GST Net
37682 Carriage Circle Common
Fremont, CA 94536 USA
Phone: 510 792 0768
Fax: 510 792 0768
Email: info@gst.net
Web site: http://www.gst.net
Levels of Connectivity Supported: PPP, ISDN, 56kb, T1

Idiom Consulting
2406 Roosevelt Ave
Berkeley, CA 94703 USA
Phone: 510 644 0441
Email: info@idiom.com
Web site: http://www.idiom.com
Levels of Connectivity Supported: Shell, SLIP, PPP

InterNex Tiara
2302 Walsh Ave.
Santa Clara, CA 95051 USA
Phone: 408 496 5466
Fax: 408 496 5485
Email: info@internex.net
Web site: www.internex.net
Levels of Connectivity Supported: SLIP, PPP, ISDN,
56kb, T1, Frame Relay

LanMinds, Inc.
1442A Walnut Street, #431
Berkeley, CA 94709 USA
Phone: 510 843 6389
Fax: 510 843 6390
Email: info@lanminds.com
Web site: http://www.lanminds.com
Levels of Connectivity Supported: SLIP, PPP, UUCP,
ISDN, 56kb

Liberty Information Network
446 S Anaheim Hills Road,
Suite 102
Anaheim, CA 92807 USA
Phone: 800 218 5157 or 714
996 9999
Fax: 714 961 8700 Attn: ISP
INFO
Email: info@liberty.com
Web site: http://
www.liberty.com
Levels of Connectivity Supported: Shell, SLIP, PPP,
UUCP, ISDN, 56kb, T1

LineX Communications
P.O. Box 150531
San Rafael, CA 94915
Phone: 415 455 1650
Levels of Connectivity Supported: Shell, SLIP, PPP, 56kb,
128kb

MobiusNet
243 Vallejo Street
San Francisco, CA 94111 USA
Phone: 415 821 0600
Email: info@mobius.net
Web site: http://
www.mobius.net
Levels of Connectivity Supported: SLIP, PPP, ISDN, T1

Network Solutions
1000 Ames Ave., Suite C50
Milpitas, CA 95035 USA
Phone: 408 946 6895
Fax: 408 946 6899
Email: info@inow.com
Web site: http://www.inow.com
Levels of Connectivity Supported: Shell, PPP, UUCP, T1

QuakeNet
830 Wilmington Road
San Mateo, CA 94402 USA
Phone: 415 655 6607
Fax: 415 377 0635
Email: info@quake.net
Web site: http://
www.quake.net
Levels of Connectivity Supported: SLIP, PPP, UUCP

**San Francisco Online
(Televolve, Inc.)**
221 14th Street
San Francisco, CA 94103 USA
Phone: 415 861 7712
Fax: 415 861 7562
Email: info@sfo.com
Web site: http://www.sfo.com
Levels of Connectivity Supported: Shell, SLIP, PPP,
UUCP, ISDN, 56kb, T1

Sirius
350 Townsend, Suite #425
San Francisco, CA 94107 USA
Phone: 415 284 4700
Fax: 415 284 4704
Email: info@sirius.com
Web site: http://
www.sirius.com
Levels of Connectivity Supported: SLIP, PPP, ISDN

SLIPNET
25 Stillman Street, #200
San Francisco, CA 94107
Phone: 415 281 3132
Fax: 415 281 4498
Levels of Connectivity Supported: Shell, SLIP, PPP

22 Solutions
1040 Fell, Suite 3
San Francisco, CA 94117 USA
Phone: 415 431 9903
Email: info@catch22.com
Web site: http://
www.catch22.com
Levels of Connectivity Supported: Shell, SLIP, PPP,
UUCP, ISDN, 56kb, T1

Ultima Tool
927 Hampshire Street
San Francisco, CA 94110 USA
Phone: 415 775 8960
Email: info@ultima.org
Web site: http://
www.ultima.org
Levels of Connectivity Supported: Shell, SLIP, PPP

**Value Net Internetwork
Services**
2855 Mitchell Drive, Suite 105
Walnut Creek, CA 94598
USA
Phone: 510 943 5769
Fax: 510 943 1708
Email: info@value.net
Web site: http://
www.value.net
Levels of Connectivity Supported: Shell, SLIP, PPP,
ISDN, 56kb, T1

West Coast Online

6050 Commerce Blvd.,
Suite 210

Rohnert Park, CA 94928 USA

Phone: 707 586 3060

Fax: 707 586 5254

Email: info@calon.com

Web site: http://
www.calon.com

Levels of Connectivity Supported: Shell, SLIP, PPP,
UUCP

Zocalo Engineering

2355 Virginia Street

Berkeley, CA 94709-1315
USA

Phone: 510 540 8000

Fax: 510 548 1891

Email: info@zocalo.net

Web site: http://
www.zocalo.net

Levels of Connectivity Supported: Shell, SLIP, PPP, 56kb,
128kb, 348kb, T1

ISPs for Area Code 512

@sig.net

1515 S. Capital of Texas Hwy,
Suite 400

Austin, TX 78746

Phone: 512 306 0700

Fax: 512 306 0702

Email: sales@aus.sig.net

Web site: http://
www.aus.sig.net

Levels of Connectivity Supported: Shell, SLIP, PPP

CVTV - Internet

P.O. Box 610

La Grange, TX 78945 USA

Phone: 800 247 8885

Fax: 409 247 5127

Email: cyndyz@cvtv.net

Web site: http://www.cvtv.net

Levels of Connectivity Supported: SLIP, PPP, 56kb, T1

Delta Design and Development Inc.

6448 Hwy. 290 East, Suite
F108

Austin, TX 78723 USA

Phone: 800 763 8265

Fax: 512 467 8462

Email: sales@deltaweb.com

Web site: http://
www.deltaweb.com

Levels of Connectivity Supported: PPP, ISDN, 56kb, T1

The Eden Matrix

101 W. 6th Street, Suite 210

Austin, TX 78701 USA

Phone: 512 478 9900

Fax: 512 478 9934

Email: info@eden.com

Web site: http://www.eden.com

Levels of Connectivity Supported: Shell, SLIP, PPP,
ISDN, T1

I-Link Ltd

1 Chisholm Trail

Round Rock, TX 78681 USA

Phone: 800 ILINK 99

Fax: 512 244 9681

Email: info@i-link.net

Web site: http://www.
i-link.net

Levels of Connectivity Supported: PPP, ISDN, 56kb, T1

Illuminati Online

P.O. Box 18957

Austin, TX 78760 USA

Phone: 512 447 1144

Email: info@io.com

Web site: http://www.io.com

Levels of Connectivity Supported: Shell, SLIP, PPP

Internet Connect Services, Inc.

202 W. Goodwin

Victoria, TX 77901

Phone: 512 572 9987

Fax: 512 572 8193

Levels of Connectivity Supported: Shell, SLIP, PPP,
UUCP

Onramp Access, Inc.

612 Brazos, Suite 103

Austin, TX 78701 USA

Phone: 512 322 9200

Fax: 512 476 2878

Email: info@onr.com

Web site: http://www.onr.com

Levels of Connectivity Supported: SLIP, PPP, UUCP,
ISDN, 56kb, T1

OuterNet Connection Strategies

8235 Shoal Creek, Suite #105

Austin, TX 78758 USA

Phone: 512 345 3573

Fax: 512 206 0345

Email: question@outer.net

Web site: http://www.outer.net

Levels of Connectivity Supported: Shell, SLIP, PPP, UUCP, ISDN, T1

Phoenix DataNet, Inc.

17100 El Camino Real

Houston, TX 77058 USA

Phone: 713 486 8337

Fax: 713 486 7464

Email: info@phoenix.net

Web site: http://www.phoenix.net

Levels of Connectivity Supported: Shell, SLIP, PPP, ISDN, 56kb, T1

Real/Time Communications

6721 N. Lamar, Suite 103

Austin, TX 78752

Phone: 512 451 0046

Fax: 512 459 3858

Levels of Connectivity Supported: Shell, SLIP, PPP, UUCP

Turning Point Information Services, Inc.

301 Congress Ave., Ste. 330

Austin, TX 78763 USA

Phone: 512 499 8400

Fax: 512 499 8400

Email: info@tpoint.net

Web site: http://www.tpoint.net

Levels of Connectivity Supported: SLIP, PPP, UUCP, ISDN, 56kb, T1

Zilker Internet Park, Inc.

1106 Clayton Lane, Suite 500W

Austin, TX 78723

Phone: 512 206 3850

Fax: 512 206 3852

Levels of Connectivity Supported: Shell, PPP, UUCP

ISPs for Area Code 513

Dayton Network Access

P.O. Box 31280

45437-1280

Levels of Connectivity Supported: Shell, SLIP, PPP

IgLou Internet Services

3315 Gilmore Industrial Blvd.

Louisville, KY 40213

Phone: 800 436 IGLOU

Fax: 502 968 0449

Levels of Connectivity Supported: Shell, SLIP, PPP, UUCP

Internet Access Cincinnati

P.O. Box 602

Hamilton, OH 45012-0602

Phone: 513 887 8877

Fax: 513 887 2085

Levels of Connectivity Supported: Shell, SLIP, PPP, UUCP

Local Internet Gateway Co.

2464 Rosina Drive

Miamisburg, OH 45342-6430

Phone: 510 503 9227

Levels of Connectivity Supported: Shell

OARnet

2455 North Star Road

Columbus, OH 43221 USA

Phone: 614 728 8100 or 800 627 8101

Fax: 614 728 8110

Email: info@oar.net

Web site: http://www.oar.net

Levels of Connectivity Supported: Shell, SLIP, PPP

Premier Internet Cincinnati, Inc.

3814 West Street, Suite 201

Cincinnati, OH 45227 USA

Phone: 513 561 6245

Fax: 513 272 4367

Email: pic@cinti.net

Web site: http://www.cinti.net

Levels of Connectivity Supported: Shell, SLIP, PPP, UUCP, ISDN, 56kb, T1

ISPs for Area Code 514

Accent Internet

6900 Decarie, Suite 3100
Montreal, PQ H3X 2T8
Canada
Phone: 514 737 6077
Fax: 514 737 7041
Email: admin@accent.net
Web site: http://
www.accent.net
Levels of Connectivity Supported: Shell, SLIP, PPP,
UUCP, ISDN, 56kb, T1, Web
Hosting

autoroute.net (System Technology Development Inc.)

1100 Begin Street, Suite 100
Montreal, PQ H4R 1X1
CANADA
Phone: 514 333 3145
Fax: 514 334 7671
Email: info@autoroute.net
Web site: http://
www.autoroute.net
Levels of Connectivity Supported: Shell, SLIP, PPP,
UUCP, ISDN, 56kb, T1

CiteNet Telecom Inc.

4890 Eymard
Montreal, Quebec H1S 1C5
Canada
Phone: 514 721 1351
Fax: 514 725 5110
Email: info@citenet.net
Web site: http://
www.citenet.net
Levels of Connectivity Supported: Shell, SLIP, PPP,
UUCP, ISDN, 56kb, T1

Communication Accessibles Montreal

2055 Peel, #825
Montreal, QC H3A 1V4
Canada
Phone: 514 288 2581
Fax: 514 288 3401
Email: info@cam.org
Web site: http://www.cam.org
Levels of Connectivity Supported: Shell, SLIP, PPP,
UUCP

Communications Inter-Acces

5475 Pare Street, #104
Montreal, QC H4P 1R4
Canada
Phone: 514 367 0002
Fax: 514 368 3529
Email: info@interax.net
Web site: http://
www.interax.net
Levels of Connectivity Supported: SLIP, PPP, UUCP

Cycor Communications Incorporated

P.O. Box 454
Prince Edward Island, C1A
7K7 Canada
Email: signup@cycor.ca
Web site: http://www.cycor.ca
Levels of Connectivity Supported: SLIP, PPP, ISDN,
56kb, T1

Odyssee Internet

85 de la commune east,
Suite 301
Monteal, Quebec H2Y 1J1
Canada
Phone: 514 861 3432 (help
desk)
Fax: 514 861 6599
Email: info@odyssee.net
Web site: http://
www.odyssee.net
Levels of Connectivity Supported: UUCP, ISDN,
56kb, T1

UUNET Canada Inc.

1 Yonge Street, Suite 1400
Toronto, Ontario M5E 1J9
Canada
Phone: 416 368 6621
Fax: 416 368 1350
Levels of Connectivity Supported: SLIP, PPP, UUCP,
ISDN, 56kb, T1

ISPs for Area Code 515

Freese-Notis Weather.Net

2411 Grand Avenue
Des Moines, IA 50312 USA
Phone: 515 282 9310
Fax: 515 282 6832
Email: hfreese@weather.net
Web site: http://
www.weather.net
Levels of Connectivity Supported: PPP, 56kb, T1

ia.net

3417 Center Point Road N.E.

Cedar Rapids, IA 52402 USA

Phone: 319 393 1095

Fax: 319 378 1489

Email: info@ia.net

Web site: http://www.ia.net

Levels of Connectivity Supported: Shell, SLIP, PPP, UUCP, 56kb, T1

Iowa Network Services

4201 Corporate Drive

West Des Moines, IA 50265 USA

Phone: 800 546 6587

Fax: 515 830 0345

Email: service@netins.net

Web site: http://www.netins.net

Levels of Connectivity Supported: Shell, SLIP, PPP, UUCP, 56kb, T1, Web Hosting

JTM MultiMedia, Inc.

P.O. Box 1744

Des Moines, IA 50306-1744 USA

Phone: 515 277 1990

Fax: 612 397 9717

Email: jtm@ecity.net

Web site: http://www.ecity.net

Levels of Connectivity Supported: PPP

Minnesota OnLine

23 Empire Drive, Suite 152

Saint Paul, MN 55103-1857 USA

Phone: 612 225 1110

Fax: 612 225 1424

Email: info@mn.state.net

Web site: http://www.state.net

Levels of Connectivity Supported: SLIP, PPP, UUCP, ISDN, 56kb, T1

Synergy Communications, Inc.

1941 South 42nd Street

Omaha, NE 68105 USA

Phone: 800 345 9669

Fax: 402 346 0208

Email: info@synergy.net

Levels of Connectivity Supported: PPP

ISPs for Area Code 516

ASB Internet Services

NJ, USA

Phone: 516 981 1953

Email: info@asb.com

Web site: http://www.asb.com

Levels of Connectivity Supported: Shell, SLIP, PPP

bway.net / Outernet, Inc.

626 Broadwaym, Suite 3A

New York, NY 10012 USA

Phone: 212 982 9800

Fax: 212 982 5499

Email: info@bway.net

Web site: http://www.bway.net

Levels of Connectivity Supported: Shell, SLIP, PPP, UUCP, ISDN, 56kb, T1

Creative Data Consultants (SILLY.COM)

Bayside, NY 11364 USA

Phone: 718 229 0489 x23

Fax: 718 229 7096

Email: info@silly.com

Web site: http://www.silly.com

Levels of Connectivity Supported: Shell, SLIP, PPP, UUCP

Echo Communications Group

97 Perry Street, Suite 13

New York, NY 10014

Phone: 212 255 3839

Fax: 212 255 9440

Levels of Connectivity Supported: Shell, SLIP, PPP

I-2000 Inc.

416 Main Street

Metuchen, NJ 08840 USA

Phone: 800 464 3820

Fax: 908 906 2396

Email: info@i-2000.com

Web site: http://www.i-2000.com

Levels of Connectivity Supported: SLIP, PPP, 56kb, T1

INTAC Access Corporation

256 Broad Avenue

Palisades Park, NJ 07650 USA

Phone: 800 50 INTAC

Fax: 201 944 1434

Email: info@intac.com

Web site: http://
www.intac.com

Levels of Connectivity Supported: Shell, SLIP, PPP, UUCP, ISDN, 56kb, T1

LI Net, Inc.

49 Landing Avenue

Smithtown, NY 11787-2712

Phone: 516 265 0997

Levels of Connectivity Supported: Shell, SLIP, PPP, UUCP, 56kb, T1

Lightning Internet Services, LLC

327C Sagamore Avenue

Mineola, NY 11501 USA

Phone: 516 248 8400

Fax: 516 248 8897

Email: sales@lightning.net

Web site: http://
www.lightning.net

Levels of Connectivity Supported: ISDN, 56kb, T1

Long Island Information, Inc.

P.O. Box 151

Albertson, NY 11507 USA

Phone: 516 INTERNET, 516
248 5381

Email: admin@liii.com

Web site: http://www.liii.com

Levels of Connectivity Supported: Shell, SLIP, PPP, UUCP, 56kb, T1

Long Island Internet HeadQuarters

506 Route 110

Melville, NY 11747 USA

Phone: 516 439 7800

Fax: 516 439 7321

Email: support@pb.net

Web site: http://www.pb.net

Levels of Connectivity Supported: Shell, SLIP, PPP, UUCP, ISDN, 56kb, T1

Network Internet Services

P.O. Box 819

Commack, NY 11725

Phone: 516 543 0234

Fax: 516 543 0274

Levels of Connectivity Supported: Shell, SLIP, PPP

New World Data

253-17 80th Ave., Suite 2B

Floral Park, NY 11004 USA

Phone: 718 962 1725

Fax: 718 962 1708

Email: dmk@nwdc.com

Web site: http://www.nwdc.com

Levels of Connectivity Supported: Shell, SLIP, PPP, UUCP, ISDN, 56kb, T1

NYSERNet

200 Elwood Davis Road

Liverpool, NY 13088-6147
USA

Phone: 800 493 4367

Fax: 315 453 3052

Email: sales@nysernet.org

Web site: http://nysernet.org

Levels of Connectivity Supported: Shell, 56kb, T1

Panix (Public Access uNIX)

New York, NY USA

Phone: 212 741 4400

Fax: 212 741 5311

Email: info@panix.com

Web site: http://
www.panix.com

Levels of Connectivity Supported: Shell, SLIP, PPP

Pipeline New York

150 Broadway, Suite 610

New York, NY 10038 USA

Phone: 212 267 3636

Fax: 212 267 4380

Email: info@pipeline.com

Web site: http://
www.pipeline.com

Levels of Connectivity Supported: Shell

Real Life Pictures RealNet
58 W36th Street, 2nd Floor
New York, NY 10018 USA
Phone: 212 366 4434
Email: reallife@walrus.com
Web site: http://
www.reallife.com
Levels of Connectivity Supported: Shell, SLIP, PPP,
ISDN, 56kb, 384kb, T1

ZONE One Network Exchange
304 Hudson Street
New York, NY 10013 USA
Phone: 212 824 4000
Fax: 212 824 4009
Email: info@zone.net
Web site: http://www.zone.net
Levels of Connectivity Supported: Shell, SLIP, PPP,
UUCP, ISDN, 56kb, T1

ISPs for Area Code 517

Branch Information Services
2901 Hubbard
Ann Arbor, MI 48105 USA
Phone: 313 741 4442
Fax: 313 995 1931
Email: branch-info@branch.com
Web site: http://branch.com
Levels of Connectivity Supported: SLIP, PPP, ISDN,
56kb, T1

Freeway Inc. (tm)
P.O. Box 2389
Petoskey, Michigan 49770
USA
Phone: 616 347 3175
Fax: 616 347 1568
Email: info@freeway.net
Web site: http://
www.freeway.net
Levels of Connectivity Supported: Shell, PPP, UUCP,
56kb, T1

The Internet Ramp
G-4225 Miller Road, Suite 179
Flint, MI 48507 USA
Phone: 800 502 0620 (phone
registration)
Fax: 810 732 5628
Email: newaccts@tir.com
Web site: http://www.tir.com
Levels of Connectivity Supported: PPP, T1

Mich.com, Inc.
21042 Laurelwood
Farmington, MI 48336 USA
Phone: 810 478 4300
Fax: 810 478 4302
Email: info@mich.com
Web site: http://www.mich.com
Levels of Connectivity Supported: Shell, SLIP, PPP,
UUCP, 56kb, T1

Msen, Inc.
320 Miller Avenue
Ann Arbor, MI 48103
Phone: 313 998 4562
Fax: 313 998 4563
Levels of Connectivity Supported: Shell, SLIP, PPP,
UUCP

Voyager Information Networks, Inc.
600 West St. Jospeh Hwy.,
Suite 20
Lansing, MI 48933 USA
Phone: 517 485 9068
Fax: 517 485 9074
Email: help@voyager.net
Web site: http://
www.voyager.net
Levels of Connectivity Supported: PPP, ISDN, 56kb, T1

ISPs for Area Code 518

AlbanyNet
262 Central Ave
Albany, NY 12206 USA
Phone: 518 462 6262
Fax: 518 463 0014
Email: info@albany.net
Web site: http://
www.albany.net
Levels of Connectivity Supported: Shell, SLIP, PPP,
UUCP, ISDN, 56kb, T1

epix
100 Lake Street
Dallas, PA 18612 USA
Phone: 800 374 9669
Fax: 717 675 5711
Email: karndt@epix.net
Web site: http://www.epix.net
Levels of Connectivity Supported: SLIP, PPP, ISDN, 56kb, T1

Global One, Inc.
1840 Western Avenue
Albany, NY 12203 USA
Phone: 518 452 1465
Fax: 518 452 1466
Email: lorin@global1.net
Web site: http://www.global1.net
Levels of Connectivity Supported: Shell, SLIP, PPP, ISDN, 565bk, T1

Klink Net Communications
124 Olaf Johnson Rd
Northville, NY 12134 USA
Phone: 518 725 3000
Fax: 518 863 7215
Email: admin@klink.net
Web site: http://www.klink.net
Levels of Connectivity Supported: Shell, SLIP, PPP, UUCP, ISDN, 56kb, T1

NetHeaven
1503 Saratoga Rd.
Ballston Spa, NY 12020 USA
Phone: 800 910 6671
Fax: 518 885 1335
Email: info@netheaven.com
Web site: http://www.netheaven.com
Levels of Connectivity Supported: SLIP, PPP, 56kb, T1

NYSERNet
200 Elwood Davis Road
Liverpool, NY 13088-6147 USA
Phone: 800 493 4367
Fax: 315 453 3052
Email: sales@nysernet.org
Web site: http://nysernet.org
Levels of Connectivity Supported: Shell, 56kb, T1

SoVerNet, Inc.
5 Rockingham Street
Bellows Falls, VT 05101 USA
Phone: 802 463 2111
Fax: 802 463 2110
Email: info@sover.net
Web site: http://www.sover.net
Levels of Connectivity Supported: Shell, SLIP, PPP, UUCP, ISDN, 56kb, T1

Wizvax Communications
1508 Tibbits Ave
Troy, NY 12180 USA
Phone: 518 273 4325
Fax: 518 271 6289
Email: info@wizvax.net
Web site: http://www.wizvax.net
Levels of Connectivity Supported: Shell, SLIP, PPP, UUCP, 56kb, T1

ISPs for Area Code 519

Electro-Byte Technologies
559-B Exmouth Street
Sarnia, Ontario N7T 5P6 Canada
Phone: 519 332 8235
Fax: 519 332 8307
Email: info@ebtech.net
Web site: http://www.ebtech.net
Levels of Connectivity Supported: Shell, SLIP, PPP, UUCP, 56kb, T1

Execulink Internet Services Corporation
P.O.Box 40004
London, Ontario N5W 3G3 Canada
Phone: 519 451 4288
Fax: 519 455 8805
Email: info@execulink.com
Web site: http://www.execulink.com
Levels of Connectivity Supported: Shell, SLIP, PPP

FastLane.Net Ltd.
654 Grosvenor Street
London, Ontario N5Y 3T4
Canada
Phone: 519 679 0908
Fax: 519 679 6539
Email: info@fastlane.ca
Web site: http://
www.fastlane.ca
Levels of Connectivity Supported: Shell, SLIP, ISDN,
56kb, T1

headwaters network
113 Broadway
Orangeville, Ontario L9W 1K2
Canada
Phone: 519 940 9252
Fax: 519 942 3776
Email: sales@headwaters.com
Web site: http://
www.headwaters.com
Levels of Connectivity Supported: Shell, SLIP, PPP,
UUCP, ISDN, 56kb, T1

HookUp Communications
1075 North Service Road West,
Suite 207
Oakville, Ontario L6M 2G2
Phone: 905 847 8000
Fax: 905 847 8866
Levels of Connectivity Supported: Shell, SLIP, PPP,
UUCP

HyperNet
4026 Meadowbrook Dr.,
Unit 140
London, Ontario N6L 1C8
Canada
Phone: 519 652 3790
Fax: 519 652 0569
Email: Admin@L2.lonet.ca
Web site: http://www.lonet.ca
Levels of Connectivity Supported: PPP, ISDN, 56kb

Information Gateway Services (Kitchener-Waterloo)
151 Frobisher Drive, Suite E-118
Waterloo, Ontario N2V 2C9
Canada
Phone: 519 884 7200Fax: from
Guelph, dial 648-3164
Email: info@kw.igs.net
Web site: http://
www.kw.igs.net
Levels of Connectivity Supported: Shell, SLIP, PPP,
UUCP, ISDN, 56kb, T1

Inter*Com Information Services
1464 Adelaide Street North
London, Ontario N5X 1K4
Canada
Phone: 519 679 1620
Fax: 519 679 1583
Email: info@icis.on.ca
Web site: http://
www.icis.on.ca
Levels of Connectivity Supported: Shell, SLIP, PPP,
UUCP, ISDN, 56kb, T1

Magic Online Services International Inc.
260 Richmond Street West,
Suite 206
Toronto, Ontario M5V 1W5
Canada
Phone: 416 591 6490
Fax: 416 591 6409
Email: info@magic.ca
Web site: http://www.magic.ca
Levels of Connectivity Supported: SLIP, PPP, UUCP,
ISDN

MGL Systems Computer Technologies Inc.
RR#1
Guelph, Ontario N1H 7N4
Canada
Phone: 519 836 1295
Fax: 519 836 1309
Email: info@mgl.ca
Web site: http://www.mgl.ca
Levels of Connectivity Supported: Shell, SLIP, PPP,
UUCP, ISDN, 56kb, T1

Network Enterprise Technology Inc.
20 Jackson St. W., Suite 206
Hamilton, Ontario L8P 1L2
Canada
Phone: 905 525 4555
Fax: 905 525 3222
Email: info@netinc.ca
Web site: http://
www.netinc.ca
Levels of Connectivity Supported: Shell, PPP, UUCP,
ISDN, 56kb

UUNET Canada Inc.

1 Yonge Street, Suite 1400

Toronto, Ontario M5E 1J9

Canada

Phone: 416 368 6621

Fax: 416 368 1350

Levels of Connectivity Supported: SLIP, PPP, UUCP, ISDN, 56kb, T1

Windsor Infromation Network Company (WINCOM)

4510 Rhodes Drive, Unit 905

Windsor, Ontario N8W 5K5

Canada

Phone: 519 945 9462

Fax: 519 945 9777

Email: kim@wincom.net

Web site: http://
www.wincom.net

Levels of Connectivity Supported: Shell, PPP, UUCP, ISDN, 56kb, T1

ISPs for Area Code 520

InfoMagic, Inc

11950 N. Highway 89

Flagstaff, AZ 86004 USA

Phone: 520 526 9565

Fax: 520 526 9873

Email:
mailto:info@infomagic.com

Web site: http://
www.infomagic.com

Levels of Connectivity Supported: Shell, SLIP, PPP, UUCP, ISDN, 56kb, T1

Internet Direct, Inc.

1366 East Thomas Road, Suite 210

Phoenix, AZ 85014 USA

Phone: 1 800 TRY EMAIL

Fax: 602 274 8518

Email: mailto:info@direct.net

Web site: http://
www.indirect.com

Levels of Connectivity Supported: Shell, SLIP, PPP, UUCP, ISDN, 56kb, T1

Opus One

1404 East Line Road

Tucson, AZ 85719

Phone: 602 324 0494

Fax: 602 324 0495

Levels of Connectivity Supported: Shell, SLIP, PPP

Primenet

2320 W. Peoria Avenue, Suite A103

Phoenix, AZ 85029 USA

Phone: 602 870 1010 or 800 4 NET FUN

Fax: 602 870 1010

Email:
mailto:info@primenet.com

Web site: http://
www.primenet.com

Levels of Connectivity Supported: Shell, SLIP, PPP, UUCP

RTD Systems & Networking, Inc.

177 N. Church Ave., Suite 310

Tucson, AZ 85701 USA

Phone: 520 623 9663

Fax: 520 623 9934

Email: mailto:info@rtd.com

Web site: http://www.rtd.com

Levels of Connectivity Supported: Shell, SLIP, PPP, UUCP, ISDN, 56kb, T1

Sedona Internet Services, Inc.

2675 W. Hwy 89A, Suite #1111

Sedona, AZ 86336 USA

Phone: 520 204 2247

Fax: 520 282 3061

Email: mailto:info@sedona.net

Web site: http://
www.sedona.net

Levels of Connectivity Supported: PPP, 56kb, T1

ISPs for Area Code 540

Cyber Services, Inc.

8027 Leesburg Pike, Suite 317

Vienna, VA 22182 USA

Phone: 703 749 9590

Fax: 703 749 9598

Email: mailto:info@cs.com

Web site: http://www.cs.com

Levels of Connectivity Supported: Shell, SLIP, PPP, UUCP, ISDN, 56kb, T1

ISPs for Area Code 541

aVastNet
P.O. Box 6
Canby, OR 97013 USA
Phone: 503 263 0912
Fax: 503 266 2015
Email:
mailto:info@vastnet.com
Web site: http://
www.vastnet.com
Levels of Connectivity Sup-
ported: Shell, SLIP, PPP,
UUCP

ISPs for Area Code 601

A2ZNET
141 East Highway 72, Suite 7
Collierville, TN 38017 USA
Phone: 901 854 1871
Fax: 901 854 1872
Email: webmaster@a2znet.com
Web site:
webmaster@a2znet.com

Datasync Internet
P. O. Box 399
Ocean Springs, MS 39566-0399
USA
Phone: 601 872 0001, 601 452
0011, 334 476 8155
Email: info@datasync.com
Web site: http://
www.datasync.com
Levels of Connectivity Sup-
ported: Shell, SLIP, PPP,
UUCP, 56kb, T1

Gulfcoast On-Line Develop-ment, Inc.
PO Box 406
Long Beach, MS 39560 USA
Phone: 601 864 2423
Fax: 601 864 2423
Email: info@goldinc.com
Web site: http://
www.goldinc.com
Levels of Connectivity Sup-
ported: Shell, SLIP, PPP,
UUCP, 56kb, T1

Hub City Area Access
110 Fox Run Drive
Hattiesburg, MS 39401 USA
Phone: 601 268 6156
Fax: 601 268 3799
Email: info@hub1.hubcity.com
Web site: http://
hub1.hubcity.com/~hubcity
Levels of Connectivity Sup-
ported: Shell, SLIP, PPP,
UUCP, 56kb, T1

ISPs for Area Code 602

Crossroads Communications
P.O. Box 30250
Mesa, AZ 85275 USA
Phone: 602 813 9040
Fax: 602 545 7470
Email: crossroads@xroads.com
Web site: http://
xroads.xroads.com/home.html
Levels of Connectivity Sup-
ported: Shell, SLIP, PPP,
UUCP

I-Link Ltd
1 Chisholm Trail
Round Rock, TX 78681 USA
Phone: 800 ILINK 99
Fax: 512 244 9681
Email: info@i-link.net
Web site: ="http://www.
i-link.net
Levels of Connectivity Sup-
ported: PPP, ISDN, 56kb, T1

InfoMagic, Inc
11950 N. Highway 89
Flagstaff, AZ 86004 USA
Phone: 520 526 9565
Fax: 520 526 9873
Email: info@infomagic.com
Web site: http://
www.infomagic.com
Levels of Connectivity Sup-
ported: Shell, SLIP, PPP,
UUCP, 56kb, T1

Internet Direct, Inc.
1366 East Thomas Road, Suite
210
Phoenix, AZ 85014 USA
Phone: 1 800 TRY EMAIL
Fax: 602 274 8518
Email: info@direct.net
Web site: http://
www.indirect.com
Levels of Connectivity Sup-
ported: Shell, SLIP, PPP,
UUCP, 56kb, T1

Internet Express

1155 Kelly Johnson Blvd, Ste 400

Colorado Springs, CO 80920-3959 USA

Phone: 800-592-1240

Fax: 719-592-1201

Email: service@usa.net

Web site: http://www.usa.net

Levels of Connectivity Supported: Shell, SLIP, PPP, UUCP, 56kb, T1

New Mexico Technet, Inc.

4100 Osuna NE, Suite 103

Albuquerque, NM 87109

Phone: 505 345 6555

Fax: 505 345 6559

Levels of Connectivity Supported: Shell, SLIP, PPP, UUCP

Opus One

1404 East Line Road

Tucson, AZ 85719

Phone: 602 324 0494

Fax: 602 324 0495

Levels of Connectivity Supported: Shell, SLIP, PPP

Shell access: $30/month

Phoenix Computer Specialists

3120 North 19th Avenue, Suite 130

Phoenix, AZ 85015 USA

Phone: 602 265 9188

Fax: 602 265 9357

Email: info@pcslink.com

Levels of Connectivity Supported: Shell, SLIP, PPP, UUCP, 56kb, T1

Primenet

2320 W. Peoria Avenue, Suite A103

Phoenix, AZ 85029 USA

Phone: 602 870 1010 or 800 4 NET FUN

Fax: 602 870 1010

Email: info@primenet.com

Web site: http://www.primenet.com

Levels of Connectivity Supported: Shell, SLIP, PPP, UUCP

RTD Systems & Networking, Inc.

177 N. Church Ave., Suite 310

Tucson, AZ 85701 USA

Phone: 520 623 9663

Fax: 520 623 9934

Email: info@rtd.com

Web site: http://www.rtd.com

Levels of Connectivity Supported: Shell, SLIP, PPP, UUCP, ISDN, 56kb, T1

StarLink Internet Services

7465 W. Cactus, Suite 101

Peoria, AZ 85345 USA

Phone: 602 878 7001

Fax: 602 878 0258

Email: sysop@starlink.com

Web site: http://www.starlink.com

Levels of Connectivity Supported: Shell, PPP, UUCP, 56kb, T1

Systems Solutions Inc.

2108 E. Thomas Road

Phoenix, AZ 85016 USA

Phone: 602 955 5566

Fax: 602 955 0085

Email: support@syspac.com

Web site: http://www.syspac.com

Levels of Connectivity Supported: Shell, SLIP, PPP, UUCP, ISDN, 56kb, T1

ISPs for Area Code 603

Agate Internet

31 Central Street, Suite 312

Bangor, ME 04401 USA

Phone: 207 947 8248

Fax: 207 947 4432

Email: info@agate.net

Web site: http://www.agate.net

Levels of Connectivity Supported: SLIP, PPP, 56kb, T1

The Destek Group, Inc.

21 Hinds Lane

Pelham, NH 03076-3013

Phone: 603 635 3857 or 508 363 2413

Fax: 508 363 2115

Levels of Connectivity Supported: Shell, SLIP, PPP, UUCP

Empire.Net, Inc.
127 Main Street, Suite 5
Nashua, NH 03060 USA
Phone: 603 889 1220
Fax: 603 889 0366
Email: info@empire.net
Web site: http://
www.empire.net
Levels of Connectivity Supported: telnet, Shell, SLIP, PPP, UUCP, ISDN, 56kb, T1

MV Communications, Inc.
P.O. Box 4963
Manchester, NH 03108-4963
USA
Phone: 603 429 2223
Fax: 603 424 0386
Email: info@mv.mv.com
Web site: http://www.mv.com
Levels of Connectivity Supported: Shell, SLIP, PPP, UUCP, 56kb, T1

NETIS Public Access Internet
P.O. Box 1015
Windham, NH 03087-1015
Phone: 603 437 1811
Fax: 603 437 1811
Levels of Connectivity Supported: Shell, UUCP

Rocket Science Computer Services, Inc.
601 Spaulding Turnpike,
Suite 40
Portsmouth, NH 03801 USA
Phone: 603 334 6444
Fax: 603 334 6457
Email: info@rscs.com
Web site: http://www.rscs.net
Levels of Connectivity Supported: PPP, 56kb, T1

SoVerNet, Inc.
5 Rockingham Street
Bellows Falls, VT 05101 USA
Phone: 802 463 2111
Fax: 802 463 2110
Email: info@sover.net
Web site: http://
www.sover.net
Levels of Connectivity Supported: Shell, SLIP, PPP, UUCP, ISDN, 56kb, T1

StarNet (Advanced Communication Systems, Inc.)
54 West Dane St.
Clemenzi Industrial Park
Beverly, MA 01915 USA
Phone: 508 922 8238 or
800 779 3309
Fax: 508 921 8456
Email: info@star.net
Web site: http://www.star.net
Levels of Connectivity Supported: SLIP, PPP, ISDN, 56kb, T1

UltraNet Communications, Inc.
910 Boston Post Road
Suite 220
Marlborough, MA 01752 USA
Phone: 508 229 8400 or
800 763 8111
Fax: 508 229 2375
Email: info@ultranet.com
Web site: http://
www.ultranet.com
Levels of Connectivity Supported: SLIP, PPP, ISDN, 56kb, T1

ISPs for Area Code 604

AMT Solutions Group, Inc. Island Net
P.O. Box 6201, Depot 1
Victoria, BC V8Z 7G1 Canada
Phone: 604 727 6030
Fax: 604 479 7343
Email: info@islandnet.com
Web site: http://
www.islandnet.com
Levels of Connectivity Supported: Shell, SLIP, PPP, UUCP

auroraNET Inc.
5065 Anola Drive
Burnaby, BC V5B 4V7 Canada
Phone: 604 294 1815
Fax: 604 4357 x115
Email: sales@aurora.net
Web site: http://
www.aurora.net
Levels of Connectivity Supported: SLIP, PPP, UUCP, ISDN, 56kb, T1

Cycor Communications Incorporated
P.O. Box 454
Prince Edward Island C1A 7K7
Canada
Phone: 902 892 7354
Fax: : 902-892-5600
Email: signup@cycor.ca
Web site: http://www.cycor.ca
Levels of Connectivity Supported: SLIP, PPP, ISDN, 56kb, T1

Fairview Technology Centre Ltd.

Rt. 1 S24 - C9

Oliver, BC V0H 1T0 Canada

Phone: 604 498 4316

Fax: 604 498 3210

Email: bwklatt@ftcnet.com

Web site: http://www.ftcnet.com

Levels of Connectivity Supported: Shell, PPP, UUCP, ISDN, Cablemodem

The InterNet Shop Inc.

1160 - 8th Street

Kamloops, BC V2C 1Z3 Canada

Phone: 604 376 3719

Fax: 604 376 5931

Email: info@stargazer.netshop.net

Web site: http://www.netshop.net

Levels of Connectivity Supported: Shell, PPP, UUCP, 56kb, T1

Mind Link!

BC Canada

Phone: 604 534 5663

Fax: 604 534 7473

Levels of Connectivity Supported: Shell, SLIP, PPP

Okanagan Internet Junction

Suite 1, 4216 25th Ave.

Vernon, BC V1T 1P4 Canada

Phone: 604 549 1036

Fax: 604 542 4130

Email: info@junction.net

Web site: http://www.junction.net

Levels of Connectivity Supported: Shell, SLIP, PPP, UUCP, 56kb, T1

Sunshine Net, Inc.

Box 44, 552 Reed Road

Grantham's Landing, BC V0N 1X0 Canada

Phone: 604 886 4120

Fax: 604 886 4513

Levels of Connectivity Supported: SLIP, PPP

UUNET Canada Inc.

1 Yonge Street, Suite 1400

Toronto, Ontario M5E 1J9 Canada

Phone: 416 368 6621

Fax: 416 368 1350

Levels of Connectivity Supported: SLIP, PPP, UUCP, ISDN, 56kb, T1

ISPs for Area Code 605

Internet Services of the Black Hills, Inc.

511 W Jackson Blvd.

South Dakota 57783, USA

Phone: 605 642 2244 or 605 343 3190

Fax: 605 642 3606

Email: postmaster@blackhills.com

Web site: http://www.blackhills.com

Levels of Connectivity Supported: Shell, SLIP, PPP, UUCP, ISDN, 56kb, T1

Pioneer Internet

504 4th Street

Sergeant Bluff, IA 51054

Phone: 712 271 0101

Email: info@pionet.net

Web site: http://www.pionet.net

Levels of Connectivity Supported: PPP, 56kb, T1

ISPs for Area Code 606

IgLou Internet Services

3315 Gilmore Industrial Blvd.

Louisville, KY 40213

Phone: 800 436 IGLOU

Fax: 502 968 0449

Levels of Connectivity Supported: Shell, SLIP, PPP, UUCP

Internet Access Cincinnati

P.O. Box 602

Hamilton, OH 45012-0602

Phone: 513 887 8877

Fax: 513 887 2085

Levels of Connectivity Supported: Shell, SLIP, PPP, UUCP

Mikrotec Internet Services, Inc.

1001 Winchester Rd

Lexington, KY 40505 USA

Phone: 606 225 1488

Fax: 606 225 5852

Email: info@mis.net

Web site: http://www.mis.net

Levels of Connectivity Supported: Shell, PPP, UUCP, ISDN, 56kb, T1

RAM Technologies Inc.

P.O. Box 1760

2025 13th Street

Ashland, KY 41105-1760 USA

Phone: 800 950 1726

Fax: 606 329 9203

Email: info@ramlink.net

Web site: http://www.ramlink.net

Levels of Connectivity Supported: Shell, SLIP, PPP, 56kb, T1

ISPs for Area Code 607

Art Matrix - Lightlink

PO 880

Ithaca, NY 14851-0880 USA

Phone: 607 277 0959

Fax: 607 277 8913

Email: info@lightlink.com

Web site: http://www.lightlink.com

Levels of Connectivity Supported: Shell, SLIP, PPP, UUCP

Clarity Connect, Inc.

200 Pleasant Grove Road #1F

Ithaca, NY 14850 USA

Phone: 607 257 2070

Fax: 607 257 2657

Email: chuck@baka.com

Web site: http://www.baka.com

Levels of Connectivity Supported: Shell, SLIP, PPP, ISDN, 56kb, T1

epix

100 Lake Street

Dallas, PA 18612 USA

Phone: 800 374 9669

Fax: 717 675 5711

Email: karndt@epix.net

Web site: http://www.epix.net

Levels of Connectivity Supported: SLIP, PPP, ISDN, 56kb, T1

NYSERNet

200 Elwood Davis Road

Liverpool, NY 13088-6147 USA

Phone: 800 493 4367

Fax: 315 453 3052

Email: sales@nysernet.org

Web site: http://nysernet.org

Levels of Connectivity Supported: Shell, 56kb, T1, T3

ServiceTech, Inc.

182 Monroe Ave

Rochester, NY 14607 USA

Phone: 716 263 3360

Fax: 716 423 1596

Email: info@servtech.com

Web site: http://www.servtech.com

Levels of Connectivity Supported: Shell, PPP, 56kb, T1

Spectra.net

139 Grand Avenue

Johnson City, NY 13790

Phone: 607 798 7300

Fax: 607 717 315

Email: info@spectra.net

Web site: http://www.spectra.net

Levels of Connectivity Supported: Shell, SLIP, PPP, ISDN, 56kb, fractional T1

ISPs for Area Code 608

BOSSNet Internet Services
614 East Grand Avenue
Beloit, WI 53511 USA
Phone: 608 362 1340
Fax: 608 362 4584
Email: mbusam@bossnt.com
Web site: http://www.bossnt.com
Levels of Connectivity Supported: Shell, SLIP, PPP, ISDN, 56kb, T1

Exec-PC
2105 South 170th St
New Berlin, WI 53151 USA
Phone: 414 789 4200
Fax: 414 789 1946
Email: info@execpc.com
Web site: http://
www.execpc.com
Levels of Connectivity Supported: Shell, SLIP, PPP, ISDN

FullFeed Communications
Madison, WI 53704-2488
Phone: 608 246 4239
Levels of Connectivity Supported: Shell, SLIP, PPP, UUCP

ISPs for Area Code 609

CyberComm Online Services
P.O. Box 5252
Toms River, NJ 08753-5252
USA
Phone: 908 506 6651
Fax: 908 506 6674
Email: info@cybercomm.net
Web site: http://
www.cybercomm.net
Levels of Connectivity Supported: Shell, SLIP, UUCP

Cyberenet (Kaps, Inc.)
Centennial Center, Suite#106
Cross Keys Road
Berlin, NJ 08009 USA
Phone: 609 753 9840
Fax: 609 753 9838
Email: access-
sales@cyberenet.net
Web site: http://
www.cyberenet.net
Levels of Connectivity Supported: Shell, SLIP, PPP, UUCP, ISDN, 56kb, T1

Digital Express Group, Inc.
6006 Greenbelt Road, Suite 228
Greenbelt, MD 20770 USA
Phone: 301 847 5000 or 847 5050
Fax: 301 847 5215
Email: info@digex.net
Web site: http://
www.digex.net
Levels of Connectivity Supported: Shell, SLIP, PPP, 56kb, T1

Eclipse Internet Access
P.O. Box 512
Plainfield, NJ 07061 USA
Phone: 800 483 1223
Fax: 908 755 6379
Email: info@eclipse.net
Web site: http://
www.eclipse.net
Levels of Connectivity Supported: PPP, 56kb, T1

InterActive Network Services
Four Shoppers Lane, Suite 303
Turnersville, NJ 08012 USA
Phone: 609 227 6380
Fax: 609 227 3943
Email: info@jersey.net
Web site: http://
www.jersey.net
Levels of Connectivity Supported: Shell, SLIP, PPP, UUCP, ISDN, 56kb, T1

NetK2NE
332 Ridge Road
Browns Mills, NJ 08015 USA
Phone: 609 893 0673
Email: vince-q@k2nesoft.com
Web site: http://
www.k2nesoft.com
Levels of Connectivity Supported: Shell, SLIP, PPP, 56kb, T1

Net Access
P.O. Box 502
Glenside, PA 19117 USA
Phone: 215 576 8669
Email: support@netaxs.com
Web site: http://
www.netaxs.com
Levels of Connectivity Supported: Shell, SLIP, PPP,
UUCP, 56kb, T1

NetReach, Incorporated
41 St. James Place
Ardmore, PA 19003 USA
Phone: 215 283 2300
Fax: 215 642 0453
Email: info@netreach.net
Web site: http://
www.netreach.net
Levels of Connectivity Supported: Shell, SLIP, PPP,
UUCP, ISDN, 56kb, T1

New Jersey Computer Connection
P.O. Box 6909
Lawrenceville, NJ 08648
Phone: 609 896 2799
Fax: 609 896 2994
Levels of Connectivity Supported: Shell, SLIP, PPP,
UUCP

Texel International
North Brunswick, NJ 08902
Phone: 908 297 0290
Fax: 908 940 9535
Email: info@texel.com
Web site: http://
www.texel.com

VoiceNet
17 Richard Rd.
Ivyland, PA 18974 USA
Phone: 800 835 5710
Fax: 215 674 9662
Email: info@voicenet.com
Web site: http://
www.voicenet.com
Levels of Connectivity Supported: Shell, SLIP, PPP,
UUCP, ISDN, 56kb, T1

ISPs for Area Code 610

Cheap Net
P.O. Box 22
Yorklyn, DE 19736 USA
Phone: 302 993 8420
Fax: 302 993 8419
Email: sammy@ravenet.com
Levels of Connectivity Supported: Shell

Digital Express Group, Inc.
6006 Greenbelt Road, Suite 228
Greenbelt, MD 20770 USA
Phone: 301 847 5000 or 847 5050
Fax: 301 847 5215
Email: info@digex.net
Web site: http://
www.digex.net
Levels of Connectivity Supported: Shell, SLIP, PPP,
56kb, T1

ENTER.Net
4676 Broadway, #225
PA 18104
Phone: 610 366 1300
Email: info@enter.net
Web site: http://
www.enter.net
Levels of Connectivity Supported: PPP, T1

epix
100 Lake Street
Dallas, PA 18612 USA
Phone: 800 374 9669
Fax: 717 675 5711
Email: karndt@epix.net
Web site: http://www.epix.net
Levels of Connectivity Supported: SLIP, PPP, ISDN,
56kb, T1

FishNet (Prometheus Information Corp.)
1006 West Ninth Ave
King Of Prussia, PA 10406
USA
Phone: 610 337 9994
Fax: 610 337 9918
Email: info@pond.com
Web site: http://www.pond.com
Levels of Connectivity Supported: Shell, SLIP, PPP

GlobalQUEST, Inc.
P.O. Box 443
Malvern, PA 19355-0443 USA
Phone: 610 696 8111
Fax: 610 696 8575
Email: info@globalquest.net
Web site: http://
www.globalquest.net
Levels of Connectivity Supported: PPP, UUCP, 56kb, T1

Internet Tidal Wave

1444 Hamilton Street, Suite 500

Allentown, PA 18102-4266 USA

Phone: 610 770 6187

Fax: 610 770 6186

Email: info@itw.com

Web site: http://www.itw.com

Levels of Connectivity Supported: Shell, SLIP, PPP, ISDN, 56kb, T1

InterNetworking Technologies

P.O. Box 852

Milford, DE 19963 USA

Phone: 302 398 4369

Email: itnt.com@itnt.com

Web site: http://www.itnt.com

Levels of Connectivity Supported: Shell, SLIP, PPP, ISDN, 56kb

The Magnetic Page

P.O. Box 1787

Wilmington, DE 19899 USA

Phone: 302 651 9753

Fax: 302 426 9731

Email: info@magpage.com

Web site: http://www.magpage.com

Levels of Connectivity Supported: Shell, SLIP, PPP, UUCP, ISDN, 56kb, T1

Microserve Information Systems

222 Temperance Hill

Plymouth, PA 18651 USA

Phone: 800 380 INET or 717 821 5964

Fax: 717 779 5490

Email: info@microserve.net

Web site: http://www.microserve.net

Levels of Connectivity Supported: Shell, PPP, UUCP

Net Access

P.O. Box 502

Glenside, PA 19117 USA

Phone: 215 576 8669

Email: support@netaxs.com

Web site: http://www.netaxs.com

Levels of Connectivity Supported: Shell, SLIP, PPP, UUCP, 56kb, T1

NetReach, Incorporated

41 St. James Place

Ardmore, PA 19003 USA

Phone: 215 283 2300

Fax: 215 642 0453

Email: info@netreach.net

Web site: http://www.netreach.net

Levels of Connectivity Supported: Shell, SLIP, PPP, UUCP, ISDN, 56kb, T1

Network Analysis Group

7540 Windsor Drive, Suite 90

Allentown, PA 7540 USA

Phone: 800 624 9240

Fax: 800 607 9548

Email: nag@good.freedom.net

Web site: http://webmart.freedom.net

Levels of Connectivity Supported: 56kb, T1

Night Vision

4676 Broadway, Suite 214

Allentown, PA 18104-3214 USA

Phone: 610 366 9767

Fax: 610 366 9767

Email: info@n-vision.com

Web site: http://www.n-vision.com

Levels of Connectivity Supported: PPP

Oasis Telecommunication, Inc

1541 Alta Drive, Suite 303

Whitehall, PA 18052 USA

Phone: 610 439 8560

Fax: 610 435 6114

Email: info@ot.com

Web site: http://www.ot.com

Levels of Connectivity Supported: Shell, PPP

OpNet
901 Glenbrook Av
Bryn Mawr, PA 19010 USA
Phone: 610 520 2880
Fax: 610 520 2881
Email: info@op.net
Web site: http://www.op.net
Levels of Connectivity Supported: Shell, SLIP, PPP, 56kb, T1

RaveNet Systems Inc
P.O. Box 22
Yorklyn, DE 19736 USA
Phone: 302 993 8420
Fax: 302 993 8419
Email: waltemus@ravenet.com
Web site: http://www.ravenet.com
Levels of Connectivity Supported: PPP, UUCP, ISDN, 56kb, T1

SSNet, Inc.
1254 Lorewood Grove Road
Middletown, DE 19709
Phone: 302 378 1386
Fax: 302 378 3871
Levels of Connectivity Supported: Shell, SLIP, PPP, UUCP

VivaNET, Inc.
1555 East Henrietta Road
Rochester, NY 14623 USA
Phone: 800 836 UNIX
Fax: 716 272 7627
Email: info@vivanet.com
Web site: http://www.vivanet.com
Levels of Connectivity Supported: Shell, SLIP, PPP, UUCP, ISDN, 56kb, T1

VoiceNet
17 Richard Rd.
Ivyland, PA 18974 USA
Phone: 800 835 5710
Fax: 215 674 9662
Email: info@voicenet.com
Web site: http://www.voicenet.com
Levels of Connectivity Supported: Shell, SLIP, PPP, UUCP, ISDN, 56kb, T1

You Tools Corporation / FASTNET
Two Courtney Place, Suite 140
3864 Courtney Street
Bethlehem , PA 18017 USA
Phone: 610 954 5910
Fax: 610 954 5925
Email: info@fast.net
Web site: http://www.youtools.com
Levels of Connectivity Supported: SLIP, PPP, UUCP, ISDN, 56kb, T1

ISPs for Area Code 612

Cloudnet
411 3rd St. N., Suite 210
Waite Park, MN 56387 USA
Phone: 612 240 8243
Email: info@cloudnet.com
Web site: http://www.cloudnet.com
Levels of Connectivity Supported: Shell, SLIP, PPP

DCC Inc.
10 Second Street NE, Suite 400
Minneapolis, MN 55413 USA
Phone: 612 378 4000
Fax: 612 378 4401
Email: kgastony@dcc.com
Web site: http://www.dcc.com
Levels of Connectivity Supported: PPP, ISDN, 56kb, T1

Freese-Notis Weather.Net
2411 Grand Avenue
Des Moines, IA 50312 USA
Phone: 515 282 9310
Fax: 515 282 6832
Email: hfreese@weather.net
Web site: http://www.weather.net
Levels of Connectivity Supported: PPP, 56kb, T1

GlobalCom
4820 Excelsior Blvd, Ste 10
St. Louis Park, MN 55416 USA
Phone: 612 920 9920
Email: info@globalc.com
Web site: http://www.globalc.com
Levels of Connectivity Supported: Shell, SLIP, PPP, 56kb

James River Group Inc
125 N First St
Minneapolis, MN 55401 USA
Phone: 612 339 2521
Email: jriver@jriver.jriver.com
Levels of Connectivity Supported: SLIP, 56kb, T1

Millennium Communications, Inc.

1300 Nicollet Mall, Suite 5083
Minneapolis, MN 55403
Phone: 612 338 5509
Fax: 507 282 8943
Levels of Connectivity Supported: Shell, SLIP, PPP, UUCP

Minnesota OnLine

23 Empire Drive, Suite 152
Saint Paul, MN 55103-1857
USA
Phone: 612 225 1110
Fax: 612 225 1424
Email: info@mn.state.net
Web site: http://www.state.net
Levels of Connectivity Supported: SLIP, PPP, UUCP, ISDN, 56kb, T1

Minnesota Regional Network

511 - 11th Avenue South, Box 212
Minneapolis, MN 55415
Phone: 612 342 2570
Levels of Connectivity Supported: SLIP, UUCP

Orbis Internet Services, Inc.

475 Cleveland Avenue North, Suite 205
St. Paul, MN 55104 USA
Phone: 612 645 9663
Fax: 612 227 2218
Email: info@orbis.net
Web site: http://www.orbis.net
Levels of Connectivity Supported: SLIP, PPP, ISDN, T1

pclink.com

P. O. Box 47974
Plymouth, MN 55447 USA
Phone: 612 541 5656
Fax: 612 541 1586
Email: infomatic@pclink.com
Web site: http://www.pclink.com
Levels of Connectivity Supported: SLIP, PPP

Primenet

2320 W. Peoria Avenue, Suite A103
Phoenix, AZ 85029 USA
Phone: 602 870 1010 or 800 4 NET FUN
Fax: 602 870 1010
Email: info@primenet.com
Web site: http://www.primenet.com
Levels of Connectivity Supported: Shell, SLIP, PPP, UUCP

Protocol Communications, Inc.

6280 Highway 65 NE, Suite 401
Minneapolis, MN 55432-5136
USA
Phone: 612 541 9900
Fax: 612 541 1586
Email: info@protocom.com
Web site: http://www.protocom.com
Levels of Connectivity Supported: Shell, SLIP, PPP, 56kb, T1

Sihope Communications

8944 Darnel Road
Eden Prairie, MN 55344USA
Phone: 612 829 9667
Fax: 612 829 5880
Email: info@sihope.com
Web site: http://www.sihope.com
Levels of Connectivity Supported: Shell, SLIP, PPP, UUCP, ISDN, 56kb, T1

Sound Communications Internet

5344 37th Ave South
Minneapolis, MN 55417 USA
Phone: 612 722 8470
Fax: 612 381 6794
Email: root@scc.net
Web site: http://www.scc.net
Levels of Connectivity Supported: Shell, SLIP, PPP, UUCP, 56kb, T1

StarNet Communications, Inc.

9971 Valley View Road, Suite 211
Eden Prairie, MN 55344
Phone: 612 941 9177
Levels of Connectivity Supported: Shell, SLIP, PPP

Synergy Communications, Inc.

1941 South 42nd Street
Omaha, NE 68105 USA
Phone: 800 345 9669
Fax: 402 346 0208
Email: info@synergy.net
Levels of Connectivity Supported: PPP

Vector Internet Services Inc.
12 South Sixth Street,
Suite M115
Minneapolis, MN 55402 USA
Phone: 612 288 0880
Fax: 612 288 0889
Email: info@visi.com
Web site: http://visi.com
Levels of Connectivity Supported: Shell, SLIP, PPP, UUCP, ISDN, 56kb, T1

ISPs for Area Code 613

autoroute.net (System Technology Development Inc.)
1100 Begin Street
Suite 100
Montreal (St-Laurent), Quebec
H4R 1X1 Canada
Phone: 514 333 3145
Fax: 514 334 7671
Email: info@autoroute.net
Web site: http://
www.autoroute.net
Levels of Connectivity Supported: Shell, SLIP, PPP, UUCP, ISDN, 56kb, T1

Cyberius Online Inc.
99 Fifth Avenue, Unit 406
Ottawa, Ontario K1S 5P5
Canada
Phone: 613 233 1215
Fax: 613 233 0292
Email: info@cyberus.ca
Web site: http://
www.cyberus.ca
Levels of Connectivity Supported: SLIP, PPP, UUCP, ISDN, 56kb, T1

Cycor Communications Incorporated
P.O. Box 454
Prince Edward Island C1A 7K7
Canada
Phone: 902 892 7354
Fax: : 902 892 5600
Email: signup@cycor.ca
Web site: http://www.cycor.ca
Levels of Connectivity Supported: SLIP, PPP, ISDN, 56kb, T1

HookUp Communications
1075 North Service Road West,
Suite 207
Oakville, Ontario L6M 2G2
Phone: 905 847 8000
Fax: 905 847 8866
Levels of Connectivity Supported: Shell, PPP, UUCP

Information Gateway Services (Ottawa)
300 March Road, Suite 101
Kanata, Ontario K2K 2E2
Canada
Phone: 613 592 5619
Fax: 613 592 3556
Email: info@igs.net
Web site: http://www.igs.net
Levels of Connectivity Supported: Shell, SLIP, PPP, UUCP, ISDN, 56kb, T1

Interactive Telecom Inc.
190 Colonnade Rd., Suite 204
Nepean, Ontario K2E 7J5
Canada
Phone: 613 727 5258
Fax: 613 727 5438
Email: info@intertel.net
Web site: http://
www.intertel.net
Levels of Connectivity Supported: SLIP, PPP, UUCP, ISDN, 56kb, T1

Magma Communications Ltd.
Unit 201
52 Antares Drive
Nepean, Ontario K2E 7Z1
Canada
Phone: 613 228 3565
Fax: 613 228 8313
Email: info@magmacom.com
Web site: http://
www.magmacom.com
Levels of Connectivity Supported: Shell, SLIP, PPP, ISDN

o://info.web - Internet access and Training
100 - 20 Colonnade Road,
North
Nepean, Ontario K2E 7M6
Canada
Phone: 613 225 3354
Fax: 613 225 2880
Levels of Connectivity Supported: SLIP, PPP, UUCP

UUNET Canada Inc.

1 Yonge Street, Suite 1400
Toronto, Ontario M5E 1J9
Canada
Phone: 416 368 6621
Fax: 416 368 1350
Levels of Connectivity Supported: SLIP, PPP, UUCP, ISDN, 56kb, T1

ISPs for Area Code 614

ASCInet

3520 Snouffer Road, Suite 203
Columbus, OH 43235-2776
USA
Phone: 614 798 5321 or 800 843 5321
Fax: 614 793 0261
Email: info@ascinet.com
Web site: http://www.ascinet.com
Levels of Connectivity Supported: Shell, SLIP, PPP, UUCP, 56kb

Branch Information Services

2901 Hubbard
Ann Arbor, MI 48105 USA
Phone: 313-741-4442
Fax: 313-995-1931
Email: branch-info@branch.com
Web site: http://branch.com
Levels of Connectivity Supported: SLIP, PPP, ISDN, 56kb, T1

Internet Access Cincinnati

P.O. Box 602
Hamilton, OH 45012-0602
Phone: 513 887 8877
Fax: 513 887 2085
Levels of Connectivity Supported: Shell, SLIP, PPP, UUCP

OARnet

2455 North Star Road
Columbus, OH 43221 USA
Phone: 614 728 8100 or 800 627 8101
Fax: 614 728 8110
Email: info@oar.net
Web site: http://www.oar.net
Levels of Connectivity Supported: Shell, SLIP, PPP

RAM Technologies Inc.

P.O. Box 1760
2025 13th Street
Ashland, KY 41105-1760 USA
Phone: 800 950 1726
Fax: 606 329 9203
Email: info@ramlink.net
Web site: http://www.ramlink.net
Levels of Connectivity Supported: Shell, SLIP, PPP, 56kb, T1

ISPs for Area Code 615

accessU.S. Inc.

P.O. Box 985
1500 Main Street
Mt. Vernon, IL 62864 USA
Phone: 800 638 6373
Fax: 618 244 9175
Email: info@accessus.net
Web site: http://www.accessus.net
Levels of Connectivity Supported: SLIP, PPP, ISDN, 56kb, T1

The Edge

205 Research Park Drive
P.O. Box 417
Tullahoma, TN 37388
Phone: 615 455 9915
Fax: 615 454 2042
Levels of Connectivity Supported: Shell, SLIP, PPP

First Internet Resources

7511 Chapman Highway
Knoxville, TN 37920 USA
Phone: 800 577 5969
Fax: 615 577 1505
Email: jcarter@1stresource.com
Web site: http://www.1stresource.com
Levels of Connectivity Supported: SLIP, PPP, UUCP, ISDN, 56kb, T1

GoldSword Systems
P.O. Box 31945
Knoxville, TN 37923-1945
Phone: 615 691 6498
Levels of Connectivity Supported: Shell, SLIP, PPP, UUCP

ISDN-Net Inc.
5115 Maryland Way
Brentwood, TN 37027-7512
USA
Phone: 615 377 7672
Fax: 615 377 3959
Email: info@isdn.net
Web site: http://www.isdn.net
Levels of Connectivity Supported: Shell, SLIP, PPP, UUCP, ISDN, 56kb, T1

MindSpring Enterprises, Inc.
1430 West Peachtree St NW, Suite 400
Atlanta, GA 30309 USA
Phone: 800 719 4332
Fax: 404 815 8805
Email: info@mindspring.com
Web site: http://www.mindspring.com
Levels of Connectivity Supported: SLIP, PPP, UUCP, ISDN, 56kb

Preferred Internet, Inc.
5925 Cochise Trail
Kingsport, TN 37664 USA
Phone: 615 323 1142

Fax: 615 323 6827
Email: info@preferred.com
Web site: http://www.preferred.com/pis
Levels of Connectivity Supported: Shell, SLIP, PPP, UUCP, ISDN, 56kb, T1

The Telalink Corporation
110 30th Avenue North, Suite 5
Nashville, TN 37203 USA
Phone: 615 321 9100
Fax: 615 327 4520
Email: sales@info.net
Web site: http://www.internet.net
Levels of Connectivity Supported: SLIP, PPP, UUCP, ISDN, 56kb, T1

The Tri-Cities Connection
1008 Executive Park Blvd #102
Kingsport, TN 37660-4619
USA
Phone: 615 378 5355
Fax: 615 378 0117
Email: info@tricon.net
Web site: http://www.tricon.net
Levels of Connectivity Sup-

ported: Shell, SLIP, PPP, UUCP, ISDN, 56kb

U.S. Internet
1127 North Broadway
Knoxville, TN 37917 USA
Phone: 615 522 6788
Fax: 615 524 6313
Email: info@usit.net
Web site: http://www.usit.net
Levels of Connectivity Supported: Shell, SLIP, PPP, UUCP, ISDN, 56kb, T1

Virtual Interactive Center
P.O. Box 31571
Knoxville, TN 37930 USA
Phone: 423 544 7902
Fax: 423 691 5131
Email: info@vic.com
Web site: http://www.vic.com
Levels of Connectivity Supported: Shell, SLIP, PPP, UUCP, ISDN, 56kb, T1

ISPs for Area Code 616

Branch Information Services
2901 Hubbard
Ann Arbor, MI 48105 USA
Phone: 313-741-4442
Fax: 313-995-1931
Email: mailto:branch-info@branch.com
Web site: http://branch.com
Levels of Connectivity Supported: SLIP, PPP, ISDN, 56kb, T1

Freeway Inc. (tm)
P.O. Box 2389
Petoskey, Michigan 49770 USA
Phone: 616 347 3175
Fax: 616 347 1568
Email: info@freeway.net
Web site: http://
www.freeway.net
Levels of Connectivity Supported: Shell, PPP, UUCP, 56kb, T1

The iserv Co.
2130 Enterprise Drive
Kentwood, Michigan 49508
USA
Phone: 616 281 5254
Fax: 616 281 2268
Email: info@iserv.net
Web site: http://
www.iserv.net
Levels of Connectivity Supported: PPP, UUCP, 56kb, T1

Mich.com, Inc.
21042 Laurelwood
Farmington, MI 48336 USA
Phone: 810 478 4300
Fax: 810 478 4302
Email: info@mich.com
Web site: http://www.mich.com
Levels of Connectivity Supported: Shell, SLIP, PPP, UUCP, 56kb, T1

Msen, Inc.
320 Miller Avenue
Ann Arbor, MI 48103
Phone: 313 998 4562
Fax: 313 998 4563
Levels of Connectivity Supported: Shell, SLIP, PPP, UUCP

NetLink Systems L.L.C.
P. O. Box 541
Kalamazoo, Michigan 49081
USA
Phone: 616 345 LINK
Fax: 616 345 0763
Email: mailto:info@serv01.net-link.net
Web site: http://www.net-link.net
Levels of Connectivity Supported: Shell, PPP, UUCP, ISDN, 56kb, T1

Novagate Communications Corp.
235 Fulton Street, Suite 204
Grand Haven, MI 49417 USA
Phone: 616 847 0910
Fax: 616 847 0792
Email: info@novagate.com
Web site: http://
www.novagate.com
Levels of Connectivity Supported: Shell, SLIP, PPP, UUCP, ISDN, 56kb, T1

RustNet, Inc.
6905 Telegraph Rd., Suite 315
Bloomfield Hills, MI 48301
USA
Phone: 810 642 2276
Fax: 810 642 3676
Email: info@rust.net
Web site: http://www.rust.net
Levels of Connectivity Supported: Shell, PPP, ISDN, 56kb, T1

Traverse Communication Company
223 Grandview Parkway, Suite 108
Traverse City, MI, 49684
Phone: 616 935 1705
Email: info@traverse.com
Web site: http://
www.traverse.com
Levels of Connectivity Supported: SLIP, PPP, ISDN, 56kb, T1

Voyager Information Networks, Inc.
600 West St. Jospeh Hwy., Suite 20
Lansing, MI 48933 USA
Phone: 517 485 9068
Fax: 517 485 9074
Email: help@voyager.net
Web site: http://
www.voyager.net
Levels of Connectivity Supported: PPP, ISDN, 56kb, T1

ISPs for Area Code 617

Alternet (UUNET Technologies, Inc.)

3110 Fairview Park Drive, Suite 570

Falls Church, VA 22042

Phone: 703 204 8000

Fax: 703 204 8001

Email: info@alter.net

Levels of Connectivity Supported: SLIP, PPP

Argo Communications

129 North Main Street

Mansfield, MA 02048 USA

Phone: 508 261 6121

Fax: 508 261 0221

Email: info@argo.net

Web site: http://www.argo.net

Levels of Connectivity Supported: Shell, SLIP, PPP, UUCP, ISDN, 56kb, T1

Channel 1

1030 Massachusetts Ave

Cambridge, MA 02138 USA

Phone: 617 864 0100

Fax: 617 354 3100

Email: support@channel1.com

Web site: http://www.channel1.com

Levels of Connectivity Supported: Shell, SLIP, PPP, ISDN, T1

CompUtopia

205 Hallene Road, Unit A6

Warwick, RI 02886 USA

Phone: 401 732 5588

Fax: 401 732 5518

Email: allan@computopia.com

Web site: http://www.computopia.com

Levels of Connectivity Supported: ISDN, 56kb, T1

Cyber Access Internet Communications, Inc.

422 Salem St.

Suite #152

Medford, MA 02155 USA

Phone: 617 396 0491

Fax: 617 396 0854

Email: info@cybercom.net

Web site: http://www.cybercom.net

Levels of Connectivity Supported: shell, SLIP, PPP, 56kb, T1

FOURnet Information Network

P.O. Box 38

West Wareham, MA 02576-0038 USA

Phone: 508 291 2900 code 2954139

Email: info@four.net

Web site: http://www.four.net

Levels of Connectivity Supported: shell, Telnet, SLIP, PPP, UUCP, Domain Hosting

The Internet Access

7 Railroad Avenue

Bedford, MA 01730

Phone: 617 276 7200

Fax: 617 275 2224

Levels of Connectivity Supported: Shell, SLIP, PPP

The Internet Connection, Inc.

Brookside Office Park

272 Chauncy St, Suite 6

Mansfield, MA 02048 USA

Phone: 508 261 0383

Fax: 508 730 1049

Email: info@ici.net

Web site: http://www.ici.net

Levels of Connectivity Supported: Shell, SLIP, PPP, UUCP, ISDN, 56kb, T1

intuitive information, inc.

P.O. Box 10

Ashburnham, MA 01430

Phone: 508 342 1100

Fax: 508 342 2075

Levels of Connectivity Supported: Shell, SLIP, PPP, UUCP

Pioneer Global Telecommunications, Inc.

811 Boylston Street

Boston, MA 02116 USA

Phone: 617 375 0200

Fax: 617 375 0201

Email: info@pn.com

Web site: http://www.pn.com

Levels of Connectivity Supported: SLIP, PPP, UUCP, ISDN, 56kb, fractional T1

Plymouth Commercial Internet eXchange
190 Old Derby Street,
Suite #115
Hingham, MA 02043 USA
Phone: 617 741 5900
Fax: 617 741 5416
Email: info@pcix.com
Web site: http://www.pcix.com
Levels of Connectivity Supported: Shell, SLIP, PPP, UUCP, ISDN, 56kb, T1

Saturn Internet Corporation
151 Pearl Street, 4th Floor
Boston, MA 02110 USA
Phone: 617 451 9121
Fax: 617 451 0358
Email: info@saturn.net
Web site: http://www.saturn.net
Levels of Connectivity Supported: SLIP, PPP, 56kb, T1

Shore.Net
145 Munroe Street, Suite 405
Lynn, MA 01901 USA
Phone: 617 593 3110
Fax: 617 593 6858
Email: info@shore.net
Web site: http://www.shore.net
Levels of Connectivity Supported: Shell, SLIP, PPP, UUCP, ISDN, 56kb, T1

StarNet (Advanced Communication Systems, Inc.)
54 West Dane St.
Clemenzi Industrial Park
Beverly, MA 01915 USA
Phone: 508 922 8238 or 800 779 3309
Fax: 508 921 8456
Email: info@star.net
Web site: http://www.star.net
Levels of Connectivity Supported: SLIP, PPP, ISDN, 56kb, T1

TerraNet, Inc.
729 Boylston Street, Flr 5
Boston, MA 02116 USA
Phone: 617 450 9000
Fax: 617 450 9003
Email: info@terra.net
Web site: http://www.terra.net
Levels of Connectivity Supported: SLIP, PPP, ISDN, 56kb, T1

UltraNet Communications, Inc.
910 Boston Post Road,
Suite 220
Marlborough, MA 01752 USA
Phone: 508 229 8400 or 800 763 8111
Fax: 508 229 2375
Email: info@ultranet.com
Web site: http://www.ultranet.com
Levels of Connectivity Supported: SLIP, PPP, ISDN, 56kb, T1

USAinternet, Inc.
99 Rosewood Drive,
Mailstop 265
Danvers, MA 01923-1300 USA
Phone: 800 236 9737
Fax: 508 777 0180
Email: info@usa1.com
Web site: http://www.usa1.com
Levels of Connectivity Supported: SLIP, PPP, ISDN, 56kb, T1

The World
Software Tool & Die
1330 Beacon Street
Brookline, MA 02146 USA
Phone: 617 739 0202
Email: info@world.std.com
Web site: http://www.world.std.com
Levels of Connectivity Supported: Shell, SLIP

Wilder Systems, Inc.
400 W. Cummings Park,
Suite 2350
Woburn, MA 01801
Phone: 617 933 8810
Fax: 617 933 8648
Levels of Connectivity Supported: Shell, SLIP, PPP

The Xensei Corporation
270 Quarry Street, Suite 10
Quincy, MA 02169 USA
Phone: 617 376 6342
Fax: 617 376 6343
Email: info@xensei.com
Web site: http://www.xensei.com
Levels of Connectivity Supported: SLIP, PPP, 56kb

ISPs for Area Code 618

accessU.S. Inc.
PO Box 985
1500 Main Street
Mt. Vernon, IL 62864 USA
Phone: 800 638 6373
Fax: 618 244 9175
Email: info@accessus.net
Web site: http://
www.accessus.net
Levels of Connectivity Supported: SLIP, PPP, ISDN, 56kb, T1

Allied Access Inc.
1002 Walnut Street
Murphysboro, IL 62966 USA
Phone: 618 684 2255 or 800 INETDOM
Fax: 618 684 5907
Email: sales@intrnet.net
Web site: http://
www.intrnet.net
Levels of Connectivity Supported: Shell, SLIP, PPP

Applied Personal Computing Inc.
1218 Paragon Dr, Suite 2
O'Fallon, IL 62269 USA
Phone: 618 632 7282
Fax: 618 632 7287
Email: spider@apci.net
Web site: http://www.apci.net
Levels of Connectivity Supported: SLIP, PPP, UUCP, ISDN, 56kb, T1

MVP-Net, Inc.
5494 Brown Road, Suite 109
Hazelwood, MO 63042 USA
Phone: 314 731 2252
Fax: 314 731 2260
Email: info@MO.net
Web site: http://www.mo.net
Levels of Connectivity Supported: Shell, SLIP, PPP, UUCP, ISDN, 56kb, T1

Online Information Access Network
3 Sunset Hills Executive Park
Edwardsville, IL 62025 USA
Phone: 618 692 9813
Fax: 618 692 9874
Email: info@oia.net
Web site: http://www.oia.net
Levels of Connectivity Supported: Shell, SLIP

ISPs for Area Code 619

CONNECTnet Internet Network Services
6370 Lusk Blvd., Suite F-208
San Diego, CA 92121 USA
Phone: 619 450 0254
Fax: 619 450 3216
Email: info@connectnet.com
Web site: http://
www.connectnet.com
Levels of Connectivity Supported: Shell, SLIP, PPP, UUCP, 56kb, T1, ISDN

CTS Network Services
4444 Convoy St., Suite 300
San Diego, CA 92111 USA
Phone: 619 637 3637
Fax: 619 637 3630
Email: support@cts.com
Web site: http://www.cts.com
Levels of Connectivity Supported: Shell, SLIP, PPP, UUCP, ISDN, 56kb, T1

Cyberg8t Internet Services
225 Yale Ave., Suite D
Claremont, CA 91711 USA
Phone: 909 398 4638
Fax: 909 398 4621
Email: sales@cyberg8t.com
Web site: http://
www.cyberg8t.com
Levels of Connectivity Supported: PPP, UUCP, 56kb, T1

The Cyberspace Station
204 N. El Camino Real, Suite E626
Encinitas, CA 92024
Phone: 619 634 2894
Levels of Connectivity Supported: Shell, SLIP, PPP

Delta Internet Services
731 E. Ball Rd., Suite 204
Anaheim, CA 92805 USA
Phone: 714 778 0370
Fax: 714 778 1064
Email: info@delta.net
Web site: http://
www.delta.net
Levels of Connectivity Supported: Shell, SLIP, PPP, UUCP, ISDN, 56kb, T1

Electriciti

2271 India Street, Suite C
San Diego, CA 92101
Phone: 619 338 9000
Fax: 619 687 3879
Levels of Connectivity Supported: SLIP, PPP, UUCP

I-Link Ltd

1 Chisholm Trail
Round Rock, TX 78681 USA
Phone: 800 ILINK 99
Fax: 512 244 9681
Email: info@i-link.net
Web site: ="http://www.
i-link.net
Levels of Connectivity Supported: PPP, ISDN, 56kb, T1

Liberty Information Network

446 S Anaheim Hills Road,
Suite 102
Anaheim, CA 92807 USA
Phone: 800 218 5157 or 714
996 9999
Fax: 714 961 8700 Attn: ISP
INFO
Email: info@liberty.com
Web site: http://
www.liberty.com
Levels of Connectivity Supported: Shell, SLIP, PPP,
UUCP, ISDN, 56kb, T1

Primenet

2320 W. Peoria Avenue,
Suite A103
Phoenix, AZ 85029 USA
Phone: 602 870 1010 or 800 4
NET FUN
Fax: 602 870 1010
Email: info@primenet.com
Web site: http://
www.primenet.com
Levels of Connectivity Supported: Shell, SLIP, PPP,
UUCP

RidgeNET

P.O. Box 986
Ridgecrest, CA 93555 USA
Phone: 619 371 3501
Fax: 619 371 3503
Email: saic@ridgecrest.ca.us
Web site: http://
www.ridgecrest.ca.us
Levels of Connectivity Supported: Shell, SLIP, PPP,
ARAP, 56kb, T1

Sierra-Net

P.O. Box 3709
Incline Village, NV 89450 USA
Phone: 702 832 6911
Fax: 702 831 3970
Email: giles@sierra.net
Web site: http://
www.sierra.net
Levels of Connectivity Supported: Shell, SLIP, PPP,
UUCP, ISDN, 56kb, T1

WANet, Software Design Associates, Inc.

12642-16 Poway Road,
Suite 314
Poway, CA 92064 USA
Phone: 619 679 5900
Fax: 619 679 2327
Email: info@WANet.net
Web site: http://
www.WANet.net
Levels of Connectivity Supported: Shell, SLIP, PPP,
UUCP, ISDN, 56kb, T1

ISPs for Area Code 701

NorthWestNet

15400 S.E. 30th Place,
Suite 202
Bellevue, WA 98007 USA
Phone: 206 562 3000
Fax: 206 562 4822
Email: info@nwnet.net
Web site: http://
www.nwnet.net
Levels of Connectivity Supported: Frame Relay, Fractional
T1, 10mbps, DS3

Red River Net

P.O. Box 388
Fargo, ND 58107
Phone: 701 232 2227
Levels of Connectivity Supported: Shell, SLIP

ISPs for Area Code 702

@wizard.com

3355 Spring Mountain Rd.,
Suite 267
Las Vegas, NV 89102 USA
Phone: 702 871 4461
Fax: 702 871 4249
Email: custserv@wizard.com
Web site: http://
www.wizard.com
Levels of Connectivity Supported: Shell, SLIP, PPP,
UUCP, 56kb, T1

Connectus, Inc.

200 South Virginia Ave.,
Suite 553
Reno, Nevada 89501-2415 USA
Phone: 702 323 2008
Fax: 702 323 9088
Email: info@connectus.com
Web site: http://
www.connectus.com
Levels of Connectivity Supported: Shell, SLIP, PPP,
UUCP, ISDN, 56kb, T1

Great Basin Internet Services

1155 W Fourth Street,
Suite 225
P.O. Box 6209
Reno, NV 89513-6209
Phone: 702 348 7299
Fax: 702 348 9412
Levels of Connectivity Supported: Shell, SLIP, UUCP

InterMind

1304 S. Jones Blvd.
Las Vegas, NV 89102 USA
Phone: 702 878 6111
Fax: 702 871 1325
Email:
support@terminus.intermind.net
Web site: http://
www.intermind.net
Levels of Connectivity Supported: Shell, SLIP, PPP,
UUCP, ISDN, 56kb, T1

NETConnect

P.O. Box 3425
Cedar City, UT 84720 USA
Phone: 800 689 8001
Fax: 801 865 7079
Email: office@tcd.net
Web site: http://www.tcd.net
Levels of Connectivity Supported: SLIP, PPP, UUCP,
56kb, T1
Credit Cards ——>: Visa,
MasterCard, AMEX, Discover

Sierra-Net

P.O. Box 3709
Incline Village, NV 89450 USA
Phone: 702 832 6911
Fax: 702 831 3970
Email: giles@sierra.net
Web site: http://
www.sierra.net
Levels of Connectivity Supported: Shell, SLIP, PPP,
UUCP, ISDN, 56kb, T1

Skylink Networks, Inc.

4850 West Flamingo Road,
Suite 23
Las Vegas, NV 89103USA
Phone: 702 368 0700
Fax: 702 368 0880
Email: sales@skylink.net
Web site: http://
www.skylink.net
Levels of Connectivity Supported: Shell, SLIP, PPP, ISDN,
56kb, T1

ISPs for Area Code 703

Alternet (UUNET Technologies, Inc.)

3110 Fairview Park Drive,
Suite 570
Falls Church, VA 22042
Phone: 703 204 8000
Fax: 703 204 8001
Email: info@alter.net
Levels of Connectivity Supported: SLIP, PPP

ARInternet Corporation

8201 Corporate Drive,
Suite 1100
Landover, MD 20785 USA
Phone: 301 459 7171
Fax: 301 459 7174
Email: info@ari.net
Web site: http://www.ari.net
Levels of Connectivity Supported: Shell, SLIP, PPP, ISDN,
56kb, T1, Web Hosting

CAPCON Library Network
1320 - 19th Street, NW,
Suite 400
Washington, DC 20036 USA
Phone: 202 331 5771
Fax: 202 797 7719
Email: info@capcon.net
Levels of Connectivity Supported: SLIP, PPP

Charm.Net
2228 E. Lombard Street
Baltimore, MD 21231 USA
Phone: 410 558 3900
Fax: 410 558 3901
Email: info@charm.net
Web site: http://
www.charm.net
Levels of Connectivity Supported: Shell, SLIP, PPP

**Clark Internet Services, Inc.
ClarkNet**
10600 Route 108
Ellicott City, MD 21042 USA
Phone: 410 995 0691
Fax: 410 730 9765
Email: info@clark.net
Web site: http://
www.clark.net
Levels of Connectivity Supported: Shell, SLIP, PPP,
UUCP

Cyber Services, Inc.
8027 Leesburg Pike, Suite 317
Vienna, VA 22182 USA
Phone: 703 749 9590
Fax: 703 749 9598
Email: info@cs.com
Web site: http://www.cs.com
Levels of Connectivity Supported: Shell, SLIP, PPP,
UUCP, ISDN, 56kb, T1

Digital Express Group, Inc.
6006 Greenbelt Road, Suite 228
Greenbelt, MD 20770 USA
Phone: 301 847 5000 or
847 5050
Fax: 301 847 5215
Email: info@digex.net
Web site: http://
www.digex.net
Levels of Connectivity Supported: Shell, SLIP, PPP,
56kb, T1

**Genuine Computing
Resources**
5429 Mapledale Plaza,
Suite 122
Woodbridge, VA 22193
Phone: 703 878 4680
Fax: 703 878 4220
Levels of Connectivity Supported: Shell, SLIP, PPP,
UUCP

Internet Online, Inc.
4925 St. Elmo Avenue
Bethesda, MD 20814 USA
Phone: 301 652 6100
Fax: 202 301 703
Email: info@intr.net
Web site: http://www.intr.net
Levels of Connectivity Supported: Shell, SLIP, PPP,
56kb, T1

Interpath
P.O. Box 12800
Raleigh, NC 27605 USA
Phone: 800 849 6305
Fax: 919 890 6319
Email: info@interpath.net
Web site: http://
www.interpath.net
Levels of Connectivity Supported: Shell, SLIP, PPP,
UUCP

KIVEX, Inc.
3 Bethesda Metro Center, Suite
B-001
Bethesda, MD 80214 USA
Phone: 800 47 KIVEX
Fax: 301 215 5991
Email: info@kivex.com
Web site: http://
www.kivex.com
Levels of Connectivity Supported: Shell, SLIP, PPP, ISDN,
56kb, T1, Web Hosting

LaserNet
11200 Waples Mill Road,
Suite 210
Fairfax, VA 22020
Phone: 703 591 4232
Fax: 703 591 7164
Email: info@laser.net
Web site: http://
www.laser.net
Levels of Connectivity Supported: Shell, SLIP, PPP, 56kb, T1

Preferred Internet, Inc.
5925 Cochise Trail
Kingsport, TN 37664 USA
Phone: 615 323 1142
Fax: 615 323 6827
Email: info@preferred.com
Web site: http://
www.preferred.com/pis
Levels of Connectivity Supported: Shell, SLIP, PPP, UUCP, ISDN, 56kb, T1

Quantum Networking Solutions, Inc.
2022 Cliff Drive, Suite 121
Santa Barbara, CA 93109
Phone: 805 538 2028 or
703 878 4680
Fax: 805 563 9147 or 703 878 4220
Levels of Connectivity Supported: Shell, SLIP, PPP, UUCP

RadixNet Internet Services
6230 Oxon Hill Road
Oxon Hill, MD 20745 USA
Phone: 301 567 9831
Fax: 301 839 0836
Email: info@radix.net
Web site: http://
www.radix.net
Levels of Connectivity Supported: Shell, SLIP, PPP, 56kb, T1

Smartnet Internet Services, LLC
8562A Laureldale Drive
Laurel, MD 20724 USA
Phone: 301 470 3400 or 410 792 4555
Fax: 410 792 4571
Email: info@smart.net
Web site: http://
www.smart.net
Levels of Connectivity Supported: PPP, 56kb, T1, Web Hosting

SONNETS, Inc.
13904 Stonefield Lane
Clifton, VA 22024 USA
Phone: 703 502 8589
Fax: 703 502 8564
Email: office@sonnets.net
Web site: http://
www.sonnets.net
Levels of Connectivity Supported: Shell, SLIP, PPP, 56kb, T1, Web Hosting

UltraPlex Information Providers
P.O. Box 626
Laurel, MD 20725-0626 USA
Phone: 301 598 6UPX or
410 880 4604
Email: info@upx.net
Web site: http://www.upx.net
Levels of Connectivity Supported: Shell, PPP, UUCP, ISDN, 56kb

Universal Telecomm Corporation
3008, Franklin Corner Lane
Herndon, VA 22071 USA
Phone: 703 758 0550
Fax: 703 758 0549
Email: root@utc.net
Web site: http://www.utc.net
Levels of Connectivity Supported: SLIP, PPP, T1

US Net, Inc.
3316 Kilkenny Street
Silver Spring, MD 20904
Phone: 301 572 5926
Fax: 301 572 5201
Levels of Connectivity Supported: Shell, SLIP, PPP, UUCP

World Web Limited
906 King Street
Alexandria, VA 22314 USA
Phone: 703 518 5005
Fax: 703 838 2002
Email: info@worldweb.net
Web site: http://
www.worldweb.net
Levels of Connectivity Supported: PPP, ISDN, 56kb, T1

Xpress Internet Services
18825 Birdseye Drive
Germantown, MD 20874 USA
Phone: 301 601 5050
Fax: 301 601 5055
Email: info@xis.com
Web site: http://xis.com
Levels of Connectivity Supported: SLIP, PPP

ISPs for Area Code 704

Interpath
P.O. Box 12800
Raleigh, NC 27605 USA
Phone: 800 849 6305
Fax: 919 890 6319
Email: info@interpath.net
Web site: http://www.interpath.net
Levels of Connectivity Supported: Shell, SLIP, PPP, UUCP

SunBelt.Net
P.O. Box 10630
Rock Hill, SC 29730
Phone: 803 328 1500
Fax: 803 324 6134
Levels of Connectivity Supported: Shell, SLIP, PPP, UUCP

Vnet Internet Access
P.O. Box 31474
Charlotte, NC 28231
Phone: 704 334 3282 or 800 377 3282
Fax: 704 334 6880
Levels of Connectivity Supported: Shell, SLIP, PPP, UUCP

ISPs for Area Code 705

Barrie Connex Inc.
55 Cedar Pointe Drive, Unit 606
Barrie, Ontario L4N 7T3 Canada
Phone: 705 725 0819
Fax: 705 725 1287
Email: info@bconnex.net
Web site: http://www.bconnex.net
Levels of Connectivity Supported: Shell, SLIP, PPP, UUCP, ISDN, 56kb, T1

Magic Online Services International Inc.
260 Richmond Street West, Suite 206
Toronto, Ontario M5V 1W5 Canada
Phone: 416 591 6490
Fax: 416 591 6409
Email: info@magic.ca
Web site: http://www.magic.ca
Levels of Connectivity Supported: SLIP, PPP, UUCP, ISDN

Mindemoya Computing
P.O. Box 21013
1935 Paris Street
Sudbury, ON P3E 6G6 Canada
Phone: 705 523 0243
Levels of Connectivity Supported: Shell, SLIP, PPP, UUCP

SooNet Corporation
477 Queen Street East, Suite 305
Sault Ste. Marie, Ontario P6A 1Z5 Canada
Phone: 705 253 4700
Fax: 705 253 4705
Email: service@soonet.ca
Web site: http://www.soonet.ca
Levels of Connectivity Supported: Shell, SLIP, PPP, UUCP, ISDN, 56kb

ISPs for Area Code 706

Athens' ISP, Inc.
337 South Milledge Avenue, Suite 200
Athens, GA 30605 USA
Phone: 706 613 0611
Fax: 706 613 0447
Email: info@athens.net
Web site: http://www.athens.net
Levels of Connectivity Supported: Shell, SLIP, PPP, ISDN, 56kb

InteliNet

1359 Silver Bluff Road,
Suite A-1
Aiken, SC 29803 USA
Phone: 803 279 9775
Fax: 803 641 1560
Email:
administrator@intelinet.net
Web site: http://
www.intelinet.net
Levels of Connectivity Supported: PPP, ISDN, 56kb, T1

internet@Dalton

P.O. Box 1415
Rocky Face, GA 30740 USA
Phone: 706 673 4715
Fax: 706 673 4715
Email: support@dalton.net
Web site: http://
www.dalton.net
Levels of Connectivity Supported: Shell, SLIP, PPP,
UUCP

Internet Atlanta

340 Knoll Ridge Court
Alpharetta, GA 30202
Phone: 404 410 9000
Fax: 404 410 9005
Email: info@atlanta.com
Web site: http://
www.atlanta.com
Levels of Connectivity Supported: Shell, SLIP, PPP,
UUCP

MindSpring Enterprises, Inc.

1430 West Peachtree St NW,
Suite 400
Atlanta, GA 30309 USA
Phone: 800 719 4332
Fax: 404 815 8805
Email: info@mindspring.com
Web site: http://
www.mindspring.com
Levels of Connectivity Supported: SLIP, PPP, UUCP,
ISDN, 56kb

ISPs for Area Code 707

Beckemeyer Development

P.O. Box 21575
Oakland, CA 94610 USA
Phone: 510 530 9637
Fax: 510 530 0451
Email: info@bdt.com
Web site: http://www.bdt.com
Levels of Connectivity Supported: SLIP, PPP, UUCP,
ISDN, 56kb, T1

CASTLES Information Network

1425 West Texas Street
Fairfield, CA 94533 USA
Phone: 707 422 7311
Fax: 707 422 5265
Email: info@castles.com
Web site: http://
www.castles.com
Levels of Connectivity Supported: SLIP, PPP, ISDN,
56kb, T1

Datatamers

P.O. Box 2467
Menlo Park, CA 94026-2467
USA
Phone: 415 364 7919
Fax: 415 364 7919
Email: info@datatamers.com
Web site: http://
www.datatamers.com
Levels of Connectivity Supported: Shell, PPP, 56kb

InReach Internet Communications

P.O. Box 470425
San Francisco, CA 94147 USA
Phone: 800 4 INREACH
Fax: 800 399 7499
Email: info@inreach.com
Web site: http://
www.inreach.com
Levels of Connectivity Supported: PPP, UUCP, ISDN

Liberty Information Network

446 S Anaheim Hills Road,
Suite 102
Anaheim, CA 92807 USA
Phone: 800 218 5157 or 714
996 9999
Fax: 714 961 8700 Attn: ISP
INFO
Email: info@liberty.com
Web site: http://
www.liberty.com
Levels of Connectivity Supported: Shell, SLIP, PPP,
UUCP, ISDN, 56kb, T1

QuakeNet
830 Wilmington Road
San Mateo, CA 94402 USA
Phone: 415 655 6607
Fax: 415 377 0635
Email: info@quake.net
Web site: http://
www.quake.net
Levels of Connectivity Supported: SLIP, PPP, UUCP

Value Net Internetwork Services
2855 Mitchell Drive, Suite 105
Walnut Creek, CA 94598 USA
Phone: 510 943 5769
Fax: 510 943 1708
Email: info@value.net
Web site: http://
www.value.net
Levels of Connectivity Supported: Shell, SLIP, PPP, ISDN, 56kb, T1

West Coast Online
6050 Commerce Blvd.,
Suite 210
Rohnert Park, CA 94928 USA
Phone: 707 586 3060
Fax: 707 586 5254
Email: info@calon.com
Web site: http://
www.calon.com
Levels of Connectivity Supported: Shell, SLIP, PPP

Zocalo Engineering
2355 Virginia Street
Berkeley, CA 94709-1315 USA
Phone: 510 540 8000
Fax: 510 548 1891
Email: info@zocalo.net
Web site: http://
www.zocalo.net/frompocia.html
Levels of Connectivity Supported: Shell, SLIP, PPP, 56kb, T1

ISPs for Area Code 708

American Information Systems, Inc.
911 North Plum Grove Road, Suite F
Schaumburg, IL 60173 USA
Phone: 708 413 8400
Fax: 708 413 8401
Email: info@ais.net
Web site: http://www.ais.net
Levels of Connectivity Supported: Shell, SLIP, PPP, UUCP

CICNet, Inc.
2901 Hubbard Drive
Ann Arbor, MI 48105 USA
Phone: 313 998 6103
Fax: 313 998 6105
Email: info@cic.net
Web site: http://www.cic.net
Levels of Connectivity Supported: Shell, SLIP, PPP, 56kb, T1

CIN.net (Computerese Information Network)
721 West Golf Road
Hoffman Estates, IL 60194
USA
Phone: 708 310 1188
Fax: 708 885 8308
Email: info@cin.net
Web site: http://www.cin.net
Levels of Connectivity Supported: Shell, SLIP, PPP, UUCP, ISDN, 56kb, T1

Compunet Technology Consultants
P.O. Box 880
Naperville, IL 60540 USA
Phone: 708 355 XNET
Fax: 708 355 UFAX
Email: mailto:webmaster@ms.com-punet.com
Web site: http://www.com-punet.com
Levels of Connectivity Supported: SLIP, PPP, ISDN, 56kb, T1

I Connection, Inc.
2504 Washington Street, Suite 201-6
Waukegan, IL 60085 USA
Phone: 708 662 0877
Fax: 708 662 0325
Email: info@iconnect.net
Web site: http://
www.iconnect.net
Levels of Connectivity Supported: Shell, SLIP, PPP, UUCP, 56kb, T1

InterAccess Co.

3345 Commercial Ave.

Northbrook, IL 60062 USA

Phone: 708 498 2542

Fax: 708 498 3289

Email: info@interaccess.com

Web site: http://www.interaccess.com

Levels of Connectivity Supported: Shell, SLIP, PPP, UUCP, ISDN, 56kb, T1

Interactive Network Systems, Inc.

2316 West 108th Place

Chicago, Illinois 60643 USA

Phone: 312 881 3039

Fax: 312 881 3064

Email: info@insnet.com

Web site: http://www.insnet.com

Levels of Connectivity Supported: Shell, SLIP, PPP, UUCP, ISDN, 56kb, T1

MCSNet

1300 W. Belmont, Suite 405

Chicago, IL 60657 USA

Phone: 312 803 6271

Fax: 312 803 6271

Email: info@mcs.net

Web site: http://www.mcs.net

Levels of Connectivity Supported: Shell, SLIP, UUCP

The Planet Group, Inc.

1608 Milwaukee Avenue, Suite 1200

Chicago, IL 60647 USA

Phone: 312 772 8333

Fax: 312 772 9214

Email: mailto:info@www.planet-group.com

Web site: =http://www.planet-group.com

Levels of Connectivity Supported: Shell, SLIP, PPP, UUCP, ISDN, 56kb, T1

Ripco Communications, Inc.

3163 N. Clybourn Avenue

Chicago, IL 60618-6424

Phone: 312 477 6210

Levels of Connectivity Supported: Shell, UUCP

TensorNet Co.

PO Box 4364,

Wheaton, IL 60189-4364 USA

Phone: 708 665 3637

Fax: 708 665 5038

Email: info@tensornet.com

Web site: http://www.tensornet.com

Levels of Connectivity Supported: Shell, SLIP, PPP

Tezcatlipoca, Inc.

Tezcat

1573-A N. Milwaukee,

Suite 440

Chicago, IL 60622 USA

Phone: 312 850 0181

Fax: 312 850 0492

Email: info@tezcat.com

Web site: http://www.tezcat.com/export.html

Levels of Connectivity Supported: Shell, SLIP, PPP, Virtual Server, Dedicated Web Server

Wink Communications Group, Inc.

2500 W Higgins Rd, Suite 480

Hoffman Estates, IL 60195 USA

Phone: 708 310 9465

Fax: 708 310 3477

Email: sales@winkcomm.com

Web site: http://www.winkcomm.com

Levels of Connectivity Supported: ISDN, 56kb, T1

WorldWide Access

20 North Wacker Drive, Suite 766

Chicago, IL 60606 USA

Phone: 312 803 9921

Fax: 312 803 9923

Email: info@wwa.com

Web site: http://www.wwa.com

Levels of Connectivity Supported: Shell, SLIP, PPP, UUCP, ISDN, 56kb, T1

XNet Information Systems
3080 E. Ogden Ave Suite 202
Lisle, IL 60532 USA
Phone: 708 983 6064
Fax: 708 983 6879
Email: info@xnet.com
Web site: http://www.xnet.com
Levels of Connectivity Supported: Shell, SLIP, PPP,
UUCP, 56kb, T1

ISPs for Area Code 709

InterActions Limited
40 Bannister Street
P.O. Box 1000
Mount Pearl, NF A1N 3C9
Canada
Phone: 709 745 4638
Fax: 709 745 7927
Email: connect@nfld.com
Web site: http://
www.compusult.nf.ca/
InterActions
Levels of Connectivity Supported: Shell, SLIP, PPP,
UUCP, 56kb

ISPs for Area Code 712

Freese-Notis Weather.Net
2411 Grand Avenue
Des Moines, IA 50312 USA
Phone: 515 282 9310
Fax: 515 282 6832
Email: hfreese@weather.net
Web site: http://
www.weather.net
Levels of Connectivity Supported: PPP, 56kb, T1

Greater Omaha Public Access Unix Corporation
5062 So. 108th, Suite 345
Omaha, NE 68137 USA
Phone: 402 558 5030
Fax: 402 339 2327
Email: info@gonix.com
Web site: http://
www.gonix.com
Levels of Connectivity Supported: Shell, SLIP, PPP,
UUCP, ISDN

ia.net
3417 Center Point Road N.E.
Cedar Rapids, IA 52402 USA
Phone: 319 393 1095
Fax: 319 378 1489
Email: info@ia.net
Web site: http://www.ia.net
Levels of Connectivity Supported: Shell, SLIP, PPP,
UUCP, 56kb, T1

Iowa Network Services
4201 Corporate Drive
West Des Moines, IA 50265
USA
Phone: 800 546 6587
Fax: 515 830 0345
Email: service@netins.net
Web site: http://
www.netins.net
Levels of Connectivity Supported: Shell, SLIP, PPP,
UUCP, 56kb, T1, Web Hosting

The Online Pitstop
P.O. Box 1051
Bellevue, NE 68005 USA
Phone: 402 291 1542
Email: bob@top.net
Web site: http://www.top.net
Levels of Connectivity Supported: Shell, SLIP, ISDN,
56kb, T1

Pioneer Internet
504 4th Street
Sergeant Bluff, IA 51054
Phone: 712 271 0101
Fax: 712 943 4742
Email: info@pionet.net
Web site: http://
www.pionet.net
Levels of Connectivity Supported: PPP, 56kb, T1

ProLinx Communications, Inc.
P.O. Box 31185
Omaha, NE 68131-0185 USA
Phone: 402 551 3036
Email:
techsupport@nfinity.nfinity.com
Web site: http://
www.nfinity.com
Levels of Connectivity Supported: Shell, SLIP, PPP,
UUCP, 56kb, T1

Synergy Communications, Inc.
1941 South 42nd Street
Omaha, NE 68105 USA
Phone: 800 345 9669
Fax: 402 346 0208
Email: info@synergy.net
Levels of Connectivity Supported: PPP

Zelcom International, Incorporated
2819 S. 125th Ave., Suite 256
Omaha, NE 68144 USA
Phone: 402 333 2441
Fax: 402 333 4583
Email: administration-dept@zelcom.com
Web site: http://www.zelcom.com
Levels of Connectivity Supported: Shell, SLIP, ISDN, 56kb, T1

ISPs for Area Code 713

Alternet (UUNET Technologies, Inc.)
3110 Fairview Park Drive, Suite 570
Falls Church, VA 22042
Phone: 703 204 8000
Fax: 703 204 8001
Email: info@alter.net
Levels of Connectivity Supported: SLIP, PPP

The Black Box
P.O. Box 591822
Houston, TX 77259-1822 USA
Phone: 713 480 2684
Email: info@blkbox.com
Web site: http://www.blkbox.com
Levels of Connectivity Supported: Shell, SLIP, PPP

Delta Design and Development Inc.
6448 Hwy. 290 East, Suite F108
Austin, TX 78723 USA
Phone: 800 763 8265
Fax: 512 467 8462
Email: sales@deltaweb.com
Web site: http://www.deltaweb.com
Levels of Connectivity Supported: PPP, ISDN, 56kb, T1

Electrotex,Inc.
2300 Richmond
Houston, TX 77098 USA
Phone: 713 526 3456 or 800 460 1801
Fax: 713 639 6400
Email: info@electrotex.com
Web site: http://www.electrotex.com
Levels of Connectivity Supported: SLIP, PPP, UUCP, ISDN, 56kb, T1

I-Link Ltd
1 Chisholm Trail
Round Rock, TX 78681 USA
Phone: 800 ILINK 99
Fax: 512 244 9681
Email: info@i-link.net
Web site: http://www.i-link.net
Levels of Connectivity Supported: PPP, ISDN, 56kb, T1

InfoCom Networks
P.O. Box 590343
Houston, TX 77259 USA
Phone: 713 286 0399
Email: info@infocom.net
Web site: http://www.infocom.net
Levels of Connectivity Supported: Shell, SLIP, PPP, ISDN, T1

Internet Connect Services, Inc.
202 W. Goodwin
Victoria, TX 77901
Phone: 512 572 9987
Fax: 512 572 8193
Levels of Connectivity Supported: Shell, SLIP, PPP, UUCP

NeoSoft, Inc.
3408 Magnum Road
Houston, TX 77092
Phone: 800 GET NEOSOFT or 713 684 5969
Fax: 713 684 5922
Levels of Connectivity Supported: Shell, SLIP, PPP, UUCP

OnRamp Technologies, Inc.
1950 Stemmons Freeway,
Suite 5061
Dallas, TX 75207 USA
Phone: 214 672 7267
Fax: 214 713 5400
Email: info@onramp.net
Web site: http://
www.onramp.net
Levels of Connectivity Supported: SLIP, PPP, UUCP, ISDN, 56kb, T1

Phoenix DataNet, Inc.
17100 El Camino Real
Houston, TX 77058 USA
Phone: 713 486 8337
Fax: 713 486 7464
Email: info@phoenix.net
Web site: http://
www.phoenix.net
Levels of Connectivity Supported: Shell, SLIP, PPP, ISDN, 56kb, T1

South Coast Computing Services, Inc.
1811 Bering Dr., Suite 100
Houston, TX 77057 USA
Phone: 713 917 5000
Fax: 713 917 5005
Email: info@houston.net
Web site: http://
www.sccsi.com
Levels of Connectivity Supported: Shell, SLIP, PPP, UUCP, ISDN, T1

USiS
4800 W. 34th Street
Suite C-51A
Houston, TX 77092
Phone: 713 682 1666
Fax: 713 957 5525
Levels of Connectivity Supported: Shell, SLIP, PPP, UUCP

ISPs for Area Code 714

Argonet
2815 McGaw Avenue
Irvine, CA 92714 USA
Phone: 714 261 7511
Fax: 714 261 7566
Email: postmaster@argonet.net
Web site: http://
www.argonet.net
Levels of Connectivity Supported: PPP, 56kb, T1

ArtNetwork
844 S. Robertson
Los Angeles, CA 90035 USA
Phone: 800 395 0692
Fax: 310 652 7114
Email: info@artnet.net
Web site: http://
www.artnet.net
Levels of Connectivity Supported: Shell, SLIP, PPP, UUCP, ISDN, 56kb, T1

Business Access Technologies
3484 E Orangethorpe
Anaheim, CA 92806 USA
Phone: 714 577 8978
Email: Techs@batech.com
Web site: http://batech.com

Cloverleaf Communications
7862 Yorkshire
Stanton, CA 90680 USA
Phone: 714 895 3075
Fax: 310 420 7255
Email: sales@cloverleaf.com
Web site: http://
www.cloverleaf.com
Levels of Connectivity Supported: Shell, SLIP, PPP, UUCP

Cogent Software, Inc.
221 E. Walnut St., Suite 215
Pasadena, CA 91101 USA
Phone: 818 585 2788
Fax: 818 585 2785
Email: info@cogsoft.com
Web site: http://
www.cogsoft.com
Levels of Connectivity Supported: Shell, PPP, ISDN, 56kb, T1

CruzNet
215 E. Orangethorpe Ave.
Suite: 333
Fullerton, CA 92632 USA
Phone: 714 680 6600
Fax: 714 680 4241
Email: info@cruznet.net
Web site: http://
www.cruznet.net
Levels of Connectivity Supported: Shell, SLIP, PPP, UUCP, ISDN, 56kb, T1

DPC Systems Beach.Net

24681 La Plaza Ste 360
Dana Point, CA 92629 USA
Phone: 714 443 4172
Fax: 714 443 9516
Email: connect@beach.net
Web site: http://www.beach.net
Levels of Connectivity Supported: SLIP, PPP, UUCP, ISDN, 56kb, T1

Delta Internet Services

731 E. Ball Rd., Suite 204
Anaheim, CA 92805 USA
Phone: 714 778 0370
Fax: 714 778 1064
Email: info@delta.net
Web site: http://www.delta.net
Levels of Connectivity Supported: Shell, SLIP, PPP, UUCP, 56kb, T1

DigiLink Network Services

4429 W. 169th Street
Lawndale, CA 90260-3252
Phone: 310 542 7421
Web site: http://www.dfw.net
Levels of Connectivity Supported: ISDN

EDM NetWORK

17785 Sky Park Circle, Suite B
Irvine, CA 92714 USA
Phone: 714 476 0416
Fax: 714 476 8621
Email: info@edm.net
Web site: http://www.edm.net
Levels of Connectivity Supported: SLIP, PPP, ISDN, 56kb, T1

Electriciti

2271 India Street, Suite C
San Diego, CA 92101
Phone: 619 338 9000
Fax: 619 687 3879
Levels of Connectivity Supported: SLIP, PPP, UUCP

Exodus Communications, Inc.

948 Benecia Avenue
Sunnyvale, CA 94086 USA
Phone: 408 522 8450
Fax: 408 736 6843
Email: info@exodus.net
Web site: http://www.exodus.net
Levels of Connectivity Supported: ISDN, 56kb, T1

InterNex Tiara

2302 Walsh Ave
Santa Clara, CA 95051 USA
Phone: 408 496 5466
Fax: 408 496 5485
Email: info@internex.net
Web site: http://www.internex.net
Levels of Connectivity Supported: SLIP, PPP, ISDN, 56kb, T1, Frame Relay, Web Hosting

InterWorld Communications, Inc.

222 N. Sepulveda Blvd., Suite 1560
El Segundo, CA 90245 USA
Phone: 310 726 0500
Fax: 310 726 0559
Email: sales@interworld.net
Web site: http://www.interworld.net
Levels of Connectivity Supported: SLIP, PPP, UUCP, ISDN, 56kb, T1, Web Hosting

KAIWAN Internet

12550 Brookhurst Street, Suite H
Garden Grove, CA 92640 USA
Phone: 714 638 2139
Fax: 714 638 0455
Email: info@kaiwan.com
Web site: http://www.kaiwan.com
Levels of Connectivity Supported: Shell, SLIP, PPP, UUCP, ISDN, 56kb, T1

Liberty Information Network

446 S Anaheim Hills Road, Suite 102
Anaheim, CA 92807 USA
Phone: 800 218 5157 or 714 996 9999
Fax: 714 961 8700 Attn: ISP INFO
Email: info@liberty.com
Web site: http://www.liberty.com
Levels of Connectivity Supported: Shell, SLIP, PPP, UUCP, ISDN, 56kb, T1

Lightside, Inc.
101 N. Citrus, Suite #4A
Covina, CA 91723 USA
Phone: 818 858 9261
Fax: 818 858 8982
Email:
Lightside@Lightside.Com
Web site: http://
www.lightside.Net
Levels of Connectivity Supported: SLIP, PPP, 56kb, T1

The Loop Internet Switch Co.
6611 Santa Monica Blvd.
Los Angeles, CA 90038 USA
Phone: 213 465 1311
Fax: 213 469 2193
Email: info@loop.com
Web site: http://
www.loop.com/rates.html
Levels of Connectivity Supported: SLIP, PPP

NetQuest
14441 Beach Blvd, Suite 207
Westminster, CA 92683 USA
Phone: 714 379 8228
Fax: 714 379 8229
Email: info@net-quest.com
Web site: http://www.
net-quest.com
Levels of Connectivity Supported: Shell, SLIP, PPP, 56kb, T1, Web Hosting

Network Intensive
8001 Irvine Center Drive,
Suite #1130
Irvine, CA 92718 USA
Phone: 714 450 8400
Fax: 714 450 8410
Email: info@ni.net
Web site: http://www.ni.net
Levels of Connectivity Supported: Shell, SLIP, PPP, UUCP, ISDN, 56kb, T1

Primenet
2320 W. Peoria Avenue,
Suite A103
Phoenix, AZ 85029 USA
Phone: 602 870 1010 or 800 4 NET FUN
Fax: 602 870 1010
Email: info@primenet.com
Web site: http://
www.primenet.com
Levels of Connectivity Supported: Shell, SLIP, PPP, UUCP

OutWest Network Services Inc.
440 Western Avenue, Suite 101
Glendale, CA 91201 USA
Phone: 818 545 1996
Email: info@outwest.net
Web site: http://outwest.net
Levels of Connectivity Supported: Shell, SLIP, PPP, UUCP, 56kb, T1

QuickNet, Inc.
7401 Seabluff Drive, Suite #110
Huntington Beach, CA 92648-2433 USA
Phone: 714 969 1091
Email: sales@quick.net
Web site: http://
www.quick.net
Levels of Connectivity Supported: Shell, PPP, UUCP, ISDN, 56kb, T1

SoftAware
4676 Admiralty Way, Suite 410
Marina del Rey, CA 90292 USA
Phone: 310 305 0275
Email: info@softaware.com
Web site: http://
www.softaware.com
Levels of Connectivity Supported: T1

ISPs for Area Code 715

FullFeed Communications
Madison, WI 53704-2488
Phone: 608 246 4239
Levels of Connectivity Supported: Shell, SLIP, PPP, UUCP

Minnesota OnLine
23 Empire Drive, Suite 152
Saint Paul, MN 55103-1857
USA
Phone: 612 225 1110
Fax: 612 225 1424
Email: info@mn.state.net
Web site: http://
www.state.net
Levels of Connectivity Supported: SLIP, PPP, UUCP, ISDN, 56kb, T1

ISPs for Area Code 716

Blue Moon Online System Internet Services

P.O. Box 651
Buffalo, NY 14207 USA
Phone: 716 447 5629
Fax: 716 447 5629
Email: sales@net.bluemoon.net
Web site: http://
www.bluemoon.net
Levels of Connectivity Supported: Shell, SLIP, PPP, ISDN, 56kb, T1

BuffNET

10 Center Road
West Seneca, NY 14224 USA
Phone: 800 463 6499
Fax: 716 825 2718
Email: info@buffnet.net
Web site: http://
www.buffnet.net
Levels of Connectivity Supported: Shell, SLIP, PPP, ISDN

E-Znet, Inc.

1128 Sibley Tower Building
25 Franklyn Street
Rochester, NY 14604 USA
Phone: 716 262 2485
Fax: 716 262 3766
Email: info@eznet.net
Web site: http://
www.eznet.net
Levels of Connectivity Supported: Shell, SLIP, PPP, UUCP, ISDN

epix

100 Lake Street
Dallas, PA 18612 USA
Phone: 800 374 9669
Fax: 717 675 5711
Email: karndt@epix.net
Web site: http://www.epix.net
Levels of Connectivity Supported: SLIP, PPP, ISDN, 56kb, T1

NYSERNet

200 Elwood Davis Road
Liverpool, NY 13088-6147 USA
Phone: 800 493 4367
Fax: 315 453 3052
Email: sales@nysernet.org
Web site: http://nysernet.org
Levels of Connectivity Supported: Shell, 56kb, T1

ServiceTech, Inc.

182 Monroe Ave
Rochester, NY 14607 USA
Phone: 716 263 3360
Fax: 716 423 1596
Email: info@servtech.com
Web site: http://
www.servtech.com
Levels of Connectivity Supported: Shell, PPP, 56kb, T1

VivaNET, Inc.

1555 East Henrietta Road
Rochester, NY 14623 USA
Phone: 800 836 UNIX
Fax: 716 272 7627
Email: info@vivanet.com
Web site: http://
www.vivanet.com
Levels of Connectivity Supported: Shell, SLIP, PPP, UUCP, ISDN, 56kb, T1

ISPs for Area Code 717

epix

100 Lake Street
Dallas, PA 18612 USA
Phone: 800 374 9669
Fax: 717 675 5711
Email: karndt@epix.net
Web site: http://www.epix.net
Levels of Connectivity Supported: Shell, SLIP, PPP, ISDN, 56kb, T1

The Internet Cafe

342 Adams Ave
Scranton, PA 18503 USA
Phone: 717 344 1969
Email:
info@lydian.scranton.com
Web site: http://
www.scranton.com
Levels of Connectivity Supported: Shell, PPP, 56kb

Keystone Information Access Systems

P. O. Box 32
Dallastown, PA. 17313 USA
Phone: 717 741 2626
Fax: 717 741 2626
Email: office@yrkpa.kias.com
Web site: http://
yrkpa.kias.com
Levels of Connectivity Supported: Shell, SLIP, PPP,
UUCP, 56kb

Microserve Information Systems

222 Temperance Hill
Plymouth, PA 18651 USA
Phone: 800 380 INET or 717
821 5964
Fax: 717 779 5490
Email: info@microserve.net
Web site: http://
www.microserve.net
Levels of Connectivity Supported: Shell, PPP, UUCP

PenNet - A Subsidiary of Smith's (Bahamas) Ltd.

342 Broad Street
Montoursville, PA 17754 USA
Phone: 717 368 1577
Fax: 717 368 8837
Email: safrye@pennet.net
Web site: http://
www.pennet.net
Levels of Connectivity Supported: PPP, ISDN, 56kb, T1

Red Rose SuperNet

4139 Oregon Pike
Ephrata, PA 17522 USA
Phone: 800 222 2517
Fax: 717 738 7030
Email: info@redrose.net
Web site: http://
www.redrose.net
Levels of Connectivity Supported: PPP, ISDN, 56kb, T1

Spectra.net

139 Grand Avenue
Johnson City, NY 13790
Phone: 607 798 7300
Fax: 607 717 315
Email: info@spectra.net
Web site: http://
www.spectra.net
Levels of Connectivity Supported: Shell, SLIP, PPP, ISDN,
56kb, Fractional T1

VoiceNet

17 Richard Rd.
Ivyland, PA 18974 USA
Phone: 800 835 5710
Fax: 215 674 9662
Email: info@voicenet.com
Web site: http://
www.voicenet.com
Levels of Connectivity Supported: Shell, SLIP, PPP,
UUCP, ISDN, 56kb, T1

You Tools Corporation / FASTNET

Two Courtney Place, Suite 140
3864 Courtney Street
Bethlehem, PA 18017 USA
Phone: 610 954 5910
Fax: 610 954 5925
Email: info@fast.net
Web site: http://
www.youtools.com
Levels of Connectivity Supported: SLIP, PPP, UUCP,
ISDN, 56kb, T1

ISPs for Area Code 718

Advanced Standards, Inc advn.com

19 W 44 St, Suite 615
New York, NY 10036 USA
Phone: 212 302 3366
Email: kolian@advn.com
Levels of Connectivity Supported: Shell, PPP, UUCP,
56kb

Blythe Systems

39 West 14th Street, #206
New York, NY 10011 USA
Phone: 212 226 7171
Fax: 212 274 8712
Email: infodesk@blythe.org
Levels of Connectivity Supported: Shell

BrainLINK
87-90 118 St
Richmond Hill, NY 11418 USA
Phone: 718 805 6559
Fax: 718 805 6564
Email:
info@beast.brainlink.com
Web site: http://
www.brainlink.com
Levels of Connectivity Supported: Shell

bway.net / Outernet, Inc.
626 Broadway, Suite 3A
New York, NY 10012 USA
Phone: 212 982 9800
Fax: 212 982 5499
Email: info@bway.net
Web site: http://www.bway.net
Levels of Connectivity Supported: Shell, SLIP, PPP,
UUCP, ISDN, 56kb, T1, Web
Hosting

Creative Data Consultants (SILLY.COM)
Bayside, NY 11364 USA
Phone: 718 229 0489 x23
Fax: 718 229 7096
Email: info@silly.com
Web site: http://
www.silly.com
Levels of Connectivity Supported: Shell, SLIP, PPP,
UUCP

escape.com - Kazan Corp
16 East 55th Street, 5th Floor
New York, NY 10022
Phone: 212 888 8780
Fax: 212 832 0344
Levels of Connectivity Supported: Shell, SLIP, PPP,
UUCP

Ingress Communications Inc.
538 2nd Avenue
New York, NY 10016
Phone: 212 679 2838
Fax: 212 213 0736
Levels of Connectivity Supported: Shell, SLIP, PPP,
UUCP

INTAC Access Corporation
256 Broad Avenue
Palisades Park, NJ 07650 USA
Phone: 800 50 INTAC
Fax: 201 944 1434
Email: info@intac.com
Web site: http://
www.intac.com
Levels of Connectivity Supported: Shell, SLIP, PPP,
UUCP, ISDN, 56kb, T1

Intellitech Walrus
90 John Street, 27th Fl.
New York, NY 10038 USA
Phone: 212 406 5000
Email: info@walrus.com
Web site: http://
www.walrus.com
Levels of Connectivity Supported: Shell, SLIP, PPP,
UUCP, 56kb, T1

Intercall, Inc
33 Route 17 South
Rutherford, NJ 07073
Phone: 800 758 7329
Fax: 201 939 2507
Email: sales@intercall.com
Web site: http://
www.intercall.com
Levels of Connectivity Supported: SLIP, PPP

InterCom Online
1412 Avenue M, Suite 2428
Brooklyn, NY 11230
Phone: 212 714 7183
Levels of Connectivity Supported: Shell

Internet QuickLink Corp.
415 West 57th Street, Suite 1D
New York, NY 10019 USA
Phone: 212 307 1669
Fax: 212 586 1303
Email: info@quicklink.com
Web site: http://
www.quicklink.com
Levels of Connectivity Supported: Shell, SLIP, PPP, ISDN,
56kb, T1

Interport Communications Corp.
1133 Broadway Avenue
New York, NY 10010
Phone: 212 989 1128
Levels of Connectivity Supported: Shell, SLIP, PPP

Lightning Internet Services, LLC
327C Sagamore Avenue
Mineola, NY 11501 USA
Phone: 516 248 8400
Fax: 516 248 8897
Email: sales@lightning.net
Web site: http://www.lightning.net
Levels of Connectivity Supported: ISDN, 56kb, T1

Long Island Information, Inc.
P.O. Box 151
Albertson, NY 11507 USA
Phone: 516 INTERNET or 516 248 5381
Email: admin@liii.com
Web site: http://www.liii.com
Levels of Connectivity Supported: Shell, SLIP, PPP, UUCP, 56kb, T1

Long Island Internet HeadQuarters
506 Route 110
Melville, NY 11747 USA
Phone: 516 439 7800
Fax: 516 439 7321
Email: support@pb.net
Web site: http://www.pb.net
Levels of Connectivity Supported: Shell, SLIP, PPP, UUCP, ISDN, 56kb, T1

Mordor International BBS
Jersey City, New Jersey
Fax: 201 433 4222
Levels of Connectivity Supported: Shell

Mnematics, Incorporated
P.O. Box 19
Sparkill, NY 10976-0019 USA
Phone: 914 359 4546
Fax: 914 359 0361
Email: service@mne.com
Web site: http://www.mne.com
Levels of Connectivity Supported: Shell, SLIP, PPP, UUCP

New World Data
253-17 80th Ave, Suite 2B
Floral Park, NY 11004 USA
Phone: 718 962 1725
Fax: 718 962 1708
Email: dmk@nwdc.com
Web site: http://www.nwdc.com
Levels of Connectivity Supported: Shell, SLIP, PPP, UUCP, ISDN, 56kb, T1

Panix (Public Access uNIX)
New York, NY USA
Phone: 212 741 4400
Fax: 212 741 5311
Email: info@panix.com
Web site: http://www.panix.com
Levels of Connectivity Supported: Shell, SLIP, PPP

Phantom Access Technologies, Inc. / MindVox
1133 Broadway, Suite 1126
New York, NY 10010 USA
Phone: 212 843 5529
Fax: 212 843 5531
Email: info@phantom.com
Web site: http://www.phantom.com
Levels of Connectivity Supported: Shell, SLIP, PPP

Pipeline New York
150 Broadway, Suite 610
New York, NY 10038 USA
Phone: 212 267 3636
Fax: 212 267 4380
Email: info@pipeline.com
Web site: http://www.pipeline.com
Levels of Connectivity Supported: Shell

Real Life Pictures RealNet
58 W36th Street, 2nd Floor
New York, NY 10018 USA
Phone: 212 366 4434
Email: reallife@walrus.com
Web site: http://www.reallife.com
Levels of Connectivity Supported: Shell, SLIP, PPP, ISDN, 56kb, T1

Spacelab.Net
60 Spring Street, Suite 1208
New York, NY 10012 USA
Phone: 212 966 8844
Fax: 212 966 9873
Email: mike@mxol.com
Levels of Connectivity Supported: Shell, SLIP, PPP, ISDN, 56kb, T1

ThoughtPort of New York City

95 Horatio Street, Suite 401
New York, NY 10014-1530
USA
Phone: 212 645 7970
Fax: 212 924 4360
Email: info@precipice.com
Web site: http://
www.precipice.com
Levels of Connectivity Supported: SLIP, PPP, UUCP, ISDN, 56kb, T1

tunanet/InfoHouse

151 1st Ave, #34
New York, NY 10009 USA
Phone: 212 229 8224
Fax: 212 228 7051
Email: info@tunanet.com
Web site: http://
www.tunanet.com
Levels of Connectivity Supported: PPP, UUCP

ZONE One Network Exchange

304 Hudson Street
New York, NY 10013 USA
Phone: 212 824 4000
Fax: 212 824 4009
Email: info@zone.net
Web site: http://www.zone.net
Levels of Connectivity Supported: Shell, SLIP, PPP, UUCP, ISDN, 56kb, T1

ISPs for Area Code 719

Colorado SuperNet, Inc.

999 18th Street, Suite 2640
Denver, CO 80202 USA
Phone: 303 296 8202
Fax: 303 296 8224
Email: mailto:info@csn.org
Web site: http://www.csn.net
Levels of Connectivity Supported: Shell, SLIP, PPP, UUCP, ISDN, 56kb, T1, Web Hosting

Internet Express

1155 Kelly Johnson Blvd,
Suite 400
Colorado Springs, CO 80920-3959 USA
Phone: 800-592-1240
Fax: 719-592-1201
Email: service@usa.net
Web site: http://www.usa.net
Levels of Connectivity Supported: Shell, SLIP, PPP, UUCP, 56kb, T1

Old Colorado City Communications

2473 Garden Way
Colorado Springs, CO 80918-4021
Phone: 719 528 5849
Fax: 719 528 5869
Levels of Connectivity Supported: Shell, UUCP

Rocky Mountain Internet

2860 S. Circle Drive,
Suite 2202
Colorado Springs, CO 80906
USA
Phone: 800 900 7644
Fax: 719 576 0301
Email: info@rmii.com
Web site: http://www.rmii.com
Levels of Connectivity Supported: Shell, SLIP, PPP, UUCP

ISPs for Area Code 770

Digital Service Consultants Inc.

3688 Clearview Ave, Suite 211
Atlanta, GA 30340 USA
Phone: 770 455 9022
Fax: 770 455 7714
Email: info@dscga.com
Web site: http://
www.dscga.com
Levels of Connectivity Supported: PPP, ISDN, 56kb, T1

MindSpring Enterprises, Inc.

1430 West Peachtree St NW,
Suite 400
Atlanta, GA 30309 USA
Phone: 800 719 4332
Fax: 404 815 8805
Email: info@mindspring.com
Web site: http://
www.mindspring.com
Levels of Connectivity Supported: SLIP, PPP, UUCP, ISDN, 56kb

Paradise Communications, Inc.

1000 Circle 75 Pkwy, Suite 120

Atlanta, GA 30339 USA

Phone: 404 980 0078

Fax: 404 984 1796

Email: info@paradise.net

Web site: http://www.paradise.net

Levels of Connectivity Supported: Shell, SLIP, PPP, UUCP, ISDN, 56kb, T1

Random Access, Inc.

6160 Peachtree-Dunwoody Rd., #A-100

Atlantam, GA 30328 USA

Phone: 404 804 1190 or 800 910 1190

Fax: 404 804 4546

Email: sales@randomc.com

Web site: http://www.randomc.com

Levels of Connectivity Supported: Shell, SLIP, PPP, UUCP, ISDN, 56kb, T1

vividnet

2400 Herodian Way, Suite 170

Atlanta, GA 30080 USA

Phone: 770 933 0999

Fax: 770 951 1881

Email: webadmin@vivid.net

Web site: http://www.vivid.net

Levels of Connectivity Supported: SLIP, PPP, ISDN, 56kb, T1

ISPs for Area Code 801

I-Link Ltd

1 Chisholm Trail

Round Rock, TX 78681 USA

Phone: 800 ILINK 99

Fax: 512 244 9681

Email: info@i-link.net

Web site: ="http://www.i-link.net

Levels of Connectivity Supported: PPP, ISDN, 56kb, T1

Internet Technology Systems (ITS)

1018 South 350 East

Provo, UT 84606 USA

Phone: 801 375 0538

Fax: 801 373 4095

Email: admin@itsnet.com

Web site: http://www.itsnet.com

Levels of Connectivity Supported: Shell, SLIP, PPP, 56kb, T1

NETConnect

P.O. Box 3425

Cedar City, UT 84720 USA

Phone: 800 689 8001

Fax: 801 865 7079

Email: office@tcd.net

Web site: http://www.tcd.net

Levels of Connectivity Supported: SLIP, PPP, UUCP, 56kb, T1

The ThoughtPort Authority Inc.

2000 E. Broadway, Suite 242

Columbia, MO 65201 USA

Phone: 800 ISP 6870

Fax: 314 474 4122

Email: info@thoughtport.com

Web site: http://www.thoughtport.com

Levels of Connectivity Supported: SLIP, PPP, ISDN, 56kb, T1

Utah Wired/The Friendly Net

350 west 300 south, Suite #111

Salt Lake City, Utah 84101 USA

Phone: 801 532 1117

Fax: 801 532 8478

Email: sales@utw.com

Web site: http://www.utw.com

Levels of Connectivity Supported: Shell, SLIP, PPP, ISDN, 56kb, T1

Vyzynz International

6995 South Union Park Center, Suite 475

UT 84037 USA

Phone: 801 568 0999

Fax: 801 568 0953

Email: info@vii.com

Web site: http://www.vii.com

Levels of Connectivity Supported: Shell, SLIP, PPP, 56kb, T1

XMission

51 East 400 South Suite 200
Salt Lake City, UT 84111 USA
Phone: 801 539 0852
Fax: 801 539 0853
Email: info@xmission.com
Web site: http://
www.xmission.com
Levels of Connectivity Supported: Shell, SLIP, PPP, UUCP, 56kb, T1

ISPs for Area Code 802

The Plainfield Bypass

P.O. Box 188
Plainfield, VT 05667 USA
Phone: 802 426 3963
Fax: 802 426 3963
Email:
questions@plainfield.bypass.com
Web site: http://
plainfield.bypass.com
Levels of Connectivity Supported: SLIP, PPP, ISDN, 56kb, T1

SoVerNet, Inc.

5 Rockingham Street
Bellows Falls, VT 05101 USA
Phone: 802 463 2111
Fax: 802 463 2110
Email: info@sover.net
Web site: http://
www.sover.net
Levels of Connectivity Supported: Shell, SLIP, PPP, UUCP, ISDN, 56kb, T1

ISPs for Area Code 803

A World of Difference, Inc.

P.O. Box 31788
1 Carriage Lane Suite J
Charleston, SC 29417 USA
Phone: 803 769 4488
Fax: 803 556 3044
Email: info@awod.com
Web site: http://www.awod.com
Levels of Connectivity Supported: PPP

CetLink.Net

325 S. Oakland Ave., Suite 2A
Rock Hill, SC 29730 USA
Phone: 803 327 2754
Fax: 803 327 0481
Email: info@cetlink.net
Web site: http://
www.cetlink.net
Levels of Connectivity Supported: PPP, 56kb, T1

Global Vision Inc.

201 East North Street
Greenville, SC 29601 USA
Phone: 803 241 0901
Fax: 803 241 9999
Email: info@globalvision.net
Web site: http://
www.globalvision.net
Levels of Connectivity Supported: SLIP, PPP, ISDN, 56kb, T1

Hargray Telephone Company

P.O. Box 5519
856 William Hilton Pkwy
Hilton Head Island, SC 29938 USA
Phone: 803 686 5000
Fax: 803 686 1251
Email: info@hargray.com
Web site: http://
www.hargray.com
Levels of Connectivity Supported: PPP, 56kb, T1

InteliNet

1359 Silver Bluff Road,
Suite A-1
Aiken, SC 29803 USA
Phone: 803 279 9775
Fax: 803 641 1560
Email:
administrator@intelinet.net
Web site: http://
www.intelinet.net
Levels of Connectivity Supported: PPP, ISDN, 56kb, T1

SIMS, Inc.

1209 Midvale Avenue
Charleston, SC 29412
Phone: 803 762 4956
Fax: 803 762 4956
Levels of Connectivity Supported: Shell, SLIP, PPP, UUCP

South Carolina SuperNet, Inc.
1901 Main St. Suite 1125
Compartment 400
Columbia, SC 29201 USA
Phone: 803 212 4400
Fax: 803 212 4444
Email: info@scsn.net
Web site: http://www.scsn.net
Levels of Connectivity Supported: SLIP, PPP, UUCP, ISDN, 56kb, T1

SunBelt.Net
P.O. Box 10630
Rock Hill, SC 29730
Phone: 803 328 1500
Fax: 803 324 6134
Levels of Connectivity Supported: Shell, SLIP, PPP, UUCP

Teleplex Communications, Inc.
P.O. Box 1211
Spartanburg, SC 29304 USA
Phone: 803 585 PLEX
Fax: 803 585 0850
Email: info@teleplex.net
Web site: http://www.teleplex.net
Levels of Connectivity Supported: Shell, SLIP, PPP, UUCP, ISDN, 56kb, T1

ISPs for Area Code 804

Widomaker Communication Service
700 Maupin Place
Williamsburg, VA 23185
Phone: 804 253 7621
Levels of Connectivity Supported: Shell, SLIP, PPP, UUCP

ISPs for Area Code 805

The Central Connection
31194 LaBaya Drive, Suite 100
Westlake Village, CA 91362 USA
Phone: 818 735 3000
Fax: 818 879 9997
Email: info@centcon.com
Web site: http://www.centcon.com
Levels of Connectivity Supported: Shell, SLIP, PPP, UUCP, ISDN, 56kb, T1

Cogent Software, Inc.
221 E. Walnut St., Suite 215
Pasadena, CA 91101 USA
Phone: 818 585 2788
Fax: 818 585 2785
Email: info@cogsoft.com
Web site: http://www.cogsoft.com
Levels of Connectivity Supported: Shell, PPP, ISDN, 56kb, T1

Delta Internet Services
731 E. Ball Rd., Suite 204
Anaheim, CA 92805 USA
Phone: 714 778 0370
Fax: 714 778 1064
Email: info@delta.net
Web site: http://www.delta.net
Levels of Connectivity Supported: Shell, SLIP, PPP, UUCP, ISDN, 56kb, T1

Fishnet Internet Services, Inc
5960 Valentine Road, Suite 8
Ventura, CA 93003 USA
Phone: 805 650 1844
Fax: 805 650 5948
Email: info@fishnet.net
Web site: http://www.fishnet.net
Levels of Connectivity Supported: SLIP, PPP, UUCP, ISDN, 56kb, T1

Hi-Desert Online
3053 Rancho Vista Blvd., Suite H-125
Palmdale, CA 93551 USA
Phone: 805 722 4119
Fax: 805 722 4119
Email: sysop@hidesert.com
Web site: http://www.hidesert.com
Levels of Connectivity Supported: Shell, SLIP, PPP, Web Hosting

Internet Access of Ventura County

1320 Flynn Road, Suite #403
Camarillo, CA 93012 USA
Phone: 805 383 3500
Fax: 805 383 3519
Email: info@vcnet.com
Web site: http://www.vcnet.com
Levels of Connectivity Supported: SLIP, PPP, ISDN, 56kb, Fractional T1

Instant Internet Corporation (InstaNet)

21010 Devonshire St.
Chatsworth, CA. 91311 USA
Phone: 818 772 0097
Fax: 818 772 9941
Email: charlyg@instanet.com
Web site: http://www.instanet.com
Levels of Connectivity Supported: PPP, UUCP, ISDN, 56kb

KAIWAN Internet

12550 Brookhurst Street, Suite H
Garden Grove, CA 92640 USA
Phone: 714 638 2139
Fax: 714 638 0455
Email: info@kaiwan.com
Web site: http://www.kaiwan.com
Levels of Connectivity Supported: Shell, SLIP, PPP, UUCP, 56kb, T1

KTB Internet Online

P.O. Box 3121
Glendale, CA 91221 USA
Phone: 818 240 6600
Fax: 818 240 6600
Email: info@ktb.net
Web site: http://www.ktb.net
Levels of Connectivity Supported: Shell, SLIP, PPP, UUCP, ISDN, 56kb, T1

Lancaster Internet (California)

P. O. Box 1988
Lancaster, CA 93539-1988 USA
Phone: 805 943 2112
Fax: 805 943 5649
Email: dennis@gargamel.ptw.com
Web site: http://www.ptw.com/index.html
Levels of Connectivity Supported: PPP

Liberty Information Network

446 S Anaheim Hills Road, Suite 102
Anaheim, CA 92807 USA
Phone: 800 218 5157 or 714 996 9999
Fax: 714 961 8700 Attn: ISP INFO
Email: info@liberty.com
Web site: http://www.liberty.com
Levels of Connectivity Supported: Shell, SLIP, PPP, UUCP, ISDN, 56kb, T1

The Loop Internet Switch Co.

6611 Santa Monica Blvd.
Los Angeles, CA 90038 USA
Phone: 213 465 1311
Fax: 213 469 2193
Email: info@loop.com
Web site: http://www.loop.com/rates.html
Levels of Connectivity Supported: SLIP, PPP

Netport Internet Access

343 East Palmdale Blvd., Suite 8
Palmdale, CA 93550 USA
Phone: 805 538 2860
Fax: 805 273 9334
Email: info@netport.com
Web site: http://www.netport.com
Levels of Connectivity Supported: Shell, SLIP, PPP, UUCP, 56kb, T1

Network Intensive

8001 Irvine Center Drive, Suite #1130
Irvine, CA 92718 USA
Phone: 714 450 8400
Fax: 714 450 8410
Email: info@ni.net
Web site: http://www.ni.net
Levels of Connectivity Supported: Shell, SLIP, PPP, UUCP, ISDN, 56kb, T1

OutWest Network Services Inc.

440 Western Avenue, Suite 101
Glendale, CA 91201 USA
Phone: 818 545 1996
Email: info@outwest.net
Web site: http://outwest.net
Levels of Connectivity Supported: Shell, SLIP, PPP, UUCP, 56kb, T1

Regional Alliance for Information Networking

P.O. Box 2683
Santa Barbara, CA 93120-2683
Phone: 805 967 7246
Fax: 805 967 2420
Levels of Connectivity Supported: Shell, SLIP, PPP, UUCP

Quantum Networking Solutions, Inc.

2022 Cliff Drive, Suite 121
Santa Barbara, CA 93109
Phone: 805 538 2028 or 703 878 4680
Fax: 805 563 9147or 703 878 4220
Levels of Connectivity Supported: Shell, SLIP, PPP, UUCP

Saigon Enterprises

P.O. Box 3121
Glendale, CA 91221-0121 USA
Phone: 818 246 0689
Fax: 818 240 6600
Email: info@saigon.net
Web site: http://www.saigon.net
Levels of Connectivity Supported: Shell, SLIP, PPP, UUCP, ISDN, 56kb, T1

Silicon Beach Communications

1216 State St. #602
Santa Barbara, CA 93101 USA
Phone: 805 730 7740
Fax: 805 882 2431
Email: help@silcom.com
Web site: http://www.silcom.com
Levels of Connectivity Supported: Shell, SLIP, PPP, UUCP, ISDN, 56kb, T1

Tehachapi Mountain Internet

204 South Green Street
Tehachapi, CA 93561 USA
Phone: 805 822 7803
Fax: 805 822 1163
Email: info@tminet.com
Web site: http://www.tminet.com
Levels of Connectivity Supported: PPP, 56kb

ValleyNet Communications

2300 Tulare, Suite 100
Fresno, CA 93721-2226 USA
Phone: 800 426 8638 or 209 486 8638
Fax: 209 495 4940
Email: info@valleynet.com
Web site: http://www.valleynet.com
Levels of Connectivity Supported: Shell, SLIP, PPP, UUCP, ISDN, 56kb, T1, Web hosting

WestNet

4572 Telephone Road, Suite 918
Ventura, CA
Phone: 805 289 1000
Fax: 805 289 1001
Email: info@west.net
Web site: http://www.west.net
Levels of Connectivity Supported: Shell, SLIP, PPP, ISDN, 56kb

ISPs for Area Code 806

HubNet

3060 34th Street
Lubbock, TX 79410 USA
Phone: 806 792 4482
Fax: 806 792 3937
Email: info@HUB.ofthe.NET
Web site: http://www.HUB.ofthe.NET
Levels of Connectivity Supported: PPP, ISDN, 56kb, T1

OnRamp Technologies, Inc.
1950 Stemmons Freeway,
Suite 5061
Dallas, TX 75207 USA
Phone: 214 672 7267
Fax: 214 713 5400
Email: info@onramp.net
Web site: http://
www.onramp.net
Levels of Connectivity Supported: SLIP, PPP, UUCP, ISDN, 56kb, T1

ISPs for Area Code 807

Pronet Internet Services
1184 Roland Street
Thunder Bay, Ontario P7B
5M4 Canada
Phone: 807 622 5915
Fax: 807 622 2082
Email: info@mail.procom.net
Web site: http://
www.procom.net
Levels of Connectivity Supported: Shell, PPP, UUCP, 56kb

ISPs for Area Code 808

FlexNet Inc.
P.O.Box 22481
Honolulu, HI 96823-2481 USA
Phone: 808 732 8849
Fax: 808 733 2000
Email: info@aloha.com
Web site: http://
www.aloha.com
Levels of Connectivity Supported: Shell, SLIP, PPP, 56kb

Hawaii OnLine
737 Bishop St., Suite 2350
Honolulu, HI 96813 USA
Phone: 808 533 6981
Fax: 808 534 0089
Email: info@aloha.net
Web site: http://
www.aloha.net
Levels of Connectivity Supported: Shell, SLIP, PPP, UUCP, ISDN, 56kb, T1

Inter-Pacific Network Services
180 Kinoole Street,
Suite 106A-2
Hilo, HI 97620 USA
Phone: 808 935 5550
Fax: 808 935 5534
Email: sales@interpac.net
Web site: http://
www.interpac.net
Levels of Connectivity Supported: Shell, SLIP, PPP, UUCP, 56kb, T1

LavaNet, Inc.
733 Bishop Street, Suite 1590
Honolulu, HI 96813 USA
Phone: 808 545 5282
Fax: 808 545 7020
Email: info@lava.net
Web site: http://www.lava.net
Levels of Connectivity Supported: Shell, SLIP, PPP

Pacific Information Exchange, Inc.
1142 Auahi Street, Suite 2788
Honolulu, HI 96814
Phone: 808 596 7494
Fax: 808 593 1403
Levels of Connectivity Supported: Shell, SLIP, PPP, UUCP

SenseMedia
P.O.B. 228
Felton, CA 95018 USA
Phone: 408 335 9400
Email: info@sensemedia.net
Web site: http://
sensemedia.net/info
Levels of Connectivity Supported: SLIP, PPP

ISPs for Area Code 810

Branch Information Services
2901 Hubbard
Ann Arbor, MI 48105 USA
Phone: 313-741-4442
Fax: 313-995-1931
Email: branch-info@branch.com
Web site: http://branch.com
Levels of Connectivity Supported: SLIP, PPP, ISDN, 56kb, T1

Freeway Inc. (tm)
P.O. Box 2389
Petoskey, Michigan 49770 USA
Phone: 616 347 3175
Fax: 616 347 1568
Email: info@freeway.net
Web site: http://
www.freeway.net
Levels of Connectivity Supported: Shell, PPP, UUCP, 56kb, T1

Great Lakes Information Systems
P.O. Box 189216
Utica, Michigan 48318-9216 USA
Phone: 810 786 0454
Fax: 810 786 0325
Email: info@glis.net
Web site: http://www.glis.net
Levels of Connectivity Supported: PPP, UUCP, 56kb, T1

ICNET / Innovative Concepts
2901 Hubbard
Ann Arbor, MI 48105
Phone: 313 998 0090
Fax: 313 998 0816
Levels of Connectivity Supported: Shell, SLIP, PPP, UUCP

The Internet Ramp
G-4225 Miller Road, Suite 179
Flint, MI 48507 USA
Phone: 800 502 0620
Fax: 810 732 5628
Email: newaccts@tir.com
Web site: http://www.tir.com
Levels of Connectivity Supported: PPP, T1

Michigan Internet Cooperative Association (MICA.net)
P.O. Box 40899
Redford, MI 48240 USA
Phone: 810 355 1438
Email: info@coop.mica.net
Web site: http://www.mica.net
Levels of Connectivity Supported: SLIP, PPP, 56kb, T1

Mich.com, Inc.
21042 Laurelwood
Farmington, MI 48336 USA
Phone: 810 478 4300
Fax: 810 478 4302
Email: info@mich.com
Web site: http://www.mich.com
Levels of Connectivity Supported: Shell, SLIP, PPP, UUCP, 56kb, T1

Msen, Inc.
320 Miller Avenue
Ann Arbor, MI 48103
Phone: 313 998 4562
Fax: 313 998 4563
Levels of Connectivity Supported: Shell, SLIP, PPP, UUCP

RustNet, Inc.
6905 Telegraph Rd., Suite 315
Bloomfield Hills, MI 48301 USA
Phone: 810 642 2276
Fax: 810 642 3676
Email: info@rust.net
Web site: http://www.rust.net
Levels of Connectivity Supported: Shell, PPP, ISDN, 56kb, T1

Voyager Information Networks, Inc.
600 West St. Jospeh Hwy, Suite 20
Lansing, MI 48933 USA
Phone: 517 485 9068
Fax: 517 485 9074
Email: help@voyager.net
Web site: http://www.voyager.net
Levels of Connectivity Supported: PPP, ISDN, 56kb, T1

ISPs for Area Code 812

accessU.S. Inc.
P.O. Box 985
1500 Main Street
Mt. Vernon, IL 62864 USA
Phone: 800 638 6373
Fax: 618 244 9175
Email: info@accessus.net
Web site: http://www.accessus.net
Levels of Connectivity Supported: SLIP, PPP, ISDN, 56kb, T1

HolliCom Internet Services

6810 West 400 South
Russiaville, IN 46979 USA
Phone: 317 883 4500
Fax: 317 883 7669
Email: cale@holli.com
Web site: http://
www.holli.com
Levels of Connectivity Supported: Shell, SLIP, PPP,
UUCP, ISDN, 56kb, T1

IgLou Internet Services

3315 Gilmore Industrial Blvd.
Louisville, KY 40213
Phone: 800 436 IGLOU
Fax: 502 968 0449
Levels of Connectivity Supported: Shell, SLIP, PPP,
UUCP

World Connection Services

2009 Lincoln Avenue
Evansville, IN 47714 USA
Phone: 812 479 1700
Fax: 812 479 3439
Email: info@evansville.net
Web site: http://
www.evansville.net
Levels of Connectivity Supported: Shell, SLIP, PPP,
UUCP, 56kb, T1

ISPs for Area Code 813

Bay-A-Net

P.O. Box 290261
Tampa, FL 33687 USA
Phone: 813 988 7772
Fax: 813 988 5511
Email: info@bayanet.com
Web site: http://
www.bayanet.com
Levels of Connectivity Supported: SLIP, PPP, ISDN,
56kb, T1

Centurion Technology, Inc.

4175 E. Bay Dr., Suite 142
Largo, FL 34624 USA
Phone: 813 538 1919
Fax: 813 524 2909
Email: info@tpa.cent.com
Web site: http://tpa.cent.com
Levels of Connectivity Supported: PPP, UUCP, 56kb

CFTnet

@cftnet.com
P.O. Box 291783
Tampa, FL 33687 USA
Phone: 813 980 1317
Fax: 813 982 1992
Email: info@cftnet.com
Web site: http://
www.cftnet.com
Levels of Connectivity Supported: Shell, PPP

CocoNet Corporation

1031 Cape Coral Pkwy
Cape Coral, FL 33904 USA
Phone: 813 945 0055
Fax: 813 466 6692
Email: info@coconet.com
Web site: http://
www.coconet.com
Levels of Connectivity Supported: Shell, SLIP, 56kb, T1

Florida Online

3815 N US 1, $59
Cocoa, FL 32926 USA
Phone: 407 635 8888
Fax: 407 635 9050
Email: info@digital.net
Web site: http://digital.net
Levels of Connectivity Supported: Shell, SLIP, PPP,
UUCP

CyberGate, Inc.

662 South Military Trail
Deerfield Beach, FL 33442 USA
Phone: 305 428 4283
Fax: 305 428 7977
Email: sales@gate.net
Web site: http://www.gate.net
Levels of Connectivity Supported: Shell, SLIP, PPP,
UUCP

Intelligence Network Online, Inc.

P.O. Box 727
Clearwater, FL 34617
Phone: 813 442 0114 x22
Levels of Connectivity Supported: Shell, SLIP, PPP,
56kb, T1

PacketWorks, Inc.
1100 Cleveland St. #900P
Clearwater, FL 34615 USA
Phone: 813 446 8826
Fax: 813 447 1585
Email: info@packet.net
Web site: http://www.packet.net
Levels of Connectivity Supported: PPP, ISDN

Shadow Information Services, Inc.
2000 Nw 88 Court
Miami, FL 33172 USA
Phone: 305 594 2450
Fax: 305 599 1140
Email: admin@shadow.net
Web site: http://www.shadow.net
Levels of Connectivity Supported: Shell, SLIP, PPP

The ThoughtPort Authority Inc.
2000 E. Broadway, Suite 242
Columbia, MO 65201 USA
Phone: 800 ISP 6870
Fax: 314 474 4122
Email: info@thoughtport.com
Web site: http://www.thoughtport.com
Levels of Connectivity Supported: SLIP, PPP, ISDN, 56kb, T1

WebIMAGE, Inc an internet presence provider
1900 S.Harbor City Blvd, Suite 328
Melbourne, FL 32901 USA
Phone: 407 723 0001
Email: info@webimage.com
Web site: http://www.webimage.com
Levels of Connectivity Supported: 56kb, T1

ISPs for Area Code 814

North Coast Internet
4509 West Ridge Road
Erie, PA 16428 USA
Phone: 814 838 6386
Fax: 814 833 2293
Email: info@ncinter.net
Web site: http://www.ncinter.net
Levels of Connectivity Supported: Shell, SLIP, PPP, UUCP, 56kb

Penncom Internet Co.
210 Liberty St.
Warren, PA 16365 USA
Phone: 814 723 4141
Email: admin@penn.com
Web site: http://www.penn.com
Levels of Connectivity Supported: Shell, SLIP, PPP

PenNet - A Subsidiary of Smith's (Bahamas) Ltd.
342 Broad Street
Montoursville, PA 17754 USA
Phone: 717 368 1577
Fax: 717 368 8837
Email: safrye@pennet.net
Web site: http://www.pennet.net
Levels of Connectivity Supported: PPP, ISDN, 56kb, T1

ISPs for Area Code 815

American Information Systems, Inc.
911 North Plum Grove Road, Suite F
Schaumburg, IL 60173 USA
Phone: 708 413 8400
Fax: 708 413 8401
Email: info@ais.net
Web site: http://www.ais.net
Levels of Connectivity Supported: Shell, SLIP, PPP, UUCP

BOSSNet Internet Services
614 East Grand Avenue
Beloit, WI 53511 USA
Phone: 608 362 1340
Fax: 608 362 4584
Email: mbusam@bossnt.com
Web site: http://www.bossnt.com
Levels of Connectivity Supported: Shell, SLIP, PPP, ISDN, 56kb, T1

CIN.net (Computerese Information Network)

721 West Golf Road

Hoffman Estates, IL 60194 USA

Phone: 708 310 1188

Fax: 708 885 8308

Email: info@cin.net

Web site: http://www.cin.net

Levels of Connectivity Supported: Shell, SLIP, PPP, UUCP, ISDN, 56kb, T1

InterAccess Co.

3345 Commercial Ave.

Northbrook, IL 60062 USA

Phone: 708 498 2542

Fax: 708 498 3289

Email: info@interaccess.com

Web site: http://www.interaccess.com

Levels of Connectivity Supported: Shell, SLIP, PPP, UUCP, ISDN, 56kb, T1

The Software Farm

P.O. Box 477

120 S. Ottawa

Earlville, IL 60518 USA

Phone: 815 246 7295

Fax: 815 246 7296

Email: info@softfarm.com

Web site: http://www.softfarm.com

Levels of Connectivity Supported: PPP

T.B.C. Online Data-Net

P.O. Box 547

Cortland, IL 60112 USA

Phone: 815 758 5040

Fax: 815 758 5040

Email: info@tbcnet.com

Web site: http://www.tbcnet.com

Levels of Connectivity Supported: Shell, SLIP, PPP, 56kb

Wink Communications Group, Inc.

2500 W Higgins Rd, Suite 480

Hoffman Estates, IL 60195 USA

Phone: 708 310 9465

Fax: 708 310 3477

Email: sales@winkcomm.com

Web site: http://www.winkcomm.com

Levels of Connectivity Supported: ISDN, 56kb, T1

ISPs for Area Code 816

fyi@unicom.net

7223 W. 95th St., Suite 325

Overland Park, Kansas 66212 USA

Phone: 913 383 8466

Fax: 913 383 1998

Email: fyi@unicom.net

Web site: http://www.unicom.net

Levels of Connectivity Supported: SLIP, PPP, UUCP, ISDN, 56kb, T1

Interstate Networking Corporation

2700 Rockcreek Parkway, #302

North Kansas City, MO 64117 USA

Phone: 816 472 4949

Email: staff@interstate.net

Web site: http://www.interstate.net

Levels of Connectivity Supported: Shell, SLIP, PPP, UUCP

Primenet

2320 W. Peoria Avenue, Suite A103

Phoenix, AZ 85029 USA

Phone: 602 870 1010 or 800 4 NET FUN

Fax: 602 870 1010

Email: info@primenet.com

Web site: http://www.primenet.com

Levels of Connectivity Supported: Shell, SLIP, PPP, UUCP

ISPs for Area Code 817

ANET (American Internet)

2225 E. Randol Mill Rd, Suite 209

Arlington, TX 76011 USA

Phone: 800 776 8894

Fax: 817 633 4816

Email: sales@anet-dfw.com

Web site: http://www.anet-dfw.com

Levels of Connectivity Supported: Shell, PPP, ISDN, 56kb, T1

CompuTek

1005 Business Parkway

Richardson, TX 75081 USA

Phone: 214 994 0190

Fax: 214 994 0350

Email: info@computek.net

Web site: http://
www.computek.net

Levels of Connectivity Supported: SLIP, PPP, ISDN, 56kb, T1

Connection Technologies - ConnectNet

14651 Dallas Parkway, Suite 424

Dallas, TX 75240 USA

Phone: 214 490 7100

Fax: 214 490 7108

Email: sales@connect.net

Web site: http://
www.connect.net

Levels of Connectivity Supported: SLIP, PPP, UUCP, ISDN, 56kb, T1

Delta Design and Development Inc.

6448 Hwy. 290 East, Suite F108

Austin, TX 78723 USA

Phone: 800 763 8265

Fax: 512 467 8462

Email: sales@deltaweb.com

Web site: http://
www.deltaweb.com

Levels of Connectivity Supported: PPP, ISDN, 56kb, T1

DFW Internet Services, Inc.

204 East Belknap, Suite 200

Ft. Worth, TX 76103 USA

Phone: 817 332 5116 or Metro 817 429 3520

Fax: 817 870 1501

Email: info@dfw.net

Web site: http://www.dfw.net

Levels of Connectivity Supported: Shell, SLIP, PPP, UUCP, ISDN, 56kb, T1

Texas Metronet, Inc.

860 Kinwest Pkwy, Suite 179

Irving, TX 75063-3440

Phone: 214 705 2900

Fax: 214 401 2802

Levels of Connectivity Supported: Shell, SLIP, PPP, UUCP

OnRamp Technologies, Inc.

1950 Stemmons Freeway, Suite 5061

Dallas, TX 75207 USA

Phone: 214 672 7267

Fax: 214 713 5400

Email: info@onramp.net

Web site: http://
www.onramp.net

Levels of Connectivity Supported: SLIP, PPP, UUCP, ISDN, 56kb, T1

PICnet

12801 North Central Expressway, Suite 1518

Dallas, TX 75243 USA

Phone: 214 789 0456

Fax: 214 789 0460

Email: info@pic.net

Web site: http://www.pic.net

Levels of Connectivity Supported: SLIP, PPP, 56kb, T1

WorldNet of Central Texas

2210 E. Central Texas Expressway, Suite 205

Killeen, TX 76543 USA

Phone: 817 526 8481

Fax: 817 526 8830

Email: centraltexas@sat.net

Web site: http://
www.centraltx.net

Levels of Connectivity Supported: Shell, SLIP, PPP, ISDN, 56kb, T1, Web Hosting

ISPs for Area Code 818

ArtNetwork

844 S. Robertson

Los Angeles, CA 90035 USA

Phone: 800 395 0692

Fax: 310 652 7114

Email: info@artnet.net

Web site: http://
www.artnet.net

Levels of Connectivity Supported: Shell, SLIP, PPP, UUCP, ISDN, 56kb, T1

BeachNet Internet Access

BeachNet, Inc.

Marina Del Rey, CA 90292 USA

Phone: 310 823 3308

Fax: 310 823 1390

Email: info@beachnet.com

Web site: http://www.beachnet.com

Levels of Connectivity Supported: SLIP, PPP, T1

The Central Connection

31194 LaBaya Drive, Suite 100

Westlake Village, CA 91362 USA

Phone: 818 735 3000

Fax: 818 879 9997

Email: info@centcon.com

Web site: http://www.centcon.com

Levels of Connectivity Supported: Shell, SLIP, PPP, UUCP, ISDN, 56kb, T1

Cogent Software, Inc.

221 E. Walnut St., Suite 215

Pasadena, CA 91101 USA

Phone: 818 585 2788

Fax: 818 585 2785

Email: info@cogsoft.com

Web site: http://www.cogsoft.com

Levels of Connectivity Supported: Shell, PPP, ISDN, 56kb, T1

CruzNet

215 E. Orangethorpe Ave.

Suite: 333

Fullerton, CA 92632 USA

Phone: 714 680 6600

Fax: 714 680 4241

Email: info@cruznet.net

Web site: http://www.cruznet.net

Levels of Connectivity Supported: Shell, SLIP, PPP, UUCP, ISDN, 56kb

Cyberg8t Internet Services

225 Yale Ave., Suite D

Claremont, CA 91711 USA

Phone: 909 398 4638

Fax: 909 398 4621

Email: sales@cyberg8t.com

Web site: http://www.cyberg8t.com

Levels of Connectivity Supported: PPP, UUCP, 56kb, T1

Cyberverse Online

2221 Rosecrans Avenue, Suite 130

El Segundo, CA 90245 USA

Phone: 310 643 3783

Fax: 310 643 6137

Email: info@cyberverse.com

Web site: http://www.cyberverse.com

Levels of Connectivity Supported: Shell, SLIP, PPP

Delta Internet Services

731 E. Ball Rd., Suite 204

Anaheim, CA 92805 USA

Phone: 714 778 0370

Fax: 714 778 1064

Email: info@delta.net

Web site: http://www.delta.net

Levels of Connectivity Supported: Shell, SLIP, PPP, UUCP, ISDN, 56kb, T1

DigiLink Network Services

4429 W. 169th Street

Lawndale, CA 90260-3252

Phone: 310 542 7421

Web site: http://www.dfw.net

Levels of Connectivity Supported: ISDN

Exodus Communications, Inc.

948 Benecia Avenue

Sunnyvale, CA 94086 USA

Phone: 408 522 8450

Fax: 408 736 6843

Email: info@exodus.net

Web site: http://www.exodus.net

Levels of Connectivity Supported: ISDN, 56kb, T1

Flamingo Communications Inc.

19401 So. Vermont Ave., Suite D-104

Torrance, CA 90502 USA

Phone: 310 532 3533

Fax: 310 532 3622

Email: sales@fcom.com

Web site: http://www.fcom.com

Levels of Connectivity Supported: Shell, SLIP, PPP

InterNex Tiara
2302 Walsh Ave
Santa Clara, CA 95051 USA
Phone: 408 496 5466
Fax: 408 496 5485
Email: info@internex.net
Web site: http://
www.internex.net
Levels of Connectivity Sup-
ported: SLIP, PPP, ISDN,
56kb, T1, Frame Relay

**Instant Internet Corporation
(InstaNet)**
21010 Devonshire St.
Chatsworth, CA 91311 USA
Phone: 818 772 0097
Fax: 818 772 9941
Email: charlyg@instanet.com
Web site: http://
www.instanet.com
Levels of Connectivity Sup-
ported: PPP, UUCP, ISDN,
56kb

KAIWAN Internet
12550 Brookhurst Street,
Suite H
Garden Grove, CA 92640 USA
Phone: 714 638 2139
Fax: 714 638 0455
Email: info@kaiwan.com
Web site: http://
www.kaiwan.com
Levels of Connectivity Sup-
ported: Shell, SLIP, PPP,
UUCP, ISDN, 56kb, T1

KTB Internet Online
P.O. Box 3121
Glendale, CA 91221 USA
Phone: 818 240 6600
Fax: 818 240 6600
Email: info@ktb.net
Web site: http://www.ktb.net
Levels of Connectivity Sup-
ported: Shell, SLIP, PPP,
UUCP, ISDN, 56kb, T1

**InterWorld Communica-
tions, Inc.**
222 N. Sepulveda Blvd., Suite
1560
El Segundo, CA 90245 USA
Phone: 310 726 0500
Fax: 310 726 0559
Email: sales@interworld.net
Web site: http://
www.interworld.net
Levels of Connectivity Sup-
ported: SLIP, PPP, UUCP,
ISDN, 56kb, T1, Web Hosting

Leonardo Internet
927 6th Street
Santa Monica, CA 90403 USA
Phone: 310 395 5500
Fax: 310 395 9924
Email: jimp@leonardo.net
Web site: http://leonardo.net
Levels of Connectivity Sup-
ported: Shell, PPP, 56kb, T1

Liberty Information Network
446 S Anaheim Hills Road,
Suite 102
Anaheim, CA 92807 USA
Phone: 800 218 5157 or 714
996 9999
Fax: 714 961 8700 Attn: ISP
INFO
Email: info@liberty.com
Web site: http://
www.liberty.com
Levels of Connectivity Sup-
ported: Shell, SLIP, PPP,
UUCP, ISDN, 56kb, T1

Lightside, Inc.
101 N. Citrus, Suite #4A
Covina, CA 91723 USA
Phone: 818 858 9261
Fax: 818 858 8982
Email:
Lightside@Lightside.Com
Web site: http://
www.lightside.Net
Levels of Connectivity Sup-
ported: SLIP, PPP, 56kb, T1

**The Loop Internet Switch
Co.**
6611 Santa Monica Blvd.
Los Angeles, CA 90038 USA
Phone: 213 465 1311
Fax: 213 469 2193
Email: info@loop.com
Web site: http://
www.loop.com/rates.html
Levels of Connectivity Sup-
ported: SLIP, PPP

Network Intensive

8001 Irvine Center Drive,
Suite #1130
Irvine, CA 92718 USA
Phone: 714 450 8400
Fax: 714 450 8410
Email: info@ni.net
Web site: http://www.ni.net
Levels of Connectivity Supported: Shell, UUCP, SLIP, PPP, ISDN, 56kb, T1

Online-LA

8671 Wilshire Blvd.
Beverly Hills, CA 90211 USA
Phone: 310 967 8000
Fax: 310 358 5610
Email: sales@online-la.com
Web site: http://www.online-la.com
Levels of Connectivity Supported: PPP, ISDN, 56kb, T1

OutWest Network Services Inc.

440 Western Avenue, Suite 101
Glendale, CA 91201 USA
Phone: 818 545 1996
Email: info@outwest.net
Web site: http://outwest.net
Levels of Connectivity Supported: Shell, SLIP, PPP, UUCP, 56kb, T1

Primenet

2320 W. Peoria Avenue,
Suite A103
Phoenix, AZ 85029 USA
Phone: 602 870 1010 or 800 4 NET FUN
Fax: 602 870 1010
Email: info@primenet.com
Web site: http://www.primenet.com
Levels of Connectivity Supported: Shell, SLIP, PPP, UUCP

QuickCom Internet Communcations

5724 W. Third St. Ste.# 507
Los Angeles, CA 90036 USA
Phone: 213 634 7735
Fax: 213 634 7722
Email: info@quickcom.net
Web site: http://www.quickcom.net
Levels of Connectivity Supported: PPP, ISDN, 56kb, T1

Regional Alliance for Information Networking

P.O. Box 2683
Santa Barbara, CA 93120-2683
Phone: 805 967 7246
Fax: 805 967 2420
Levels of Connectivity Supported: Shell, SLIP, PPP, UUCP

Saigon Enterprises

P.O. Box 3121
Glendale, CA 91221-0121 USA
Phone: 818 246 0689
Fax: 818 240 6600
Email: info@saigon.net
Web site: http://www.saigon.net
Levels of Connectivity Supported: Shell, SLIP, PPP, UUCP, ISDN, 56kb, T1

SoftAware

4676 Admiralty Way, Suite 410
Marina del Rey, CA 90292 USA
Phone: 310 305 0275
Email: info@softaware.com
Web site: http://www.softaware.com
Levels of Connectivity Supported: T1

ViaNet Communications

800 El Camino Real West,
Suite 180
Mountain View, CA 94040
Phone: 415 903 2242
Fax: 415 903 2241
Levels of Connectivity Supported: Shell, SLIP, PPP, UUCP

ISPs for Area Code 819

Information Gateway Services (Ottawa)

300 March Road, Suite 101

Kanata, Ontario K2K 2E2

Canada

Phone: 613 592 5619

Fax: 613 592 3556

Email: info@igs.net

Web site: http://www.igs.net

Levels of Connectivity Supported: Shell, SLIP, PPP, UUCP, ISDN, 56kb, T1

Interactive Telecom Inc.

190 Colonnade Rd., Suite 204

Nepean, Ontario K2E 7J5

Canada

Phone: 613 727 5258

Fax: 613 727 5438

Email: info@intertel.net

Web site: http://www.intertel.net

Levels of Connectivity Supported: SLIP, PPP, UUCP, ISDN, 56kb, T1

Magma Communications Ltd.

Unit 201

52 Antares Drive

Nepean, Ontario K2E 7Z1

Canada

Phone: 613 228 3565

Fax: 613 228 8313

Email: info@magmacom.com

Web site: http://www.magmacom.com

Levels of Connectivity Supported: Shell, SLIP, PPP, UUCP, ISDN

o://info.web - Internet access and Training

100 - 20 Colonnade Road, North

Nepean, Ontario K2E 7M6

Canada

Phone: 613 225 3354

Fax: 613 225 2880

Levels of Connectivity Supported: SLIP, PPP, UUCP

ISPs for Area Code 860

Connix: The Connecticut Internet Exchange

Suite 33

6 Way Road

Middlefield, CT 06455 USA

Phone: 860 349 7059

Fax: 860 349 7058

Email: office@connix.com

Web site: http://www.connix.com

Levels of Connectivity Supported: Shell, SLIP, PPP, UUCP, 56kb, T1

imagine.com

92 Weston Street, Suite #12

Hartford, CT 06120 USA

Phone: 860 527 9245

Fax: 860 293 0762

Email: Postmaster@imagine.com

Web site: http://www.imagine.com

Levels of Connectivity Supported: SLIP, PPP, ISDN, 56kb, T1

MCIX, Inc.

5 Roosevelt Ave

Mystic, CT 06355 USA

Phone: 860 572 8720

Fax: 860 572 8720

Email: info@mcix.com

Web site: http://www.mcix.com

Levels of Connectivity Supported: Shell, SLIP, PPP, UUCP, ISDN, 56kb, T1

Mindport Internet Services, Inc.

P.O. Box 208

Norwich, CT 06360 USA

Phone: 860 892 2081

Fax: 860 892 2084

Email: staff@mindport.net

Web site: http://www.mindport.net

Levels of Connectivity Supported: Shell, SLIP, PPP, UUCP, ISDN, 56kb, T1

Paradigm Communications, Inc.

416 Highland Avenue

P. O. Box 1334

Cheshire, CT 06410-1334 USA

Phone: 203 250 7397

Fax: 203 250 2250

Email: info@pcnet.com

Web site: http://www.pcnet.com

Levels of Connectivity Supported: PPP, UUCP, ISDN, 56kb, T1

ISPs for Area Code 864

Global Vision Inc.

201 East North Street

Greenville, SC 29601 USA

Phone: 803 241 0901

Fax: 803 241 9999

Email: info@globalvision.net

Web site: http://
www.globalvision.net

Levels of Connectivity Supported: SLIP, PPP, ISDN, 56kb, T1

ISPs for Area Code 901

accessU.S. Inc.

P.O. Box 985

1500 Main Street

Mt. Vernon, IL 62864 USA

Phone: 800 638 6373

Fax: 618 244 9175

Email: info@accessus.net

Web site: http://
www.accessus.net

Levels of Connectivity Supported: SLIP, PPP, ISDN, 56kb, T1

A2ZNET

141 East Highway 72,
Suite 7

Collierville, TN 38017 USA

Phone: 901 854 1871

Fax: 901 854 1872

Email: webmaster@a2znet.com

Web site: http://
www.a2znet.com

Levels of Connectivity Supported: Shell, SLIP, PPP, UUCP, ISDN, 56kb, T1

ISDN-Net Inc.

5115 Maryland Way

Brentwood, TN 37027-7512
USA

Phone: 615 377 7672

Fax: 615 377 3959

Email: info@isdn.net

Web site: http://www.isdn.net

Levels of Connectivity Supported: Shell, SLIP, PPP, UUCP, ISDN, 56kb, T1

Magibox Incorporated

1873 Hidden Oaks Drive

Germantown, TN 38138

Phone: 901 757 7835

Fax: 901 757 5875

Levels of Connectivity Supported: Shell, SLIP, PPP, UUCP

U.S. Internet

1127 North Broadway

Knoxville, TN 37917 USA

Phone: 615 522 6788

Fax: 615 524 6313

Email: info@usit.net

Web site: http://www.usit.net

Levels of Connectivity Supported: Shell, SLIP, PPP, UUCP, 56kb, T1

ISPs for Area Code 902

Cycor Communications Incorporated

P.O. Box 454

Charlottetown, Prince Edward
Island C1A 7K7 Canada

Phone: 902 892 7354

Fax: : 902-892-5600

Email: signup@cycor.ca

Web site: http://www.cycor.ca

Levels of Connectivity Supported: SLIP, PPP, ISDN, T1

ISPs for Area Code 903

Cloverleaf Technologies

P.O. Box 6185

Texarkana, TX 75505-6185
USA

Phone: 903 832 1367

Email:
helpdesk@clover.cleaf.com

Levels of Connectivity Supported: Shell, SLIP

Delta Design and Development Inc.

6448 Hwy. 290 East, Suite
F108

Austin, TX 78723 USA

Phone: 800 763 8265

Fax: 512 467 8462

Email: sales@deltaweb.com

Web site: http://
www.deltaweb.com

Levels of Connectivity Supported: PPP, ISDN, 56kb, T1

Phoenix DataNet, Inc.

17100 El Camino Real

Houston, TX 77058 USA

Phone: 713 486 8337

Fax: 713 486 7464

Email: info@phoenix.net

Web site: http://
www.phoenix.net

Levels of Connectivity Supported: Shell, SLIP, PPP, ISDN, 56kb, T1

Rapid Ramp, Inc.

3543 Gilmer Road

P.O. Box 150662

Longview, TX 75615-0662 USA

Phone: 903 759 0705

Fax: 903 759 7896

Email: help@rapidramp.com

Web site: http://
www.easttexas.com

Levels of Connectivity Supported: PPP, UUCP, ISDN, 56kb, T1

StarNet Online Systems

3365 Lamar Avenue

Paris, TX 75460 USA

Phone: 903 785 5533

Fax: 903 784 1259

Email:
lrhea@stargate.1starnet.com

Web site: http://
www.1starnet.com

Levels of Connectivity Supported: Shell, SLIP, PPP, UUCP, ISDN, 56kb, T1

ISPs for Area Code 904

CyberGate, Inc.

662 South Military Trail

Deerfield Beach, FL 33442 USA

Phone: 305 428 4283

Fax: 305 428 7977

Email: sales@gate.net

Web site: http://www.gate.net

Levels of Connectivity Supported: Shell, SLIP, PPP, UUCP

Florida Online

3815 N US 1, $59

Cocoa, FL 32926 USA

Phone: 407 635 8888

Fax: 407 635 9050

Email: info@digital.net

Web site: http://digital.net

Levels of Connectivity Supported: Shell, SLIP, PPP, UUCP

Gulf Coast Internet Company

41 North Jefferson Street

Rhodes Building Suite 401

Pensacola, FL 32501 USA

Phone: 904 438 5700

Fax: 904 438 5750

Email: info@gulf.net

Web site: http://www.gulf.net

Levels of Connectivity Supported: Shell, SLIP, PPP, UUCP, ISDN, 56kb, T1

Internet Connect Company

11 West University Ave,
Suite #200

Gainesville, FL 32601 USA

Phone: 904 375 2912

Fax: 904 375 2702

Email: info@atlantic.net

Web site: http://
www.atlantic.net

Levels of Connectivity Supported: Shell, SLIP, PPP, UUCP, ISDN, 56kb, T1

Jax Gateway to the World,

Technology Corp.

2532 West University Blvd

Jacksonville, FL 32217 USA

Phone: 904 730 7692

Fax: 904 730 8045

Email: sales@gttw.com

Web site: http://www.gttw.com

Levels of Connectivity Supported: SLIP, PPP, ISDN, 56kb, T1

MagicNet, Inc.

10149 University Blvd.

Orlando, FL 32817 USA

Phone: 407 657 2202

Fax: 407 679 8562

Email: info@magicnet.net

Web site: http://
www.magicnet.net

Levels of Connectivity Supported: Shell, SLIP, PPP, UUCP, 56kb, T1

Polaris Network, Inc.

Polaris Network, Inc.

433 North Magnolia Drive

Tallahassee, FL 32308 USA

Phone: 904 878 9745

Fax: 904 656 1539

Email: staff@polaris.net

Web site: http://
www.polaris.net

Levels of Connectivity Supported: Shell, SLIP, PPP, 56kb, T1

PSS InterNet Services

2455 West International Speedway Blvd, Suite #807

Daytona Beach, FL 32114 USA

Phone: 800 463 8499

Fax: 904 253 1006

Email: support@america.com

Web site: http://
www.america.com

Levels of Connectivity Supported: Shell, SLIP, PPP

SymNet

P.O. Box 20074

Tallahassee, FL 32316-0074

Phone: 904 385 1061

Levels of Connectivity Supported: Shell, SLIP, PPP

WebIMAGE, Inc an internet presence provider

1900 S.Harbor City Blvd, Suite 328

Melbourne, FL 32901 USA

Phone: 407 723 0001

Email: info@webimage.com

Web site: http://
www.webimage.com

Levels of Connectivity Supported: 56kb, T1

ISPs for Area Code 905

ComputerLink/Internet Direct

5415 Dundas Street #301

Etobicoke, ON M9B 1B5 Canada

Phone: 416 233 7150

Fax: 416 233 6970

Email: info@idirect.com

Web site: http://
www.idirect.com

Levels of Connectivity Supported: SLIP, PPP, UUCP, ISDN, 56kb, T1

Cycor Communications Incorporated

P.O. Box 454

Charlottetown, Prince Edward Island C1A 7K7 Canada

Phone: 902 892 7354

Fax: : 902-892-5600

Email: signup@cycor.ca

Web site: http://www.cycor.ca

Levels of Connectivity Supported: SLIP, PPP, ISDN, 56kb, T1

eagle.ca - Northumbria Associates

Suite 26

1011 William Street

Cobourg, ON K9A 5J4 Canada

Phone: 905 373 9313

Fax: 905 373 1801

Email: info@eagle.ca

Web site: http://www.eagle.ca

Levels of Connectivity Supported: Shell, SLIP, PPP, UUCP, 56kb, T1

HookUp Communications

1075 North Service Road West, Suite 207

Oakville, Ontario L6M 2G2

Phone: 905 847 8000

Fax: 905 847 8866

Levels of Connectivity Supported: Shell, SLIP, PPP, UUCP

iCOM Internet Services

7 Mary St., Suite 201

Hamilton, Ontario L8R 1J6 Canada

Phone: 905 522 1220

Fax: 905 546 1996

Email: sales@icom.ca

Web site: http://www.icom.ca

Levels of Connectivity Supported: Shell, SLIP, PPP, UUCP, ISDN, 56kb, T1

InterLog Internet Services

1235 Bay Street, Suite 400

Toronto, Ontario M5R 3K4 Canada

Phone: 416 975 2655

Fax: 416 532 5015

Levels of Connectivity Supported: Shell, SLIP, PPP

Internet Access Worldwide

15 Burgar Street, 2nd floor
Welland, Ontario L3B 2S6
Canada
Phone: 905 714 1400
Fax: 905 732 0524
Email: info@iaw.on.ca
Web site: http://
www.iaw.on.ca
Levels of Connectivity Supported: Shell, SLIP, PPP,
UUCP, 56kb

Internet Connect Niagara Inc

25 Church St.
St. Catharines, Ontario L2R
3B1 Canada
Phone: 905 988 9909
Fax: 905 988 1090
Email: info@niagara.com
Web site: http://
www.niagara.com
Levels of Connectivity Supported: Shell, SLIP, PPP,
UUCP, ISDN, 56kb, T1

Internex Online, Inc.

1801 - 1 Yonge Street
Toronto, Ontario M5E 1W7
Canada
Phone: 416 363 8676
Levels of Connectivity Supported: Shell, SLIP, PPP

Magic Online Services International Inc.

260 Richmond Street West,
Suite 206
Toronto, Ontario M5V 1W5
Canada
Phone: 416 591 6490
Fax: 416 591 6409
Email: info@magic.ca
Web site: http://www.magic.ca
Levels of Connectivity Supported: SLIP, PPP, UUCP,
ISDN

Neptune Internet Services

465 Davis Dr , Suite 404
Newmarket, Ontario L0G 1E0
Canada
Phone: 905 895 0898
Fax: 905 863 4679
Email: info@neptune.on.ca
Web site: http://
www.neptune.on.ca
Levels of Connectivity Supported: Shell, SLIP, PPP,
UUCP, 56kb, T1

Network Enterprise Technology Inc.

20 Jackson St. W., Suite 206
Hamilton, Ontario L8P 1L2
Canada
Phone: 905 525 4555
Fax: 905 525 3222
Email: info@netinc.ca
Web site: http://
www.netinc.ca
Levels of Connectivity Supported: Shell, PPP, UUCP,
ISDN, 56kb

Times.net

Box 1570
32 Holland St., E
Bradford, Ontario L3Z 2B8
Canada
Phone: 905 775 4471
Fax: 905 775 4489
Email: rfonger@times.net
Web site: http://
www.times.net
Levels of Connectivity Supported: Shell, SLIP, PPP,
UUCP, 56kb, T1

Vaxxine Computer Systems Inc.

P.O. Box 279
4520 Jordan Road
Jordan Station, Ontario L0R
1S0 Canada
Phone: 905 562 3500
Fax: 905 562 3515
Email: admin@vaxxine.com
Web site: http://
www.vaxxine.com
Levels of Connectivity Supported: Shell, SLIP, PPP,
UUCP

ISPs for Area Code 906

Branch Information Services

2901 Hubbard
Ann Arbor, MI 48105 USA
Phone: 313 741 4442
Fax: 313 995 1931
Email: branch-info@branch.com
Web site: http://branch.com
Levels of Connectivity Supported: SLIP, PPP, ISDN,
56kb, T1

Mich.com, Inc.

21042 Laurelwood

Farmington, MI 48336 USA

Phone: 810 478 4300

Fax: 810 478 4302

Email: info@mich.com

Web site: http://www.mich.com

Levels of Connectivity Supported: Shell, SLIP, PPP, UUCP, 56kb, T1

Msen, Inc.

320 Miller Avenue

Ann Arbor, MI 48103

Phone: 313 998 4562

Fax: 313 998 4563

Levels of Connectivity Supported: Shell, SLIP, PPP, UUCP

The Portage at Micro + Computers

506 Shelden Ave

Houghton, MI 49931 USA

Phone: 906 487 9832

Fax: 906 487 9690

Email: admin@mail.portup.com

Web site: http://www.portup.com

Levels of Connectivity Supported: Shell, SLIP, PPP, ISDN, 56kb

ISPs for Area Code 907

Alaska Information Technology

P.O. Box 92439

Anchorage, AK 99509 USA

Phone: 907 258 1881

Fax: 907 258 9552

Email: info@anc.ak.net

Web site: http://www.ak.net

Levels of Connectivity Supported: SLIP, PPP, UUCP, 56kb, T1

Internet Alaska

4050 Lake Otis Pkwy., Suite 107A

Anchorage, AK 99508 USA

Phone: 907 562 4638

Fax: 907 562 1677

Email: info@alaska.net

Web site: http://www.alaska.net

Levels of Connectivity Supported: Shell, SLIP, PPP, UUCP, ISDN, 56kb, T1

Micronet Communications

505 West Northern Lights Blvd., Suite 108

Anchorage, AK 99503 USA

Phone: 907 333 8663

Fax: 907 337 4186

Email: info@micronet.net

Web site: http://www.lasertone.com

Levels of Connectivity Supported: PPP, UUPC, 56kb, T1

NorthWestNet

15400 S.E. 30th Place, Suite 202

Bellevue, WA 98007 USA

Phone: 206 562 3000

Fax: 206 562 4822

Email: info@nwnet.net

Web site: http://www.nwnet.net

Levels of Connectivity Supported: T1, Frame Relay

ISPs for Area Code 908

BLASTNET Internet Service

472 Route 22 West

Whitehouse Station, NJ 08889 USA

Phone: 908 534 5881

Fax: 908 534 6928

Email: mcp@blast.net

Web site: http://fireball.blast.net/blast.html

Levels of Connectivity Supported: Shell, SLIP, PPP, 56kb, T1

Castle Network, Inc.

385 Main Street #2

Metuchen, NJ 08840 USA

Phone: 908 548 8881 or 800 577 9449 (within New Jersey)

Email: request@castle.net

Web site: http://www.castle.net

Levels of Connectivity Supported: Shell, SLIP, PPP, UUCP

Crystal Palace Networking, Inc.
287 Newton-Sparta Road
Newton, NJ 07871 USA
Phone: 201 300 0881
Fax: 201 300 0691
Email:
info@crystal.palace.net
Web site: http://
www.palace.net
Levels of Connectivity Supported: Shell, PPP

CyberComm Online Services
P.O. Box 5252
Toms River, NJ 08753-5252
USA
Phone: 908 506 6651
Fax: 908 506 6674
Email: info@cybercomm.net
Web site: http://
www.cybercomm.net
Levels of Connectivity Supported: Shell, SLIP, UUCP

Digital Express Group, Inc.
6006 Greenbelt Road, Suite 228
Greenbelt, MD 20770 USA
Phone: 301 847 5000 or 847 5050
Fax: 301 847 5215
Email: info@digex.net
Web site: http://
www.digex.net
Levels of Connectivity Supported: Shell, SLIP, PPP, UUCP, 56kb, T1

Eclipse Internet Access
P.O. Box 512
Plainfield, NJ 07061 USA
Phone: 800 483 1223
Fax: 908 755 6379
Email: info@eclipse.net
Web site: http://
www.eclipse.net
Levels of Connectivity Supported: PPP, 56kb, T1

I-2000 Inc.
416 Main Street
Metuchen, NJ 08840 USA
Phone: 800 464 3820
Fax: 908 906 2396
Email: info@i-2000.com
Web site: http://www.
i-2000.com
Levels of Connectivity Supported: SLIP, PPP, 56kb, T1

INTAC Access Corporation
256 Broad Avenue
Palisades Park, NJ 07650 USA
Phone: 800 50 INTAC
Fax: 201 944 1434
Email: info@intac.com
Web site: http://
www.intac.com
Levels of Connectivity Supported: Shell, SLIP, PPP, UUCP, ISDN, 56kb, T1

Intercall, Inc
33 Route 17 South
Rutherford, NJ 07073
Phone: 800 758 7329
Fax: 201 939 2507
Email: sales@intercall.com
Web site: http://
www.intercall.com
Levels of Connectivity Supported: SLIP, PPP

Internet For 'U'
24 North 3rd Ave., Suite 20
Highland Park, NJ 08908 USA
Phone: 800 NETWAY1
Fax: 908 435 0566
Email: info@ifu.net
Web site: http://ifu.net/
home.html
Levels of Connectivity Supported: Shell, SLIP, PPP, UUCP, T1

Internet Online Services
294 State Street
Hackensack, NJ 07601
Phone: 201 928 1000 x226
Fax: 201 928 1057
Levels of Connectivity Supported: Shell, SLIP, PPP, UUCP

Lightning Internet Services, LLC

327C Sagamore Avenue
Mineola, NY 11501 USA
Phone: 516 248 8400
Fax: 516 248 8897
Email: sales@lightning.net
Web site: http://
www.lightning.net
Levels of Connectivity Supported: ISDN, 56kb, T1

Openix - Open Internet Exchange

25 Green Village Rd
Madison, NJ 07940USA
Phone: 201 443 0400
Fax: 201 377 0418
Email: info@openix.com
Web site: http://
www.openix.com
Levels of Connectivity Supported: Shell, SLIP, PPP,
UUCP, 56kb, T1

Planet Access Networks

7 Waterloo Rd, Suite 202
Stanhope, NJ 07874 USA
Phone: 201 691 4704
Fax: 201 691 7588
Email: info@planet.net
Web site: http://
www.planet.net
Levels of Connectivity Supported: Shell, SLIP, PPP,
UUCP, ISDN, 56kb, T1

TechnoCore Communications, Inc.

P.O. Box 106
Jackson, NJ 08527 USA
Phone: 908 928 7400
Fax: 908 928 7402
Email: info@thecore.com
Web site: http://
www.thecore.com
Levels of Connectivity Supported: Shell, SLIP, PPP, 56kb

Texel International

North Brunswick, NJ 08902
USA
Phone: 908 297 0290
Fax: 908 940 9535
Email: info@texel.com
Web site: http://
www.texel.com
Levels of Connectivity Supported: Shell, SLIP, PPP

You Tools Corporation / FASTNET

Two Courtney Place, Suite 140
3864 Courtney Street
Bethlehem, PA 18017 USA
Phone: 610 954 5910
Fax: 610 954 5925
Email: info@fast.net
Web site: http://
www.youtools.com
Levels of Connectivity Supported: SLIP, PPP, UUCP,
ISDN, 56kb, T1

ISPs for Area Code 909

Cogent Software, Inc.

221 E. Walnut St., Suite 215
Pasadena, CA 91101 USA
Phone: 818 585 2788
Fax: 818 585 2785
Email: info@cogsoft.com
Web site: http://
www.cogsoft.com
Levels of Connectivity Supported: Shell, PPP, ISDN,
56kb, T1

CONNECTnet Internet Network Services

6370 Lusk Blvd.
Suite F-208
San Diego, CA92121 USA
Phone: 619 450 0254
Fax: 619 450 3216
Email: info@connectnet.com
Web site: http://
www.connectnet.com
Levels of Connectivity Supported: Shell, SLIP, PPP,
UUCP, ISDN, 56kb, T1

CruzNet

215 E. Orangethorpe Ave.
Suite: 333
Fullerton, CA92632 USA
Phone: 714 680 6600
Fax: 714 680 4241
Email: info@cruznet.net
Web site: http://
www.cruznet.net
Levels of Connectivity Supported: Shell, SLIP, PPP,
UUCP, ISDN, 56kb, T1

Cyberg8t Internet Services
225 Yale Ave., Suite D
Claremont, CA 91711 USA
Phone: 909 398 4638
Fax: 909 398 4621
Email: sales@cyberg8t.com
Web site: http://
www.cyberg8t.com
Levels of Connectivity Supported: PPP, UUCP, 56kb, T1

DiscoverNet
826 Brookside Ave, Suite B
Redlands, CA 92373 USA
Phone: 909 335 1209
Fax: 909 335 1480
Email: info@discover.net
Web site: http://
www.discover.net
Levels of Connectivity Supported: SLIP, PPP, ISDN,
56kb, T1

DPC Systems Beach.Net
24681 La Plaza Ste 360
Dana Point, CA 92629 USA
Phone: 714 443 4172
Fax: 714 443 9516
Email: connect@beach.net
Web site: http:/www.beach.net
Levels of Connectivity Supported: SLIP, PPP, UUCP,
ISDN, 56kb, T1

Delta Internet Services
731 E. Ball Rd., Suite 204
Anaheim, CA 92805 USA
Phone: 714 778 0370
Fax: 714 778 1064
Email: info@delta.net
Web site: http://
www.delta.net
Levels of Connectivity Supported: Shell, SLIP, PPP,
UUCP, ISDN, 56kb, T1

EmpireNet
3637 Canyon Crest Drive,
Suite H105
Riverside, CA 92507 USA
Phone: 909 787 4969
Fax: 909 787 4987
Email: support@empirenet.com
Web site: http://
www.empirenet.com
Levels of Connectivity Supported: Shell, SLIP, PPP, ISDN

InterWorld Communications, Inc.
222 N. Sepulveda Blvd.,
Suite 1560
El Segundo, CA 90245 USA
Phone: 310 726 0500
Fax: 310 726 0559
Email: sales@interworld.net
Web site: http://
www.interworld.net
Levels of Connectivity Supported: SLIP, PPP, UUCP,
ISDN, 56kb, T1, Web Hosting

KAIWAN Internet
12550 Brookhurst Street,
Suite H
Garden Grove, CA 92640 USA
Phone: 714 638 2139
Fax: 714 638 0455
Email: info@kaiwan.com
Web site: http://
www.kaiwan.com
Levels of Connectivity Supported: Shell, SLIP, PPP,
UUCP, ISDN, T1

Keyway Internet Access
P.O. Box 1427
Ontario, CA 91762 USA
Phone: 909 933 3650
Email: sales@keyway.net
Web site: http://
www.keyway.net
Levels of Connectivity Supported: Shell, SLIP, PPP,
UUCP, ISDN, 56kb, T1

Liberty Information Network
446 S Anaheim Hills Road,
Suite 102
Anaheim, CA 92807 USA
Phone: 800 218 5157 or 714
996 9999
Fax: 714 961 8700 Attn: ISP
INFO
Email: info@liberty.com
Web site: http://
www.liberty.com
Levels of Connectivity Supported: Shell, SLIP, PPP,
UUCP, ISDN, 56kb, T1

Lightside, Inc.

101 N. Citrus, Suite #4A
Covina, CA 91723 USA
Phone: 818 858 9261
Fax: 818 858 8982
Email:
Lightside@Lightside.Com
Web site: http://
www.lightside.Net
Levels of Connectivity Supported: SLIP, PPP, 56kb, T1

Network Intensive

8001 Irvine Center Drive,
Suite #1130
Irvine, CA 92718 USA
Phone: 714 450 8400
Fax: 714 450 8410
Email: info@ni.net
Web site: http://www.ni.net
Levels of Connectivity Supported: Shell, SLIP, PPP,
UUCP, ISDN, 56kb, T1

Primenet

2320 W. Peoria Avenue,
Suite A103
Phoenix, AZ 85029 USA
Phone: 602 870 1010 or 800 4
NET FUN
Fax: 602 870 1010
Email: info@primenet.com
Web site: http://
www.primenet.com
Levels of Connectivity Supported: Shell, SLIP, PPP,
UUCP

Saigon Enterprises

P.O. Box 3121
Glendale, CA 91221-0121 USA
Phone: 818 246 0689
Fax: 818 240 6600
Email: info@saigon.net
Web site: http://
www.saigon.net
Levels of Connectivity
Supported: Shell, SLIP, PPP,
UUCP, ISDN, 56kb, T1

ISPs for Area Code 910

Interpath

P.O. Box 12800
Raleigh, NC 27605 USA
Phone: 800 849 6305
Fax: 919 890 6319
Email: info@interpath.net
Web site: http://
www.interpath.net
Levels of Connectivity Supported: Shell, SLIP, PPP,
UUCP

KIVEX, Inc.

3 Bethesda Metro Center, Suite
B-001
Bethesda, MD 80214 USA
Phone: 800 47 KIVEX
Fax: 301 215 5991
Email: info@kivex.com
Web site: http://
www.kivex.com
Levels of Connectivity Supported: Shell, SLIP, PPP, ISDN,
56kb, T1, Web Hosting

NetDepot Inc.

1310 Cumberland Court
Smyrna, GA 30080 USA
Phone: 770 434 5595
Fax: 770 953 6830
Email: info@netdepot.com
Web site: http://
www.netdepot.com
Levels of Connectivity Supported: SLIP, PPP, ISDN,
56kb, T1

Netpath, Inc

2466 Corporation Pkwy
Burlington, NC 27215 USA
Phone: 910 226 0425 or 919
304 4309
Fax: 910 226 1688
Email: info@netpath.net
Web site: http://
www.netpath.net
Levels of Connectivity Supported: Shell, SLIP, PPP, ISDN,
56kb, T1

Online South Inc.

P.O. Box 178
Tobaccoville, NC 27050 USA
Phone: 910 983 7212
Fax: 910 983 0980
Email: support@ols.net
Web site: http://www.ols.net
Levels of Connectivity Supported: Shell, SLIP, PPP,
56kb, T1

SpyderByte Communications

P.O. Box 35421
Greensboro, NC 27425 USA
Phone: 910 643 6999
Fax: 910 643 3480
Email: info@spyder.net
Web site: http://
www.spyder.net
Levels of Connectivity Supported: PPP, UUCP, 56kb

Vnet Internet Access

P.O. Box 31474
Charlotte, NC 28231
Phone: 704 334 3282 or 800 377 3282
Fax: 704 334 6880
Levels of Connectivity Supported: Shell, SLIP, PPP, UUCP

Red Barn Data Center

131 Old Indian Trail
Lexington, NC 27292 USA
Phone: 910 750 9809
Fax: 704 798 1595
Email: tom@rbdc.rbdc.com
Web site: http://www.rbdc.com
Levels of Connectivity Supported: Shell, PPP, UUCP

ISPs for Area Code 912

Hargray Telephone Company

P.O. Box 5519
856 William Hilton Pkwy
Hilton Head Island, SC 29938 USA
Phone: 803 686 5000
Fax: 803 686 1251
Email: info@hargray.com
Web site: http://
www.hargray.com
Levels of Connectivity Supported: PPP, 56kb, T1

Homenet Communications, Inc.

806 Russell Parkway
Warner Robins, GA 31088 USA
Phone: 912 329 8638
Fax: 912 329 0838
Email: info@hom.net
Web site: http://www.hom.net
Levels of Connectivity Supported:Shell, SLIP, PPP, UUCP, ISDN, 56kb

Internet Atlanta

340 Knoll Ridge Court
Alpharetta, GA 30202
Phone: 404 410 9000
Fax: 404 410 9005
Email: info@atlanta.com
Web site: http://
www.atlanta.com
Levels of Connectivity Supported: Shell, SLIP, PPP, UUCP

MindSpring Enterprises, Inc.

1430 West Peachtree St NW, Suite 400
Atlanta, GA 30309 USA
Phone: 800 719 4332
Fax: 404 815 8805
Email: info@mindspring.com
Web site: http://
www.mindspring.com
Levels of Connectivity Supported: SLIP, PPP, UUCP, ISDN, 56kb

ISPs for Area Code 913

Flint Hills Computers, Inc.

1344 Westloop
Manhattan, KS 66503 USA
Phone: 913 776 4333
Fax: 913 776 1409
Email: gil@flinthills.com
Web site: http://
www.flinthills.com
Levels of Connectivity Supported: Shell, SLIP, PPP, UUCP, ISDN, 56kb

fyi@unicom.net

7223 W. 95th St., Suite 325
Overland Park, Kansas 66212 USA
Phone: 913 383 8466
Fax: 913 383 1998
Email: fyi@unicom.net
Web site: http://
www.unicom.net
Levels of Connectivity Supported: SLIP, PPP, UUCP, ISDN, 56kb, T1

Interstate Networking Corporation
2700 Rockcreek Parkway, #302
North Kansas City, MO 64117
USA
Phone: 816 472 4949
Email: staff@interstate.net
Web site: http://
www.interstate.net
Levels of Connectivity Supported: Shell, SLIP, PPP, UUCP

Tri-Rivers Internet
P.O. Box 3711
Salina, KS 67402 USA
Phone: 913 826 2595
Email: staff@tri.net
Web site: http://www.tri.net
Levels of Connectivity Supported: Shell, SLIP, PPP, UUCP, ISDN, 56kb, T1

ISPs for Area Code 914

bway.net / Outernet, Inc.
626 Broadway, Suite 3A
New York, NY 10012 USA
Phone: 212 982 9800
Fax: 212 982 5499
Email: info@bway.net
Web site: http://www.bway.net
Levels of Connectivity Supported: Shell, SLIP, PPP, UUCP, ISDN, 56kb, T1, Web Hosting

Cloud 9 Internet
15 Lake Street
White Plains, NY 10603-3851
USA
Phone: 914 682 0626
Fax: 914 682 0506
Email: info@cloud9.net
Web site: http://
www.cloud9.net
Levels of Connectivity Supported: Shell, SLIP, PPP, UUCP

Computer Net
P.O. Box 518
Mahopac Falls, New York
10542 USA
Phone: 914 773 1130
Fax: 914 628 6251
Email: paul@computer.net
Web site: http://
www.computer.net
Levels of Connectivity Supported: SLIP, PPP, UUCP, ISDN, 56kb, T1

Creative Data Consultants (SILLY.COM)
Bayside, NY 11364 USA
Phone: 718 229 0489 x23
Fax: 718 229 7096
Email: info@silly.com
Web site: http://
www.silly.com
Levels of Connectivity Supported: Shell, SLIP, PPP, UUCP

epix
100 Lake Street
Dallas, PA 18612 USA
Phone: 800 374 9669
Fax: 717 675 5711
Email: karndt@epix.net
Web site: http://www.epix.net
Levels of Connectivity Supported: SLIP, PPP, ISDN, 56kb, T1

GBN InternetAccess
83A Burlews Court
Hackensack, NJ 07601 USA
Phone: 201 343 6427
Fax: 201 343 6110
Email: gbninfo@gbn.net
Web site: http://www.gbn.net
Levels of Connectivity Supported: Shell, SLIP, PPP, UUCP, ISDN, 56kb, T1

I-2000 Inc.
416 Main Street
Metuchen, NJ 08840 USA
Phone: 800 464 3820
Fax: 908 906 2396
Email: info@i-2000.com
Web site: http://www.
i-2000.com
Levels of Connectivity Supported: SLIP, PPP, ISDN, 56kb, T1

ICU On-Line
167 RT 304
Bardonia, NY 10954 USA
Phone: 914 627 3800
Fax: 914 627 3811
Email: info@icu.com
Levels of Connectivity Supported: PPP, 56kb

INTAC Access Corporation
256 Broad Avenue
Palisades Park, NJ 07650 USA
Phone: 800 50 INTAC
Fax: 201 944 1434
Email: info@intac.com
Web site: http://
www.intac.com
Levels of Connectivity Supported: Shell, SLIP, PPP, UUCP, ISDN, 56kb, T1

InteleCom Data Systems, Inc.
East Greenwich, RI
Phone: 401 885 6855
Email: info@ids.net
Web site: http://www.ids.net
Levels of Connectivity Supported: Shell, SLIP, PPP, UUCP

Lightning Internet Services, LLC
327C Sagamore Avenue
Mineola, NY.11501 USA
Phone: 516 248 8400
Fax: 516 248 8897
Email: sales@lightning.net
Web site: http://
www.lightning.net
Levels of Connectivity Supported: ISDN, 56kb, T1

Long Island Internet HeadQuarters
506 Route 110
Melville, NY 11747 USA
Phone: 516 439 7800
Fax: 516 439 7321
Email: support@pb.net
Web site: http://www.pb.net
Levels of Connectivity Supported: Shell, SLIP, PPP, UUCP, ISDN, 56kb, T1

MHVNet (Computer Solutions by Hawkinson)
P.O. Box 314
Hyde Park, NY 12538 USA
Phone: 914 473 0844
Fax: 914 229 0197
Email: info@mhv.net
Web site: http://www.mhv.net
Levels of Connectivity Supported: Shell, SLIP, PPP, UUCP, ISDN, 56kb, T1

Mnematics, Incorporated
P.O. Box 19
Sparkill, NY 10976-0019 USA
Phone: 914 359 4546
Fax: 914 359 0361
Email: service@mne.com
Web site: http://www.mne.com
Levels of Connectivity Supported: Shell, SLIP, PPP, UUCP

New World Data
253-17 80th Ave, Suite 2B
Floral Park, NY 11004 USA
Phone: 718 962 1725
Fax: 718 962 1708
Email: dmk@nwdc.com
Web site: http://www.nwdc.com
Levels of Connectivity Supported: Shell, SLIP, PPP, UUCP, ISDN, 56kb, T1

NYSERNet
200 Elwood Davis Road
Liverpool, NY 13088-6147
USA
Phone: 800 493 4367
Fax: 315 453 3052
Email: sales@nysernet.org
Web site: http://nysernet.org
Levels of Connectivity Supported: Shell, 56kb, T1

Panix (Public Access uNIX)
New York, NY
Phone: 212 741 4400
Fax: 212 741 5311
Email: info@panix.com
Web site: http://
www.panix.com
Levels of Connectivity Supported: Shell, SLIP, PPP

Pipeline New York
150 Broadway, Suite 610
New York, NY 10038 USA
Phone: 212 267 3636
Fax: 212 267 4380
Email: info@pipeline.com
Web site: http://
www.pipeline.com
Levels of Connectivity Supported: Shell

TZ-Link Internet

47 Summit St.

Nyack, NY 10960 USA

Phone: 914 353 5443

Fax: 914 353 5443

Email: info@j51.com

Web site: http://www.j51.com

Levels of Connectivity Supported: Shell, SLIP, PPP

WestNet Internet Services

40 Redfield St.

Rye, NY 10580 USA

Phone: 914 967 7816

Email: info@westnet.com

Web site: http://
www.westnet.com

Levels of Connectivity Supported: Shell, SLIP, PPP,
UUCP, 56kb

ZONE One Network Exchange

304 Hudson Street

New York, NY 10013 USA

Phone: 212 824 4000

Fax: 212 824 4009

Email: info@zone.net

Web site: http://www.zone.net

Levels of Connectivity Supported: Shell, SLIP, PPP,
UUCP, ISDN, 56kb, T1

ISPs for Area Code 915

Delta Design and Development Inc.

6448 Hwy. 290 East, Suite
F108

Austin, TX 78723 USA

Phone: 800 763 8265

Fax: 512 467 8462

Email: sales@deltaweb.com

Web site: http://
www.deltaweb.com

Levels of Connectivity Supported: PPP, ISDN, 56kb, T1

New Mexico Technet, Inc.

4100 Osuna NE, Suite 103

Albuquerque, NM 87109

Phone: 505 345 6555

Fax: 505 345 6559

Levels of Connectivity Supported: Shell, SLIP, PPP

Primenet

2320 W. Peoria Avenue, Suite
A103

Phoenix, AZ 85029 USA

Phone: 602 870 1010 or 800 4
NET FUN

Fax: 602 870 1010

Email: info@primenet.com

Web site: http://
www.primenet.com

Levels of Connectivity Supported: Shell, SLIP, PPP,
UUCP

TexNet Internet Services

1974 Pueblo Nuevo Circle

El Paso, TX 79936-3710 USA

Phone: 915 857 1800

Fax: 915 857 9683

Email: jcoving@tnis.net

Web site: http://
www.tnis.net/index.html

Levels of Connectivity Supported: SLIP, PPP, 56kb, T1

WhiteHorse Communications, Inc.

5812 Cromo Dr. Suite 202

El Paso, TX 79912 USA

Phone: 915 584 6630

Fax: 915 585 2569

Email: info@whc.net

Web site: http://www.whc.net

Levels of Connectivity Supported: Shell, SLIP, PPP,
56kb, T1

ISPs for Area Code 916

**CASTLES Information
Network**

1425 West Texas Street

Fairfield, CA 94533 USA

Phone: 707 422 7311

Fax: 707 422 5265

Email: info@castles.com

Web site: http://
www.castles.com

Levels of Connectivity Supported: SLIP, PPP, ISDN,
56kb, T1

Connectus, Inc.

200 South Virginia Ave.,
Suite 553
Reno, Nevada 89501-2415 USA
Phone: 702 323 2008
Fax: 702 323 9088
Email: info@connectus.com
Web site: http://
www.connectus.com
Levels of Connectivity Supported: Shell, SLIP, PPP,
UUCP, ISDN, 56kb, T1

Great Basin Internet Services

1155 W Fourth Street,
Suite 225
P.O. Box 6209
Reno, NV 89513-6209
Phone: 702 348 7299
Fax: 702 348 9412
Levels of Connectivity Supported: Shell, SLIP, PPP,
UUCP

InterStar Network Services

1805 Hilltop Drive, Suite 203B
Redding, CA 96002 USA
Phone: 916 224 6866
Fax: 916 224 6866
Email: gfrank@shasta.com
Web site: http://
www.shasta.com
Levels of Connectivity Supported: Shell, SLIP, PPP,
UUCP, ISDN, 56kb, T1

mother.com

P.O. BOX 4466
Davis CA 95617
Phone: 916 757 8070
Email: info@mail.mother.com
Web site: http://
www.mother.com
Levels of Connectivity Supported: Shell, SLIP, PPP,
UUCP, ISDN, 56kb, T1

NetLink Data-Communications, Inc

905 23rd Street
Sacramento, CA 95816 USA
Phone: 916 447 3025
Fax: 916 447 0199
Email: info@netlink.net
Web site: http://www.sacto-business.net
Levels of Connectivity Supported: PPP, ISDN, 56kb, T1

ORONET

P.O. Box 1199
Penn Valley, CA 95946 USA
Phone: 916 477 6650
Fax: 916 274 2833
Email: info@oro.net
Web site: http://www.oro.net
Levels of Connectivity Supported: Shell, SLIP, PPP,
UUCP, ISDN, 56kb, T1

Psyberware Internet Access

1508 Sixth Street
Lincoln, CA 95648-1514 USA
Phone: 916 645 4567
Email: info@psyber.com
Web site: http://
www.psyber.com
Levels of Connectivity Supported: Shell, SLIP, PPP,
UUCP, ISDN, 56kb, T1

R C Concepts Foothill-Net

P.O. Box 1427
24388 Main Street
Foresthill, CA 95631 USA
Phone: 916 367 3818
Fax: 916 367 4140
Email: sales@foothill.net
Web site: http://
www.foothill.net
Levels of Connectivity Supported: Shell, SLIP, PPP,
UUCP, ISDN, 56kb, T1

Sacramento Network Access

1765 Challenge Way, #125
Sacramento, CA 95815 USA
Phone: 916 565 4500
Fax: 916 565 4501
Email: info@sna.com
Web site: http://www.sna.com
Levels of Connectivity Supported: Shell, SLIP, PPP, ISDN,
56kb, T1

Sierra-Net

P.O. Box 3709

Incline Village, NV 89450 USA

Phone: 702 832 6911

Fax: 702 831 3970

Email: giles@sierra.net

Web site: http://
www.sierra.net

Levels of Connectivity Supported: Shell, SLIP, PPP, UUCP, ISDN, 56kb, T1

SnowCrest Computer Specialties

527 McCloud Ave

Mt. Shasta, CA 96067 USA

Phone: 916 926 6888 or 916 245 4698

Fax: 916 926 2526

Email: root@snowcrest.net

Web site: http://
www.snowcrest.net

Levels of Connectivity Supported: Shell, SLIP, PPP, UUCP, ISDN

Sutter Yuba Internet Exchange

229-A Clark Avenue

Yuba City, CA 95991 USA

Phone: 916 755 1751

Fax: 916 755 3565

Email: dave@syix.com

Web site: http://www.syix.com

Levels of Connectivity Supported: Shell, SLIP, PPP, UUCP, ISDN, 56kb, T1

TTCI.net

452 Manzanita Avenue

Chico, CA 95926 USA

Phone: 916 895 1609

Fax: 916 895 3204

Email: info@ttci.net

Web site: http://www.ttci.net

Levels of Connectivity Supported: Shell, PPP, ISDN, 56kb, T1

VFR, Inc.

P.O. Box 351

Loomis, CA 95650 USA

Phone: 916 652 7237

Email: vfr@vfr.net

Web site:

Levels of Connectivity Supported: Shell, SLIP, PPP, UUCP, 56kb, T1

West Coast Online

6050 Commerce Blvd., Suite 210

Rohnert Park, CA 94928 USA

Phone: 707 586 3060

Fax: 707 586 5254

Email: info@calon.com

Web site: http://
www.calon.com

Levels of Connectivity Supported: Shell, SLIP, PPP, UUCP

Email: info@calon.com

Website: http.//www.calon.com

Zocalo Engineering

2355 Virginia Street

Berkeley, CA 94709-1315 USA

Phone: 510 540 8000

Fax: 510 548 1891

Email: info@zocalo.net

Web site: http://www.zocalo.net/
frompocia.html

Levels of Connectivity Supported: Shell, SLIP, PPP, 56kb, T1

ISPs for Area Code 917

ZONE One Network Exchange

304 Hudson Street

New York, NY 10013 USA

Phone: 212 824 4000

Fax: 212 824 4009

Email: info@zone.net

Web site: http://www.zone.net

Levels of Connectivity Supported: Shell, SLIP, PPP, UUCP, ISDN, 56kb, T1

ISPs for Area Code 918

Galaxy Star Systems

P.O. Box 580782

Tulsa, OK 74158

Phone: 918 835 3655

Levels of Connectivity Supported: Shell, SLIP, PPP, UUCP

Internet Oklahoma

9500 Westgate, #120
Oklahoma City, OK 73162
Phone: 405 721 1580 or 918 583 1161
Fax: 405 721 4861 or 918 584 7222
Levels of Connectivity Supported: Shell, SLIP, PPP

South Coast Computing Services, Inc.

1811 Bering Dr., Suite 100
Houston, TX 77057 USA
Phone: 713 917 5000
Fax: 713 917 5005
Email: info@houston.net
Web site: http://www.sccsi.com
Levels of Connectivity Supported: Shell, SLIP, PPP, UUCP, ISDN, T1

ISPs for Area Code 919

Interpath

P.O. Box 12800
Raleigh, NC 27605 USA
Phone: 800 849 6305
Fax: 919 890 6319
Email: info@interpath.net
Web site: http://www.interpath.net
Levels of Connectivity Supported: Shell, SLIP, PPP, UUCP

KIVEX, Inc.

3 Bethesda Metro Center, Suite B-001
Bethesda, MD 80214 USA
Phone: 800 47 KIVEX
Fax: 301 215 5991
Email: info@kivex.com
Web site: http://www.kivex.com
Levels of Connectivity Supported: Shell, SLIP, PPP, ISDN, 56kb, T1, Web Hosting

MCS Internet Services

309 North Spence Ave.
Goldsboro, NC 27534 USA
Phone: 919 751 5777
Fax: 919 751 5777
Email: shultz@mail.gld.com
Web site: http://www.gld.com
Levels of Connectivity Supported: SLIP, PPP, UUCP, 56kb, T1

Vnet Internet Access

P.O. Box 31474
Charlotte, NC 28231
Phone: 704 334 3282 or 800 377 3282
Fax: 704 334 6880
Levels of Connectivity Supported: Shell, SLIP, PPP, UUCP

ISPs for Area Code 941

Centurion Technology, Inc.

4175 E. Bay Dr., Suite 142
Largo, FL 34624 USA
Phone: 813 538 1919
Fax: 813 524 2909
Email: info@tpa.cent.com
Web site: http://tpa.cent.com
Levels of Connectivity Supported: PPP, UUCP, 56kb

Net Sarasota

3235 Pafko Drive
Sarasota, FL 34232 USA
Phone: 941 371 1966
Email: info@netsrq.com
Web site: http://www.netsrq.com
Levels of Connectivity Supported: SLIP, PPP

PacketWorks, Inc.

1100 Cleveland St. #900P
Clearwater, FL 34615 USA
Phone: 813 446 8826
Fax: 813 447 1585
Email: info@packet.net
Web site: http://www.packet.net
Levels of Connectivity Supported: PPP, ISDN

USA Computers

5240 Bank Street, Suite 17
Fort Myers, FL 33907 USA
Phone: 941 939 5630
Fax: 941 939 0891
Email: info@usacomputers.net
Web site: http://www.usacomputers.net
Levels of Connectivity Supported: PPP, ISDN, 56kb, T1

ISPs for Area Code 954

Acquired Knowledge Systems, Inc.

817 SW 8 Terrace

Fort Lauderdale, FL 33315 USA

Phone: 954 525 2574

Fax: 954 462 2329

Email: info@aksi.net

Web site: http://www.aksi.net

Levels of Connectivity Supported: Shell, SLIP, PPP, ISDN

ICANECT

1020 NW 163 Drive

Miami, FL 33139 USA

Phone: 305 621 9200

Fax: 305 621 2227

Email: sales@icanect.net

Web site: http://www.icanect.net

Levels of Connectivity Supported: Shell, SLIP, PPP, ISDN, 56kb, T1, Web Hosting

Safari Internet

1137 North Federal Highway

Ft Lauderdale, FL 33304 USA

Phone: 954 537 9550

Fax: 954 537 7959

Email: sales@safari.net

Web site: http://www.safari.net

Levels of Connectivity Supported: Shell, SLIP, PPP, 56kb, T1, Web Hosting

Shadow Information Services, Inc.

2000 Nw 88 Court

Miami, FL 33172 USA

Phone: 305 594 2450

Fax: 305 599 1140

Email: admin@shadow.net

Web site: http://www.shadow.net

Levels of Connectivity Supported: Shell, SLIP, PPP

Zimmerman Communications

1061 SW 75 Ave

Plantation, FL 33317 USA

Phone: 954 584 0199

Fax: 954 584 0199

Email: bob@zim.com

Web site: http://www.zim.com

Levels of Connectivity Supported: PPP, ISDN, 56kb

ISPs for Area Code 970

EZLink Internet Access

1304 Westward Drive

Fort Collins, CO 80521 USA

Phone: 970 482 0807

Fax: 970 224 1933

Email: ezadmin@ezlink.com

Web site: http://www.ezlink.com

Levels of Connectivity Supported: Shell, SLIP, PPP, UUCP

Frontier Internet, Inc.

777 Main Avenue, Suite 201

Durango, Colorado 81301 USA

Phone: 970 385 4177

Fax: 970 385 6745

Email: info@frontier.net

Web site: http://www.frontier.net

Levels of Connectivity Supported: Shell, SLIP, PPP, UUCP, 56kb, T1

Rocky Mountain Internet

2860 S. Circle Drive, Suite 2202

Colorado Springs, CO 80906 USA

Phone: 800 900 7644

Fax: 719 576 0301

Email: info@rmii.com

Web site: http://www.rmii.com

Levels of Connectivity Supported: Shell, SLIP, PPP, UUCP

Verinet Communications, Inc.

315 West Oak Street, Suite 300

Fort Collins, CO 80521 USA

Phone: 970 416 9152

Fax: 970 416 9174

Email: info@verinet.com

Web site: http://www.verinet.com

Levels of Connectivity Supported: Shell, SLIP, PPP, ISDN, 56kb

1-800 ISPs

Allied Access Inc.

1002 Walnut Street
Murphysboro, IL 62966 USA
Phone: 618 684 2255 or 800
INETDOM
Fax: 618 684 5907
Email: sales@intrnet.net
Web site: http://
www.intrnet.net
Levels of Connectivity Supported: Shell, SLIP, PPP

American Information Systems, Inc.

911 North Plum Grove Road,
Suite F
Schaumburg, IL 60173 USA
Phone: 708 413 8400
Fax: 708 413 8401
Email: info@ais.net
Web site: http://www.ais.net
Levels of Connectivity Supported: Shell, SLIP, PPP,
UUCP

ARInternet Corporation

8201 Corporate Drive,
Suite 1100
Landover, MD 20785 USA
Phone: 301 459 7171
Fax: 301 459 7174
Email: info@ari.net
Web site: http://www.ari.net
Levels of Connectivity Supported: Shell, SLIP, PPP ISDN,
56kb, T1

Association for Computing Machinery

P.O. Box 21599
Waco, TX 76702 USA
Phone: 817 776 6876
Fax: 817 751 7785
Email: account-info@acm.org
Web site: http://www.acm.org
Levels of Connectivity Supported: Shell, SLIP, PPP

CICNet, Inc.

2901 Hubbard Drive
Ann Arbor, MI 48105 USA
Phone: 313 998 6103
Fax: 313 998 6105
Email: info@cic.net
Web site: http://www.cic.net
Levels of Connectivity Supported: Shell, SLIP, PPP,
56kb, T1

Colorado SuperNet, Inc.

999 - 18th Street, Suite 2640
Denver, CO 80202 USA
Phone: 303 296 8202
Fax: 303 296 8224
Email: info@csn.org
Web site: http://www.csn.net
Levels of Connectivity Supported: Shell, SLIP, PPP,
UUCP, ISDN, 56kb, T1, Web
Hosting

Concentric Research Corporation

400 41st Street
Bay City, MI 48708 USA
Phone: 800 745 2747
Fax: 517 895 0529
Email: info@cris.com
Web site: http://www.cris.com
Levels of Connectivity Supported: Shell, SLIP, 56kb, T1

Cyberius Online Inc.

99 Fifth Avenue, Unit 406
Ottawa, Ontario K1S 5P5
Canada
Phone: 613 233 1215
Fax: 613 233 0292
Email: info@cyberus.ca
Web site: http://
www.cyberus.ca
Levels of Connectivity Supported: SLIP, PPP, UUCP,
ISDN, 56kb, T1

EarthLink Network, Inc.

3171 Los Feliz Blvd., Suite 203
Los Angeles, CA 90039 USA
Phone: 213 644 9500
Fax: 213 644 9510
Email: info@earthlink.net
Web site: http://
www.earthlink.net
Levels of Connectivity Supported: SLIP, PPP, ISDN,
56kb, T1

Global Connect, Inc.
497 Queens Creek Road
Williamsburg, VA 23185
Phone: 804 229 4484
Fax: 804 229 6557
Levels of Connectivity Supported: SLIP, PPP, UUCP

Global Enterprise Services, Inc. (The JvNCnet)
3 Independence Way
Princeton, NJ 08540 USA
Phone: 1 800 35 TIGER
Fax: 1 609 897 7310
Email: market@jvnc.net
Web site: ="http://www-ges.jvnc.net
Levels of Connectivity Supported: SLIP, ISDN, 56kb, T1

Internet Express
1155 Kelly Johnson Blvd,
Suite 400
Colorado Springs, CO 80920-3959 USA
Phone: 800-592-1240
Fax: 719-592-1201
Email: service@usa.net
Web site: http://www.usa.net
Levels of Connectivity Supported: Shell, SLIP, PPP, UUCP, 56kb, T1

Iowa Network Services
4201 Corporate Drive
West Des Moines, IA 50265
USA
Phone: 800 546 6587
Fax: 515 830 0345
Email: service@netins.net
Web site: http://www.netins.net
Levels of Connectivity Supported: Shell, SLIP, PPP, UUCP, 56kb, T1, Web Hosting

Micron Internet Services
8000 S Federal Way
P.O. Box 6
Boise, ID 83707-0006 USA
Phone: 208 368 5400
Fax: 208 368 5640
Email: sales@micron.net
Web site: http://www.micron.net
Levels of Connectivity Supported: SLIP, PPP, 56kb, T1

Mnematics, Incorporated
P.O. Box 19
Sparkill, NY 10976-0019 USA
Phone: 914 359 4546
Fax: 914 359 0361
Email: service@mne.com
Web site: http://www.mne.com
Levels of Connectivity Supported: Shell, SLIP, PPP, UUCP

Msen, Inc.
320 Miller Avenue
Ann Arbor, MI 48103
Phone: 313 998 4562
Fax: 313 998 4563
Levels of Connectivity Supported: Shell, SLIP, PPP, UUCP

NeoSoft, Inc.
3408 Magnum Road
Houston, TX 77092
Phone: 800 GET NEOSOFT or 713 684 5969
Fax: 713 684 5922
Levels of Connectivity Supported: Shell, SLIP, PPP, UUCP

NETCOM On-Line Communications Services, Inc.
3031 Tisch Way
San Jose, CA 95128 USA
Phone: 800 353 6600 or 408 983 5950
Fax: 408 241 9145
Email: info@netcom.com
Web site: http://www.netcom.com
Levels of Connectivity Supported: Shell, UUCP, 56kb, T1

New Mexico Technet, Inc.
4100 Osuna NE, Suite 103
Albuquerque, NM 87109
Phone: 505 345 6555
Fax: 505 345 6559
Levels of Connectivity Supported: Shell, SLIP, PPP

Pacific Rim Network, Inc.
P.O. Box 5006
Bellingham, WA 98227 USA
Phone: 360 650 0442 x 11
Fax: 360 738 8315
Email: info@pacificrim.net
Web site: http://
www.pacificrim.net
Levels of Connectivity Supported: PPP, ISDN, 56kb, 128kb, T1

Rocky Mountain Internet
2860 S. Circle Drive, Suite 2202
Colorado Springs, CO 80906 USA
Phone: 800 900 7644
Fax: 719 576 0301
Email: info@rmii.com
Web site: http://www.rmii.com
Levels of Connectivity Supported: Shell, SLIP, PPP, UUCP

Safari Internet
1137 North Federal Highway
Ft Lauderdale, FL 33304 USA
Phone: 954 537 9550
Fax: 954 537 7959
Email: sales@safari.net
Web site: http://
www.safari.net
Levels of Connectivity Supported: Shell, SLIP, PPP, 56kb, ISDN

Synergy Communications, Inc.
1941 South 42nd Street
Omaha, NE 68105 USA
Phone: 800 345 9669
Fax: 402 346 0208
Email: info@synergy.net
Levels of Connectivity Supported: PPP

VivaNET, Inc.
1555 East Henrietta Road
Rochester, NY 14623 USA
Phone: 800 836 UNIX
Fax: 716 272 7627
Email: info@vivanet.com
Web site: http://
www.vivanet.com
Levels of Connectivity Supported: Shell, SLIP, PPP, UUCP, ISDN, 56kb, T1

VoiceNet
17 Richard Rd.
Ivyland, PA 18974 USA
Phone: 800 835 5710
Fax: 215 674 9662
Email: info@voicenet.com
Web site: http://
www.voicenet.com
Levels of Connectivity Supported: Shell, SLIP, PPP, UUCP, ISDN, 56kb, T1

WLN
P.O. Box 3888
Lacey, WA 98503-0888 USA
Phone: 800 342 5956 or 360 923 4000
Fax: 360 923 4009
Email: info@wln.com
Levels of Connectivity Supported: Shell, SLIP, PPP

INDEX

Symbols

Q–R

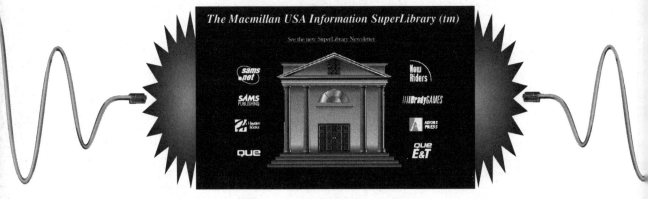

Check Us Out Online!

New Riders has emerged as a premier publisher of computer books for the professional computer user. Focusing on CAD/graphics/multimedia, communications/internetworking, and networking/operating systems, New Riders continues to provide expert advice on high-end topics and software.

Check out the online version of *New Riders' Official World Wide Yellow Pages, 1996 Edition* for the most engaging, entertaining, and informative sites on the Web! You can even add your own site!

Brave our site for the finest collection of CAD and 3D imagery produced today. Professionals from all over the world contribute to our gallery, which features new designs every month.

From Novell to Microsoft, New Riders publishes the training guides you need to attain your certification. Visit our site and try your hand at the CNE Endeavor, a test engine created by VFX Technologies, Inc. that enables you to measure what you know—and what you don't!

http://www.mcp.com/newriders

WANT MORE INFORMATION?

CHECK OUT THESE RELATED TOPICS OR SEE YOUR LOCAL BOOKSTORE

CAD and 3D Studio

As the number one CAD publisher in the world, and as a Registered Publisher of Autodesk, New Riders Publishing provides unequaled content on this complex topic. Industry-leading products include AutoCAD and 3D Studio.

Networking

As the leading Novell NetWare publisher, New Riders Publishing delivers cutting-edge products for network professionals. We publish books for all levels of users, from those wanting to gain NetWare Certification, to those administering or installing a network. Leading books in this category include *Inside NetWare 3.12*, *CNE Training Guide: Managing NetWare Systems*, *Inside TCP/IP*, and *NetWare: The Professional Reference*.

Graphics

New Riders provides readers with the most comprehensive product tutorials and references available for the graphics market. Best-sellers include *Inside CorelDRAW! 5*, *Inside Photoshop 3*, and *Adobe Photoshop NOW!*

Internet and Communications

As one of the fastest growing publishers in the communications market, New Riders provides unparalleled information and detail on this ever-changing topic area. We publish international best-sellers such as *New Riders' Official Internet Yellow Pages, 2nd Edition*, a directory of over 10,000 listings of Internet sites and resources from around the world, and *Riding the Internet Highway, Deluxe Edition*.

Operating Systems

Expanding off our expertise in technical markets, and driven by the needs of the computing and business professional, New Riders offers comprehensive references for experienced and advanced users of today's most popular operating systems, including *Understanding Windows 95, Inside Unix, Inside Windows 3.11 Platinum Edition, Inside OS/2 Warp Version 3*, and *Inside MS-DOS 6.22*.

Other Markets

Professionals looking to increase productivity and maximize the potential of their software and hardware should spend time discovering our line of products for Word, Excel, and Lotus 1-2-3. These titles include *Inside Word 6 for Windows, Inside Excel 5 for Windows, Inside 1-2-3 Release 5*, and *Inside WordPerfect for Windows*.

Orders/Customer Service **1-800-653-6156**   Source Code **NRP95**

New Riders Publishing   201 West 103rd Street ◆ Indianapolis, Indiana 46290 USA